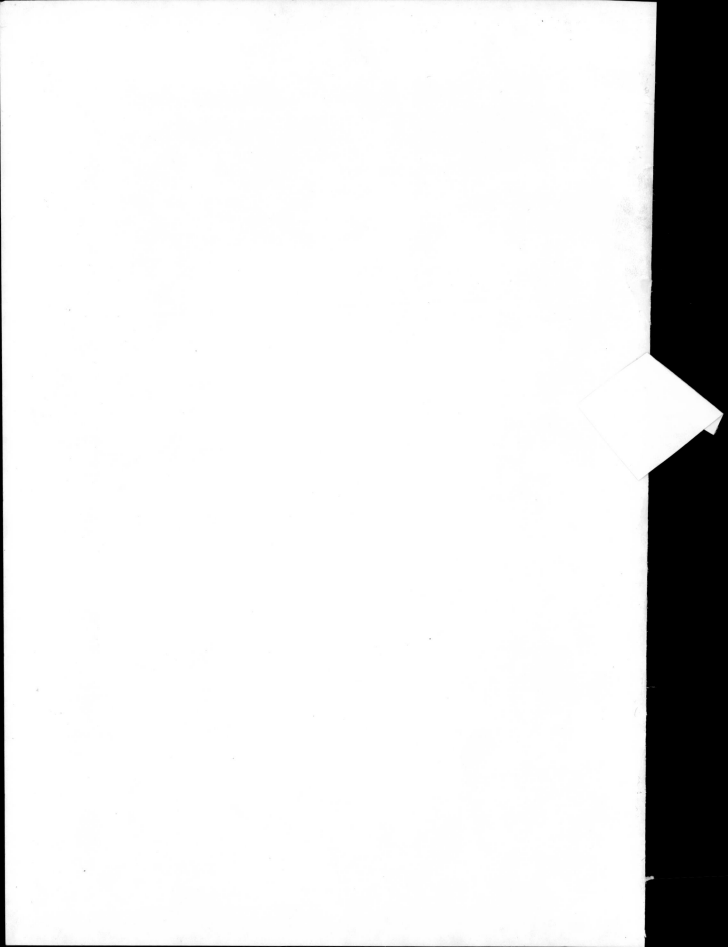

The Complete Guide to Furniture Styles

Louise Ade Boger

THE COMPLETE GUIDE TO

FURNITURE STYLES

THE COMPLETE GUIDE TO

FURNITURE STYLES

Enlarged Edition

by

LOUISE ADE BOGER

New York

CHARLES SCRIBNER'S SONS

THE COMPLETE GUIDE TO

FURNITURE STYLES

CHAPTER ONE

GRECIAN & ROMAN

GRECIAN FURNITURE

To understand the daily life of civilized people we must know something of domestic furniture. Practically all of our knowledge of the daily life of the ancient Greeks is derived from references in literature and, more importantly, from innumerable scenes of Grecian life found on vases and marbled reliefs, for unfortunately the furniture used by the Greeks in their daily living has almost entirely disappeared. This is due to the damp atmosphere which makes it impossible for wood, the natural material for furniture, to survive. Specimens of Egyptian wooden furniture, which belong to an earlier civilization, have survived because the climate is dry. In the early archaic period Grecian art was still very dependent on Egyptian and the great oriental arts, preceding her own. This is evident in ornament in the use of the palmette, the anthemion and above all the sphinx, which in its Greek form became a favorite Renaissance motif. It is also discernible in the use of Egyptian forms for furniture. However, during the fully developed period of the 5th century B.C., which marked the acme of Greek creative genius, the Greeks evolved original creations, and whatever they had borrowed from earlier civilizations they perfected and made their own. Perfection was achieved in every branch of Greek art. In furniture the forms became more pure and the proportions were perfected. In the ensuing 4th and 3rd centuries B.C., a general deterioration set in, when the earlier purity of line and simplicity of form yielded to overelaboration.

It is apparent that the same Greek conservatism displayed in their architecture and sculpture was also mirrored in their furniture. Although Grecian furniture is confined to a few fundamental pieces there is a wealth of detail which prevents any feeling of monotony. In the study of Grecian furniture nothing is more striking than the relative simplicity of the life of

3

the Greeks. All the many possessions which complicate and clutter our modern existence were unknown to the Greeks. Chairs, stools, couches, tables and chests were all the furniture they possessed. The Grecian home with its sparse furnishings presented an atmosphere of quiet dignity, ease and refinement and offers an interesting contrast to our modern crowded interiors burdened with countless possessions. The interior of a Grecian house was enlivened and enriched with coverlets and cushions made of richly embroidered silks and with brilliantly colored rugs. Throughout Greek classical times from the 7th century to the 2nd century B.C., there were three principal forms of seats, namely, the throne chair, chair and stool.

The Greek throne chair or thronos was always a dignified and stately chair. It is depicted in sculpture and painting as a seat reserved for gods and goddesses and for princes and other dignitaries. As a result of its use the word throne has become through the centuries synonymous with royal power. Since the throne chair was a lofty seat it was provided with a foot stool. It was a seat of great splendor and elaborateness. Occasionally it was made of gold or silver and was elegantly draped with handsome embroidered fabrics. As a rule the legs of the throne chair were joined with stretchers and apparently it most frequently had a back of varying height. The open arms and arm supports showed a great diversity in design. It was also designed without arm rests. The throne chair can be best identified by its legs; namely, legs terminating in animals' paws, or legs either rectangular in form or turned. In another type the seat of the chair rested on a solid underframing extending to the floor. The throne chair with legs terminating in animals' paws

was of Egyptian inspiration. A variant of this chair derived from an Egyptian prototype (FIGURE 2) had the entire chair leg modeled in the form of an animal's leg. Occasionally the chair leg was in the form of a winged animal, a sphinx or some similar motif. A characteristic feature obviously copied from Egyptian prototypes was the addition of figures, such as a sphinx, a lion, an imaginary creature or some similar decorative ornament extending from the seat rail to the stretcher or from the seat rail to the floor. The throne chair with a straight rectangular leg was apparently a Grecian innovation and owed nothing to Eastern models. The leg was generally decorated with a rosette and a double palmette, one palmette pointing upward and the other downward. The space around the stem of the palmette was most often carved away, leaving two deep incisions which resembled C-scrolls. Knobs were added on the stem to restore the width to the leg lost by the incisions. This decorative treatment was generally around or below the middle of the leg and it gave lightness and elegance to what would otherwise have been a rather heavy and clumsy leg (15). In the early models of Greek throne chairs with turned legs the influence of Egyptian turning was readily discernible. However, by the 5th century B.C., the Greeks had developed original models of turned legs notable for their graceful simplicity and fine proportions.

Undoubtedly the most characteristic Grecian chair is the klismos (3), a variety of light side chair deriving its beauty from its fine proportions and lines. The klismos was the principal inspiration for the late 18th century and early 19th century European chair designed in the French Directoire and English Regency styles.

The chair, which was a Grecian innovation, was perfected by the 5th century B.C., and remained in vogue through the 4th century B.C., and even later. The klismos is distinctive for its sweeping curving lines and for its elegant simplicity. Although slight variations in design occurred, in the principal perfected variety the uprights of the open chair back and the rear legs generally formed one continuous graceful curve and were made from a single piece of wood. The front legs curved forward correspondingly. The open chair back had a solid splat and a concave broad and flat crest rail, which extended beyond the uprights and was about the height of the shoulders. The seat rail was never higher than the top of the legs and was generally slightly lower. It seems that the top of the seat was plaited and that a piece of fabric or the skin of an animal was thrown over it and on this was placed a pillow. In an early variation of this chair the uprights rolled over and terminated in swans' heads or a similar decorative motif.

The stool or diphros was a practical Grecian seat and it was used equally by persons of importance and those of humble birth. The rectangular seat of the stool was mounted on four turned legs which were occasionally joined with a stretcher. The Greeks borrowed this form from the Egyptians. Another variety of stool favored by the Greeks and also of Egyptian inspiration was the folding stool or okladias with its crossed legs resembling our modern camp stool. The Egyptian folding stool commonly had plain legs crossing around the center and terminating on a horizontal side bar resting on the floor (1). In the Greek specimens the legs generally terminated in animals' feet. It has never been ascertained whether the Grecian folding stool actually folded like the Egyptian

model or simply gave that appearance, although it is reasonable to assume that it did. The Grecians also had another type of stool having the part under the rectangular seat enclosed to the floor.

The Grecian couch or kline, serving as a combination bed, couch and sofa, is an interesting category of Grecian furniture. It was used not only for sleeping and reposing but also for reclining on at meals. It was principally made of wood. The top was generally of interlaced cords, and on this interlacing the Grecians placed the mattress, cover and pillows. The richly embroidered silk cover and pillows added color and beauty. The couch was a relatively high piece of furniture and its length seems to have been around six feet. The legs were similar to those found on a throne chair, namely legs terminating in animals' feet, rectangular legs or turned legs. An important distinction between the Grecian and the Egyptian couch was that the former regularly had a low head-rest and sometimes a foot-rest, while the latter only had a foot-rest. The separate head-rest so common in Egypt was apparently never used in Greece.

The footstool was a favorite and necessary household article. It was used as a foot-rest for the throne chair and to mount the high couches. Its use in this latter respect was similar to the 18th century bedsteps. One principal variety was designed with a rectangular top mounted on four short rectangular legs, occasionally terminating in lions' paws. A stool of box-like construction with either straight or curving sides was also in general use. A more interesting variety of footstool was designed with finely curved legs and with a decorative pendant motif centered at each end. Pillows or hassocks also served as footstools.

The table was principally used in Greek classical times for the serving of meals. Each person had his own individual table which was carried in laden with food. It was generally placed next to the couch on which the dinner guest was reclining. The table was usually low enough to be pushed under the couch after the dinner was completed. One principal form of table in general use from the 6th to the 4th century B.C. had an oblong top resting on three rectangular tapering straight legs generally terminating in lions' paws and joined with a stretcher. One end of the table had a leg at each corner and was placed at the head of the couch; the other end had a leg in the middle. Four-legged rectangular tables were also known, but were not in general use, while in Egypt the custom was just the opposite. The Egyptian table having a round top and mounted on a central support was also found in Greece, but was relatively rare. In the 4th century the Greeks introduced a table with a circular top resting on three legs of animal form. This table, which can be regarded as a Grecian innovation, became very fashionable and finally supplanted the table with a rectangular top.

The chest, either large or small, was an indispensable household article both in Greece and in Egypt. The Egyptian chest had a flat, curved or gabled lid, and the body of the chest often rested on four rectangular short feet, formed by the prolongation of the stiles. The chest was plain, panelled or richly decorated and the lid was secured by winding string around two knobs. The characteristic 6th and 5th century Greek chest was evolved from the Egyptian chest. It generally was designed with a flat lid. Sometimes the rectangular feet ended in lions' paws. Small chests for jewelry were miniatures of the large chests.

ETRUSCAN FURNITURE

Etruscan furniture is essentially similar and almost entirely dependent on Greek furniture. The ornament and forms are repetitions of Greek ornament and forms with only slight variations to satisfy any particular individual taste. They did introduce a new variety of throne chair having the back and sides designed as one continuous unit, giving a rounded effect (4). The part under the seat of the chair was enclosed to the floor and was either round or rectangular in shape (4). Practically all the other forms of seats and couches were in the Grecian taste. Beds were frequently made of bronze (13); however, they undoubtedly were also made of wood. In addition to the characteristic Grecian tables they designed a table having an oblong top mounted on crossed curved legs. However, this table, which was generally of bronze, had been previously used in Assyria and other Eastern countries. Etruscan chests were also from Grecian prototypes. The cista, which served as a chest, was much favored by the Etruscans and can be regarded as an Etruscan innovation. As a rule it was made of bronze and its round body was mounted on four short feet in the form of animals' paws. The domed lid was surmounted by decorative figures serving as a handle.

ROMAN FURNITURE

Roman furniture is especially interesting to us since we have borrowed primarily from Roman rather than from Grecian furniture. All branches of Greek art are continued in Roman art, for Rome through her ascendancy became the logical transmitter of Greek art. The Romans possessed few artistic ideas, so they simply repeated and elaborated or enriched the forms and ornament developed by the Greeks. When the Roman borrowing began, the art of Greece had lost its perfection and purity of form, and in its decline had become ornate and over-elaborated. The Romans with their innate love of pomp and splendor understood this ornateness, while the earlier Greek simplicity would not have been appreciated to the same extent. It is only natural that the Romans carried the ornament and forms toward a greater elaboration. In appraising Roman contribution to furniture design, it must be allowed they did furnish several important innovations including the couch with a back and several distinctive forms of tables.

It is regrettable that Roman wooden furniture has shared the same fate as that of Greece. The study of Roman furniture is principally derived from fresco paintings at Pompeii and Herculaneum, representations on Roman tombstones and sarcophagi and actual examples in marble and in bronze. Latin writers talk about the Roman desire for luxury and deplore the extravagant and expensive tastes. They also describe the different woods of which there were about twenty varieties in common use by the ancients. Among the principal woods were maple, willow, beech, citron, cedar, oak, juniper, fir, holly and lime. Citron was the most prized of all woods and Latin writers were eloquent about its color and texture. Maple was also a favorite wood. One variety was an imported curly maple while another variety of extreme whiteness came from northern Italy. Ebony was much favored for veneering. The lavish use of veneering, plating and inlay work was a feature of Roman furniture. The Greeks also had used veneering and inlay but in a less pretentious manner. Exotic and costly woods,

tortoise shell, ivory, gold, silver and bronze were all employed by the Romans in inlay work. The plating of furniture with ivory, silver, gold and bronze became a rather ordinary practice for costly furniture. In some extremes the furniture was made entirely of one of these materials; however, in the majority of examples the semblance of such splendor was sufficient. We also learn from Latin writers that the practice of painting ordinary woods to simulate the graining of more expensive woods was employed in these early times.

The Roman throne chair or solium followed its Grecian predecessors and was designed with animal feet or with animal legs terminating in animal feet (2), with rectangular legs having decorative incisions (15), or with turned legs. The throne chair with animal legs displayed many variant forms. Occasionally the animal leg was surmounted by a fabulous winged figure, or an entire winged figure was used in place of the animal leg (5). One interesting variety of Roman throne chair resembled the 18th century tub-shaped chair with its back and sides designed in one continuous unit. The influence of the Roman throne chair is apparent in later European chair design, especially so in the Italian Renaissance and French Empire periods. In comparing the Roman chair with the earlier Grecian models it is patent that the Roman taste was inclined to elaboration. The ornament was more florid and grandiose and the forms were more cumbrous. The turned legs were generally heavy and uninteresting, since the turning was marred by a badly balanced profile. The sella curulis or the folding stool with curved legs of X-form was often made of bronze (6). Occasionally the folding stool was designed with a low back and was an interesting contribution to

Roman furniture design. The Greek klismos or Roman cathedra was not a particularly distinctive variety of Roman seat furniture. The Roman adaptation was inclined to be heavy and it was sometimes designed with straight legs as well as with arms.

The footstool persisted throughout the Roman period as a necessary article of furniture. Its function remained the same for throne chairs and for couches as in the Grecian period. The Romans were particularly partial to a variety of footstool essentially resembling a long and low rectangular box, the sides of which were often richly decorated. Sometimes at each corner there was an entire figure of a sphinx, an imaginary winged animal or some similar motif (12).

The Roman couch (10) or lectus designed with turned legs was much favored by the Romans. The legs often rested on runner feet or horizontal bars resting on the floor (10). The fulcrum or head-rest rolled over and the upper end most commonly terminated in a horse's or mule's head, while the lower end generally terminated in a medallion head (9). The upper end of the fulcrum occasionally terminated in a swan's head (8), and sometimes figure subjects were employed for enrichment (7). The railings of the bronze couches as well as the fulcrum were frequently richly decorated with conventionally treated designs of flowers and leaves and with subjects from mythology inlaid in silver (9). The fulcrum with its gently curving lines was completely pleasing. It was customary in the Roman dining room to have three couches placed at right angles to each other. The upper couch had a head-rest, the lower couch a foot-rest and the middle couch was devoid of either. It may be that in extant examples of these

couches depicting two fulcra (11) that one of the fulcrum originally belonged to a similar couch, since these couches have been incorrectly reconstructed in the past as seats with two arm-rests. Toward the end of the first century B.C., the Grecian type of couch was supplanted by another variety of couch which still retained the turned legs, but was designed with both a head-board and a foot-board that were higher than the earlier ones and the curves of which were less pronounced. The novel and interesting feature of this couch is the addition of a back.

The Romans made their most valuable contribution to furniture design in the category of tables or mensae. The characteristic Grecian table with an oblong top and four straight legs terminating in lions' paws was adopted by the Romans. However, in the surviving Roman examples the legs are curved and enriched with decorative detail. The Romans also designed a table with either a round or oblong top mounted on a central standard. The most original table introduced by the Romans, and apparently a Roman innovation, was a large and massive table designed with an oblong top mounted on solid end supports elaborately carved and ornately shaped (17). The outline of these end supports was generally the profile of a winged monster, an imaginary bird or some similar motif (17). As a rule the supports were of marble and the top was of wood. The table had a singular overwhelming richness and it became a favorite form during the Renaissance for the refectory table with solid truss end supports reinforced with a stretcher (45).

Another type of table which was especially favored by the Romans, and which was derived directly from Greek models, had a circular top mounted on three legs modelled in the form of animal's legs. These tables or tripods varied considerably in design. Of great interest are the bronze tripods with slender shaped supports displaying exquisite workmanship in their richly modelled ornament. The top was in the form of a basin or bowl and was generally of bronze and occasionally of gold, and was very often fitted with three rings which served as handles (15, 16). Extant bronze examples of this type which were found at Pompeii in the 18th century were extensively copied in the latter part of the 18th century when the pursuit of the antique became more exacting (203). Another interesting category was of more massive and simple design and had a flat circular top mounted on three animal legs terminating in paw feet. Extant Roman bronze examples are practically identical to late Grecian models depicted in reliefs where they are seen placed in front of the long side of the couch. Apparently the majority of these tables were relatively low. Related to this type and especially characteristic is a more massive table or tripod made of stone or marble. Each of the three animal legs, which terminate in a paw foot, is surmounted with the head of a lion (18). This form of animal leg occurred frequently at a much later time in English Regency cabinetwork borrowed from the antique (434, 437). It seems a reasonable assumption that these massive stone or marble tripods served also as an altar or seat such as the celebrated Delphic tripod.

The Romans also adopted the sideboard or abacus, which was introduced from Asia around the 2nd century B.C. It has not been possible to identify its form other than in the Roman tables already described.

The chest or arca was similar in form to the chest developed by the Egyptians and the Grecians except that the short rectangular feet upon which it was mounted were no longer a prolongation of the stiles.

The movable cupboard or armarium was known to the Romans and it was not too unlike our own. It had a rectangular body mounted on short feet and was fitted with shelves and cupboard doors. The cupboard was apparently also used as a bookcase as is seen in representations in which rolled manuscripts are neatly stacked on the shelves.

CHAPTER TWO

GOTHIC FURNITURE
in England, France & Italy

GOTHIC

The period between the breakup of the Roman Empire in the west and the Crusades, approximately from the 6th century to the 11th century, is generally referred to as the Dark Ages. These five centuries were marked by wars, invasions and upheavals, which plunged the people of western Europe into chaos and darkness. Unfortunately, due to our meager information we are also in considerable darkness about these years. We do know, however, that we are strongly indebted to the monastic communities, which came into existence as early as the 6th century, for through their efforts to preserve and create an interest in ancient Greek and Roman art they richly served civilization. To a great extent the art of Western Europe for this period lapsed into a lethargy from which it was briefly aroused by the efforts of Charlemagne. Probably the most interesting feature to us in any art expression of this period is the conflicting influences and the

resultant lack of uniformity. Undoubtedly this was due to some extent to the tremendous differences existing among the people themselves. We must remember that the Teutonic tribes, the Goths, Danes, Vandals, Vikings and others, were constantly sweeping through Europe and their impact cannot be disregarded. It was not until the end of this period that any strong semblance of blending and uniformity developed among these different peoples in their style of art and architecture. By this time practically all the nations of Europe had struggled into existence and from the 11th century onwards new buildings gradually began to appear. It became increasingly evident that Western Europe was gradually awakening from her long sleep.

This fusion of the preceding five centuries finally resulted in the Romanesque style of architecture, the name indicating the principal influence in its evolution. Although this style had some characteristics common to all regions, it exhibited wide variations in the different Western European countries as well as within each country. Geographical position and the character of the inhabitants exercised a strong formative influence on Romanesque architecture in each respective country and determined many of its peculiarities. Apart from its Roman origin the Romanesque style was indebted to Byzantine art, composed of Greco-Roman and Oriental influences. Byzantine art, which was carried along the trade routes, was more pronounced in some sections than in others. The Italian cities of Venice and Ravenna, which were the connecting trade links between the East and West, were strongly influenced. The city of Venice is particularly rich in Byzantine architecture, while the Byzantine mosaic work in the churches of Ravenna is unrivalled. The Romanesque style of architecture flourished in Western Europe from the beginning of the 11th century until around the middle of the 12th century, when it was gradually supplanted by the Gothic style and the general use of the pointed arch. The Romanesque style, achieving its highest standards in the 12th century, possessed a striking barbaric vigor, particularly in the north, undoubtedly resulting from the times in which it developed. Vegetable and animal forms conventionally treated were the favorite ornament, which was often very roughly executed since craftsmanship was to a great extent at a low point.

The Christian Church was the principal source of education and culture. During this era the Papacy had great powers and influence, and rivalled or sometimes even controlled any existing form of civil government. Everywhere the Church predominated. This religious zeal and enthusiasm was mirrored in the many imposing cathedral churches and monastic buildings, which were really a more typical

outgrowth of this period than the fortified feudal castles. This same religious ardor led to the Crusades and the long warfare between the Christians of the West and the Mohammedans of the East had its effect on Western art. During the 11th century the monastic communities were remarkably developed and they played an important role in the life of the people of all countries, particularly in the country districts. Until around the middle of the 12th century, the science, art and letters of this period were controlled by the different religious orders, such as the Benedictines and the Cistercians. They wielded a great influence on architecture, many of the cathedrals, as well as the secular buildings, being the designs of monks and their pupils. Schools belonging to these monasteries trained the pupils for a full life of religious service, including both spiritual and temporal occupations. The plans for these monasteries reveal the numerous buildings found in one of these monastic communities. In addition to the church and sacristy, there were the dormitories, the refectory and kitchen, the infirmary or hospital, a granary, guest lodgings, a house for the abbot, a library, a scriptorium for writing and illuminating, all kinds of workshops for making furniture, metal and pottery wares, a prison and a court and numerous other buildings. They also had vegetable gardens, orchards and fish ponds. The monks were instrumental in developing new methods in agriculture, in fact they furnished an incentive to civilizing influences of all kinds.

Domestic architecture in the early Middle Ages in western Europe reflected the instability and insecurity of the times. The castles of the feudal lords and barons were strongly fortified, for the only relative security was behind thick walls. They were picturesque and imposing but cold and uncomfortable according to modern standards. The people chiefly lived in rural communities and were attached as serfs to the estate of some feudal lord. Their cottages were generally made of clay matted with straw and twigs. Western Europe changed a great deal in the hundred years between the 13th and 14th centuries. When the Gothic style, which was the glory of the Middle Ages, first began to develop, the monasteries and feudal castles were still the principal centers of learning and of power. However, in the ensuing one hundred and fifty years towns grew in number and in power. They became lively centers of trade. Commerce was expanded and the trade guilds were organized. The powers of the Church and the feudal lords gradually diminished as the burghers, merchants and citizens became more independent and prosperous. The nobles no longer lived a life of seclusion in their fortified castles. Many of them moved into the cities where they built imposing houses. The Gothic cathedral became the symbol of town solidarity. All the enthusiasm of a vigorous town life in which religious zeal and civic pride were interwoven found expression in the erection of magnificent buildings, both ecclesiastical and municipal. Architecture was the dominating form of art throughout the Gothic period, and it was principally employed in the service of the Church.

From the Middle Ages to the 19th century the development in furniture has been from the simple to the complex, from scarcity to plenty and from crudely made to skillfully wrought. Unfortunately, extant furniture from medieval times is exceedingly rare. We gain most of our knowledge about this furniture from il-luminated manuscripts, carved reliefs in wood, ivory or stone, and contemporary accounts and inventories. The powerful feudal lord, who usually owned several castles, took all his valuable possessions with him as he travelled from one castle to another. Chests were used to carry clothes, tapestries, fabrics, cushions, coverlets, small boxes and toilet articles and sometimes folding stools. Only crudely made large pieces, such as the long dining tables made of boards and placed on trestles, the beds, which were little more than wooden frames covered with curtains, and such built-in pieces as cupboards and benches were left in the castle. In this manner if a neighboring feudal lord paid an unexpected visit to the castle and pillaged it in the owner's absence there was little to tempt the unwelcome guest. Even when the times became secure the removal of personal furniture and furnishings from one castle to another continued. This is particularly interesting, for it reveals how limited the supply of such articles were as well as how costly.

Domestic furniture during the Gothic period was essentially confined to comparatively few pieces, which were of simple and crude construction. The furniture was solid and massive and severe in character. Ecclesiastical influence was evident in this medieval furniture, both in the severity of its form and in its decorative detail. The forms of the furniture were generally rectilinear with emphasis on the vertical. The use of curved lines was limited to the folding chair of curule form. In the northern countries the furniture was chiefly made of oak, a wood of great durability. Walnut was also used in France and other local woods were used in each country to some extent. The craftsman who made the furniture was completely influenced by the architecture that surrounded him. The decorative details for ornamenting the furniture were borrowed from the architecture. Carving was the favorite process for decorating the surface of the furniture. Foliage was much favored as a decorative motif in Gothic ornamentation. The plants were always selected from the native plant life and included vine leaves with grapes, maple leaves, parsley and cress leaves. Tracery work either solid or pierced was extensively employed by the wood carver in decorating Gothic furniture and was copied from the great tracery windows first developed in Gothic architecture. Panels with fenestrations, which also had their origin in architecture, were widely used on the façades of chests. Figure subjects, animals and birds employed in Gothic ornament were often treated in a humorous and exaggerated manner.

ENGLISH GOTHIC

The Gothic rooms in England, as seen in pictorial representations, were bare and were provided with only a few forms of furniture. The great hall was principally used for entertaining and for dining. It was generally furnished with a long table placed in front of a dossier, with chests, benches and forms comprising the other dining seats. A low side table for serving was generally placed on either side of the principal seat. A settle and perhaps a couple of chairs were found near the big fireplace. A cupboard of some variety or a dresser with open shelf space for the display of silver generally completed the furniture. Colorful fabrics were draped over the furniture and cushions were placed on the settle, stools and benches to provide a little comfort and some feeling of luxury. The walls were enlivened by rich wall hangings and handsome tapestries. Heavy draperies gave additional color and beauty and, more importantly, made the big room less drafty. The most important room was a combination dining and bedroom belonging to the lord and lady of the castle. It was chiefly furnished with a dining table, dossier, a table or chest for toilet articles, a tall cupboard, bed, stools and a prie-dieu.

The framework of medieval furniture was held together with mortise and tenon joints. In panelled pieces the panels were grooved into the framework. No glue was used in construction. The tenons were secured by square oak pegs which were driven through round holes into the joints. Woodwork fastened in this manner is referred to as joined. Hence the term *joyned* or *joynt* for stools and tables is constantly found in early inventories.

Early English furniture lacked the taste and artistic quality found in the contemporary furniture of France and Italy. Prior to the late 15th century furniture of any decorative quality was confined to the royal palaces, to the monasteries and to the castles of the nobility. However, from that time onwards furniture of a more decorative character was gradually found in simpler homes. This sudden advancement in domestic civilization dates from the termination of the civil war, known as the War of the Roses, with the victory of Henry Tudor in 1485, marking the end of feudalism in England. From this time domestic architecture was gradually developed. The feudal castle yielded to the Tudor country mansion and thought was given to the decoration of the interiors of these mansions. More furniture was made and the ornament was more elaborate and more finished in detail. Gradually the finer furniture, which had previously been imported from the Continent, was made in England. In the beginning these pieces were chiefly rather coarse reproductions of the foreign models. It was not until around the middle of the 16th century that furniture of a distinctive English character was produced in any quantity. The accession of Queen Elizabeth I in 1558, who was the last reigning member of the House of Tudor, marked the beginning of the Renaissance style in England and approximately corresponds with the development of a vernacular style of English cabinetwork.

The English furniture maker during the Gothic style borrowed his decorative motifs from contemporary Gothic architecture. Carving was by far the favorite method for decorating the surface of furniture. Tracery work, either solid or pierced, was constantly employed. The linen-fold motif, having a resemblance to linen arranged in narrow vertical folds, was apparently introduced in England by Flemish craftsmen. It was much favored for decorating the panels of furniture such as chairs and chests. The treatment of the motif was almost infinite and varied from the simple to the elaborate. In England it was generally treated in a rather simple manner, with the folds being ogee shape at top and bottom. Small panels of checker carving or carved spandrels were done above and below the lock plates. Carved geometrical network or honeycombing was also used. Other popular Gothic motifs included the Gothic trefoil, quatrefoil and cinquefoil, cusping, heraldic devices and a stylized floral motif having three or four lobes with a ball in the hollow center, known as the ball-flower. The dogtooth motif having four leaves grouped together in a conical manner and joined at the point, and the Tudor rose with its five open petals were both fashionable forms of ornament. Arcaded work and foliated and floral scrollwork were also used. Around 1530 there was an infiltration of Italian Renaissance motifs, such as wreathed medallion heads, and they were mingled with Gothic ornament in decorating the Gothic forms of furniture. These profile portraits in the Renaissance taste, which were very popular, were referred to by the English as Romayne medallions. In order to provide the cabinetwork with a touch of color, both painting and gilding were occasionally employed. Furniture was occasionally painted with heraldic devices and sacred subjects in bright colors. The painting, in tempera or wax, has long since disappeared. The iron lock plates and hinges were generally plain.

ARTICLES OF FURNITURE

Chairs   Until late in the 16th century chairs were relatively rare. The chair, during medieval times, was regarded as a symbol of authority and its use was restricted to the master of the house and to distinguished guests. The finest castles seldom had more than two chairs. Chests, forms, dossiers, settles, stools and benches were generally used for seats. The principal and typical English Gothic chair was made of oak and had a rectilinear, box-like form, with a high panelled back, sides and arms. It was notable for the solidity of its construction. The portion below the seat usually formed a box, the seat being hinged to give access to the box. During the Gothic period a few chairs of the curule form appeared in England, undoubtedly copied from Italian models.

Another variety of oak chair, found at an early date in England, was a three-legged turned wooden chair with a triangular wooden seat (FIGURE 263). (A chair of this variety has been used by the president of Harvard University when conferring degrees since the 18th century and is referred to as the Harvard chair.) This chair continued to be used in the succeeding Elizabethan style.

Stools   The joint or joined stool was the usual form of seating for all but the chief persons in a household. The stool was of trestle form and the deep underframing was keyed through the solid splayed end supports (21). Occasionally the underframing was boxed in to form a shallow chest (25).

Benches   The form or backless bench differed only from the stool in its greater length. Its primary function was to seat guests at the long dining table. Another type of bench also mounted on truss-end supports was provided with a back (28).

The dossier was the name given in England during the Gothic period to a wooden bench with a high back and canopy built in the wainscot. It was elaborately panelled and carved. The bench was used primarily as a seat for dining, generally holding four persons. It was also used as a day bed.

The settle was a long wooden bench having a high panelled back, sides and arms, designed to seat several persons. It was a massive piece of Gothic furniture and sometimes it was so heavy that it was almost unmovable. Generally the part between the seat and floor was solidly enclosed with panelling, the seat being hinged to form a chest. It was frequently placed before the fire, and with cushions added it was the nearest thing to comfort in the English Gothic home.

Beds   Until the 16th century the bed was simply a boarded box, completely surrounded by curtains. Cords were attached to the ceiling to hold the draperies; however, sometimes a light framework was constructed for that purpose. In the palaces and castles these draperies were sometimes made of rich fabrics. In the 16th century the bed began to assume the contour of the Elizabethan bed, having four wooden posts and a headboard. It is doubtful if the wooden tester was added until after the middle of the 16th century.

Prie-dieux   The Gothic bedroom generally contained a small prayer stand or prie-dieu. The term *prie-dieu* was not given to a prayer stand until the early part of the 17th century, at which time in France a small room or oratory was sometimes known by the same name. The form of the prie-dieu varied. Essentially it consisted of an upright vertical

15

portion supporting a narrow shelf serving as an arm rest or book rest and a flat portion close to the floor used for kneeling.

Tables

Tables during the Gothic period were primarily used for dining. Occasionally they were used as a serving table in the dining hall and as a dressing table in the bedroom. They varied in size and character according to their use. As a rule the table was of trestle construction and had a massive, oblong, removable top of oak resting upon solid end supports. Another variety of Gothic table was the low side table (24), having a heavy, fixed oblong top extending well over the underframing which was often enclosed to form a long, shallow cupboard. It rested on four massive supports or legs.

Writing Furniture

The desk, which was exceedingly rare in medieval times, combined the functions of a book rest and writing desk. In general the desk derived its form from the contour of the ecclesiastical lectern, being characterized by a sloping top to hold the book. Due to the invention of printing and the substitution of linen paper for parchment, the books were made smaller and the lectern type was no longer needed to support the large books. As a result, the craftsmen started to design portable desks with a sloping surface, which remained the characteristic form for desks in England throughout the 16th century.

Chests

During medieval times the domestic chest was the most important piece of furniture and served many purposes. It was used as a receptacle for storing clothes, wall hangings and other possessions, and as a travelling box for carrying these possessions on a journey. As an article of furniture, it was used as a seat, bed or table. The coffer was generally smaller in size and was strongly made for the safekeeping of valuables and documents. This distinction is not always observed, with the result the terms *coffer* and *chest* are frequently used interchangeably. The early English chest of the 13th century was crudely carved with tracery work. The chest during the 14th century was often carved with an arcade of decorated tracery while the chest in the 15th century was carved with an arcade of perpendicular tracery. Chests with carved linen-fold panels were popular about the middle of the 15th century. The tilting chest having deeds of combat or chivalry portrayed on the façade was characteristic of that era. The coffret or little strong box was used as a receptacle for deeds and small valuable possessions.

The hutch, which is derived from the French word *huche,* is defined as a domestic chest, box or coffer. In early England the name was applied to a household chest of very crude construction. The name was also usually given to a more decorative receptacle with the general contour of a chest, raised on supports or legs and having a fixed top, with one or more doors in front. Undoubtedly the hutch was used for different purposes, such as for storing clothes and other possessions. It is generally believed that the hutch of rough construction was used as a bin for storing grains and as a kneading trough.

Dressers

The dresser or dressoir (29) as a piece of furniture was in general use throughout the Middle Ages in France, the Netherlands and England. The word *dressoir* frequently appears in medieval inventories. The dresser occupied an important position in the medieval hall. It was chiefly intended to display the owner's fine plate, such as gold and silver cups and tankards. The dresser was essentially an open framework of shelves, a cupboard according to the medieval connotation of the word *cupboard*. On the Continent the dressoir often grew to towering heights, and according to contemporary records it was sometimes taken down and removed after the banquet. Apparently the medieval dresser was very colorful with its polychrome carvings and its magnificent hangings. Canopies were a feature on the more elaborate models. A later variety having a panelled back surmounted with a canopy, superimposed on a cupboard portion, gradually evolved into one of the principal varieties of the English hall and parlor cupboard. It seems that the dresser was also sometimes used as a sideboard or buffet, for an early record mentions that during the feasting there was sufficient plate so that it was not necessary to use any of the pieces on the dresser. In England the distinction between a cupboard and dresser was never very clearly made in early times.

Cupboards

Originally the term *cupboard* was used to describe an open framework or an open structure fitted with boards or shelves to hold cups. Around the second quarter of the 16th century the term began to acquire its modern meaning and was used to describe a piece of furniture of similar structure fitted with shelves and enclosed with doors, being either fixed or movable. However, the term was still often applied to designate a structure formed of superimposed shelves. The term *cupboard* has a fairly comprehensive meaning and is generally used to describe a number of different pieces of furniture which, in the majority of examples, are entirely enclosed with doors and are fitted with shelves to hold dishes, linen, food and clothes.

During the Gothic period in England a large cupboard enclosed with doors and having shelves, being movable or built in the wall, was commonly called an ambry. The word *ambry,* also spelled aumbry, was the English equivalent of the French word armoire, which was used to describe a large cupboard or wardrobe. In a general sense it was used as a repository for arms and other possessions, and was especially used as a place for keeping food. The ambry was rectilinear in form and it was usually designed with more than one door (27). The term was also chiefly used to describe a cupboard or closed recess in a wall for books and for ceremonial vessels belonging to the Church. A compartment of a cupboard was also occasionally called an ambry.

In the second half of the 15th century cupboards with ambries were mentioned in inventories, which, it seems reasonable to assume, implied that part of the open shelves was provided with doors. It appears that early in the reign of Henry VIII the term *cupboard* was given to what had been previously called an ambry and that around the end of the 16th century the terms *ambries, cupboards* and *presses* were more or less interchangeable.

The food cupboard (22) with the front pierced for ventilation of the contents was one of the most important of the few varieties of domestic furniture in use toward the end of the medieval period. It was known as a livery cupboard since it is believed to have contained the allowance of food, wine and candles which were each night delivered (livré) to the members of a household, guests and servants.

The press, which was a cupboard with solid doors, was fitted with either shelves for linen or pegs for clothes. It was found only in the extremely wealthy homes after the middle of the 16th century. It was a variety of an ambry.

During medieval times the English called the small room fitted for the reception of clothes and other possessions a wardrobe or garderobe. It adjoined the private combination dining and bedroom apartment on the first floor. It also served as a dressing room.

FRENCH GOTHIC

From the 12th to the 14th centuries France assumed a leading role in the development of western Europe, particularly during the reigns of Louis Augustus, 1180–1223, and Louis IX or Saint Louis, 1226–1270. Gothic architecture was purely a native growth. It originated in Ile de France, an old province in northern France with Paris as its capital, shortly after the middle of the 12th century. From northern France it spread over all of western Europe and reached its acme of perfection in the 14th century. When France had exhausted all her creative ideas for Gothic art she turned to Italy for new inspiration. This blending of Italian and French art was to continue for three centuries. The first fusion occurred late in the 15th and early 16th centuries when the elements in the French Flamboyant Gothic style with its flowing, flame-like lines and the Early Renaissance style of northern Italy were brought together. This finally resulted in the emergence of the Early Renaissance in France or the François I style, 1515–1547. It is generally accepted that the finest examples of Gothic furniture were made in France. French carving was praiseworthy for the precise clean-cut detail which gave it a flat and finished effect. Foliage, especially vine leaves and grapes, tracery and arcaded work were constantly employed. The fleur-de-lis, the Gothic trefoil and cinquefoil, rosettes, real and fantastic birds and animals, grotesque figures were included among their favorite decorative motifs. Human figures were rarely used for decorative purposes on furniture. Polychromy was occasionally used to accent the delicate richness of the tracery designs. Metal mountings, hasps and lock cases were veritable works of art. Exquisite motifs having their origin in Gothic architecture, imaginary animals and birds and pictorial scenes, all of jewel-like quality, were worked on the metal fittings. France also excelled in the art of tapestry weaving, which was perfected during the 14th century at Arras and Paris, the great tapestry centers. The technique of tapestry weaving displayed in French Gothic tapestries has never been surpassed.

ARTICLES OF FURNITURE

Chairs Chairs were rare during the Gothic period in France. The typical French armchair had a rectilinear, box-like form with a high panelled back and arms. The portion below the seat was usually enclosed to form a coffer, the seat being hinged to give access to the box (FIGURES 19, 20). The French also had the curule or folding variety of chair resembling a camp stool with its crossed legs, and it was undoubtedly of Roman inspiration.

Stools The French stool or escabeau or escabelle was the most common of all seats. It was generally of trestle form with two solid end supports. It was also called a placet.

Benches The French bench or banc was usually designed with a back, sometimes with a canopy, and was known as a banc à dos and a banc à ciel respectively.

The French term *forme* was given to a long narrow bench designed without arms or a back. At a much later time this particular type of French bench when upholstered was called a banquette.

The bancelle was a long and narrow bench. Essentially it was a smaller variety of a banc. It was generally designed with a low back and side pieces, or simply with side pieces. The distinction between a banc and bancelle is difficult to observe. Generally the term *bancelle* was reserved for a bench of lighter appearance.

The archebanc or coffre-bench was the equivalent of the English settle. It was a massive wooden bench with a back and arms, designed to seat several persons. The portion between the seat and the floor was enclosed to form a coffre.

Beds The French bed until the end of the 15th century was crudely constructed and was completely covered by draperies. The dossier or headboard and the tester or canopy were generally made of fabric.

Tables Tables were primarily used for dining in medieval times. The table was usually of trestle construction, having a removable top resting on trestle supports. The trestles were made of wood or of iron or brass and frequently folded. The characteristic dining table in the large hall was long and narrow, since only one side was used for dining while the other side was reserved for the serving of food. When it was necessary to increase the size of the dining table another similar table was placed at a right angle to it. If this was not large enough

19

a third table was placed on the opposite end making a U-shaped arrangement. Many of the earliest tables were of the folding type and it seems that they evolved from the table of trestle form (26).

An early form of dressing table was known as a demoiselle à atourner. It was principally designed with a round table top supporting a short columnar shaft, surmounted with a carved feminine head upon which the coiffure was placed. Essentially it was an early form of a wig-stand.

Chests   The French chest or coffre of the 13th century was crudely made of thick boards held together by braces of wrought iron which covered the surface of the chest with scrollwork. The wood was generally painted red, or covered with hide or painted canvas, providing a contrast for the ironwork. By the 14th century the coffre was decorated with carving, the carved detail being borrowed from Gothic architectural motifs (23). The iron mountings, such as the hasp and case of the lock, were remarkable for their minute detail and artistic quality.

Originally the bahut was a rather shallow oblong box with a hinged lid and was attached to a coffre or a chest. The combined piece was called a coffre à bahut and was used in travelling, the immediate articles needed for the trip being placed in the bahut. Later the term *bahut* was applied to a coffre with an arched or convex lid used in travelling and finally to any coffre.

Buffets   The buffet, which is of French origin, varied greatly in design, and it appears that the name was given to almost any dining room piece provided with one or more flat spaces or shelves, such as a sideboard or a dressoir (29), for holding valuable silver and other similar pieces necessary in the dining service. The buffet was partly or completely opened or closed. An early form of French buffet was designed with an oblong shallow horizontal body fitted with doors, mounted on a stand having a low display shelf and a panelled back.

Crédences   Originally the crédence or crédence table was a small side table, placed near the dining table in the palaces of royal or noble families. The food prior to serving was placed on this table for tasting to guard against poisoning. This custom originated in Italy where the tasting of the food and drink for poisons was done by an official of the household called the credentarius. In France both the ceremony and table were called crédence, and in Italy, credenza. After the need for the ceremony had disappeared the name still survived. The table developed a back and several shelves for the display of silver and from the 14th century it was made in several different forms. During the Renaissance the crédence developed into an elaborate variety of buffet, principally used to display valuable silver. From the 15th century the characteristic variety (31) was designed with a massive oblong horizontal upper section which was generally panelled and richly carved and was usually fitted with one or more doors. It was mounted on an open stand usually having a panelled back and a carved frieze resting on four heavy carved supports which were secured to a display shelf close to the floor (31). The traceried iron mounts were of lace-like quality and were often backed with red velvet in order to enhance the detail work of the delicate traceries. The rings securing the bolts were large and beautifully executed. The term *credence* in England was used only as an ecclesiastical term to describe a small altar table holding the bread and the wine.

Cupboards   The armoire or French domestic cupboard in the Gothic period was rectilinear in form and was either movable (30) or built in the wainscoting. Originally the armoire served as a repository for arms, and in a general sense it was used to store all kinds of household possessions and supplies. Essentially the contemporary English equivalent piece of furniture was the ambry.

ITALIAN GOTHIC

The Gothic style, introduced in Italy in the 13th century from France, never flourished to the same degree in Italy as it did in the other European countries. Italy combined the Gothic style with her then flourishing Lombard, Tuscan and Byzantine-Romanesque styles. Probably the most notable Gothic buildings were the town halls of Florence and Siena and the fanciful Gothic Venetian palaces. Antique culture was so much a heritage of the Italian people that the Gothic style declined first in Italy. By the end of the 14th century Renaissance motifs were sometimes found mingled with Gothic ornament on Gothic or Romanesque forms. It was evident that Italy was preparing early for the Renaissance and that her memories of classic architecture had impaired her development of the Gothic style. The Italians of the Renaissance, in particular the writer Vasari, were the first to apply the name *Gothic* derisively to this style of architecture, which was the only Western style that did not look into the classic traditions of the past to achieve

its perfection. They regarded the style as belonging to the barbarous tribes from the north and as being introduced into Italy by the descendants of the Goths who had ravaged the Roman Empire.

The 13th century in Italy was an age of simplicity. The dwellings and furniture were simple and relatively crude. However, from the 14th century this frugality gradually yielded to sumptuousness and by the 16th century the Italians achieved a standard of magnificence only duplicated in France in the 17th and 18th centuries under the Bourbon kings. Individuality of expression received an early impetus in Italy due to the social and political life of the democratic communes and free towns. The Italians benefited from extensive trade relations which were a deadly foe to feudalism and which brought great wealth to Italy. As early as the 14th century the Italian nobleman enjoyed a life of domestic comfort and refinement far in advance of the noblemen living in the northern countries. He found time for artistic and intellectual pursuits. The humanistic influence was apparent in literature by the 14th century. However, it was not until the following century that the influence of antique culture was evident in architecture and in furniture. The city of Florence even in medieval times was an important art center. Contemporary literature around 1280 mentions her prosperity and refinement. Venice was in her glory during the Middle Ages when her ships controlled the richest trade routes in the world. Venetian noblemen during the 14th century lived in fanciful Gothic palaces built along the canals, and contemporary records tell about their furnishings. Fine goldsmith work, paintings on wooden panels, drawings, bronze medals, remains of antique sculpture and manuscripts were all recorded. The social and domestic life in northern Italy was far less developed. Probably Siena, after Venice, had the finest palaces for that period, and they were furnished with some of the best examples of Italian Gothic furniture. Rome and Naples contributed little during this period to the development of a more gracious and worldly manner of living.

The interior of an Italian 14th century palace as compared to the interior of a Renaissance or a Baroque palace was bare and ascetic. The furniture was limited to a few pieces which were simple in form and substantially made. Almost all of the furniture was found in the living room which generally had a beamed ceiling, rough plaster walls and a tiled floor. The huge hooded chimneypiece was probably the most prominent feature in the living room, and with its friendly warmth and soft light reflected from the burning logs was the natural center for the family grouping. The living room was generally furnished with one or more cassone, a few chairs, benches and stools, a long table and sometimes a cupboard. The bed was in a smaller adjoining apartment. The walls of these principal rooms were often colorful and gay with their tempera frescoes depicting wall hangings and draperies. One of the most interesting features of Italian furniture is the emphasis the Italians placed on horizontal line effects both in the form of furniture and in the composition of its decoration instead of the emphasis on vertical line effects which is so characteristic of Gothic art. For decorating the surface of furniture the Italians used intarsia, which is a kind of inlay work, pastiglia, gilding, painting and carving. The painted decoration often depicted stories from mythology, romantic scenes and other similar subjects. The Florentine lily was a favorite floral motif. Tracery work was much used when the surface of the furniture was enriched with carved detail. Metal mountings were occasionally used for decorative purposes such as the scrolled brass bands sometimes found on the cassone.

ARTICLES OF FURNITURE

Chairs   Chairs were relatively few in Italian medieval times. Pictorial representations of that era depict wall benches with panelled backs and chairs of rectangular form without arms and having rush seats. The first important armchair for domestic use was of ancient Roman curule form or a folding chair of X-form. It was similar in construction to a camp stool with curved legs and was designed in two principal varieties, namely the dantesca and the savonarola. The dantesca had two front and two rear supports of curule or curved X-form.

The front and rear lower supports were secured on each side by runner feet and the upper supports by down-curving arms. The seat and back panel were of leather and were stretched between the supports. The savonarola consisted of about seven serpentine X-shaped staves instead of a single front and rear support. The lower staves were secured with runner feet while the upper staves or supports were secured by straight arms. It had a flat-arched back rail made of wood which was joined to the rear ends of the arms. The narrow seat was made of slats and was placed slightly above the intersection of the supports. A loose cushion was usually placed on the seat. The early examples of the savonarola and dantesca were plain and relatively crude. They were not handsomely decorated until toward the end of the 15th century (FIGURES 32, 33).

Beds
The bed before the Renaissance as depicted in representations generally was designed with a rectangular headboard and footboard, decorated with intarsia work, painting or small rectangular panelling, and was enclosed to the base. The bed was on a dais which had a hinged top that opened to reveal compartments for storage purposes.

Tables
The majority of tables were simply made of long boards laid on trestles.

Chests
The cassone, which is a form of chest, was the most important piece of Italian domestic furniture and served many purposes. It was used as a receptacle for clothes and for other possessions and with the addition of pillows it served as a seat and even as a bed. The cassone differed from the characteristic chest in that it was generally longer and not as high and its decoration also showed a more horizontal composition. The surface of the cassone during the 14th century was usually enriched with painted decoration or with intarsia or pastiglia work. The more elaborate decoration was always found on the façade of the cassone, with the sides and top more simply decorated. The earliest and finest cassoni were generally enriched with pastiglia work, which is a kind of plaster composition worked in low relief and usually gilded and occasionally painted. Sometimes the façade of the cassone was decorated with pastiglia panels of figures depicting stories from mythology. Frequently the façade of the cassone was ornamented with a beautiful painted panel inserted in a frame of pastiglia. The painted panels were often done by celebrated painters. In the northern part of Italy they also made chests elaborately carved with Gothic tracery, which strongly resembled those made on the other side of the Alps.

Cupboards
The principal domestic cupboard was built into the thick walls of the different rooms and was either with or without cupboard doors. It is generally believed that the only early movable cupboard was the sacristy cupboard. It was often made in two sections, both the upper and lower sections being fitted with cupboard doors.

CHAPTER THREE

ITALIAN

EARLY RENAISSANCE

The Renaissance, which literally means a rebirth, is a widespread movement of complex character that had its inception in Italy in the 14th century. The scope of the Renaissance is of such magnitude that it is not possible to define it in a few words. Various phrases are used to describe it and many suggest some of its phases. At least two general aspects of the Renaissance are apparent which affect its art expression. One is the discovery of man as an individual and a realization of the beauty that surrounds him in his temporal existence and the other is the discovery of the classic past. This interest in mankind on earth or humanism was divergent from the medieval point of view which stressed the future life. Individualism was greatly stimulated by the study of classic literature, which was the earliest manifestation of the new energy that was to dominate all fields relating to the intellect and to the arts and sci-

ences in the 15th century. This new approach toward life, which stressed the development of the individual, resulted in a greater freedom of thought and a natural curiosity about man and the world in which he lives. As a result of this aroused interest an era of scientific research, inventions and voyages of discovery was inaugurated. These voyages of discovery led to colonizing enterprises and expansion of trade, resulting in an ever-increasing wealth, which was reflected in the continuous growth of towns and industry. Advances were made in astronomy and geography, and movable type and paper were introduced in connection with the invention of the printing press.

Late in the 14th century the Italians discovered their classic past. The Italians realized that the Roman remains of sculpture and architecture that lay everywhere about them were their own national art, recalling the glory and achievements of their people in ancient times. Instinctively and deliberately the Italians returned to this ancient Roman culture as the only acceptable source of civilization. From around the end of the 14th century examples of ancient Roman sculpture and architecture found in Rome and in other cities were zealously scrutinized and studied by scholars and artists. The outstanding feature of this revived interest in classic architecture was the use of the classic Roman Orders which were again reintroduced, having been in abeyance for almost one thousand years. In the beginning the architects only borrowed classical details from the antique and they were found on buildings constructed on Romanesque or Gothic plans, for it was not possible to assimilate everything immediately. The transition from medieval to Renaissance expression in architecture is seen in the dome of the Tuscan Gothic cathedral at Florence, which was the first great architectural work of the Renaissance. It was designed by Filippo Brunelleschi, 1377–1446, who was the first architect to convey the spirit of classic art in his work. Essentially the 15th century, which is generally referred to as the Early Renaissance, was an intellectual age of preparation and experimentation. Artists and craftsmen in every branch of art began to experiment with classic culture. It was this spirit of adventure and new vitality in art that marked the break with the Middle Ages. This great movement in art began in Florence early in the 15th century. And during this century sculpture, architecture, painting, furniture and the other decorative arts were transformed by an overwhelming enthusiasm for classic culture. Perfection in all the arts was achieved in the High Renaissance of the early 16th century.

Florence, the cradle of the Renaissance, was the dominating influence in all the arts during the 15th century. The Medici family were largely responsible for her enviable position. First Cosimo de Medici laid the foundation for the development of Early Renaissance culture, and he was succeeded in 1464 by Lorenzo the Magnificent. Even after that family rose to high ecclesiastical positions in the papal court at Rome and the art center of the Renaissance moved to Rome, the city of Florence maintained a high standard and continued to exert considerable influence throughout the entire Renaissance. Her work was still widely emulated in many of the leading Italian art centers. By the end of the 15th century Florence had built numerous fine churches, many stately town palaces and country villas, complete with enchanting gardens, statuary, fountains and aviaries. Lorenzo the Magnificent encouraged all branches of art. He attracted to his court illustrious painters, sculptors, architects and scholars. These distinguished men of art and letters met and mingled in the society of noblemen, popes and tyrants. The fine relationship or bond existing between patron, artist and humanist accounted for many of the great Renaissance achievements. Proud and prosperous Venice, which was the most powerful state in Italy during the 15th century, was second only to Florence in importance as an art center. Venice, whose trade connections linked her closely with the colorful Near East, was later than the other earlier art centers in embracing the Renaissance styles. When she did develop the new style, it was imbued with a singular spirit of gaiety, charm and splendor. The Houses of Ferrara, Mantua and Urbino all excelled at this time in gracious and refined social standards. Of these three Ferrara became the most renowned center of art and learning. The papacy, which dominated the culture at Rome, first began to devote time to art and culture around the middle of the 15th century under Pope Nicholas V, who was one of the great humanists of the 15th century. He founded the Vatican library for which he collected about five thousand volumes and also established the first tapestry atelier in Rome.

The Renaissance in Italy was an age of pomp and pageantry. It was colorful, extravant and spectacular. The pageantry of festivals, the silks and velvet costumes and gold jewelry of the citizens, the shining armor of the soldiers and the bright colored silk banners provided a never-ending display of spectacle and color. Great splendor and magnificence were exemplified in the furnishings of the palaces, which were rich in masterpieces of sculpture, paintings and tapestries. These palaces were furnished with the finest of Italian walnut furniture, remarkable for its finished craftsmanship. Draperies and cushions were made of figured cut silk velvets, brocaded satins and embroidered silks. Additional richness and elegance were provided by the carved and gilded chandeliers and mirrors, beautifully wrought gold and silver plate, the finest of linens, exquisite Venetian point laces, delicate Venetian glass vessels and colorful Della Robbia plaques and majolica plates. The floors in the great hall and principal apartments were sometimes covered with bright and finely woven Oriental carpets. The culmination of all this brilliance and splendor was found in Venice. Only the Romans and the French during the 17th and 18th centuries ever achieved such elegance and magnificence. The principal rooms and the great hall in these Early Renaissance palaces were planned according to the principles of Roman classic architecture and were remarkable for their richness. Sometimes the walls were decorated with pilasters supporting gilded and polychromed cornices. Other walls were panelled with a wainscoting of intarsia above which were frescoes and tapestries. Entire walls were sometimes covered with colorful frescoes, depicting landscapes with villas and towns in the distance and terraces with beautiful gardens. In some Venetian palaces the state apartments and the great hall had panelled walls of different colored marbles. During the Early Renaissance the beamed ceilings became more refined and were enriched with painted decoration in gold and in colors. Coffered and panelled ceilings were also developed and were praiseworthy for their elegance and richness.

In order to design furniture successfully in the new classic manner the cabinetmaker had to understand and also had to know how to apply the principles of classic architecture to his work. It was not until about the middle of the 15th century that domestic furniture designed in the new classic style came into general use and then it was found only in the princely palaces. Practically all of the fine furniture was made of walnut and was distinctive for its imposing and dignified character. It was massive and essentially rectilinear in form with emphasis on the horizontal effect. Occasionally curved lines were used, such as in the dantesca and savonarola chairs. Architectural detail, such as pediments, pilasters, cornices and moldings, borrowed from classic architecture, were incorporated into the designs for furniture. Due to the desire for luxury and comfort, new forms were gradually introduced in cabinetwork.

However, in comparison with the later 18th century standards the number of pieces in the different categories were still very limited and offered little comfort.

The study of Renaissance furniture begins with Tuscany whose capital was Florence. Her furniture designs, which were distinguished by simplicity, dignity and reticence of line, became the models which later art centers tried to emulate. This early Renaissance furniture was notable for its purity of line and fine classic proportions and for its sparing but effective use of carving, which was sometimes combined with delicate designs of intarsia or enhanced with gilding and color. Equally praiseworthy was the classic purity of its decorative motifs and the minuteness of its detail. When carving was used to enrich the surface of furniture it was generally executed in low relief and gave a flat effect. The carved decoration was remarkable for its graceful delicacy and for the fineness of its composition. Carving in high relief did not appear until the 16th century. The preference for intarsia or inlay work to carving encouraged the designing of furniture with large smooth surfaces for the inlay work and with a certain simplicity which would not detract from the intarsia.

Intarsia or inlay work in multicolored woods was one of Italy's great artistic achievements. Its finest period was from about 1475 to 1525. It is generally accepted that intarsia was first developed in Siena. In the most elaborate specimens of intarsia the designs were composed of landscapes, interiors of rooms, garden scenes, human figures, fanciful arabesques and other similar subjects. It was extensively employed on the panels of choir stalls, on the wainscoting of principal rooms and in a more limited manner on domestic furniture. It was also worked in minute and delicate bandings on furniture. Intarsia enjoyed its greatest popularity in the late 15th and early 16th centuries, since carving was the preferred method for decorating the surface of furniture in the 16th century. However, intarsia continued to be used to some extent throughout the 16th century. Another fashionable form of inlay work used in the 15th century was called certosina work. It consisted of an intricate inlaid decoration of geometrical and conventionalized designs made of minute pieces of ivory or bone. Venice is often credited with its origin because its designs are strongly tinged with Near Eastern influence. It seems that ivory and precious woods were frequently used at Cairo and Damascus for inlay work on tables, screens and similar articles as early as the third quarter of the 14th century. Undoubtedly articles having this so-called Damascus work were imported into Italy as a result of her growing trade with the Near East. The influence of these wares is patent on furniture inlaid with certosina work. This unusual style of inlay work is especially identified with the Carthusian Monasteries (Certose) of Lombardy. Pastiglia work as a form of decoration is chiefly identified with the 15th century, although the process continued to be used for the next two centuries. Painting and gilding were also used in the decoration of furniture. Moldings employed on Early Renaissance furniture were few and modest and were carved with classic repetitive motifs, such as the egg and dart or guilloche. During the High Renaissance moldings became more prominent and were often vigorously carved, and in the Late Renaissance the furniture was characterized by prominent, boldly carved projecting moldings. Turning was occasionally employed in the 15th century, although it was not until the following century that its decorative value was appreciated to any great extent. Escutcheons or key-plates employed on furniture were beautifully wrought of iron or bronze.

During the Renaissance the entire alphabet of classic ornament was employed by the Italians. Repetitive running motifs, which were a legacy of ancient architecture, were much in evidence, such as the guilloche, egg and dart and bead and leaf. Included among the favorite decorative motifs were the acanthus leaf, the anthemion, all forms of flowers, fruit and foliage, arabesques, rosettes, roundels, scrolls, vase forms, medallions, swags or festoons, paterae, lozenges, cartouches, cornucopiae, banderoles, candelabra and grotesques. Cherubs, cupids, atlantes, caryatids, terms, masks, dolphins, chimeras, satyrs, human and animal figures were all included among the innumerable classic motifs employed in their style of ornament. Religious subjects, historical, mythological and allegorical stories, as well as garden scenes and marriage processions, were all favorite decorative themes for the painter and for the carver. Mythological stories though pagan in sentiment were in accordance with the taste of the age. Scenes depicted from mythology were kept within the bounds of refinement and were neither coarse nor sensual.

HIGH RENAISSANCE

The first three or four decades of the 16th century is the most celebrated period of Italian art and one of the great periods of all times. It was the time of Leonardo da Vinci, Michelangelo, Raphael, Titian and a host of other artists of equal renown. During this golden age, which is called the High Renaissance, architecture, painting, sculpture and the decorative arts achieved their highest degree of perfection. In brief, this period represented the culmination of the art movement begun in the 15th century. The interiors of the palaces were magnificent and splendid, and the furniture was as elegant and dignified as the architectural background to which it was closely related. The cabinetmaker endeavored to achieve perfection in his workmanship. The simplicity and ecclesiastical dignity of the Early Renaissance were still apparent in furniture design, with the utmost care expended on the refinement of detail. Proportions were further perfected. The ornament, moldings and such architectural detail as pilasters and cornices were notable for the classic purity of their composition. Carving, which was the preferred method for decorating the surface of furniture during the High Renaissance, was richly modelled and revealed a remarkable delicacy in its composition. Intarsia, pastiglia and painting were all of the most finished workmanship. Motifs designed in a Raphaelesque manner, such as delicate arabesques, playful grotesques and other fanciful forms, were especially charming and pleasing. The artistic reserve displayed in the furniture design of this period is one of its most striking features.

Not since the days of the Roman Empire had Italy enjoyed such great prosperity as she did early in the 16th century. She was also rich in fine cities, patrician families and illustrious artists and men of letters. Life was joyous, pleasurable and beautiful and not until the invaders were at the gates of Rome was she aware of any impending disaster. The artistic energies of Florence during this period contributed much to the development of the brilliant court at Milan and later at Rome. The art of Milan and Lombardy achieved its highest standards shortly after the death of Lorenzo the Magnificent, when Lombardy became the leading art center. The splendid court of Lodovico il Moro, Duke of Milan, a man of letters and great wealth, and his duchess, Beatrice d'Este, attracted the greatest of contemporary artists. This glorious page in the art history of Milan was brought to a sudden end by the French invasion shortly after the death of Beatrice d'Este in 1497. Artists and men of letters seeking more fruitful art centers found their way to the courts of Mantua and Ferrara and later of Rome. The art center of Mantua was greatly stimulated by Isabella d'Este, Duchess of Mantua, who is often called the most illustrious and aristocratic lady of the Renaissance. She was a great patroness of the arts and her palace with its rare tapestries, paintings, sculptures and manuscripts was one of the most famous of the High Renaissance. Ferrara, which was the court of the Este dukes, had long been, like Mantua, a leading center for culture and aristocratic social life. The marriage of Alfonso d'Este to Lucrezia Borgia brought great renown to this art center, for Lucrezia, an ardent patroness of the arts and a woman of considerable charm, lured many outstanding artists to her court. Worldly Venice was more magnificent and sensuous during the first half of the 16th century than ever before. Her most brilliant contributions to Renaissance art were made at this time. Luxury and splendor became the Venetians and they were never stifled by it. Contemporary records tell us that the Venetian interiors were the richest in all Italy and that they were in harmony with the magnificent architecture of the exterior. Venetian fêtes and festivals attracted patricians from all parts of Italy.

The art of the High Renaissance culminated in Rome. Gradually, after the decline of Florence and Milan as art centers, Rome became the mecca for the great artists. As her appreciation for art and for the humanities grew she became more worldly and intensified her pursuit of culture, and with her increasing wealth, she was in a position to attract great masters. Michelangelo, Raphael and scores of others of equal renown were drawn to her court. A marked change became increasingly evident in her social life toward the end of the 15th century. Wealthy popes, cardinals, princes and aristocratic families began to build imposing palaces and villas in Rome and to accumulate fabulous works of art. These palaces, which were literally storehouses of paintings, tapestries, antique and modern sculpture, manuscripts, gold plate and furniture, reflected the worldly grandeur of the High Renaissance. Unfortunately all this brilliance was brought to a sudden halt in 1527 when Rome was sacked by the Imperial Army, a horde of Germans and Spaniards thirsty for plunder, who ravaged the city for eight days. Of all the great masters who were in Rome during the early years of the 16th century, Michelangelo especially stands out for he inaugurated a new school of art that marked the beginning of the Baroque. He enriched art with unsuspected new effects but his style was pernicious to art and ultimately led to the Baroque. Later artists who did not possess the spirit or the lofty conceptions of a Michelangelo could not successfully imitate his heroic forms. Michelangelo's influence became evident in art from the latter half of the 16th century. Sculptors tried to effect his style in heroic forms and painters covered vast walls with frescoes of boldly painted forms but they were unable to capture his skill and mastery of the human figure.

The different art centers of the High Renaissance showed strong individual tastes in their style of architecture and ornament which was reflected in their furniture designs. The designs for Florentine or Tuscan furniture reflected a classic purity and a pedantic correctness. The furniture was dignified and restrained and revealed a less frequent use of ornament, especially of figures, such as caryatids, grotesques and human figures. The furniture of Siena, which was also in the province of Tuscany, was simple and severe in form and was distinctive for its rich and dignified simplicity. During the first half of the 16th century the furniture of Ferrara and Mantua was influenced by Venetian art. Especially favored were decorative pilasters and panels with arabesques and pleasing grotesques. In the second half of the century the ornament reflected the influence of Michelangelo and Sansovino. Their furniture designs always revealed a graceful elegance. Venetian furniture offers an interesting contrast to Florentine furniture, for while the latter was serious and correct the former was more rich and graceful. The Venetians displayed a taste for painted and gilded furniture with fanciful designs in low relief. However, after Sansovino's arrival from Rome in 1527, furni-

ture in natural wood richly carved in high relief and slightly touched with gilt became the vogue. The carved decoration included such favorite motifs as pleasing grotesques, cherubs or putti, scrolls and arabesques composed of foliage, executed with a graceful rhythm. The furniture of Liguria, which displayed intricate and elaborate carved decoration, was similar to contemporary French designs. A close artistic bond existed between northern Italy and France which resulted in a frequent exchange of influence. In fact in Piedmont and Savoy the Gothic traditions were retained as late as the 16th century. The furniture of Rome, which was ponderous and massive, was influenced at first by Tuscan designs and the art work of Raphael and later by her own antique ruins. Even her characteristic cassone resembled an ancient sarcophagus in form. The furniture, which was distinctive for its grandeur and bronze-like finish, displayed vigorously carved moldings and decorative motifs, the latter consisting chiefly of human figures, caryatids and grotesques. Furniture made at Urbino, Bologna, Verona, Naples, as well as other art centers during the High Renaissance, all manifested some individual character. The majority of the art centers displayed more homogeneity in their furniture designs after the middle of the 16th century. This was essentially due to the fact that Rome became the center for developing and disseminating styles in architecture, furniture and the other arts during the Late Renaissance.

LATE RENAISSANCE

Certain historical events hastened the cultural decline in Italy. The Spanish victory at the battle of Pavia in 1525 marked the beginning of Spanish domination in Italy, and, although hardly noticeable at first, by the middle of the 16th century the Spanish domination had a telling effect on the fine intellectual zest of the Italians which had made the Early and High Renaissance in Italy such a brilliant and creative period. The spontaneity, vitality and aesthetic inventiveness expressed with such striking originality in Italian art was stifled by the pomp and stilted grandeur of the Spanish nobles who came to live in Italy. Only Venice was free from the influence of Spain and the Papacy who directed the course of art for this era. She still maintained the worldly grandeur and brilliance of the High Renaissance. Shortly after Charles V was crowned Emperor of Rome in 1530 the Papacy displayed renewed strength and vigor and continued to increase in power. Rich papal families and cardinals tried to outrival each other in the splendor of their palaces. Rome became second only to Venice in the extravagance of her fêtes and festivals. However, it was not until about the last two decades of the 16th century that Rome had sufficient wealth to begin to build those sumptuous and imposing palaces for her papal nobility, such as the Palazzo Borghese and the Palazzo Colonna. During the Late Renaissance Genoa became very prosperous due to her alliance with Spain and she built many fine palaces and filled them with costly furnishings. Enormous country villas and estates were built in the environs of Rome, Florence, Genoa and in various parts of Italy during the second half of the 16th century. Many of these villas adhered to the Palladian school of architecture with its emphasis on correctness of proportions, giving the work a decided academic flavor. The for-

mality and restraint in the exterior architectural designs were also mirrored in the interior decoration. Lofty ceilings and vast wall spaces gave the interior of these palaces a stateliness that was an admirable background for formal society, which in all probability explains their popularity at a later date in Georgian England. The walls were often covered with frescoes sometimes painted en grisaille with elaborate architectural details of pilasters and cornices. Stucco decoration was much favored and rich decorative effects were often achieved in this medium. Ceilings molded in gilt and painted stucco were often of indescribable richness.

During the Late Renaissance, as in the preceding periods, architecture strongly influenced the furniture designs to which it was closely allied. The influence of the architectural designs and paintings of Michelangelo was evident in the furniture designs from around the middle of the 16th century. Michelangelo's love of figures, his skill in creating a race of supermen and his complete mastery of the naked figure, as portrayed in the paintings of the ceiling of the Sistine chapel, inspired the cabinetmaker to decorate the furniture with carved human figures. And however debatable was the taste exhibited in some of these carved decorations, the quality of the workmanship was of a high standard. The exaggerated scale and some weak architectural features used by Michelangelo in his work is regarded as having led architecture and furniture into the ways of the Baroque. Running parallel with the taste developed by the followers of Michelangelo was the work of the architect Andrea Palladio, 1518–1580. His designs, which were executed with scholarly accurateness, adhered to the classic proportions of the buildings of ancient Rome. His work, which was stamped with formality and restraint, was notable for its stateliness, simplicity of line and fine proportions. Italian cabinetwork of the Late Renaissance influenced by Palladio was more in accordance with fine classic tradition. It was characterized by a more sparing and concentrated use of ornament and by undecorated moldings and heavy bases.

Although the furniture of the Late Renaissance displayed many excellent qualities of design, the fine classic proportions and the classic purity of ornament of the High Renaissance were very often overlooked. Carving in high relief was the preferred method for decorating furniture, and occasionally touches of gold would be added to further enhance the carving which was of a sculpturesque and florid character. Practically all of the furniture was marked by an excessive use of carving. Human figures of a sculpturesque quality, grotesques of a less pleasing design, and boldly modelled caryatids were all favorite subjects for the carver. The stiles, such as on cabinets, were often decorated with several tiers of figures carved in the round. Although all the Renaissance motifs were used there was a marked preference for heraldic devices and coats-of-arms, for banderoles and cartouches, as well as for human figures, masks, grotesques and caryatids. Generally the ornament was of an increased scale and treated in a heavily ornate manner. The influence of Michelangelo was evident in the bold and heavy moldings, which were usually elaborately carved and often of an exaggerated scale. The taste for elaborate and pretentious furniture found an appropriate outlet in pietra dura, a form of inlay work, composed of cut and polished semi-precious stones inlaid in furniture made of ebony or a dark-toned wood. Sometimes the furniture was further enriched with inlays of ivory, exotic woods, mother-of-pearl, tortoise shell and various metals and with gilded bronze appliqués. Pietra dura was principally found on tall cabinets and tables. It did not achieve its greatest perfection and popularity until the first half of the 17th century, at which time it was almost mandatory for every elegant home in Italy and Europe to possess at least one fine example of pietra dura work.

ARTICLES OF FURNITURE

Chairs   Until the end of the 15th century chairs were relatively scarce. Benches, stools and cassoni were plentiful and were used for seats. One variety of chair prior to the 16th century was the rectangular, stately, solid throne chair, with a high panelled back, enriched with intarsia and carving. It was usually raised on a dais and was placed under a canopy of costly fabric. Its use was reserved for the master of the house or for a person of high rank. Prior to 1500 the first important armchairs for domestic use were the folding chairs of X-form. They were made in two principal varieties, namely the savonarola and the dantesca (FIGURES 32, 33). They were used by the Italians for dining, reading and writing. By the end of the 15th century these chairs were quite plentiful. Their surfaces were enriched with intarsia, certosina (32) or carving (33). The carving became more elaborate as the 16th century progressed. A loose cushion was often placed on the seat of the savonarola. The dantesca had a seat and back panel of fine velvet or tooled leather. Toward the close of the 16th century these armchairs of X-form were almost entirely supplanted by the armchair of rectangular form.

The sgabello (34) or stool chair, which was introduced in the 15th century, was a popular variety of Renaissance side chair. It was a relatively small chair and was generally made of walnut. It consisted of a small wooden seat which was often octagonal in shape and which rested on a shallow, box-like section that was mounted on a solid front support and a solid back support in place of legs (34). The chair back, which was practically fan-shaped or almost triangular in form, was usually made from a single piece of wood and slanted slightly backward (34). In another variety the seat rested directly on the solid front and on the solid back supports. The early sgabello was often enriched with intarsia work, since carving was only sparingly employed as a medium for surface enrichment until the time of the High Renaissance. The sgabello during the Late Renaissance had an ornately shaped back and supports, and was elaborately carved with all the prevailing classic motifs.

The panchetto, which in all probability developed from the three-legged Gothic stool, resembled to some extent the sgabello, but was more crude in both construction and decoration. It had a small seat supported on three splayed legs and a shaped back, which was generally fan-shaped. It was often embellished with chip carving.

The principal variety of chair during the 16th century was the tall armchair of rectangular form with an upholstered velvet seat and with a velvet panel stretched between the two uprights (35). The early 16th century chair had a relatively high and deep upholstered seat; the velvet in some specimens extended about one third down the legs. The four quadrangular legs rested on side runners which usually terminated in carved lion feet. The quadrangular uprights were sometimes surmounted with carved finials. The armposts continued to form the two front legs. Carving was used effectively but sparingly. The upholstery was often enhanced with fringe. Later this chair was designed with a broad carved front stretcher, slightly beneath the seat, and the base runners were generally discarded. In their place was a plain narrow back stretcher and two plain side stretchers. Sometimes the legs were joined with a continuous stretcher near the floor. Occasionally the finials and front stretcher were parcel-gilded. Some of these armchairs were designed with relatively low backs, and some were made in the form of side chairs. Those of the Late Renaissance had either ornately carved or turned supporting members with wide flat arms and elaborate and prominent broad front stretchers (37).

Another characteristic variety of Late Renaissance chair was a tall, rectangular, side chair with quadrangular supports and a wooden seat (36). The uprights were surmounted with carved finials. The raked back consisted of two or three ornately shaped and richly carved ornamental crosspieces. The quadrangular front legs were joined with a broad front stretcher which conformed in shape and in decoration with the decorative crosspieces.

An interesting type of folding chair without arms was the so-called monastery chair (48). Extant examples dating from the 16th century were generally formed of two sets of seven square channeled standards crossing and pivoting at the intersection so as to fold. The shaped back rail was sometimes enriched with carving.

The faldistorium, a variety of curule chair, was of ecclesiastical origin and early extant examples belong principally to the Late Renaissance. It had a wrought-iron curule frame with four upright supports, usually of turned brass, terminating in brass knob hand grips.

Stools

Stools were plentiful throughout the Renaissance. The principal variety was designed with a rectangular and sometimes octagonal wooden seat resting on a box-like section which was mounted on a solid front and on a solid back support in place of legs. Occasionally the underframing was fitted with a small drawer. The carving on the supports reflected the taste of the period in which it was done. This variety of stool was essentially similar to the sgabello without a back.

Benches

Benches or forms without backs or arms designed with carved trestle-end supports continued to be plentiful throughout the High Renaissance.

The cassapanca (38) was a combination seat and chest made to seat several persons. It was introduced around the middle of the 15th century in Florence, where it retained its popularity for over a century. The cassapanca was stately and monumental in character. It was used as a seat of honor in the houses of the upper classes, and, like all such seats, it was generally raised on a dais with one or two steps. It was made more comfortable with soft cushions. The part between the seat and floor was solidly enclosed, the seat being hinged to form a chest. The early cassapancas were usually panelled and enriched with intarsia. The later ones were ornamented with carving and moldings in accordance with the taste of the period.

There was also a type of chest-bench which resembled the cassapanca in form and in decoration, except that it was without arms. Occasionally the chest portion was almost of sarcophagus shape.

Beds

During the Early Renaissance the bed most commonly used was designed with a moderately low, rectangular headboard and footboard and low sides. Instead of legs it was either raised on a platform, called a predella or dais, or was simply enclosed with panelling to the floor. The headboard, footboard and sides were covered with small, rectangular panels; later the headboard and footboard were done in a single broad panel. As a rule the bed was sparingly decorated with intarsia and carving. However, the Venetian prototype was elaborately decorated with intarsia, painted designs and gilding. Contemporary pictures also depict a form of bed having a headboard and a canopy which was supported on four slender tall posts. It was mounted on a dais. At the beginning of the 16th century the bed was designed with legs. One characteristic variety consisted of a canopy, with a carved and molded cornice and a carved frieze, supported on four tall slender posts which were usually fluted. It had a richly carved headboard and was mounted on legs which were frequently of vase form terminating in lion feet. Another principal variety had a carved headboard and a low carved footboard with four medium-height posts which were usually enriched with spiral flutings and bands carved with classic motifs. The posts were surmounted with carved finials. During the Late Renaissance the two principal varieties of beds continued to be the tall-post bed with a tester and draperies and the bed with four posts of medium height. Occasionally variations occurred in their form. A late 16th century bed which displayed Baroque influence had an arcaded headboard which was surmounted with a richly carved cresting. Iron beds were used in Italy from the 16th century. The iron framework was frequently decorated with gilded ornaments.

Tables   The name *refectory table* (45) was generally given to the very long, narrow, oblong dining table. It was so called because originally it was used in the refectory or dining room in a monastery. The early refectory table followed the traditional lines of the trestle table, being constructed with truss-end supports which were usually reinforced with a stretcher. Toward the end of the 15th century the designs for tables became more elaborate and more finished in detail. The trusses were more elaborately carved and ornately shaped. Sometimes the trusses terminated in lion feet (45) instead of resting on floor runners. The horizontal stretcher became more important and was often either valanced or arcaded and was placed at different heights under the table. Sometimes the table was mounted on a colonnaded plinth or a base of H-form. (*See page* 90, FIGURES 76, 118.) The early table top had a plain edge; however, as the 15th century advanced, a molding was placed under the edge to give it additional thickness. Finally the edge was heavily molded and richly carved. A carved apron or frieze gradually developed under the table top and was frequently fitted with one or more drawers. Later, in place of the truss-end supports, the table was designed with four or more massive legs which were joined with a continuous stretcher close to the floor. By the end of the 16th century the table with legs had practically supplanted the table with trestle-end supports. The smaller table developed in the same manner as the long table.

The ingeniously devised draw-top table was introduced during the Renaissance. It was a large, massive, oblong table. The top was made in three pieces, that is, two lower sliding leaves under a center top. It was so designed that the main top was held in place by two blocks of wood and was not permanently fixed. The two leaves were fitted on two tapered runners, so that when they were drawn out the runners supported them and held them level with the center table top. In this manner the table was elongated to double its length.

The center or occasional table of medium size began to develop in the late 15th century. It was designed with a round, square, hexagonal or octagonal top, the last being the favorite shape. In one variety the top was supported by richly carved, scroll-shaped supports which radiated from a central shaft. In another variety the top was supported by a square, molded pedestal which rested on a broader molded base. The frieze on both these types of tables was often fitted with shallow drawers. During the 16th century the center table was designed with either quadrangular or turned legs which were always joined with a continuous floor stretcher. One characteristic variety had an octagonal top with a deep frieze supported on eight legs, which were joined with a continuous floor stretcher. As the 16th century progressed center tables became more plentiful and displayed further variations in their designs. During the Late Renaissance the center table designed with console supports radiating from a central shaft was less in demand.

Writing Furniture Furniture designed for writing was made in a variety of forms. One early variety of desk resembled the English 18th century slant-front desk. It had an oblong top and a slant-front over two rows of long drawers. It was mounted on a bracket base. The slant-front opened to reveal an interior of small drawers and compartments. In the 16th century a small portable desk of similar design with a sloping surface was also made. It was usually handsomely ornamented with intarsia work or was covered with tooled leather.

A characteristic 15th century flat-top writing table was the bancone. It had an oblong top which extended well beyond the deep frieze which was fitted with two drawers. The frieze was over a recessed box-like section which was fitted with end drawers. It rested on runner feet. Variations in design occurred. The bancone retained its popularity well into the 16th century.

Cabinets The tall, rectilinear, double-bodied writing cabinet was the favorite form of writing furniture and was among the luxuries introduced toward the end of the 15th century in Italy. It incorporated many architectural features in its principles of design. The upper body had a drop-front which when let down revealed many ingeniously designed small drawers and compartments (39). Occasionally it was designed with two doors in place of the drop-front. The lower portion was designed with two doors, the interior being fitted with either cupboard shelves or several rows of long drawers. During the Late Renaissance the upper body was recessed, sometimes only in the front, but more often in both the front and sides. The writing cabinet in the Early Renaissance was sometimes covered with certosina work. It was always distinctive for its fine classic proportions and for the classic purity of its carved decoration. The interior of the upper portion was often richly embellished with "picture" intarsia work (39). The Late Renaissance writing cabinet was usually characterized by excessive ornamentation. It was generally richly carved in high relief with foliage, arabesques, birds and mascarons, and the stiles were often enhanced with sculptured caryatids. One characteristic variety, often designed to be placed on a stand or table, had the stiles on the upper body decorated with several tiers of sculptured figures, while the small drawers and compartments displayed elaborate architectural detail. A great demand for these elaborate cabinets spread throughout Europe. Late in the 16th century the lower body was usually designed simply as a stand upon which the upper body rested. The craftsman exerted all his skill in designing and decorating these splendid cabinets made of walnut and ebony. They were sometimes handsomely enriched with inlays of exotic woods, semi-precious stones, tortoise shell, mother-of-pearl and ivory. (*See pages* 32, 69, 90, 91.)

Chests The cassone (41, 42) was by far the most important article of domestic furniture, and its popularity continued until the Late Renaissance when the demand for an all-purpose piece had greatly diminished. This was due to the advancement in household comfort and luxury which provided an impetus for the development of specialized pieces of domestic furniture. The lid of the cassone was flat, shaped or arched. The plain flat lid usually extended slightly beyond the sides. The shaped lid had a center portion raised or shaped with plain or carved moldings, and the arched lid was slightly curved. The cassone was made in several forms. The simplest had a long, rectangular form with a flat lid; sometimes this variety was very low, when it was to be used as a bench, and sometimes relatively high, when it undoubtedly was used as a table. An early and rather uncommon form was the boat-shaped cassone, the front of which was slightly convex like the hull of a boat. The sarcophagus-shaped cassone had the contour of an ancient Roman sarcophagus, and rested on a molded base or lion feet. Occasionally the cassone rested directly on the ground; however, it was more frequently mounted on either a molded base or on feet. The early cassone was usually mounted on bracket feet and the later usually on lions' feet. When the surface of the cassone was carved or inlaid, it was made of walnut. A less costly wood was used when its surface was completely covered with painting or pastiglia work. The cassone had the greatest artistic value of all contemporary domestic furniture. Great artists and the most skillful of craftsmen exerted all their talents in creating cassoni, which were veritable works of art. Their surfaces were enriched with pastiglia work, painted panels, gilding, intarsia, certosina and carving. The façade of the cassone was divided into panels or treated as one long continuous design. Characteristic of the 15th century was the long, rectangular cassone, the façade of which was decorated with beautifully painted panels, inserted in a classic architectural background. Equally fine was the gilt pastiglia cassone (41), with its entire surface enriched with delicate designs in low relief. Sometimes mythological subjects were depicted in gilt and painted pastiglia work. Very handsome was the cassone decorated with certosina work or with intarsia work. During the 16th century, the cassone was generally enriched with carved decoration and was very often of sarcophagus form. The carving on the façade, which was in high relief, depicted stories from Roman history and mythology and was either divided into panels or treated as one continuous carving. This carved walnut cassone was notable for the fine finish of its wood and for the beautiful quality of its carvings. The Late Renaissance cassone (42) was elaborately carved in high relief and was heavily molded. Carved in the round figure subjects at each end as well as bold gadrooning were characteristic features of this cassone which as a rule was of either rectangular or sarcophagus form.

During the Renaissance in Italy it was the custom for every great family to order a pair of cassoni as wedding gifts for the bride and bridegroom. These marriage cassoni (41) were always choice articles of furniture, since the most celebrated craftsmen lavished their skill on the decoration of these magnificent pieces. The coat-of-arms of each family was usually found on the façade of each cassone. Favorite subjects for the scenes which were carved, painted or inlaid on the front panels included a wedding feast or a bridal procession.

The cassette was a small chest or casket. Its form was often similar to that of the contemporary cassone, and was usually ornamented with delicate pastiglia and painted decorations. In the Middle Ages the cassette, occasionally in the form of a Gothic tomb, was used as a reliquary for preserving the relics of saints.

Chests of Drawers   The chest of drawers (43) was introduced toward the end of the 16th century, and its florid decoration was typical of that era. The principal variety was designed with two small top drawers over three long drawers. Each drawer, which was divided by a carved horizontal member, was prominently molded and was fitted with handles generally made of carved wood grotesque figures and with an elaborately wrought bronze keyplate. The stiles were generally decorated with several tiers of sculptured figures. It rested on a molded base, generally surmounted on lions' paws.

Cupboards   Many of the cupboards during the Early Renaissance were set in the wall and were fitted with shelves and panelled doors, the latter being occasionally enriched with either intarsia work or paintings. The sacristy cupboard, which was the earliest Italian movable cupboard, was an ecclesiastical piece of furniture. It served as a receptacle for the sacred utensils which were used in church ritual. The characteristic variety during the Early Renaissance was rectilinear in form and was longer than it was tall. It was designed with two or three doors which were divided either by narrow vertical panels or pilasters. It rested on a molded base.

The credenza (47) or domestic cupboard was an important piece of Italian furniture and strongly resembled the early ecclesiastical sacristy cupboard (50). As a rule the credenza during the 16th century was rectilinear in form and its length exceeded its height. Architectural features were incorporated in its principles of design. The principal variety of credenza had an oblong top over a frieze which was fitted with two or three drawers that were separated by carved brackets or modillions. Beneath the frieze were two or three doors; the number of doors corresponded to the number of drawers in the frieze. Each door was divided by either a narrow vertical panel or by a fluted pilaster that was directly under each modillion in the frieze. It rested on a carved and molded base which was often mounted on carved lions' feet. The base was frequently boldly carved, usually with gadrooning. The credenza was only occasionally designed with a recessed superstructure fitted with a row of small shallow drawers or cupboard doors. Equally rare was the credenza having a superstructure of one or more shelves. The credenza was made of walnut and its surface was enriched either with intarsia work or with carving. The narrow vertical panels were often carved with graceful arabesques, playful grotesques, vase forms and other similar motifs. Fluted pilasters were often used in place of the narrow vertical panels. Although the features of design were essentially the same, the credenza (47) during the Late Renaissance lacked the fine classic proportions and refinement of detail that characterized the earlier credenza. It was often ornately carved with classic motifs of a larger scale. Sculptured caryatids and human figures largely supplanted the pilasters, which, when used, were often tapered in form. The frieze drawers were often separated by grotesque masks of a less pleasing character. The moldings became very prominent. The moldings around the frieze and base usually broke around the stiles. There was an undecorated variety of late 16th century credenza which reflected the influence of Palladio in its design. This variety displayed finer classic proportions and it was more sparingly decorated. The Late Renaissance credenza was sometimes taller and not as long as its predecessor. Variations in design frequently occurred. In some examples the base of the credenza was sometimes designed with a row of drawers.

The credenzina (44) or small credenza was a favorite and useful piece of furniture. It was essentially similar in form and decoration to the credenza. In fact, it often resembled in appearance one section of the credenza. The credenzina was designed with one or two cupboard doors.

The name *madia* was given to a piece of kitchen furniture used to store loaves of bread. It was a kind of bread-cupboard or large bread-box. It was usually fitted with cupboard doors, variously arranged, and sometimes with a row of narrow drawers above or below the cupboard doors. It was generally mounted on legs of varying height. One variety had a hinged lid instead of a fixed top. Since the madia was a piece of kitchen furniture it was not considered worthy of the rich decoration characteristic of this era. However, its simplicity often gave it a great deal of individual charm. In a broad sense the madia in its general appearance, as well as to some extent its general purpose, resembled the English hutch or French huche.

The armadio which was a tall, rectilinear, single-bodied, movable cupboard or wardrobe, incorporated architectural detail in its design. One principal variety was designed with a molded cornice and frieze over two or four panelled long doors, resting on a molded base. It was decorated according to the taste of the period in which it was made. The armadio corresponded in its function and general form to the French armoire.

Bookcases   The bookcase of the Late Renaissance was a rare piece of furniture and was found only in the homes of the most wealthy and cultured. It was a large, double-bodied article of furniture and incorporated architectural features in its principles of design. The receded upper body, which was surmounted with a frieze and cornice, contained two or more rows of shelves, which were divided into sections by upright members, frequently in the form of pilasters. The lower body was composed of four or more cupboard doors and rested on a molded base. Sometimes the lower body was fitted with a row of narrow frieze drawers above the cupboard doors.

Mirrors   Wall mirrors (49) were first introduced during the Renaissance, although hand mirrors had been made during the medieval period.

The characteristic Renaissance wall mirror was almost square, with a slight emphasis on the vertical, and was made of a sheet of highly polished metal, with a richly carved frame which was frequently gilded. Two sliding doors, often ornamented with painted designs, covered from sight the unpleasing surface of the mirror. The early Venetian wall mirror was round, and curtains were often used in place of the sliding doors. The frame of the Venetian mirror was frequently decorated with pastiglia work as well as with carving. Later, the Venetians preferred the mirror of rectangular form. As the 16th century advanced the carved frame of the mirror became more elaborate and ornate. Around the middle of the 16th century the Venetians perfected the technique of silvering glass with an amalgam of tin and mercury.

Accessories   Richly carved and gilded pedestals and wall brackets figured prominently in the decorative scheme of the fine palaces. This was especially true in the Late Renaissance when bronze and marble antique sculptures figured prominently in the interior decoration. These sculptures were placed on either pedestals or wall brackets or were arranged in wall niches.

Carved and gilded candlesticks, bronze candlesticks and bronze candelabra all exhibited workmanship of the highest quality. They were exquisitely and richly decorated in accordance with the prevailing fashion.

Résumé of
ITALIAN BAROQUE, ROCOCO AND
NEO-CLASSIC FURNITURE
during the 17th and 18th Centuries

The history of furniture, like all art, is sometimes described as a story of different successive styles. The Gothic was followed by the Renaissance, which in turn was supplanted by the Baroque, Rococo and Neo-Classic in that order. In these styles from the time of the Renaissance the basic forms for architecture, such as orders, pilasters, cornices and moldings, had their origin in classical architecture. Only the Rococo style did not lend itself to architecture and was best suited for the decoration of interiors and for the decorative arts. Sometimes this whole period from the days of Brunelleschi to the early 19th century is referred to as the Renaissance. However, it is a long period of time and it is helpful to give different names to designate certain changes in style which occurred during that time. The word *baroque*, which is taken from the Italian word *barocco* meaning a misshapen pearl, was given by later critics to the period following the Renaissance. It was used in censure against the style of architecture of the 17th century by the believers in pure classic tradition who regarded any violation of proportions and forms as established in ancient Greek and Roman architecture to be bad taste.

Rome was the fountainhead of Baroque art and it is referred to as the Baroque city.

Baroque art was essentially the continuation of the art of the late 16th century. The dominating personality for Italian Baroque was undoubtedly the sculptor and architect Giovanni Bernini, 1598–1680, who was closely associated with the art of Rome in the 17th century. The papal aristocracy and Spanish noblemen continued to be the predominating society. Their insatiable appetite for luxury, pomp and grandeur resulted in the building of splendid palaces, sumptuously decorated and furnished. The interior decoration and furniture in these imposing palaces reflected Bernini's taste for he was greatly favored by the court at Rome. It was during this time that the Roman Church realized the power of art to overwhelm and impress. The interiors of the churches were transformed into dramatic displays of glittering wealth and dazzling pageantry. They were gorgeously decorated with colored marbles, bronzes, sculptures, paintings, frescoes and masses of gilding. The magnificence of these interiors created a vision of the greater glory awaiting the faithful in the life of the future. Bernini's influence was evident in much of this decoration full of rapturous splendor and movement. In his sculptures to add to the effect of excitement, restlessness and movement, which were typical Baroque features, he treated the draperies in a whirling and writhing manner rather than in the early smooth and soft classical folds. Although the feeling for stone is lost in this treatment, it was highly theatrical and it was soon imitated in all parts of Europe. From Rome the Baroque style spread throughout Italy and later into the other European countries. The Roman churches kindled the Baroque spirit and every Catholic church and monastery wanted to vie with the splendor of Bernini's work.

Italian Baroque reached its culmination around the middle of the 17th century when Spanish influence was supplanted by French. This change was brought about by the accession of Louis XIV to the throne of France in 1643, and by the defeat of Spain by France in 1659 when France became the leading Continental power. French art and French manners and customs, all expressed in the magnificent and strong personality of Louis XIV, came to influence and finally dominate the taste of Europe by the end of the 17th century. Italy, toward the end of the century, along with the other countries of Europe, found herself accepting the French interpretation of her own Baroque style, which had been so homogeneously developed by the craftsmen of France under the patronage of Louis XIV. This shrewd and powerful ruler also realized the power of art to overwhelm and impress. In building Versailles he hoped to display the might and splendor of royalty. And as the Roman churches served as an inspiration, so we find that every European royal prince wanted his own Versailles. French Baroque possessed a stateliness and nobility quite different from Italian Baroque. It reached its culmination toward the end of the 17th century, and it was supplanted early in the 18th century by the French Rococo, also perfected in France, which depicted a fantastic, frivolous and artificial world in its style of ornament and decoration. The era around 1700 was a remarkable period for building activity, providing a great impetus for the designing of much furniture and for the introduction of many new forms.

Italian furniture of the 17th century, until it was tempered by French influence, displayed many of the features found in the late 16th century. It was massive in form and was essentially of rectilinear construction. It was excessively and heavily ornamented. Carving was the preferred method for decorating the surface of furniture and it was of a sculpturesque and florid character. Boldly carved, prominent moldings were typical of the style. There was an air of splendid vitality about this furniture which offset to some extent its violation of pure classic proportions and ornament. The finest pieces of furniture in the Baroque taste were made by the Venetians (51, 52). The classic ornament, which was generally of an exaggerated scale, displayed a more complicated composition and a greater complexity of curved forms. It was characterized by dramatic contrast and extravagant movement. Cartouches, banderoles, volutes, large foliated scrolls, C-scrolls, S-scrolls, showy coats-of-arms and heraldic devices, putti and grotesques were all favorite decorative motifs and were characterized by their heavily plastic quality. When the exuberance of Baroque ornament was under control, especially as is evident in the later French Baroque, it had a distinctive quality of sweeping rhythm.

As has already been mentioned, by the end of the 17th century France had entirely supplanted Spanish domination in Italy. Due to a certain artistic bond which seemed to link France and Italy together, the Italians took quite naturally to the French arts and manners. The artificiality, frivolity and gaiety of the French court supplanted the stilted grandeur of the Spanish court. Italian furniture design followed the development of the Rococo style as perfected in France, where it was known as the Louis XV style. Although the Italian furniture could not be compared with the finely detailed, exquisitely ornamented French pieces, it

did capture the spirit of the style and interpreted it in many charming, graceful pieces. This furniture frequently displayed good workmanship in its nice sense of balance and proportion and in its wide range of decorative motifs. However, Italy never embraced the Rococo style as completely as France for she still found many interesting features in the Baroque.

Undoubtedly Italy's finest contribution during this period was her charming painted Venetian Rococo furniture (55, 56, 57, 58), the most exquisite pieces being made around the middle of the 18th century. Venice was the leading art center in the 18th century and she made much fine furniture during that period. The painted Venetian Rococo furniture was admirable for its graceful lines, for its unrivalled harmonious colors and velvet-like texture, and for the composition of its rich decoration, which was made more interesting with exotic birds, flowers and chinoiseries. All types of furniture were made and the models were borrowed from the fashionable Louis XV forms. Bombé and serpentine-shaped commodes (55, 56), generally with marble tops, and many delightful small pieces such as wall cabinets and bookshelves, small boxes and mirrors and sconces of fantastic outline, were especially outstanding. The painted decoration was often executed in water colors for economical reasons. When it was painted in water colors the surface first received a coat of gesso, which gave the surface a velvet-like texture and absorbed the water colors exceptionally well. Finally a coat of varnish was applied over the painted decoration to make it more lasting and durable. Although the decoration in water colors was not as permanent as the decoration in oil paints, it surpassed oil paints in its freshness of color and in its velvet-like texture.

During the 18th century Italy once again became the scene of archaeological activities, and, as in the Renaissance, Rome was the center of all this archaeological research and study and abounded with scholars from all parts of Europe. This second Renaissance, which is called the Classic Revival or Neo-Classic, was stimulated by excavations commenced in 1738 at Pompeii and Herculaneum. Numerous scholarly publications retold the great achievements of classic art and created a new interest in it. French and English classic designs were indebted to the archaeological researches of Johann Winckelmann, 1717–1768, the celebrated German archaeologist, who went to Rome in 1755 and gradually acquired an unrivalled knowledge of ancient culture. He was a prolific writer and his books covered all phases of ancient Greek and Roman art. Scholars gained their first real information about the treasures excavated at Pompeii and Herculaneum from his books. The style of the decorative arts in Italy for this period was largely inspired by the publications of Giovanni Piranesi, 1704–1784, the renowned Venetian architect, etcher and draughtsman, who studied at Rome and was greatly inspired by the classic works of art. This prolific genius wrote many books; however, his outstanding contribution to furniture and the other decorative arts was a book of engravings entitled DIVERSE MANIERE, published in 1769. This book, which was an endless source of supply and inspiration, was filled with the Neo-Classic style of ornament for mural decorations, for furniture and for such decorative appointments as vases and candelabra. Piranesi is now given credit

for having strongly influenced French and English designs as well as Italian.

Although the Classic Revival had its inception in Italy, it was not until after the new style was fully developed in France and in England that it became fashionable in Italy. The founding of the Academy of Milan in 1775 played an important part in establishing the Louis XVI style in Italy. The Academy was fortunate in having as one of its directors Giocondo Albertolli, 1742–1839, who was the famous organizer of Neo-Classic art in Italy and was instrumental in continuing its high standard of designs. Neo-Classic art was adopted throughout Italy, and, as in the Renaissance, each state displayed to some extent certain individual characteristics. Venetian furniture was notable for its delicate coloring and fine detail, for its simplicity of form and for its skillful blending of antique art with some features held over from her own graceful Rococo style. The furniture of Rome, which was of fine craftsmanship, usually reflected a certain heaviness in its designs. The furniture of Naples was notable for the artful manner in which the Louis XVI style and Pompeiian art were frequently combined.

A tremendous amount of furniture was made by the Italians during the Neo-Classic period. The Italians expressed virtually all their enthusiasm for the new style in furniture, for there was little building. The interiors of the old palaces and villas, when redecorated to harmonize with the Neo-Classic style, introduced classic architectural detail and classic motifs in place of Rococo scrollwork and ornament. Mirrors, chandeliers and sconces were important decorative appointments and gave additional brilliance to the principal apartments. Although the Italian Neo-Classic furniture was inferior to the French and English in quality of workmanship and materials, it was distinctive for its unmistakable individuality and for its artful blending of antique and Renaissance motifs, expressed in the lighter form of the 18th century. The furniture of this era is often considered to be the finest Italian work since the Renaissance. The furniture was essentially rectilinear in form. Architectural details, such as pilasters and columns, were again incorporated in the designs for furniture. The curves of the circle, oval and ellipse replaced the sinuous curves of the Rococo. Ornamental bronze appliqués were seldom used, although there was an increased use of hardware in the form of wrought metal keyplates and handles. The finest Italian marquetry work was done at this time. Painted furniture, frequently brightened by touches of gilt, came into general use. Caned chairs and settees, which were especially suitable to the warm Italian climate, were very fashionable. The Italians made many fine pieces in this so-called Italian Louis XVI style. They also made numerous articles of furniture inspired by the designs of Robert Adam, Hepplewhite and Sheraton. A difference in technique as well as in materials made these pieces easy to distinguish from their English models. All their cabinetwork for this era displayed a striking individuality and a delightful interpretation of designs whether borrowed from French or English designs.

During the latter part of the 18th century a more pronounced taste for the antique and its closer imitation resulted in the Directoire style which ultimately developed into the Empire style. The Italian cabinetmaker returned to direct classical sources for his inspiration and began to formulate more original designs for furniture based upon antique classic models. The Italians designed many articles of furniture in the Directoire style which were admirable for their unique charm and striking originality. Especially outstanding were the chairs with rolled over and concave crest rails inspired by the distinctive Grecian side chair, the klismos. Antique Grecian sofas used for reclining and dining furnished the inspiration for the design of numerous interesting Directoire settees.

The principles of the Empire style were forecast in Italian furniture design before it was established in France by Fontaine and Percier. However, as in the previous 18th century styles, the Empire style was not adopted in Italy until after it had been organized in France. Outside of France the Empire style was most effectively interpreted in Italy. Napoleon during his brief reign, 1804–1814, chose Rome, after Paris, as the fitting scene for his second court, where he embarked upon a period of lavish display. Several members of Bonaparte's family were given positions of high rank in Italy, and wherever each member established himself he successfully inaugurated the new style. Napoleon's sister Caroline married Joachim Murat, Marshal of France, and together they ruled as King and Queen of Naples from 1808 to 1814 where a delightful Empire style was fully developed. His sister Pauline married a Borghese Prince, and they were instrumental in making the Empire style fashionable in Italy, not only in furniture and interior decoration, but in dress as well. They lived in Rome and spent a fortune in remodelling and refurnishing palaces in the new mode for their own pleasure. Napoleon's sister Elsie became Grand Duchess of Tuscany which also embraced the Empire style. Other relatives, including Napoleon's mother, were all given princely palaces in Italy newly redecorated in the Empire taste. Venice was virtually the only state which did not contribute to the Empire style. Her social, economic and art life was at its lowest ebb. Venice had been shamelessly looted by Napoleon and her art treasures had all been carried by him to Paris.

Italian furniture designed in the Empire style was inferior in quality to that designed in France. Nevertheless, it often achieved a more pleasing effect, for although the Italians copied the style they interpreted it in their own technique and materials, which dispelled to some extent the stiffness and formality inherent in the French designs. Some of the costly Italian pieces, which were principally made at Rome, were direct copies of the French Empire and were made of ma-

hogany. However, most of the furniture was made either of walnut or was painted. Ormolu mounts, which were seldom used in the former styles, were more extensively employed. Occasionally carved and gilt wood mounts were substituted for the chased and gilded bronze mounts because they were less costly. The Italians in their interpretation of the Empire style often incorporated some features of Piranesi in their designs which contributed more variety and creative charm to their work. Decorative war-like motifs were used less frequently and when they were used they were less ostentatious. White and gold was the dominating color scheme in several states, especially in Rome and Naples. The painted furniture designed in the Empire taste was very striking. Especially impressive were the many finely designed console tables. Chairs designed from antique Roman curule models were equally effective with their pleasing graceful lines.

CHAPTER FOUR

SPANISH

SPANISH GOTHIC

Undoubtedly the most distinctive feature of Spanish art during practically the entire period of the Middle Ages was the concurrent existence in Spain of two schools of art. This was due to the fact that in the 8th century, while the Spanish people were still in an early formative stage, they were conquered by the Mohammedan Moors from Africa across the straits of Gibraltar. So complete was the Mohammedan victory that scattered Christian groups were able to maintain their freedom only in the northern mountainous regions. Courageously through the ensuing centuries these Christians slowly pushed the enemy southward toward the sea. Finally, with the conquest of Granada in 1492 they terminated a most hated rule which had lasted for almost eight centuries. However, although the state of the Moors had vanished, the Moors themselves still remained in certain sections, chiefly along the southern coast, where they constituted an important urban element. The final expulsion of the Moors occurred in 1607 during the reign of Philip III. This was a great loss to the handicrafts and commerce of southern Spain, for the industrious Moors had been the chief factor contributing to its prosperity. As a result of this Moorish occupation all the Spanish decorative arts were imbued with a peculiar exotic touch and this influence persisted to a greater or less extent in all their later work.

The Moors, who were supreme ornamentalists and the world's finest geometricians, greatly influenced the artistic taste and customs of Spain even beyond the boundaries of their own political spheres of influence. The naturalistic representation of men, animals and plants was forbidden in the Mohammedan style of ornament. This resulted in the development of a conventionalized leaf design, which was often used as a background for inscriptions in Arabic characters, and of an endless variety of geometrical designs and of patterns worked on a geometrical basis. The Spaniards accepted from Mohammedan art that which was in harmony with Christian principles. This fusion of the art of Christian Spain with Moorish art, with all its colorful exuberant fancy, resulted in a style of ornament known as Mudéjar. These Oriental precepts were so deeply rooted in Spanish art that even after the Moors were finally expelled and Spanish art was subjected to European influence, in the ensuing centuries the influence of Moorish art, with its colorful exuberance, was always present to a greater or less degree. This combination of Hispano-Moresque art is a striking feature of Spanish cabinetwork. Many Spanish craftsmen were conquered Moors who incorporated Moorish styles of ornament and methods of construction in their designs for furniture. The Moors were expert workers in wood and their finest skill was displayed in furniture design and in carved wooden ceilings.

When the Gothic style was introduced into Spain from France, in the first half of the 13th century, the style of ornament for that period was characterized by strong Moorish influence. Architects were also brought into Spain from France and from the Low Countries, who brought with them their own development of Gothic ornament. Since there are few extant examples of Gothic furniture it is necessary to resort to early paintings, illustrated manuscripts and records for any knowledge of the furnishings during this era. It seems that the early Gothic Spanish home, as well as the Moorish, was practically devoid of tables and chairs. The Spanish chest or arca was the principal all-purpose piece of domestic furniture. Cushions were in great favor as seats, in accordance with Moorish customs. Although in the Late Gothic period stools, benches, settles or chest-benches, tables and other elementary forms were found in the Spanish home, not much Spanish furniture was made before 1500. The ornament was largely influenced by the ecclesiastical architecture found in northern Europe, with Spanish Flamboyant Gothic tracery being much in evidence. Fabrics were draped over the simple, crudely carved wooden frames. Wrought-iron mounts on the Late Gothic chests were executed in a flamboyant manner, and were remarkable for their elaborate and delicate workmanship. Spain was always rich in all kinds of decorative ironwork.

SPANISH RENAISSANCE

The 16th century marked the most brilliant era in Spanish history, when the history of Europe seemed to revolve around Spain. Ferdinand and Isabella, through the voyages of Columbus, had acquired title to the New World, with its promise of untold wealth and opportunity. Spain was preeminent during this Age of Discovery. The Spaniards were both bold and successful navigators and traders, and as a result of their exploits and enterprises fabulous amounts of gold and silver bullion poured into Spain from the New World. Toward the middle of the century Spain reached the height of her power as the leading European country. By the end of the century Spain was practically bankrupt, largely due to her costly campaigns to maintain her possessions and her spendthrift policy to maintain Catholic imperialism. The reigns of Charles V, 1519–1556, and his son Philip II, 1556–1598, covered almost the entire century, which was the golden age of Spanish history. During this century, Spain, with her vast hereditary possessions and military conquests and her discovery of new lands, was the dominating power in Europe.

Spanish Renaissance architecture from around 1492 to 1650 is generally divided into two phases. The early phase, introduced into the country from France and Italy, is known as the Plateresque or Silversmith's style because its minute and delicate ornament resembled the delicate work of the silversmith. This early phase of classic architecture in Spain, with its rich decoration, was essentially of a transitional character since the ornament was usually engrafted on Spanish Flamboyant Gothic forms and the exuberance of the work reflected Moorish influence. The second phase, introduced by Philip II in 1556, was based on the work of the celebrated Italian Renaissance architects, Palladio and Vignola. This Italian style of Renaissance architecture is frequently referred to as the style of Herrera, since Juan de Herrera, the state architect to Philip II, was its chief exponent. The style was characterized by its severe classic forms, plain surfaces and sparse decorations. Due to its coldness and formality the Spaniards did not find it particularly pleasing, and as a result early in the 17th century the Baroque style of ornament began to make itself evident. Baroque ornament appealed much more to the Spanish temperament with its love of elaboration and its religious zeal. The architectural style of Herrera, with its close adherence to ancient Roman designs, prevailed until around 1650, when a reaction against this severe formalism developed. Baroque architecture in Spain is sometimes known as the Churri-

gueresque style, deriving its name from the architect José Churriguera, d.1725, who was the principal leader of the movement and under whose influence the style reached a climax of elaboration. This extravagant Baroque style with its never-ending movement, curved lines and overwhelmingly rich decoration was much more compatible with the innate Spanish love of lavish decoration. The Churrigueresque style, which remained in fashion until about 1800, took greater freedom with the Classic Orders than any other style of Baroque architecture and employed many fantastic forms very often divorced from good taste. Nevertheless, it did reveal a remarkable freedom of treatment and daring in its designs and cannot be regarded as entirely without artistic value. The climax of all this Churrigueresque richness was principally found in the interior decoration of churches, altarpieces and metal work.

After the cessation of racial wars many town palaces were built during the Spanish Renaissance by the aristocracy, who moved from their feudal fortresses into such leading cities as Madrid, Seville and Barcelona. In addition to these palaces numerous modest rural houses were built in the regional districts by families of lesser wealth and social position. The typical early style of Spanish Renaissance domestic architecture reflected the influence of earlier Moorish work, which enhanced the value of rich decorations in the patios, galleries, doorways and windows by contrasting them against plain walls. The Spanish home was built around a central patio or court, with all of the rooms of simple rectangular construction. The rooms were long and narrow and were practically of similar design, with the exception of the salon which sometimes was designed with a fireplace. Among the most beautiful and artistic features of a Spanish house were the magnificent and superb iron grilles, sometimes enhanced with gilding, used at the windows and the openings. Handsome wrought-iron handrails were also an important decorative feature and were notable for their finished craftsmanship. The built-in decorations found in the Spanish house were always rich and colorful and they seemed even more striking against the plain white smooth plaster walls. The most exotic interiors were found in the south of Spain where the Moorish influence survived the longest. The built-in decorations based on Mudéjar principles were used in most Spanish interiors and made these interiors completely different from those found in any other part of Europe. They generally consisted of colored tiles or azulejos, a painted wooden ceiling or artesonado and plasterwork or yesería.

The use of colored pottery tiles for wall decoration had its origin in the Near East, where the earliest specimens date from the 9th century. Seville was an important center for the production of tiles, and a mosaic tilework, introduced from the Near East, was made there in the 14th century. Noteworthy examples of this mosaic tilework are found at the Alcazar at Seville dating from the time of Peter the Cruel, 1350 to 1366. In this process of mosaic tilework, known as alicatados in Spain, the designs were composed of many small pieces of tin-glazed earthenware assembled with mortar. Around the middle of the 15th century in Spain this technique was followed by the cuerda seca process, simulating the earlier process by dry lines of grease and manganese which kept the

colored glazes from running together. The cuenca process of the early 16th century used stamped lines of relief to achieve the same purpose. During the Renaissance painted tiles in the Italian majolica technique supplanted the earlier methods and were employed as wall decoration early in the 16th century. The designs for these tiles in the 14th and 15th centuries were of Moorish derivation, while in the 16th century Spanish Gothic and Renaissance motifs became more prominent. These polychrome pottery tiles were used for dadoes and frequently for the facings of doorways, windows and window seats. They were also used to line the interior of niches, and for the enrichment of stairs, generally only for the risers but occasionally for the treads as well. The Spanish also made tile pictures which were patent imitations of wall tapestries. The fashionable Dutch monochrome tiles in blue and white or in manganese purple and white were made during the 17th and 18th centuries in Spain; however, the traditional polychrome tiles continued to be made in the regional districts where the latest fashions were of little concern to the inhabitants.

Pine-panelled ceilings, which were often the principal decorative feature in many old Spanish interiors, were traditionally Moorish and indigenous to Spain alone. These ceilings displayed a pattern of minute divisions and intricate geometrical shapes and were generally enriched with painted and gilded carved decoration of Moorish inspiration. When the pine-panelled ceilings were not embellished with carved and painted decoration they were simply oiled and were remarkable for their soft warm patina. Frequently the doors and window shutters were treated in a similar manner, but they were rarely enriched with painted and carved decoration. The plasterwork or yesería, which in those days was always carved and never cast in molds, was white in all the Spanish Christian houses. It was principally used as a decorative border or frame around the doors and window openings and as a frieze band under the carved wooden cornice. Occasionally the chimneypiece in the salon would be decorated with plasterwork. This plasterwork was very often richly carved with decorative motifs remarkable for fine composition and finished detail. The designs were chiefly of Moorish inspiration, although during the Renaissance many Italian classic motifs appeared, but these were frequently tinctured with an Oriental flavor. Spanish floors were laid in tile, stone, brick or wood, with the latter being generally reserved for the upper floors. Tile floors were frequently laid in a basket weave and their coloring was subdued.

In the great houses of the aristocracy the walls were sometimes hung with colorful silk velvet or damask hangings, frequently exquisitely embroidered or appliquéd with armorial bearings or family crests and enriched with gold braid and fringe. The Spanish were also partial to hangings of tooled Cordova leather brilliantly painted and gilded, for Spain was one of the leading centers in fine leather work. Fine Renaissance tapestries and oil paintings in richly carved massive gold frames provided additional elegance and richness in some Spanish interiors. Magnificent handmade cut pile Spanish carpets and elaborately designed Moorish rugs and mats were sometimes laid on the tile or stone floors. In this atmosphere of rich elegance the Spanish carefully arranged a few dignified pieces of wal-

nut furniture and always showed a preference for placing furniture against the wall. The number of pieces of furniture found in a Spanish room were relatively few in comparison to the amount found in the other countries for the same period. Traditionally, Moorish was the prevailing fashion for canopies, cushions and the numerous small coffers placed on every table. The vogue for fringes, braids, cords, tassels and decorative nailheads, of the finest workmanship, also had its source of origin in Moorish customs. Spanish cabinetwork of the 16th century possessed a singular artistic charm that was completely pleasing and satisfying. Undoubtedly much of this charm was due to its peculiar structural simplicity and to its style of ornament, which frequently displayed considerable originality in its composition.

Spanish Renaissance furniture was essentially rectilinear in contour with the exception of a few chairs of curule form. A pronounced feature of Spanish furniture design was the marked absence of architectural detail, such as cornices, friezes and pilasters, which were extensively employed in contemporary Italian Renaissance furniture design. The furniture was to a large extent even devoid of moldings. The simplicity displayed in the structure and design of this furniture harmonized with the simple structure of the Spanish room in which it was to be placed. In comparison to the quality of craftsmanship with contemporary Italian cabinetwork it was much inferior. The intrinsic charm of Spanish furniture was not in any great elegance or finished craftsmanship but rather in its simplicity, its boldness of design and vigorous lines. A unique feature of its construction was the frequent use of ornamental wrought-iron underbraces for tables and benches. Walnut was the fashionable Spanish wood, for the Spanish cabinetmaker liked its warm coloring and smooth texture. Oak was second in popularity for cabinetwork. Pine and chestnut were also used and exotic fruit woods were occasionally employed in inlay work. A striking feature of Spanish cabinetwork was the limited number of different pieces. The Spanish always seemed satisfied with the more or less basic and elementary pieces, such as chairs, stools, benches, tables, chests, beds, vargueños and cupboards. This distinguishing feature of Spanish taste continued into the 17th and 18th centuries. The Spanish were cognizant of the almost endless number of new forms introduced in the different categories by the French and the English cabinetmakers, yet many of these articles, such as commodes, different kinds of writing furniture, day beds and many other pieces both decorative and useful were seldom found in the Spanish home. Spanish Renaissance furniture and the later 17th and 18th century regional furniture had the greatest appeal. This cabinetwork, with its Mudéjar influence, embraced all those interesting features identified with traditional Spanish furniture design, which the cabinetmaker of the 18th century working in the more fashionable Continental designs tried to erase.

The Spanish cabinetmaker employed various methods to decorate the surface of furniture, such as inlay work, carving, painting and gilding. Inlay work was one of Spain's finest artistic achievements. The Eastern art of inlay work, which is called taracea, consisted of minute pieces of bone, ivory, exotic woods, mother-of-pearl and metal worked in intricate and innumerable combinations of geometrical designs and highly stylized leaf and floral designs. One kind of taracea work was inlaid with minute dots of ivory and because of its resemblance to grains of wheat it was sometimes called granos de trigo. Especially characteristic was the use of many intricate geometrical small panel divisions to form striking surface designs. Undoubtedly this feature was inspired by the pine-panelled ceilings with their intricate geometrical patterns. Lozenge-shaped and rectangular panelling was also employed to decorate the surface of furniture. Carving was also used to enrich the surface of furniture. Provincial pieces were frequently decorated with incised or chip carving. Almost every variety of turning was developed. Spiral and baluster-turned supports were especially popular. Painting and gilding were also practiced. The interior of the vargueño was one of the finest examples of Spanish painted and gilded furniture. The Spanish, who were unrivalled leather workers, sometimes covered the surface of chests with finely tooled leather. Chests were also occasionally covered with velvet or silk and their surface was then frequently enhanced with geometrical designs composed of decorative nailheads. The Spaniards were superb metallists and were unsurpassed in producing elaborate and delicate wrought-iron work of lace-like quality. Decorative nailheads or chatónes, ingeniously designed and used for decorating furniture, locks and hasps, ornamental mounts and bands were of the finest artistic quality. Especially praiseworthy were the exquisitely pierced ornamental mounts used on the façade of the vargueño. Graceful wrought-iron braces for tables and benches were also distinctive and decorative. Frequently the wrought-iron work was enriched with gilding.

The Spanish style of ornament during

the Renaissance continued to reflect to a greater or less extent the influence of Moorish art, which was characterized by its rich vivid coloring and its prolific combinations of geometrical motifs. The Moorish artist, who was gifted with a fanciful imagination, was unrivalled in his ability to artistically interweave and interlace geometric ornament. His technical drawings were executed with such consummate skill that each part of the ornament was always distinct and well-defined. The Moors also used as ornament fine Arabic lettering. As has already been mentioned, one of the unique features of Spanish art was the so-called Mudéjar style of ornament. In the beginning of the 16th century the influence of the Italian Renaissance was barely perceptible. The Spanish cabinetmaker preferred the Moorish and Spanish traditional styles of ornament. Spanish Gothic motifs were used on many early Renaissance pieces. This overlapping of different styles of ornament was quite pronounced in Spain, and was probably due to the fact that Spain did not have any great art center to establish and dictate its fashions. Even when the influence of the Italian Renaissance was felt to some appreciable extent, the Spanish Renaissance furniture never displayed the wealth of classic motifs found on Italian Renaissance furniture. The Spanish interpretation of Renaissance motifs was essentially geometrical and conventionalized and was never completely free of Moorish precepts. Included among the characteristic and favorite Spanish Renaissance motifs were stylized leaf and flower motifs, highly conventionalized rosettes treated in many various ways, simplified scroll designs, shells, interlaced fret ornament, armorial bearings, lozenge motifs, wheel medallions, cherubs and various figure subjects.

ARTICLES OF FURNITURE

Chairs   In all probability the oldest extant examples of Spanish chairs are those of ancient Roman curule form or the folding chair of X-form, generally called by the Spanish sillón de caderas, hip-joint chair or sillón de tijera, X-form chair (FIGURE 59). This Spanish chair was similar to the Italian dantesca and savonarola chairs, and is commonly regarded to have been of Moorish origin, where it was reserved as a seat of honor. The sillón de caderas was usually richly ornamented with a minute, geometrical inlay design of ivory, bone and exotic woods. The seat and back panel were generally of leather, sometimes richly tooled or merely stitched in a geometrical pattern. A loose cushion was often placed on the seat. By the time of the Renaissance the X-form chair had lost much of its popularity.

The favorite and characteristic Spanish Renaissance armchair or sillón was the frailero (60) or monk's chair. It was a walnut armchair of simple rectangular form made of plain quadrangular supports with a leather seat and back panel. The chair was designed with a medium to moderately high back and with a broad front stretcher. The leather back panel stretched between the upright supports and the leather seat stretched between the side rails were securely fastened with decorative nailheads. Frequently the upright supports were surmounted with finials. Occasionally the leather seat was provided with a loose cushion. Generally the arms were straight and frequently very wide. This chair was the prototype for the Mission chair so profusely and cheaply manufactured in America. However, the latter had neither the dignity nor the grace which made the original distinctive. It seems that when the Spanish missionaries settled in California and Mexico, they furnished their monasteries in a style similar to those at home. Unfortunately, the furniture was a poor reproduction of the original Spanish pieces, with the result that the so-called Mission furniture of this country, which further accentuated the weak points, was destined to be a fiasco. The frame of the earliest frailero (60) was often collapsible, so that it could be carried on a journey. Later it was made of permanent construction. The leather seat and back panel were frequently elaborately tooled. When the frailero was to be used in a more elegant and formal room, the leather was generally covered with velvet and enhanced with braid and a deep fringe, the back panel often being embroidered in gold thread. As the 16th century advanced the frailero became more ornate (61). The broad front stretcher, which was always its most distinguishing feature, was more elaborately carved or fretted. The side stretchers, which were usually close to the floor, often had a shaped lower edge. The finials were sometimes made of molded brass and the armposts supporting the broadened flat arms were often carved or turned. Occasionally the seat of the frailero had the usual frame of four seat rails instead of just the two side rails, and sometimes it was designed with an arcaded wooden back in place of the leather panel. The runner feet, which were found on many Italian Renaissance chairs, were only occasionally used on Spanish chairs.

A variety of Late Spanish Renaissance rectangular, tall-back armchair, showing Baroque influence, is usually referred to as the Portuguese chair, since it is believed to have been of Portuguese origin. It was characterized by elaborately turned armposts, legs and stretchers and by an ornately carved and arched broad front stretcher. As a rule the arms were shaped, and the feet were in the form of scrolls, known as a Spanish foot. The chair had a finely tooled leather seat and a deep back panel, fastened to the frame with a solid row of large ornamental nailheads or chatónes. The seat was wider in the front. The deep back panel, which was usually arched at the top and shaped at the base, was frequently surmounted with two brass finials. The Portuguese chair was also designed as a side chair.

The Spanish side chair or silla, which was also rectangular in form, was made in a variety of designs. The low back side chair with an upholstered seat and back panel and turned members (62) displayed a family resemblance to the rectilinear French chair with spirally turned members which was fashionable in France in the first half of the 17th century. The different provinces, such as Aragon, Catalonia, Santander, Andalusia, Navarre, Castile and the island of Majorca, all contributed many distinctive designs for side chairs. One form of side chair had a wooden seat with an arcaded back and a broad front stretcher (64). In some examples the open back and front stretcher were of conforming design (63). Occasionally the chair was made with a rush seat or a corded seat, the latter being worked in intricate and ingenious designs. Frequently the side chair was simply carved with incised or merely gouged geometric designs or conventionalized leaf and flower motifs. The originality of design, simplicity of form and sturdy construction combined to give these provincial side chairs a unique peasant charm, which was innately Spanish in character. In all probability the most colorful and distinctive provincial side chair was developed in Catalonia toward the end of the 17th century or early 18th century. It was a rectangular, tall-back chair, with elaborately turned supports and a rush seat. The backposts were surmounted with long pointed finials. The back consisted of three ornamental crosspieces. The top crosspiece was arched and elaborately decorated, and the two remaining crosspieces, as well as the broad front stretcher, were of conforming design, but less elaborate in detail and with the arch more modified. The legs were connected with turned stretchers. The chair was brilliantly painted in red, green or ivory and then partially gilded.

Benches   The bench (69) or banco was a popular article of furniture and was found everywhere. It must be remembered that the bench, chair and stool composed all the seating facilities in the Spanish Renaissance home. The characteristic variety was of simple construction, and was made to seat about three persons (69). The back was made of a solid, oblong piece of wood, with a similar piece of wood being used for the seat. The height of the back and the depth of the seat were about equal. The seat rested on trestle-end supports. Frequently a scrolled wrought-iron underbrace was attached beneath the middle of the seat and was fastened to the stretcher of each trestle-end support (69). The back was sometimes sparingly carved or enhanced with wrought-iron appliqués. Occasionally the top of the back was shaped. When the bench was to be used in a more formal setting, it was covered in leather or velvet, often quilted or stitched in geometrical patterns, and fastened to the wooden back and seat with ornamental nailheads (69). Another form of bench had a wooden seat with either an arched back or a spindled back, designed in a manner similar to the provincial chair backs already described. The early benches were generally without arms. Some of the later benches were designed with arms. The characteristic Gothic chest-bench (65, 66) or settle, having a panelled back and arms, was also found in Spain toward the close of the 15th century. Extant examples are notable for their wealth of carved ornament (66).

Stools

The low stool or banqueta was also popular and plentiful. It was of simple construction. The stool usually had a rectangular wood seat. Occasionally the seat was covered with leather or velvet and fastened with decorative nailheads. The seat rested either on trestle-end supports or on turned or carved legs.

Beds

The Spanish bed or cama, until about the 17th century, was crudely constructed. It was completely concealed by draperies, the quality and quantity of which depended upon the affluence of the owner. By the 17th century the bed with tall posts and the bed with medium-height posts had both been designed. The Spanish were inherently fond of lavish and elaborate beds. The Spanish bed was generally made of either walnut or mahogany. Occasionally it was painted and gilded. It was often designed without a footboard. A distinctive Spanish bed was a splendid Baroque model, originating in the province of Catalonia, in the 17th century. The solid headboard, which was separate, was attached to the wall. It was elaborately ornamented and generally brilliantly painted and gilded, and was outlined in bold Baroque scrolls. A low four-post bed was used with this headboard. Another type of bed had four tall slender spirally turned posts, surmounted with long pointed finials, with a turned spindled headboard. This type usually had a shallow fabric valance.

Tables

The Spanish table or mesa was made in a variety of forms and sizes. In all probability the most characteristic Spanish table is the one with splayed legs and an ornamental wrought-iron underbrace (73, 74). Practically all the early, long, Spanish dining tables originated in the monasteries and were usually of walnut. They were generally constructed with thick, massive removable tops, which rested upon trestle-end supports. The Renaissance table had either turned or carved legs or splayed trestle-end supports, frequently of lyre shape. The table with trestle-end supports was especially characteristic and usually had a scrolled wrought-iron underbrace, attached beneath the center of the table and joined at the stretcher of each trestle-end support (73, 74). The turned or carved legs were generally connected with a continuous stretcher or one of H-form, which sometimes had an arcaded crosspiece; the stretcher was usually close to the floor. The edge of the Renaissance table was always square. Carved or molded edges did not appear, and then only occasionally, until late in the 17th century. A Renaissance table was also made with a carved frieze, which was fitted with drawers. In this type of table the top sometimes extended well over the frieze. The ingeniously devised draw-top table was also made by the Spanish cabinetmaker, but in a limited quantity. The richly carved table with its ornately shaped truss-end supports, which was so fashionable in Italy (45) and France in the 16th century, was only seldom found in Spain (76). Small Renaissance tables were made in the same forms as the large ones, as well as in several designs of their own. Small gate-leg tables were popular in the 17th century. Especially fashionable and plentiful in the 17th century Spanish home were diminutive walnut tables, fashioned after the large ones, and having an average height of about two feet.

Cabinets The vargueño (72, 75), an oblong walnut cabinet, which was essentially designed as a receptacle for documents and other valuables and could also be used as a desk, was Spain's most distinctive, as well as finest, piece of cabinetwork. It was notable for its skillfully executed and exuberantly rich decorations. The vargueño was designed with a hinged drop-front, which opened to disclose a richly ornamented interior of drawers and doors. In the early vargueño the interior, and frequently the exterior, was generally elaborately inlaid with ivory and various woods in designs executed in either the Moorish or Mudéjar styles (72). The ivory was often brilliantly painted in red, blue, green and gold, and the pieces in natural ivory color were often etched with designs in black. Later, due to the influence of the Italian Renaissance, the interior usually displayed an architectural façade, incorporating colonnettes and pilasters, made of ivory or carved and gilded (75). The small drawers and doors were handsomely carved and brilliantly painted and gilded with classic motifs, or richly inlaid with exotic woods or ivory (75). The interior was ornamented in many other combinations of elaborate designs, and it was always notable for its rich and exuberant ornamentation, which represented the highest degree of Spanish craftsmanship. As a rule, the only exterior decoration of the vargueño was the exquisite wrought-iron mounts, which were sometimes gilded. These usually consisted of delicately pierced wrought-iron appliqués, generally backed with crimson velvet, and an elaborate lock, hasp and pulls. Also at each end were drop handles. The vargueño was also designed in miniature form.

The vargueño rested on one of several varieties of table stands or bases. One typical variety was an elaborately carved table trestle stand, called a puente (72). It was especially designed to support the vargueño and was fitted with two long slides, which, when pulled out, supported the drop-front of the vargueño. The end of each slide was usually decorated with a carved shell motif or a grotesque animal mask (72). At each end of the stand there were three fluted or spiralled columns, which rested on a runner base, and had a high, richly carved, arcaded stretcher, which connected the two middle columns of each trestle end support (72). By extension the term *puente* is frequently applied to any table trestle stand which is used to support a vargueño or papelera. A variant of this type was a graceful, narrow, table stand with turned splayed trestle-ends and with an ornamental wrought-iron brace (71). Another characteristic base designed to support a vargueño is called a taquillón (75), and was approximately of the same dimensions as the vargueño. The façade was designed in four equal compartments (75), being fitted with two upper drawers and two lower cupboard doors, or four of each. Above the compartments were two slides, which when pulled out supported the drop-front of the vargueño (75). The façade of the taquillón was richly but not as lavishly designed as the interior of the vargueño. It was frequently parcel gilded and inlaid with ivory ornament and carved with lozenge motifs (75). The façade was decorated in many combinations of beautiful designs, all of which were invariably geometrical in character. The taquillón was mounted on four feet. Another variety of table stand was a scissors stand or one of X-form. This type was of Moorish origin and was rare. It was usually ornamented with intricate geometrical patterns of ivory inlay.

The Spanish term *papelera* was given to a cabinet designed as a receptacle for documents and papers and all kinds of writing materials. In particular, the name *papelera* was applied to an oblong cabinet, similar to the vargueño, but without a drop-front (71). In this article of furniture the richly decorated interior was the actual front. The papelera was usually mounted on ball feet (71). As a rule it was placed on a narrow, graceful, trestle table stand with an ornamental wrought-iron underbrace.

Writing Furniture It seems that the Spanish did most of their writing at tables, so that the desk was not a characteristic piece of Spanish furniture. During the Renaissance they did design a limited number of double-bodied writing cabinets, which were found in a few of the wealthy houses. The double-bodied writing cabinet was essentially an architectural piece and reflected the influence of the Italian Renaissance. One characteristic variety had a hinged fall-front, which opened to reveal an interior of drawers, doors and pigeonholes, richly decorated and generally incorporating architectural detail such as colonnettes, pediments and pilasters. The stiles on the upper body were often decorated with several tiers of fully sculptured figures. The lower body was fitted with plain molded cupboard doors and rested on an undecorated molded base.

Chests The Spanish chest or arca (67, 79, 80) was by far the most important and necessary piece of Spanish domestic furniture. And, unlike in other countries where it was supplanted by more specialized pieces for specific purposes, such as a chest of drawers, its popularity continued throughout the following centuries. The chest varied greatly in height, width and length. It was usually designed with a flat hinged lid. Occasionally the lid was arched but this more frequently occurred in the designs for small coffers. The early Spanish chest was usually decorated in characteristic Gothic, Moorish or Mudéjar taste. The Gothic chest (67) was carved, painted or gilded. Tracery work (67) or linen-fold panels were favorite motifs for the decorative carvings. Painted heraldic panels and religious emblems were widely used. Especially characteristic was the use of elaborate, wrought-iron mounts and decorative bands, finely executed in flamboyant Gothic designs. The chest decorated in Moorish taste displayed an elaborate inlay of bone or ivory, worked in rich and varied minute geometrical designs (80). Distinctively Spanish was the chest covered in either plain or handsomely tooled leather or in fine velvet or damask, crimson being the favorite color. A chest covered in leather or fabric was generally trunk-shaped and usually had an arched lid, and was frequently decorated in chatónes or ornamental nailheads worked in beautiful geometrical designs. Due to the influence of the Italian Renaissance many new combinations of designs, incorporating classic motifs, were used in decorating the Renaissance chest. Occasionally in the most ambitious examples the inside of the lid of the chest was inlaid, carved or painted (79). This chest was usually fitted with another plain lid, which covered the contents of the chest and permitted the top lid to rest against the wall, in order to display its decoration. Provincial chests were distinctive for the charming simplicity of their decoration. The Spanish term *arqueta* was frequently given to a miniature chest, such as one used as a receptacle for jewels. The Spanish fondness for table boxes was an old Moorish legacy. These early boxes, profusely placed on tables, were rarely more than a foot in length, and were usually richly decorated in different combinations of elaborate surface ornamentation.

Cupboards   The early domestic cupboard was set in the wall and was fitted with shelves. A characteristic variety of built-in cupboard had the interior lined with tiles, with a border of tiles generally outlining the opening. This type of cupboard was especially decorative and has retained its popularity down to the present day. It is generally believed that the oldest movable cupboard or armario was the sacristy cupboard, which was rectilinear and usually upright in form. The principal Renaissance variety was double-bodied in construction (78). The upper body was fitted with two doors, and each door was panelled into two sections, the upper section being designed with a row of turned spindles; sometimes each section had a row of spindles. The lower body was fitted with two cupboard doors, with each door panelled into two or more divisions and carved with geometrical ornament. The use of the turned spindles was a marked feature of design of this form of sacristy cupboard (78). Another variety of sacristy cupboard had an oblong rectangular body, fitted with two doors, with a single row of drawers beneath, and rested on four supports which were secured to a shelf close to the floor. This cupboard was frequently decorated with an inlay of various woods. There was also a low cupboard having a resemblance to the Italian sacristy cupboard. The Spanish sacristy cupboard found its way into many Spanish homes where it was often used as a buffet.

The Renaissance armario (70), which corresponded in its general function and design to the Italian armadio and the French armoire, was rectangular and upright in form and was generally designed with either two or four cupboard doors. Of interest was the double-bodied armario which was similar to the French armoire à deux corps, and which in all probability often served as a buffet in the Spanish home. Another form of armario was purely of Moorish inspiration in its method of joinery and design. It was enriched with small interlaced panel divisions and painted decoration resembling the cabinetwork in a traditional Moorish carved and painted ceiling. The armario was a relatively rare piece of Spanish Renaissance furniture. However, in the ensuing 17th and 18th centuries it became more popular and plentiful.

The fresquera was the name given to a ventilated domestic food cupboard. A characteristic variety was rectangular in form and rather shallow, and hung on the wall. The upper division in each of the two cupboard doors was designed with a row of turned spindles or lattice work. There was a graceful simplicity attached to this well-proportioned piece, which gave it considerable individual charm.

Accessories   Wrought-iron and bronze candlesticks and candelabra all displayed workmanship of the highest quality. A distinctive decorative appointment was the Spanish pole lantern, also called a farol. It was a relatively large, many-sided lantern, made of tin, which was painted and gilded and cut into elaborate, openwork designs. Generally, various colored pieces of glass were fitted in back of or into these openwork designs. The lantern was mounted on a long red pole or one covered with crimson velvet. Occasionally instead of surmounting a pole it was suspended on a heavy silk cord from the ceiling.

The lavabo, a French term meaning a wash-basin, was the name given to a basin placed beneath a wall fountain. The wall fountain, which was usually affixed to the wall, was a container for water, with a spigot at the bottom. It was generally made of copper, pewter or pottery, and the lavabo was of similar material. In the Spanish home the wall fountain and lavabo were made of colorful faïence, and were invariably placed in a niche lined with colored tiles. They were often used in the dining room, and provided a striking note in the décor of the room. Sometimes the lavabo and water vessels were provided with their own stands (77).

Résumé of SPANISH
17th and 18th Century FURNITURE

The Baroque spirit permeated the Spanish decorative arts of the 17th century and its influence became more noticeable as the century progressed. Much Spanish furniture of the 17th century still reflected traditional Spanish and Moorish influence in its style of ornament and simplicity of structure. This was especially noticeable in the provincial cabinetwork made by the village cabinetmaker. Spanish furniture reflecting the Baroque influence, as developed in Italy and later in France under Louis XIV, was chiefly found in the fashionable cabinetwork made in the principal cities. This furniture displayed a more extensive use of classic motifs, especially those in vogue during the Late Renaissance in Italy. The classic ornament was larger in scale and less geometrical and stylized than in the preceding 16th century. There was a more pronounced use of vigorous curves. Cartouches, large foliated scrolls, volutes, C-scrolls and S-scrolls, banderoles, coats-of-arms and heraldic devices, human figures, birds and animal figures were all included among the favorite Spanish motifs. Spanish Baroque furniture often displayed more carving, and painting and gilding were used more extensively. Bold and vigorous scrolls and elaborate turning were much in evidence. The elaborate Baroque bedsteads were especially characteristic. A greater variety of more elegant chairs was made. Benches and settees were often more elaborate, some being carved and gilded. Cabinets frequently incorporated more architectural detail in their designs, and were often lavishly painted and gilded or inlaid. Tables occasionally had valanced aprons and scrolled trestle-end supports. The decorative appointments became more sumptuous. Especially typical were the elaborate velvet or brocaded wall hangings blazoned with armorial bearings, the heavily carved and gilded Baroque wall mirrors often with scrolled crestings, the carved, gilded and polychromed torchères, the fine Venetian glass chandeliers and the ornate sconces, candlesticks and candelabra made of gilded bronze or wood.

Since Spain was governed by the Bourbons in the 18th century it was only natural that French art and customs should prevail. Philip V, 1700–1746, who was the first Bourbon to sit on the Spanish throne, brought with him from his palace in Paris much of its furnishings, and in so doing he created a vogue among the Spanish noblemen for French furniture. These noblemen, emulating the tastes of their French King, proceeded to have their furniture imported from France. Soon the Spanish cabinetmakers in the principal cities began to reproduce these French imports for their less wealthy clients, who also wanted the newest designs in fashionable furniture. As a result of this vogue for French furniture, the Louis XV style was evident in much contemporary Spanish cabinetwork. Then, at a later date, Charles III, 1759–1788, established a royal workshop at Madrid where some fine examples of Spanish cabinetwork were designed in the succeeding Louis XVI style. Later, during the Napoleonic era, the Spanish cabinetmaker produced some excellent cabinetwork interpreting the Empire style. All the fashionable 18th century English styles were also interpreted in Spanish furniture design. A difference in technique as well as very often in materials made all this Spanish cabinetwork easy to distinguish from its French and English prototypes. In addition to this fashionable furniture there was also made in the regional districts much Spanish furniture decorated with the prevailing French and English 18th century styles of ornament but designed and constructed in the traditional Spanish and Moorish manner, such as provincial chests, painted chairs and tables. Some regional cabinetmakers completely ignored the new styles of ornament and persisted in using ornament of Moorish inspiration.

The different categories for Spanish furniture in the 18th century essentially remained the same, although there was a greater diversity within each category. Some of the wealthy aristocracy did adopt many of the new forms introduced by the French and English during the 18th century. However, this custom was confined to a relatively small group and some of the forms were never interpreted by the Spanish cabinetmaker. The craftsmanship found in French and English cabinetwork was superior in quality to Spanish, although the Spanish did do some excellent work. As in the earlier Baroque style, the Spanish cabinetmaker working in these 18th century styles imbued them with certain peculiarities which made them distinctively Spanish. For example, chair backs with high crestings and cabriole legs with conspicuous curves were much in evidence. The Spanish Rococo furniture was generally marred by ostentatious ornamentation and by exaggerated curves, resulting in an incorrect sense of balance and proportion. The Spanish Louis XVI, Empire and English Sheraton were more pleasing since they adhered more closely to the original models. Especially fine were some pieces designed in the French Empire style, which were often painted and gilded. Lacquered furniture, particularly with a red ground, was quite popular. All the fashionable decorative processes, such as veneering, marquetry, carving, painting and gilding, were employed for decorating the surface of furniture. The metal mounts used on the cabinetwork displayed the highest quality of craftsmanship. Although some of this later Spanish cabinetwork possessed real merit, it was in the earlier Renaissance work with its structural simplicity and vigorous lines that the Spanish cabinetmaker achieved his renown in the history of European furniture design.

CHAPTER FIVE

DUTCH & FLEMISH

DUTCH AND FLEMISH GOTHIC

The Low Countries, comprising what is now known as Holland and Belgium, are pressed in closely between countries inhabited by Teutonic and Latin races. This dual influence has been reflected through the centuries in their religion and politics and in all their branches of art. In a broad sense Belgium was influenced by France and Holland by Germany. The history of this section of Europe is very checkered and to try to fit in all the different influences contributing to its art is almost like solving a jigsaw puzzle. The dominating influence for this group of provinces during the Gothic period was the House of Burgundy. The dynastic events uniting the affairs of the Netherlands early in the 14th century with the House of Burgundy and which finally united the Netherlands with Spain under Emperor Charles V, 1516–1556, are exceedingly complicated and it will not be necessary from a cultural viewpoint to discuss these burdensome details. However, since the Burgundian court exerted great influence on the development of the decorative arts in the Netherlands, it is of considerable significance to realize that the Burgundian Court in those days was renowned for its luxury, magnificence and opulence.

Contemporary records give vivid descriptions of the wealthy Burgundian princes, their sumptuous palaces, their magnificent dress and their stiff and splendid liveries. Philip the Bold, 1363–1404, and Philip the Good, 1419–1467, were both ardent patrons of the arts. Under their patronage all branches of the arts flourished. No court in Europe surpassed the court of Philip the Good in luxury and magnificence. The finest in paintings, manuscripts, gold plate, furniture and tapestries were all made for the Dukes of Burgundy. Artistically unimportant were the French kings Charles VI, 1380–1422, and Charles VII, 1422–1461,

63

when compared to their relatives, the wealthy and powerful Dukes of Burgundy. Contemporary literature reveals that travelers going from France to Flanders felt as if they were entering the Promised Land. Commercial and industrial towns like Bruges, Ghent, Brussels, Antwerp, Utrecht and Amsterdam became thriving art centers and abounded with the most skillful of craftsmen. It is recorded that in 1340 the city of Ghent had over 40,000 weavers, while the city of Bruges was noted for its goldsmiths. The severance of the Netherlands from Burgundy occurred in 1477 when Charles the Bold was killed in battle. The French King, Louis XI, promptly seized the Duchy of Burgundy which remained from that time onwards united to the French crown. The Netherlands passing from the dominion of the House of Burgundy to the House of Austria, which also numbered Spain among its possessions, continued to prosper, with wealth pouring in from all quarters. And, although the Netherlands were cut off politically from Burgundy, the Burgundian influence continued to be an important factor in the arts of the Lowlands throughout the 16th century.

The commercial and industrial superiority enjoyed by the Netherlands with its resultant social progress had a stimulating effect on medieval architecture. The wealth and prosperity of the merchants and weavers in the thriving industrial and commercial centers were reflected in the numerous Guild houses and Town Halls. It is easy to understand that the influence of French Gothic architecture was felt at an early date in that part of the Netherlands near to France. The French character was particularly evident in Flanders. German and Spanish ingredients could also be detected in some Flemish work. Flemish architecture was rich in sculptured ornament executed in either stone or wood. It was marked by a prominent use of sculptured human figures. A striking feature of Flemish architecture was the exacting care given to the entire work, even to the smallest detail. The Gothic style was later in developing in Holland than it was in Flanders. The influence of the German Gothic style was evident in Dutch architecture. However, the seeds of the Dutch national quality of simplicity notable in their later work were visible in their Gothic architecture.

The fame of the Flemish wood carvers spread far beyond their own domains. Their skillful carvings, which were copied from the stone sculpture work on the beautiful cathedrals, ornamented many Flemish ecclesiastical and domestic pieces of furniture. The Flemish Gothic furniture was fundamentally similar to the contemporary French Gothic furniture in its general function, construction, forms and style of ornament. Chests, tables made of removable boards and trestle supports, rectangular stools, the so-called box-chair, with the portion beneath the seat forming a chest, and folding chairs were found among the essential pieces of domestic furniture. Much of the early furniture, such as cupboards, benches, beds and settles, was built into the walls. As the 15th century progressed the furniture became more elaborately carved. Burgundian furniture, which is always distinctive for its wealth of ornament, was richly and vigorously carved with the fashionable Gothic motifs. Fine examples of this Burgundian manner of ornamentation can be found on some Flemish chests and buffet-dressoirs. Wall hangings of magnificent tapestries and brilliantly painted and gilded leather decorated the walls of the medieval castles. Some of the great tapestries of the world were of Flemish origin. Tournay was renowned for its Gothic tapestries. The art of embossing leather as perfected by the Moors in Spain was another Flemish achievement. France, Venice and the Netherlands were the leading centers for gilded leathers during the Gothic era. Beautifully wrought gold plate, fine enamel work, exquisite embroideries, silk velvets and damasks were all executed with the highest skill by the Flemish craftsmen. Finely wrought brass and copper wares or dinanderie were made at Dinand in the Netherlands and were remarkable for their finished craftsmanship. Paintings by Van Eyck and his contemporaries and followers convey the atmosphere of a Late Gothic interior with notable success. Perhaps the perfect example is Van Eyck's *John Arnolfini and His Wife* with its exquisitely painted details. The mirror with its frame decorated with miniatures, the one lighted candle in the chandelier and the carved detail on the furniture become almost tangible in this enchanting example of beautifully finished art.

DUTCH AND FLEMISH RENAISSANCE

We have already seen that the life of the Netherlands was based on commerce and industry, for she was favorably located on the sea and she had deep wide rivers penetrating into the interior. During the 16th century the fine trade and industry, which had enjoyed such an auspicious beginning in the Gothic period, prospered prodigiously. The Burgundian heritage, with its love of splendor and opulence, was an important influence in the Netherlands in the 16th century. The nobility vied with royalty in acquiring such luxuries as tapestries, gold and silver plate, enamels, gilded leathers, finely engraved and enamelled glass, colorful majolica dishes and vessels, and fine furniture. Because of this taste for all kinds of decorative art objects, the thriving cities of the Netherlands abounded with craftsmen, who were highly skilled as weavers, goldsmiths, glass engravers, cabinetmakers, wood carvers, enamellers, leather workers, lace makers, embroiderers and ceramic workers. Cities like Antwerp, Lille, Bruges, Ghent, Brussels, Haarlem and Amsterdam were the wonder and envy of the other European cities, not only because of their wealth but also because of the intellectual culture of their people. Early in the 16th century Antwerp became the leading center of art and industry, occupying the position held by Bruges in the preceding century. Brussels was unrivalled for its Renaissance tapestries. Charles V, who was born and reared in the Netherlands, always retained a high esteem and sincere affection for his native country. He made Brussels the capital of the Netherlands. Unfortunately, he drew heavily upon the resources of the Netherlands to support his imperial policies. This fact, plus his suppression of Protestantism, resulted in a growing discontent boding ill for his successor, who was his son, Philip II of Spain, 1556–1598.

This impending religious and political struggle with Spain finally broke out in open revolt, with the southern Catholic Netherlands remaining loyal to the Spanish crown. The seven northern Protestant provinces, which were destined to be a great maritime and commercial power, continued their struggle against Spain until their independence was recognized in 1609. Undoubtedly the most striking cultural feature in this part of the history of the Netherlands is the revelation that the division of Europe into Catholic and Protestant camps affected the art of even small countries like the Netherlands. This fact becomes patent in the ensuing 17th century when the southern Netherlands accepted the exuberant painter Rubens whose art work so typically represented the Baroque movement in Catholic Europe. On the other hand, the inhabitants of the northern provinces were almost all Protestants. They had little toleration for the sensuous Baroque style and disliked the exuberant pomp and splendor associated with the Catholic Church. The Dutch showed little inclination for any artistic expression of their religion. And, although their almost puritanical outlook on art mellowed with their increasing wealth, they never accepted the full Baroque style, which ruled over Catholic Europe until about 1700 when it reached its culmination.

A closer relationship between Italy and the south Netherlands became increasingly evident in the 15th century. This was largely due to common trade interests and to the Flemish artists who journeyed more frequently to Venice and Florence to study classical culture. Gradually in architecture Renaissance ornament and detail began to supplant the Gothic ornament. This transitional character of the early Renaissance continued during practically the entire first half of the 16th century. It was not until around the middle of the 16th century that the Renaissance style was fully developed. Flemish architecture of the 16th century, as well as of the ensuing 17th and 18th centuries, was essentially similar to that of France, but was characterized by a greater freedom and extravagance in design. Flemish Renaissance ornament never did achieve the high standard that the Flemish Gothic ornament had attained. The Flemings seemed unable to assimilate with the same degree of success the principles of Renaissance architecture. Their work was usually overburdened with a profusion of ornament amounting to almost riotous extravagance. For this reason the Baroque style gained an early foothold in the south Netherlands. Actually, all the Renaissance architecture was exuberant and ornate, and any feeling of restraint or reserve was almost always disregarded. In view of this fact it is difficult to say just how early the Baroque spirit was felt in that part of the Lowlands. To the Flemings the Baroque style seemed to be a normal method of expression, and this expression reached its pinnacle in the paintings of that great genius, Rubens.

The Renaissance style developed later and flourished longer in Holland than in Flanders; it was not until the last quarter of the 16th century that the Renaissance style was felt to any great extent. Renaissance architecture in Holland displayed a distinctive sober restraint. A peculiar solid and matter-of-fact quality, which is associated with the Dutch people, was visible in their architecture. This Dutch style or taste became more pronounced in the following 17th century and was mirrored in the plain and serviceable red brick houses built for the wealthy burghers and in the almost barn-like churches. Fine proportions, an interesting spatial relationship and a sensitive use of materials were principal features in this essentially severely plain and regular style of classic architecture. Occasionally certain Oriental features were introduced, which undoubtedly resulted from their trade relations with the Far East and which added a novel and interesting note to their work. Then, too, the Spanish occupation, which continued until 1713, and its resultant influence sometimes added a small element of richness. However, the Dutch character is most directly shown in its buildings of very simple structure and not in the ones on a grander scale displaying rich ornament. The Dutch did not possess the talent for integrating ornament, with the result that it was often heavy, excessive and obvious.

Much of the early Renaissance furniture was of a transitional nature. Renaissance motifs were blended with a few favorite Gothic motifs and were grafted on Gothic forms. The 16th century Flemish Renaissance furniture was essentially similar to the French styles of François I and Henri II. The furniture was rectilinear in contour and massive in form. Certain details borrowed from architecture were incorporated in its principles of design, such as pediments, pilasters, cornices and moldings. Unfortunately a large part of their cabinetwork revealed the same inability to grasp Renaissance principles that was evident in their architecture. For example, the moldings were seldom in scale with each other or with the article of furniture they were decorating. Then, too, the ornament, which should be subordinate to the structure and should complement and emphasize the lines of the structure, frequently concealed or obscured the lines. It is important to remember that in all cabinetwork displaying a high level of design the moldings, ornament and structure are invariably in harmony with each other and are skillfully adapted to the scale of the piece of furniture. During the Renaissance the majority of Flemish cabinetwork was in walnut, superseding the oak furniture of the Gothic period. Ebony was occasionally employed for some ambitious pieces of cabinetwork, such as the well-known Flemish cabinets with their beautifully carved decoration. Carving was by far the most fashionable method for decorating the surface of furniture. The fame of the Flemish wood carver was known throughout Europe, for his carvings were artistic achievements of rare skill. The French king Henri IV sent French cabinetmakers to the Netherlands to learn the art of carving in ebony. Inlay work, painting and gilding were all practiced by the Flemish cabinetmaker. Occasionally, very costly and elaborate cabinets were inlaid with semi-precious stones, precious metals and various exotic woods.

Flemish furniture was always characterized by its great wealth of carved ornament and much of it was excessively burdened with rich ornament. The composition of the ornament, which was assertively Flemish, lacked the refinement and finish for which the Italian craftsmen of the High Renaissance were unsurpassed. During the late 16th century some Flemish furniture was more restrained in its design as well as in its ornamentation, and displayed a less frequent use of human figures. This became more apparent in the early 17th century when the vogue for turning resulted in a further diminishing of the number of carved figures for supports. Included among the favorite Flemish Renaissance motifs were classical heroes and pagan deities, animal figures, birds, grotesques, caryatids, terms, cartouches, arabesques, all kinds of foliage, flowers and fruit, foliated scrolls, C-scrolls, S-scrolls, vase forms, medallions, swags, trophies, cornucopias, candelabra, mascarons, strapwork, banderoles, cherubs' heads and winged angels. The influence of Jan Vredman de Vries, b.1527, Dutch architect, sculptor and designer of ornament and furniture, and his son, Paul, was evident in contemporary furniture designs. In 1577 Jan de Vries published a book on designs and style of ornament in Antwerp. Especially characteristic of his work were elaborately carved pilasters, heavy cornices, rich scrollwork, curling and twisted flowers and leaves, pierced crestings, strapwork and all kinds of figures. Numerous Flemish pattern books, such as the one by De Vries, were published around the third and last quarters of the 16th century. These books, which also included designs for chimneypieces, doorways and windows, were exported to England and were a principal source of supply and inspiration for Renaissance ornament during the long reign of Queen Elizabeth. Their influence was evident in the work of Hugues Sambin who established a distinctive school of furniture making in Burgundy.

ARTICLES OF FURNITURE

Many pieces of Flemish furniture in the 16th century were of a permanent nature, such as cupboards, benches, settles and beds. Especially distinctive were the numerous beds resembling huge cupboards which were built into the panelling of rooms. They had a rather cramped uncomfortable appearance, but on a cold night in a room without heat they undoubtedly were entirely satisfactory. The movable pieces were not too unlike the contemporary pieces found in northern France.

Chairs   The Flemings designed a wide variety of richly carved armchairs, essentially using Italian chairs as prototypes. Wooden side chairs were characterized by ornately carved and shaped backs. There was a marked preference for chairs of curule form designed either with or without arms. These chairs retained their popularity during the 17th century, as can be seen in the Flemish and Dutch paintings.

Beds   The Flemish tester bed found in the homes of the nobility was elaborately carved, inlaid, painted or gilded. It was always an imposing and massive article of furniture, and it generally displayed architectural detail in its principles of design. Occasionally the bed was enclosed with panelling extending to the floor, in place of legs. The headboard was lavishly ornamented and sometimes the richly carved wooden tester was supported by either massive columns or terms. A distinctive feature of the Flemish bed was the pomme or the decorative finial surmounting each corner of the cornice. The pomme designed as a plume of feathers was most fashionable.

Tables   The Flemish Renaissance table was principally inspired by Italian Renaissance models. The top of the table was most often rectangular and it was supported on truss-ends, a pedestal, brackets or legs; the latter were often designed in the form of human figures, crouching animals, terms or vases. The Flemish also had developed the ingenious draw-top table.

Chests   The Flemish chest was an important piece of domestic furniture and was richly carved in Renaissance motifs. The chest was very often decorated with carved figures of a sculpturesque quality and with prominent vigorously carved moldings. Occasionally the chest was covered with embossed painted and gilded leather.

Cabinets   The Flemish cabinet (FIGURES 103, 104) possessed the greatest artistic value of all the Flemish Renaissance cabinetwork. The cabinet-maker lavished all of his skill in carving and decorating this choice piece of furniture. Sculptors, painters, stone and ivory cutters, marqueteurs, enamellers and goldsmiths frequently contributed their talent to its enrichment. Cabinets displaying this ambitious workmanship had their provenance in Italy, and their prototypes were later found at Antwerp, at Augsburg and Nuremberg in Germany and at Paris. These elaborately decorated cabinets which were often mounted on a decorative stand with figural supports, were fitted with secret drawers and with numerous small compartments and doors for displaying and storing priceless objects of virtú. The vogue for these luxury cabinets continued into the 17th century. Cabinets made of ebony designed in two sections and with each section generally fitted with two doors were also remarkable for their workmanship. These cabinets, having the interior of their upper section fitted with numerous small cupboard doors and drawers, attested to the unrivalled skill of the Flemish wood carver.

Résumé of FLEMISH
17th and 18th Century FURNITURE

The paintings of Peter Paul Rubens influenced the art of Catholic Europe for the first half of the 17th century. After studying in Italy and Spain for eight years Rubens returned to Antwerp in 1608 and in the following year he was appointed court painter. During his years of study he had acquired such facility in arranging large scale compositions, of placing figures, of handling draperies, of using light and color to increase the general effect of more movement and contrast that he had no rival north of the Alps. His paintings expressed his conceptions, as well as the Flemish conception, of the fullness and richness of life. He possessed the magic skill to make any subject intensely and joyously alive. The art of Rubens became very fashionable, for it was suited to enhance the splendor of palaces and to glorify the powers of this world. He accepted commissions from the contemporary Catholic rulers for Flanders, Spain and France and England, and, in so doing, he was instrumental in spreading Roman Baroque art through Europe. Rubens devoted much time to the study of antique carvings, in which field he became a leading authority. This same vitality, richness, fullness and movement was also evident in his ornament. It is easy to understand why Rubens is regarded as the originator of

69

the Baroque style in the Netherlands and one of its principal transmitters in Europe. It is difficult to ascertain just when the Baroque style developed in Antwerp and Brussels. Undoubtedly an important milestone in the development of Baroque decorative art in Belgium was the completion of Rubens' home in 1620 in Antwerp. The architecture, interior decoration and furniture reflected strong Italian Baroque influence.

Until about the third or fourth decade of the 17th century Flanders continued to dominate Holland in the decorative arts. However, due to the commercial ascendancy of Holland in the Netherlands in the 17th century, the Dutch style gradually asserted itself in certain preferences both in ornament and form over the prevailing Flemish style. The Flemish furniture for the first half of the 17th century was essentially similar to the French style of Louis XIII, 1610–1643 (*see pages* 85, 86, 87). Spanish decorative art also supplied a small source of inspiration for the Flemish style of ornament. During the second half of the 17th century the French Baroque, as perfected in the style of Louis XIV, was the principal influence. Chairs, stools, benches, settles, beds, tables, chests, double-bodied cupboards, cabinets and buffets were included among the characteristic pieces of Flemish 17th century furniture. There was less furniture of a permanent nature. The fashionable furniture was profusely ornamented; however, furniture made in the provinces was sparingly decorated, as is apparent in the 17th century Flemish paintings. Later in the 17th century there was evident a growing tendency to introduce curved members into the furniture forms, such as scrolled front legs for chairs. Toward the end of the century upholstered furniture became more prevalent. Carving, turning, marquetry, painting, lacquering, gilding and inlaying of semiprecious stones and exotic woods were all included among the favorite decorative methods for ornamenting the surface of furniture. Carving was employed on much fine furniture; however, the vogue for turning and marquetry substantially reduced the amount of carving. Assertively Flemish Baroque were elaborate carvings, crestings and scrolled ornaments. All kinds of rich and extravagant scrollwork, such as floral and leaf scrolls, C-scrolls and S-scrolls, were a conspicuous feature of the Flemish Baroque spirit. The Flemish scroll, which was two Baroque reverse C-scrolls joined at an angle, was extremely popular. Flemish furniture throughout the 18th century essentially followed the French styles of the Régence, Louis XV, Louis XVI and Empire, and like all of the Flemish cabinetwork of the preceding centuries it was always characterized by a wealth of decorative detail.

ARTICLES OF FLEMISH FURNITURE

Chairs   Among the principal 17th century Flemish chairs were the rectangular chair, the spirally turned chair and the tall so-called Flemish chair with the Flemish scrolled front legs. The principal rectangular armchair (FIGURE 82) of the late 16th and early 17th centuries was designed with plain uprights surmounted with finials, very often in the form of a lion's head. It generally had turned and blocked legs connected with two rows of stretchers. The lower row of stretchers was close to the floor and its lower edge was usually shaped. The seat and back panel were of leather and were fastened to the frame with ornamental nailheads. It was made with either straight or scrolled arms. The chair frequently varied in design (81). Sometimes two crosspieces connected the two uprights instead of a leather panel. It was also designed as a side chair. In its general design the chair incorporated many features of the Spanish frailero. This chair when designed with a low back and without arms was very popular (82).

Another form of armchair (84) resembled the Louis XIII spirally turned armchair. The spirally turned open arms usually terminated in the form of carved female heads. It had a spirally turned front stretcher, and the spirally turned legs, which rested on small ball or bun feet, were connected with a turned stretcher, usually of H-form. The chair had a seat and back panel of fabric. As a rule this chair had a relatively low back. Variations in design as well as in the kind and amount of turning sometimes occurred. This chair was also designed as a side chair.

A characteristic Flemish armchair (85), which showed strong Baroque influence, was a tall upright chair, being finely turned and carved and pierced with leaf scrolls and foliations. The turned uprights were surmounted with finials and were connected with a crested carved top rail and a carved bottom crosspiece, several inches above the seat rail, between which extended a carved openwork panel with a cane center. The arms were frequently carved and scrolled with carved and scrolled armposts. The seat was frequently caned and was broader in the front. The two front Flemish scrolled legs were connected with a broad, ornately carved, arched front stretcher, while a serpentine X-shaped stretcher connected the four legs. Variations in design as well as in its decorative treatment sometimes occurred; it was also designed as a side chair. Many of the Baroque features characteristic of this chair were later incorporated in the English Charles II Restoration chair and later Carolean chairs. This chair with scrolled supports was sometimes upholstered (86).

Tables   Tables revealed a greater diversity in their size as well as in their design. Especially interesting were the variety of supports. Some tables were mounted on ornately carved and shaped truss-end supports, connected with either an arcaded or a carved horizontal stretcher. Other tables were designed with massive carved bulbous-shaped legs joined with a continuous stretcher close to the floor. A later form of table was designed with more slender turned supports connected with an X-shaped stretcher, frequently surmounted with a turned and carved finial in the center.

Cupboards   Cupboards were an interesting category of 17th century furniture.

In one characteristic variety of double-bodied cupboard (98), with each section provided with two doors, the lower portion was noticeably tall, which emphasized the horizontal effect of the upper portion. A popular type of single-bodied cupboard (93) was similar to the lower portion of the double-bodied cupboard.

The articles of Flemish furniture during the ensuing 18th century were essentially similar to those found in France. All the many new forms in the different categories originating in France were to a greater or less extent copied in 18th century Flemish cabinetwork and were interpreted in the Louis XV, Louis XVI and Empire styles.

Résumé of DUTCH
17th and 18th Century FURNITURE

The Dutch were a seafaring nation, and, as a result of their daring exploits on the seas, they became the carrier nation of the world early in the 17th century. The Dutch East India Company was formed in Holland in 1602 and was granted a monopoly of trade in the Far East. The vast trade resulting from the activities of this company was a great impetus in developing Chinese influence in all branches of European art. Dutch prosperity resulting from their profitable world commerce continued into the second half of the 17th century when her powerful neighbors, England and France, took certain commercial and political measures which marked the beginning of a gradual Dutch decline. All this commercial success was mirrored in the Town Halls, the churches and in the serviceable red brick houses with gabled roofs of the wealthy burghers, who were the patrons of art. This was the Golden Age of Dutch painting when Rembrandt and a host of others of equal renown contributed their great genius to this glorious page in Dutch art. The Dutch school of painting which began late in the 16th century was a national art. Its inspiration was a realistic portrayal of its native soil. Dutch canvases revel in scenes of everyday life and constitute an unsurpassed record of contemporary customs and fashions. Dutch interiors were eloquently portrayed in the work of such artists as Pieter de Hooch.

A specific Dutch style developed in Holland during the 17th century in architecture and in furniture as well as in painting. We have already observed the development of a distinctive national style in Dutch classic architecture. The Dutch cabinetmaker continued to stamp his cabinetwork with more and more Dutch peculiarities until it finally had a distinctive Dutch character. This divergence in Dutch and Flemish furniture, with the latter being content to follow the French styles and the former developing into a national style, dates from around 1640. It must be remembered, however, that the Dutch style was far from divorced from the French style, for later in the century, due to the Revocation of the Edict of Nantes in 1685, many highly skilled French craftsmen sought refuge in Holland, the foremost among whom was Daniel Marot, French architect, furniture designer and engraver of ornament. Marot's designs were based on the style of Louis XIV and his later work showed a blending of Dutch and French designs. He was taken into the service of William of Orange, who was later crowned King William III of England in 1689. Marot, who was architect to William of Orange, later followed him to England, where he remained from 1694 at least until 1698, when he apparently returned to Holland. Marot, who was born in Paris around 1666, spent the remaining years of his long life in Holland, where he died around 1752. As was proper for an artist of the time of Louis XIV, the prevailing characteristics of Marot's style were splendor and elaboration. In Holland he made designs for furniture, decorative appointments and textiles. His designs for furniture were characterized by their lavish display of Louis XIV style classic motifs, which he interpreted with remarkable refinement and finish. His designs also included a room entirely decorated in the Chinese taste. His books of engraved designs exerted wide influence on contemporary English taste, and he was undoubtedly responsible for introducing into England new forms and style of ornament from abroad. This resulted in producing a similarity between the contemporary Dutch styles and the English styles of William and Mary and Queen Anne.

It is not difficult to understand the close ties existing between Holland and England if we remember the geography, climate and a certain racial resemblance in character in these two seafaring nations. This commercial, political and social relationship naturally led to a fairly continuous and general interchange of ideas between the two countries. Due to this close understanding the furniture of England was more influenced during the second half of the 16th and 17th centuries by Holland than by any other European country. At some times these ties were more intensified than at others, depending on current wars, politics and religion. In such a time of political confluence, as in the reign of William and Mary, the furniture developed along almost parallel lines. English walnut and marquetry furniture from the time of the Restoration in 1660 until about 1700 bears the unmistakable imprint of Dutch influence. And, although Dutch influence persisted in England as long as walnut remained the fashionable wood for cabinetwork, the influence was less marked from around 1700. It is generally accepted that the finest Dutch cabinetwork was made from around 1660 to 1690, after which date Dutch furniture gradually declined in quality. As a rule the Dutch furniture for that period was more elaborately ornamented than the English furniture which usually revealed more restraint in the general character of its design and ornament. The carving on the Dutch chairs very often had more intricate detail than similar English specimens. A peculiar heaviness and overelaboration, which characterized so much of the 17th century Dutch furniture, was also evident in their 18th century furniture designs. Articles of furniture, such as desks of bombé contour, which was a feature of Dutch cabinetwork, were marred by exaggerated curving lines. Much of the early 18th century Dutch furniture was similar to the furniture designed in England during the Queen Anne and Early Georgian styles. As in the Flemish cabinetwork, the Dutch 18th century style of ornament and furniture designs were influenced by the great French designers and essentially followed the styles of Louis XV, Louis XVI and Empire. Dutch cabinetwork lacked the refined elegance which stamped the French originals, for unhappily the Dutch did not possess the finished taste to interpret artistically the French designs.

Included among the favorite methods for decorating the surface of Dutch furniture were turning, marquetry, veneering, applied ornament, carving, lacquering, painting and gilding. The decorative value of turning was fully appreciated and was developed in various forms, such as baluster, ball and ring, blocked and spiral turning. Turned supports were profusely employed in the construction of chairs and tables. Especially distinctive was the use of applied wooden ornament, very often in a contrasting darker wood, in the form of bosses, lozenges, split spindles and moldings worked in various geometrical designs. The Dutch, who were always fond of marquetry, have produced some remarkable specimens of cabinetwork in that medium. The reputation of the Dutch marqueteur was so great that several were engaged to work in Paris early in the 17th century. A distinctive variety of Dutch marquetry developing later in the 17th century consisted of large designs of flowers, birds and foliage worked in a realistic manner in various exotic colored woods enriched with inlays of ivory. Typically Dutch were the large realistic floral designs worked in marquetry. Dutch carving was often more lavish and extravagant than the Flemish; however, they employed it much less frequently. The Dutch East India Company, who often brought lacquered woodwork articles, especially screens, to Europe from the Orient, was largely responsible in creating a vogue for all kinds of lacquered articles. In the beginning, panels of lacquer work were imported and were set into the framework of Western furniture. Later the Dutch merchants sent parts of the Western furniture to the East to be lacquered. And finally, because of this flourishing industry, it seems that Oriental workers were brought to Holland to practice their art and to teach it to the Dutch craftsmen. It must be remembered, however, that European lacquer was made in a different manner from the method practiced in the Orient. Lacquered woodwork, with its exquisite and delicate designs of Chinese figures and scenes, flowers and exotic birds painted in colors and gold on a green, yellow, red or black ground, was found on numerous articles. Cabinets, tables, chairs and chests, screens, trays, small boxes and many other similar articles were richly decorated. Especially colorful and handsome were the tall lacquered secretary bookcases and oblong cabinets mounted on richly carved and gilded stands.

The influence of the lucrative Dutch trade with the Orient was reflected in the Dutch decorative arts. We have already seen the popularity of lacquered woodwork which spread throughout Europe and about which we shall read more later. All kinds of bibelots from the Orient, such as carved ivories, jades and bronzes, were found in the wealthy burgher's home. The increased importation and popularity of Chinese porcelain was an important incentive for the Delft faïence industry which developed so handsomely from about the middle of the 17th century and which became famous for its imitations in faïence of Chinese porcelain. All kinds of shelves and special articles of furniture were designed for the display of porcelain. Apart from the direct influence of imported wares was the more scattered interest in the Far East to which can be attributed the fantastic chinoiseries. These fanciful compositions, depicting an imaginary world of pseudo-Chinese figures and scenes, became fashionable as a decoration in all branches of the decorative arts. These motifs, drawn from a Chinese fairy-tale world, were gradually found on lacquered woodwork, silver, pottery, wallpaper and on cotton and linen prints from around the end of the 17th century or early 18th century onwards. Travel books, chiefly Dutch, purporting to portray the life and customs of the Chinese, published from about the third quarter of the 17th century, were an important source for disseminating this Chinese taste. Numerous engravings by Peter Schenck of Amsterdam at the end of the 17th century, and several German houses, inspired some of the earlier chinoiseries in the late Baroque taste, while the chinoiseries in the Rococo taste were principally attributed to the French school of decorative designers led by François Boucher. A much later phase of chinoiseries occurred in England at the end of the 18th century during the Regency style.

ARTICLES OF DUTCH FURNITURE

Chairs   There was a great variety of Dutch 17th century armchairs. The rectangular chair (FIGURE 82), the chair with spirally turned members (84), generally having a lower back in the Dutch examples, and the tall, turned, carved and pierced chair (85) were especially characteristic of Dutch chair design. These chairs have already been described in the Flemish section. The fashion for turning structural members of chairs was a marked feature. Folding armchairs inspired by ancient Roman curule models and folding side chairs, frequently with arcaded wooden backs (83), were plentiful.

Toward the end of the 17th century and at the beginning of the 18th century the Dutch cabinetmaker introduced a number of novel features in chair design (88) which influenced the design of the characteristic Queen Anne splat-back chair (313). The chair leg became cabriole in form. At first the cabriole leg, which was quite narrow in form, terminated in a graceful cloven hoof foot (88). Later the cabriole leg was made chiefly with the Dutch foot, which, as a rule, was a club foot made in the form of a thickened disc resting directly on the floor or slightly raised on a wooden pad or shoe. The cabriole leg with the claw and ball foot was also designed. The uprights of the back of the chair were curved. An approximate hoop-shaped back having the top rail and the two uprights constructed as one continuous arch was also discernible in these Dutch model chairs (88, 297). (*See page* 239.) The shaped splat was finally extended to the seat frame and was joined to it. The characteristic broad front stretcher disappeared. The horizontal crosspiece of the H-form stretcher was sometimes elaborately carved and scrolled instead (88). Later, the chair with cabriole legs was designed without any stretcher. The seat was broad and the front was wider than the back. An early feature was the ornament, often in the form of a shell, carved on the curved knee of the cabriole leg.

A characteristic chair first made in walnut in Holland about 1700, was popularly called the Burgomaster chair (89) and was designed with a circular frame. The chair had a semi-circular arched back, usually with three oval panels, enriched with carved and pierced motifs, often reflecting Oriental influence. It generally had a caned compass seat. The seat rails were sometimes carved, and often revolved on a central pivot. The six cabriole legs were connected with turned cross stretchers, usually resembling in arrangement the spokes of a wheel.

Accompanying the armchairs were numerous side chairs, stools and benches. Characteristically Dutch were the many foot warmers which could also be used for footstools. The tabouret was also much in evidence. Oriental influence was generally perceptible in its design and in its style of ornament. Upholstered chairs and settees became more plentiful toward the end of the century. In one principal variety of upholstered settee the back was divided into two shaped chair backs. The settee designed with two or three open chair backs was introduced around the end of the 17th century. This variety essentially followed the development of the contemporary open chair back both in form and in style of ornament.

Tables   The Dutch had a variety of tables. The principal type was a large, oblong, massive table with heavy vase (97) or bulbous-shaped legs, usually elaborately carved, joined by a continuous stretcher or one of H-form, close to the floor. The table designed with ornately shaped and carved trestle-end supports and the table made with spirally turned legs joined with a shaped stretcher (95) were also plentiful. Dutch ball and bun feet were much in evidence in the contemporary work. (95, 99). Gate-leg tables with drop-leaves were designed around the middle of the century. The social custom of drinking tea resulted in the development of a tea table for serving tea. As the century advanced the heavier forms for tables were superseded by lighter and more graceful forms. The Dutch table with cabriole legs and club feet was designed around the end of the century. Small side tables, dressing tables, center tables and variously shaped little tables, often with folding tops that could be converted into gaming tables, were all designed and grew in popularity during the ensuing 18th century, when many new forms for specialized purposes were introduced.

Chests   The chest which was often relatively tall and wide was an exceedingly important article of Dutch domestic furniture (90). It was used as a receptacle for their many fine linens and clothes. Lacquered chests provided an interesting note of color in a Dutch room.

Cabinets   The cabinet was also exceptionally popular, due to the Dutch pre-dilection for collecting all kinds of small objects of art and curios. One principal 17th century variety had an oblong rectangular body, fitted with two doors, which rested on spirally turned legs, mounted on ball or bun feet; the four legs were connected with a stretcher often of H-form. Another type was the tall double-bodied cabinet, the upper section sometimes having a fall-front. Both varieties had only slightly projecting cornices and were designed with large plain surfaces, which were often beautifully decorated with ingenious compositions of stars and circles in various exotic woods. These cabinets are frequently referred to as star cabinets and according to tradition their provenance was Zeeland. Other cabinets (102) were colorfully decorated with floral marquetry or blomwerk. These more ambitious examples with floral marquetry retained their popularity well into the 18th century. The oblong lacquered cabinets imported from the Orient, which were usually placed on carved and gilded stands, were especially colorful and handsome, particularly when the designs were on a red ground.

Cupboards   The cupboard or kas, correctly spelled *kast* by the Dutch, usually an enormous piece, was a familiar article of furniture in a Dutch household. It commonly incorporated architectural features in its design, and was ornamented according to the taste of the period. One characteristic variety was a large, massive, rectangular, upright, double-bodied cupboard, with a small recessed upper section, surmounted by a heavy overhanging cornice supported on columns, which rested on the top of the lower section; it was generally mounted on large ball feet. Each section had two cupboard doors. Another type was a tall rectangular, single-bodied cupboard (99), having two long cupboard doors, the base being fitted with a row of two drawers. A distinctive feature of this single-bodied variety was also its large overhanging cornice (99). The kas was often handsomely decorated.

Buffets and dressoirs were also used for the disposition of gold and silver plate, as well as for fine engraved glass.

Accessories   Among the different decorative appointments were included the tall folding screens, mirrors, wall brackets, shelves and pedestals. The richly carved ebony or rosewood frames of the tall folding screens were usually filled with beautiful panels of lacquer work, fine fabrics or gilded leathers. The wall mirror frames were generally ornately carved and gilded. Especially fine were the richly carved frames designed in the taste of Daniel Marot.

The articles of furniture during the early 18th century were fundamentally similar to those designed in England in the Queen Anne and Early Georgian styles. The pieces of furniture throughout the remaining years of the 18th century were to a large extent in the contemporary fashionable French styles. Many of the new forms originating in French 18th century cabinetwork were found in Dutch cabinetwork, but were adapted to the Dutch taste (94). Cabinets (100) and secretary bookcases (96) of kettle-shape form were much favored by Dutch cabinetmakers working around the mid-18th century.

CHAPTER SIX

FRENCH RENAISSANCE
François I, Henry II & Louis XIII

The influence of the Renaissance movement spread into France in the second half of the 15th century. The close contact established with Italy by the recurrent French invasions of Charles VIII, 1483–1498, Louis XII, 1498–1515, and François I, 1515–1547, led to the revelation of the great wealth of classic treasures in Italy, and considerably accelerated the flow of Italian Renaissance influence into the kingdom of France. However, due to the vitality of the Flamboyant Gothic style, this influence was able in the beginning only to modify the decorative detail. The Renaissance style in France is not one single style; it consists of several successive styles overlapping one another. In studying the furniture of the French Renaissance it is convenient to divide it into three principal styles, namely, the François I style, 1515–1547, the Henri II style, 1547–1589, and the

Louis XIII style, 1589–1643, for during the reigns of these three kings the greatest changes in the development of French Renaissance art were discernible. The François I style was essentially a transitional style in furniture design in which Italian Renaissance ornament and detail were found on Gothic forms. This style corresponded in principal to the English Elizabethan style. During the reign of Henri II and his Florentine wife, Catherine de' Medici, the Italian influence was more pronounced, as Italian classic design began to exert its influence on forms. The French cabinetmaker acquired a better understanding of the principles of Renaissance architecture, which knowledge he applied to his designs for furniture. Finally, around the last decade of the 16th century, France gave up her last vestige of Gothic preference and Paris definitely and wholeheartedly embraced the Renaissance. Everything from Italy was in vogue. During the Louis XIII style France began to prepare the foundation for her own great national Baroque style of Renaissance art, which was to be so magnificently expressed in the style of Louis XIV.

We have already seen that the earliest manifestation of the Renaissance in Italy was in literature, in the writings of Dante, Petrarch, Boccaccio and others. This newly discovered interest in classic literature prepared the foundation for a revolt against medieval art in favor of classic Roman culture. The outstanding feature of this revived interest in classic architecture was the employment of the five Roman Orders, which were reintroduced after having been in abeyance for almost one thousand years. No two styles of architecture could be more different in purpose and in spirit than Gothic and Renaissance architecture. And, while Italy embraced these classic forms most readily, considerable time elapsed before they were adopted north of the Alps. In fact in the beginning these countries complied only superficially with the new requirements by adding Renaissance motifs and classic detail on Gothic forms. When this Renaissance in classic architecture did spread into Europe it was first felt in France, a country which has always been receptive to any new ideas in artistic expression. France had become, since the Gothic period, one united kingdom with Paris as the center. French royal princes and noblemen who visited Florence and Venice, having seen the wonders of the Italian Renaissance in all its brilliant and colorful splendor, were instrumental in introducing the Renaissance in France.

Early traces of Renaissance influence were perceptible in the reign of Louis XII, when Renaissance ornament, such as wreathed and medallion heads, were found mingled with the fashionable Gothic ornament on Gothic forms. The new art made rapid progress under François I who was a great patron of all the arts. He maintained a brilliant court at Paris, which achieved preeminence in art and literature. He delighted in attracting foreign artists to his court and service and he was able to induce such renowned Italian artists as Leonardo da Vinci and Cellini to come to France and to execute commissions for him. François I's liberal patronage of the arts also enabled many French artists to study in Italy. The reign of François I is well known for its famous châteaux of kings and courtiers, such as Blois and Chambord, which were built in the country around Paris and in the Loire Valley. These great country palaces had a singular picturesque quality in which both Gothic and Renaissance features were combined and displayed with a striking originality that is inseparable from all French artistic work. The great attraction of many of these châteaux depended not so much on the actual exterior of these great houses as on the formal gardens and radiating vistas, the courts and terraces, the arbors, lakes and fountains and on the elaborate architectural features of the interiors with their sumptuous appointments and furnishings.

The development of French 16th century furniture was influenced by French Renaissance secular architecture. The cabinetmaker, as in the preceding centuries, continued to borrow his decorative motifs and detail from the architecture that was everywhere around him. Exterior architecture and architectural features of the interior were the inspiration for the ornamentation and designs for furniture. During the François I style there was apparent an ever-increasing proportion of Renaissance motifs until finally the Gothic ornament was virtually eliminated. The style of François I was notable for the varied and graceful composition of its ornament and for its exuberant and fanciful motifs. The style displayed an endless variety of exquisite and delicate detail and was remarkable for the beauty and refinement of its carvings. In the beginning there was a tendency frequently to overlook the refinement of proportions and to indulge in an overabundance of ornamentation. However, this was largely corrected by the last decade of François I, for the style was being constantly purified and perfected. The François I style was always varied and vivid with its abundant decorative fancy which imbued it with a singular charm and fascination.

French furniture of the 16th century was characterized by simplicity and stability of construction, and was essentially massive and rectilinear in form. Gothic form was present to a greater or less extent throughout the entire 16th century. The furniture, as in the Middle Ages, was for the most part made to be transportable or mobile, as the French word *mobilier* implies. Even the inventory of the furniture belonging to Catherine de' Medici, dated 1589, mentions very little furniture which could not be readily taken apart for packing. In the 17th century the mode of living became more stable and the transportation of furniture was of less importance. However, it is interesting to note that there are extant armoires made in the workshop of Boulle which are so constructed that they can be readily taken apart for transport. Furniture became a little more plentiful under Francois I. The forms remained practically similar to Late French Gothic,

and, although the ornament belonged to the Italian Renaissance, it possessed a distinctive French feeling in its manner of treatment. French ornament was always praiseworthy for its inventive and graceful elegance, for whatever the French artist borrowed he thoroughly assimilated and transformed into a piece of French work stamped with an unmistakable French touch. Even in the subsequent Henri II style, when the Italian influence was more pronounced and the cabinetwork adhered more closely to Italian Renaissance models, which were sculptured, elaborate and architectural in style, certain innate artistic French qualities of originality and good taste persisted with sufficient strength to give the work a French flavor. Since the civil and religious wars of the 16th century were not conducive to nurturing native craftsmanship, much of the luxury furniture was imported to France from Italy, Flanders, Spain and Germany. It was this lack of native products which led Henri IV in 1608 to establish workshops at the Louvre to foster the luxury arts in France.

During the reign of Henri II, 1547–1559, Italian classic architectural principles began to exert their influence on furniture forms, and resulted in a kind of family resemblance in the contemporary French and Italian cabinetwork. Many details borrowed from classic architecture, such as slender columns, fluted pilasters, cornices, moldings and friezes, were incorporated into the designs for furniture. The style of Henri II was fundamentally one of refinement and restraint. The forms were generally simple and severe. The furniture displayed a high level of design in its excellent proportions and balance, which undoubtedly was due to its adherence to the principles of classic architecture. The ornament and the moldings were in scale with the piece they decorated as well as with each other. The moldings, which were copied from sections of moldings in classic architecture, were noteworthy for their classic profile. The ornament was well distributed and not as abundant as in the earlier style, and the carvings were delicate and refined and generally executed in low relief. The brief reign of Henri II covered approximately the central years of the Henri II style and its finest work was achieved at that time. The Henri II style was greatly influenced by Androuet du Cerceau, French architect, designer and engraver of ornament whose publications became available in the last quarter of the century. His designs for furniture were remarkable for their elegance and for their originality of treatment. After studying in Italy he returned to the French court around 1558 where he remained until his retirement around 1580.

The furniture of this period falls into either one or the other of two principal schools of art. The one school, described in the preceding paragraph, was characteristic of the furniture designed around Paris and its environs and reflected the classic architectural influence of such celebrated French architects as Pierre Lescot and Philibert de l'Orme and Jean Goujon who was sculptor to Henri II. The other principal school included the regions around Burgundy. This Burgundian style of Renaissance furniture was marked by an overabundance of carved ornament in high relief, which often concealed the form, by its massive construction and by its richly carved prominent moldings. It is commonly thought that Hugues Sambin of Dijon, architect and designer of ornament and furniture,

through his architectural work and his book of engraved ornament, published in 1570 at Lyons, was largely responsible for the Renaissance style of Burgundian furniture. However, he was obviously inspired, in turn, by du Cerceau. The composition of his ornament, which was notable for its fantasy, was dominated by figure subjects, grotesques and caryatids surrounded with a profusion of garlands. The beauty of this furniture was not in its design, for it very often lacked the fine proportions and balance essential for harmonious lines, but rather in its bold and vigorous carvings which gave the furniture a certain vital and dramatic quality. The caryatids, grotesques and other figures were animated with a forceful energy that was striking and unique. Some pieces of Burgundian furniture of finished craftsmanship, combining this style of carving with well-balanced proportions, were remarkable for their singular richness. Especially characteristic of Burgundian furniture were the tall and massive armoire à deux corps richly carved with mythological figures in high relief and the handsomely carved beds resembling large cupboards, being either completely or partly enclosed.

After the reign of Henri II there was evident a gradual decline in furniture design. This can probably be partially explained by the religious wars between the Huguenots and Catholics which prostrated the country from 1558 to 1598. Some Huguenot craftsmen fled to England after the St. Bartholomew Massacre in 1572. It seems that all branches of the arts lost their strength and vitality during the reign of Henri III, 1574–1589, and although the art of the Renaissance was to continue a precarious existence up to the end of the Louis XIII period it was incontestably impoverished by the end of the 16th century. The source of inspiration for ornament was almost exhausted and the same motifs were being repeated constantly and were becoming coarser and dryer because of this repetition. The fine sense of classical proportions which had been so carefully developed under Henri II was lacking in this later cabinetwork. The furniture became burdened with useless architectural detail, such as the delicate too-long pillars frequently employed on cupboards. Traces of Flemish influence were perceptible in the coarser ornament and in the heavier forms. Toward the end of the century architectural details, such as columns and pilasters, were supplanted to a great extent by caryatids and various other carved figure subjects. During the reign of Henri IV peace was again restored, which resulted in a resumption of commercial activities. Increasing quantities of imported furniture came into France from the Netherlands, Italy and Spain. The vogue for Flemish cabinets grew to such proportions among French noblemen that Henri IV sent French cabinetmakers to the Netherlands to learn the art of decorating cabinets, especially the art of carving in ebony. From the time that Henri IV sent cabinetmakers to the Netherlands to study the work being done in ebony, the French cabinetmaker was called a menuisier en ébène or joiner in ebony. It is interesting to note that the name *ébéniste*, which was later applied to the French cabinetmaker, was derived from menuisier en ébène.

Carving was the principal decorative process for ornamenting the surface of furniture. There was apparent in the cabinetwork an ever-increasing appreciation for the play of light and shade, which is effected by varying the degrees of the relief of the carved decoration and by combining various kinds of moldings. Walnut gradually superseded oak as the fashionable wood in cabinetwork, for walnut, with its smooth surface and warm texture, was admirably suited for the finely executed carved decoration. Ebony was also used in some ambitious pieces of cabinetwork. The carved decoration on such articles of furniture, as cupboards, was often further enriched with insets of marble plaquettes and cabochons. Polychromy and gilding were used much less frequently than in the Gothic style; this apparently was due to a growing preference for well-waxed and polished furniture in the natural finish. Wrought-iron pierced mounts, which had also been a feature of the Gothic style and in which period they had been so exquisitely fashioned, were rarely used as ornamental appliqués on furniture after the reign of François I. Of interest was the abundance and richness of woven stuffs. Contemporary inventories, such as the inventory of Catherine de' Medici written in 1589, revealed the predominance of rich textiles. In addition to upholstered hassocks, folding chairs covered entirely with fabric and beds almost concealed with hangings, rich stuffs were thrown over chairs, benches and stools when in use and were extensively used for wall hangings. The nomadic habits of Gothic times did not disappear in 16th century France. Scarcity of furniture, especially carved furniture, even in the richest châteaux, and the abundance of fabrics which were easily transportable were characteristic features of this era.

During the French Renaissance the entire alphabet of classic motifs was substituted for the Gothic style of ornament. However, in the early days of the

Renaissance such popular Gothic motifs as carved linen-fold panels, pierced Flamboyant tracery and fenestrations were freely combined with classic motifs. Included among the favorite Renaissance motifs were acanthus leafage, all kinds of foliage, flowers and fruit, arabesques, rinceaux, rosettes, roundels, foliated scrolls, vase forms, lozenges, palmettes, swags, cornucopiae, cartouches, banderoles, candelabra, shells, volutes, strapwork, martial trophies, plumes and medallions. The medallion was especially characteristic of the style of François I, and was designed as a head or bust of a man or woman in profile or in full face and was carved in varying degrees of relief. It was usually enclosed in a round frame fashioned as a wreath of foliage, such as the laurel wreath, or the round frame was simply made from a turned molding. Mythological, historical, allegorical and religious stories were all used as decorative subjects by the carver; also all kinds of figure subjects and animal subjects, caryatids, terms, mascarons, grotesques, winged cherubs' heads, swans, eagles usually with outspread wings, dolphins, the heads of animals, half figures terminating in scrolls and all forms of fanciful conceptions or monstrous beings, such as chimeras, satyrs, tritons, sirens, sphinxes and griffons. All the ingredients of Italian Renaissance architecture such as columns, pilasters, cornices, moldings with carved repetitive designs, arches and friezes were incorporated into the principles of furniture design.

LOUIS XIII STYLE

The assassination of Henri III in 1589 marked the end of the Valois dynasty and the beginning of the Bourbon dynasty in the person of Henri IV, 1589–1610. The establishment of the Bourbons was an important turning point in French history and in France's cultural development. In the ensuing years the government became more centralized and the increasing influence and power of the crown became more evident. The Bourbon policy in art was developed, which was a milestone of great cultural significance. The Bourbon monarchs regarded art as one of the essential factors contributing to the dignity and prestige of the state. They wished to express through art their personal glorification, and, with this in mind, they developed a well-conceived plan to organize all branches of art under the control of the central government. Gradually, as this plan began to crystallize, France became a center of great activity and dissemination in all branches of the arts. Paris developed into the social and intellectual center of the nation. The fashions and opinions of Paris became a dominating influence throughout France and later throughout Europe. This ascendancy of France in the arts, which had its inception during the reign of Henri IV, reached its fulfillment under Louis XIV, and French influence to a greater or less extent continued to be a dominating factor in European art throughout the 18th century. Henri IV began the practice of providing free workshops and apartments in certain parts of the Louvre for painters, sculptors, goldsmiths, cabinetmakers, enamellers, engravers and a host of other craftsmen. While these artists did not work directly for the crown, they entered into direct relations with it and enjoyed many special privileges. Henri IV also incorporated the tapestry manufactory at the Gobelins in 1607, extended patronage to the Savonnerie carpet manufactory and encouraged new industries, such as the silk industry.

The style of Louis XIII, 1589–1643, corresponds roughly to the first half of the 17th century. It spans approximately that time from the founding of the Bourbon dynasty to the establishment of the Baroque Louis XIV style, or that time during which the essence of the Louis XIV style was gradually developing. The art of this epoch does not possess a strong national character, is full of contradictions, and comprises many incongruous elements. Sometimes this era is further divided into the Henri IV style, but this seems only to add further complexities, since the art of this period is so difficult to characterize. Foreign influence was especially dominant in this period. French decorative art consisted principally of an assortment of prevailing fashions borrowed from Flemish, Spanish and particularly Italian sources. Both Cardinal Richelieu and the Italian Cardinal Mazarin, who served as chief ministers to Louis XIII and Louis XIV respectively, were enthusiastic patrons of the arts. They encouraged French artists to travel in foreign countries and they attracted as many foreign artists as possible to live in Paris. As a result Italian, Spanish and Flemish influences were all at work and produced a curious intermingling and exchange of ideas. The French artist gradually assimilated all that he borrowed and he modified it in accordance with his inherent good taste. The result was the emergence of the sumptuous and resplendent Baroque style of Louis XIV, triumphant in scale and remarkable for the skillful originality of its planning, which reached its culmination around 1700.

The furniture for the first half of the 17th century had a cosmopolitan character due to the prevailing foreign influences. Italian, Spanish and Flemish influences were dominant factors during this era. For about the first four decades of

the century the French cabinetmaker was particularly subjected to the art of the Netherlands. Flemish furniture and decorative appointments enjoyed a great vogue among the French. Fortunately the French cabinetmaker, due to his innate good taste, avoided much of the Flemish excesses in his style of ornament. Although some of the French furniture was elaborately carved, the overcharged and turgid style of carved decoration which characterized Flemish cabinetwork was generally avoided by the French cabinetmaker. Toward the end of the reign of Louis XIII Italian Baroque art became fashionable and the ratio between Flemish and Italian influence was reversed. However, it is important to remember that Flemish art had been strongly influenced by Italian art through the work of Rubens. And, keeping this fact in mind, it is easy to appreciate that Italian influence was indirectly a principal factor throughout the Louis XIII style. In addition to the foreign influences, some of the French furniture displayed evidence of the traditions of the French school of Henri II. These pieces, which still showed the influence of du Cerceau, were inferior in the quality of their carved decoration and in their design to the Henri II style of cabinetwork of the previous century. The Louis XIII style of furniture was heavy and massive and of solid construction. It was essentially rectilinear in form and was rather simple and austere. The number of pieces of furniture in the different categories remained practically the same as in the previous Henri II style. Some furniture, especially pietra dura cabinets and tables from Italy and ebony cabinets from the Netherlands, were still imported into France.

Carving, turning, inlay work, painting and gilding were all included among the principal methods for decorating the surfaces of furniture. The two favorite methods were carving and turning. Undoubtedly the outstanding feature of the Louis XIII style was the use of turning. This method was never more employed than in this period, nor was the best work of this period ever surpassed. Legs of tables, the entire framework of chairs, ornamental finials and pendants, decorative corner columns, such as on cupboards, split columns glued on the central upright of cupboards with two doors, were all popular subjects for the cabinetmaker's lathe. Turning was done in many varieties, the most common being spiral turning. Occasionally in spiral turning a narrow fillet or band was arranged in the bottom of the groove so that the deeper depressions were not too dark. Spiral turning almost always turned from left to right. Spiral turning in opposite directions, such as might be employed on the two front legs of a chair, was used for symmetrical perfection and was found only on pieces of fine craftsmanship. Baluster turning had the greatest artistic quality, since the outlines could be executed in an endless variety in accordance with the skill of the craftsman. Some pieces of 17th century furniture simply had moldings as their only decoration. Cupboards with heavily molded projecting cornices and bases and with doors strongly enframed in moldings were typical. Occasionally cupboards were decorated with both moldings and turning. Apart from lathe turning, the use of fabrics, often of a very rich quality, was a most important part in furnishing. Lists of fabrics are given a more important place in contemporary inventories than the chairs with their rectilinear lines and the great box-like beds which they were to cover. The framework of a large proportion of the chairs and stools as well as of the beds was covered entirely with fabric that was very often velvet and sometimes damask. Perhaps this explains why so little of the furniture used by the well-to-do classes of the period of Louis XIII remains, since the most important factor was of an impermanent character and the framework made of common wood and rather crudely constructed has long since been destroyed. Luxury pieces, in particular veneered ebony cabinets, were occasionally decorated with an inlay of marquetry reflecting Italian influence in their style of decoration. These cabinets decorated with a marquetry of either brass and tortoise shell or of brass in combination with rosewood and other exotic woods were probably the work of foreign craftsmen residing in Paris and afforded examples of a technique which French craftsmen were soon to develop with remarkable success. Other cabinets made of ebony are praiseworthy for their magnificent carvings (FIGURE 117).

The style of ornament under Louis XIII was essentially similar to the Flemish Baroque. The visit of Rubens to Paris around 1620 to decorate the Luxembourg Palace afforded a great impetus toward developing a taste for the Baroque style of ornament and decoration. Furniture and interiors were often laden with exaggerated and unappropriate detail of carved ornament. Nevertheless, although the ornament was often florid in execution, it was always vigorous and intolerant of restraint, expressing a certain spontaneity and a desire for novelty of design. The Flemish Baroque ornament which chiefly affected furniture and interior decoration was generally characterized by the prominent use of cartouches, intricate and elaborate strapwork, protuberant and ovoid-shaped shields, banderoles, ponderous draperies, well-rounded cherubs, grotesques, masks, luxuriant swags composed of fruit and flowers, twisted and curling palm branches and elaborate scrollwork. Geometrical ornament was also used to decorate furniture and it is especially identified with the cabinetwork of the province of Gascogne, where it was a favorite decoration for cupboards or armoires. Naturally the geometrical ornament could be combined into many different designs. Undoubtedly the diamond point and star diamond point were the most pleasing and effective as well as the most popular. The diamond point, which was framed in a rectangular panel, was sometimes composed of a diamond-shaped pyramid flanked by four small triangular-shaped pyramids. The star diamond point, which was also enclosed in a rectangular panel, consisted of eight elongated pyramids, with the four center ones being triangular and the four corner ones quadrangular. The sharp long apexes of the eight pyramids converged toward the center, in which there was generally a small round boss.

ARTICLES OF FURNITURE

Chairs   The chair under François I retained its massive Gothic box-like form and was decorated with carved Renaissance motifs. The principal variety had a rectilinear, box-like form, with a high panelled back and arms (FIGURE 105). The portion beneath the seat was usually enclosed to form a coffre, the seat being hinged to give access to the box. This chair of state or throne stall, as it was frequently called, was designed throughout the 16th century. However, in the second half of the century, by embodying architectural features in its principles of design, it was given a simple architectural form. The French also had from early times a folding chair of X-form, similar to the ancient Roman curule chair.

Toward the middle of the century the chair began to grow lighter in form and the characteristic upright rectangular chair with open arms was introduced (106, 107). Essentially it was severe and simple in form and sparingly decorated. The principal variety was generally designed with a vertical back of medium height and a narrow seat. It was made either entirely of wood (106) or it had a seat and back panel of fabric (107). The earliest type had a panelled wood back, carved with Renaissance motifs. Later the back was designed with a carved solid splat (106); sometimes it had either an arcaded or turned spindled back. Especially typical were the down-curving arms terminating in scrolls and occasionally in rams' heads (106, 107) which were gracefully shaped and gave a maximum of comfort. The armposts were usually baluster-turned or scroll-shaped (106, 107). The early chairs were frequently designed with chamfered quadrangular supports. Later the legs were usually baluster-turned or designed as slender round plain columns (106, 107). The legs, which were sometimes mounted on small knob or bun feet (106, 107), were joined with either a continuous stretcher (107) or one of H-form (106) close to the floor. The ornate front stretcher did not appear until the reign of Henri IV, when it became a marked feature in contemporary Italian (37) and Spanish chair (61) design. Frequently the armchairs belonging to the second half of the 16th century were entirely covered in fabric.

The caquetoire (108), a distinctive type of wooden armchair introduced around the middle of the 16th century, derived its name from the French word *caqueter* meaning to chatter or to gossip, or in other words a chaise de femme. It was designed with a high narrow upright panelled back, with the top of the arms forming a U-shape. The arms rested on baluster-turned supports continuing to conformingly shaped legs, which were joined with a continuous stretcher close to the floor and mounted on bun feet. The seat was much wider in front since it followed the curves of the arms. The width of the seat in the back was only as wide or slightly wider than the narrow back panel which joined the seat. The back legs were also much closer together than the front legs since they were a continuation of the back panel. The name with its allusion to gossip has always made it a popular term.

The French term *chaise à vertugadin* (109) was used to describe a chair without arms. In particular, it was used to describe a chair similar to the English farthingale chair, which was a rectangular-shaped, small chair introduced in the Early Jacobean style. It was designed with turned legs, joined with a continuous stretcher close to the floor, and it had an upholstered seat and a back panel stretched between the two uprights.

The chauffeuse, a variety of wooden chair characterized by its very low seat, was introduced in the 16th century. It was used by the mother or nurse in the dressing and care of babies and small children. This type of chair with its low seat permitted the mother to reach conveniently all the things around her. Later in the following century the term was also given to a form of upholstered chair used by a lady. It was designed with a relatively high narrow back and a low seat. It appears that in a chair of this type the occupant could enjoy more warmth from the hearth when her chair was placed near it.

The characteristic Louis XIII chair was rather stiff and austere in appearance due to its severely rectilinear lines. The low back, which was occasionally raked, featured a padded and upholstered back panel secured to the two uprights. The seat was also padded and upholstered and the legs were of columnar form and were joined with stretchers. Sometimes the framework was covered entirely with fabric to match the back panel and seat. It was designed with or without arms. The French engraver Abraham Bosse, 1602–1676, often represented this chair in his charming engravings of domestic French interiors. In design this chair closely resembled contemporary Flemish and Dutch examples. A similar square upholstered chair was also fashionable in England. Especially characteristic of the Louis XIII period was this upholstered rectilinear model with spirally turned members (110). The spirally turned open arms, which terminated in a turned knob, or sometimes in the form of a carved female head or lion or ram's head, rested on spirally turned armposts. The legs, the H-form stretcher, which connected the four legs and was close to the ground, and the front stretcher, which connected the two front legs just beneath the seat, were all spirally turned. The legs rested on small bun feet. This chair was also designed as a side chair. Sometimes baluster turnings were employed in place of the spiral turnings.

Stools   Stools and benches were made in great numbers throughout the 16th century. Many stools were still of Gothic construction, having a molded oblong seat with traverses keyed through the truss-end supports. Stools were square, round, rectangular and sometimes triangular, and they usually rested on truss-end supports, on four turned and blocked legs, or on plain round columns. Benches were designed both with and without backs and with and without arms. Some were still fitted with chests under the seat, while the others rested on supports similar to those used for stools. Cushions were widely used on chairs, benches and stools. They were made of rich and costly fabrics, and were handsomely trimmed with braid and tassels. They gave the furniture an added air of luxury, as well as providing a little much needed comfort.

Beds   There are few extant 16th century French beds. The principal variety was the lit à colonnes having a tester supported on four posts, usually in the form of four elaborately carved and turned pillars. Sometimes terms or caryatids were used in place of the pillars, especially when the rear posts were an extension of the headboard. The massive wooden tester had a richly carved cornice and frieze, and the headboard was also lavishly carved. It was without a footboard. By the end of the 16th century a growing preference was apparent for beds completely covered in a rich silk fabric. The tester was surmounted with four large richly carved finials. The Burgundian clos or mi-clos bed resembling a huge cupboard was notable for its richly carved ornament and panel work.

Tables   French Renaissance tables were handsome and decorative. The table of trestle construction, with its massive removable top, was the principal variety until about the middle of the century and continued in use into the time of Louis XIV. Along with these tables were the richly decorated massive tables (118) which became fashionable from around the middle of the 16th century onwards. The majority of these tables were rectangular in form and were more Italian in their general appearance than any other piece of French furniture. One principal type had a massive oblong top with a carved and molded edge, the frieze being richly carved and sometimes fitted with a row of drawers. It rested on elaborately carved and ornately shaped truss-end supports, mounted on scrolled runner feet. The horizontal stretcher, which was usually close to the floor, was often arcaded or colonnaded. Sometimes the table was supported on colonnaded ends (118) enriched with figures resting on an H-shaped molded base, the traverse supporting an arcade of three turned columns. Occasionally the table top rested on four turned round columns, joined with a continuous stretcher close to the floor and mounted on bun feet.

Another form of table (113), which is especially identified with the style of Louis XIII, had a massive oblong top, over a frieze with turned corner pendants, often in the form of acorns, resting on seven columnar supports, joined on a molded stretcher and mounted on bun feet. Two pairs of the legs were placed about one fourth of the distance in from each end; one leg was in the center of the table, while another leg was placed in the center of each end. The traverse stretcher extended the length of the table and was intersected by two side stretchers which joined the other two pairs of legs. The table was also designed with six, eight or nine legs. When it was designed with nine legs, two legs instead of one were at each end. When it was designed with six or eight legs, the leg in the center of the table was omitted.

Chests   The carved decoration on the façade of the coffre or chest (114) in the second half of the 16th century frequently revealed the influence of Hugues Sambin, whose designs for furniture were strongly influenced at times by the pattern books of such Northern European designers as Dietterlein and De Vries. Strapwork, cartouches, swags of fruit and flowers, grotesque masks and bold caryatids were characteristic features of this Northern European Renaissance style.

Cabinets   The cabinet was an extremely fashionable and choice article of 16th century furniture. It was originally imported from Italy and later from Flanders and Germany. It was always a costly and richly ornamented piece, and was used as a receptacle for the owner's rarest possessions, such as enamelled boxes, jewels, pieces of carved ivory, medals and other small objects of art. The essential difference between a cupboard and a cabinet is that the latter is characterized by an interior fitted with many small drawers, secret panels and small doors. These interiors were handsomely enriched with carving, painting, gilding and inlay work and were remarkable for their perfected craftsmanship. One early form of cabinet consisted of an oblong rectangular body, fitted with two doors or a drop-front. This variety of cabinet was placed on a table or stand, frequently of trestle construction. Sometimes the cabinet was designed as a double-bodied piece, the upper section being fitted with two doors, which opened to disclose an interior of richly carved small drawers and doors. It is generally believed that the cabinet was either imported into France from abroad or was made by foreign craftsmen residing in Paris until around the middle of the 17th century. The Italian cabinet was sometimes handsomely enriched with inlays of exotic woods, semi-precious stones, metals, ivory, tortoise shell and mother-of-pearl. There was also a great demand around the time of Henri III for the ebony cabinets carved in low relief from Flanders. As a rule the Italian cabinet was of a more pronouncedly architectural form than the cabinet from Flanders.

Dressoirs   Essentially the Renaissance dressoir (111, 116) was a descendant of the Gothic dressoir. The upper portion consisted of a rectangular, horizontal body fitted with hinged doors, which rested on an open lower portion, being designed either with or without frieze drawers. It seems that in the second half of the 16th century although the dressoir continued its own existence, there was little distinction made between a cabinet and dressoir. It is interesting to note that in the inventory of Catherine de' Medici, 1589, the term *dressoir* was not mentioned.

Buffets   Reference to buffets occur frequently in early French inventories. Buffet avec armoires, or a buffet with cupboard compartments, appeared in inventories at least as early as 1426. "Grande" and "petite" buffets and buffets with cupboards and drawers are all mentioned. Apparently dressoirs and armoires à deux corps were sometimes referred to as buffets depending on their use. One form of buffet was a variety of sideboard in three tiers used chiefly for the disposition of plate. It was entirely open and the top and median tiers were generally fitted with drawers. Essentially it was similar to the English court cupboard (270) which until very recently was described in literature on English furniture as a buffet. Frequently in this model the upper portion was closed in with doors to form cupboard compartments.

Cupboards   The armoire (112, 115) or cupboard grew more plentiful as the 16th century progressed. In the second half of the 16th century the principal variety was the tall and imposing armoire à deux corps, incorporating architectural features in its principles of design. As a rule the front and sides of the upper body were recessed, and the lower body, which was generally more oblong in appearance, was mounted on ball feet. The upper body was often surmounted by a pediment or some other form of decorative treatment. In the majority of extant examples the upper and lower parts each contain two cupboard doors which are divided and flanked by columns, pilasters or panels carved in low relief. The lower part sometimes has one or two frieze drawers with either carved lions' heads holding the loose iron ring handles or simply iron drop handles. Each door is carved with rectangular panels, or sometimes ovals, containing carvings in low relief of classical deities or other suitable subjects executed in the most supple refinement. It is often inset with plaques of veined marble. This type of armoire à deux corps (112) with its architectural façade reflecting the classical influence of Philibert de l'Orme and with its carvings in low relief mirroring the elegant and graceful stone sculptures associated with the name of Jean Goujon, embodied the finest qualities of French Renaissance craftsmanship. The Burgundian walnut armoire à deux corps (115) in the style of Hugues Sambin with its vigorous and exuberant carvings which almost always covered the entire surface, even including the moldings, was equally praiseworthy when combined with craftsmanship of the highest merit.

CHAPTER SEVEN

LOUIS XIV

French art of the 17th and 18th centuries has been accorded an illustrious place in the history of the world's art. Celebrated sculptors, painters, architects, decorative artists, cabinetmakers, goldsmiths, potters, engravers and a host of craftsmen in every branch of the decorative arts contributed to this glorious age of French art. The House of Bourbon regarded art as one of the essential ways of giving dignity and prestige to the state. This policy toward art, which had its inception under Henri IV, was zealously pursued by all the Bourbon monarchs. The style of Louis XIV and the succeeding styles reflected the influence of the King and his court and his royal workshops. The Baroque style developed in France during the reign of Louis XIV, 1643–1715, with its heavy and heroic classicism, was a sumptuous one. This style, which had its origin in Italy, was characterized by exaggerated and restless movement, dramatic planning and contrast and by often massive forms. Under the gifted French artists the Baroque

style was skillfully planned and was tempered by their innate good taste. They imbued the French Baroque with the remarkable air of triumphant and stately elegance and imposing grandeur which was so magnificently expressed in the palace of Versailles. The style of Louis XIV may be divided into three phases which essentially correspond to the three periods in the life of that monarch. The early phase under Cardinal Mazarin, 1643–1661, was dominated by Italian influence. During the second phase, under Louis XIV's personal rule, the foreign elements were eliminated or transformed and the Louis XIV style was unified. It reached its perfect maturity around 1685–1690. The last phase and decline became evident after 1690. In the final years of the 17th century a new style, known as the Régence, began to develop considerably before the death of Louis XIV.

When Louis XIII died in 1643, the five-year-old Louis XIV was proclaimed King of France; however, he had to wait sixteen years before he began to rule. During that time the power was in the hands of the Queen Mother, Anne of Austria, and in those of her first minister, Cardinal Mazarin. When Cardinal Mazarin died in 1661, France was unquestionably the first state in Europe. Louis XIV instead of appointing another first minister assumed the reigns of government, and announced that he would be his own first minister. He kept his word, and while he lived the government rested squarely on his shoulders. Whatever great qualities he lacked, he was always aware of his royal duties, and he discharged them with patience and industry. It has often been reported that Louis XIV once boasted, "l'état c'est moi," or I am the State. And, although he perhaps never did use the phrase, it did express the spirit of his reign, for he regarded himself as the absolute head of the State. He chose the sun as his emblem, for it pleased him to think that as the earth drew its sustenance from the sun, so the life of France emanated from his person. His admiring courtiers gave him the title, le Roi Soleil or Sun King. His court from the beginning was one of great brilliance. It is to the credit of Louis XIV that France became the first state in Europe in art, as well as in arms. Louis XIV was singularly well suited for his role of the grand monarque. He surrounded himself with well-chosen and capable ministers who were completely under his control. He built Versailles which symbolized to all the world the magnificent splendor of the king and his court. In 1667 Louis XIV resolved upon a career of conquest, which after a few brilliant victories, led to a succession of disasters. The decade between 1678 and 1688 was the turning point in his reign. The long series of wars, which were concluded in

1713, had been very costly. The government was burdened with debt, the aristocracy was discontented, the middle class was impoverished and the peasants were hungry. The reign of Louis XIV is the longest recorded in European history, and upon his death he was succeeded by his great-grandson, the five-year-old Duke of Anjou, who was to reign as Louis XV.

In a general sense, French art for the first half of the 17th century until Louis XIV assumed the reigns of government in 1661 had little national character. During that time French decorative art consisted principally of an assortment of prevailing fashions borrowed from Flemish, Spanish and particularly Italian sources. The Spanish influence was largely explained by the marriage of Louis XIV to his cousin the Infanta Maria Theresa, which strengthened the friendship between France and Spain. Flemish influence persisted to some extent; however, it must be remembered that Flemish art had been strongly influenced by Italian art through the work of the Flemish painter Peter Paul Rubens. Cardinal Mazarin, who was an Italian by birth, was to a large extent responsible for the predominance of the Italian influence. He was a renowned collector of all works of art, and his palace was filled with a magnificent collection of paintings, sculptures, furniture, rich wall hangings and finely wrought plate. Almost the entire collection came from Italy. A few pieces in the collection were made in Paris largely by craftsmen brought to Paris from the Lowlands and Italy by Mazarin. Pierre Golle, who made most of Mazarin's inlaid furniture, was brought from Holland. Among those summoned from Italy were Domenico Cucci, the wood carver, and Philippe Caffieri, the first of that celebrated family of bronze workers; also Megliorini, Branchi and Grachetti who were skilled in mosaics. Nicolas Fouquet, Viscount of Melun and of Vaux, was also a distinguished connoisseur. His palace at Vaux in splendor and magnificence afforded a preview of Versailles. The sculptor Puget and the painter Lebrun were in his employ. When Louis XIV came into power he decided that the development of a national art should be one of his great achievements. He took into his service the most gifted of artists, and his long reign was marked by a continuous effort to develop a French style of art in architecture, painting, sculpture, and in the decorative arts. From around 1660 the French artists instead of simply copying Italian Baroque ornament and forms began to display in their work a daring originality and skillful planning which is inseparable from all French artistic work. They started to eliminate all those elements that were not in accord with the essence of French art, which has always been praiseworthy for its fine sense of proportions, for its clarity, and for its refined and finished elegance. By removing excessive ornament they clarified the forms and gave them more definite outlines. They assimilated those features which were compatible with the inherent French genius for good taste. In the course of this work of elimination, modification and assimilation these great craftsmen, who were in the service of Louis XIV, created the Baroque style in France, which is known by the name of that most magnificent of French monarchs.

Although the style of Louis XIV affected public taste to some extent in the second half of the 17th century, it was never in a general manner adopted throughout France. The Louis XIV style was too elaborate and costly to be found in the homes of the middle class. It is true that the principles of design identified with the Louis XIV style of cabinetwork were also found in a simplified form in some cabinetwork of a plainer variety. However, the sumptuous interiors and the elegant cabinetwork so characteristic of the Louis XIV style were confined to the royal palaces and to the splendid mansions of the aristocracy located in and around Paris. The interiors and furniture of the homes in the provinces in the second half of the 17th century did not differ to any great extent from those during the first half of the 17th century. Louis XIV firmly believed that magnificent palaces were essential to the renown of a great monarch, and in the palace of Versailles with its formal gardens embellished with fountains and statues he realized all his dreams of dazzling splendor. The interior was gorgeously decorated with painted and gilded ceilings, the walls glittering with mirrors and masses of gilding, plus the additional brilliance of paintings, sculptures and bronzes. Louis XIV realized that the furniture and the furnishings had to display a magnificence unknown until that time to harmonize with such a setting. He was aware of the fact that the cabinetmaking and the other furnishings could be entrusted only to great craftsmen. In order to surround himself with the most skillful of artists he granted apartments and workshops in the gallery at the Louvre to such artists who had already made their reputations. To acquire lodgings in these galleries was not only a singular mark of royal favor, but it also gave the workers certain important privileges of freedom from the trade guilds. This great gallery was divided into small lodgings and was filled with every kind of artist, such as painters, sculptors, enamellers and cabinetmakers. These privileged artists lived there with their families. Then in 1662 Louis XIV centralized a series of workshops at the Gobelins and made the Gobelins a state institution. And, in order that the work of each artist should be submitted to the guidance of one person, he placed the Gobelins under the direction of the painter Lebrun. Other manufactories, such as the Beauvais Tapestry Manufactory founded in 1664, were subsidized by the French Crown. Through these different policies the decorative arts were placed on the same level as painting, sculpture and architecture. Fortunately this practice was continued throughout the 18th century. And, as a result of this policy, cabinetmaking developed into an art in France and was unique in its perfection of workmanship.

The successful endeavors of Louis XIV to create a national style of art were largely due to the resourcefulness of Jean Baptiste Colbert, 1619–1693, the great French statesman. He was undoubtedly Louis XIV's most important collaborator. Between them they won for France from Italy the artistic supremacy which she had held since the Renaissance. Colbert, who enjoyed much power under Louis XIV, had great schemes for the commercial, industrial and financial reorganization of France. He was always willing to employ the money of France to glorify the external magnificence of his King. He was an excellent financier, but unfortunately his financial reforms were later ruined by Louis XIV's militarism. He favored the development of home industries and he encouraged exports. He was successful in promoting the manufacture of certain luxury articles suited to the French genius, such as tapestries, silks, brocades, laces, furniture and glass. He

brought many manufactures into existence by means of special privileges, and he encouraged foreign workers to live in France. For example, Venetian glassmakers came to France and taught the French how to make large sheets of glass, and Flemish weavers were encouraged to work at the Gobelins. French workmen were not permitted to emigrate. Colbert was greatly interested in textiles and he enforced regulations guaranteeing the quality of the fabrics, which established a fine reputation for the industry. He was interested in art and in literature, and he reorganized the Academy of Painting and Sculpture, originally founded in 1648. He purchased the Gobelins in 1662 for the Crown, and he converted it into a series of workshops and ateliers, which was definitely organized in 1667 under the title of "Manufacture Royale des Meubles de la Couronne," or a Royal Manufactory of Court Furniture. The majority of the magnificent furniture and furnishings required by Louis XIV for his royal palaces were produced at the Gobelins.

The artistic success enjoyed by the Royal Manufactory can to a great extent be attributed to Colbert, who served in the capacity of superintendent. He always gave it his careful attention. He selected Charles Lebrun, the great decorative artist, who had formerly been in the service of Fouquet, for the position of Art Director. In 1669 the King granted letters patent to the Manufactory. These letters patent explained the entire plan of the establishment which represented the work of Colbert and Lebrun. The document is generally considered to be an almost perfect plan for the administration of the arts. In the preamble Louis XIV mentioned the effort made by Henri IV to establish royal workshops in France, thus hoping to revive "the commerce and the manufactures which civil and foreign wars had almost destroyed in the kingdom." Next was outlined the history of the weaving of tapestries, and it was stated that the manufactory for tapestries and for other works should be established in the Hôtel known as the Gobelins. The King's First Painter received the title of Director of the Manufactory, as being "a person capable and intelligent in the art of painting, to make the designs for tapestry, sculpture and other works, to cause them to be correctly carried out, and to have the general direction and supervision over all workers to be employed in these manufactures." The establishment was to be filled with "good painters, master weavers, goldsmiths, metal workers, engravers, mosaic workers, lapidaries, enamellers, joiners in ebony and in other woods, dyers and other good workers in every kind of art or craft." To insure a supply of craftsmen a school was established for sixty children under the King's protection. Their preliminary education was under the care of a master painter. Then they were apprenticed by the Director to the masters of the different arts and crafts, each being placed in accordance with his respective talent. After serving an apprenticeship for six years and a further period of four years as workmen they were classed as "Masters" of their craft. Under this admirable system of training the Louis XIV style was unified and perfected.

Part of the credit for the success of the Gobelins should also be given to Charles Lebrun, the French painter and decorative artist, who was born at Paris in 1619. He studied at Rome and upon his return to Paris he executed numerous decorative works for the great mansions owned by the aristocracy. His most important early patron was Nicolas Fouquet, who commissioned him to execute the mural decorations in his château at Vaux. Colbert, who was familiar with Lebrun's work, recognized Lebrun's ability as an organizer and as a leader, and promptly engaged him in his service. Lebrun did not recognize any division between the fine arts and the decorative arts, and in all his work he always endeavored to unite them. He had a wide conception of art and he never considered it beneath him to design for the metal workers or locksmiths, for he felt that every detail was a part of a harmonious scheme and that only in this manner could a complete and accordant result be achieved. A similar attitude was later held by the English architect, Robert Adam. Lebrun was appointed First Painter to the King in 1662, and from that time the decorative work in all the royal palaces was under his supervision. In 1667 he was appointed Art Director of the Manufacture Royale des Meubles de la Couronne. He also held different posts in the Academy of Painting and Sculpture. From 1662 until his death in 1690 he was virtually the arbiter of the arts of France. Although his color and drawings had little merit he did possess great artistic talent. Lebrun's art work was praiseworthy for its splendor and for its balance. Above all he was gifted with the imagination to form conceptions of a gigantic scale and the talent to realize them in the most minute detail. In this respect he was like a few of the universal artists of the Renaissance. His chief work was Versailles. Among his more celebrated works were the Apollo Gallery at the Louvre and the Mirror Gallery at Versailles. Practically all of his compositions were reproduced by celebrated engravers. Lebrun's style of art inspired a peculiar solemnity that was heavily reminiscent of classical Rome.

The decorative engravings of Jean Bérain, 1638–1711, who was a designer, painter and engraver of ornament, exerted an important formative influence on the Louis XIV style. His name has become especially attached to a fantastic style of decoration that was exceedingly fashionable and was widely but not slavishly copied. After 1677 he had his apartments at the Louvre near those of André Charles Boulle for whom he made many designs. Although he did not possess any remarkable originality he was particularly gifted in assimilating the work of those who had preceded him and in adapting that work to the prevailing French taste. He particularly followed the manner of Raphael. His delicate arabesques and playful grotesques and other fanciful forms and devices, which he treated in a Raphaelesque manner, were very fine and completely pleasing. Scrollwork, festoons and slender architectural motifs forming a delicate web and enclosing figures, classical busts, vases, coats-of-arms, singeries and birds were all included in his repertory of ornament. Bérain executed the designs used for court festivals and for the decoration and costumes employed in the opera. He also provided the designs for tapestries. He was much in demand to furnish the designs for ceilings and for panels, and those which he did not design himself were done in a Bérainesque manner. His designs also served as an inspiration for the decoration of furniture. A large part of his collection of designs were published in three folio volumes. He had a brother, Claude Bérain, who was also an engraver and executed a number of plates of ornament, which included various kinds of arabesques. His son, Jean Bérain the Younger, c.1678–1726, was also a decora-

tive artist and carried on the work of his gifted father. He is probably best known as an engraver. His style was remarkably similar to that of his father's.

The architectural and decorative designs of Daniel Marot, c.1662–c.1752, and Jean Le Pautre, 1618–1682, as well as the work of the former's father, Jean Marot, and the latter's son, Pierre Le Pautre, c.1648–1716, greatly influenced the style of art work of this era. Jean Marot, 1619–1679, was also an architect, designer and engraver and he was a contemporary of Jean Le Pautre. Their early work was characteristic of the reign of Louis XIII, when the influence of the Italian Baroque predominated. Their work was carried on by their respective sons, and the prolific engraved designs of these two generations represent a complete repertory of the prevailing fashions for mural decorations and for the decorative arts during the reign of Louis XIV. They made designs for practically every detail in the interior decoration of a house, such as chimneypieces, doorways, window openings, ceilings, wall panelling, cornices, valances, sconces and wall brackets. They engraved ornament suitable for ceramic work, bronze work and for gold and silver plate. They made numerous designs for many pieces of furniture, such as tables, consoles, cabinets, tiered shelves and frames for mirrors. The work of Jean Le Pautre was often over-elaborated. His style of ornament was characterized by the pronounced use of swags, cartouches, amorini and arabesques. However, although he used the same motifs over and over again, he was especially gifted in developing new treatment in his compositions. Daniel Marot was the pupil of Jean Le Pautre. His work, which was characteristic of the second phase of the Louis XIV style, was distinctive for its splendor and elaboration. He made many designs for André Charles Boulle, especially for long case and bracket clocks. Marot, who was an artist of remarkable talent, possessed a thorough knowledge of French design, as is evidenced in his works of designs later published in Holland. After the Revocation of the Edict of Nantes he migrated to Holland and later worked in England where he exerted a powerful influence on contemporary taste. In addition to these outstanding decorative artists there were a host of others whose work was instrumental in developing the Louis XIV style. Toward the end of the 17th century both the furniture and the mural decorations became more graceful and less formal. This tendency was to be further developed in the Régence. The later work of Pierre Le Pautre, as well as the later work of Bérain, was prophetic of this trend. Their decorative compositions, such as their light and animated forms of arabesques, are now considered to be an important creative factor in developing the style of the Régence. The decorative work of Le Pautre derived much from the delightful painted arabesques by Bérain, who also especially favored the use of singeries. The playful character of Bérain's decorative designs introduced a new vivacity in the solemn and heroic classical style of Louis XIV as exemplified in the work of Lebrun.

The engraved designs of these decorative artists provided the cabinetmaker, as well as the craftsmen in the other branches of the decorative arts, with an almost endless supply of ideas from which they could select those compositions most appropriate to their work. Such engravings continued to be widely used as a source of inspiration for ornament throughout the 18th and early 19th centuries. It seems that it became a rather common practice for some of the large cabinet shops to keep a stock of engravings for reference. Undoubtedly the use of these engraved designs assured a high standard of design as well as a certain consistency, and fortunately, because of the French genius for originality, they were never slavishly copied. Due to the insistence of Louis XIV that the furniture for the royal palaces should be as elegant as its background, the craft of cabinetmaking made remarkable artistic progress and the skill of the cabinetmaker was perfected. Philippe Caffieri, Domenico Cucci, Jean Oppenord, Jean Macé, André Charles Boulle, as well as Pierre Golle, the Poitous and Jacques Sommer are but a few of the outstanding cabinetmakers working in the Louis XIV style. Philippe Caffieri, 1634–1716, who was born in Italy, entered the service of Louis XIV around 1660. He was the first member of that gifted family of bronze workers, the most celebrated being his fifth son, Jacques Caffieri, 1678–1755, whose consummate skill in the Rocaille style is well known. Philippe Caffieri was also a cabinetmaker and he was particularly skilled in executing the carved ornament for chairs, tables, guéridons, pedestals and mirror frames. The Italian, Domenico Cucci, was a cabinetmaker, wood carver and bronze worker. His work was representative of that group of craftsmen whose work formed a connecting link between Italian and French art. His ebony cabinets and tables decorated in the Italian pietra dura manner for the royal palaces were exceedingly fine and elaborate. Jean Oppenord, who was a Flemish marqueteur, became a French citizen in 1679. Much of his work resembled that of André Charles Boulle. Jean Macé of Blois lived at the Louvre from around 1644 until his death in 1672. He is generally regarded as one of the earliest of French marqueteurs, having learned the art in the Netherlands.

Undoubtedly André Charles Boulle, 1642–1732, was the outstanding cabinetmaker working in the Louis XIV style, and the most celebrated member of a noted family of ébénistes, who apparently were of Swiss origin. André Charles Boulle, who was born in Paris, was the son of Jean Boulle, a carpenter. (It is not known whether there was any relationship between Jean Boulle and a Pierre Boulle, d.1636, a Swiss cabinetmaker, who had his lodgings at the Louvre.) In 1672, at the age of thirty, André Charles Boulle was granted his lodgings in the Louvre, which happened to be those formerly occupied by Jean Macé. Boulle, who is probably the best known of French marqueteurs, achieved his greatest artistic triumphs in the marquetry of metal and tortoise shell combined with beautifully sculptured bronze mounts, on an ebony surface. This form of marquetry, which dates in France from the time of Louis XIII, had its provenance in Italy, especially in Neapolitan work. However, this form of art, in which the surfaces are enriched with ebony, tortoise shell and metal, attained its apogee in the work of André Charles Boulle, and rightfully bears his name. In this work very thin layers of brass and tortoise shell of equal thickness were glued together and designs of arabesques, rinceaux, foliage and other motifs were traced on the surface. These ornaments were cut out with a fine saw and produced exact corresponding pieces in the two materials, which could then be counterchanged. In other words, the ground was both in tortoise shell and brass, and the ornament was also duplicated. The tortoise shell ground and the brass ornament were glued on the wooden foundation. This is described as inlay of "the first part", or première partie as distinct from the "counter inlay" or contre partie which is the reverse combination of the materials. The inlay of "the first part" was considered to be more artistic and was therefore more to be desired. Usually on a piece of ebony furniture both the "first part" and the "counter part" were combined. The brass of the "first part" was often enhanced with elaborate gravings of the burin. Occasionally Boulle placed gold leaf or a similar material beneath the tortoise shell to make it more brilliant. Sometimes in this form of marquetry very thin layers of wood of the exact thickness as the brass were used in place of the tortoise shell.

In order to provide the final touch of magnificence Boulle ornamented this marquetry work with exquisitely modelled gilt bronze appliqués of mythological figures, masks and acanthus foliage. Simpler bronze mounts were applied at the corners to resist the strain, and metal moldings of varying width were used to prevent the marquetry from being loosened. Undoubtedly the admirable unity existing between the bronze mounts and the marquetry was due to the fact that Boulle was a draftsman and sculptor as well as an ébéniste. Boulle supplied the models for his bronze mounts which were praiseworthy for their perfected elegance and sculpturesque quality. The work of Boulle marked the beginning of the era of French marquetry, which technique was to continue supreme until the end of the Ancien Régime. Boulle work was especially suitable for enriching the surfaces of cabinets, armoires, bureaux plats, marriage chests, commodes, tall case clocks and bracket clocks. Unfortunately this form of marquetry work is not very durable and is greatly affected by atmospheric changes. Boulle's furniture with its monumental character was admirably suited to the sumptuous interiors of the royal palaces. In addition to the enormous amount of furniture he made for the Crown, he received commissions to do work for all the important aristocracy of his time. He occupied twenty workshops at the Louvre. Boulle had four sons who carried on the work of their illustrious father. Jean-Philippe and Charles-Joseph continued at the Louvre, while Pierre-Benoît and André-Charles worked independently. The death of Charles-Joseph in 1754 brought to an end the work of this distinguished family of marqueteurs. Although their work as well as that of Boulle's numerous followers was similar in technique it lacked the artistic perfection, particularly in the chasing and gilding of the bronzes, of the original work. From around 1775 onwards the taste for Boulle work flourished with considerable vitality. Such well-known ébénistes as Etienne Levasseur and Philippe-Claude Montigny provided fine reproductions. An observation made around 1780 that "fashion has not exercised its caprice on his works" was still valid almost a century later, since the vogue for Boulle work continued through a greater part of the 19th century, resulting in both good and bad imitations. Authenticated pieces of Boulle work rank among the furniture treasures of the world.

French architects, such as Marot, were completely responsible for the rich and elegant interior decoration found in the royal palaces and in the homes of the aristocracy. They furnished the designs for the panelled walls, ceilings, chimney-pieces, doors and windows. The earlier wood-panelled walls, finished in the natural color of the wood and enhanced with touches of gilt, were superseded by wood-panelled walls painted white and embellished with carved and gilded moldings. Especially characteristic of the Baroque interiors was the use of carved ornament emphasized by gilding and accompanied by sculptured figures often in strained or contorted attitudes. The walls were designed as an architectural composition and the panelling was distinctive for its fine proportions which were carefully computed in relation to the height of the room and in accordance with the dimensions of the door and window openings. Occasionally the walls were hung with tapestries. Mirrors framed in carved and gilded moldings were a fashionable form of mural decoration. Generally in the state apartments the floors were covered with parquetry worked in rich geometrical designs. The carved and gilded molded ceilings were divided into compartments and the polychrome painted decoration was very often in the style of Jean Bérain. Toward the end of the 17th century the carved ornament began to lose some of its heroic classicism, and it became less formal and more graceful, and the use of human figures became less pronounced.

The cabinetwork designed to harmonize with these Baroque interiors was majestic, magnificent and massive. The Louis XIV style of furniture was distinctive for its stately and imposing grandeur and for its elegant formality. Much of the furniture was designed to be placed against the wall. There was an abundance of side tables, console tables and cabinets. The furniture displayed excellent proportions and a fine sense of balance. Unity of design was a pronounced feature. The forms as well as the decorative details of this cabinetwork possessed a singular quality of greatness. The panelling was always exact and sharply defined and the moldings were firm and strong. The spirit of the French Baroque, which was both boastful and triumphant, was adroitly expressed in this furniture. Essentially the furniture was rectilinear in form, although curved lines were frequently found even before the style reflected the influence of the incoming Régence. Curved lines appeared in the Baroque scrolls employed on the legs and stretchers of chairs and tables. The Louis XIV style curve was firm and brief and in this respect was quite different from the long gracefully swept curve of the Louis XV style. In all probability the finest pieces of furniture executed in the Louis XIV style harmoniously combined the straight line and the curved line. This was evident in the console tables with their oblong tops and their richly carved scrolled legs, and in the tall rectangular armchairs with their scrolled arms and scrolled legs and matching stretchers. The quadrangular tapering pillar leg with its bold capital was typical of the era. The leg of cabriole form terminating in a cloven hoof foot also appeared before the end of the 17th century. Symmetry was a marked feature of the Louis XIV style. As the end of the century approached, the forms of the furniture as well as the style of ornament began to grow lighter and more graceful and less sumptuous, and the curves gradually became more drawn out, which presaged the approach of the Louis XV style.

Louis XIV and his Court displayed a strong predilection for Chinese art. This taste for imported Chinese wares received an important early stimulus through the Dutch East India Company who carried on a most lucrative trade with the Orient from early in the 17th century. The English and French East India Companies also played an increasing part in bringing Japanese and Chinese wares to Europe. All the gorgeously colored embroidered and painted silks woven in China were used in the upholstery work on the Court furniture as well as for window draperies and bed hangings. These magnificent silks with their white, gold, blue and rose grounds were sprinkled with flowering shrubs, birds, butterflies and other fashionable Chinese motifs. Eastern lacquered wares were greatly admired by Louis XIV and there was a great demand in France for lacquered cabinets and for lacquered panels for screens. Because of this vogue for lacquered wares, workshops were allocated in the Gobelins to improve this medium of decoration. Later, in the following century, French lacquer achieved a remarkable standard of excellence, particularly in the exquisitely executed Vernis Martin work. The vogue for Chinese porcelains was carried to the extreme and led to their subsequent imitation in Europe, although fewer close copies were made in France than in some of the other European countries. Especially famous were the Japanese Kakiemon wares made at Chantilly and the Chinese blanc de chine made at Saint Cloud. The French designers, such as Marot and Le Pautre, illustrated lavish designs of tiered shelves arranged in a pyramid manner to be placed above doors and chimneypieces for the reception of fine porcelains. Elaborate brackets for the display of porcelain were also featured. As a result of this genuine enthusiasm for Chinese art, a great interest in Oriental art developed to which can be partially attributed that remarkable phenomenon of European chinoiseries. These chinoiseries, with their fantastic compositions depicting an imaginary world of pseudo-Chinese figures and scenes, first appeared mingled with Baroque ornament around the end of the 17th century. The development of chinoiseries was particularly suited to the French genius. These charming figure subjects were found in the later work of both Bérain and Marot. Jean Bérain was particularly instrumental in developing the early phase of chinoiseries in France, where they became fashionable as a decoration on lacquered woodwork, furniture, silver, wallpaper, porcelain and cotton and linen textiles. Cabinetwork displaying this style of ornament is considered to be in the style of the Régence, which was essentially a transitional style between the Louis XIV and the Louis XV.

Among the principal woods used in the reign of Louis XIV were ebony, walnut, oak, beechwood and various woods employed in marquetry work, such as box, almond, holly and pear wood. Ebony was extensively used for the magnificent court furniture. Much of the finest furniture made by Boulle and his numerous imitators was of ebony. The richly carved and gilded furniture, such as the chairs, settees and console tables, was made from different semi-hard or soft woods. Especially characteristic of the Louis XIV style was the ebony cabinetwork and the carved giltwood furniture. The use of walnut and oak was restricted to a greater or less extent to large panelled pieces of cabinetwork, such as cupboards and other pieces of a similar nature. Chairs and tables, generally of a plainer variety with turned members, were also made of walnut. The veneered cabinetwork was also executed in walnut. Quite a few plain, inexpensive light chairs were made of beechwood or wild cherry and were finished in a lacquer varnish. A pronounced feature of the Louis XIV style was the use of rare and richly veined and colored marbles such as for the tops of the elaborately carved giltwood side tables. Upholstered chairs and canapés were extremely fashionable. As a rule the colors of the textiles were warm and brilliant, crimson being a favorite. The different rich and strong colors provided an effective contrast to the dark woods used by Boulle and to the ebony cabinets encrusted with stone mosaics. Late in the reign of Louis XIV the colors began to grow softer. Embroidered silks from the Orient, plain and figured velvets, damasks, brocades, satins and taffetas were all included among the fashionable textiles. Around 1680 imported chintz and muslins made their initial appearance and they rapidly gained in favor. Different kinds of needlework, especially point de hongrie or the flame stitch, were also popular. Toward the end of the reign of Louis XIV tapestries came into use for furniture coverings. An inventory of 1653 lists a suite of furniture covered in floral tapestry belonging to Mazarin. Although the 18th century was the great period for furniture tapestries they did not become plentiful until around 1750. The splendor and magnificence of the textiles used in upholstery work and for wall hangings was one of the outstanding features of the Louis XIV style. From around 1662 onward all of the great tapestries were woven in France. The magnificent wall tapestries woven at the Gobelins under the direction of Charles Lebrun provide an invaluable source of information pertaining to the customs of that period, especially that monumental set of fourteen pieces called the Story of the King.

The decorative processes employed during the Louis XIV style were essentially the same as those used in the first half of the 17th century. However, certain practices which had been relatively rare, such as marquetry and gilding, came into general use. Carving was undoubtedly one of the favorite methods for decorating the surface of furniture. Profusely carved giltwood furniture was a marked feature of the Louis XIV style. The marquetry of brass and tortoise shell combined with magnificent bronze appliqués was regarded as the supreme artistic expression of the Louis XIV style. The marquetry of various colored woods was also employed, but to a much lesser extent, to decorate the surface of furniture. Much of this work was inspired by the contemporary Dutch floral marquetry, with tulips and anemones being fashionable floral motifs. In order to gain a greater variety of colors the different woods were often shaded and tinted. As a rule the shading was done by means of a hot iron while the tinting was done by chemical washes. Occasionally in this marquetry of various colored woods, other materials such as ivory, different kinds of metals and tortoise shell were used to provide additional color and contrast. However, it is questionable whether the work was enhanced by combining these other materials with the various colored woods. A form of stone mosaic work, originating in Italy where it was known as pietra dura, was much favored for the Court furniture, in particular for ebony cabinets and for the tops of elaborately carved giltwood side tables. In this form of inlay work the designs were made of stone tesserae, such as agate, amethyst, lapis lazuli, onyx, carnelian, jasper and chalcedony. The decorative motifs, which included birds, flowers and butterflies, were realistically depicted in their brilliant natural colors. The tops of the side tables, which were ornamented in this manner, were generally of black basalt. The vogue for cabinetwork decorated in this overwhelmingly rich fashion continued until practically the end of the reign of Louis XIV. Applied mounts of bronze doré were employed on all the various kinds of marquetry and inlaid furniture and were veritable works of art. Female masks, winged masks, acanthus foliage, heads of sphinxes and satyrs were all included among the fashionable motifs modelled in gilded bronze.

The practice of gilding furniture was freely employed. Richly carved chairs, canapés and tables in the royal suites were generally entirely gilded. The carved ornament on painted furniture was usually picked out in gilt in order to give it a rich and brilliant effect. The prevailing taste for rich and strong colorful decoration resulted in the painting of many articles of furniture. Oriental lacquer work was held in high esteem and the French craftsmen constantly endeavored to improve their technique in that medium of decoration. The practice of turning as a decorative process was largely eclipsed by the more elaborate methods during the Louis XIV style. However, turning was often employed on the legs of chairs and tables. When the legs of the chairs were turned the armposts and stretchers were generally finished in a similar manner. Baluster-turned members were quite popular, while spirally turned members were relatively few. Panelling was found on walnut and oak cupboards and on other similar articles of furniture. Rectangular panelling was the most common, and occasionally the four corners were hollowed out. A typical form of panelling during the

Louis XIV style retained its four right angles, with the center portion of the upper line changed to a semicircle. Sometimes the bottom line was rounded in a similar manner. In addition to the rectangular panels, circular and oval panels were also employed. The subdivision of panels and the use of moldings on cupboard doors were often most effective. The moldings used on the Louis XIV style of cabinetwork were always emphatic and strong. Unfortunately they were sometimes complicated and heavy, such as the heavily molded and projecting cornices found on cupboards. The moldings which were often used on the arms and legs of chairs were characterized by their suppleness and refined proportions.

The classic Baroque ornament of the Louis XIV style was praiseworthy for the symmetry of its composition and for its finished elegance. The French artists drew deeply for their inspiration on Italian Baroque art. Fortunately they carefully avoided the excesses of Italian Baroque ornament and they purified the composition in accordance with their own good taste. Symmetry was an all-important principle and only in the Empire style was the principle of symmetry more exactingly observed. Heavy heroic Roman ornament and war-like trophies were employed in the early phase of the Louis XIV style. Included among the fashionable motifs were arabesques, rinceaux, lambrequins, cartouches, rosettes, strapwork and C- and S-scrolls. A favorite background design was the diamond pattern, with each diamond or lozenge often centering a dot or some small conventionalized motif. The shell motif was everywhere and was always symmetrically treated. Human and animal grotesques of a pleasing design were widely used. Especially fine were the grotesque as well as the arabesque compositions of Bérain. Female masks were much employed and they frequently had radiating crowns. Satyr masks often had long plaited beards. Included among the popular animal motifs were the lion's head and paws, the ram's head and horns and the cloven hoof of the stag. Various kinds of fanciful conceptions and monstrous beings, such as satyrs, winged genii, dolphins, sphinxes, griffons and chimeras were found in the repertory of ornament. Groups of children, cupids and the winged heads of cherubs were all used. Figure subjects taken from mythology were sometimes found in ambitious pieces of cabinetwork. The acanthus leaf was the favorite form of foliage and was worked into many compositions. Waterlily leaves, palm leaves, branches of laurel, olive and oak were also found. Garlands and festoons were made of fruit and flowers. Certain decorative details were also borrowed from architecture. The Doric triglyphs taken from the frieze of Doric columns were used by Boulle and his followers. Other decorative motifs, which were used in a limited manner and which were to become very popular in the 18th century, included ancient weapons, thunderbolts and tridents of mythological gods, trophies of musical instruments and the implements of fishing, hunting and agriculture.

ARTICLES OF FURNITURE

Chairs   The description of the articles of furniture is restricted to a few characteristic pieces which displayed the principal features of the Louis
XIV style. The majority of the different types of furniture, such as
commodes, were in the process of development and did not attain
their most characteristic forms until the succeeding style. The characteristics of the Louis XIV style were well expressed in the stately
armchair (FIGURES 120, 121, 122, 123). The high rectangular back, the
down curving arms terminating in massive volutes and the legs solidly
joined with heavy stretchers gave it an air of imposing size, strength
and immobility. The back of the chair was almost always entirely upholstered, and was either joined to the seat rail or was several inches
above the seat rail (121, 122, 123). The richly carved and molded
quadrangular tapering pillar leg with a bold capital was much used
(120, 121). This leg is often called a term leg. The console or bracket
leg (122), that is a leg having a scroll-shaped profile, was also a characteristic form. Baluster-turned legs with a matching stretchered underframe were occasionally employed on the more elegant chairs as well
as on the plainer models. Many forms of feet were used, such as bun
feet (121), shaggy paw feet and rectangular molded and carved feet.
Occasionally the scroll tip of the console-shaped leg rested on a
small square piece of plain wood which was called a shoe; the shoe
served as an added protection. Toward the end of the century the
leg of cabriole form was introduced, and terminated in the pied de
biche or cloven hoof foot (123). The early cabriole legs were usually
stretchered (123). The majority of early stretchers were of H-form.
Sometimes there was an additional front stretcher slightly beneath the
seat. When the legs were joined with an H-form stretcher, each crosspiece was generally made of two raised consoles (121). Saltire stretchers
or stretchers of X-form were typical of the Louis XIV style (120,
122). The X-stretcher was made of four carved and molded consoles,
which were arranged in either an arched (120) or flat manner (122).
The flat X-shaped stretcher often had a decorative centerpiece. The
seat rail of the chair was generally upholstered (121, 122). The open
arms were of wood; the manchette or armpad was introduced late in
the century and was only occasionally used. The favorite armposts were
molded and scroll-shaped (121, 122). Some were straight and baluster-
turned, especially when the legs were baluster-turned. The open molded
arms almost always terminated in volutes (121, 122). The finest arm
had a free down-sweeping curve that terminated in a wide volute
designed to harmonize with the scrolled or console-shaped armpost
(121, 122). These chairs were gilded, painted and parcel-gilded or
made of walnut. The upholstery was usually secured to the frame with

large gilt or silvered decorative nailheads. The seat of the chair was often finished in long fringe. They were also made as side chairs.

The term *confessional* was given to a large upholstered wing chair.

Settees   Upholstered canapés and sofas came into use during Louis XIV. They were made en suite with the tall upholstered armchairs. It seems that the earliest canapés were designed with upholstered "cheeks" or wings called joues. Banquettes, bancelles, placets or tabourets were much used and were richly upholstered. Pliants or ployants or folding stools with X-shaped legs were also fashionable. The carreau, which was a large flat cushion stuffed with horsehair or down, also often served as a seat. Sometimes several were piled one above another.

Beds   The 17th century was an age of monumental beds of indescribable magnificence. The splendor of the bed was in its overwhelming display of costly fabrics. The carved framework was covered in fabric and the bed was heavily draped so that its occupant was completely protected against any drafts. In the palaces belonging to the aristocracy the lit de parade or state bed was purely ornamental. It was in the state bedroom which was part of that suite of rooms in which the owner displayed all his finest possessions. This suite of rooms called the suite de parade was used for gala dinner parties and receptions. Naturally, ordinary people were content with less imposing beds and less expensive hangings. However, in all homes the bed was an important article of furniture and was believed to reflect the affluence of its owner. Many homes of the wealthy merchants had beds of remarkable beauty. The lit à colonnes having four very tall posts remained in fashion until the end of the reign of Louis XIV and was revived in the reign of Louis XVI. Late in the 17th century the lit à colonnes was designed with a footboard and in back of the headboard a piece of rich material the width of the tester was hung flat from the tester against the wall. The chantourné de lit with its headboard outlined in pronounced Baroque C-scrolls was a fashionable form of the Louis XIV style lit à colonnes. In the following reign of Louis XV the lit à colonnes practically disappeared when the lit à la duchesse and the lit d'ange, which were introduced late in the 17th century, enjoyed the greatest popularity.

Cradles   The two principal types of cradles, namely the low cradle mounted on rockers and the swing cradle suspended between upright posts, were both found in France from medieval times. The frame for this latter type was called a bersouère, and the phrase "un berseil (cradle) et une bersouère" occurred in French inventories as early as 1388. From medieval times the infant princes often had two cradles, a plain cradle for ordinary use and a richly decorated cradle with costly coverings for display, which corresponded to the lit à gésir and the lit de parade used by their royal parents. French Crown inventories frequently list berceaux de parement or decorated cradles. A French record of 1400 mentions un bersel d'or (a gold cradle) and un bersel d'argent (a silver cradle) which had belonged to Isabelle of France, 1292–1358, who had married the English king, Edward II. These princely cradles continued to be made in the following centuries. Undoubtedly one of the most magnificent extant cradles is a silver gilt cradle which Napoleon I had made for his infant son, the King of Rome (212, 213). Especially typical of the Louis XIV period was a low cradle mounted on rockers richly ornamented with extravagant Baroque carvings and provided with an ornately shell-shaped headboard.

Day Beds   The lit de repos or day bed, which was introduced around 1625, came into general use in the reign of Louis XIV and from early in the 18th century this category of furniture began to display a variety of forms.

Tables   There was a great abundance of tables. The majority of tables were placed against the wall and were regarded as a permanent part of the decoration of a room. They were extremely elaborate and massive. The top was often decorated with a marquetry of either wood or metal and tortoise shell. Frequently the top was ornamented with a brilliant stone mosaic. The use of imported marbles was characteristic of the era, and very often the top consisted of a slab of costly and beautifully colored marble (124). The frieze, legs and stretchers were profusely carved and generally gilded (124). Either quadrangular tapering legs with bold capitals (124) or scroll-shaped legs joined with elaborately scrolled stretchers (124) were typical of the Louis XIV style. Legs of cabriole form were also employed toward the end of the century. Other tables of a less sumptuous character were either painted and parcel-gilded or made of walnut. The legs on the less costly tables were often baluster-turned with a matching stretchered underframe. Tables of a plainer variety with a plain wood top and simply turned supports were also made. Various kinds of tables designed for specialized purposes were in the process of evolution during the Louis XIV style, such as card and gaming tables, work tables and dressing tables. However, although they began to assume definite form in the 17th century, they did not attain their most typical form until the 18th century.

Writing   Especially notable were the numerous writing tables made by Boulle
Furniture   ornamented with metal and tortoise shell marquetry. It is often thought that the writing table or bureau plat (133), of which a number were made by Boulle and his sons, was a Boulle creation. The bureaux plats fashioned by Cressent in the style of the Régence were especially praiseworthy (150). A serre-papiers with either open compartments or drawers was often added to the bureau plat.

The bureau semainier (136) having a drawer for each day of the week was in general use in the reign of Louis XIV. This kneehole form of writing table was designed with eight legs.

Cabinets The ornately decorated oblong ebony cabinet, mounted on a gilded or ebony stand, with its elaborate interior was typical of the display of richness which characterized the Louis XIV furniture. These cabinets were richly encrusted with stone mosaic work or were decorated with a marquetry of wood, metal and tortoise shell (127) with magnificent chased and gilded bronze mounts. The vogue for these cabinets greatly diminished toward the end of the 17th century.

Chests An interesting article of Boulle furniture, also regarded as a Boulle creation, was the coffret de mariage (128) or marriage chest enriched with a marquetry of metal and tortoise shell. It comprised an arched coffre mounted on a stand having a frieze and four scroll-shaped legs joined with a stretcher. It is generally thought that the serre-bijoux derived from the coffret de mariage.

Commodes It is generally believed that the table commode en tombeau (134) had its provenance in the Italian cassone of sarcophagus form. The original pair of commodes of sarcophagus form were executed by Boulle for the chamber of Louis XIV at the Palais de Trianon, for which he received payment in 1708 and 1709. It is generally accepted that they are the only extant pieces of furniture which are identifiable from contemporary records as being the work of Boulle himself. They were done in ebony with a marquetry of metal and tortoise shell combined with magnificent gilded bronze mounts. The top of the table extended beyond the two large and long superimposed drawers of swelling form, which were mounted on four short and straight legs. Four large curved legs richly mounted in bronze appliqués enclosed the corners. The backs of the commodes were also finished, so it was not necessary to place them against a wall.

Cupboards The bas d'armoire or low cupboard was also in use in the reign of Louis XIV. An inventory for Versailles in 1708 mentions "un bas d'armoire à deux battants." The low cupboard generally designed with two and sometimes three doors became a fashionable and elegant piece of 18th century furniture. It is often referred to as an entre-deux since it was incorporated into the architecture of a room. The height was determined by the dado of the panelling and it was placed in the space left entre-deux, that is between two windows or doors. Probably the first indication of its disposition as a piece of furniture occurs in a Toulouse inventory of 1562, "ung petit dressoer de coral entre deulx fenestres." The entre-deux, which belongs to that category of French furniture referred to as meubles d'appui or meubles à hauteur d'appui, meaning furniture of elbow height, was generally mounted on four short legs. However, the entre-deux designed in the Empire style generally had a plinth base. Frequently in French furniture literature the entre-deux is simply called a commode, which seems to be less confusing and also sufficiently accurate. Of interest were the Louis XIV Boulle cabinets (129) which from around 1760 were mounted on four short legs in place of the earlier high supports or stands. In this manner they conformed to the fashionable 18th century armoire of elbow height.

Apparently Boulle was either the first or one of the earliest ébénistes to design large armoires for storing prints, drawings and medals (132). These tall rectilinear cupboards with their uninterrupted surfaces were especially suitable for lavish displays of marquetry enriched with gilded bronze appliqués.

Accessories   Many other articles of furniture contributed to the dazzling display of overwhelming richness which characterized the Louis XIV style. Pedestals, pedestal clocks (130) and mantel clocks decorated with a marquetry of metal and tortoise shell embellished with bronze doré appliqués were of unrivalled magnificence. Crystal chandeliers and elaborately carved giltwood guéridons for the reception of candelabra all contributed to this brilliant pageantry. It is stated that there were 455 guéridons (126, 135) listed in the crown inventories of Louis XIV. Handsome folding screens with panels of figured silk, tapestry or lacquer were extremely rich and decorative. Especially symbolic of all the glitter of the Louis XIV style were the enormous mirrors with their richly carved and pierced giltwood frames and the walls of the reception rooms with their colorful and rare marbles. The abundant use of mirrors was one of the special features of the Louis XIV style which was unsurpassed for its dazzling splendor. Only the ancients and the Italians of the Renaissance achieved such magnificence as the French did in the 17th and 18th centuries. Louis XIV surrounded himself with a magnificence unprecedented in Europe. A great deal of the furniture at Versailles in the Grande Galerie, the king's bedchamber and to some extent in other state rooms was made entirely of silver. Unfortunately almost all this furniture was melted down in Paris in an effort to avert national bankruptcy caused by the king's vainglorious wars and disastrous policies. Probably only about six pieces are extant from the entire collection of silver furniture.

Of immeasurable importance as a source of information for the study of French furniture is the preservation, almost complete, of the archives pertaining to the furniture belonging to the French Crown. These inventories of Crown furniture are without parallel in any other country. The system of inventories was established by Louis XIV in order to prevent the further distribution or scattering of the inherited possessions of the Crown. In the letters patent, dated 1663, he appointed an

Intendant et Contrôleur Générale des Meubles de la Couronne who was charged with the order, upkeep and conservation of the furniture of the Crown. The first inventory was completed in 1673. The system of recording this furniture was replaced in 1685 by the Journal du Garde Meuble, a more detailed and complete system of keeping these records. This Journal was kept from that time onwards to the end of the Ancien Régime and comprises 3,600 pages in 18 volumes, of which only about 250 pages are missing at the present time. Almost every piece of furniture made for one of the royal palaces was recorded in the Journal. Each piece was given an inventory number, and the number entered in the Journal was also marked on the piece of furniture itself and on any part of the furniture easily detachable from it, such as a marble top on a commode. Accompanying the inventory number in the Journal, details were also provided pertaining to the date of delivery, the name of the maker or furnisher supplying it, a detailed description of that particular piece, the royal residence to which it was to be delivered and where it was to be placed in that residence. The subsequent history of a piece of furniture as it was moved from palace to palace can also often be traced in the Journal. More than 9,000 pieces of furniture were described in the Journal du Garde Meuble. In addition to the invaluable academic character of these records, the Journal also provides interesting auxiliary information on different aspects of the Crown furniture. According to the accounts it appears that supplying the royal household did not necessarily guarantee prompt payments. The combination of petty economy and extravagant spending is evident in an item recording the purchase of very costly chair frames upholstered with fabric salvaged from discarded draperies.

CHAPTER EIGHT

RÉGENCE & LOUIS XV

THE STYLE OF THE RÉGENCE

The name *Régence* is given to a style of furniture retaining certain features of the Louis XIV and displaying some new features of the Louis XV. The Régence style is rather difficult to define. It seems that the Régence style as well as the later Directoire style have been arbitrarily used in the literature on French cabinetwork as convenient terms to designate the work of a particular era marked by certain transitional qualities. It is important to understand that, not only in these transitional styles but in all styles, specific dates are arbitrary and can be interpreted only in a general sense. A style cannot be treated like a historical event, such as the date of a battle, for it is foolish to assume that a style ended one year and another style began the following year. It is true that the years for some styles are easier to determine than for other styles. For example, in the transition between the Rococo

and the Classic Revival it is possible to feel the rather rapid and conscious reaction against the former. But the line of demarcation between the Louis XIV and the Régence, and the Régence and the Louis XV, is not too clearly defined since each is a rather slow and unconscious evolution from one to the other. Essentially the Régence covers those years, roughly from around 1700 to 1720, when the Louis XIV principles were being modified or used in a new way and the Louis XV principles were being developed. In an article of Régence furniture the old and the new were combined, and the combination was almost always in perfect harmony. The Régence cabinetwork possessed the rich elegance and dignity of the Louis XIV style but that singular quality of formal grandeur was gone and in its place was an indication of a graceful suppleness which was so characteristic of the Louis XV style cabinetwork. During the Régence a completely new principle known as "le style Rocaille" appeared in French design. This Rocaille or Rococo as it is now generally called differs essentially from the Baroque in its lightness and in its avoidance of the characteristic symmetry of the latter. In the perfected Louis XV style the Rocaille became considerably purified, and the early harshness yielded to a more ample rhythm. Historically the Régence covers that period of time from 1715 to 1723, when Philippe, the Duke of Orléans, was appointed Regent for Louis XV. It appears that Louis XIV in his later years favored a less formal style of decoration, and it was this easing in formality that permitted the introduction of fresh and exuberant forms of ornament. Jean Bérain, Pierre Le Pautre, J. Bernard Toro and Claude Audran were among the early pioneers in creating these new decorative compositions full of fantasy and imbued with a gay and graceful spirit. Robert de Cotte, 1656–1735, the King's First Architect, Jacques Gabriel, 1667–1742, who succeeded Cotte as First Architect, and Germain Boffrand, 1667–1754, who was the principal architect of the Hôtel de Soubise, greatly influenced the interior decoration found in the mansions of Paris and the châteaux of the countryside in the first half of the 18th century. These architects planned the entire ensemble for the interior decoration, while the ornamentistes created and designed in detail the mural decorations, the furniture, the gilded bronze mounts and fitments and the decorative accessories.

The celebrated painter Antoine Watteau, 1648–1721, was the founder of a new school of painting which marked a revolt against the stately and heroic classicism of the Louis XIV style and which initiated the Louis XV style. The influence of Watteau was to persist in French art until the vogue for classic antiquity

was established, when French art became completely dominated by the painter Jacques Louis David. François Boucher, Jean-Honoré Fragonard, Jean-Baptiste François Pater and Nicolas Lancret, as well as many other well-known French artists, were all followers of Watteau and the spirit of the Rococo was immortalized in their work. Watteau lived most of his life during the reign of Louis XIV. He depicted in his paintings a world that was gay, graceful and gallant, and dedicated to pleasure. It was his visions of a dream life divorced from hardships that helped to mold the fashion known as the Rococo and enables us more than two hundred years later to understand the spirit of this epoch. Watteau was also a great decorative artist. He, together with Claude Gillot, Jean Pillement and especially François Boucher, were probably the most prolific inventors of ornament during the Régence and Rococo eras. They designed decorative fantasies, chinoiseries and other figure compositions which were reproduced by celebrated engravers. Watteau gained much of his knowledge of decorative designing in the atelier of the brilliant painter and decorative artist Claude Gillot, 1673–1722, who succeeded Jean Bérain as the designer of the scenery and costumes for the opera. Gillot introduced the decorative fêtes champêtres in which he was later excelled by Watteau. The decorative designs of Watteau and Gillot were undoubtedly inspired to some extent by the work of Bérain and Audran; however, they imparted far more vivacity to their work. The use of numerous curves in the work of Gillot and Watteau anticipated the Rocaille style. Especially fashionable were their chinoiseries and singeries and their decorative designs of ingenious compositions in which Turks and other quaint doll-like figures from the Italian Comedy figured prominently.

During this time of transition in France a new spirit was developing which was to be the spirit of the 18th century. The arts were undergoing a vital change from the majestic and heroic forms of the Louis XIV style to the gayest and most imaginative forms of the Louis XV style. In decorative design the former mythological themes, which were devoted in a large measure to the glorification of Louis XIV, were superseded by mythological themes of a romantic nature, such as the Loves of Psyche. In the search for something gay, amusing, and stimulating, an entire new world of fabulous figures made their appearance in ornamental design inspired by Oriental as well as Near Eastern art. This interest in Oriental art, which began to be the fashion in literature and in the theatre, was originally inspired by the importation of Chinese wares. Europeans were curious to know more about this part of the world and as early as the third quarter of the 17th century Dutch travel books began to appear, endeavoring to depict the life and the customs of the Chinese. The chinoiserie wood cuts in Johan Nieuhof's EMBASSY TO THE GRAND TARTAR CHAM published in 1669 were typical of some of this early literature. The French decorative artists elaborating on this fashionable theme of Orientalism created fantastic doll-like figures of pseudo-Chinese, Turks, Hindus and Persians resembling masqueraders at a fancy dress ball, who were completely captivating in their bizarre costumes. Chinese art was given all the accessories considered appropriate, such as dragons, parasols, peacock feathers, pagodas and weirdly shaped rocks, tree-trunks and bridges. To this array of imaginary picturings of foreign peoples,

which was so characteristic of the Rococo era, Gillot and Watteau created and added a repertory of piquant and exquisite figures from the Italian Comedy. Columbine, Silvia, Gilles and the Serenader were all included in these charming figure subjects. It was in the work of Watteau that these delightful figures were given immortality as well as French nationality. Amusing monkey-pieces or singeries, which had already been introduced by Bérain in his grotesque compositions, were also further elaborated and became more whimsical and lively in the 18th century compositions.

All these new themes, which are closely related to the Rococo style, were mingled with the classic motifs of Louis XIV and were employed in every form of decoration from wall panelling to small jewel boxes. During the Régence the decorative artists conferred far more vivacity and grace upon the classic motifs than was evident in the preceding Louis XIV style. The shell motif was constantly employed, but it was now generally pierced and elaborated in many different ways. The acanthus leaf was longer, thinner and more supple. Especially characteristic of the Régence was the upright shell with acanthus leafage starting from both sides of the base of the shell. The profile of the folded water leaf with its wavy edge and strongly marked ribbings was a favorite decorative motif. Flowers and garland compositions were also used. A diaper arrangement of the lozenge motif centering a small flower was much favored for a background. Attributes of pastoral life, hunting, fishing and music were increasingly evident. Symbols of love, such as bows and arrows and quivers, were also becoming more popular. C-scrolls and S-scrolls lost their Baroque quality. The busts of charming and smiling young women in the manner of Watteau were worked in bronze and were typical of the Régence. These delightful bronze figure subjects, which were called espagnolettes, were found at the tops of the cabriole legs of bureau tables, on the stiles of commodes and on other bronze mounts, such as the escutcheons and handles. Symmetry was observed during the Régence until the advent of the Rocaille, which is virtually synonymous with the Louis XV style. The forms as well as the decorative motifs lost much of their stiffness and began to grow softer and lighter.

The work of Charles Cressent, 1685–1768, the distinguished French cabinetmaker, sculptor and bronze worker, is closely identified with the style of the Régence. Naturally during his long life his style changed in accordance with the prevailing fashion. Cressent, who was the most famous ébéniste of the Régence, was primarily a sculptor and metal worker. He not only designed and made the furniture, but he also made the wax models for the bronze mounts which were so characteristic of his work. Color strongly appealed to Cressent and he introduced a new element of color in his cabinetwork. He completely discarded ebony and he favored amaranth, palissandre and violet wood. These woods covered the entire range of purples from a reddish wine-tone mahogany to a violet brown inclining to black. His favorite combination was veneered amaranth and palissandre, for these warm tones afforded a superb background for his gilded bronze mounts. His ornament was largely inspired by the decorative designs of Bérain, Cotte, Gillot and Watteau. He especially borrowed from Watteau his amusing singeries with monkey acrobats and musicians, which the latter so often

introduced in his arabesques. His bronze espagnolettes retained all the graceful charm and suppleness of the originals as done by Watteau and are considered among the artistic triumphs of French metal work. In Cressent's furniture, the cabinetwork was essentially subordinate to his gilded bronze mounts, which were praiseworthy for their flexible and masterful modelling and for their exquisite chasing. His cabinetwork displayed a fine sense of perfectly balanced proportions. Due to his particular talent for harmoniously combining wood and metal, his furniture had a remarkable quality of unity. Cressent possessed the special genius to unite nobility and gracefulness in his furniture, which were symbolic of the Louis XIV and Louis XV styles respectively. This combination of nobility and gracefulness exemplified the spirit of the Régence when Cressent produced his finest cabinetwork. The large writing table or bureau plat made by Cressent is generally considered to be his most perfected work.

The prevailing taste in cabinetwork during the Régence featured the use of veneering and the marquetry of brilliantly colored woods combined with rich chased and gilded bronze appliqués. This was particularly evident in such fashionable pieces as commodes, occasional tables, writing tables, tall case clocks, bracket clocks and other articles of a similar nature. Carving was a favorite decorative process for articles enriched with gilding or partial gilding such as chairs, settees, guéridons, console tables and mirror frames. Chairs and settees made of walnut were generally richly carved. Although Boulle and his sons continued to use ebony in their marquetry of tortoise shell and brass it was no longer regarded as a fashionable wood. The prevailing taste, which was undoubtedly due to Cressent, was for amaranth and other woods, such as palissandre, having various gradations of purple in their coloring. Chased and gilded bronze mounts were rich and abundant and were a meritorious feature of Régence cabinetwork. The work of casting, chasing and gilding was carried out by two different guilds. One guild was in charge of the sculpturing and founding, while the other executed the chasing and gilding. In order to gild these mounts the bronze was covered with an amalgam of mercury and gold and then fired to vaporize the amalgam. An ébéniste had to have special permission to execute his own bronze mounts. Especially characteristic of the Régence were the large writing tables and commodes handsomely mounted in bronze doré. Metal mounts served a dual purpose for they were both decorative and utilitarian, since in the latter capacity they protected the veneer. The leg of cabriole form introduced late in the Louis XIV style was employed on all fashionable furniture. Many features of Louis XV cabinetwork as well as the different forms in the various categories began to crystallize at the time of the Régence.

ARTICLES OF FURNITURE

The articles of furniture are restricted to several characteristic pieces, such as chairs, tables and commodes, which display certain principles of design associated with the style of the Régence.

Chairs

During the Régence chairs became more graceful and more comfortable. They were gradually becoming smaller and lighter (FIGURE 138), and were therefore more easy to move about. As a rule the open armchair or fauteuil had a somewhat lower upholstered back (138) which did or did not join the seat rail. The back of the chair was either entirely upholstered (137) or it had a carved and molded frame (138). The top of the back was commonly arched (137, 138). As a rule the uprights were straight (137, 138). Straight uprights persisted the longest of any of the Louis XIV features of chair design. Undulating uprights that curved in toward the center of the back were principally a feature of the Louis XV style rather than of the Régence. The open arms were either scrolled (137) or practically straight; the latter usually had armpads (138). The scrolled armposts set back on the upholstered seat which was a new feature of design (137, 138). The seat rail was generally exposed and was commonly valanced and curved into the cabriole legs (137, 138). It very often centered an upright shell with acanthus leafage (137). Straight legs were discarded except for the chair with a straw seat, known as a chaise à capucine, which had simply turned straight legs. In all other chairs the cabriole leg was always used and commonly terminated in a small volute or whorl foot which usually rested on a shoe (137, 138). The knee of the cabriole leg was often ornamented with a carved shell and scrolling leafage (137). Serpentine-shaped stretchers were occasionally used

(137); however, stretchers were gradually abandoned (138). The frame of the chair was finely molded and was richly carved with shells and scrolling foliations (137, 138). The fauteuil was usually gilded, painted and parcel-gilded, or finished in natural walnut. Caned fauteuils made of beechwood were extremely fashionable. They were either painted or finished in the natural wood, and were fitted with loose cushion seats. These chairs were often distinctive for their delicate carved details. The confessional or large wing chair continued to be made during the Régence. The bergère, which is characterized by its solid or closed upholstered sides, was gradually being developed. Canapés, which were relatively few in the preceding style, came into general use. They followed the same features of design found in the contemporary armchair. The back of the canapé essentially resembled three chair backs. It had either open arms or closed sides, and occasionally it had winged sides. The canapé was generally designed with eight cabriole legs. Benches and stools were still much used. All kinds of needlework, tapestry, cut silk velvets, damasks, brocades and satins were considered fashionable as coverings for chairs and canapés. Crimson was a very popular color.

Tables   In accordance with the general tendency to make everything lighter and more graceful the tables gradually became less massive. Straight legs and stretchers were discarded. All the tables were designed with cabriole legs with the exception of console tables which were mounted on scrolled and carved supports that were generally connected with a stretcher. The gilded console table with its handsome marble top and valanced frieze was elaborately carved and pierced with leaf scrolls and shells to harmonize with the richly carved and pierced gilded frame of the mirror beneath which it was placed. Especially outstanding was the large oblong writing table or bureau plat (150). The top was covered with tooled leather and the edge of the table was finished with a gilded bronze molding that was effectively reinforced at the rounded corners. The valanced frieze, which curved into the cabriole legs, was fitted with a row of three drawers which were framed with gilded bronze moldings and were often richly fitted with escutcheons and bail handles. The projecting cabriole legs were headed by espagnolettes and terminated in sabots. A narrow bronze fillet along the sharp edge of the cabriole leg protected the veneer from ripping off. The rear of the table was conformingly ornamented and the frieze was fitted with three mock drawers. Especially praiseworthy were the bureaux plats made by Cressent.

Commodes   The characteristic Régence commode or chest of drawers (158) was massive and its lines were heavy. It had a handsome marble top and was usually designed with three rows of drawers. It generally had a valanced base and it rested on heavy splayed feet or shaped bracket

117

feet which were a continuation of the stiles. The bombé-shaped commode with its rounded surface of convex form was introduced around 1700, and although this characteristic shape was to continue through the Louis XV style it was gradually improved and perfected. The profile of the curves on each stile resembled a cabriole outline, while the façade appeared slightly rounded. The applied bronze doré mounts were magnificent and plentiful and were superbly chased. The drawers were often framed with gilded bronze moldings and were fitted with elaborate escutcheons and bail handles. Beneath each drawer there was often a horizontal groove which extended the length of the drawer and which was lined with brass. The projecting bowed stiles, the feet and valanced base were richly ornamented with gilded bronze appliqués.

LOUIS XV STYLE

The long reign of Louis XV was disastrous to France and brought discredit to the monarchy. Louis XV endeavored to imitate Louis XIV and he tried to establish a personal autocracy. However, he lacked the tenacity of purpose and intellect to unify the administration. The different wars and alliances, the humiliating termination of the colonial struggle with England in which France lost both Canada and India, and the system of taxation, which rested heavily upon the middle classes, tended to spread discontent. The Royal Court, which was maintained at Versailles on a scale of reckless magnificence, became a favorite object for criticism. However, much more serious was the intrigue, vice and licentiousness existing at the Court. The names of such royal mistresses as Madame de Pompadour and Madame du Barry are indelibly associated with this polished and corrupt society. As a result of the pursuit for mundane pleasures there was an ever-increasing amount of criticism against the Crown, which never ceased until the Monarchy was finally overthrown. The reign of Louis XV was the perfect expression of a voluptuous era spent in the gratification of every kind of refinement and luxury. It was an amorous, artificial and frivolous world dedicated to the enthronement of pleasure. This spirit, which is so symbolic of Rococo art, was immortalized in the brilliant creative work of the contemporary artists. Fortunately the King and his Court were but a small minority. France of the 18th century was peopled with professional men, financiers, merchants, the provincial nobility, the middle class and the farmer, who were all rapidly coming to the foreground as they became more prosperous and better informed. The era witnessed the rise of the upper bourgeoisie to a decisive role. Under Louis XV France produced a unique array of French philosophers, economists and scientists who criticized the government. Voltaire, Diderot, J. J. Rousseau and Montesquieu are among the best known names of this Age of Reason. Intellectually the period was one of ferment. The indifference of the Court of Louis XV to the almost inevitable consequences of their mismanagement found expression in the saying "après moi le déluge," as these various forces, comprising the aristocracy, the upper bourgeoisie and the writers, continued to play their allotted parts until the early days of the Revolution.

The Louis XV furniture, of which there was an enormous amount produced, was easily adapted to suit the needs of all the different classes. The cabinetmaker created many new forms of furniture in the different categories and adapted them to every conceivable use, for convenience was very important. Every refinement in comfort was attained and great care was given to the upholstery work in order to achieve the maximum of comfort. In fact during the succeeding reign of Louis XVI the cabinetmaker could do little or nothing to improve on either the comfort or the convenience of the cabinetwork made in the preceding style. The technique of the cabinetmaker achieved its highest standard of perfection. Masterpieces of unrivalled elegance were produced. The celebrated Bureau du Roi, which required nine years to complete, is considered to be the greatest achievement in cabinetwork of all time. Unfortunately some of this cabinetwork was marred by the overwhelming richness of its decoration, for the essence of Louis XV cabinetwork is in the graceful suppleness of its lines and in its delicate moldings rather than in its sumptuous elegance. The aristocracy and the rich bourgeoisie were possessed with a mania for fine cabinetwork. The King and his Court filled their palaces and mansions with richly decorated cabinetwork. Furniture of a less pretentious nature was very often found in the fashionable rustic retreats or "folies" and pavilions of which the King and the aristocracy had many. This furniture, which the cabinetmaker frequently copied for his clients of more modest circumstances, often had as much or more beauty than the sumptuous cabinetwork. The fine proportions and the graceful curving lines, so firm and pleasant, could be fully appreciated and enjoyed in this less elaborate furniture. The size and wealth of the middle class throughout France were increased many times under Louis XV and the demand for furniture by this group was proportionately increased. The rank of the lower middle class was greatly swelled by the prosperous farming element, which had scarcely existed before the 18th century. As a result of this prosperity, the farms and houses in the provinces began to acquire all those characteristic provincial pieces, such as huge cupboards, kneading troughs and buffet-vaisseliers, made in solid walnut or oak, which kept the provincial cabinetmakers busy throughout the 18th century. The provincial furniture was admirable for its good constructional methods and materials. The carved decoration, inspired by the fashionable Rococo style of ornament, displayed a fresh originality that was entirely satisfying.

The term *Rococo*, which is virtually synonymous with Louis XV style, is now used as an equivalent term for the French word *Rocaille*, meaning rockwork. However the term *Rocaille* was not given its present meaning until late in the 18th century in France. At the time when the Louis XV style was in fashion, the term *Rocaille* was used to describe the artificial grottoes found in French gardens, which were in imitation of marine grottoes, decorated with natural stones of irregular outline and stalactites and other ornamentation made of colored pebbles and all kinds of shells. These rocailles or grottoes had been fashionable in France for almost two centuries from the time of Catherine de' Medici. The term *Rocaille* or *Rococo* is now given to a singular form of asymmetrical ornament evolved from the Baroque in France during the Régence. It was widely used by French craftsmen from around 1720 to 1760. From around 1730 the movement was intensified and accelerated in the work of such designers as Oppenord and Meissonnier, who were among the principal designers of these more extravagant forms. This extreme phase, which carried the Louis XV style to its culmination, was marked by an extravagant and more complete and organic use of asymmetry. Sometimes the word *Rococo* is restricted in its use to this later and more advanced phase. It is generally accepted that the Louis XV style achieved its finest expression in the decorative arts from around 1740 to 1755–60. The finished and perfected Louis XV style possessed a charming gracefulness and a light and inventive elegance which were typically French. The Louis XV style as interpreted by the gifted French decorative artists was remarkable for its spontaneous gaiety and for its lively and fanciful qualities. There was evident, however, during the entire time that the Rococo style was in fashion, a certain amount of protest against the excessive use of sinuous curves and the principle of asymmetry. The final phase of the Louis XV style was marked by a more moderate use of curved lines and by ornament of a less fanciful quality. Finally, due to the discoveries at Pompeii and Herculaneum, which resulted in a universal enthusiasm for the antique, the Louis XV style began to go out of fashion. Naturally there was a period of transition when numerous pieces, such as chairs and commodes, retained all or some of their curved lines, but were decorated with ornament in the Neo-Classic taste. This evolution in cabinetwork leading from the Rocaille to the Neo-Classicism of the Louis XVI style began around 1755–1760. It is important to realize that the Louis XVI style was established before that king's reign. Too often the designation is reserved for French art after 1774. In fact the great moment of the art of Louis XV's reign is distinguished by the revival of classical art. The furniture made at that time displaying a compromise between Rocaille and Classicism, in a French guise, is regarded by many as the finest of all French cabinetwork.

The principal designers whose ideas created the fashion for the Rocaille style were Oppenord and Meissonnier. These artists are best known for their numerous collections of designs which were interpreted by the cabinetmakers, goldsmiths, metal workers and other craftsmen. Their work was characterized by the principle of asymmetry, by complicated curves and by the predominance of shell work in their ornament. Gilles Marie Oppenord, 1672–1742, who was the son of a Dutch cabinetmaker established in Paris and working for Louis XIV, was an architect and designer. He spent his early years studying in Italy. His designs at times retained some of the grandeur of the previous century. He was appointed Architect in Chief to the Regent. Juste Aurèle Meissonnier, 1693–1750, who was born in Turin, Italy, and who was a disciple of the Italian architect Borromini, was an architect, goldsmith, sculptor, painter and designer. It is generally accepted that he was the most extreme of all the designers working in the Rocaille style. His work was popular not only in France but in all the European countries which adopted the Rococo style of ornament. His work was excessively ornate, and he rarely left any undecorated space. Due to his remarkable imagination he created many novel compositions in his designs. His best work was imbued with a quality of freedom and pliability that was distinctively bold and striking. Unfortunately his work was often marred by his fondness for complicated curves suggesting waves suddenly stopped in their breaking, twisted branches and swirling lines which gave his designs a feeling of restlessness and endless movement. In 1726 Louis XV appointed him Dessinateur de la Chambre et du Cabinet du Roi. After Meissonnier's death different members of the Slodtz family succeeded to this position. There were five brothers Slodtz, three of whom, Antoine Sébastien, c.1695–1754, Paul Ambroise, 1702–1758, and René Michel, 1705–1764, called Michel-Ange, worked for the Crown both as sculptors and designers. The latter, Michel-Ange, was appointed Dessinateur de la Chambre et du Cabinet du Roi in 1758. He, in collaboration with his brothers Antoine Sébastien and Paul, produced many decorative works. Although the majority of their designs were similar to those of Meissonnier, some of their designs, especially those for furniture, were more moderate and restrained. In addition to these outstanding names there were numerous other ornamentistes whose engraved designs were adapted by the different craftsmen in their respective fields. The names of Nicolas Pineau, 1684–1754, and Jacques de Lajoue, 1686–1761, are sometimes linked with Meissonnier as being the three principal creators of the more intensified phase of the Rococo dating from around 1730. The ornamental designs of François de Cuvilliés, 1695–1768, an important ornamentiste, were chiefly inspired by the work of these three men. There was also Jean Mondon the Younger, whose designs in the Rocaille style were published in Paris around 1738.

The 18th century was the age of the celebrated French ébénistes. From the middle of the 17th century or earlier until 1743 they had been members of the menuisiers' guild, but in that year this guild was officially renamed the corporation of menuisiers-ébénistes, and, at the same time, cabinetmaking was divided into two groups, namely the menuisiers d'assemblage or the joiners of solid wooden furniture, such as chairs and beds, and the menuisiers de placage et de marqueterie or the veneerers and marqueteurs. This latter group adopted the name ébéniste deriving from menuisier en ébène. The craft guild system, which existed in France from medieval times until the Revolution, resulted in a very high standard of technical excellence. Furniture-making under this system enjoyed conspicuous success. At the age of twelve or fourteen an apprentice entered the workshop of a maître-menuisier or maître-ébéniste. After serving an apprenticeship for six years, he became a compagnon and began his compagnonage which lasted at least three years and very often longer. He was then qualified to be admitted into the Paris Communauté des Maîtres Menuisiers-Ébénistes providing he could pay a rather heavy fee, that an example of his cabinet-work upon examination showed sufficient evidence of skill, and lastly that a vacancy in the guild existed. Because of these rules some remained compagnons for their entire lives. If he became a maître he was permitted to have his own workshop. The king also had the absolute right to create maîtres.

There were more than one thousand maîtres in the 18th century in Paris who stamped their work. The first guild statutes of 1467 ordered the members of the corporation to stamp their work, but the ruling was not strictly enforced and relatively few maîtres placed their marks on their work. The order was given again in 1741, and new guild statutes issued between 1744 and 1751 compelled each maître to possess an iron stamp, having his name or occasionally his initials, with which he must stamp every piece of his furniture made for sale. He was also required to deposit an impression of his stamp on a lead bar which was kept at the guild's headquarters. Failure to comply resulted in various penalties. As a rule the maître stamped his furniture under the marble tops of commodes, on the underframing of chairs and tables or some similar place which would not mar the appearance. After the guilds were dissolved in 1790 the stamp was no longer compulsory. In order to maintain the guild's standard of craftsmanship a committee comprising the syndic and six jurors inspected four times annually all of the work in each maître's shop, the syndic and three of the jurors being elected annually from among the senior maîtres. If the furniture passed inspection, each piece also bore the stamped monogram of the committee which sometimes read ME or JME, and is often interpreted as menuisier-ébéniste or juré des menuisiers-ébénistes. If the piece of furniture failed to pass the examination it was sold by the guild and the money went toward guild maintenance. In addition to the menuisiers-ébénistes working under guild regulations there were two other groups. The more important of these two comprised those craftsmen of great skill who were given workshops in buildings in Paris owned by the French Crown, such as the Louvre or the Gobelins, and who were free of guild regulations. Much of their work was made for the Crown and sometimes was not stamped by the maker. The second group comprised those "free craftsmen" who managed to work in a few places still protected by certain medieval rights of refuge which freed them from guild supervision.

It is generally accepted that the most celebrated cabinetmaker of the Louis XV period was Jean François Oeben, c.1720–1763. A German by birth, the date of his arrival in France is unknown. In 1754 he was appointed ébéniste du Roi and granted lodgings in the Gobelins, and in 1756 he moved to the Arsenal. He was primarily a marqueteur and the bronzes for his furniture were largely executed by Philippe Caffieri the younger. His cabinetwork possessed remarkable grace and beauty and was executed in the highest degree of craftsmanship. His delicate and exquisite floral marquetry, which was inlaid in a veneer of choice woods, was unrivalled. Toward the end of his life he favored a return to classic principles and his later work was essentially of a transitional nature. Undoubtedly his great fame was due to the fact that he was commissioned by the King in 1760 to produce the celebrated Bureau du Roi. This remarkable piece of furniture was completed after his death by his pupil, Riesener, whose signature appears on it. It is generally believed, however, that Oeben had completed the construction and the designs for the marquetry before his death. One of his principal patrons from around 1745 until his death was Madame de Pompadour. He produced furniture for her houses at Versailles, Paris and Fontainebleau, for her suites of apartments at Versailles and Marly and for her country "folies" and pavilions. Madame de Pompadour, who possessed faultless taste, shunned all the florid magnificence in favor of purity of line and perfection in execution. It is frequently believed that her rather severe taste was instrumental in molding the final phase of the Louis XV style.

The work of the French ébéniste Antoine-Robert Gauderau, c.1680–c.1751, was also held in the highest esteem. Some time after 1726 he was attaché au service du Garde-meuble de la Couronne, as well as director of interior decoration of the Bibliothèque Royale and the palace of the Tuileries. Unfortunately, like other ébénistes of his time he neglected to sign his pieces. He produced the celebrated médaillier or medal cabinet for Louis XV which is in the Bibliothèque Nationale. Another praiseworthy piece is an elaborately veneered commode made by Gaudreau from drawings by Michel-Ange Slodtz for the chamber of Louis XV at Versailles in 1738. The chased and gilt bronze mounts on this superb commode in the Rococo style were by Jacques Caffieri. Gaudreau produced many fine pieces for the aristocracy, the Dauphin, Mme. de Pompadour, as well as for the King. There was Pierre Garnier, born c.1720, who received his master in 1742 and who is regarded as one of the most famous ébénistes of his time. Especially noteworthy were his veneered pieces decorated with a marquetry of flowers. Pierre Migeon II, 1701–1758, a member of a well-known family of ébénistes, worked successfully for Louis XV and Mme. de Pompadour. Jacques Dubois, c.1693–1763, was made a maître ébéniste in 1742. He worked a great deal in lacquer and enriched his elegantly shaped furniture with female figure subjects in the manner of Falconet. Upon his death his business was carried on by his two sons.

Gilles Joubert, 1689–1775, who was one of the most celebrated of royal cabinetmakers, was appointed in 1758 ébéniste ordinaire du Garde-meuble de la Couronne. In 1763 he succeeded Oeben as ébéniste du Roi and until his retirement in 1774, when he was succeeded by Riesener, he made a great number of pieces of furniture for the King, the royal family and members of the Court. Perhaps his best known pieces are the two encoignures designed en suite with the médaillier by Gaudreau. They were made for the King's private apartments at Versailles in 1755 and are now in the Bibliothèque Nationale. The ébéniste who stamped his work B.V.R.B. has recently been identified as Bernard van Risenbourgh, whose father, a Dutchman, was also an ébéniste working in Paris. He died around 1767. His work, which was of a fine quality, was chiefly in the Rococo style, and some later pieces displayed the features characteristic of the transitional period between Louis XV and Louis XVI. He favored furniture veneered with either lacquer panels in the Chinese taste or a marquetry of realistically treated flowers in a light ground. The work of the ébéniste Joseph Baumhauer, d.1772, called Joseph, displayed admirable skill. He was of German birth, but came to Paris early in life. Shortly after 1764 he obtained the rank of ébéniste privilégé du Roi. Among the extant examples stamped Joseph are commodes veneered with marquetry or decorated with lacquer panels in the Chinese taste. Roger Vandercruse, called Lacroix, 1728–1799, who received his master in 1755, was one of the foremost French ébénistes. He worked for Louis XV, Madame du Barry at Louveciennes and for the Duc d'Orléans. His work from around 1755 to 1770 displayed moderate curves and was decorated in the Neo-Classic taste. The cabinetwork of Claude Charles Saunier, m.1752, and Jean François Leleu, m.1764, also displayed a more sedate use of curves and was admirable for its graceful Neo-Classic decoration and for the broad modelling of its bronzes. Both of these ébénistes adopted the Louis XVI style before the advent of that king. Leleu, 1729–1807, worked for the Court and for private patrons. His principal patron was the Prince de Condé. Unfortunately in this present work it is possible to mention only a few of the great ébénistes. Nor will space permit any mention of the menuisiers who made the seat furniture and brought to their work a very high degree of technical skill as wood carvers.

Aside from the corporation of menuisiers-ébénistes, there were other guilds whose work was especially well represented in furniture making. Of particular importance were the fondeurs and the doreurs who made all the gilt bronze accessories and fitments, including clock cases, sconces, chandeliers, candelabras, fireplace furnishings, door fitments and the mounts which were applied to so much of the furniture. Toward the end of the 18th century there were about three hundred maîtres fondeurs and about three hundred and seventy maîtres doreurs working in Paris. For all of this metal work a model of either wood or wax was first made by a sculptor. A cast was made by a fondeur from the model, and, after casting, the rough bronze was tooled to the necessary degree of finish with very delicate instruments. This finishing or chasing work, known as ciselure, was carried to a remarkable standard of excellence by the 18th century French ciseleurs. After the chasing was completed, gilding was applied by the doreurs if required. The gilding was generally applied to the bronze by the mercury method. In this process the bronze was coated with an amalgam of gold dissolved in heated mercury forming a paste-like substance. The bronze with its coated surface was heated, which evaporated the mercury and left the gold deposited on the bronze. The gilt bronze was then either burnished or given a matt finish. Occasionally the burnished gilding almost resembled in texture and in color pure gold. Gilding was only applied to the finest bronzes, the majority were simply cleaned in acid and lacquered. Undoubtedly the two great bronze workers belonging to the period of Louis XV were Jacques Caffieri, 1678–1755, and his son, Philippe, 1714–1774, the former very often being regarded as the greatest of all fondeurs. Their skill as decorative sculptors and bronze founders was unsurpassed and they executed many masterpieces for the royal family, members of the Court and the aristocracy. They held the title successively of Sculptor, Founder and Chaser to the King. The influence of Meissonnier was evident in the work of both. Since they were primarily bronze workers the chased and gilt bronze mounts on their furniture played a more important role in the ornamentation than any other decorative practice. Their chased and gilt bronze mounts, which freely and boldly flowed into one another on a piece of furniture with consummate skill, were unrivalled for their vigorous curves and for the dexterity of their execution. Undoubtedly Jacques Caffieri was the great inventor of Rocaille bronzes, which he conceived with admirable taste. He possessed the special genius to subordinate the capricious forms of the Rocaille to the harmony of the whole. His son, Philippe, at a later date abandoned the Rocaille in accordance with the prevailing taste.

During the Louis XV style much fine furniture was lacquered in the Chinese manner. The taste for Chinese art had been strongly developed in France during the reign of Louis XIV, and Oriental lacquer ware because of its vivid beauty and great decorative value was especially prized. Lacquered panels were imported from the Orient and set into the framework of European furniture and later panels made in Europe were sent to the Orient to be decorated in lacquer. Because of this enthusiasm for lacquered wares, European craftsmen started to imitate Eastern lacquer work as early as the 17th century. Painter-varnishers were quite active in France from around 1660 and workshops were allocated at the Gobelins to improve this medium of decoration. European lacquer work, which is done in an essentially different method from that practiced in the Orient, reached its acme of perfection in the work of the Martin brothers, who were members of a distinguished family of French artists-artificers. There were four brothers, namely Guillaume, Simon Etienne, Julien and Robert. It is generally accepted that Robert Martin, 1706–1765, produced the most finished and artistic work. Originally these brothers were coach painters. The term *vernis martin* has been given to the varnish which they perfected, *vernis* being the French word for varnish. They did not invent the varnish, but they perfected it and improved the methods for applying the varnish, which they jealously guarded. They successfully imitated every variety of Chinese lacquer, and at a later date they even produced compositions of elaborate pictures, the themes for which were often borrowed from mythology. The Martin brothers made a large amount of exquisite lacquered furniture, such as tables, cabinets, bureaus and commodes enhanced with magnificent bronze Rococo appli-

qués. Their famous lacquer work was regarded as the acme of luxurious decoration. By 1748 the Martins had at least three manufactories in Paris, which were incorporated into a Royal Manufactory of Lacquer in the Chinese Manner. The vogue for lacquer work continued until the Revolution.

Early in the reign of Louis XV the aristocracy developed an intense dislike for the pompous manner of living as it had been under Louis XIV. They aspired to a life of sociability, comfort and even relative intimacy. Everything had to be pleasing and convenient. The French adjectives *agréable* and *charmant* were much used and aptly expressed the new fashion. One result of this tendency was the creation of small rooms within the great palaces and Paris mansions and the building of pavilions and "folies" in the country side for recreation. These small rooms or apartments were designed for special uses, such as a music room, boudoir, game room and sitting room. Special rooms or cabinets were also designed for serving coffee, for conversation and for reading, and were generally decorated in accordance with their use. The walls of the music room were frequently painted with appropriate stories from mythology and with trophies of musical instruments such as the guitar, flageolet, violin and bagpipe elaborated in charming compositions. The mural decoration was always delightful, playful and gallant, and sometimes the walls were covered with all those fanciful doll-like subjects introduced in the Régence. Everything was carried out to the smallest detail to give the room a charming intimacy in response to the fastidious demand for more comfort. As the rooms continued to decrease in size in the second half of the 18th century the amount of small furniture proportionately multiplied. The dining room was also a creation of the 18th century. However, even under Louis XVI the dining room was generally found only in the great palaces and the mansions belonging to the aristocracy. Until the time of the Revolution, the rich bourgeois served their meals in the ante-chamber just as the kings had formerly done. The marble and stuccoed walls with their cold and formal grandeur found in the state apartments of the palaces and mansions in Louis XIV's reign were largely supplanted by panelled walls in the 18th century. These wood-panelled walls were very often painted white and the carved Rococo decoration and moldings were gilded. Especially fashionable were gilded reliefs with their subjects inspired from mythological themes of a romantic nature. These same subjects were also found in the overdoor paintings. Occasionally colorful silks, such as damask or brocade, or painted papers were arranged in the panels. Tapestries were not used as extensively for wall hangings as in the previous century.

The furniture, which had been gradually losing its massiveness during the Régence, became noticeably smaller and lighter. It was extremely comfortable and was delightfully adapted to every need. There were many delicate and easily movable small articles, such as the almost endless variety of little tables. The furniture was characterized by its curved contours, for straight lines were employed only when necessary, such as for the vertical members of an armoire. Legs of cabriole form were typical of the style and were invariably used. The extravagant use of various forms of ornamental curves, such as serpentine curves and C-scrolls, practically abolished the use of right angles, for the Louis XV style was marked by a dislike for rectangles and everything that could be rounded always was rounded. All the curves were slender, drawn out and extremely graceful. They were distinctive for their verve and elasticity and for their perfect blending. An outstanding feature of the Louis XV style was the continuity of its parts. This was particularly evident in chair design, in which each member seemed to flow into one another without any feeling of separation. Delicate moldings were expertly employed to develop this feeling of continuity. Bronze mounts, such as on the fronts of commodes, skillfully flowed into one another so that the division of the rows of drawers was not apparent. Graceful and delicate moldings were a pronounced feature of the Louis XV style and they were remarkable for their supple quality. The Louis XV style was characterized by the principle of asymmetry and consequently it was more suitable for interior decoration and for the decorative arts than for architecture. In articles of furniture, such as chairs, tables and commodes, which require a symmetrical basis, the principle of asymmetry was expressed in the elaboration of surface ornament. It is important, however, to remember that some of the ornament was symmetrical, for asymmetry was not an invariable rule of the style. The great French craftsmen achieved many artistic triumphs in this new style of design. This was due to their rich imagination in creating novel forms and their unfailing ability to combine novelty of design with good taste. In addition they possessed the supreme technical ability to achieve asymmetry without loss of balance. For example, on a molded panel, one generally has to look very closely to realize that the opposite sides of the axis do not exactly repeat one another. Combination pieces, which became a marked feature from around 1750 onwards, testified to the improvement in mechanical devices. They owed their success to fashionable society who were always searching for the novel, the amusing and unexpected. Certain ébénistes, especially those of German origin, excelled in creating all kinds of mechanical devices for transforming furniture. A taste for secrecy, which pervaded society, resulted in multiple hiding places incorporated in articles of furniture which opened with springs.

It is generally accepted that acajou or mahogany was imported into France from the time of the Régence. The first mention of mahogany furniture in French inventories occurs around 1740, and from 1755–60 onwards mahogany enjoyed a great vogue, as the supply became more plentiful and since it was less costly than other exotic woods. Under Louis XVI it became the customary wood for fine furniture for the third estate. In every respect mahogany is a very satisfactory wood, for it is an excellent medium for carving, it takes varnish very well, it can be finely polished and it possesses a pleasing depth of tone. Ebony was practically discarded, except for cabinetwork such as commodes decorated with panels of black and gold Chinese lacquer. In all probability Cressent was responsible for the popularity of amaranth which he employed with palissandre in much of his cabinetwork. Rosewood with its fine warm tones was also fashionable and it was often harmoniously blended with palissandre. Satinwood was also used in conjunction with other woods in veneering. There were almost one hundred exotic woods, covering practically the entire range of different colors used in marquetry work. Many native woods, such as oak, walnut, beech, elm and wild cherry, were especially found in provincial cabinetwork. Oak was plentiful in Normandy and Brittany, while there was an abundant supply of walnut in central and southern France. Woods of numerous fruit trees, such as cherry, apricot, pear and plum, were also popular in provincial cabinetwork. Occasionally plum wood and cherry wood were found in more elegant cabinetwork for which the use of mahogany or rosewood would be more customary. Cherry wood, which has a fine grain and is a good medium for carving, was used for chairs, tables, commodes, cupboards and other similar articles. Pear wood, which has a poor grain, was generally stained black. Much of the provincial furniture was made of solid wood, since veneering and marquetry work principally flourished in Paris, where there was a sufficient concentration of wealth to purchase these more ambitious pieces of cabinetwork.

Veneering and the marquetry of multicolored woods were fashionable decorative processes for ornamenting the surface of cabinetwork and they were remarkable for their perfection of craftsmanship. Due to the characteristic undulating surfaces of the Louis XV style more technical skill was required in veneering than in the succeeding Louis XVI style. Most of the marquetry and veneered work was done in Paris. Especially favored for marquetry work were all kinds of writing furniture, tables and commodes, which were all richly mounted in bronze doré appliqués. Since the marquetry was executed in almost one hundred different kinds of exotic woods, the work was extremely colorful and brilliant. Shaped panels of floral marquetry were particularly characteristic of the Louis XV style. Bouquets of flowers realistically depicted in all their natural colors were arranged in baskets or in vases. Delicate compositions of garlands in the manner of Watteau were especially noteworthy. Musical trophies, symbols of love and attributes from pastoral life were all fashionable themes. The pastoral scenes with shepherds and shepherdesses in the manner of Boucher were of incomparable beauty. In another variety of marquetry especially favored in the succeeding Louis XVI style, the surface was veneered with an all-over trellis pattern either centering a small blossom or having a blossom to mark the points of intersection. This floriated trellis marquetry was sometimes used in the decoration of small tables and particularly on commodes with straight fronts designed in the later phase of the Louis XV style. Parquetry, especially cube parquetry, was also fashionable and was frequently employed in the decoration of commodes and tables. Magnificent bronze doré mounts, which were a pronounced feature of the Louis XV style, were used in conjunction with lacquer work, veneering and marquetry. These mounts were distinctive for the unrivalled beauty of their chasing. Unfortunately, some articles of furniture, especially commodes, were overwhelmed by the glitter of their lavish curves of twisting foliage. The metal workers primarily copied their Rocaille style of ornament from the engraved designs of Meissonnier and Oppenord. Their ornament was also inspired by the decorative art work of Gillot and Watteau, such as the singeries and espagnolettes. Later, due to the approaching fashion for the antique, the gilded bronze mounts were less ornate, as was evidenced in some of the later work by Oeben.

Although gilded furniture was not as popular as in the preceding Louis XIV style, carved giltwood chairs and settees were still customary in the elegant state apartments. Elaborately carved giltwood console tables and mirrors retained all of their popularity and were practically essential in any well-appointed drawing room. Painted furniture harmonizing with the painted panelled walls was much favored for chairs and canapés and also for many small pieces, such as toilet tables, screens and writing furniture designed for feminine use. The ground color was generally in white or in a natural tint, while the carved decoration and the moldings were picked out in gold or in a strong contrasting color such as blue, green or yellow. The painted decoration in Louis XV cabinetwork was relatively strong and bright and should not be confused with the more delicate tones preferred in the Louis XVI style. Caned chairs and canapés were extremely fashionable under Louis XV, and they were fitted with loose seat cushions, which, depending upon the height of the seat, were either thick or flat. The flat cushions were generally used only during the winter and were tied to the seat. The frames were generally made of beech, walnut or cherry, and they were often painted and occasionally gilded. When the frames were gilded the caning was also painted in gilt. The carved decoration found on such articles as chairs, canapés, console tables, mirror frames and armoires was spirited, light and elegant, and was deftly executed. Floral carvings, especially roses, were a favorite theme. Even the most modest chair very often had a flower carved on the center of the top rail, on the knees of the cabriole legs and in the center of the valanced front seat rail. The practice of using porcelain plaques to enrich certain articles of furniture was introduced during this era and reached its peak around 1766 to 1786. They were largely found on delicate and small pieces of veneered and marquetry cabinetwork designed for feminine use, such as various types of small tables. The taste for using porcelain plaques on cabinetwork, the propriety and suitability of which is always debatable, persisted up to the time of the Revolution, and recurred in some 19th century cabinetwork. Madame du Barry possessed numerous pieces of furniture decorated with porcelain plaques at Louveciennes, and it is reputed that the cabinetmaker Migeon, who possessed a special talent for this kind of work, received a pension of 1000 livres a year from Madame de Pompadour. The variety of marbles, which were widely used for the tops of commodes and different kinds of tables, was almost as extensive as the different woods. These finely veined marbles provided a superb touch of color and elegance, and they were an important decorative accessory in Louis XV cabinetwork.

The upholstery, which was never more comfortable, was a feature of the Louis XV style, and the work of the upholsterer achieved a high standard of perfection. The 18th century was the great century for tapestry furniture coverings and much of the ambitious furniture was upholstered in this manner. Fine sets for furniture coverings were woven at the Gobelins, at Beauvais, and at the different manufactories located within the city of Aubusson. The illustrations of La Fontaine's fables by Jean Baptiste Oudry, the French animal painter, inspired a large majority of the designs for the tapestry furniture coverings. The delightful pastoral scenes with shepherds and shepherdesses by Boucher, who undoubtedly was the great tapestry

designer of the 18th century, were equally favored. Various kinds of needlework, such as needlework on canvas, were also used in upholstery, for in almost every period the French women from the Queen to the humble peasant's wife found occupation in this manner. All the heavy and stiff brocades and damasks with metallic threads woven in with the silk, which were so fashionable during the Louis XIV period, were no longer in vogue. Plain and figured cut silk velvets were still used for chair coverings, but more supple fabrics, which could be arranged in smaller folds, were preferred for draperies, such as a light-weight pure silk damask or brocade. Probably the most admired was the silk damask, especially when it was imported from Genoa, where also were woven the richest figured velvets. Crimson damask was the favorite color, and then green, while blue and yellow were still further down the list of popular colors. Drawing rooms and state bedrooms with crimson damask panelled walls and draperies were decidedly the haute mode. A silk painted with flowers, taffeta, and plain, striped or figured satin were fashionable summer textiles. Other stuffs, such as brocatelle and satin of Bruges, which were not made of pure silk and were therefore less costly, were also favored. Utrecht velvet and other velvet-like fabrics were recommended for seat coverings subject to constant wear. For the caned writing table or dressing table chairs red morocco leather was preferred. Chintz and painted linens, having the outline of the design printed in black and then painted in by hand, were popular summer fabrics. Somewhat later the printed cotton or linen toile de jouy was widely used in upholstery.

Certain natural forms were the foundation for the Rocaille or Rococo style of ornament. Rocks and shells with foliage and flowers dominated the theme of the ornament which was richly fantastic. Many motifs employed in the Louis XIV style were discarded and others were completely transformed. For example, the haricot or kidney bean motif of the Louis XV style had been the C motif of the Louis XIV style. This kidney bean shape was also a favorite form for the tops of small marquetry tables. Decorative details borrowed from classic architecture were in disfavor. The shell, which was often pierced, was given many fanciful new forms. In accordance with the prevailing taste for serrated foliage, the acanthus leaf was often elaborately serrated and fringed, and it became very long and narrow. There was a profusion of light flowers, blossoms, sprays and tendrils. Bouquets of flowers tied with ribbons and flowers gracefully arranged in baskets were everywhere. All of the flowers were studied from the native countryside. The rose was a particularly favorite flower. Branches of palm and laurel were popular decorative motifs. Reeds and palms were often decorated with delicate wreaths or garlands of flowers. As in the Gothic period plants were selected from the native flora, such as endive, parsley and cress leaves. Especially fashionable themes were trophies of musical instruments, such as the violin, flageolet and tambourine, implements associated with hunting and fishing, symbols of love, such as bows, arrows and torches, and pastoral emblems, such as crooks and the large straw hats of shepherdesses. Mythological stories of a romantic nature and animals and groups of game in the style of Oudry were all included in the Rococo repertory of ornament. All the chinoiseries, singeries, the fantastic doll-like figures of foreign people and the charming figures from the Italian Comedy introduced during the Régence were very characteristic of the Rococo era. They were a favorite decoration not only on furniture but also on porcelains, lacquered woodwork, silver, fabrics and wallpaper. François Boucher, who was a principal exponent of the Rococo style, was a prolific inventor of decorative fantasies as well as numerous fantastic chinoiseries which are closely related to the Rococo style and attained their apogee around 1750.

ARTICLES OF FURNITURE

Chairs   Louis XV chairs were designed in a great variety of forms in order to attain every refinement in comfort. The chairs designed in this style can invariably be identified by the curving character of all their lines. By 1720 the chair did not possess a single straight line (FIGURE 142). The frame of the chair, which was almost always visible, was distinctive for the continuity of its curves which were accentuated by graceful and supple moldings (142). The molded frame was very often enhanced with carved leaf and floral ornament (140). Usually the carved detail was centered on the crest rail and on the valanced front seat rail and on the knees of the cabriole legs (140, 143). All the fashionable furniture designed in the Louis XV style had legs of cabriole form (140, 141, 142, 143). The majority of cabriole legs terminated in a small volute or whorl (141), which commonly rested on a small square piece of plain wood, called a shoe. Occasionally the cabriole leg terminated in a graceful projection (139) which was a kind of modification of a cloven hoof foot. Very frequently a carved acanthus leaf occurred at the foot (139, 140, 141). The back and seat of the chairs were either upholstered or caned. As a rule the upholstered chairs were gilded, painted or lacquered and parcel-gilded, or were waxed in the natural wood. Caned chairs which were extremely fashionable were made in the same shapes as the upholstered chairs and were much used in dining. The frames were generally made of beech, walnut or cherry and were often painted and some were gilded. All the armchairs, whether they were upholstered or caned, usually had upholstered elbow rests or manchettes (139, 140, 141, 142, 143).

The curvilinear molded back of the fauteuil, which rarely if ever extended to the seat, was designed in different shapes. The cartouche-shaped back was a favorite form (142). The medallion or oval back (143) was in existence later in the Louis XV style; however, it is principally identified with the succeeding Louis XVI style. When the shaped back of the fauteuil was concave (142), the back was described as *cabriolet*. The shaped arms were set back and rested on shaped arm supports which were connected to the side seat rails (142). This was done so that the women with their fashionable panniers could sit comfortably in the chairs. In other chairs the supports were joined to the front legs (143). However, in these chairs the arms and supports effectively curved outward to permit the panniers of the ladies to spread about them. The design for the side chair was similar to that for the armchair.

The bergère (140), which is a form of upholstered armchair, was perfected during the Louis XV style. It was characterized by its closed arms and loose seat cushion. It was a very comfortable and charming armchair, and it was undoubtedly the most characteristic piece of Louis XV seat furniture. Although the bergère was made in a variety of forms there were three principal types. One form was closely related to the contemporary fauteuil, except that the seat was generally wider and deeper, the arms were closed and it was provided with a loose seat cushion. Another type often referred to as a bergère en gondole (140) had an arched horseshoe-shaped back continuing to form the arms. The back and sides were rounded about the seat and were upholstered as one unit. This type of bergère is described as gondola-shaped. A third type, called bergère confessional (139), was designed with shallow wings and a higher back. It was essentially similar to the earlier confessional chair.

The marquise, which was a form of upholstered armchair, was characterized by a very wide and deep seat. It was extremely comfortable and was generally fitted with a loose seat cushion. It appears that the marquise was often used before the fireplace and was quite popular in the 18th century. Essentially it corresponded to the English courting chair or love seat.

The chaise encoignure or corner chair designed in the Louis XV style featured a molded curvilinear frame. The gracefully curving valanced front seat rail centered a cabriole leg. Occasionally when the corner chair was very large it was called a marquise d'alcove.

As a rule the small writing table and dressing table chairs (chaise à bureau and chaise à poudreuse) were much alike and were usually caned. One principal variety was a kind of corner chair with a low back (141). It was designed with an arched horseshoe-shaped back that continued to form the arms, which rested on curved arm supports. The front of the seat between the two arm supports was serpentine-shaped, while the rest of the seat was semicircular. The chair had four cabriole legs; one was centered in the front, one was placed directly under each arm support and the fourth was centered in the back. The seat was fitted with a leather cushion. Sometimes the front of the caned back was covered in leather and occasionally the back and seat were upholstered in leather. Another type of desk chair had a similar rounded back and sides with a circular revolving seat.

Settees

The principal features of design incorporated in the bergère and fauteuil were essentially found in the contemporary canapé (145) for it was usually designed en suite with the chairs. The length of the canapé varied; the longer ones were usually designed with eight cabriole legs. The canapé was designed in a variety of forms. One principal variety of upholstered canapé had a gracefully swept arched horseshoe-shaped back which continued to curve around the front, forming semicircular ends. This variety is often described as a canapé à corbeille, because of its supposed resemblance to the shape of a round basket. The valanced front seat rail was slightly rounded. The back and arms were upholstered as one unit and it had the upholstered armpads. Occasionally a cushion was placed at each end. This form of canapé is also called an ottomane. Another fashionable type of canapé resembled a caned or upholstered fauteuil (145). The back, which was sometimes divided into three chair backs, did not extend to the seat rail. It was designed with open arms.

Sofas

The French term *confidente* was given to an unusual type of large upholstered sofa which had rounded-off ends separated from the main part by arms, so that a small triangular seat was formed at each end.

Day Beds

The upholstered and sometimes caned day bed or chaise longue was a fashionable piece of furniture. It was fitted with a long loose seat cushion and extra back cushions. The chaise longue designed with a gondola-shaped back was much in favor from about 1740 to 1780 and was called a duchesse. The duchesse was constructed either in one piece or in two or three pieces when it was called a duchesse brisée (144). Sometimes the duchesse designed in one piece had two gondola-shaped ends, the one at the foot being very much lower. The duchesse brisée designed in two parts was made in several different forms. One type was designed with two gondola-shaped bergères which had elongated seats. Another kind had a gondola-shaped bergère and a long bench seat with a gondola-shaped end (144). The duchesse brisée in three parts comprised two gondola-shaped bergères and a stool. The chaise longue was also made in a variety of forms. One principal type of chaise longue designed in one piece had a winged-bergère end. The turquoise (146), a form of day bed introduced around 1750, was designed with out-scrolled sides of equal height and was provided with a long seat cushion.

Beds   The vogue for the four-post bed greatly diminished under Louis XV. The beds which were regarded as most fashionable were the lit à la duchesse, the lit d'ange and the lit à la polonaise, or Polish bed. The lit à la duchesse, having a flat oblong tester extending the length of the bed, was designed without posts and simply had a low headboard. The flat oblong tester of the lit d'ange did not extend the entire length of the bed. It was designed without posts and had a low headboard and footboard, the latter as a rule being lower than the headboard. Variations occurred. The Polish bed had a headboard and a footboard of equal height. Each one of the four corners of the woodwork supported an iron rod which curved inward and upward. The four iron rods centered and supported a dome from which fell four draperies, and each one of the draperies was gracefully fastened to one of the iron rods. There were many other kinds of beds. Of particular interest were the beds which could be converted into lounges or couches in the daytime, such as the so-called Turkish beds. This form of bed, the lit à la Turque, was placed lengthwise against the wall and had a shaped backpiece and two side or end pieces. Although it was actually a bed, it essentially differed from a sofa only in its dimensions. When the bed was dressed each end was fitted with a rolled cushion. The lit à la Turque, which generally seems to have had a small and narrow arched canopy, was in vogue from around 1755 to 1785. Essentially similar to the lit à la Turque was the lit d'Anglais. With the general adoption of the duchesse bed and angel bed, beds once again were made with the wood showing. The molded and carved frames were gilded, painted and sometimes partially gilded or finished in the natural wood. The valanced and molded side rails rested on four short cabriole legs. The headboard and footboard were either completely upholstered or had a molded frame.

Tables   The rafraîchissoir, a kind of servante, enjoyed great popularity. It was a small table primarily used for chilling wine and was frequently designed with a separate top which was over a frieze well, provided with a metal liner. It had several undershelves which were used for extra dishes and cutlery. The rafraîchissoir was much used for intimate supper parties and one was placed at each person's chair. In this manner the guest could serve himself and the presence of the butler could be discreetly dispensed with.

The size of the decorative carved and gilded console table depended upon its position. It was generally placed in the middle of a panelled wall or in the space between two windows, under a trumeau. The manner in which the excessively ornate carving was executed was similar to that used by the contemporary metal workers for their sculptured bronzes (149). The shaped marble top of the console table was over a carved and pierced valanced frieze which boldly curved into the scroll-shaped supports that were usually joined with a carved stretcher. Of all the furniture the console table displayed the most extravagant excesses of the Rocaille style.

There was an almost endless variety of graceful and delicate small occasional tables which were exquisitely decorated and mounted. The tops of these small tables were often beautifully decorated in marquetry work, while others had marble tops, and occasionally the top was fitted with a porcelain plaque. The tops were generally circular, oval, serpentine, cartouche-shaped or haricot-shaped. The conformingly shaped frieze, which was generally fitted with a drawer, gracefully curved into the slender cabriole legs. Occasionally the small table was designed with a rising candle screen, and some were skillfully adapted for reading and writing. Tables of every sort were designed for the bedroom, the boudoir and those many delightful small rooms or cabinets. Night tables, breakfast tables with removable trays, the serre-bijoux or jewel box table and the vide-poche or pocket-emptier were all found in the bedroom and boudoir. (*See page* 141.)

Gaming Tables

Since card playing was almost a mania during the reign of Louis XV there was a great variety of card tables. The principal French card table had a folding top mounted on a pivot. All the tops of card tables were lined with green baize or some other suitable fabric. Many were handsomely inlaid with marquetry work combined with metal mounts. Piquet, which was a card game played by two persons, inspired the designs for a number of small elegant tables. A triangular table was designed for tri or three-handed ombre. Quadrille was a fashionable card game for four persons and a number of square tables were especially made for that game. These tables often had circular dished corners for candlesticks. For five-handed reversi and brelan, which were both popular card games, tables with five sides were designed. Of special interest was the table designed for tric-trac or backgammon.

The tric-trac table had an oblong removable top which frequently centered an inlaid checkerboard. The reverse side of the top was inset with green baize. The frieze was designed with a well and two end drawers. The well contained an inlaid tric-trac or backgammon board. The drawers opened on opposite sides of the table for the convenience of the players. The table was mounted on four legs.

Toilet Tables   The toilette or toilet table was a fashionable and necessary article of furniture. The term *toilette* was derived from the small square linen cloth or toilette, upon which in Gothic times were placed the different articles used in beautifying the hair and face. After these different beauty articles and preparations had been used, they were wrapped in the toilette and put away in a chest. Gradually the articles became known as toilet articles and finally the table which was especially designed to hold these articles was given the same name. The toilet table now called a poudreuse (155) was a fashionable and necessary article of 18th century French furniture. As a rule the poudreuse was designed in the same manner; naturally, slight variations occurred. It had an oblong top over a valanced frieze. The top was divided into three hinged parts; the two end sections which opened outward, that is left and right, were used as shelves for the toilet articles. The center section lifted up and was fitted with a framed mirror which moved forward on two grooves. Under the center panel was a pull-out slide beneath which was a drawer. Below each end panel there was a false drawer to correspond to the wells and a real drawer. It was designed with four legs. The toilet table is generally considered to be one of the choice articles of 18th century French furniture. In the more costly examples the wells were lined with silk and the toilet articles were made of fine French porcelain, cut glass and lacquer. This characteristic type remained in fashion till the end of the Ancien Régime. There were also numerous other forms for toilet tables which seemed to multiply under Louis XVI. Especially fashionable in the time of Louis XVI were the combination toilet tables, which were made necessary to some extent by the small rooms that reduced the amount of furniture to a minimum. An advertisement in 1789 mentioned "une toilette à six fins." From around the middle of the 18th century onwards all kinds of combination pieces serving different purposes became increasingly popular as a result of the growing fastidious demand for comfort and convenience (151). Mechanical devices for transforming furniture reached their peak of complexity under Louis XVI (196). Secret hiding places, such as in cabinets and writing furniture, controlled by mechanical devices were also very fashionable.

Work Tables   In the social gatherings of the time, women still observed the custom of sewing while seated in the drawing room near a round table. The individual small work table or table à ouvrage with the necessary equipment for needlework developed from around 1750–60 onwards. One variety designed with two or three superimposed drawers essentially resembled a very small commode or table and was called a chiffonnière. It was generally used by ladies to "keep their needlework or trifles in." Another form of work table, called a tricoteuse, was characterized by a high solid or pierced gallery of either metal or wood designed to contain the spools or balls of wool. Work tables were listed in the inventory of Marie Antoinette, showing that needlework was also a fashionable occupation for royalty. Sometimes the work table had a rising screen in the rear. It was also designed as a combination piece, when it could also be used for reading, writing, or some other use depending on its equipage. (*See page* 141.)

Writing Furniture

The bureau plat or large writing table with a flat top was a fashionable piece of Louis XV furniture. As a rule the bureau plat was found in the library. It was usually veneered in mahogany and enriched with handsome gilded bronze mounts. The oblong top of the table was covered with leather and was edged with a gilded bronze molding. The bureau plat was often equipped with a serre papiers or paper holder which was placed at one end of the leather writing surface. It consisted of several lateral tiers of small shelves and pigeonholes which were sometimes fitted with small doors. It was either detachable or was designed as a part of the table and was used for the reception of papers. The serre papiers was sometimes mounted on a stand, which conformed in design to the bureau plat, and which was placed next to it.

The bureau à cylindre (151) was introduced toward the middle of the 18th century. It had an oblong top over a solid wooden cylinder which, when rolled back, revealed a fitted interior and a pull-out leather-lined slide. Very often a three-quarter pierced metal gallery extended around the oblong top. The valanced frieze contained two or three drawers. It was mounted on four cabriole legs. It was usually veneered in mahogany and was often handsomely inlaid with marquetry work combined with bronze doré mounts. The celebrated Bureau du Roi (152) was designed as a cylinder desk. Occasionally a cabinet section enclosed with two doors was mounted on the oblong top of the cylinder desk. This variety is usually called a cabinete-secrétaire de cylindre.

A wide variety of bureaux were designed for feminine use. These were distinctive for their beautiful marquetry or lacquer work combined with exquisitely chased bronze mounts. One principal type was called a bureau à pente or slant-front desk. It had a narrow oblong top and hinged slant lid which opened to a fitted writing interior. The valanced frieze was fitted with a row of drawers and it was mounted on four cabriole legs. A variant and popular form of the bureau à pente is now commonly called a bureau à dos d'âne (153) or donkey's back. It is so called because the contour of the slanting front and slightly slanting back resembled to some degree the device placed on a donkey's back for carrying articles. The bureau à dos d'âne was distinctive for its gracefully curving outline. Occasionally at the back of these desks there was a rising screen made of silk or India paper which served to protect the writer from any glaring light.

The bonheur du jour (157) which was the most fashionable feminine bureau during the succeeding Louis XVI style was introduced late in the Louis XV style. It had a small oblong recessed superstructure designed with doors which were often of tambour construction and which opened to a series of small drawers and compartments. The top was usually surmounted with marble and a three-quarter pierced metal gallery. The table generally had either a hinged writing lid or a pull-out writing board. Occasionally the narrow frieze drawer contained a writing panel in tooled leather or blue velvet. The table was mounted on four slender legs. The bonheur du jour reflected the influence of the incoming classical style in its moderately curving lines and classical style of ornament.

Due to the penchant for letter writing the French ébénistes ingeniously incorporated into different types of furniture, in addition to various forms of tables, the necessary equipage for such writing (156).

The secrétaire à abattant, which was a tall upright secretary with a drop-front, was introduced around the middle of the 18th century, and it retained its popularity until the time of Louis Philippe. It had an oblong top, often of marble, over a cavetto frieze which was fitted with a long drawer. Beneath the frieze was a drop-front, which, when let down, revealed an interior of small drawers, secret compartments and pigeonholes. The lower portion was enclosed with two cupboard doors. It rested on a valanced base which curved into very short cabriole legs. The stiles were generally either rounded or chamfered. It was usually finely decorated with either marquetry or lacquer work combined with bronze doré mounts. Although the secrétaire à abattant was designed in the Louis XV style, it did not achieve its characteristic classical form until the following Louis XVI style, when it enjoyed a great vogue.

Commodes   Undoubtedly the commode (159, 160, 161, 162) was one of the most fashionable and ambitious pieces of 18th century French cabinetwork. The marqueteur, the lacquer worker and the metal worker expended their greatest skill in its decoration. As a rule the commode was placed beneath a mirror or trumeau, and it generally occupied the same position in a room as a console table. The origin of the commode is not known. The early commodes, which date from the end of the 17th century, were massive (158). However, as the Louis XV style progressed the commode became lighter and more graceful. The length of the commode greatly varied. The very large commodes were around 50 to 60 inches in length. It had already been stated under the Régence that the commode of bombé form was the characteristic shape of the commode designed in the Louis XV style. The front and sides of the bombé commode were very often serpentine-shaped also. In other words the body of the commode combined both vertical and horizontal curves. The commode almost always had a handsome marble top. The front and sides of the commode were valanced. It was designed with projecting bowed stiles that continued to the angular splayed supports. The commode was usually designed with two, three or four drawers which were arranged in two or three rows. Commodes designed with two long drawers were exceptionally elegant and graceful. From around 1725 onwards the division between the drawers was generally concealed as much as possible by either the marquetry or lacquer work and by the chased and gilded bronze mounts. The Rococo gilded bronze mounts were richly magnificent. The front was often enhanced by gilded bronze Rococo leaf scrolls which flowed vigorously into one another. The floral marquetry or lacquer panels were sometimes framed in shaped gilded bronze surrounds of scrolling leafage. The drawers were fitted with Rococo gilded bronze bail handles and escutcheons, and the projecting bowed stiles were embellished with gilded bronze appliqués extending to the sabots. The best commodes revealed a lightness and refinement demonstrating the elegance of which the Rococo style was capable. Since the commode played an important part in the architectural decoration of a room, the wall decoration or panelling was echoed to a greater or less extent on its façade; for example, a capricious border of gilded bronze on the façade of the commode harmonized with the panelling above it.

One principal type of commode displaying transitional features in its design between the Louis XV and Louis XVI styles (164) had an oblong marble top over a straight front. The center portion of the straight front generally had a slight rectangular projection that made a break in the front. The frieze, which contained one or three narrow drawers, was over two deep long drawers. The stiles, which were either canted or rounded, continued to the cabriole legs. Its slightly curved legs were its chief identification with the Louis XV style. The chased and gilded bronze mounts mirrored the revival of classical ornament (163, 164).

Cupboards   The encoignure or armoire d'encoignure basse, the low corner cupboard, became fashionable around the middle of the 18th century as an article of drawing room furniture. However, the encoignure was also found in other rooms. The encoignure generally had a handsome marble top and was richly decorated. As a rule it was designed in pairs. The façade of the encoignure was either serpentine-shaped or bowed; it was designed with either one or two cupboard doors. It usually had either slightly projecting bowed stiles or straight convex stiles. It was mounted on a valanced base which curved into the short cabriole legs. The encoignure, like all corner cupboards whether hanging or standing on the floor, attained its greatest vogue under Louis XV when there was a strong aversion to rectangles. The encoignure, entre-deux and commode, which belong to that family of furniture called meubles d'appui, often matched each other since they were incorporated into the architectural treatment of a room.

Chiffonniers

The chiffonnier, which was a tall chest of drawers, was essentially a feminine piece of furniture. The name, which is derived from *chiffonnier* meaning a collector of scraps or odds and ends, was given to this piece of furniture in which the ladies kept their work, such as needlework and cuttings of cloth. The chiffonnier, which rested on a base with very short legs, was about four to five feet in height, and was generally fitted with five and occasionally six drawers of equal depth. It was of costly workmanship and was principally made of rosewood or violet ebony. The chiffonnier was introduced around the middle of the 18th century and retained its popularity through the Empire style.

Bookcases

The bibliothèque or bookcase did not come into general use until the 18th century. In one characteristic type the length considerably exceeded the height. This bookcase, which was about five or six feet in length, had an oblong marble top with a three-quarter pierced metal gallery. The two or more long doors were generally designed with shaped wire grille panels that were lined with silk. It had a valanced base and short cabriole legs. In the more ambitious examples this bookcase was finely veneered and enriched with bronze appliqués.

Clocks

The régulateur or tall case clock was a fashionable and important article of furniture. It was finely veneered and sumptuously mounted in bronze doré. The tall case clock was always one of the most elegant articles of French cabinetwork and the finest craftsmanship was lavished on it. Equally superb in its craftsmanship was the bronze doré cartel, which was a wall or mural clock of French origin. It was a veritable masterpiece of the ciseleur's art. The round dial was framed in vigorously wrought bronze doré asymmetrical leaf scrolls and scrolling stems which bore realistically modelled blossoms and leaves. It was often surmounted by figures of a shepherd playing a flageolet and a shepherdess with an open book posed before two flowering trees. Mantel clocks and bracket clocks were also remarkable for the magnificence of their bronze doré mounts.

Accessories

Mirrors were magnificent and plentiful. The upright giltwood frame was carved and pierced with Rococo scrolls and floral festoons and was surmounted with an openwork cresting.

Bronze doré sconces were remarkable for their fanciful shapes. The sconce was often composed of a leaf stalk which boldly flowed into two asymmetrical scrolled candle arms.

Bronze doré chenets or andirons, like the sconces, were typical of the exuberant style of the Rocaille and were distinctive for their boldly flowing leafage scrolls. Frequently scantily draped cherubs were seated upon the pierced and foliated scrolls.

The écran à éventail, which is a fan-shaped fire screen made of bronze doré, was an interesting decorative accessory. It was designed with an upright fan-shaped case, enclosing nine pierced and pivoted foils or leaf-shaped parts, mounted on a Rococo base. When the very thin pierced metal foils were opened it resembled an open fan.

The écran à coulisse, a cheval type of fire screen, having a vertical upright frame which enclosed a panel sliding in grooves on the inner sides of the uprights, was introduced in the reign of Louis XIV. The panel was easily pulled up and down and in that manner the heat from the fireplace was regulated. Frequently the fire screen had a shelf near the floor joining the two arched supports, serving as a foot rest. Occasionally the écran à coulisse was designed with a shelf which could be let down by means of metal quadrants. This shelf was used to hold a cup of coffee or tea, an inkstand or a needlework case. The shelf could also be slanted to serve as a reading desk. This type of fire screen was sometimes provided with two adjustable metal candle arms. The sliding panel was made of different materials, such as tapestry, painted paper or canvas and lacquered wood. Sometimes the fire screen had a fixed panel enclosed in an elaborately carved upright frame, when it is simply referred to as an écran, since the French term *coulisse* means a groove. Both the écran and écran à coulisse enjoyed great popularity in the 18th century.

Decorative folding screens became much smaller and they were generally designed with three or four panels. Some of the very small ones were not much taller than a fire screen. The carved wooden frame was generally gilded, painted or entirely covered in fabric. The panels were generally made of a colorful fabric, lacquer or painted Chinese paper. Frequently the upper part of each panel was fitted with a shaped mirror.

Stands　　The decorative candlestand or guéridon has been found in French inventories since 1640. The original model had a circular top and central standard, which was often in the form of a young Moor in brilliant attire, who served as a page at the French court and was given the name of *guéridon*. Typical examples of the taste for exoticism which prevailed well into the 18th century were those in the form of an Indian or Negress (135). The French craftsmen soon designed innumerable forms of guéridons of a more elegant and artistic quality inspired by the prevailing fashion in decoration (126). When the torchère developed in the 18th century the guéridon became the small movable table or table ambulante of many uses. Many of these small tables designed in the Louis XV style (147, 148) and the succeeding Louis XVI style were remarkable for the delicacy of their marquetry and for the jewel-like quality of their gilded bronze mounts. Some with two shelves were rather similar to the so-called tables à dejeuner. From around 1785 the original model of the guéridon, having a round top on a central standard, was gradually supplanted by guéridons in the form of antique tripods.

The reading stand or pupitre was made in every conceivable form, either to stand alone or incorporated in furniture that was quite alien to reading, such as toilet tables or fire screens. The vogue for all kinds of tables à pupitre dates from around 1750 onwards. The majority were designed as tables de dame, but lecterns were also occasionally found in large masculine desks. Work tables with an adjustable easel so that the top could be raised to form a reading stand or perhaps on which to write a brief note were very fashionable and choice articles of furniture. They combined the purpose of a chiffonnière and a small desk.

CHAPTER NINE

LOUIS XVI

It is generally accepted that the revival of interest in the arts of Rome and Greece, which occurred in the latter part of the 18th century and the new classic style based upon them, was due to the excavations of Pompeii and Herculaneum as well as to certain publications on antiquities. Undoubtedly the success of the movement was equally due to a reaction against the Rococo, because the taste for the antique had never been entirely stifled in France during the Rococo style. Even at the height of its popularity there was an undercurrent of protest in certain circles against asymmetry and the sinuous curves of le style Rocaille, for it was felt that they did not express the finer artistic instincts of the French, which were always inclined to moderation and restraint. The distinguished architect Jean François Blondel, 1681–1756, was a leading opponent of the Rocaille style. In 1737 he published an important work entitled DE LA DISTRIBUTION DES MAISONS DE PLAISANCE in which he derided asymmetrical ornament although he did give several designs of such ornament in this work in deference to the prevailing fashion. Other articles also appeared, such as those by Charles-Nicolas Cochin in the Mercure Galant in 1754, attacking the exaggerations of the Rocaille style. All this mounting criticism coincided with and was intensified by the discoveries made at Pompeii and Herculaneum, which attracted scholars and archaeologists from all over Europe to Rome. These excavations revealed how the ancients really lived. Their temples, ceramics, bronzes and above all their houses and furniture were made known through actual remains as well as through mural paintings and reliefs. This greatly stimulated the imagination of scholars and archaeologists, who, possessed with the zeal of missionaries, issued numerous publications between 1750 and 1765 in which they eulogized antique art. Especially praiseworthy were the writings of Johann Winckelmann, the distinguished pioneer in historic and scientific archaeology. These publications reached France and were an important factor in developing this new classic movement. Archaeology became a fashionable and absorbing subject, and French architects, such as Germain Soufflot, who was to be one of the principal supporters of the antique style, went to Italy to study Renaissance art and above all to study Roman antiquities. A series of collections lauding the beauties of Imperial Rome issued from 1748 on by Piranesi, 1704–1784, the noted Venetian architect and etcher, were also influential. French publications on Greek and Roman art began to appear, such as the illustrious works of the Comte de Caylus. As the arts of Greece and Rome gradually became better understood the enthusiasm for the antique became universal. Even such French writers on philosophy as Diderot and Rousseau became captivated with the works of Plutarch and other classical writers.

It was inevitable that the Rocaille style had to yield before such a general onset. Neo-Classicism was brought into fashion by such men as the architect Gabriel and the ornamentiste Delafosse. Architecture was the first to respond to this revived interest in classicism. Jacques-Ange Gabriel, 1699–1782, who succeeded his father as First Architect to the King, was well skilled in the Neo-Classic style from 1753 on, as was evident in the new wings of the Château de Compiègne. Between 1762–1764 he constructed for Louis XV the Petit Trianon which anticipated the style of Louis XVI. Furniture followed architecture, as it always does, but more slowly. Finally painting and sculpture returned to the classic style toward the end of the 18th century under the powerful influence of the painter Jacques Louis David. It is not possible to fix an exact date when furniture began to return to the classic style of ornament and to the straight line. Contemporary documents support the belief that the fashion for furniture designed in le style à la Grecque or le style à l'antique, as it was then called, began around 1760. Naturally the Rocaille style was not banished immediately. There was a period of transition from about 1760 to 1770 in which certain principles of the Louis XV style and the Louis XVI style were harmoniously combined in furniture design. The classic influence was first reflected in the ornament. Classic motifs, principally borrowed from Renaissance art, were found mingled with French flowers and with the different attributes of love, music, science and pastoral life. In the beginning the forms of furniture underwent little or no change, as was evident in the contour of chairs. Gradually by slight changes the contour of the furniture was modified. The number of curves decreased and the remaining curves were less pronounced, such as in the commode designed with a straight front but still mounted on cabriole legs. Finally, when the transition was complete, the structural lines were chiefly based on the rectilinear, and the curves of the circle, oval and ellipse supplanted the sinuous and complicated curves of the Rococo. The straight leg superseded the cabriole leg, which in an attenuated form persisted the longest on the very delicate small table enriched with marquetry and gilded bronze appliqués. The transitional furniture possessed all the qualities of fine proportions, balance and gracefulness which are the essence of the charm of French cabinetwork. The Louis XVI style, which remained in fashion in Paris until the days of the French Revolution, was firmly established in Paris by the time Louis XVI actually ascended the throne in 1774.

After the middle of the 18th century the inspiration for French art was derived from antiquity. This return to or imitation of the antique, which is referred to as the Classic Revival or the Neo-Classic style, was marked by two distinct phases. The early phase of the Neo-Classic was the lighter and graceful Louis XVI style, while the last phase was the pompous and more solemn Empire style, in which imitation of the antique was observed with uncompromising rigor. Between these two phases was an era of transition which is now generally referred to as the Directoire style, in which certain features of both the Louis XVI and the Empire styles were artfully combined. During the Louis XVI style the cabinetmaker was content to confine his imitation of the antique to classic architectural detail such as pilasters and columns, and to certain classic motifs, which he interpreted in accordance with the French taste for graceful elegance and refinement. The decorative artists who created these designs for the Louis XVI style gave new life and beauty to their compositions, which were in the lighter form of the 18th century. These compositions were imbued with a spirit of light and refined originality, which was typical of that era and which made them so decidedly French. At first the ornament was borrowed from the Renaissance interpretation of the antique. However, in a short space of time as antique Roman ornament became better understood, it was found artfully blended with the Renaissance ornament. For example, arabesques both ancient and Raphaelesque appeared in decorative compositions. Thus Roman architecture

and ornament were the dominating theme in this new style. From about 1770 to 1785 the style of Louis XVI remained essentially the same, but toward the end of the reign of Louis XVI the taste for the antique became more exacting and widespread. A translation of Johann Winckelmann's HISTORY OF ART, the collection of engravings by Piranesi and his son, and Sir William Hamilton's books on Greek and Etruscan vases were all contributing factors and had great influence in France. The French decorative artists introduced new classic motifs derived from the antique art of Rome, Pompeii, Herculaneum and Greece, as the art of the latter country became better understood. Gradually the Louis XVI style of classic ornament was buried under this accumulation of new material for decoration. Furniture copied from antique models appeared in the collection of designs for cabinetwork. This pronounced taste for the antique and its closer imitation resulted in the Directoire style, which ultimately and logically evolved into the style of the French Empire, when the antique was pursued with meticulous accuracy.

The manners and customs of society were much the same under Louis XVI as they had been under his predecessor. Royalty, the aristocracy and the wealthy bourgeoisie were all eager for a life of luxury and pleasure. Everything had to be pleasing and convenient for this sophisticated society. However, there was another side to this society which explains to some extent a sentimental mode linked with the Neo-Classic movement, which was exemplified in the art of Greuze, Angelica Kauffmann and other contemporary artists. This fashion for virtue, simplicity and reason seems to have been dictated by a sentimental idealization of the ancient world. The virtue and simplicity of ancient days were regarded as noble and inspiring subjects. This worldly society derived great pleasure in finding these emotions in others, although they themselves never changed their habits to acquire finer feelings. It was all a part of the new fashion, but it never penetrated beneath the surface. They found it so delightful to exclaim over simplicity and so refreshing to visit a farm at noon and eat bread and honey, but they carefully forgot to mention the fine cuisine waiting for them after their return from the farm. In the same manner their enthusiasm for the antique in furniture never permitted any sacrifice in material comfort and convenience. They liked to see the simple beauty of antiquity in their furniture, but not if it conflicted with pleasant living. This almost dual character of fashionable society lasted as long as the Ancien Régime, when it all became a part of a vanished world. The paintings of Hubert Robert depicting Roman ruins with crumbling colonnades amidst landscapes and human figures evoked a dream of antiquity which contemporary society found very exhilarating and which flattered their sentimental philosophy.

The delicate beauty, the exquisite refinement and the restrained and graceful elegance, which were the essence of the Louis XVI style, represented the acme of French cabinetwork. Much of this grace and beauty were achieved through the perfection of proportions, the faultless balance of all the parts and the harmonious division of the surface into panels and the accuracy of their framing. Never in the history of French cabinetwork did the cabinetmaker display more assuredness in his technique. He displayed this same sureness of taste in his selection of orna-

ment which gave the required richness but still stayed within the boundary of delicate sobriety. In achieving his goal of refined simplicity and restrained elegance, he imbued his cabinetwork with neatness and precision but he softened it with an abundance of graceful and delicate ornament. During the Louis XVI style the decorative artist and cabinetmaker borrowed heavily from Roman architecture for his inspiration, because it was the best understood of all the ancient arts. The new style, which reasserted the taste for classic form and ornament, was completely dominated by the principle of symmetry. Only in such incidental decorative details as flowers, ribbons and bowknots was any deviation from the principle of symmetry permitted. Rectilinear forms and classic detail interpreted in the light manner of the 18th century were typical. The cabinetmaker endeavored to relieve the severity of the simple rectilinear outlines by a profusion of delicate and graceful ornament, such as the carved moldings on chairs and canapés and the exquisite marquetry work and finely chased gilded bronze mounts on tables and commodes. The work of Riesener and Carlin with its abundance of graceful ornament exemplified this principle. Other cabinetmakers working in the Louis XVI style, who had more affection for stiff lines, did not endeavor to lessen the severe rectilinear and at times almost angular aspect of their cabinetwork to the same degree as Riesener and Carlin. Although some of the cabinetwork was composed entirely of straight lines, the curve of the circle, ellipse and oval was introduced in many articles of furniture, such as the chair with a medallion-shaped back and the commode and side table of semi-circular plan. Many semi-circular arches, which had originated in Roman architecture, were found on the crest rails of chairs and on the upper lines of panelled woodwork. However, when curving lines were employed, they did not detract from the directness of the horizontal and vertical structural lines found in the same article of furniture.

Another characteristic feature of the Louis XVI style, which also had its provenance in classic architecture, was the treatment of a plain surface framed with a border or several parallel borders in place of ornamentation. Undecorated mahogany surfaces were extremely fashionable during the Louis XVI style, and many articles of furniture, such as commodes, tables and bureaus, depended entirely upon their framed panels for their decoration. These panelled borders were generally in the form of finely chased narrow bronze moldings. Toward the end of the Louis XVI style narrow strips of brass were frequently inlaid in the mahogany surface in place of the bronze moldings, and occasionally narrow bands of a contrasting wood were substituted for the bronze moldings or metal strips. These molded or banded panels were generally entirely composed of straight lines, in fact the majority of panels during the Louis XVI style were rectangular in form. Occasionally the four corners of the panel were cut off and either squared-in or incurvate corners were substituted, and the space was filled with a rosette. Panels in the form of ovals, ellipses and circles were occasionally centered within the rectangular panels. This was often evident in the decoration of a commode, with the façade of the commode centering an oval panel decorated with a basket or vase of flowers worked in marquetry. The use of moldings was less pronounced than in the pre-ceding style. The moldings, which were flatter, more precise and more uniform, were generally embellished with a delicate repetitive pattern, such as bead and leaf, husk chain or beads. The combination of moldings was in accordance with classic architecture and they were used in conjunction with fillets. The very small or reduced scale on which the ornament was treated by the wood carver and especially by the bronze worker was a pronounced feature of the Louis XVI style. The bronze mounts with their precise and delicate ornament had a jewel-like quality which resembled the work of the goldsmith more than that of the bronze worker. They were remarkable for their minute detail and perfected workmanship. Running motifs, such as entrelacs, which also had their origin in classic architecture, were a marked feature of the style and were extensively found on the friezes of tables and commodes. The ornament, especially in marquetry work, was often diapered. Mechanical devices for transforming furniture were especially characteristic and attained their peak of complexity under Louis XVI. Certain ébénistes, especially those from the Rhineland such as Röntgen and Riesener, excelled in this kind of locksmithing.

The era abounded with great craftsmen, and ébénistes from across the Rhine played an even more important role than in the preceding Louis XV style. Undoubtedly Jean Henri Riesener, 1734–1806, was the great cabinetmaker working in the style of Louis XVI. He was born at Gladbach near Essen and at an early age he came to Paris. He entered the workshop of Oeben, his fellow countryman, and upon the latter's death in 1763 he worked as foreman for Oeben's widow. Several years later he married Madame

Oeben and in 1768 he was admitted as a master cabinetmaker. He finished the celebrated Bureau du Roi in 1769 which had been begun by Oeben and Riesener's name alone was stamped upon it. In 1774 he was appointed ébéniste ordinaire du Mobilier de la Couronne. All the qualities of the Louis XVI style such as perfection in proportions, exquisite refinement and a graceful elegance were combined in his work. His marquetry of dainty garlands, delicate bouquets of flowers, showers of blossoms and draperies with gently flowing graceful curves were imbued with the spirit of French grace. He also especially favored a marquetry comprising a network of lozenges enclosing realistically treated flowers such as a rose or narcissus. Riesener's supremacy among his contemporaries was undisputed and he executed many commissions for Marie Antoinette and for members of the court. The chased and gilded bronze mounts found on his furniture were unrivalled for their finished detail. Some of the mounts, possessing an extreme refinement almost similar to a jeweler's technique, seem to have been chiefly the creation of Gouthière, although no documents have been found up to the present time linking the names of these two craftsmen. In addition to his furniture enriched with marquetry he also produced veneered mahogany furniture, which, like all his work, was unexcelled in its faultless proportions and technical perfection. Combination pieces and pieces with secret compartments designed by Riesener were a miracle of accuracy and attest to his German heritage. Many of Riesener's works as well as Oeben's bear no stamp, since much of their work was undertaken for the Crown which permitted them to dispense with such guild regulations. The French ébéniste Martin

Carlin, like Riesener, was also a perfect exponent of the Louis XVI style. He was admitted as a master cabinetmaker in 1766 and he is often regarded as the best known cabinetmaker working in the style of Louis XVI. Carlin did much work for Madame du Barry for her château at Louveciennes. His furniture displayed exquisite taste in all its details and possessed all the delicacy, refinement and graceful elegance which were so characteristic of the Louis XVI style. Both he and Riesener decorated some of their furniture with panels of Chinese lacquer work. He also worked in ebony, because he felt that the deep black and polished surface brilliantly set off his delicate gilded bronze mounts of garlands, wreaths of roses and bowknots. His marquetry and veneered furniture revealed his special talent for effectively combining the various colored woods and bronze mounts to achieve a maximum of beauty. Carlin sometimes decorated his cabinetwork with porcelain plaques. He was also adept in producing combination pieces, such as small work tables equipped with reading and writing boards.

There was also the work of the French ébéniste Nicolas Petit, 1732–1791, who received his master in 1761. He executed many fine pieces, especially in marquetry work and in black lacquer decorated in the Chinese taste. One of his most outstanding pieces is a commode decorated with exquisite floral marquetry which is in the Bibliothèque at Versailles. René Dubois, 1737–1799, a distinguished ébéniste to Marie Antoinette, received his master in 1755. Among his many notable pieces is a famous commode in black lacquer in the Chinese taste and exquisitely mounted in bronze doré. This piece was made by request for the marriage of Marie Antoinette. The work of such ébénistes as Leleu, Avril and Saunier was representative of that phase of the Louis XVI style which displayed large uniform unbroken surfaces and a closer affiliation with Roman architectural details in its decoration. Claude-Charles Saunier, 1735–1807, who was admitted as a master cabinetmaker in 1752, was an expert marqueteur at the beginning of his career. His work admirably illustrates the development in French cabinetwork from the use of certain details and motifs borrowed from Roman architecture to the closer imitation of antiquity which ultimately triumphed in the style of the French Empire. It is generally accepted that Jean François Leleu, who was admitted as a master cabinetmaker in 1764, was the first to inlay the grooves of flutings with thin strips of brass and to put metal rings around pilasters and columns. The work of Etienne Avril, who was admitted as a master ébéniste in 1774, is chiefly identified with plain and uniform veneered surfaces framed in very narrow gilded bronze moldings. Sharp and angular lines were very noticeable in much of his work, such as commodes. Although the cabinetwork of the different members of the Jacob family essentially belongs to the succeeding Empire style, the elder Georges Jacob, who received his master in 1765, also worked for various members of the royal family and aristocracy until the Revolution. Of particular interest were his carved pieces, such as chairs, sofas and day beds, which were his speciality. The deftness with which he executed his carved decoration has rightfully earned for him the reputation as one of the great wood carvers of the 18th century.

David Röntgen or Roentgen, 1741–1809, who was a German cabinetmaker, had his principal workshop at Neuwied-on-the-Rhine, near Coblenz. He had only limited facilities in Paris where he could receive orders and deliver his furniture. He was patronized by Marie Antoinette and was admitted as a master cabinetmaker in 1780. Although his cabinetwork was of an excellent quality it lacked the delicate execution and refinement found in the finest French work. His taste was heavier and his bronze mounts did not possess the same quality of French grace found in the contemporary work of Carlin or Riesener. However, his marquetry work was above reproach. The vivid coloring, the vigorous and original manner in which he treated his flowers, and the expressiveness that he gave to his figure subjects were truly remarkable. It seemed impossible for anyone to improve on the marquetry work of the Louis XV period, but Röntgen developed a technique that brought his work even closer to the art of painting. Prior to Röntgen the light and shade found in pictures depicted in marquetry were obtained by burning or engraving the wood. He achieved a better effect of light and shade, which gave his marquetry a quality of new depth and vividness, by skillfully arranging the minute pieces of darker woods in the manner of very small stone mosaics or pietra dura work. His favorite themes for marquetry work were stories from classical mythology. He produced numerous pieces of furniture for the royalty of Europe and Russia, such as cylinder desks, secretaries, tables and cabinets that were praiseworthy for their perfection of joinery. Undoubtedly his great contemporary reputation was due to a large extent to his mechanical genius. Early in his career, Marie Antoinette appointed him as her ébéniste-mécanicien. He was expert in designing harlequin pieces of furniture equipped with complex mechanisms, which, when set in motion, controlled their transformations and secret hiding places. Some of his commodes and tables were amazing for their mechanical precision. It is generally thought that the almost horological precision found in some of these ingenious interior fittings was due to Röntgen's partner, Peter Kinzing, who was a clockmaker. Röntgen also made some mahogany furniture with rectangular panels framed in narrow bronze doré moldings.

Toward the end of the reign of Louis XVI many pieces of furniture varied from the typical Louis XVI style as exemplified in the work of Riesener and Carlin. Much of this work displayed a strong resemblance in its quality of grandeur to the Louis XIV style of cabinetwork. It chiefly comprised richly decorated furniture, such as large commodes and console tables and tall case clocks, especially made for the royal palaces. Some of the work of the German cabinetmaker Guillaume Beneman illustrated the influence of this earlier style. Beneman, who was admitted as master cabinetmaker in 1785, was the principal cabinetmaker to the Court of France during the last years of the reign of Louis XVI. Of particular interest were his monumental marble-top mahogany commodes (FIGURE 192) which were remarkable for their quality of grandeur. The façade, which was fitted with two cupboard doors, was divided into three shaped panels framed in bronze moldings. The large center panel, which was in the form of an elliptical arch shaped like the handle of a basket, extended practically the length of the commode. The frieze and the shaped panels were covered with bronze doré appliqués of delicate foliage scrolls and other classic motifs. The large center panel centered a large figured medallion

in the classical taste made of biscuit or unglazed porcelain. It had half-round cable-fluted pilasters over short vase-shaped legs. Also during this era several cabinetmakers devoted part of their talent to making reproductions of the sumptuous marquetry pieces of André Charles Boulle. Excellent reproductions were made by such maître-ébénistes as Philippe-Claude Montigny, Etienne Levasseur (131) and Nicolas-Pierre Séverin. They cast their bronze mounts from Boulle models. In fact some of the Boulle work of the late 18th century was executed with such consummate skill that it is very difficult to distinguish the reproductions from the original Boulle work. In direct contrast to the cabinetwork that was strongly reminiscent of the Louis XIV style, other cabinetwork toward the end of the reign of Louis XVI forecast the Directoire and Empire styles. This increasing taste for the antique, in which a closer imitation was sought, was expressed in much of the work of the German cabinetmaker Adam Weisweiler, who was admitted as a master cabinetmaker in 1778. Weisweiler, who used a wide range of materials, including exotic woods, lacquer and porcelain, very often designed the slender supports for his tables and desks in the form of delicate caryatids and canephoroi. The composition of his ornament and bronze mounts belong to the style called Pompeiian or Etruscan, which under Louis XVI became more and more fashionable for interior decoration and furnishings. He was one of the most appreciated of the contemporary ébénistes and he worked for Marie Antoinette at her château at Saint-Cloud.

Undoubtedly the two outstanding metal workers of this era were Pierre Gouthière, 1740–1806, and Pierre Philippe Thomire.

Gouthière executed a great quantity of metal work of the utmost variety. In addition to his bronze doré mounts for marquetry and lacquer furniture, he also mounted in bronze such pieces as vases and bowls made of jasper, choice marbles and French or Oriental porcelain. He executed many articles in bronze such as magnificent cartels, chandeliers, candelabra, sconces and andirons. It is generally believed that some of the bronze mounts on furniture attributed to Gouthière were the work of Thomire. Gouthière was selected by Madame du Barry to make the bronze fitments for her château at Louveciennes which was regarded as the most exquisite masterpiece of the Louis XVI style. Much of the fame of her château was due to the magnificent bronze embellishments of Gouthière. All of Gouthière's work was not of the highest quality. His best work was admirable for its delicacy and refinement, while his superlative work was unexcelled for its artistry and perfected workmanship. Especially praiseworthy was the gilding on his bronzes which was of a superb quality. The French Revolution and the Napoleonic wars ruined the career of Gouthière as they did the careers of so many other great craftsmen belonging to that era. Thomire also produced metal work of the finest quality. Later in his career he worked in the style of the French Empire and some of his bronze appliqués for furniture designed in the Empire style were remarkable for their precise and jewel-like quality.

The different woods employed during the Louis XVI style were similar to those used in the preceding style. Mahogany was extremely fashionable and was much used in veneering. Ebony, which had been used only occasionally in Louis XV cabinet-work, was employed more frequently for some ambitious pieces of furniture. Late in the reign of Louis XVI small elaborate occasional tables with marble tops were sometimes entirely made of bronze. The different decorative processes for ornamenting the surface of furniture were essentially the same as those employed in the Louis XV style, and since the cabinetmaker working in the style of Louis XV had skillfully developed the technique of these decorative processes to such a high standard the Louis XVI cabinetmaker could make no significant improvement. The new method employed by Röntgen for creating light and shade was the only appreciable advancement. The practice of enriching small choice articles of furniture with porcelain plaques was increasingly employed. They were chiefly found on such articles as writing furniture designed for feminine use, on jardinières and small occasional and work tables. In addition to the small flower plaques of Sèvres porcelain, occasionally biscuit medallions or plaques of Wedgwood's blue jasper ware with their characteristic white reliefs were inserted. The practice of ornamenting furniture, such as commodes, with painted decorative panels of flowers or classical figure subjects was also sometimes employed late in the style of Louis XVI.

There was little change in the choice of fashionable textiles employed in upholstery. The general tendency toward more delicate tones in interior decoration was carried out in the fabrics, which were also of a lighter weight. Tapestry was still preferred for the fine suites of drawing room furniture and many fine tapestry coverings were designed by Jean Baptiste Huet, whose work was largely inspired by Boucher and Oudry. Of particular interest were the linen and cotton printed fabrics woven at Jouy by Philip Oberkampf, 1738–1815, a German cloth printer and dyer. He founded his celebrated print works at the village of Jouy, near Versailles, in 1760. The designs, which were generally pictorial, were usually done in a single soft French tone on a light or natural-colored ground. His printed fabrics became fashionable almost immediately and in 1783 Louis XVI made his workshop a Manufacture Royale. His early prints were mostly in a deep rose and the designs were chiefly inspired by Chinese art. His later prints were principally scenes of pastoral life and stories from mythology. Many of his greatest designs were executed by Jean Baptiste Huet.

Decorative motifs having their provenance in Roman art and French flowers were the principal inspiration for the Louis XVI style of ornament. Running motifs, which were a legacy of ancient architecture, were much used, especially on the classic moldings made of either wood or bronze and on the friezes of tables or commodes. Included among the popular running motifs were dentils, gadrooning, entrelacs or two interlaced ribbons, guilloches, vitruvian scrolls, leaf bands such as acanthus, bay or oak, bead chains and bead and olive chains, spiralled ribbon and leaf, ribbon and bead or leaf and bead, husk chains, fret bands, reeds fastened with an interlacing ribbon, imbricated coin bands and above all short rows of fluting. Decorative details such as columns and pilasters, borrowed from Roman architecture, were incorporated in the designs for furniture and were remarkable for their refinement. Later in the Louis XVI style caryatids were occasionally used as supports in place of the

columns. Included among the favorite classic motifs were Roman eagles, the head of the ram, goat and lion, the cloven-hoof foot, dolphins, cherubs and cupids, winged cupids, cherubs' heads, human and animal masks and fanciful beings such as sphinxes, griffins, chimeras, satyrs and sirens. The acanthus leaf was much used, for instance in rinceaux and in combination with human and animal masks. Also much used were wreaths and garlands of acanthus, ivy and bay leaves, festoons such as drapery, floral, husks or bead festoons, rosettes, lyres, pine cones, paterae, husk trails, arabesques, grotesques, lambrequins, medallions, classic urns often of tripod form, vases of classical form frequently decorated with garlands of acanthus leaves or drapery festoons, urns with a flaming finial, perfume burners and tripods. Due to the artistic genius of the French designer these antique motifs were harmoniously combined with the relatively modern floral arrangements which were common to the styles of Louis XV and Louis XVI. Flowers gracefully arranged in baskets or vases, or charming bouquets of roses and lilies, and sprays of laurel and oak leaves tied with ribbons were typical of the era. All of the flowers found in a French garden were used in the floral compositions. Cornflowers or barbeaux were much favored by the ébénistes as well as full-blown roses. Graceful bowknots of ribbon and streamers were very fashionable and they were effectively used to hold the flowers in position on the panels. Subjects from Roman mythology and the different attributes appropriate to war, love, music, pastoral life, science, astronomy, agriculture, hunting and fishing were all included in the fashionable repertory of Louis XVI ornament.

Chairs   The Louis XVI style chair was not as comfortable as its predecessor. While the Louis XV style chair was composed entirely of curved lines, the Louis XVI style chair always had at least straight legs (FIGURES 167, 168, 169, 170). The manner in which the different members of the Louis XV style chair flowed into one another in continuous curves was entirely changed in the Louis XVI style chair. Due to the classic influence the point of juncture where two different members were joined was well defined (167, 168, 169, 170). This feature, which often detracted from the beauty of the chair, was evident in the chair designed with vertical baluster-shaped arm supports, where the meeting of the base of the baluster with the top of the leg was generally awkward. The molded frame of the chair was usually delicately carved with the different classic running patterns (167, 168), such as bead chains, leaf bands and imbricated coin bands. The frames were gilded (167, 169), painted and parcel-gilded (170) or finished in the natural wood, which was often beech (168) or walnut.

In a broad sense the fauteuil can be divided into two general classes, namely those with oval medallion backs (167) and those with rectangular backs (168). The oval back chair, when its members were in absolute harmony and its back a true oval, was admirable for its refined and graceful elegance. Fortunately the severity of the rectangular construction of the other type of Louis XVI chair was generally softened by some curving lines, such as incurvate arm supports and a bowed front seat rail, and by an abundance of delicate carved detail (168). The back of the open armchair did not extend to the seat rail (167, 168) and was often cabriolet or slightly concave (167). The cartouche-shaped back, which was so typical of the Louis XV style, enjoyed a short vogue at the beginning of the Louis XVI style. The oval medallion back was often crested with a bowknot (167). The rectangular back was generally square or almost square. A variation of this type of back, which was much used, had vertical uprights, which sometimes slanted slightly outward (168), and an arched (168) or flat-arched crest rail. The two uprights were often surmounted with finials (171), such as a pine cone or plume finials. The arms had upholstered armpads or manchettes (168) and their contour followed the shape of the side seat rails. The arms were very often joined to the uprights in a more or less graceful downsweeping curve (168) which sometimes started from the top of the uprights (169, 171). The armposts were almost always joined to the tops of the vertical legs (168). Rarely did they set back on the side rails. In order to provide for the panniers, which were still worn by the ladies, the armposts were incurvate (168) or curved inward and sometimes curved gracefully outward as well. This feature was also found in Louis XV chair design (142, 143). Later when panniers were no longer fashionable the armposts were often vertical (170) and baluster-shaped. The upholstered seat with its molded and carved seat rail and rosetted dies was made in different shapes. The seat was generally circular, semi-circular with a bowed front (168), or it was made entirely of straight lines with the seat being wider in the front; sometimes this angular seat had a bow-shaped front rail. Each vertical leg was headed by a die or square which centered a carved motif, usually a rosette (167, 168). As a rule the leg was round and tapered (167, 168) and was fluted vertically (167) and occasionally spirally; the fluting was plain or cabled. The leg was molded at the top and at the foot (167, 168). This round tapering leg was often called a quiver leg because of its supposed resemblance to the case in which arrows were carried (169). Sometimes the leg was carved with arrow feathers at the top (169). Occasionally the chair leg was quadrangular and tapering.

The upholstered bergère continued to be a fashionable article of furniture. It was characterized by its closed sides and loose cushion seat (169, 170). One type was similar to the fauteuil with a square or almost square back. It had the characteristic closed sides and angular seat (169). Another type of bergère, which is often referred to as gondola-shaped, had a more rounded back and sides which curved around the semi-circular seat. The back and sides were upholstered as one unit. This type had either a back designed with vertical uprights, which sometimes slanted slightly outward, and an arched or flat-arched crest rail, or it had an arched horseshoe-shaped back which continued in an unbroken curve to form the arms. A third type of bergère was designed with winged sides. Toward the close of the period chair design sometimes reflected the increasing taste for the antique; for example, armposts and front legs were designed as one continuous unit, such as in the form of an elongated terminal figure (170).

The characteristic caned dressing table or desk chair was essentially similar to that of the Louis XV style. It had a low arched horseshoe-shaped back continuing to form the arms which rested on incurvate arm supports. As a rule the seat was circular and often revolved. It was mounted on four tapering cylindrical fluted legs.

In addition to the chairs with upholstered backs many fine armchairs and side chairs were made during the Louis XVI style with open backs. These chairs were very often made of mahogany and had either a caned seat or upholstered seat of leather or some other serviceable fabric, since they were principally used in the dining room. Mahogany chairs were an innovation of the Louis XVI style. Occasionally the frames were made of a less costly wood and were gilded.

The molded frames were often enriched with carved detail. Undoubtedly the lyre-back chair was the most fashionable form. Other designs were also used for the pierced splats and occasionally the splats were of solid wood. These splat-back chairs often had a hoop-back; that is, the uprights and crest rail were designed in one continuous arch. The chair was designed with tapering cylindrical fluted legs which were headed with rosetted dies.

Settees   The upholstered canapé (171) essentially followed the same features of design found in the contemporary fauteuil. As a rule it was designed en suite with the fauteuil. One type of canapé had a rectangular back which might or might not extend to the seat rail. When the back did extend to the seat rail the arms generally had closed sides and the seat was fitted with a long loose cushion. This canapé with a rectangular back sometimes had an arched or flat-arched (171) crest rail. Another variety of canapé had a shaped back panel and was designed en suite with the oval medallion-back chair. Another characteristic type of canapé had a gracefully arched back that continued in an unbroken curve to form the arms which rested on incurvate arm supports. The back and sides were upholstered as one unit. This canapé retained the graceful lines of the canapé à corbeille designed in the Louis XV style. The majority of canapés were designed with eight round and tapering legs.

Beds   All the different types of beds described in the Louis XV style continued in vogue and were designed with either short cylindrical or quadrangular tapered and fluted legs. The lit à la duchesse (172) and the lit d' ange were especially fashionable. New types of beds were also introduced and the fashion for the lit à colonnes was revived at this time. The so-called Turkish bed or the lit à la Turque (173), introduced in the Louis XV style, also continued in fashion.

Tables   The various kinds of tables introduced in the Louis XV style continued in fashion. Serpentine-shaped tops and valanced friezes, so characteristic of the Louis XV style, were discarded. Pierced metal galleries extending either completely or three-quarters around the tops of the tables (178) were typical of the era, as well as straight tapered legs of either cylindrical or quadrangular form (175). Toward the close of the period new forms of supports were occasionally introduced (181). The description of the following tables with the exception of the carved and gilt wood side tables will be restricted to several new characteristic forms introduced in the Louis XVI period. Descriptions of such tables as the chiffonnière (175), tricoteuse (176, 177), guéridon-table (181, 182) and the table à pupitre (178, 180) have already been given in the Louis XV chapter. (*See pages* 135, 136, 140, 141.) The many small luxury tables distinguished by the elegance of their proportions and the masterly skill displayed in their decoration and gilded mounts is a feature of the Louis XVI style. Combination pieces revealed all those brilliant technical and versatile qualities which characterized the achievements of the Parisian ébénistes belonging to the periods of Louis XV and Louis XVI. Mechanical devices for transforming furniture were a striking feature of this period (180, 196).

Furniture designed to be a part of the decorative scheme of a room and adapted by its form and proportions to a particular place was multiplied from around 1750 onwards. Included in this general category of furniture which forms a unit with the walls were such pieces as commodes (191, 192, 193), low cupboards or entre-deux (194), encoignures (195) and carved and gilt wood side tables and consoles with marble tops. One principal type of console table had a demilune marble top over a conformingly shaped frieze that was carved with a running motif, such as entrelacs. The frieze, which often centered a tablet of musical trophies or some other carved decoration, was draped with finely carved floral festoons. The two straight legs, which were either cylindrical or quadrangular, were joined with an incurvate stretcher that centered a classic urn draped with festoons of flowers. The console table with heavy swags and consoles or brackets in the style popularized by Delafosse was very fashionable (174). The very small console table was usually mounted on a single shaped support or console. Massive carved and gilt wood side tables with oblong marble tops mounted on four legs were also designed in the Louis XVI style and reflected the influence of the earlier Louis XIV style in their quality of splendor.

The athénienne, a variety of small decorative stand or table introduced under Louis XVI, was in the form of an antique Pompeiian tripod and its decoration was similar to that of the classical originals. The three slender incurvate metal supports were often headed with "Egyptian" caryatids above a quadrangular leg terminating in a paw foot. Sometimes they were headed with rams' heads terminating in cloven hoof feet. The athénienne had a bowl-shaped top made of onyx or some other material. A feature of the Louis XVI period was the great number of athéniennes, jardinières, cassolettes and guéridons made at this time and which continued until the end of the Empire. It seems that the athénienne served several purposes. Its use as a perfume burner or cassolette was especially typical.

The tables à déjeuner (179) belong to that large family of small movable tables or tables ambulantes that flourished under Louis XVI. These light and convenient small tables were chiefly used as coffee tables and occasionally perhaps for tea. The top was generally of marble and was partially surrounded with a pierced metal gallery. One characteristic form was designed with a small circular top mounted on a standard and with a median shelf of similar circumference. It seems that the term *déjeuner* was first mentioned in an inventory of 1728. Originally it referred to the vessels and dishes necessary for a small meal. The principal pieces in a déjeuner comprised the tray, cups and saucers, coffee pot, chocolate pot, sugar bowl and cream jug.

Gaming Tables

The bouillotte table, which was a kind of circular card table, was first designed in the Louis XVI style. The French card game of bouillotte became very fashionable at the time of the Revolution. It was played with three, four or five persons. The characteristic bouillotte table was made of veneered mahogany. It had a circular marble top and a pierced metal gallery over a panelled frieze which was fitted with two small drawers and with two pull-out slides. It was mounted on four fluted cylindrical and tapered legs that terminated in sabots.

Writing Furniture

All the characteristic forms of bureaux designed in the Louis XV style continued in vogue, such as the bureau plat, bureau à cylindre (151), bureau à caissons latéreaux (154), bonheur du jour (157), secrétaire à abattant and the numerous harlequin tables with their skillfully concealed writing interiors. The bureau à cylindre, which was generally veneered in mahogany, was more fashionable during the Louis XVI style than the bureau plat. The surface was often delicately inlaid with marquetry combined with bronze mounts. Very often the surface of the bureau à cylindre was divided into rectangular panels framed with finely chased narrow bronze moldings which was a favorite method for decorating the surfaces of furniture during the Louis XVI style. The narrow oblong top of the bureau à cylindre was often surmounted with a plateau of three small drawers, above which was a marble top and a three-quarter pierced metal gallery. The part beneath the solid roll top was very often fitted with five narrow drawers of equal depth. It was arranged with a long center drawer which was flanked by two rows of small lateral drawers. It was mounted on four straight and tapering legs.

The characteristic and popular large veneered mahogany bureau à caissons latéreaux or writing table with lateral compartments was essentially similar to the lower portion of the bureau à cylindre. It had an oblong top inset with a leather panel and rimmed with bronze doré, and it was fitted with pull-out slides at each end inset with leather panels. The front was usually designed with five or seven narrow drawers of equal depth. The long front center drawer was flanked by two or three rows of small lateral drawers. This arrangement provided ample space for the knees of the writer. The panelled drawers were framed with bronze doré moldings. It was mounted on four tapered legs of either cylindrical or quadrangular form. The rear of the table was designed to conform with the front and was fitted with mock drawers. It is often thought that this writing table derived from the Louis XIV style bureau semainier (136).

The secrétaire à abattant (183, 184, 186) enjoyed a great vogue during the Louis XVI period. The more costly examples were notable for the superb skill displayed in their surface decoration and gilded bronze mounts. Their ample surfaces present some of the most perfected ornament belonging to this era. Sometimes the secrétaire à abattant was designed en suite with a commode or with one or a pair of encoignures. In some instances the suite comprised all three.

Cabinets

Cabinets (185, 188) also furnished a notable category of luxury pieces remarkable for the elegance of their proportions and technical brilliance. The interior of these cabinets was almost a miracle of precise construction and was often provided with many small drawers and secret compartments. Secret hiding places, frequently found in cabinets, writing furniture and other similar pieces, controlled by mechanical devices, were very fashionable during the reign of Louis XVI.

Dessertes

The term *commode-desserte* (197) is generally given to a kind of commode, fitted with drawers and shelves, which had an oblong top with quadrant-shaped returns or rounded ends. Essentially its construction was similar to that of a rectangular commode to which had been added shelves in the shape of a quarter of a circle at each end. The frieze was fitted with a long central frieze drawer and usually lateral convex frieze drawers which often swung out. There were two deep long drawers beneath the central frieze drawer and two open shelves under each lateral frieze drawer. It had a marble top and a pierced metal gallery and the two shelves at each end had a pierced gallery and sometimes a marble top. The central drawers were flanked by pilasters headed by dies. The four short legs were frequently vase-shaped, as they were on so many commodes designed in the Louis XVI style. The commode-desserte was usually veneered in mahogany, and occasionally it was made of ebony. Sometimes the mahogany commode-desserte was inlaid with oblong panels. The façade was divided into panels that were framed with bronze doré moldings. The panelled frieze was often enhanced with a bronze doré running pattern, such as interlaced ribbons, and the dies were enriched with bronze rosettes. The commode-desserte was also designed with a demilune top. Its use is generally interpreted as a buffet with the shelves for display.

The term *desserte* (198, 199) is generally given to a similar article of furniture of demilune shape frequently provided with intermediate shelves in place of the two long deep central drawers. Occasionally the rear panel was covered with a mirror. Variations occurred. Frequently the rear panel was completely omitted and the number of shelves and their arrangement varied considerably. The desserte side table was sometimes designed with an oblong top and incurvate returns or ends that curved inward over a conformingly shaped frieze and a low and matching galleried undershelf. This category of furniture was derived from the commode. The ornamentiste Albert, père, referred to these pieces as "commodes ouvertes dans le goût anglais" or "commodes ouvertes dans le goût nouveau." He observed that they were used for the reception of porcelains and other objects. The specimens with numerous shelves were easily adaptable to this use. It seems almost a certainty that this general category of furniture was intended for the dining room, since some of the models are referred to as servantes in literature on French furniture. They must also have been used to display the beautiful vessels made of metal or porcelain and in this manner they replaced the buffet à gradins of the 17th century which in turn had replaced the Renaissance dressoirs.

Accessories In addition to hanging étagères and standing étagères, sets of shelves were incorporated into the design of different articles of furniture, such as the secrétaire à étagère (189), the commode à étagère and the servante à étagère. It seems that these shelves were designed as much to receive dishes as to exhibit precious objects and their use for either display or utilitarian purposes was largely determined by the article of furniture. For example, the shelves sometimes found on the bonheur du jour were for display, while a commode with shelves was generally used as a buffet.

The vitrine was especially designed for the reception and display of fine porcelains and other small objects of art. It was fitted with shelves and provided with one or two glazed doors. As a rule the vitrine was a rather plain article of furniture so that it would not detract from the contents. The vitrine varied in size, and the very small vitrine was sometimes placed on a table or commode.

During the Louis XVI style the table à fleurs, which was later known as a jardinière, was introduced. It was designed to hold flowers and plants and was a costly article of veneered furniture. The characteristic jardinière had a narrow oblong frieze fitted with a metal-lined well. It was mounted on four legs. It was usually enriched with delicate marquetry work and was frequently decorated with Sèvres porcelain plaques.

The delicate refinement and graceful elegance which characterized the Louis XVI cabinetwork was also evident in the decorative accessories made of bronze doré. Cartels, mantle clocks, candelabra, sconces and andirons were unexcelled for their exquisite detail and finished workmanship. Other decorative objects, such as bowls and vases and bracket clocks, were made of choice marbles, jasper and malachite and were finely mounted in bronze doré. Tall case clocks were remarkable for the masterly skill displayed in their decoration and for the exceptional quality of their chased and gilded bronze mounts (187, 190).

The name *annular clock* was given to a kind of mantle clock mounted in bronze doré having an annular or horizontal ring-shaped dial which was usually of white enamel with Roman numerals. The annular clock had been introduced during the Louis XV style. Of particular interest and beauty was a Louis XVI annular clock having a black enamelled orb-shaped case with an annular dial which was upheld by the figures of the Three Graces garlanded with flowers. The figures stood on an incurvate triangular marble base, decorated with Neo-Classic bronze appliqués, mounted on bronze cone-shaped feet.

The perfume burner, also called a cassolette, essence vase or essence pot, in which various perfume-giving substances were burned, became an elaborate decorative accessory in France around the middle of the 18th century. It was called a brûle parfum and was usually designed in pairs. It was usually in the form of a covered classic urn made of choice marble, alabaster or malachite and was richly mounted in bronze doré. The bronze bands at or near the top were perforated. The interior of the body was fitted with a metal liner in which the charcoal was placed and sprinkled with a perfumed substance. Very often the Louis XVI style brûle parfum was of tripod form. One characteristic type was designed in the shape of a shallow covered urn with a bronze doré pierced rim. The urn had an exquisitely chiseled flower or a fruit finial and a matching pendant. The urn was held on three incurvate bronze supports headed with rams' heads and terminating in cloven hoof feet. It was mounted on an incurvate triangular marble base ornamented with Neo-Classic bronze appliqués.

CHAPTER TEN

DIRECTOIRE

The history of France from the opening days of the Revolution in 1789 through the rise and fall of Napoleon in 1814–15, with its shattering impact on all Europe, covers some of the best known pages in French history. During the violent and turbulent days of the Revolution, French politicians formulated laws for Liberty, Equality and Fraternity derived from a study of the ancient republics, which this new group of leaders so strongly admired. France was ruled by the National Convention from 1792 to 1795, and in the same year the Directory or Directorate was established, which was to be overthrown by Napoleon four years later. Napoleon then formed the Consulate and appointed himself First Consul, and in 1804 he removed the last vestige of a Republican pretense in the form of government by assuming the title of Emperor of France. The coronation of Napoleon and Josephine on December 2nd, 1804, before the high altar of the Cathedral Church of Paris, at which Pope Pius VII officiated, was ironically reminiscent of the dazzling splendor associated with the earlier coronations of the Bourbon monarchs, to eradicate which so much French blood had been shed. With the establishment of the First Empire these legend-like days in French history were to continue for another decade. The art of this epoch was also dramatic and swift moving. And although the Revolution did not result in a rapid change in art, for actually the Empire style was being gradually evolved under Louis XVI, it decidedly abetted it and hastened its arrival.

As in the earlier style of the Régence, the name *Directoire* has been given in the literature on cabinetwork to a transitional style of furniture, which extends roughly from about 1793 to 1804. This style, which formed a connecting link between the Louis XVI and Empire styles, derived its name from the Directory, although the articles grouped under this style appeared earlier and also outlived this form of government. It is difficult to give any exact dates to the Directoire style, because from the time of Louis XVI the prevailing fashion in art was toward a closer imitation of the antique and each of these styles evolved from one to the other. From around 1790 collections of designs for furniture featured the characteristic Directoire chair of Grecian origin with its back either concave or rolled-over, stools of ancient curule form with X-shaped supports, bedsteads with triangular pediments and antique Roman bronze tripods. Contemporary articles appearing in a newspaper stated that everyone was making "Greek pieces more and more Greek." By the time of Napoleon's coronation the Empire style had been established in Paris by Percier and Fontaine. The cabinetmaker working in the provinces did not adopt either the Directoire or Empire styles to any appreciable extent. The dual character of the furniture made during the Directoire style recalls the earlier transitional style of the Régence. Much of the furniture was designed in the tradition of the Louis XVI style; however, the lines were gradually modified and more severely treated. The angular aspect of these pieces became more pronounced. As a rule this furniture was decorated with Revolutionary symbols. Other articles of furniture were more or less exactly copied after Greco-Roman models derived from the antique art of Rome, Pompeii, Herculaneum and Greece. These pieces displayed the prevailing fashion for a closer imitation of the antique in their many novelties of design and in their style of ornament. Gradually the French designer and cabinetmaker discarded the exaggerations of these many antique novelties but retained their essence, gave their work uniformity

and finally perfected the Empire style.

From the days of the French Revolution the ideal of the artist was to capture the true spirit of the antique. This devotion to the antique, which became practically a fetish, emanated from Italy, particularly in the publications of learned archaeologists such as Winckelmann, who were constantly eulogizing the art of the ancients and recommending its exact imitation. During the frenzied days of the Revolution these artistic doctrines, which amounted almost to the worship of antiquity, were avidly embraced by the French artists. In France the principal exponent of this more intense classic revival was the painter Jacques Louis David, 1748–1825, who completely dominated the art of his time. Around 1775 he went to Rome to pursue his studies, and while he was there his taste for severe classicism fully matured. Upon his return to Paris in 1789 he was made painter to Louis XVI. At the outbreak of the Revolution he accepted all the principles of the Revolution professing a new era of equality for all and later as a member of the Convention he voted for the execution of Louis XVI. He became an ardent admirer of Napoleon and when the Bourbons were restored to power after the downfall of Napoleon he was compelled to spend the remaining years of his life in exile. One of David's most celebrated paintings was the Coronation of Napoleon I. In all probability he is best remembered today for his portraiture, such as the well-known portrait of Madame Récamier which he painted in 1800. The fashion for imitating the ancients was even extended to the style of dress as is evident in the gown of Madame Récamier. The costumes which David designed for his portraits as appropriate for his antique furniture were arranged in the classical folds of Grecian statuary.

During the last quarter of the 18th century the art of Greece was gradually becoming better understood as the archaeologists continued to discover fresh material that clarified the study of all the ancient arts. Up to that time Roman art had been the principal source of inspiration because it was the best understood of all the arts of antiquity. But now with this knowledge of Grecian art becoming more accurate and widespread, its influence became increasingly apparent in all the contemporary 18th century work, and the ideal of Grecian severity was the predominating factor of the Directoire style. Because of this intensified interest in the antique, which was the pronounced feature of this later phase of the Neo-Classic movement, the cabinetmaker was no longer content simply to decorate his furniture with antique ornament, and in the closing years of the 18th century he began to use antique models for the actual forms of his furniture. Antique articles made of bronze, which had been brought to light from the excavations at Pompeii around 1780, were exactly copied. Legs of tables and couches, the frames for folding seats, Grecian and Roman marble throne chairs were carefully studied. Figures on Grecian and Roman bas-reliefs and vases, Pompeiian mural decorations and colored stucco ornamentation were zealously scrutinized as a source for forms and style of ornament. David, who was also an important political figure as well as an antiquarian and painter, was chiefly responsible for imposing these new forms on furniture design. The antique pieces which he depicted in his paintings had been made by the celebrated French ébéniste Georges Jacob from designs by David. Especially typical was the day bed depicted in the portrait of Madame Recamier, with its two graceful out-scrolled sides of equal height. The chair of curule form having curved X-shaped supports headed with lions' heads and terminating in lions' feet, and a large armchair decorated in bronze appliqués having a completely round mahogany back were also characteristic of David's furniture. One of the fabrics David designed for his furniture was inspired by the Grecian black figure pottery and featured a red ground with stiff black palm leaves. David gave the order for the furniture for the new Salle de la Convention at the Tuileries to Georges Jacob and to two architects, Percier and Fontaine, who were then unknown. These men, working under the instructions of David, were instrumental in establishing these new forms which forecast the incoming Empire style.

Georges Jacob, 1739–1814, who was the founder of a celebrated family of cabinetmakers, was born at Cheny. He served an apprenticeship in Paris and received his master in 1765. He gained an excellent reputation as a maker of chairs, sofas and day beds, which he matched with guéridons and fire screens. The carved detail was in admirable taste and was executed with remarkable virtuosity. From around 1775 he worked for various members of the royal family. Much of his work reflected the evolution in taste from the Louis XVI style to the Empire style. His best work was praiseworthy for its charming elegance. During the days of the Revolution he went along with the leaders of that time. He was a fervent disciple of the antique, and through his work at the Salle de la Convention he played an important part in laying the foundation for the Empire style. In 1796 he gave his large furniture factory on the Rue Meslée to his two oldest sons, Georges and François-Honoré, the latter under the name of Jacob Desmalter becoming the outstanding cabinetmaker at the time of the Empire. The firm was called Jacob Frères, and the older Jacob continued in an active artistic and advisory capacity. When the son, Georges, died in 1803, the firm became Jacob-Desmalter et Cie. The firm enjoyed its greatest period under Desmalter, who was Napoleon's favorite cabinetmaker. At that time they occupied fifteen shops and employed three hundred workmen. After the Restoration the firm was reorganized, and from 1825 to 1847 it was conducted by Georges-Alphonse, a grandson of the elder Jacob.

The vogue for Revolutionary emblems as a theme for decorative motifs had its inception at the time of the Convention. Included among the favorite Revolutionary symbols were the cap of Liberty or the Phrygian bonnet, the fasces symbolizing strength through union, levels signifying equality or the same level of importance, pikes of free men, the tricolor cockade of the Republic, the oak symbolic of social virtues, clasped hands signifying fraternity and symbols of the three orders of the nation, namely the cross for the clergy, the sword for the nobility and the spade topped by the Phrygian bonnet for the third estate. These Revolutionary emblems appeared on furniture, fabrics and mural decoration. In cabinetwork they were principally found on such articles as tables and commodes of Louis XVI contour, which displayed a further simplicity and severity in their principles of design. The popularity of these Revolutionary emblems was of rather short duration and by the time of the Directory the enthusiasm for them

began to diminish. During the Directory antique Greek motifs as well as antique Greek forms became the prevailing fashion. The lyre, daisy, lozenge and star were all included in the popular repertory.

With the establishment of the Consulate, Napoleon also reestablished French traditions of luxury and splendor. Although Napoleon did not build any new palaces for his personal use, he did redecorate many of those already in existence in a manner suitable to his achievements and to his regime. He employed the architects Percier and Fontaine to redecorate Malmaison, which Josephine had purchased in 1798. Later these two architects, who always did all of Napoleon's work, redecorated Saint Cloud, the Tuileries, the Louvre and other palaces and apartments on a scale compatible with and expressive of this epoch imposed on France by Napoleon and his conquests. With this in mind it is easy to understand that the majority of favorite motifs employed in the style of the French Empire made their initial appearance during the Consulate. There were the symbols of War and Victory, such as the figures of Victory with widespread wings and flowing robes, and there were the antique motifs borrowed from Greek and Roman as well as Egyptian, Pompeiian and Etruscan art, such as chimeras, caryatids, terminal figures, winged heads of lions, dolphins and swans. Later, Imperial emblems such as the eagle were introduced. It can readily be appreciated that Greek art with its exquisite and almost quiet simplicity could not adequately express the spirit of Napoleon and his lofty conception of his power. The era required a more imposing and grandiose form of art as is found in Roman art. And it is to the lasting credit of Percier and Fontaine that this spirit of national pride and conquest was captured in their style of ornament which became the official style of the French Empire. They possessed the special genius to interpret the spirit of the antique and the spirit of the epoch in a style in which simplicity and grandeur were harmoniously combined.

As a result of Napoleon's Egyptian campaign in 1798 and 1799 there was a vogue for Egyptian style of ornament. This was chiefly due to the archaeological studies of the French artist, architect and archaeologist Baron Dominique Vivant de Denon, 1747-1825. Denon during his early diplomatic career spent seven years in Italy. He was a friend of David's, who gave him the assignment to submit designs for republican costumes. Napoleon invited him to accompany the military expedition to Egypt. While in Egypt, Denon gathered the material for his most important work which he published in 1802. This work, entitled VOYAGE DANS LA BASSE ET LA HAUTE EGYPTE, was in two volumes and contained one hundred and forty-one plates. The art of Egypt, which was clear and exact, was characterized by its cold and stiff formality. In addition to the purely geometrical, Egyptian ornament principally comprised a rigid stylized treatment of certain native plants. The lotus flower and the lily appeared most frequently, while other favorite plants were the papyrus flower, the date palm and reeds. Fontaine and Percier in their collections of designs gave numerous examples of Egyptian decoration. Among the fashionable Egyptian motifs borrowed by the French designers were the Egyptian terminal figures, the sphinx, the lotus capital and the lion-headed supports for chairs and tables.

Since the Directoire style was in existence for only about a decade, and since much of that time was of a turbulent nature, the different articles of furniture given new forms were relatively few. This intensified interest in the antique is best exemplified in the new forms given to chairs and to day beds or couches. The best pieces designed with these new forms were outstanding for the clarity of their designs and for the purity of their lines. Their slender forms were well proportioned and they displayed a refined and graceful simplicity that was entirely pleasing. Such articles as the Madame Récamier day bed possessed a remarkable quality of quiet dignity and elegant simplicity which unfortunately vanished in the more pompous Empire style. Essentially all the characteristic pieces designed in the new taste were relatively simple, because it was not until after the establishment of the Consulate that the more ambitious pieces of cabinetwork were produced. Fortunately, many of the novelties of design inspired by antique models never developed beyond the drawing board, and a few which did materialize displayed all kinds of extravagances which were not truly representative of the furniture produced in this era. Much of the ambitious furniture, limited as it was during the Directoire style, was in the Louis XVI style, such as commodes veneered in mahogany and decorated with bronze appliqués in the form of fasces and other Revolutionary symbols. Many fauteuils and bergères also retained their Louis XVI forms but the angular rear legs became concave in form and were in one piece with the uprights, and the moldings were generally flatter and devoid of any carved decoration.

ARTICLES OF FURNITURE

The description of the articles of furniture is restricted to several characteristic pieces which illustrate the principal features of design employed in the Directoire style.

Chairs   The antique Grecian chair or klismos (FIGURE 3) with its broad and concave flat crest rail which in the early examples sometimes rolled over, was the principal model for the Directoire style chair. Although there was a variety of upholstered open armchairs made in the Directoire style, there were two types of chairs which appeared most frequently, namely, the chair with a slightly concave back and the chair with a rolled-over back. Both of these chairs were still near the Louis XVI chair. The uprights of the chair with the slightly concave back flared outward and backward toward the top, making pronounced corners. The arms rested on baluster-shaped or vase-shaped arm supports that were directly above the cylindrical and tapering ring-collared front legs. The back legs, which were a continuation of the uprights, were quadrangular and curved outward, with no separation between the leg and foot. This type of rear leg is a feature of Directoire chair design. Interesting variations of this chair distinguished by its slightly concave back occurred, especially in models with an open back (200).

The other characteristic chair designed in the Directoire taste had a rolled-over back (201). The uprights which curved backward continued to form the rear concave splayed and quadrangular legs (201). The back of the chair did not extend to the seat rail. The back and sides of the seat rail were straight and the front was bowed. The arms rested on turned supports that were directly above the tapering and turned cylindrical legs. In some carved mahogany specimens the armposts were in the form of terms and the front legs were quadrangular and tapering. This chair was also designed with an open back. One favorite open back chair had a broad rolled-over top rail made of solid wood which centered a carved classic urn within a diamond-shaped panel. Between the top rail and a narrow lower crosspiece was a pierced splat. Another popular open-back chair had a slender turned top rail beneath which was a broad crosspiece of solid wood carved with a typical antique ornament. The best examples of the open back chairs were distinctive for their slender and pure lines and for the elegant simplicity of their designs. The majority of chairs with rolled-over backs were generally made of mahogany or were painted. The painted chairs were generally in a light ground and the carved details such as lozenges, stars, serrated lines and fillets or narrow flat moldings were painted in a contrasting dark color.

The principal bergère usually had either a rectilinear or rolled-over back. The arm supports were generally detached or free standing, and were in the form of turned balusters that continued to the round taper-ing and ring-collared legs. The so-called gondola-shaped bergère was also made in the Directoire style. In some examples the armposts were in the form of terms, swans (202) or some similar fashionable motif. The front legs of these chairs were commonly straight, quadrangular and tapering (202). The canapé essentially followed the same features incorporated in the contemporary chair design. The back was generally either straight or rolled-over. The arms rested on the characteristic detached baluster-turned arm supports. Detached arm supports of columnar form were also favored for chairs and canapés.

Day Beds   The fashionable duchesse of the preceding Louis XVI style was sup-planted by a couch or day bed designed in the antique style. This new form was derived from the couches used in classical times for sleeping or for reclining at meals. The two ends or the head and foot gracefully scrolled outward. The out-scrolled sides of these day beds were either of equal height, such as the day bed depicted in the por-trait of Madame Récamier by David, or they were of unequal height. As a rule the legs were shaped like a top or they curved outward.

Beds   The principal early bed designed in the Directoire style had dossiers of equal height which were surmounted with triangular pediments (204). Later the characteristic bed had rolled-over dossiers of equal height. The vertical uprights for both types of beds were generally in the form of turned balusters detached from the vertical framework of the dossiers. Sometimes each upright was in the form of an elongated terminal figure. This type of support having the bust of a woman mounted on a pillar resting on two feet (204) was very fashionable in the French Empire.

Tables   The dining table was generally round or oval and was made of mahogany. The tapered legs were either quadrangular or cylindrical and were commonly finished with brass toe caps and wheel casters. The mahogany oval breakfast table was often designed with drop-leaves and gate-legs. Card tables, writing tables and desserte side tables (205) were essentially a continuation of the Louis XVI style but were more severely treated. The leg, such as on the small oblong desserte side table, was often headed with a bronze plaque which was either plain or grooved. This decorative feature which had been introduced late in the Louis XVI style was frequently employed in the Directoire style. The tops of the stiles of commodes were sometimes treated in the same manner (206). Decorative center tables having massive round marble tops were typical of the era and the incoming Empire style. Circular tops having a diameter of around 25 to 30 inches were extremely popular. In one type the marble top rested on three incurvate bronze supports with a small median round marble under-shelf. Athé-niennes and guéridons of antique tripod form were much in vogue (203).

Commodes   The Directoire commode (206), like many other articles of furniture, was essentially a continuation of the Louis XVI style treated with
greater severity. It can chiefly be distinguished from its predecessor
by its decorative detail. The characteristic commode had an oblong
marble top, which sometimes had outset rounded corners, over three
rows of drawers flanked by fluted stiles that continued to the short
toupie or peg-topped legs (206). Plain angular bronze bail handles
were much in evidence (206), and occasionally bronze loose-ring
handles were employed. The rectangular panelled drawers were sometimes inlaid with string-bandings of bronze or brass and sometimes
narrow bandings of a contrasting wood were substituted.

CHAPTER ELEVEN

EMPIRE and later 19th century phases including Biedermeier

The Empire style, which is named after the period of the First Empire, 1804–1814, but survived for about ten to fifteen more years, was created largely by Fontaine and Percier, who were Napoleon's architects. Pierre François Léonard Fontaine, 1762–1853, went to Rome in 1785 to pursue his studies and he was accompanied by his friend, Charles Percier, 1764–1838. Upon their return to Paris, their work attracted the attention of David and after the Consulate was formed he presented them to Napoleon. Apparently upon David's recommendation, Napoleon engaged them to redecorate and refurnish the palace Malmaison, which Josephine had purchased in 1798, and it was their designs which officially established the Empire style in Paris. Both Fontaine and Percier were fervent disciples of antiquity and their devotion to Greek and Roman ideals dominated the Empire style. They possessed the special genius and imagination to blend harmoniously the simplicity of the antique with the imperial grandeur

of the Napoleonic era, and although the style was chilling, stiff and formal, it was admirably suited to the times. There was something peculiar about the style that recalled ancient empires and conquerors, and it almost seemed that if Caesar were alive he would have been most comfortable sitting in the chairs created by Percier and Fontaine. These two architects collaborated on a number of books and their first book, which was published in 1802, was entitled PALAIS, MAISONS ET AUTRES ÉDIFICES DE ROME MODERNE. In 1813 Fontaine was appointed first architect to Napoleon, and later as architect to Louis XVIII and Louis Philippe he was engaged in the principal architectural works erected in Paris during that time. In 1812 Percier and Fontaine published a book entitled RECUEIL DE DÉCORATIONS INTÉRIEURES. This work is of particular interest because in the preface Fontaine and Percier present, in the form of a doctrine, their ideas on the Empire style.

In the preface of this book they expressed their strong contempt for the earlier styles of French art. They particularly despised 18th century French art, while they were more lenient toward the art of the 16th century. They arrived at the dogma that true beauty had been realized once and forever by the Greeks and the Romans and that no one could improve upon it. They preached the exact imitation of antiquity. "It would be vain to seek for shapes preferable to those handed down to us by the ancients . . . in them can be seen the reign of the power of reason which more than anyone thinks is the true genius of architecture, of ornamentation and furniture." However, there were several reasons or obstacles to prevent the fulfillment of their ideals in which all the furniture would be copied from Greek and Roman articles. First there were all the refinements in furniture which had since the days of the Renaissance been gradually developing to meet the needs of a more complex mode of living unknown to the ancients. What Frenchman would now be content with only those fundamental articles used by the ancients, such as chairs, stools, couches, chests, small tables for dining and tripods. Then, too, the scarcity of actual knowledge about the furniture used by the ancients presented another problem. All the Grecian and Roman furniture made of wood had long since disappeared, because of the damp climate. All that remained in the 18th century were articles made of bronze such as tripods, legs of tables, frames of folding stools and marble throne chairs. Most of the knowledge of this furniture had to be acquired from bas-reliefs, pictures on vases and mural decorations. Fontaine and Percier appreciated these almost insurmountable handicaps and realized the necessity for compromise. They wrote, "We have followed the models of antiquity, not blindly but with discrimination entailed by the manners, customs and materials of the moderns. We have striven to imitate the antique in its spirit, its principles and its maxims, which are of all times."

Percier and Fontaine in creating the Empire style with its air of austere and imposing grandeur rejected all those features which had made the earlier 18th century styles of Louis XV and Louis XVI so charming, refined, graceful and comfortable. The Empire style, which displayed the ideal for severe forms in its simple and rigid lines, was cold, artificial and uninviting, and offered little in comfort. And while the Louis XVI style had been content with the elimination of many curving elements, the Empire style practically carried on a campaign against them. In this style curved lines were largely restricted to chairs and sofas. The use of moldings, which gives interest to even the simplest furniture, was almost abandoned. When moldings did occur they were of a diminutive character, such as a fillet or a narrow flat band. The use of both engaged and disengaged smooth round columns having a bronze base and a capital was an architectural ornamental feature of the Empire style. These small columns were frequently employed on the façade of the commode and on other articles of a similar nature. When the columns were engaged they were affixed to the flat surface in such a manner that they did not interfere with or soften the sharp corners. Probably the most outstanding feature of the Empire style was its clear-cut silhouette. The corners were sharp and clear and any attempt to soften the sharp right angles, such as by chamfering or engaged columns, was discarded. In the preceding Louis XVI style sharp angles also existed but they were invariably softened by moldings, flutings, engaged columns extending around the corners or by other methods, while in the Empire style everything was done to accent its severe and angular form. The block-like appearance of the cabinetwork was further emphasized by the large uninterrupted flat surfaces of veneered mahogany. This use of flat uniform surfaces of polished mahogany gave the cabinetwork a singular massive look that no form of ornamentation could ever relieve. The use of heavy bases were also introduced to accentuate further the massive and block-like appearance of the cabinetwork.

Another pronounced feature of the Empire style was the principle of symmetry, which was followed more closely in the Empire style than in any of the other previous styles. It was observed with uncompromising rigor, and everything, even to the smallest detail, had to be in perfect balance to the right and left of center. If one decorative motif was not symmetrical with another, such as the bronze appliqués used on furniture, then the composition of the single motif had to be symmetrical. For example, if only one bronze appliqué in the form of a winged victory was to be used, both of her arms were upraised, she held a wreath in each hand, and the folds in her flowing gown were exactly the same on each side of the center. This principle of symmetry was also extended to the arrangement of furniture, which undoubtedly explains the stiff and formal look associated with so many interiors decorated in the Empire style. At no other time in the history of French cabinetwork was mahogany more extensively used. Both solid and veneered

mahogany with a finely polished surface prevailed in every category of cabinetwork. A considerable amount of furniture was also made of knot elm. The popularity of this wood was undoubtedy due to its warm reddish color which was similar to the color of mahogany. Maple and lemon wood were fashionable for light colored bedroom furniture. Walnut and the majority of other native woods, such as beech, lost all of their popularity. Marble was much favored and choice pieces were carefully selected for the tops of tables, commodes, secrétaires à abattant and for other similar articles. Carving was sparingly employed and its use was generally restricted to chairs and sofas. As a rule the carved detail was in low relief and was occasionally gilded. Sometimes the chairs were painted in a white, grey or straw-colored ground, with the carved detail picked out either in gold or in a strong contrasting color. Marquetry and lacquer work were completely discarded. The inlaying of bands of contrasting wood such as ebony with mahogany was occasionally employed. Some of the ambitious pieces of mahogany cabinetwork were inlaid with bronze and even silver, while brass and steel were substituted in less costly pieces. The best cabinetwork of this era, such as the work of Desmalter, was unexcelled for its perfected workmanship, while the less ambitious pieces made for the middle class were rather commonplace.

The practice of decorating the surface of furniture with gilded bronze appliqués was an outstanding feature of the Empire style. Although gilded bronze mounts had been extensively used in cabinetwork since the time of Boulle, in no period were they more often employed than in the present style. It is also interesting to note that in the earlier styles many of the mounts served a useful purpose and were therefore generally found in the same position, while in the Empire style they were entirely decorative and therefore did not appear in any definite place. The French cabinetmaker realized the necessity for decorating the large flat surfaces of polished mahogany and he placed the gilded bronze mounts in accordance with his own artistic taste. As a rule each bronze mount was isolated in its own particular place, and its selection did not depend upon the other bronze mounts found on the same piece of furniture or on the article of furniture it was to decorate. In other words, identical mounts were used on different articles of furniture, for they were not designed for one particular piece. These bronze appliqués, which were generally flat, were remarkable for the purity of their outline and composition and for the jewel-like quality of their workmanship. They were precise and extremely neat, and their chiselled perfection and their superb chasing and gilding were exquisitely complimented by the dark polished surfaces. They were found on practically every article of furniture, and they even appeared on chairs and sofas, where their use is always of doubtful taste. Unfortunately, on some of the massive pieces of furniture these bronze mounts often seemed too delicate and too meager for the amount of mahogany surface they were required to decorate. The French cabinetmaker in achieving his goal of flat uninterrupted surfaces frequently omitted handles on the drawers, and it was necessary to pull out the drawers by means of a key placed in the keyhole, which was also almost invisible. When handles were used they were in the form of either round and flat small knobs ornamented with rosettes or loose-ring handles attached to a circular back plate at the top.

Undoubtedly the Empire style, with its lack of pleasing lines, no marquetry or lacquer work, few moldings and little carving, would have been completely poverty-stricken if it had not been for the gilt bronze appliqués and for the strange creatures used as supports for chairs and decorative tables. These fabulous creatures, which were made of bronze, wood or a combination of both, were largely borrowed from antiquity and were a marked feature of the Empire style. Winged sphinxes, winged lions and chimeras with the heads of eagles were frequently used for armposts on chairs and for the front legs of chairs and for the legs of decorative tables. Then there were the really fantastic animals, such as the lion monopodium, composed of the head and chest of a lion that continued to an animal's paw. Almost as popular as the sphinx was a creature resembling an elongated terminal figure. It was designed with the bust of a woman mounted on an elongated plain and quadrangular tapering pillar that rested on two human feet. Sometimes the head and feet were made of gilt bronze. Swans were also very fashionable and they were frequently found as armposts for chairs and sofas as well as for the entire arm. There were also numerous other forms appearing in this repertory of weird creatures. It scarcely seems necessary to say that these decorative supports in order to possess artistic merit had to be superbly designed and executed. Keeping these supports within the realm of good taste was a rare achievement that only a few of the great contemporary French cabinetmakers could accomplish. These decorative supports were acceptable only in cabinetwork of the most finished workmanship, for in any average cabinetwork they were purely ridiculous extravagances.

The Empire style was principally borrowed from antique Greek and Roman art. Egyptian motifs became more and more fashionable following Napoleon's successes in that country. Etruscan motifs and some Italian Renaissance motifs were also occasionally employed. In accordance with Fontaine's outspoken contempt for French art under the Bourbon monarchs, the decorative artists discarded many classic motifs and architectural details employed in the Louis XVI style, such as triglyphs and flutings. Included among the favorite Empire motifs were acanthus foliage of a stiff and formal character, tightly woven wreaths, Greek palm leaves of stiff design, rinceaux especially of palm leaves, rosettes, stars, swags, arabesques and medallions. Winged classical figures in flowing gowns and victories presenting laurel crowns and blowing trumpets were much in evidence. Olympian gods and goddesses, Greek and Roman heroes, mythological or allegorical subjects were all favorite decorative themes. Emblems of victory, war-like emblems and imperial emblems were all popular subjects. The imperial eagle was much used. Animals and fanciful monsters, such as archaic lion masks, chimeras, lions, winged lions, swans, griffins, dolphins, rams' heads and the paw feet of lions and other real or fanciful beasts were fashionable decorative motifs. Greek and Roman caryatids and terms were much used as decorative supports. From the art of Egypt the decorative artists introduced lotus capitals, the sphinx, Egyptian terminal figures, winged globes, vases and other Egyptian detail. Other fashionable motifs included the winged thunderbolt of Jupiter, antique heads of helmeted warriors, Roman chari-

ots, trumpets and winged trumpets, cornucopias, Neptune's trident, swords, lances and other weapons, lyres and sistrums and other musical instruments, winged torches, Grecian urns, antique Roman tripods, and vessels from classic antiquities such as kraters and amphorae. Flowers, garlands, vines, laurel boughs and bay leaves were also employed to some extent and were characterized by their stiff and formal designs.

The interiors of the mansions and châteaux were all redecorated in the Empire style, and the drawing rooms with their grandiose and pompous decorations were in complete harmony with the Empire furniture. The rooms, like the furniture, were stiff and uninviting, and all that charming intimacy conducive to comfortable living, so characteristic of the earlier Louis XV and Louis XVI styles, completely vanished in these more heavy and solemn interiors. The walls were often enriched with stucco decoration and pilasters having gilded capitals and bases. Classic figure subjects and other classic motifs were frequently painted on the walls. Pale blue ornament on a chocolate or cocoa brown, sometimes called Etruscan brown, was a fashionable color combination. Sometimes the walls were completely hung in lightweight silks falling in loose folds. This treatment, like so much of Empire work, was just the opposite from the earlier 18th century treatment with panelled silk fabric walls. In less pretentious interiors the walls were covered with wallpaper skillfully designed to simulate the silk wall hangings arranged in folds. Windows and alcoves were heavily and excessively draped, and fringes of gold, silver and silk were very popular. Elaborate valances, such as valances of fringed swags, were most fashionable. The decorative motifs for mural decorations, fabrics and wallpaper were all in the prevailing taste. Figured and striped silks made at Lyons were extensively used in upholstery work. Jean Baptiste Huet executed numerous celebrated designs depicting mythological scenes which were printed on the cotton and linen fabrics made at Jouy. The typical Empire salon was characterized by a heavy round center table with a marble top, which was placed directly under the bronze or crystal chandelier, by imposing console tables beneath large mirrors and by massive sofas and chairs symmetrically arranged. The mantel for the marble chimneypiece was usually supported by winged lions or caryatids, made of bronze or mounted in bronze. A handsome mirror was hung over the mantel. A marble and bronze mantel clock with figures depicting some appropriate allegorical or mythological subject was extremely fashionable. The bronze candelabra upon the mantel were in the form of classical figures, who held the candle branches which were finished in a contrasting gilded bronze. Porcelain vases of antique form, with elaborate pictorial work in the manner of oil painting completely concealing the white glaze and wide surfaces of gilding, were much in vogue.

The Empire style, which was the last of the great classical styles, attained its highest development in the time of Napoleon, 1804–1814. And, although the Empire style continued in fashion until around 1825–1830, this later phase revealed a gradual decline in furniture design, as the forms became more heavy and cumbrous and the ornament more coarse. In order to analyze this decline in French furniture design it is necessary to go back to the opening days of the French Revolution. At that time the trade guilds had been suppressed by the Revolution, which meant that all the rules and regulations by which the trade guilds had governed the careful and thorough training of the craftsmen were abolished. The splendid traditions, such as perfection of technique, personal pride and integrity, which had been the foundation of 18th century French cabinetwork, were ultimately lost in this reform permitting complete freedom of production in all the artistic crafts. The furniture from that time onwards, except for the ambitious Empire pieces made by cabinetmakers trained in the traditions of 18th century craftsmanship, gave evidence of this decline from the very high standards displayed in the earlier work. Some of the craftsmen from the days of the Ancien Régime adapted themselves to the changed conditions of the 19th century and continued to flourish under the Empire. The sons of the ébéniste Georges Jacob and especially one son, Jacob Desmalter, produced cabinetwork of unexcelled workmanship. On the other hand the unbroken domination exercised by the trade guilds had obstructed industrial progress. And, as much as the passing of this golden age of French cabinetwork is regretted, the democratic ideas of the Revolution did destroy forever that form of despotism in France which had continued from the days of Louis XIV. The Industrial Revolution of the 19th century with the introduction of the factory system around 1814, the constant improvement of machinery, and the division of labor, had a far-reaching effect on all the crafts. By the middle of the 19th century the Industrial Revolution had progressed to such a degree that factory-made furniture could be made more cheaply than handmade furniture, and consequently the workshops making handmade furniture were gradually forced to close one by one. With the advent of factory-made furniture, the history of artistic cabinetwork so skillfully fashioned by hand comes to an end.

After the downfall of Napoleon, the Bourbons were restored to the throne of France in the person of Louis XVIII, 1814–1824, who was succeeded by Charles X, 1824–1830. This restoration period was not marked by any new decorative movement. The French Empire style was continued in a more or less desultory fashion and late in the second decade of the 19th century a revival in the Gothic style with Gothic arches was essayed, but this Neo-Gothic cabinetwork was without artistic merit. This era following so closely the glorious Napoleonic epoch seemed rather uneventful. The Bourbon royalty were stripped of all their splendor and the bourgeoisie, who were an important part of society, were nouveaux riches and did not possess the refined taste necessary to appreciate artistic cabinetwork. This rather characterless spirit of society was mirrored in the cabinetwork, which kept growing more impoverished and uninteresting. Then, too, the majority of cabinetmakers trained in the splendid traditions of the Louis XVI epoch were fast disappearing, and in this new generation of cabinetmakers there were no truly worthy successors to the great 18th century ébénistes with their perfected technique. With these facts in mind it is not too difficult to understand why the cabinetwork and furnishings of this era reflected an absence of taste and were without vitality. Undoubtedly the outstanding and redeeming feature of this cabinetwork was its fine materials and good workmanship. Some of the best work of this later phase of the French Empire

style was in chair design. Chairs with rolled over or concave backs, arms that scrolled over and under to form the armposts, and saber legs were characteristic features found in chair design. Chairs of gondola-form were also favored. The rectangular and block-like forms of the Empire style were maintained in commodes, secrétaires à abattant and other similar pieces. Tables with lyre-shaped or X-shaped end supports were very fashionable. Naturally, the ambitious or de luxe cabinetwork of the Napoleonic era with its jewel-like bronze appliqués and decorative supports of chiselled bronze was seldom found. In addition to mahogany, light-colored woods became quite popular, such as citronnier, sycamore, érable, frêne and orme. Especially fashionable for chairs, commodes and tables was citronnier combined with an inlay of amaranth. The majority of designs for this inlay work essentially resembled a simplified version of Empire bronze appliqués. Stiff palm leaves, formal acanthus foliage and rosettes were favorite motifs for this precise and delicate inlay work which was largely found in the same positions on an article of furniture formerly occupied by the bronze appliqués. Stringing lines and narrow bandings of a contrasting wood were also employed. Many small pieces, such as tables and stands, were quite popular. In the literature on French cabinetwork this later phase of the Empire style is also arbitrarily known by the names of the two respective reigning monarchs.

Undoubtedly any appraisal of the cabinetwork from 1830 to around 1850, which includes the Louis Philippe in France, the Biedermeier in Germany and the Early Victorian in England and in America, should not be based on its worst examples, which is so often what happens. It is true that none of this work possessed the uniformity of a style nor did the designs have any artistic merit, but we can acknowledge the fine materials and the good workmanship displayed in most of this cabinetwork. In France the so-called Charles X style outlived the reign of that monarch, who was deposed in the July Revolution in Paris and was succeeded by another Bourbon in the person of Louis Philippe, 1830–1848. In the early years of the Louis Philippe reign the French cabinetmakers continued to use the Empire forms with which they were most familiar. Due to the influence of the romantic literature popular in France at that time the ébénistes essayed shapeless imitations of the Gothic (221), Renaissance and the Baroque Louis XIV, with a predilection for the marquetry of Boulle. Gothic arches, which were much favored, appeared in everything from the backs of chairs to bracket clocks. All this potpourri of furniture was found in the homes of the rich bourgeois society. Around 1840 or earlier there was a revival in France of the Louis XV style, with which the Louis Philippe cabinetwork is closely associated. This furniture in the Revived Rococo style was ill-proportioned and the lines were both beggarly and too generous at the same time. It was characterized by exaggerated cabriole legs, a profusion of curved lines, marquetry of light-colored woods and very ornate ornament of a coarse quality. Dark-colored veneered woods, such as mahogany, combined with excessive bronze mounts lacking in refinement, were also a feature of the cabinetwork. Plaques of Sèvres porcelain and biscuit medallions were popular forms for decorating the surface of furniture.

The cabinetwork belonging to the Second Empire, 1852–1870, like all 19th century cabinetwork after 1815, was principally an imitative art displaying no fresh sources of inspiration (223, 224, 225). The designs for chairs, which were of a wide variety, were borrowed from numerous styles. Frequently they were made of black wood and inlaid with mother-of-pearl. Lavishly upholstered, corded and fringed chairs and sofas, with no wood showing, were especially typical. The tufted and upholstered confidente at this time was generally of S-form and was a popular article of furniture. Renaissance models of buffets, dressoirs and armoires à deux corps with heavy architectural detail and richly carved figure subjects were typical of the era. Tables inspired by massive Renaissance types were also made. Over-elaborated Louis XIV pieces with gilded bronze mounts and enamel plaques displayed the same showy and flaunting quality which belonged to the art and society of the Second Empire. A characteristic feature of the Louis XIV style pieces was the frequent use of an urn with a cover and finial placed at the intersection of the X-form stretcher on various kinds of tables. Boulle marquetry was much practiced by the better ébénistes. A favorite piece for Boulle work was a form of table designed with an oval top over a conforming frieze with an undulating lower line, mounted on four cabriole legs. These tables were ornately mounted in gilded bronze and generally centered a large bronze mask on each side of the frieze. Articles of furniture in the Louis XV style displayed the same bad design features found in the Louis Philippe pieces. The Louis XVI style was extremely ornate, to a point where it bore little resemblance to the original models. A characteristic piece was the commode or entredeux with a center cupboard portion fitted with two doors, flanked by two narrow recessed doors. It was made in ebony or black wood decorated with semi-precious stones arranged in formally treated floral bouquets and further enriched with gilded bronze mounts. The same importance attached to the style of Charles Garnier in architecture was given to the style of furniture by Fourdinois, who made furniture for Napoleon III and the élite of society. His cabinetwork borrowed from the Renaissance styles was notable for its fine workmanship. Much of the workmanship under the Second Empire was of a fine quality, such as the metal work from the shop of Christofle, the gilded bronze appliqués from the shop of Odiot and the sculptures in bronze doré by Chapu. Also admirable were the velvets and printed cottons, and the fine detail displayed in the designs for wallpapers with naturalistic flower arrangements worked in lovely color tones. Unfortunately the gaudy and ostentatious character pervading society and art under the Second Empire destroyed to a greater or less extent the value of all the work.

In conclusion there is the Biedermeier cabinetwork (226, 227, 228, 229, 230) belonging to the 19th century, the Victorian being treated in a separate chapter. The term *Biedermeier* is derived from the name of a political caricature appearing in a German newspaper, who typified a well-to-do middle-class man without culture. Biedermeier furniture, which was in vogue from around 1815–1825 to about 1860, was always commonplace. The cabinetwork was a potpourri of some of the features, but not always the best ones, of Sheraton, Regency, Directoire and especially French Empire minus the bronze appliqués. The

best of this furniture, which undoubtedly belongs to the early period, frequently displayed an honest simplicity in its form and decorative detail, particularly in chair and table design, which many persons at the present time find interesting. The cabinetwork was marked by a preference for curving lines, such as in chair backs and in the legs for chairs and tables. From around 1830 turned supports, especially spirally turned, were much in evidence. Chairs and sofas were sometimes enriched with decorative supports in the form of swans, dolphins and griffins and the carved detail was picked out in gilt reflecting the influence of the French Empire. Cupboards, chests of drawers and other similar pieces were extremely plain and many displayed the block-like appearance of the Empire cabinetwork. The love of flowers and plants resulted in a profusion of stands to contain them. The amount of writing furniture was a marked feature and stemmed from the contemporary sentimental taste for writing long letters. Included among the favorite woods were cherry, ash, pear, birch and particularly mahogany. In the later cabinetwork the curves became more pronounced and exaggerated, and the ornament became richer and was freely used. Realistically treated flowers and fruits were fashionable motifs and were also introduced in the textiles used for furniture coverings. Carved Rococo scrollwork also began to appear and by 1840 much of the cabinetwork was in the Revived Rococo taste, which remained the principal inspiration in design until after the middle of the 19th century. Richly tufted velvet and plush upholstery became a feature from around 1850.

ARTICLES OF EMPIRE FURNITURE

Chairs Broad simple lines were typical of the Empire chair, but they were by no means always straight lines. Certain armchairs were designed with scarcely a straight line. Except for the chair of curule form the rear legs were almost always quadrangular and concave (FIGURES 207, 208). Chair backs were usually flat (207), rolled over (208), concave or hollowed into a half cylinder (215). The open arms were very often straight and they were either round or quadrangular (207, 208). They rested on supports often in the form of sphinxes, dolphins or swans made of either bronze or carved wood. Sometimes the armposts and front legs were designed in one continuous unit, such as in the form of an elongated terminal figure consisting of the bust of a woman resting on a quadrangular and tapering pillar mounted on animal or human feet (207, 208). Very often the arms were scrolled over and under to form the armposts. This type of arm resting on large volutes in place of armposts continued to be made until around the middle of the 19th century. The front legs were occasionally in the form of winged lions with paw feet. Other front legs were frequently round and ring-collared (210) or were designed in the form of square pillars; both types terminated in bronze paw feet. Concave splayed front legs of quadrangular and tapering form were not employed to any extent on Empire furniture until after 1815 (222). They were usually used on chairs of a less elaborate character frequently designed with open scrolled arms continuing to form the armposts. These concave legs in which there is no distinction between the leg and the foot are called saber legs. Chairs having low backs hollowed into a half cylinder joined to the front legs by a deep concave curve terminating directly above the tops of the legs were also a popular type of Empire chair (215). Cylinder-shaped desk chairs were typical of the style (210). Bergères were chiefly designed with either rolled over or concave backs. The gondola or tub-shaped bergère was a fashionable form. The majority of chairs were made of mahogany and the flat carved detail was sometimes gilded. Occasionally the frames were ornamented with bronze classic appliqués of rosettes, stiff palm leaves or similar stylized motifs (207, 208).

Sofas The Empire sofa or settee essentially followed the same features of design incorporated in the contemporary fauteuil or bergère. It seems that sofas were not too plentiful, which was undoubtedly due to the great popularity of the day bed or couch inspired by the ancient models used in classical times for dining and reclining. The sofa à la pommier having a low back which continued at right angles to form the sides of equal height was a favorite form.

Day Beds The day bed or couch, designed in the antique style, was an extremely fashionable piece of Empire furniture. Especially characteristic was the day bed having two gracefully outscrolled ends which were either of equal or unequal height and the *méridienne* having outscrolled ends of unequal height designed with a back panel. In the majority of examples the back panel was shaped and curved gracefully downward from the higher to the lower outscrolled end. Many variant forms of day beds were designed in the antique style. They were characterized by their massive quality and they were decorated with antique classic carved detail and occasionally with bronze appliqués.

Beds   Empire style beds were designed to be placed lengthwise against the wall and this feature determined their designs. Many were also placed in the same manner in richly draped alcoves. The inspiration for the principal and most fashionable Empire bed was derived from antiquity, with the antique fulcra (7, 8) being a striking feature in some models (211). In many respects it was more or less similar to some of the Empire day beds designed in the antique style. Because of its supposed resemblance to a boat it was called a lit en bateau or boat bed (211, 215). It was designed with dossiers or ends of equal height which usually narrowed toward the top and rolled over. The characteristic boat bed had a side piece with a concave line that continued the curves from the head and the foot in an unbroken line (215). The lower line of the side piece was straight and close to the floor (215). The lit à couronne having a small round or oval crown-shaped canopy was especially fashionable from the time of the Restauration, 1814–1815, to the end of the reign of Louis Philippe. This canopy was found over the lit en bateau and the draperies were suspended from the canopy in a soft concave curve over the two ends of the bed. Occasionally the draperies were secured by curtain holders above the ends of the bed.

Tables   Dining tables were always round and massive. They were designed either with columnar supports or with decorative supports in the form of classical figures or animals. The massive decorative center table with a round marble top was a characteristic article of Empire furniture, and it was usually found in the middle of the drawing room. The mahogany frieze was either plain or was ornamented with classic bronze appliqués. One type of round table was supported on a massive central column with a bronze capital and base, and it rested on a heavy incurvate triangular plinth. Another form of round table was supported by figures of winged lions, Egyptian sphinxes, caryatids or some other similar type of decorative support (214). The figures were made of bronze, of mahogany with or without bronze mounts. They rested on a heavy base which was designed in accordance with the number of supports. For example, a table mounted on three decorative supports rested on an incurvate triangular base (214), while a table with four supports rested on an incurvate quadrangular base. Smaller circular tables, guéridons or candlestands were principally designed with a central pillar or with three bronze incurvate supports arranged in the manner of an antique Roman tripod (216). They rested on incurvate triangular plinths (216). The majority of occasional tables in the Empire style were designed with round tops.

The typical Empire mahogany console table had an oblong marble top over a frieze decorated with bronze appliqués. The two front supports were generally in the form of caryatids, in the form of antique heads mounted on quadrangular and tapering pillars terminating in human feet, or in the form of columns each having a bronze capital and base. The supports rested on a heavy plinth. The front of the plinth between the two decorative supports was recessed. (For this form of plinth see 219.) The back of the console table between the two rear flat rectangular legs was occasionally designed with a mirror.

All the various tables and stands introduced in the 18th century such as card tables, sewing tables, jardinières, reading and music stands were all designed and decorated in the Empire style. The characteristic tricoteuse had a circular top over a conforming frieze, fitted with two drawers, that was supported on a columnar shaft which was mounted on an incurvate triangular base. It was designed with a small deep-galleried median undershelf to contain the balls of wool. The jardinières were often made of tôle or painted tin and were decorated with the popular Empire motifs.

Toilet Tables   The characteristic poudreuse introduced in the Louis XV style with its rising mirror was no longer in vogue by the end of the 18th century. The principal Empire mahogany toilet table had an oblong white marble top over a frieze fitted with drawers and was very often designed either with lyre-shaped end supports or with end supports of X-form. This toilet table, which is called a coiffeuse, was designed with two slender uprights, which supported a framed rectangular, circular or oval mirror by means of swivel screws (217). The uprights were often of bronze and were frequently fitted with bronze candle arms (217).

A fashionable and almost indispensable companion piece to the coiffeuse was the small circular basin stand or lavabo designed in the form of an antique tripod (218). The top of the table, which was dished for the reception of the basin, was mounted on three incurvate supports. The legs were joined with a small circular shelf upon which was placed the pitcher. It was often designed with two slender uprights which supported a mirror and towel rack.

Mirrors   The mahogany cheval dressing glass, or a mirror swinging in a standing frame having a mirror large enough to reflect the full length of a person, was an important and imposing article of Empire furniture. It was called a psyché and was introduced toward the end of the 18th century. The mirror was enclosed in a rectangular frame which was attached to the columnar supports by swivel screws. The uprights rested on splayed bridge feet. Bronze candle arms were generally attached to the uprights. The psyché was richly mounted in classic bronze appliqués. The psyché was also designed in miniature form and the uprights were sometimes secured to a box-like stand fitted with a long narrow drawer. These small swinging mirrors were placed on different kinds of side tables and served as a toilet table or coiffeuse.

Writing Furniture

The mahogany secrétaire à abattant was a fashionable and imposing article of Empire furniture. It had an oblong marble top over a frieze drawer. The drop-front and lower cupboard doors were very often flanked by either engaged half-colonnettes or disengaged colonnettes having bronze capitals and bases. It was mounted on a plinth base and was richly decorated with chased and gilded bronze appliqués. The fitted writing interior which was of architectural design often had a mirror panel. Bureaux designed for feminine use were principally of the bonheur du jour type (219). The bureau à cylindre and various other kinds of 18th century writing tables were all designed in the Empire style. The bureau à pente was no longer in vogue. The table à tronchin which had been introduced during the 18th century was also designed in the Empire style. It was an ingeniously designed table suitable for drawing, reading and writing and was especially favored by architects and artists. It was chiefly designed with an oblong rising top that could be supported on an easel rest. The frieze was fitted with drawers and lateral pull-out slides.

Commodes

The fashionable Empire mahogany commode (220) had an oblong marble top over three rows of long drawers flanked by stiles in the form of caryatids or some similar form of support. It rested on a plinth base. The façade was enriched with gilded bronze appliqués. The typical Empire entre-deux was designed with two doors in place of the rows of drawers.

All the different articles of 18th century furniture such as armoires, chiffonniers, glazed china cabinets and bibliothèques were designed in the Empire style and were transformed into massive and monumental pieces of mahogany furniture. The long cupboard doors of the armoires were frequently designed with rectangular mirror panels, a practice which is never considered to be in good taste.

CHAPTER TWELVE

FRENCH PROVINCIAL

Provincial furniture was made by the local cabinetmaker to meet the needs, tastes and customs of the people who were to use it, which in turn had been molded by the climate, geographical location, history and economy of the different provinces. It chiefly comprised the very simple farmhouse type or rustique furniture used by the peasants and the bourgeois furniture used by the large middle class. In French furniture literature the French term *régional* is used to describe all this furniture made in the provinces exhibiting local originality. However, in America the term *Provincial* is the more customary designation for this work. It is important to remember that the term *Provincial* is correctly applied only to those pieces displaying provincial characteristics or peculiarities as distinguished from the work regarded to be national or which is in the fashion emanating from the capital. For example, if a piece of furniture is made in one of the large cities and is finely executed and skillfully interprets the prevailing Paris style and displays no local flavor in either its form or decorative details it is no longer provincial. It is true that many provincial pieces were a more or less close interpretation of the prevailing French styles but they were more simply treated and they had a rather countrified look distinguishing them from the finished and perfected technique of a highly trained cabinetmaker. In other words, provincial furniture should display some provincial character generally held to be distinct from the national character. All the provincial furniture was inspired and influenced by the fashions originating in Paris for the King and his Royal Court. Essentially these styles were modestly interpreted in their characteristic pieces, and were generally made in solid native woods by the local cabinetmaker working in the cities, small towns and villages. In the rustique furniture, the prevailing styles, such as the Louis XV style, was more evident in their panelled pieces, such as the buffet-vaisselier and armoire with their shaped molded panels, than in their tables and chairs with wooden seats. The relationship existing between the furniture and the region in which it was made was more pronounced in some provinces than in others. Provinces near Paris lost much of their local originality, which was undoubtedly due to their proximity to this great art center and its resultant stronger influence.

The study of provincial furniture starts from around the beginning of the 17th century with the Louis XIII style, which was essentially the first French style displaying any local color developed in the provinces. Provincial household possessions prior to the 17th century were few and were very simply and often crudely made, because in most of the provinces the living conditions were still rather primitive, with beds, chests, stools and trestle tables with removable boards comprising the bulk of the furniture. However, there were exceptions, such as the province of Burgundy, which had been an important cultural center from around the middle of the 14th century. Especially outstanding were their Renaissance double-bodied cupboards in the manner of Hugues Sambin, characterized by an over-abundance of carved ornament and massive construction. The singular richness displayed in these cupboards was a distinguishing feature of all the later Burgundian cabinetwork. From around the last decade of the 16th century a large amount of furniture was imported into France from the Netherlands and Italy, and its influence was mirrored in the contemporary French work. Much of the bourgeois furniture was distinctly Dutch and Flemish in feeling. Even in the 18th century the bombé-shaped secrétaire-commode with its slant-front top was reminiscent in its contour of the Dutch and Flemish scribanne. Much of this furniture coming from the Netherlands was sent to Bordeaux, a flourishing port city. Although the Louis XIII style developed in Paris reflected both Italian and Flemish influence, it was French in feeling. It was not until the Louis XIV style that the French craftsmen evolved a style completely expressing the French genius for creative greatness, which was to mark all their work through the Empire style. In the provinces, from after the middle of the 17th century, furniture gradually became more plentiful. The homes of the bourgeois received most of this new furniture designed in the Louis XIII style, for the peasants were still content with their few and crudely made pieces, even though their financial position had improved during this period. However, around the end of the 17th century, wardrobes for clothes and linens and cupboards for dishes and vessels slowly began to appear in the cottages of the peasants.

Rural cabinetmakers working in the Louis XIII style produced chairs with straw or wooden seats, stools, benches, tables and cupboards. Turning, which was always a favorite provincial method, was the preferred method for decorating the surface of furniture during the Louis XIII style. Spiral turning was the most common and baluster turning the most artistic. The tall cupboard or armoire was undoubtedly the most important and imposing article of 17th century furniture, and it always retained its popularity in the provincial home. Geometrical carved ornament, especially the diamond point and star diamond point, was typical of the Louis XIII style and was used to decorate the pan-

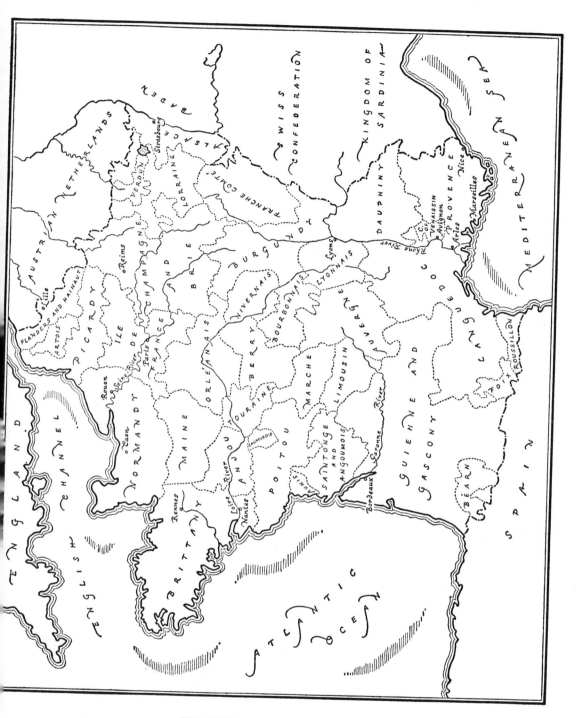

THE FRENCH PROVINCES IN 1798

elled cupboard doors. Furniture designed in the Louis XIII style was made for the middle class for practically a century until it was supplanted by the Louis XV style. In certain regions, especially in Gascogne and Guienne, it lasted much longer. In fact in these two provinces it has always remained their favorite style. Although it is generally accepted that cabinetmakers working in the provinces were familiar with the Louis XIV style it was not adopted by the people in the country to any appreciable extent because of its sumptuous and overwhelming grandeur. However, a large number of imposing Louis XIV armoires with the characteristic Louis XIV style of panelled doors and architectural details were found in the homes of the bourgeoisie. The Louis XIV style of panelling also occurred in other panelled pieces, such as the buffet bas. Plain armchairs of Louis XIV contour, with open arms, substituting simply turned members for the elaborately carved and molded members found on the court furniture, were also made. This chair was often called chaise à bec de corbin, because of the supposed resemblance of the end of the arm to a crow's beak. Tall slat-back chairs, as well as sturdy low-back chairs with wooden seats, also displayed simplified Louis XIV features of design.

The Louis XV style, which could easily be adapted to suit the needs of all classes of society, flourished in almost every province. This style, in which the local cabinetmaker achieved such remarkable results, has always been the favorite provincial style and it penetrated into the depths of practically every province. It retained its popularity in some provinces, such as Provence, into the 19th century. The Louis XV style of provincial furniture was characterized by its graceful lines and flexible moldings, by its good constructional methods and materials and by the originality of its decoration. When the Louis XVI style came into fashion the majority of provincial cabinetmakers never advanced beyond the transitional phase. In these pieces the influence of the Louis XVI style was evident only in the carved classic ornament, for the shapes retained their graceful curving lines of the Louis XV style although the curves were less pronounced and more refined. Frequently the Rococo motifs were still found mingled with the Neo-Classic motifs. These characteristics were especially apparent on such panelled pieces as armoires and buffets. This combination of the Louis XV and Louis XVI styles was prolonged indefinitely in the provinces and was mirrored in their 19th century cabinetwork. The Louis XVI style was actually more suitable for the simpler rural furniture than the preceding Louis XV style, since its straight lines were easier to execute than the Louis XV curved lines. However, as a rule, the Louis XVI style furniture without its decoration to soften the angular aspects of its contour was rather poverty-stricken, while the real charm of the Louis XV style was in its graceful contour. This fact, together with a general reluctance to change on the part of the cabinetmakers located in the depths of the provinces, were probably the chief reasons why the Louis XVI style never enjoyed the popularity of its predecessor. Many large cities, particularly those in provinces near Paris, did adopt the Louis XVI style both in form as well as in ornament. This was especially evident in chair design. Gradually the general lines of the Louis XVI style were also found in some of the furniture made in the country districts where its naïve designs gave it a purely local character that was the essence of its charm. The Directoire style and particularly the French Empire style were not adopted in the provinces to any appreciable extent.

Although the amount of provincial furniture made in the 17th century was relatively limited, it began to assume its local character as certain details inherent to different provinces gradually crystallized in the rural work. These regional traits, which were more marked in some provinces than in others, were more apparent in the following century when the furniture became plentiful for all classes. It is important to remember, however, that the similarity existing in all provincial furniture was by far more pronounced than its differences. The diversity of provincial tastes was principally found in the decorative details, for the needs of most of the people in all of the provinces were much the same. They entertained, they ate, slept and stored their possessions in much the same manner. Because of this existing similarity in demands, the same shapes, which were generally the simplest and most practical, were essentially found in all of the provinces. It is true that the homes of the affluent bourgeois in the wealthier provinces, such as Provence, Saintonge, Normandy and Poitou, had many of the fashionable pieces originating in Paris during the 18th century, such as poudreuses and different kinds of writing furniture, but these pieces were still restricted to relatively few homes. Even these articles, which were simply treated and modestly ornamented, had a marked similarity. The small work tables, occasional tables, day beds and other pieces were all much alike in the different provinces. This broad similarity existing in the 18th century provincial cabinetwork can

be attributed to some extent to the circulation of pattern books of engraved designs for furniture emanating from Paris. The local cabinetmaker copied these designs for armoires, commodes, tables, chairs and canapés not slavishly but closely enough to give the furniture a general national relationship. There were certain differences existing in the designs of some pieces, such as beds, which in the colder regions were sometimes completely enclosed with doors and resembled huge cupboards.

All the provincial furniture was practical, solid and sturdy. Its naïve ornamentation and the charming simplicity of its contours were always effective and entirely agreeable, and sometimes possessed real beauty. It was marked by good workmanship and good materials, and most of it was made in native woods, such as oak, walnut, beech, elm and wild cherry. Oak was plentiful in Normandy and Brittany, while there was an abundant supply of walnut in central and southern France. Woods of numerous fruit trees, such as cherry, apricot, pear and plum, were also popular. Cherry with its warm reddish color and fine grain was an effective substitute for mahogany and was often used in some of the better cabinetwork. Rural cabinetwork made of mahogany was quite limited and was essentially found only in some fine pieces made for the wealthy bourgeois after the middle of the 18th century. As a rule the rural furniture was made of solid wood, since most of the marquetry and veneered work was done in Paris, where there was a sufficient concentration of wealth to purchase these more ambitious pieces of cabinetwork with their finely chiselled gilded bronze mounts. Upholstered chairs and canapés were also quite limited. Loose cushions tied to the seats and backs were more customary. It is almost needless to say that the fabrics were serviceable and less costly. Woolen fabrics, part silk and woolen fabrics mixed with thread, painted and printed cottons and linens and needlework upon canvas in gros point were favorite provincial fabrics. It is often said that the ambition of every bourgeois housewife was to find enough free time in her later years to make a set of needlework coverings for her living room furniture. As in all French cabinetwork, the rural cabinetmaker displayed his innate good taste by adapting the furniture to the homes and cottages in which it was to be used. Even the simplest pieces had a singular peasant charm that was entirely satisfying for its background and appropriate for the people who were to use it.

The great century for provincial furniture, like all French cabinetwork, was the 18th century, as comfort became an important consideration in the provincial homes of both the upper and lower middle class. Undoubtedly this awareness of comfort and convenience had its provenance in Paris where everything was done to make living more pleasant and agreeable. Apparently this desire for comfortable living was contagious, for even the cottages of the peasants, which had formerly been so barren, began to have a more livable and friendly atmosphere. The middle class and the peasants were much better off financially, and they could afford to indulge in a few luxuries which would make their homes more enjoyable. The size of the lower middle class was also greatly augmented by the prosperous farmers, who had scarcely existed before the 18th century. Cabinetmakers capable of making all the different articles required by their furniture-conscious cus-

tomers soon were found in every little town and village. At this time the simple and sturdy furniture used in the peasant cottages began to develop its local originality. All the different characteristic articles of provincial furniture necessary for pleasant country living were introduced, and the amount and variety of this furniture, as well as its quality, depended upon the social standards of the people who were to use it. Comfortable chaises à capucine and canapés fitted with loose cushions covered in gay and colorful painted chintz, bergères with turned supports, armoires, buffets, dressoirs, kneading troughs enriched with carved detail, delightful small hanging wall shelves, corner cupboards, small occasional tables, tall case clocks, commodes and secretary commodes with slant fronts came into general use, as French provincial furniture finally began to flourish. The commode enjoyed great popularity and was even frequently found in the more simple interiors. Along with the commode were introduced many other pieces with drawers, such as numerous small tables serving different purposes and the bombé-shaped secretary commode with its hinged slant-front opening to reveal a fitted writing interior. The furniture designed in the Louis XV style with its gay and piquant gracefully curving lines possessed a provocative charm that endeared the style to those who were to use it as well as to those who made it. As the furniture became more plentiful the different regional traits were easier to observe. In some provinces, such as Provence, Alsace and Brittany, local originality was much more pronounced than in others.

The furniture made in Provence, which was an old province in southeastern France, displayed certain native traits which were readily discernible. The city of Arles was the great center for Provençal cabinetwork, and because its work was so popular, other cabinet shops producing similar pieces were soon flourishing at Avignon and Carpentras. Provençal furniture, which was skillfully executed, possessed a singular quality of vitality and vigor. This work was characterized by a wide variety of shapes and types. The ornament, whether of wood or of metal, was exuberant and was remarkable for its originality. The moldings, which were firm, clear-cut and rich, never concealed the framework and always contributed to the unity of design. Louis XV style panelled pieces, such as the buffet bas, armoire and commode, were remarkable for the interesting and varied treatment of their moldings which gave the work an unusual gay and pert air. Moldings were by far the favorite form of decoration; however, in the later 18th century work carved details became increasingly evident. An outstanding feature of their cabinetwork was the use of large finely wrought steel buttress hinges and fret-pierced escutcheon plates often extending the entire length of the cupboard doors. Oak, walnut, chestnut and cherry were the favorite woods. Especially characteristic pieces were the buffet-crédence or the buffet à glissants, the pétrin, the panetière, many charming small hanging wall shelves for pewter, glass tumblers and pottery, and the delightful boîte à sel and the boîte à farine. The great variety of small pieces to be hung on the walls was a pronounced feature of the Provençal interior. The buffet à glissants was undoubtedly one of the choice pieces if not *the* choice piece of Provençal furniture. In the Provençal cottages the kitchen, with its big open fireplace, was the principal room, serving

as a combination living room, dining room and kitchen. In this room was generally a large cupboard, often built-in, a low buffet, pétrin, dining table and chairs with straw or wooden seats. These cottages generally had a separate bedroom and in that respect differed from many of the cottages found in the other provinces. In addition to the bed, the armoire was the other principal piece of bedroom furniture, and occasionally a commode was also found in the bedroom.

It is difficult to believe that the provinces of Alsace and Lorraine with their geographical proximity could display such divergent tastes in their cabinetwork. Much of the furniture made in the province of Alsace reflected the influence of the cabinetwork of Germany, Austria and Switzerland. This was particularly evident in chair design. One very characteristic wooden chair was similar to the type found throughout the Tyrol. It was designed with a shaped and pierced low wooden back, carved with different geometrical motifs and emblems. The rectangular wooden seat rested on splayed legs which were joined to the seat several inches in from the edge of the seat. The Alsatians always had a curious liking for colored decoration which was revealed in their modest inlaid designs of different colored woods and in their taste for painted decoration and painted furniture. As a rule their furniture was inclined to be flowery and heavy with ornament. Some of their 19th century work was also made in a much simplified version of the Empire style as well as the later Louis Philippe style. Probably the Biedermeier style, flourishing in Germany at that time, was the inspiration for some of this work. In the peasant cottage the bedsteads were generally found in a small room or sometimes two small rooms, which were actually large alcoves within the principal room. These alcoves were often sufficiently large to hold chairs as well as an extra bedstead. The opening was attractively panelled and provided with hangings. On the other hand, the furniture made in the province of Lorraine was distinctly French in its artistic traditions and was characterized by its restraint and sobriety. Its cabinetwork in the Louis XV style was distinctive for simplicity, for graceful curving lines and for skillfully executed moldings. The carved detail was refined and sparingly employed, and the mounts were either of steel or brass. Under Louis XVI the ornament became more florid. Stylized flowers arranged in vases were much favored. Marquetry work, as well as carved decoration, was found on the panelled pieces. The chairs were slender and well-proportioned. Oak, walnut and cherry were the favorite woods. In the peasant cottages the bedstead very often formed a part of the structure of the alcove, and was provided with hangings which were drawn together at night.

Bretagne or Brittany was an old coastal province in northwestern France. Breton, which is the name applied to the natives of Brittany, was also the name of an old territory covering the western half of Brittany. Until the 19th century the population of Brittany was principally composed of peasants and a few nobility, for the middle class scarcely existed up until that time, and as a result most of their furniture had a peasant-like quality. As a rule the furniture was heavy and massive, and had a straight rectangular and solid appearance. Turning was a pronounced feature. Turned spindles were much in evidence, such as the spindled backs for chairs and benches with their heavy

wooden seats and angular splayed legs, the spindled cornices on cupboards, and the spindled galleries on the edges of the open shelves of dressoirs. A profusion of carved motifs executed in low relief, generally framed in thick and heavy moldings, was favored for the decoration of chests and other panelled furniture. In one form of dining table the massive rectangular top extended well over a shallow cupboard portion mounted on legs and was a combination table-huche. The top was removable and the under portion served as a kneading trough and grain bin. Any resemblance to the fashionable 18th century French styles was generally only vaguely suggested in most of their work. The typical Breton peasant cottage consisted of one room. Probably the most interesting piece of Breton furniture was the bed, or lit clos, resembling a huge cupboard with its solid panelled sides and often fitted with an upper berth. The panelled doors were made either with shutters or with spindles or pierced ornament. This unique bed assured the occupants of a certain amount of privacy while undressing and also served as a protection against the cold damp drafts of that climate. The lit clos was found in all the colder regions. The chest, which was found to a greater or less extent in all the provinces, was often placed in front of the lit clos, serving as a bedstep to the upper berth. The lit clos was also made without doors, when it was called a lit demi-clos. This type was provided with curtains to be drawn together. The furniture was made of oak, chestnut, wild cherry, pear wood with a dark stain and boxwood for the turned spindles.

Normandy, like Brittany, was an old coastal province in northwestern France, but her furniture was very different from that of Brittany. The furniture of Normandy was as distinctly French in feeling as that of Provence. Normandy was one of the wealthier provinces, which was an important factor in the development of her artistic tastes. The cabinetwork of Normandy was notable for its fine proportions, for its refined lines and delicate details. The tall armoire, with its two long cupboard doors, was one of the choice pieces of Normandy panelled cabinetwork, and was remarkable for its elegance, excellent proportions and richly carved decoration. It also had steel buttress hinges and elongated pierced keyplates, but they were not as florid as those found on the Provençal armoires. A feature of the Normandy panelled work, as found on armoires, buffets and commodes, was its richly carved decorative effect blending so harmoniously into the unity of design. There was also a predilection for charming small wall shelves of which a wide variety was made. The tall case clock was a popular piece of Normandy furniture. In addition to oak, much of the furniture was made of wild cherry, apple or elm, and some of the fine 18th century pieces were made of mahogany and occasionally ebony. The Louis XVI style and to some extent the Empire style were developed in Normandy. This was particularly evident in chair design. Especially fine were the slender slat-back or lyre-back chairs designed in the Louis XVI style with straw seats. They were well-proportioned and often possessed a quality of delicate refinement seldom found in much provincial work.

The bourgeois furniture of Saintonge, a former province of western France, was also plentiful and varied, since this province enjoyed an excellent economy due to her fertile lands for farming and cattle raising. Of particular interest were the many outstanding examples of Louis XV style chairs with their gracefully curving and harmonious lines and fine proportions. The provinces of Poitou, Angoumois and Vendée, whose economy was similar to Saintonge, also made a large amount of bourgeois furniture. They produced a great variety of armoires, both wide and narrow as well as those to stand in a corner. Of interest was a low corner cupboard, having a bow or swell-front, fitted with a tier of open shelves arranged pyramid fashion for the display of pottery and pewter. Commodes, buffets bas, tall case clocks and secrétaires bibliothèque were all favorite forms of panelled furniture. The furniture of the mountainous province of Auvergne, located in south central France, and that of the neighboring province of Limousin was largely similar. These provinces had a cold climate, and their land was mostly barren pasture fields. As a result the peasants were poor, and their poverty was reflected in their often crudely made and heavy furniture. Woods were plentiful and particularly so in Limousin, where they freely used oak, walnut and cherry for their better pieces. Limousin was rich in iron ore and was an important center for producing all kinds of fireplace tools and accessories to be used in all of France. Brass, copper and pewter workers were found in Auvergne, which was a leading center in central France for these wares.

The provinces of Gascogne or Gascony and Guienne have always been the principal source for the Louis XIII style of provincial furniture, and they continued to employ that style for certain pieces throughout the 18th century. The Louis XIII style double-bodied cupboard, having a recessed upper section, was a characteristic piece. The panelled doors, flanked by spirally turned columns, were carved with the diamond point or star diamond point ornament. Their carved geometrical ornament was always remarkable for its clear-cut quality, and the diamond point ornament achieved its highest degree of perfection in these provinces. It is generally accepted that the finest examples of Louis XIII style cabinetwork were executed in Périgord, an old division of the province of Guienne north of the Garonne River. The furniture of Périgord was distinctive for its good proportions, for the purity of its lines and the clarity of its carved decoration. The cabinetwork of the Basque country, situated in the southwestern section of the Pyrenees in the old province of Gascony, displayed a marked simplicity in its design. The furniture, which was nicely proportioned, had a singular quality of neatness and precision that was especially revealed in the carved decoration, executed in low relief, found on the panelled pieces. The thin and flat carved detail, chiefly comprising geometrical motifs and occasionally rather naïve designs of men and animals, practically covered the entire surface of chests and other panelled articles. Because of the precise quality of the carving the effect was entirely pleasing in the style of peasant work. In this respect it differed from the over-all carving found on Breton panelled pieces with its relatively heavy and often complicated quality giving a confusing and cluttered effect. The furniture made at the wealthy city of Bordeaux, which was also in the province of Gascony,

followed the prevailing 18th century French fashions, and her furniture largely resembled the cabinetwork made for the bourgeoisie of Saintonge and Poitou. Some of the fine cabinetwork made at Bordeaux in the second half of the 18th century was executed in mahogany.

Burgundian Renaissance furniture was characterized by its massive construction and by a pronounced use of architectural detail in its principles of design. The carved motifs were vigorously and boldly executed in high relief and the moldings were prominent and also richly carved. This taste for opulence was evident in all their subsequent work, and their furniture was always inclined to be rather massive, with heavy moldings and excessively rich carved decoration on their panelled pieces. Bresse, an old district in eastern France, originally formed a part of the feudal duchy of Burgundy. As a rule their furniture, like that of Burgundy, was massive, heavily molded and ornately carved. Their panelled pieces, such as armoires and buffets, were often executed in contrasting woods, with the framework made of walnut and the panels of oak. The picturesque vaisselier-horloge is especially identified with Bressan cabinetwork. In addition to these provinces there were numerous other provinces such as Flanders, Champagne and Picardy, whose furniture also displayed local originality. The study of regional furniture with all the factors contributing to the development of its particular tastes is an absorbing subject, but unfortunately it is not within the scope of this work.

The articles of furniture described in the following section are restricted to the outstanding characteristic pieces principally identified with provincial cabinetmaking. Some of the articles, in particular the armoire, were also found in the wealthy Parisian homes. However, in Paris the armoire was regarded as a utilitarian piece, while in the provinces it was given the place of honor in each home.

Chairs   The chaise à capucine (FIGURES 231, 232, 233, 234, 235), which was the principal provincial chair, was a turned open armchair or side chair of marked simplicity with an open back and a straw or rush seat. The legs were joined with stretchers. It was originally found in the monastery cells and was adopted by the laity in the first half of the 17th century. After the middle of the 17th century the structure gradually became more refined. It was chiefly made of oak, cherry and occasionally of walnut, and sometimes the wood was painted. The majority of these chairs owed their interest to the designs of their open backs. During the Louis XV style the open back often had two or three shaped slats (232, 233, 234) which were frequently of serpentine contour. In some of the fine Louis XV examples the uprights (234), open arms and armposts were designed with curved lines in place of the usual straight lines and the legs were cabriole in form (234). The straw seats were often provided with loose cushions covered in imported chintz and later in printed cotton or linen made at Jouy. During the Louis XVI style the straw chairs gained much in elegance and refinement. In one principal type the Louis XV serpentine-shaped slats were replaced by the characteristic Louis XVI flat-arched slats. Many of the more refined Louis XVI specimens were enriched with carving or fluting. The local character of their carved designs gave these chairs an individual charm. Sometimes the chair back had a flat arched top rail and a lower crosspiece which were connected with four or five delicately turned spindles. A carved lyre splat was also a favorite design. The chaise à capucine designed in the Directoire style often had a broad concave crest rail and a pierced splat (235).

The chair with a wooden seat was principally found in the peasant cottage. Another form of chair with a wooden seat was enclosed to the floor and the seat was hinged in order to give access to the chest-like section. This chair was called a chaise à sel since it served as a salt chest. Many of these chairs were quite small, and were often made without arms and with an open back simply consisting of two uprights and a straight top rail.

Chairs with open arms and upholstered seats (236) and sometimes upholstered backs often followed the general contour of the prevailing French styles. For example, the chaise à bec de corbin in which turned members were substituted for the carved and molded members of the characteristic Louis XIV chair was much favored and was made in some provinces into the middle of the 18th century. Other armchairs were simply made with plain turned members. Bergères with turned supports of cherry wood were especially popular.

Benches
Wood benches, either with or without backs, placed on one or both sides of the oblong dining table were much in evidence, especially in the peasant cottages. Sometimes the back worked on pivots and could be pulled forward to form a bench-table or chair-table.

Beds
The bed with four posts (239) having a tester and draperies was found in both the homes of the middle class and the cottages of the peasants. In the colder climates the bed was heavily draped with woolen hangings as a protection against drafts. Sometimes the peasant beds were built into the side of the wall or alcove in the manner of a built-in cupboard, and the side facing the living room was provided with hangings (238). The lit clos (237) or closed bed was especially identified with the furniture of Brittany and is often referred to as a Breton bed. This type of bed was found in all the colder regions, such as Auvergne, Limousin and Normandy. The lit d'ange and the lit à la duchesse were found in the wealthier homes during the 18th century.

Tables
In addition to the dining table which was generally oblong, there were many other kinds of tables such as side tables (240, 241), and tables fitted with frieze drawers (250), used occasionally as writing tables, as well as those having a specialized purpose, such as work tables. The majority of tables were rather plain. Some of the small tables of Louis XV contour with slender attenuated cabriole legs were pleasing and effective. Louis XV style console tables with a richly carved valanced frieze were also made, but were relatively few.

Writing Furniture
The bureau à pente was a characteristic type of panelled provincial furniture designed for writing. It had a narrow oblong top and a hinged slant lid which opened to an interior of small drawers and compartments. The frieze was fitted with a row of drawers and it was mounted on four legs. Another very characteristic piece of provincial writing furniture was the secrétaire-commode designed in the Louis XV style. It had an oblong top and a hinged slant lid over a bombé-shaped body fitted with a row of two short drawers over two long drawers. It was mounted on a valanced and molded base that curved into short whorl feet. The drawers had finely wrought bail handles and key-plates generally of bronze or brass. Frequently a cabinet section fitted with two panelled doors that enclosed small drawers, doors and compartments, surmounted the narrow oblong top. This type of secretary-cabinet or secrétaire-commode was closely similar to the Dutch and Flemish scribanne. Both these types of bureaux were principally made of walnut and occasionally of mahogany, especially those made around Bordeaux.

Chests   It seems almost needless to say that these chests were much in evidence, especially in the peasant cottages. They were often richly carved, and their naïve designs in the manner of peasant furniture were frequently most agreeable.

The maie or pétrin (253, 255), which were the French terms for a kneading trough, was a characteristic article of provincial kitchen furniture. A principal type of Louis XV pétrin had a flat hinged top which when opened revealed a single or double trough (255). The panelled trough, which was wider at the top than at the bottom (255), generally rested on four turned legs or on a cupboard section fitted with two shaped panelled doors. Of particular interest was the Provençal Louis XV style pétrin (255) which was often elaborately carved. Its four turned legs were generally joined with a distinctive valanced and molded broad box stretcher curving into short cabriole legs (255). Many of the finer models were made of walnut. Sometimes the maie with a hinged top resembled a chest in appearance (253).

Commodes   The commode, which was one of the most important articles of de luxe French furniture, was also a fashionable piece of 18th century provincial furniture. Provincial commodes in the Louis XV style were made with bombé and serpentine contours, and some of the later 18th century commodes in the Louis XVI style were semi-circular or demi-lune in plan. The majority were designed with three rows of drawers, which were generally mounted with brass bail handles and escutcheon plates. The Rococo shapes of these handles and plates were supplanted by angular bail handles in accordance with the Louis XVI taste. Many commodes were made of solid wood; cerisier or cherry wood was much favored.

Buffets   The tall buffet à deux corps (166) or double-bodied buffet was introduced in the Louis XIV period. It had a molded cornice over two panelled cupboard doors. The lower section, which usually projected slightly, was also fitted with two panelled cupboard doors, directly above which were occasionally two drawers. As a rule the upper section was distinctly longer than the lower section. These finely panelled buffets were especially found in Normandy, Provence and in other wealthy provinces as well as in Parisian bourgeois homes. The costly examples were enriched with handsome carved detail, the composition of which was sometimes typically Parisian.

The buffet bas (244) was more or less in general use in all the provinces and was a characteristic piece of panelled provincial furniture. It was a kind of low sideboard cupboard and was principally found in the dining room. It was also called either a demi-buffet or bas d'armoire or low cupboard. The buffet bas was introduced late in the Louis XIV style and some early ones reflected certain features of the Louis XIV style in their style of panelling and in their carved detail. The buffet bas had an oblong top over a frieze with two drawers which were directly above the two panelled cupboard doors (244). It was also designed without drawers. The Louis XV style buffet bas usually rested on a valanced and molded base curving into the short cabriole legs (244). Its average height was around 38 to 48 inches. The length of the buffet bas varied greatly. It was sometimes designed with as many as five or six panelled cupboard doors when its length reached around nine feet. As a rule the length was governed by the height; the taller ones were not as long and were generally designed with two cupboard doors. The buffet bas was often finely carved with either Louis XV or Louis XVI motifs. The buffet bas with its Louis XV style asymmetrically shaped panelling (244) was an effective and interesting piece of provincial furniture.

The name *buffet-crédence* (247) was generally given to a panelled buffet identified with the regional furniture of Provence. The majority were made at Arles. It was usually designed in the Louis XV style (247). The buffet-crédence was made in two sections. The narrow and low panelled upper section was deeply recessed and was fitted with two sliding end panels, rather than doors, that flanked a center fixed panel. The projecting lower section was fitted with two shaped panelled cupboard doors. It was mounted on a valanced base curving into short cabriole legs (247). Sometimes the lower section had a row of drawers above the cupboard doors. Other variations also occurred. As a rule it was finely carved and was fitted with fret-pierced steel escutcheons and large buttress hinges (247). The Arlesian buffet-crédence was a charming and original article of provincial furniture and was distinctive for the exuberance of its decoration. The majority were made of walnut. It was also called a buffet à glissants because of the sliding feature of its end panels in the small recessed superstructure.

The buffet-vaisselier (251) or dressoir was in common use in all provinces and was a favorite and characteristic piece of provincial furniture. In Gascony it was called an escudié; in Champagne a ménager; in Normandy a palier, and in Auvergne a vaisselier. Essentially the buffet-vaisselier was the same in all provinces. In a broad sense it consisted of a lower section fitted with two or three cupboard doors and a deeply recessed superstructure fitted with several rows of narrow open shelves (251). It is generally accepted that the buffet-vaisselier was not introduced before the Régence. As a rule it was designed in the Louis XV style. The recessed superstructure of the characteristic Louis XV buffet-vaisselier had a molded and valanced cornice. The shelves always had a back of solid wood and were frequently flanked by narrow lateral panelled cupboard doors. Each shelf was edged with either a small turned balustrade or a beading to secure the plates (251). The lower projecting portion was commonly designed with two small drawers over the two shaped panelled cupboard doors.

It rested on a molded and valanced base that curved into the short cabriole legs (251). The length of the buffet-vaisselier varied. Some of the longer models had four panelled cupboard doors and the shelves were of corresponding length. It was chiefly made of oak, cherry or walnut. Frequently, in addition to its fine molded panels, it was enriched with carved detail and with steel fret-pierced escutcheons and buttress hinges. The buffet-vaisselier was always an interesting and well-designed article of provincial furniture. The name *vaisselier-horloge* was given to a buffet-vaisselier having a tall case clock centered in its open shelves. The trunk and base of the tall case clock extended the height of the shelves and the hood of the clock was above the cornice. The vaisselier-horloge was a unique article of furniture and was particularly identified with the regional furniture of Bresse.

Cupboards   The cupboard or armoire was the pride of every provincial housewife and a visible sign of her prosperity. The majority of cupboards designed in the Louis XIII style were double-bodied, with the upper section generally recessed. Each section was fitted with one or two cupboard doors. Single-bodied cupboards having either one or two long doors were not uncommon (245, 246). Moldings were a striking feature of all of these cupboards. Straight projecting molded cornices and bases were typical (245, 246); frequently the molded base rested on globular feet (246). In the single-bodied examples each long cupboard door was enframed in moldings and was generally divided into three rectangular molded panels (245, 246). As a rule a carved geometrical or stylized motif entirely filled each panel (245, 246). The diamond point ornament was much favored at this time (246). It enjoyed a great vogue in Gascogne and Guienne, where the cabinetmakers achieved conspicuous success in this style of decoration. The doors of the cupboards designed in the Louis XIII style were frequently flanked by engaged or disengaged spirally turned columns. As a rule the cupboard designed in the Louis XIV style was single-bodied and had two long panelled cupboard doors. The Louis XV style armoire was also designed with two long panelled cupboard doors. In Provence it was called a garderobe; in the southwest around Bordeaux it was known as a lingère; in Brittany as a cabinet, and in Normandy as a corbeille de mariage. It was generally made of walnut, oak or cherry. Occasionally, especially around Bordeaux, some were made of mahogany. Each cupboard door was divided into two or three asymmetrically shaped panels; when there were three the center one was generally smaller (248). The majority were made with a molded arched cornice (248); however, some were made with a straight molded cornice. The armoire was designed with a molded and valanced base which curved into short cabriole legs (248). The Provençal wardrobe, which was usually made of walnut or cherry, had three shaped panels to each cupboard door. Much of the charm of these wardrobes was in the gay and almost frivolous shapes of their molded panels. The doors had large steel buttress hinges and fret-pierced escutcheon plates (248) sometimes extending the entire length of each door. As a rule Louis XV Provençal armoires were without carved detail. In the Louis XVI period the Provençal armoires and also those from other provinces frequently retained all or some of their Louis XV curving lines, but they were carved with Louis XVI classical detail (248, 249). The Louis XV–XVI Normandy armoire was almost always made of oak and was outstanding for the richness of its carvings. Only the surfaces of the shaped panels were free from carved ornamentation. Generally in the center of the frieze was an elaborately carved decoration or cresting extending above the arched and molded cornice. The Normandy armoire was an elegant and finely proportioned article of furniture. It also had steel hinges and fret-pierced escutcheon plates, but they were not as prominent as those on the Provençal armoire.

The bonnetière (242) was a tall and narrow cupboard generally designed with a long panelled door. It was introduced in the Louis XIV style. Some of the early examples were designed in two sections. Another popular form of cupboard was the double-bodied tall armoire designed to stand in the corner of a room. This corner cupboard, which was made with either one or two doors in each section, was called an encoignure à deux corps and was introduced during the Louis XV style.

The panetière (256, 257), which was a small hanging cupboard for bread, was an interesting and delightful article of provincial furniture. It is generally thought that the panetière had its origin in southern France and in all probability in Provence. Its height, which varied from about 33 to 43 inches, generally exceeded its width by several inches. The characteristic Louis XV Provençal panetière had an open frame with finely turned spindles surmounted by matching finials (256, 257). It had a very small central cupboard door mounted with a finely wrought steel fretwork escutcheon and a buttress hinge (256, 257). It was designed with a molded and valanced base that curved into short scrolled supports (256, 257). As a rule it was made of walnut.

The garde manger or food cupboard (243) with the sides or door spindled or pierced for the ventilation of its contents was a characteristic and popular piece of provincial furniture.

Accessories   The almost infinite variety of open hanging small wall shelves or étagères for articles of brass, pewter (258) and pottery was an outstanding feature of provincial cabinetwork. The inhabitants of Provence and Normandy were especially fond of small hanging shelves and their cabinetmakers produced some remarkably fine and charming specimens.

Provence also made a number of fine small walnut vitrines designed in the Louis XV style to be placed on tables or commodes. This type of vitrine had an arched and molded cornice over a single glazed door, beneath which was a row of two small drawers. It was mounted on a valanced and molded base that curved into short whorl feet. It was enriched with delicate carvings and a steel fret-pierced keyplate and buttress hinge.

Tall case clocks, often made of cherry wood, were quite popular in the provinces. As a rule they were rather plain and nicely proportioned. In some examples the curving lines of the Louis XV style were most pronounced, such as those made in Normandy.

Large wall fountains and basins or lavabos (261) were a distinctive accessory of provincial furniture, and they were chiefly found in the dining room. They were principally made of pewter, copper or faïence. Later they were sometimes made of tôle. The fountain was designed in different shapes, such as oval, cartouche-shaped or pear-shaped, and was fitted with one or two spigots. The lavabo was generally circular or semi-circular. Frequently they were attached to a kind of tall and narrow panelled cupboard stand. The stand had a tall narrow back panel to which the wall fountain was attached, while the basin rested on the cupboard portion which was fitted with a single cupboard door. Sometimes the basin simply rested on a shelf.

CHAPTER THIRTEEN

ELIZABETHAN

England was the last European country to be influenced by the Renaissance movement which chiefly came to the island by way of the Netherlands and France. It was practically one hundred years after its birth in Florence that Renaissance art made its initial appearance in England and that was in the famous tomb of Henry VII. This tomb, which was made by an Italian, Torrigiano, between the years of 1512 and 1518–19, was only an experimental display of a style that was in the ensuing years to secure an assured position. During the reign of Henry VIII, 1509–1547, the art of the Italian Renaissance was slowly grafted onto the vernacular style and the history of English decoration from that time onwards shows a gradual assimilation of Renaissance art. Henry VIII attracted to his court and service numerous minor Italian artists imbued with Renaissance ideas. The Italian artist Toto del Nunziata, who was employed on the palace "Nonsuch" built by Henry VIII and torn down in 1670, was instrumental in bringing the new style to England. The earliest evidence of a study of Italian Renaissance architecture also dates from the reign of Henry VIII. The English architect John Shute, whose patron was the Duke of Northumberland, visited Italy in order to study Renaissance architecture and after his return to England he published the first work in English on Renaissance architecture. This book, which exerted great influence, was entitled CHIEF GROUNDES OF ARCHITECTURE, and was published in 1563. Although there were numerous Italian artists in England during the first half of the 16th century their influence was confined to decorative details. From around 1530 onwards there was a gradual infiltration of Renaissance motifs and they were blended with Gothic motifs on Gothic forms. During the reign of Queen Elizabeth I, 1558–1603, the Renaissance was established in England and the earlier Italian influence was supplanted by that of the Netherlands.

The underlying principle of the Renaissance, with its belief in the inherent human right to the enjoyment of life, greatly appealed to Englishmen who had recently freed themselves from the domination of the Church and who were rapidly developing a free national and domestic life. A great change became apparent in England shortly after the termination of the Wars of the Roses, which had eliminated feudalism and the feudal lords. In their place was a new class of wealthy merchants and traders, who were the nucleus of a new English nobility. The wealth of this group was largely due to expanding commerce with its resultant enterprise and successful trading. These families, who required houses suitable to their wealth and position, were often given land by the Tudor kings from the confiscated properties of the monasteries. It soon became apparent that as the feudal lord had yielded to the wealthy merchant so the ancient feudal castle, with its fortified walls, yielded to the Tudor or Gothic manor house, picturesquely placed in a great park with a broad expanse of green lawn, trees and gardens. These distinctive Tudor manor houses with their air of comfort, hospitality and geniality developed into the magnificent and commodious country mansions of the Elizabethan and Jacobean periods which still remain the particular pride of every Englishman. Especially praiseworthy was the skillful planning of these great houses and their beautiful gardens, in which the house and the garden and the surrounding countryside became one harmonious scheme. Such houses, the largest of which were built in the first four decades of the 17th century, expressed and displayed all the new wealth of the new aristocracy. A marked development in domestic comfort and a more expansive social life among the aristocracy were all contributing factors in making this an era of remarkable building activity.

During the period of expansion under Queen Elizabeth I a variety of forces were at work which were responsible for developing a new national art and which were also to have a vital effect in shaping the lives of many future generations of Englishmen. Up to this time England had been an isolated island on the edge of Europe, but the discovery of America had advantageously altered her position. For the first time England looked upon the sea as opening to her the possibility of adventure, trade and colonial conquest. These were the days of Hawkins, Drake, Raleigh and many other equally adventurous Englishmen. The English exploits upon the seas ultimately dragged them into a life and death struggle with the world power of Philip II of Spain. The final outcome of this struggle, which resulted in the English defeat of the invincible Spanish Armada, marked the beginning of English sea supremacy. By the time of Elizabeth's death England was well on her way to replacing Spain as a colonial power. Already by the middle of the century an ever-increasing brilliance, splendor and love of luxury was evident in the royal court, which signified an absolute break with the frugal traditions of the Middle Ages. Under the dynamic Tudor rulers the spirit of nationalism was greatly strengthened and the people were welded into a single national unit. While all these various forces had a stimulating effect on the development of the arts of England, it was principally in literature that the essence of the age was revealed. The drama served brilliantly as the creative outlet for the energetic spirit and visionary hopes which filled the hearts of Englishmen. The literary works of Shakespeare, Jonson and their contemporaries represent one of the most glorious achievements in literature. The spirit of the age was vigorous, robust and exuberant and was reflected in its love of spectacles and pageantry.

Various foreign countries exerted their influence upon the development of the Elizabethan style. The influence of the Netherlands was the strongest and was undoubtedly due to some extent to the close religious and commercial ties existing between the two countries in the second half of the 16th and first half of the 17th centuries. Much of this influence resulted from the importation of Flemish pattern books, such as those by De Vries, with their Flemish interpretation of Italian Renaissance ornament and their designs for chimneypieces, windows and doorways. German and French influences were also contributing factors. Pattern books by the German designer Dietterlein enjoyed a wide circulation in England. Then, too, many Flemish and German craftsmen migrated to England and also some skilled Huguenots, who fled their country after the St. Bartholomew Massacre in 1572. However, irrespective of all these foreign influences the Elizabethan style possessed a genuine national character. The style like the Elizabethans themselves was turbulent and forceful. The architecture had a peculiar irregularity which gave it a singular striking quality that was much of its charm. The English architect had not up to this time grasped the principles underlying Renaissance architecture. This better understanding and appreciation of Classic Orders and forms were soon to be supplied by that great English architect, Inigo Jones.

The keynote of the Elizabethan interior was exuberance, which appropriately reflected the Elizabethan spirit. Many of these brilliantly colored interiors were almost like pageants in woodwork, plaster and stone. The Classic Orders, which were a rather frequent feature of the interior decoration, were treated in a crude manner, with the English architect freely interpreting their use through Flemish pattern books. The plan of the house remained traditionally English. The Italian symmetrically planned interior came somewhat later. The hall was still an important center of household life. After eating in the hall with their retainers the master and his family retired to their own parlor. Early in the 17th century some of the houses were designed with a separate dining room. The long gallery on the second floor, which was lighted from one side and was used for exercise and games, was a characteristic feature of these houses. This long gallery and the great hall on the first floor were used for music recitals and masquerading, which were typical Elizabethan forms of social life. The walls were often skillfully panelled in the finest quality of oak. The ceilings were especially spectacular with their elaborate ornamental plasterwork. Undoubtedly the center of interest was the great fireplace with its richly decorated overmantel. The carved decoration on the panelled walls, as well as on the chimneypiece and the molded plaster ceiling, was very often colored and gilded. These interiors formed a fitting background for the magnificent tapestries, which were regarded as essential decoration for any important room, especially if the walls were not wood panelled. Other luxurious accessories, such as fine glass, beautiful silks and velvets, laces and linens and carpets were all imported and prized by Elizabeth and her courtiers.

Until the Restoration of the Monarchy in 1660 English furniture, except for that found in royal palaces, was limited to a relatively few types, such as chairs, stools, benches, settles, bedsteads, tables, chests and cupboards. The general character of Elizabethan furniture was still of a rather primitive nature. Essentially the English cabinetmaker developed a style of furniture along native English lines, characterized by simplicity of construction and by strong and serviceable qualities. The ornament was heterogeneous and over-elaborated. The furniture was massive and essentially rectilinear in form. It was principally made of oak. Occasionally a few costly and ambitious pieces were made of walnut. The furniture during the Tudor era, from 1485 to 1558, was Gothic in form and in construction. After 1530 Renaissance motifs were often mingled with the fashionable Gothic motifs. In the Elizabethan period a few new pieces of furniture were developed from the earlier forms. Elizabethan furniture reflected strong Flemish influences. From around 1540 to 1640 Antwerp exported large quantities of both elaborate and plain furniture into England. We have already mentioned that in the second half of the 16th century craftsmen from the Netherlands, Germany and France came to live in England, and this mingling of influences was all reflected to some extent in English furniture. Heavy bulbous supports on tables, bedsteads and court cupboards were a pronounced feature of Elizabethan furniture. They were originally used on the furniture of the Low Countries. The bulbous form of these supports was designed to represent a tall silver cup and cover, and it is frequently referred to as a cup and cover support

and occasionally as a melon support. As the 16th century advanced the bulbous form expanded in circumference and was completely out of proportion to its original design. As a rule in the 17th century the girth of these supports was gradually decreased. The Elizabethan bulbous supports were richly carved or gadrooned, while in the following century they were generally baluster turned and their entire character was less bold.

Elizabethan furniture was decorated with either carving or inlay, the former being by far the favorite method. The practice of painting and gilding furniture, which had been still employed during the time of Henry VIII, declined rapidly in the Elizabethan era. Although the carving was at times skillfully executed it was more often inclined to be coarse in quality. The carving lacked the subtlety of relief found in contemporary foreign work. Elizabethan carving was always vigorous and robust and was imbued with a striking quality of barbaric richness. Inlay work was used to a considerable extent. Essentially the inlay work was coarse in quality and consisted chiefly of conventional leaf and floral motifs and simplified geometrical designs. It was often used in conjunction with carving, especially in the late 16th and early 17th centuries. Bands of geometrical inlay were extensively used to further enrich the surfaces of tables, cupboards and other articles of furniture. Generally holly or poplar was used for the lighter tones and bog oak for the darker tones, while wood such as cherry was employed to supply an occasional reddish tone in the inlay pattern. Although upholstered chairs and stools were listed in the possessions of Henry VIII in 1547, upholstered furniture was relatively scarce throughout the 16th century. It appears that the earliest upholstered chairs and stools were of X-form, and the entire frame, which was commonly of beech-wood, was covered in fabric and finished with fringe.

During the Elizabethan style the entire range of Renaissance ornament supplanted the Gothic motifs. However, survivals of late Gothic detail were still evident in some of the work. In the reign of Henry VIII the Renaissance motifs were principally borrowed from the Italian Renaissance. The English frequently used the contemporary word *Romayne* to describe these decorative motifs of Italian origin. Especially fashionable and typical were the wreathed and medallion heads. Flemish pattern books interpreting Italian Renaissance motifs were the principal source of supply and inspiration for the classic style of ornament during the long reign of Queen Elizabeth. Intricate strapwork of interlaced and arabesque ornament carved in low relief and generally worked in repetitive patterns was a favorite form of carved decoration. Strapwork was introduced into England around the middle of the 16th century, principally from Flemish and German pattern books, and was frequently employed in the panels on Elizabethan oak furniture. Included among the favorite and popular Elizabethan styles of ornament were acanthus leafage, vase forms, candelabra, swags, figure subjects, masks, grotesques, caryatids and scrolls. Decorative architectural details, such as arcadings, were often incorporated in furniture designs. Split baluster turnings were occasionally applied to the surface as a decorative detail late in the Elizabethan style. In furniture, as in architecture, the English had not yet learned the importance of unity in the composition of their designs, nor had they learned what to select and what to discard. Their chief purpose was to cover the surface with a wealth of ornamentation irrespective of the technical quality of the ornament used. As a result, their style of ornament was lacking in classic refinement and was inferior to the finished composition found in the contemporary Italian and French styles of ornament.

ARTICLES OF FURNITURE

Chairs   Chairs during the early 16th century were exceedingly rare. There were three principal varieties, namely, the chair with panelled back, arms and sides, the turned chair and the folding chair or chair of X-form. The oak chair with panelled back, arms and sides was the principal Gothic chair and was made well into the 16th century. It was massive and had a rectilinear box-like form. The portion below the seat usually formed a chest, the seat being hinged to give access to it. A characteristic early chair, which was made until the end of Elizabeth's reign, was the turned, three-legged armchair, with a triangular wooden seat and a low back (FIGURE 263). The base of the triangle formed the front of the seat. The seat, the three turned uprights and the turned back rail were all joined with turned spindles. This chair with its peculiarities of design is generally believed to have been of Byzantine origin. (A chair of this type has been used by the president of Harvard University when giving degrees since the 18th century and is referred to as the Harvard chair.) These chairs with an entirely turned structure and triangular seat displayed variations in the number, arrangement and kind of turned members (264). During the Gothic period a few chairs of curule form appeared in England, undoubtedly of Italian inspiration. This folding chair became very popular during the reign of Henry VIII and one principal variety was essentially similar in form to the Italian dantesca chair. The Glastonbury chair (265), which is a type of carved oak armchair with a folding framework, was introduced in the 16th century and has a family resemblance to some earlier Italian models. It is usually identified as a piece of ecclesiastical furniture. The frame was made of planks joined together with wooden pins. The carved back, which slanted backward, extended to the solid wood seat. The arms, which were hinged by a wooden bar, were shaped to support the elbows. A distinctive feature is the carved decoration, which is the same on all extant English examples. It comprises a stylized flower within a lozenge headed by a half sunflower and enclosed by a rounded arch enriched with a guilloche design.

The principal Elizabethan armchair was the so-called wainscot chair (262). This oak chair had a panelled back which extended to the seat rail (262). The open arms usually curved downward (262). The legs were joined with a continuous floor stretcher (262). This type of wainscot chair was designed throughout the 17th century. There was little variation in its shape. It was rectilinear in form and was of solid and massive construction. The top rail was often surmounted with an elaborate cresting, and occasionally the uprights were surmounted with scrolled finials (262). Toward the end of Elizabeth's reign the chair became lighter in form and the wooden seat was usually more narrow. The front legs and armposts were frequently fluted. The chair was richly carved, and sometimes later in the 16th century the carvings were further enhanced with an inlay of conventionalized leaf and floral motifs and checker patterns (262). This chair was also designed with an open arcaded back. However, oak chairs with this variation in design were relatively rare as the English preferred the panel-back type. The French caquetoire was also sometimes used as a prototype for a variety of English armchair. The few which were made were of oak.

The oak chair-table was known as early as the middle of the 16th century. It was designed with a large circular or rectangular back which extended beyond the uprights. The back worked on pivots and could be pulled forward to rest on the arms. When the back was let down in this manner it formed the top for a table. The chair-table, which was made throughout the 17th century, was sometimes called a monk's chair.

Stools   The Gothic stool of trestle form was still in general use throughout the Elizabethan era. The shaped or pierced underframing was keyed through the solid splayed truss-ends. The three-legged wooden stool, which was first made during medieval days, was still in evidence. The characteristic joint stool toward the end of the century was similar in design principles to the contemporary small table. The oblong wooden seat, which had an arched underframing, rested on columnar legs, which were often fluted. The legs were connected with a continuous stretcher close to the floor. This variety of joint stool with its molded wooden seat was still in use in the 18th century. A cushion was often placed on the seat to provide a little comfort. Toward the end of Elizabeth's reign the seat was occasionally padded and upholstered. Another variety of stool was designed with X-form supports, and its entire surface was sometimes covered with rich and costly fabric. This stool was comparatively rare.

The French term *tabouret,* meaning a small drum, was given to a low seat or stool without back or arms for one person. In the French court the king occupied a chair, and the privilege of sitting upon a tabouret or stool in his presence was restricted to the wives of the royalty and nobility. In England after Elizabethan times these same Continental rules were also observed and tabouret etiquette, which became very strict by the time of Charles II, was followed as late as the court of George II. The seat of the tabouret was richly upholstered in silk damask, velvet or some similar material.

Benches   The bench of trestle form, similar in design and construction to the Late Gothic stool of trestle form, was made throughout the 16th and 17th centuries. It was also designed with a back. In the 17th century the solid truss-end supports were sometimes superseded by turned splayed legs, joined with a continuous floor stretcher.

The oak settle, which was either built into the wall or was movable, was characterized by its massive and solid construction. It usually had a high panelled back, with panelled arms and sides. The portion below the seat generally formed a chest, with the seat being hinged to give access to it. It was designed to accommodate several persons. Cushions were usually placed on the seat to afford a little comfort and to provide an air of luxury. During the 17th century the settle grew lighter in form. One variety of settle combined the double purpose of seat and table. This settle-table had an oblong rectangular back which extended beyond the uprights. The back worked on pivots and could be pulled forward to rest on the arms. In this manner it served as a table. Although early examples date from the beginning of the 17th century, in all probability this variety of settle was introduced as early as the chair-table, since the two pieces were essentially similar in construction and function. The settle-table, which continued to be made in the 17th century, was sometimes referred to as a monk's table.

Beds Until the 16th century the bed was simply a boarded box completely covered with draperies. During the first half of the century the bed began to assume the contour of the Elizabethan tester bed. First the bed with four posts was designed and subsequently a headboard was added. The tester was added around 1550. Around the same time the posts at the head of the bed were omitted, since the massive panelled headboard was strong enough to support the tester. The Elizabethan bed was characterized by its rich and elaborate carvings and its monumental form (268). It consisted ·of a panelled and carved headboard and a corniced tester which rested on the two front bedposts (268). The ceiling of the tester was richly panelled and often elaborately carved and inlaid (268). The two posts were often completely detached from the bed and stood beyond it, with the front corners of the bed resting on two short legs (268). The bedposts were usually bulbous-shaped and rested on massive pedestals (268). The bed was also distinctive for its rich and colorful draperies.

Day Beds The day bed, which is a variety of couch or lounge resembling a long narrow bench having one end designed as a chair back, was probably first introduced from Italy during the time of Henry VIII. An early form of day bed around 1600 was designed with two panelled ends, each slanting slightly outward. The four legs were joined with a continuous stretcher. Early in the 17th century one of the panelled ends was omitted.

Cradles It appears that the two principal types of cradles, namely the low cradle mounted on rockers and the swing cradle suspended between upright posts, were introduced into England from France around the middle of the 15th century. Of these two principal types the low cradle mounted on rockers was by far the more numerous. Extant English examples of carved oak cradles mounted on rockers dating from about 1580 through the following century generally feature turned rocking posts and are made either with or without a hood, the former apparently being much more plentiful. This form of cradle was seldom made in mahogany. In fact there was little change in the cradle except for decorative detail until after the middle of the 18th century when this type was largely superseded by the swing cradle. As in France the royal princes often had two cradles, a cradle for ordinary use and a cradle for display. The latter, which were called Cradles of Estate in England, were mentioned in English royal inventories as early as 1522.

Tables The change from the Gothic trestle table, with its removable top and its trestle supports, to a table of permanent structure occurred around the middle of the 16th century. The principal dining table of the Elizabethan era was a long, narrow, rectangular oak table (266). It had a heavy top and a richly carved apron, and was mounted on four bulbous-shaped legs, which were joined to a continuous stretcher close to the floor (266). The ingeniously devised draw top table was introduced around 1558, and the draw top (266) sometimes replaced the fixed top. This table showed little variation in its design, and was in general use until around the 18th century. The bulbous or vase-shaped legs were of Flemish origin. They were usually richly carved, fluted or gadrooned (266). In the following 17th century the bulbous supports were usually less pronounced and were often baluster turned. The apron and stretcher were sometimes enriched with an inlaid checker pattern, in accordance with Elizabethan taste.

Elaborate small tables were all imported from the Netherlands, France and Italy. The English designed a small oblong table around 1600 with an arcaded underframing resting on four columnar supports, which were joined to a continuous floor stretcher. Of particular interest was a small table which could be used as a card table. Sometimes the top of this table was marked for chess or backgammon and was designed with two folding leaves which when opened were supported by sliding bars. Undoubtedly the earliest form of a gaming table in medieval times for chess, dice, draughts and backgammon was simply a wooden board marked out with lines and placed on a chest. Playing cards were introduced in the 15th century and were very popular along with all the other games at the Tudor courts. However, the characteristic English card table was not introduced until the end of the 17th century.

An early variety of table or chest was the counter table, having its top divided into spaces with distinctive symbols for counting money. Until the 16th century the counting of money was primitive and was done with a counter table or counter board. A characteristic variety of counter table was designed with an oblong hinged top which was hinged at one end. The top extended well over an underframing that was enclosed to form a shallow cupboard fitted with a cupboard door. It was mounted on four legs connected either with a shelf close to the floor or with a continuous floor stretcher. In another variety the top was kept in position by means of sliding bars which permitted access into the interior without disturbing the counters.

Writing Furniture

The portable desk (269) was the principal form of furniture designed for writing in the 16th century. It was designed to be placed upon a table. The desk had a slant-front top and was hinged so that the flap opened backward instead of forward (269). The interior was frequently fitted with drawers and tills. The desk was notable for its richly carved (269) or inlaid decoration.

Chests

The chest continued to be an important piece of domestic furniture throughout the 16th century. Many chests were imported from Flanders. Although the chest sometimes rested directly upon the floor, more frequently the stiles were lengthened to form supports. Toward the end of the reign of Henry VIII decorative architectural detail was frequently found on the façade of the chest. Buildings were often conventionally portrayed in inlay work. Characteristic of this fashion were the Nonsuch chests (267) which depicted in inlays of colored woods the palace of Nonsuch built by Henry VIII at Cheam. In another variety of chest the top was marked with such games as chess and tric trac. Occasionally a removable playing board was fitted inside the chest. A typical Elizabethan chest had an arcaded façade with elaborately carved rails and stiles and with the panels either plain or enriched with carving or inlay work.

Cupboards   The term *court cupboard* (270) is now employed to describe an open structure of shelves for the display of plate, introduced toward the end of the 16th century. Its form was inspired by a similar variety which had been designed earlier in France. It was rectangular and upright and was rarely above four feet in height. It was composed of three tiers and was entirely open (270). The uppermost tier had a frieze which rested on supports (270). The median tier or shelf also had a frieze and rested on four supports which were joined by a deep shelf at the base, mounted on feet (270). The two friezes were often fitted with drawers. The two pairs of front supports were bulbous in outline, while the rear supports were narrow and straight (270). It was made of oak and was richly carved (270). The court cupboard was made throughout the Carolean era. However, the later ones lacked the fine quality of workmanship both in form and decoration which had characterized the Elizabethan examples. The court cupboard was largely supplanted at the beginning of the 18th century in the wealthy homes by the alcove cupboard or the buffet and by the long side table or sideboard table. Contemporary records of foreigners travelling in England reveal that they called this article of furniture designed with three tiers of shelves a buffet. However, contemporary records prove that the English called it a court cupboard in the Elizabethan and Jacobean eras. During the 18th century the English used the term *buffet* (311) to describe an alcove in a panelled room fitted with shelves for the display of porcelain.

The name *hall and parlor cupboard* is now given to several forms of cupboards introduced in the 16th century that were known as cupboards by their original owners and that were intended by their obvious appearance for the hall or for the living room rather than for a bedroom. One variety of Elizabethan hall and parlor cupboard had a closed upper portion while the lower portion formed a stand (271). The oblong rectangular upper portion was fitted with three panelled cupboard doors surmounted with a frieze and with a cornice (271). The lower portion was designed with a frieze, sometimes fitted with drawers, resting on four legs which were joined to a heavy display shelf close to the floor (271). The two front legs were bulbous in form and the two rear supports were straight and usually plain (271). It was richly decorated with carved and inlaid work. This variety, which resembles the French crédence, is sometimes called a credence, however without any contemporary authority. Another variety of hall and parlor cupboard having the lower portion also designed as a stand was introduced late in the reign of Queen Elizabeth. In this type the upper portion was designed with a canted front. The upper section had three recessed panels, fitted with one or more cupboard doors, with the two end panels canted, surmounted with a projecting frieze and cornice which rested on two bulbous form supports. The lower portion had a frieze resting on four supports, the two front supports being bulbous in contour. The legs were joined to a deep display shelf that was mounted on feet. Both of the friezes were often fitted with drawers. It was handsomely carved. In another variety of hall and parlor cupboard both the upper and lower sections were closed. This type, which until recently has been called a court cupboard in the literature of English furniture, was introduced around the middle of the 16th century and retained its popularity until the Restoration in 1660. The principal variety of this type of cupboard during the 16th century was rectangular and upright. It had a projecting cornice above an upper cupboard section which contained three panels designed as one or more doors. The frieze of the cornice rested on two bulbous supports. The projecting lower body had a frieze band, sometimes fitted with drawers, over two panelled cupboard doors. The end stiles were lengthened to form feet. During the Elizabethan era the two end panels in the recessed upper section were often canted. Other variations in design occurred. Although this type of cupboard was no longer fashionable after the Restoration it was made by the village cabinetmaker along English traditional lines until early in the 18th century when it was gradually supplanted by the popular farmhouse dresser, with its superstructure of shelves.

In the Elizabethan period the Gothic food or livery cupboard having the front pierced for ventilation was generally superseded by one having a turned spindled front (272) which was in accordance with the Elizabethan taste. Due to insufficient records and few existing examples it is difficult to determine the nature of the livery cupboard. Essentially there were two principal varieties. One kind was a small livery cupboard which was kept in the bedroom and was either hung on the wall (272) or was placed on a table. It varied in height from about two to three feet. The other variety was a large livery cupboard, which was generally referred to as a standing cupboard, since it rested on its own supports. This cupboard was placed in the great hall. The name *dole* or *almoner's cupboard* was applied to a kind of livery cupboard used in the church in which bread was kept to be doled out to the poor. In comparing the Elizabethan livery cupboard to the hall and parlor cupboard the former was more roughly constructed and the carved detail was of a coarser quality. Its decorative value had not been developed. In the 17th century a few of the standing livery cupboards were more elaborately decorated. Essentially it was a utilitarian piece of furniture and its use was limited to important households with a large staff of retainers. After Charles I the tradition of serving liveries was discontinued and was never resumed after the Restoration.

CHAPTER FOURTEEN

JACOBEAN: Early Jacobean, Cromwellian & Late Jacobean

EARLY JACOBEAN AND CROMWELLIAN

The first four decades of the 17th century in England were very prosperous years despite all the religious and political difficulties. During the reign of James I, 1603–1625, who was the first Stuart to sit upon the English throne, and the ill-starred reign of his son Charles I, 1625–1649, English colonization was greater than that of any other European country. These colonizing enterprises naturally led to an expansion of trade resulting in increasing wealth for the already wealthy classes, who, emulating the Stuart kings, spent much of their time in the country and built many stately houses. The largest of the great houses were built during this era. The Stuarts brought England into closer contact with the Continent, especially with France and Italy. James I was an ardent follower of Renaissance culture and art. He was a patron of Inigo Jones, the celebrated English architect, whose prolonged studies in Italy were responsible for the introduction into England of Palladian principles of Renaissance architecture. Essentially the architecture of James I inherited the Elizabethan traditions. However, as Roman architecture became better understood, English work developed a sobriety and regularity which gradually supplanted the quaint and picturesque irregularity of the Elizabethan style. The Whitehall Banqueting House finished in the closing years of the reign of James I was the first complete Palladian structure erected in London.

From the reign of Charles I the Palladian style of architecture gradually began to supersede the earlier Elizabethan style of Renaissance architecture. The use of scholarly detail became increasingly evident in English work. Charles I deserves credit for developing at least to some extent this trend toward classic traditions, for he encouraged all branches of the arts. He was well versed in antique culture and was an enthusiastic collector of works of art. It is said that his personal collection required over a year to catalogue. His marriage to Henrietta Maria, sister of Louis XIII of France, was undoubtedly largely responsible for a certain amount of French influence occurring at this time. The names of several French architects and artists appear in contemporary records. Their work in all probability accounts for the French influence visible in some English ornamental detail. A marked increase in foreign travel among the wealthy classes also afforded an impetus for bringing Renaissance culture to England. This travelled aristocracy became better acquainted with the works of the great Italian masters in sculpture, painting and architecture, resulting in a more intimate appreciation of the arts. Contemporary inventories of the aristocracy reveal not only all kinds of European luxuries, such as furniture, glass, lace, velvets and silks, but also Oriental art, such as porcelain and lacquered articles. Unfortunately, all this enlightened advancement in collecting by the travelled dilettante, as well as all the building activity, was abruptly halted by the outbreak of civil war in 1642. War and strife, which marked the ensuing two decades in England until the Restoration of the Monarchy in 1660, were not conducive to developing the arts. The closing of the theaters also brought to an end the masques and pageants which were so typical of the Elizabethan and Early Stuart times and had been so brilliantly developed under the early Stuart kings.

During the reign of Charles I the interiors of the country mansions began to mirror the influence of Italian classic principles in their design. The traditional plan of the interior of a house, which had gradually developed from the Gothic era with its great hall and long gallery and the rest of the rooms in accidental arrangement, gradually yielded to the Palladian design with an entrance hall and with room leading to room according to a well-conceived plan. Inigo Jones had been the first to accept the classic principles of design, as interpreted by Palladio, in his treatment of the interior. The interior of the houses built around the middle of the 17th century, under the influence of Inigo Jones, reflected these classic principles. The new manner was evident not only in the suitability and distribution of ornament, but also in the symmetrical arrangement of doors and windows and in the introduction of definite proportions between the height, length and width of a room. The exuberant Elizabethan style of ornament yielded to carefully arranged and concentrated ornament. There was an increasing tendency to use miniature architectural forms, such as pediments, for ornamental detail over an opening. The use of color to enrich the wainscot walls and the elaborately modelled plaster ceilings was a characteristic feature of both Tudor and Early Stuart interiors. The framework of the wainscoting was often painted in red, while cartouches, strapwork and other favorite motifs were painted in blue and yellow on the panels. Additional brilliance was often provided by picking out ornamental details in gilt. After the Restoration the painting of wainscoting in several colors was less fashionable. The subdivision of the wainscot into small panels, which were almost always of rectangular shape and which were so characteristic of the Elizabethan and Early Jacobean styles, gradually yielded around the middle of the century to large unbroken oblong panels. These large panels formed a part of the decorative scheme and had always been favored by Inigo Jones. Wood panelling in the new manner was extensively employed throughout the second half of the 17th century and in many of the older houses the earlier plaster walls were covered with panelling.

The glazing of windows was an interesting feature of Early Renaissance domestic architecture. Glass windows were exceedingly rare until the reign of Henry VIII except in churches and in the finest houses. Framed cloth blinds or horn were used in place of glass. During the reign of Queen Elizabeth glass became quite plentiful and inexpensive. Some of the better grades of glass were imported from Flanders and Germany. The 16th century glazed windows were remarkable for their intricate and varied designs of the diamond pattern, which imparted to the window a strikingly rich texture. These diamond patterns were supplanted in the 17th century by square or oblong glazed panes. Sometimes openwork sections of cast lead were employed among the glazed panes for purposes of ventilation. The majority of the glazed panes were white in order to afford the most light. However, small panels of colored glass were occasionally introduced into the glazed surface. Originally this colored glass was cut from sheets of pot metal and the small pieces of different colored pot metal glass were framed in lead to form a design. Later, from around the middle of the 16th century, this earlier method for making colored or stained glass was supplanted by painting on glass. Armorial devices and coats-of-arms were fashionable motifs for these colored glass panels.

Prior to the restoration of the monarchy English furniture, except for that found in the royal palaces and in the great houses of the aristocracy, was lim-ited to the relatively few types which were in general use in the Elizabethan era. Essentially the Early Jacobean furniture was a continuation of the Elizabethan style. Until the English mastered the principles of Italian classic design the furniture necessarily suffered. It lacked the balance in proportion and harmony in lines essential to well-designed furniture. During the reign of Charles I some fine furniture was imported from Italy, especially from Venice. It was also imported from France, and large quantities of both elaborate and plain furniture were imported from the Netherlands. This imported furniture had little effect upon the English cabinetmaker whose work continued to reflect the Elizabethan taste. The Elizabethan style, which possessed a genuine national character, continued to dominate furniture design as long as the fashion for oak prevailed. Even after the Restoration, when walnut became the fashionable wood and all the fine furniture was made of walnut, whenever the cabinetmaker worked in oak those pieces were produced in the Elizabethan tradition. During the Early Stuart era a few new pieces of furniture were introduced and furniture became more plentiful. More plain furniture was designed for general use. Upholstery work was given serious consideration largely due to the new forms of upholstered furniture introduced from the French court of Louis XIII. Occasionally the framework of an article of furniture, such as a chair or stool, was completely covered in rich and colorful fabric. Especially characteristic were the elaborately covered bedsteads which were so fashionable during the reign of James I. During this era the bulbous supports on court cupboards and dining tables became less pronounced. The legs for chairs, stools and settees were frequently of columnar shape. Basically, to a great extent, the same forms, the same designs and the same ornament of the Elizabethan style were constantly repeated.

With the establishment of the Commonwealth in 1649 there was a return to simplicity and austerity. The production of furniture of a decorative quality was brought practically to a standstill throughout the Cromwellian era. Furniture made at this time was heavy in form and generally devoid of ornament. Especially favored were certain articles of furniture which could serve a double purpose, such as a combined chair-table and a settle-table. Puritan furniture was characterized by its severity and was designed for purely utilitarian purposes. Certain features of Dutch design, such as the use of ball feet, became noticeable during the Cromwellian era. The Commonwealth, with its aversion to all forms of pretentious display, was brought to an end with the restoration of the monarchy in 1660 which was to usher in an era of splendor and prodigious spending previously unknown to the English at that time. An entirely new phase, almost revolutionary in its scope, was to invade the field of English furniture design.

Carving was the favorite method for decorating the surface of furniture. The carved decoration was frequently incised or executed in low relief. There was little carving of a sculptured quality. Inlay work in different colored woods was often used and was frequently combined with the carving. Stylized leaf and floral motifs and simplified geometrical patterns were popular designs for the inlaid decoration. Toward the end of the reign of James I inlay work in bone and ivory began to be used for decorative purposes. This form of in-

lay, which was of Moorish inspiration, was often further enriched with an inlay of mother-of-pearl. Turning was also a favorite decorative process and various kinds of turning were employed. Split turnings were often applied to the surface of furniture for ornamentation. They provided a contrast to the general flatness of the surface and they were sometimes stained black. In addition to the split turnings, lozenge and oval bosses were applied to decorate the surfaces of furniture. In all probability this idea of applied oval bosses was inspired by the marble cabochons used to enrich the surfaces of Italian and French cupboards and cabinets. Applied pendants, often having a fret-cut heading, were also used for ornamentation, especially on cupboards and on the early chests of drawers. Geometrically molded panels were a popular form of decoration for the doors of cupboards and for chests. The geometrically panelled door was often further ornamented with a centered projecting bevelled panel, usually in the form of an octagon, diamond or square. The panels were often inlaid with ivory or mother-of-pearl. This decoration of Moorish inspiration was fashionable in the early part of the reign of Charles I and was revived again around the middle of the century. The practice of painting furniture in color as well as in silver or gilt was also widely used and characteristic of the Early Stuart era.

The style of Renaissance classic ornament remained essentially the same as in the Elizabethan style. Elaborate strapwork combined with grotesques and arabesques as developed in Flemish ornament literally ran riot in England from around the end of the 16th century for the next three decades. The strapwork was carved in low relief and generally worked in repetitive patterns, and was extensively employed in the friezes and panels of oak furniture. In the reign of Charles I the use of strapwork was not as pronounced. Classic repetitive patterns, such as the guilloche, were quite popular. Essentially the ornament used in furniture design in the Early Jacobean era lacked variety and imagination both in its composition as well as in the scope of the ornament. There was little that was fresh or new about the treatment of its composition or in the variety of the ornament. Figure subjects, caryatids, terms, masks and similar motifs were less frequently used on Jacobean furniture than in the preceding Elizabethan style.

ARTICLES OF FURNITURE

Chairs   The variety of wainscot chair, with its panel-back and open arms, introduced in the Elizabethan style, was made throughout the 17th century. Essentially there was little variation in design. The cresting was usually higher and was often made more ornate with scrollwork. Later the legs were frequently joined with side stretchers in place of the continuous floor stretcher. Around the middle of the century the chair sometimes had a spirally turned front stretcher, slightly beneath the seat rail, connecting the two front legs. The chair of X-form enjoyed considerable popularity in the early 17th century. Its entire framework was covered with rich fabric, finished with straight strands of silk fringe, which was fastened to the frame with decorative nail heads (FIGURE 273). A stuffed cushion was placed on the seat. The oak chair-table was made throughout the 17th century. Its practicability found special favor with the Puritans during the Cromwellian era.

Around the time of the Restoration a lighter type of chair superseded the panel-back wainscot chair in Derbyshire and Yorkshire. One variety of Derbyshire chair had an arcaded top rail and central crosspiece joined with turned spindles (275). The top rail and crosspiece were ornamented with knobbed finials (275). The two uprights were surmounted with scrolled finials curving outward (275). The two front legs were turned (275). The four legs were joined with a continuous floor stretcher in addition to two side stretchers (275). The wooden seat was usually sunk or dished in order to hold a cushion (275). A few years later another variety was introduced with broad flat rails or crosspieces connecting the two uprights (276). These crosspieces, of which there were generally two or three, were elaborately hooped and scalloped and vigorously carved, and were decorated with short pendants (276). The scrolled finials surmounting the two uprights curved inward (276). The two front legs were turned and were joined with a turned front stretcher beneath the seat rail (276). Two pairs of turned side stretchers and one back stretcher connected the legs (276). The wooden seat was usually dished to receive a cushion (276). Occasionally a head with a pointed beard was carved in the center of the top rail.

The chair of the Yorkshire-Derbyshire type was made of oak and was almost always designed as a side chair.

The farthingale chair (274) was designed around the beginning of the 17th century and was popular during the Early Jacobean period. It was essentially a lady's chair and was designed so that she could sit comfortably in her voluminous hoop skirt or farthingale. It was a rectangular-shaped small side chair. The seat was noticeably high and the back unusually low (274). The legs were quadrangular, sometimes the two front legs were of columnar shape (274). The four legs were joined with a continuous stretcher close to the floor (274). The chair had an upholstered seat and back panel (274). Frequently the frame was entirely covered with fabric and in some examples it was painted and gilded.

During the Protectorate an angular oak armchair of uncomfortable form was made and was popularly known as the Cromwellian chair. The turned armposts, front legs and front stretcher were often knobbed (277). Two plain side stretchers and a rear stretcher connected the four legs (277). The seat and back were of leather and were secured to the frame with a row of brass nail heads (277). The flat straight arms were often covered with leather. The chair was also designed as a side chair (277).

Stools The joint stool (278) was widely used during the Early Jacobean era. The wooden seat had an oblong rectangular underframe and was mounted on four splayed legs, joined with a continuous stretcher close to the floor (278). Another variety of stool was similar to the farthingale chair. It had an upholstered seat and the legs were usually painted or covered with fabric. The stool of X-form with its frame entirely covered in fabric was also made.

Benches The characteristic bench of the Early Jacobean period was similar in form and construction to the Elizabethan bench of trestle form with its solid splayed truss-end supports. Another variety of bench was similar in design to the joined wooden stool with the turned legs. It had a long, narrow seat and the splayed and turned legs were joined with a continuous floor stretcher.

The settle lost some of its massiveness in the Early Jacobean period. By the middle of the century the arms were open (279) and the seat was sometimes supported on turned legs, joined with a floor stretcher. However, the type with the seat opening into a chest was more common (279). The settle-table (279), like the chair-table, which combined the double purpose of seat and table, was made throughout the Early Jacobean era. This variety especially appealed to the Puritans.

Settees The settee was introduced early in the 17th century; however, few settees were made until after the Restoration. One early variety had a high back and straight open arms. The seat rested on four legs joined with a floor stretcher. The back and seat were upholstered and the arms were covered with fabric. The legs were often painted and gilded or covered with fabric. During the Cromwellian era an open arm settee was designed with turned supports. It was angular in form and was very uncomfortable. The legs were connected with a floor stretcher. It had a leather back-panel stretched between the two uprights and a leather seat, which was fastened to the frame with brass nail heads. The straight arms were covered with leather.

Beds   Early in the 17th century the massive oak tester bed was superseded by a bed with a lighter frame, usually made from beechwood. The entire framework, which included the tester, valance, very tall slender posts and headboard, was covered with rich and colorful fabric. The four corners of the tester were surmounted with vase-shaped finials, covered in fabric, each vase being filled with ostrich plumes (299). This extravagantly appointed bed, with its sumptuous and elaborate upholstery, retained its popularity throughout the 17th century in the wealthy houses. The oak tester bed continued to be made throughout the 17th and the first half of the 18th century. However, since it was no longer favored by the wealthy classes, it gradually became inferior in quality and was sparingly ornamented. Eventually the posts were simply turned balusters.

Day Beds   During the 17th century day beds became more plentiful in the luxuriously appointed homes. One principal early 17th century variety was designed with a solid panelled end, which slanted slightly outward. The long narrow seat was fitted with a long loose cushion and it rested on four legs joined with a floor stretcher.

Tables   From around the middle of the 17th century the side table, which is of early origin, often served the function of a sideboard table in the dining hall. At that time it was essentially similar in design to the contemporary dining table. It was massive, long and narrow and had a carved frieze mounted on four massive turned legs which were connected with a stretcher close to the floor.

By the beginning of the 17th century the number of small tables had greatly increased. The small table was used for many different purposes. It was usually made with an oblong, octagonal or oval top. Sometimes the table had a folding top. The underframing of the table was often arcaded. The legs were frequently columnar in shape; carved and fluted legs were later superseded by turned legs. The legs were joined with a floor stretcher.

It appears that the early gate-leg tables found in England dating from around the middle of the 16th century were provided with a single leaf and a single gate-leg which was secured at the top and at the bottom by wooden hinges instead of the later pivoted legs (280). In the early 17th century the legs were very often columnar in shape and later were baluster turned. The frieze was sometimes carved with strapwork (280). The gate-leg table having a fixed center portion with two drop-leaves and a pivoted gate-leg on either side was introduced around 1620.

Chests

The Early Jacobean chest was rather coarsely carved and reflected a lack of imagination in its style of ornament. The motifs were constantly repeated. Toward the end of the reign of James I oak chests, geometrically panelled and inlaid with bone, became fashionable. Although this form of decoration was of Moorish origin, it was treated in characteristic English technique. Occasionally it was further enhanced with an inlay of mother-of-pearl. Although the chest fitted with a row of drawers in the base was designed as early as the middle of the 16th century, it was almost a century later before this variety of chest was designed in any considerable numbers.

Chests of Drawers

The chest of drawers (281), like almost all new forms of furniture, originated on the Continent. Its importation from the Continent hastened its development in England. The early English chest of drawers, which was a massive piece of furniture, was often combined in two forms, such as a cupboard with drawers (281). In the early examples the doors often remained and opened to reveal a series of drawers (281). The chest of drawers having its entire façade designed with rows of drawers, which is the correct definition for a chest of drawers, was not designed until after the middle of the century. In fact, the evolution of the chest of drawers into its characteristic form was not complete until around 1680–85.

Cupboards

During the Early Jacobean period the oak cupboard used as a receptacle for clothes, linens and other possessions was made in a variety of sizes. Variations also occurred in the amount and kind of decoration and in the design. Essentially it was massive and was rectilinear in form, and was usually taller than it was wide. The stiles were generally lengthened to form the feet. The number of panelled cupboard doors varied. Occasionally it was fitted with a row of drawers in the frieze or base. One variety was very tall and was used as a press for clothes. This general variety of oak cupboard was usually crudely and simply constructed and coarsely decorated. It could not compare to the finished craftsmanship exhibited in the hall and parlor cupboard.

It has already been stated that much of the Early Jacobean furniture was similar to that of the Elizabethan period. Dining tables, desks, court cupboards, hall and parlor cupboards and livery cupboards have been described under the Elizabethan articles of furniture and can be referred to again at this time. (*See pages 205–209.*) These pieces during the Early Jacobean era revealed only slight variations in their designs from those of the preceding style, and these variations have already been pointed out in the Elizabethan articles of furniture.

LATE JACOBEAN OR CAROLEAN

Although Charles II, 1660–1685, spent part of his exile at the French court of Louis XIV, he lived the greater part of it in Holland where he was joined by many royalists. Upon his return to England he and the royalists brought with them all the new fashions and customs from continental Europe where standards of living were far in advance of those in England. In particular they brought with them ideas of art, decoration and furniture from Holland. The Englishman of the Restoration longed for luxury and gaiety after having been subjected to the hardships of a civil war and the subsequent somber and austere rule of the Puritans. The country was ready for a politer way of living which soon passed into very expensive tastes and customs. However, England could now afford more luxurious tastes, for under the later Stuarts the carrying trade of the world was transferred from Holland to England. Dutch commerce had already reached its height during the third quarter of the 17th century. Due to the subsequent and gradual decline in Dutch prosperity many skilled craftsmen migrated to England where the demand for fine furniture and decorative appointments was rapidly growing. During the Late Jacobean style, which also spanned the brief reign of Charles II's brother, James II, 1685–1688, Dutch influence was paramount in English furniture design. This is readily understandable when we remember that Holland was the headquarters for the royalists in exile and also the many Dutch craftsmen working in England. This bond was to be still further reinforced when Dutch William of Orange became King of England in 1689, with his wife Mary, who was the daughter of the deposed Stuart king, James II.

Classic principles in English architecture were still further developed by the English architect, Sir Christopher Wren, 1632–1723. Because he studied in Paris rather than in Rome there was more French influence in his work than Italian. At this period the work of the celebrated Italian Renaissance architect Vignola exerted great influence in France, while Palladian principles were paramount in England, largely due to the dominating personality of Inigo Jones. Sir Christopher Wren attempted to unite both of these styles in his work. The interiors reflecting the influence of designs by Inigo Jones were stately and formal while those which adhered to the methods encouraged by Wren were comfortable and friendly and were distinctive for their warm and inviting quality. The style of panelling identified with the work of Sir Christopher Wren and other contemporary English architects after the Restoration was influenced more by the contemporary style of Dutch and French interior woodwork than that by Inigo Jones. The Dutch influence was the predominating factor. Both the schools of Inigo Jones and Sir Christopher Wren designed the wall as an architectural composition. The panelling of the walls was divided into large panels. Their proportions were determined by calculation according to which one of the Five Orders, such as Doric or Ionic, had been applied to the room. After the Restoration the moldings enclosing the panels became more pronounced and were more richly carved with classic ornament. The panelling was generally finished in the natural wood.

The interior of the room was wood-panelled from floor to ceiling and the ceiling was of plasterwork. The finest examples of English plasterwork art, which had been introduced in the reign of Henry VIII by Italian craftsmen, were in these modelled ceilings. The ornamental detail of plasterwork ceilings during the second half of the 17th century was treated in a more natural manner and was less spectacular and stylized than in the earlier period. Sash windows, which had been introduced from Holland around 1670, were set within deep-panelled recesses. The panelled wall surface was characterized by long and broad panels defined by prominent moldings, by a molded dado and usually by a molded member which separated the upper panels from the dado or lower panels. The doorways were important. Each door was enclosed with a molded architrave which was generally ornamented by a frieze, cornice and broken pediment. The opening of the fireplace was surrounded with marble and had a wood-panelled overmantel in which a mirror was frequently placed. Occasionally the overmantel was designed with a fixed frame made from either moldings or applied carvings in which an oil painting was hung. A profiled cornice joined the panelled walls and plaster ceiling. This general conception of the interior lent itself to an endless variety of combinations. The carved details of the wood and the plasterwork enrichments were often of French origin. They were spirited and fanciful in their composition and were executed in a fine quality of craftsmanship. The amount of carved detail varied in accordance with the importance of the room. The acanthus leaf, which was characteristic of the Louis XIV style, was a fashionable carved motif for the frieze and moldings. Included among the other favorite motifs employed by the wood carver were pendants of fruit and flowers, all kinds of flowing scrolls, festoons of flowers, fruit and foliage, masks and cartouches.

The richest period of wood carving in English history was the last thirty years of the 17th century. This high development of the art of wood carving was centered in one man, Grinling Gibbons, 1648–1720, who was born in Rotterdam and came to England when he was about fifteen years old. By the time he was twenty-five years old his remarkable skill as a wood carver was well known. Gibbons is credited as the leader or a prominent member of a style of wood carving which lasted in England until about the end of the reign of Queen Anne. The work of the English school of wood carving for that period is generally referred to as the work of Grinling Gibbons because of the great influence he exerted in developing this style. However, much of the work attributed to him has since been revealed to have been the work of other wood carvers. He was employed by Charles II and Sir Christopher Wren. His wood carvings adorn many of England's great churches, palaces and colleges, such as St. Paul's Cathedral and the Church of St. James in Piccadilly, Trinity Colleges at both Oxford and Cambridge and St. George's Chapel at Windsor Castle. His carvings of flowers, fruit, birds and foliage have rarely been equalled. His work is unsurpassed for its minute detail, its delicate refinement and graceful realism. Until Grinling Gibbons the English style of wood carving had a solid and compact quality. His carvings, although they reveal real strength, are imbued with an airy lightness and lace-like quality. Gibbons was also an excellent draftsman, a fine designer and a skillful sculptor. Recent evidence reveals that he collaborated with Vanbrugh at Blenheim Palace and that some of the finest stone carving and sculpture on the exterior was his workmanship.

After the accession of Charles II there was a decided change, almost revolutionary in its scope, in the character of English furniture. New forms and finer examples of furniture were needed to meet the demands of a more elaborate social system and a higher standard of living. Charles and many royalists, having spent their exile on the Continent, had acquired a taste for luxury, refinement and foreign fashions. They rejected the older and more English types of solid oak furniture. The simple tables, chairs and cupboards were no longer adequate for the more elegant and polite manner of living. Chests of drawers, cabinets, candlestands, writing cabinets with fall-fronts and tall case clocks were all included among the new types of furniture found in the English home after the Restoration. At first these pieces of furniture were restricted to the royalty and nobility, but they were soon adopted by the wealthy middle class. An interesting point to observe is that from the time of the Restoration the fashions for English furniture were almost completely dictated by foreign influence. The history of furniture design reveals that continental Europe has consistently taken the lead and that England has always slowly followed the initiative and examples established in Europe. Only in the outlying country districts was the furniture still constructed and decorated along traditional English methods and made of oak. Since fine imported furniture was very expensive, the English cabinetmaker was called upon to copy the foreign pieces for the wealthy middle class. Encouraged by this patronage the English cabinetmaker began to develop his skill in designing and making finer examples of furniture. French and Dutch cabinetwork exerted the strongest influence, with the latter predominating. Numerous factors resulting from the close commercial and social ties existing between Holland and England at this time contributed to this Dutch influence. A large amount of Dutch furniture was also imported into England. English walnut and marquetry furniture from 1660 to 1700 bore the unmistakable imprint of Dutch influence. And, although this Dutch influence persisted in England as long as walnut remained the fashionable wood for cabinetwork, the influence was less marked after 1700 as the cabinetwork gradually became more Anglicized. The ascendancy of France in all branches of art under the Bourbon monarchs began to affect English work. This French influence became more apparent in the succeeding style of William and Mary.

The furniture was chiefly rectilinear in form. During the reign of Charles II there was a growing tendency to introduce scrolls into the structure. Arms, armposts, legs and stretchers were often shaped in the form of scrolls. Scrolls were worked in a variety of combinations, with the S-scroll, C-scroll and Flemish scroll being the most commonly employed. The cabinetmaker was constantly striving to obtain greater elegance in the structure and in the decoration of the furniture. The taste for rich decorative effects was evident in the vogue for brilliant floral marquetry, colorful lacquer work and richly upholstered furniture. It was also apparent in the gilt gesso furniture, which first became fashionable in the reign of Charles II and which was much used for French chairs and settees designed for the court of Louis XIV. Especially striking and elaborate were the English carved and gilded stands on which were placed oblong lacquered cabinets. Charles II's reign was marked by the introduction of glazed doors on bookcases and cabinets, copied from the new windows, with small rectangular panels of glass within a wooden framework. The characteristic feet on furniture were turned ball feet or bun feet, the latter being a flattened form of ball foot. Caned seats and back panels for chairs and day beds were in fashion during the Carolean style. Undoubtedly the use of caning in conjunction with walnut was introduced from the Continent. The Charles II furniture was characterized by its ornately decorated frames and florid leaf carving. The furniture, except for the traditional English oak pieces, was Baroque both in form and in ornament. Carving prevailed as the principal method for decorating the surface of furniture. Its exuberant treatment was very characteristic of the Charles II era.

Walnut became the fashionable wood for cabinetwork after the Restoration. The English cabinetmaker liked its warm soft color and its smooth texture. The vogue for walnut continued in England into the following century, when it was superseded by mahogany. Oak was still used, especially for furniture constructed and decorated along traditional English lines. A limited amount of plainer furniture was also made from many other woods, such as beech, elm, cedar, chestnut and pear. Lime wood was especially used by Grinling Gibbons and his school for applied carvings, such as for picture frames. Pear wood was often stained black to imitate ebony. Various exotic woods and fruit woods were used in the floral marquetry work. Ivory was also used in marquetry and inlay

work. In oysterwood parquetry, the oyster pieces were usually cut from walnut and laburnum saplings. A few pieces of furniture, such as candlestands, were made entirely from silver in emulation of the French. The fashion for silver furniture, which was regarded as evidence of prodigal extravagance, reached its height toward the end of the Carolean style and was followed only by a few of great wealth. Candlestands of silver were typical.

Veneering was practiced in England only to a very limited extent before the Restoration. However, its possibilities for producing surfaces remarkable for richness in tone and color were quickly appreciated by the cabinetmaker during the reign of Charles II. In the more ambitious pieces of cabinetwork veneers were chosen which displayed the greatest variety and richness of figures. Then, too, by selecting woods of pronounced markings the veneered surface could be artistically arranged to form ingenious decorative effects. Parquetry, employed as a veneer on furniture, was chiefly used in the early period of walnut veneered furniture and was often found in conjunction with marquetry. English parquetry was worked into simple geometrical forms made from thin pieces of wood. Occasionally lines of holly or boxwood and sometimes ivory worked in the form of circles, stars and similar simplified designs were laid into the parquetry veneer, such as for table tops. This kind of inlay with stars and circles was undoubtedly inspired by the contemporary Dutch work. (*See page* 77.) A distinctive form of parquetry employed in English cabinetwork during the Carolean and William and Mary styles was called oystering because the effect produced in this kind of veneering resembled an oyster in design. These so-called

oyster pieces were generally cut from laburnum and walnut saplings. The pieces
were circular or oval and were produced
by cutting transversely or diagonally
through small branches of about two or
three inches in diameter. They were
joined together as parquetry in the form
of irregular polygons and were laid on as
a veneer. Oystering was used in several
different ways. It was used as a border,
as a ground design when accompanied
with patterns of simple geometrical inlays of light colored wood, and as a veneering or facing for the entire ground of a
piece of furniture.

It is generally believed that marquetry
was introduced from Holland into England where it was first used in conjunction with veneered walnut after the
Restoration. In marquetry work the design and background are a combination
of veneers which are cut together and
glued to the surface. Especially favored
in England were floral and seaweed or
arabesque marquetry. Floral marquetry
was in vogue during the Charles II era
while seaweed marquetry was in fashion
in the subsequent William and Mary
style. Marquetry was especially used to
decorate walnut chests of drawers and
cabinets. The floral marquetry worked in
several different colored woods was contained in a shaped panel generally of walnut. Occasionally the dark panels were of
ebony and in the more ambitious and
elegant pieces of furniture these panels
were surrounded by walnut oystering
within bandings of a light wood. The effectiveness of floral marquetry depended
chiefly upon the strong contrasting tones
of the various colored woods. Sometimes
extra shading was obtained by dipping
the pieces in hot sand, and occasionally
ivory was also used, such as for the petals

of flowers. It is generally surmised that
much of this marquetry furniture was
made by Dutch craftsmen who had migrated to England.

The vogue for lacquered furniture did
not develop until after the Restoration
when it largely superseded painted furniture. European lacquer work was done in
an essentially different method from that
practiced in the Orient. Apparently the
imitation of Eastern lacquer work was
started in Europe at least as early as
the 17th century. Contemporary English
records mention furniture painted with
"Chinese work" early in the 17th century.
The taste for this kind of decoration in
Europe received an important early stimulus through the Dutch East India Company who were successful importers of
Oriental lacquer wares. In France, where
lacquer work achieved a remarkable
standard of excellence, workshops were
allocated in the Gobelins Manufactory to
improve this medium of decoration. An
important impetus for developing English
lacquer work was a publication by Stalker
and Parker published in 1688, entitled
A TREATISE OF JAPANNING AND VENEERING.
The authors gave their readers full instructions in the art of lacquering or
japanning, as it was called in England,
and as a result of this publication lacquering became a fashionable hobby. The
vogue for lacquered articles reached its
zenith early in the 18th century in England. Especially favorite and characteristic
pieces for japanned decoration during the
Charles II era were the tall case clocks
and the oblong cabinets mounted on ornately carved and gilded stands. The motifs for this japanned decoration comprised
an incongruous assortment of ornament,
including foliated scrollwork and pseudo-
Chinese motifs. Much of the English lac-

quered work was done by amateurs and although it had an attractive decorative effect it possessed little merit either in the quality of its workmanship or in the composition of its designs. The decoration was chiefly copied from designs in pattern books and was lacking in originality and vitality.

Turning was also a popular decorative process. Spiral turnings and baluster turnings were the two principal forms and were effectively used in many various combinations. Geometrically molded panels were also a favorite method for decorating the surface of furniture, especially furniture made of oak, such as chests of drawers, doors of cupboards and the drawers on dressers. Sometimes the panelling was overlaid with a false centered projecting beveled panel, generally in the form of an octagon, diamond or square, and with small bolection moldings mitered around the centered panel in different geometrical patterns. This form of panelling was sometimes further enriched with conventionalized flowers and simplified geometrical patterns inlaid in ivory and mother-of-pearl. The surface of oak furniture was also sometimes decorated with applied wooden ornament, such as split balusters, pendants and bosses which were often stained black.

Silk velvets and brocaded silks from Genoa were used in upholstering work. Chinese silks and embroideries were also used for coverings. Because the imported fabrics were so costly different kinds of domestic needlework were more commonly employed. Needlework had been done by the English women in large households since the early Tudor days. The principal and most durable material used in upholstery work was wool needlework upon canvas. It was generally worked in

gros point and occasionally some of the small designs were worked in petit point. Crewelwork was a popular kind of embroidery work and some very fine examples of crewelwork were made during the Jacobean era. Turkey work was also extensively employed for seat coverings. Plain or tooled leather was favored for its durability as well as for its beauty. Fringes were used to create a rich decorative effect, in addition to their practical purpose of concealing where the material was tacked down to the wooden frame. The early fringe with its straight silk threads was not as popular after the Restoration as the tasselled or tufted fringe with its balls or tassels of silk floss. The use of fringes in the upholstering of beds reached its extreme limit early in the 18th century. Fringes remained in fashion until after Queen Anne, and were revived late in the 18th century according to the latest French fashions in upholstery work.

Brass mounts were introduced after the Restoration to conform with the lighter forms of furniture. Prior to that time they had been made from wrought iron. The characteristic Carolean brass handle was in the form of a bulbous drop or pendant which was suspended from a square-shaped eye that was fastened through the back plate to the drawer by means of a split metal tang. Similar handles of bulbous form but richly decorated were also made of silver and were employed on the more ambitious pieces of cabinetwork. Simpler varieties of the pendant type include the acorn and tear drop which were fitted with a small circular plate. The pendant handle remained in vogue throughout the 17th century. Early in the 18th century the brass loop or bail handle attached to a flat-shaped back plate was introduced, and remained the principal type for the first half of the 18th century. The classic ornament in the Late Jacobean style was treated in a Baroque manner. Especially fashionable were such decorative motifs as pendants and swags of fruit, flowers and foliage, all kinds of foliated scrolls, the S-scroll, C-scroll and Flemish scroll worked in various combinations, draperies, cartouches, vase forms, arabesques, dolphins, birds, especially the eagle, masks, grotesques, cherubs' heads, amorini or putti, the coronet or crown, and human figures terminating in scrolls. The acanthus leaf was a popular decorative motif in English cabinetwork from around 1660 to 1760.

ARTICLES OF FURNITURE

Chairs   At the time of, or shortly after the Restoration, a spirally turned walnut armchair (FIGURE 282) was introduced which was probably the forerunner of the very popular carved and caned chair known as the Restoration or Charles II chair. In some extant examples of this turned chair the back and seat panels have a wide mesh caning, while in other examples the back panel is filled with vertical spirally turned members and the seat is dished for a cushion (282).

The principal walnut armchair (283) of the Restoration was a tall rectangular upright chair. It was finely turned and was richly carved and pierced with leaf scrolls and foliations, and it had a fine mesh back panel and seat (283). The uprights, armposts, legs and H-form stretcher were spirally turned. The turned uprights were surmounted with carved finials and were connected with a crested top rail and a lower crosspiece several inches above the seat rail (283). Between the carved and pierced crested top rail and the carved and pierced lower crosspiece extended a carved openwork rectangular panel, which was separated from the uprights and had a cane center (283). The arms were frequently scroll-shaped and carved (283). A broad carved and pierced front stretcher connected the two front legs (283) which were occasionally carved as well as spirally turned. As a rule the legs rested on bun feet. The top and side of the seat rail were carved. The elaborate cresting and the ornately carved broad front stretcher were the outstanding features (283). A crown, sometimes held by cupids, was often carved in the center of each. This motif, which had been copied from the Continent, had the additional significance in England of complimenting the restored monarchy. This chair when it was ornamented with a carved crown was popularly called the Restoration chair. This type of chair was also known as the Charles II or Carolean chair. Variations occurred both in structural design as well as in decorative treatment. The back panel was sometimes oval-shaped. Around 1675 S-scrolls were introduced in both the form and decoration of the chair. The front legs, the armposts and the stretcher connecting the four legs were usually scroll-shaped (283). As a rule turned balusters superseded the spirally turned uprights. Around 1685 the Charles II chair became much lighter in form and the carved and pierced decoration was more delicate. The arms began to turn outward. This chair was still in vogue after the accession of William III, although further variations in design and decoration occurred. The Charles II chair was also designed as a side chair. Around 1688 the chair was sometimes designed with a slat-back, with the carved and caned back panel being replaced by four or five carved and shaped horizontal slats or crossrails. In another variation in the design of this chair, occurring about the same time, the back panel was made of several split balusters in place of the cane.

The tall and large well-padded and upholstered wing chair, which was introduced in England from the Continent around 1680, was called an easie chair in contemporary English inventories. The wings were undoubtedly intended to protect the occupant against the drafts which were plentiful in the houses of those times. A special type of wing chair was called a sleeping chair which had ratchets to let down the back (284). The spirally turned armposts and legs, the latter being also often carved, and the richly carved scroll-shaped stretcher were in accordance with the prevailing fashion (284).

The upholstered walnut open armchair with its high rectangular raked back was introduced about 1680 (286). The back, which extended almost to the seat rail, was well padded and upholstered (286). The upholstered seat was usually finished with fringe (286). The chair was elaborately carved in a Baroque manner (286). The arms were out-scrolled and rested on scrolled armposts (286). The legs were scroll-shaped and were joined with a low H-form scrolled stretcher (286). The two front legs were joined with a high ornately carved broad front stretcher (286). The chair, which was frequently gilded, was upholstered in an elegant fabric, such as a rich cut silk velvet. Upholstered chairs varied in design, but they were always typical of the contemporary taste for Baroque splendor in their wealth of carved detail. In some extant examples the arms terminate in dolphins' heads and the legs are carved with the interlaced bodies of fish (285).

Stools The characteristic oak joint stool with its molded wooden seat and rectangular underframing, which rested on four turned and splayed legs joined with a floor stretcher, was made throughout the 17th century and was in use in the 18th century. However, it was gradually relegated to the servants' quarters. At the time of the Restoration the stool was essentially designed to match the chair and was made of walnut. The seat was usually rectangular, and was richly upholstered and finished with fringe. In one principal variety the legs were scroll-shaped and were joined, slightly beneath the seat, with a broad, elaborately carved front and rear stretcher and with a low, H-form, turned stretcher.

Benches   After the Restoration the bench became more decorative in character. It was essentially similar in form and ornament to the walnut stool, only of larger proportions. The plain oak bench was used throughout the 18th century. In the wealthier homes the bench was largely superseded by settees and day beds.

The settle continued to grow lighter in form after the Restoration. It was usually designed with a high back, downcurving open arms and turned legs joined with a stretcher. By the 18th century the settle lost its importance and was relegated to more humble surroundings.

Settees   The settee was made in an ever-increasing number and variety after the Restoration. One early variety of walnut settee was made by combining two or three chair backs, with the arms placed at each end of the seat. The seat was often caned and rested on six legs. The three front legs were joined with a broad front stretcher, while the six legs were joined with side stretchers and the three back legs with a rear stretcher. The walnut settee was largely supplanted around 1680 by an upholstered settee, designed with a high back, projecting wings and closed outscrolled arms. The seat was fitted with two loose cushions and rested on six legs. The three front legs were joined with an elaborate stretcher. The carved frame of the settee essentially followed the development of the contemporary chair. It was often made "en suite" with the chairs and stools. Toward the end of the reign of Charles II the upholstered back was divided into the distinct shape of two chair backs.

Beds   The richly draped, elaborately upholstered bed, with the four corners of the tester surmounted by vase-shaped finials holding a plume of feathers, retained its popularity into the 18th century (299). During Charles II the height of the bed gradually increased and an ornately shaped and carved wooden cornice surmounting the tester and completely covered in fabric was introduced (300).

Day Beds   The walnut day bed after the Restoration was usually designed with a hinged and adjustable rest at one end (287). It was turned, richly carved and caned and was fitted with loose cushions (287). The day bed followed the evolution of the contemporary chair in its principles of design and style of decoration. Around 1685 the back rest and seat were completely upholstered. The upholstered back rest slanted outward in a graceful curve and was permanently fixed. This variety was usually designed with six or eight scroll-shaped legs joined with scroll-shaped stretchers.

Tables   The massive long oak dining table characteristic of the Elizabethan and Early Jacobean eras was used throughout the 17th century. The top was either fixed or of draw-top construction and rested on a carved apron which was supported on four or six heavy baluster turned legs. The legs were joined with a floor stretcher. This dining table was gradually superseded by the oval or round table, made of walnut or oak and generally of the gate-leg variety with two leaves. This table was often very large in size and was sometimes designed with four gate-legs, each flap being supported by two gates. The legs and stretchers were usually spiral or baluster turned, sometimes the stretchers were plain. It became fashionable during the reign of Charles II to serve meals at several small tables, instead of at one large table.

Long side tables were designed in oak and in walnut and were sometimes used as sideboard tables for serving meals. Small walnut side tables with either spirally turned or baluster turned legs, joined with a shaped, flat stretcher, were made in large numbers. A few were elaborately carved with cherubs' heads and swags of fruit and flowers, in accordance with the taste of Grinling Gibbons. Decorative tables or center tables designed to stand in the middle of the room became more plentiful. One principal variety around 1680 had an oblong top and frieze drawer which rested on four S-scrolled legs, joined with a shaped, flat stretcher. It was mounted on bun feet.

Gaming Tables

In most instances the game table fitted for both backgammon and chess was made of walnut. The frieze beneath the rectangular top was often provided with a drawer. In an extant example of this period the top was designed with a panel which opened to a well inlaid for backgammon (290). The open spiral twist legs found on this model are typically Dutch and indicate that it was the work of a Dutch cabinetmaker.

Stands

The candlestand, as its name implies, was designed to support a candlestick or lamp and was used to augment the lighting arrangement in a room. It originated on the Continent. In France the candlestand was called a guéridon since the early stand was in the form of a young negro and that was the name given to a young Moor brought from Africa to serve as a page. The Moor in his brilliant costume was made either of painted and gilded carved wood or of bronze, and he held a candleholder in either of his hands. Sometimes he supported a small top on his head with his raised hands. In England these stands were known as blackamoor stands and were mentioned in English inventories as early as 1679. A characteristic walnut or oak candlestand in the time of Charles II was designed with a circular or octagonal top, supported on a turned shaft resting on a tripod base. Sometimes the carved detail on the shaft and tripod base was in the taste of Grinling Gibbons. The candlestand was frequently gilded and occasionally it was made entirely of silver.

The name *wig* or *powder stand* was given to a small turned stand having a top, which was often circular in shape, supported on a short shaft, resting on a circular base. It was used to hold the wig while the owner was not wearing it and also to hold the wig while powdering it. Although wearing a wig is of early origin, the ladies in England did not wear them until the 16th century and the men until after the Restoration. The wig stand was chiefly utilitarian and had no special decorative importance. The stand was usually a little over a foot in height and could in a broad sense be compared to a modern hat stand.

Writing Furniture

The small portable desk and the oblong writing cabinet with a fall-front were essentially the only furniture designed for writing in the Carolean era. The fall-front writing cabinet was introduced during the reign of Charles II, as the first form of English writing cabinet (292). The early examples were supported on turned stands (292). Frequently these early stands had four spirally turned supports joined with a shaped, flat stretcher and mounted on ball feet (292). The oblong cabinet around 1685 was frequently mounted on a chest of drawers and was decorated with floral marquetry.

Cabinets

The cabinet with its small drawers and secret compartments was known as early as Henry VIII; however, it was not until after the Restoration that it became a characteristic piece of English furniture. The principal walnut cabinet after the Restoration was oblong and was mounted on a walnut stand or chest of drawers (291). The cabinet was fitted with two doors, above which were a frieze and cornice (291). The stand, which projected slightly, had a frieze fitted with drawers, which most commonly rested on four front and two rear spirally turned legs, joined with a shaped, flat stretcher. It was mounted on bun feet. After 1680 the legs were frequently S-scrolled in form (310). In the luxury examples the walnut cabinet was usually decorated with floral marquetry (291) or was veneered with oysterwood parquetry.

A variety of cabinet was also designed with two glazed doors, fitted with small rectangular panels of glass within a wooden framework and having shelves for the display of porcelain. The cabinet, which had a frieze and cornice, was mounted on a stand, and, later, occasionally on a chest of drawers. Although the term *cabinet* is principally reserved for a piece of furniture fitted with small drawers, doors and secret compartments, it is also generally applied to a piece of furniture having an upper portion glazed and fitted with shelves for the display of china. According to the definition of a cabinet it would be more accurate to call the china cabinet a china cupboard; however, china cabinet is the more accepted name.

The brilliantly lacquered oblong cabinet generally mounted on an ornate gilt wood stand was a characteristic piece of Carolean furniture (293). There was a great demand for Oriental or European lacquered cabinets. The two doors of the lacquered cabinet, which were generally decorated on the interior as well as the exterior, opened to reveal a series of small drawers and doors all colorfully lacquered. The cabinet stand designed to support the lacquered cabinet was distinctive for its exuberant carvings, which were influenced by the school of Grinling Gibbons (293). Each leg had a pronounced outward curve at the knee and the lower portion was usually scroll-shaped (293). The four legs were richly decorated in a Baroque manner, often with human figures terminating in foliated scrolls (293). The deep apron, which was carved in the florid manner characteristic of the Late Jacobean style, was decorated with festoons of flowers, elaborate scrollwork, acanthus leaves and cherubs (293). In the center of the apron, amorini with trumpets or amorini supporting a crown were often carved. The stand was frequently of limewood and was coated with gesso before it was gilded.

Chests   The chest became less important as the 17th century progressed, due to the development of more specialized pieces of furniture. The oak chest was often decorated with geometrical panels inlaid with ivory and mother-of-pearl and with applied pendants on the stiles. The chest, which was mounted on ball feet, was sometimes fitted with a row of drawers in the base. It appears that the oak chest was used in the outlying districts well into the 18th century. It was largely superseded in the wealthy homes by walnut and lacquered chests. The walnut chest was occasionally decorated with marquetry. It was mounted on ball feet and sometimes was fitted with a drawer in the base. The lacquered chest was usually mounted on a low stand. One variety of stand was made of walnut and consisted of six S-scrolled supports joined with a shaped, flat stretcher, which rested on ball feet. Another form was richly carved and gilded.

Chests of   At the time of the Restoration the chest of drawers was still in the
Drawers   process of evolution and one principal variety of an oak chest of drawers combined drawers with cupboard doors. This variety was usually geometrically panelled and inlaid with ivory and was further decorated with applied pendants and bosses (281). By around 1680–1685 the last trace of evolution from the chest had entirely disappeared and the entire façade was designed with drawers. A rather early form of chest of drawers consisted of two rows of drawers mounted on a low stand, which was supported on S-scroll shaped legs joined with a flat, shaped stretcher (289). Veneered walnut chests of drawers, usually consisting of four rows of graduated long drawers mounted on straight bracket feet, were most fashionable. The drawers were frequently enriched with a border band of veneer and in some of the ambitious examples the top, sides and drawers were decorated with a floral marquetry of various colored woods (288). The oak chest of drawers was simply decorated with geometrical panels and usually rested on ball or straight bracket feet.

Dressers   The dresser is of early origin. It was known during medieval times, when the name was generally applied to an open framework of shelves used to display the owner's fine plate, such as silver cups, flagons and tankards. The distinction between a cupboard and a dresser was never too clearly made in early English times. After the Restoration the term *dresser* was usually applied to a long, shallow, oblong body fitted with a row of drawers, which rested on spirally turned or baluster turned legs. The legs were occasionally joined with a continuous floor stretcher which was later discarded. Sometimes there were more than two legs across the front; the two back legs were always quadrangular and plain. It was usually made of oak and the drawers were decorated with geometrical panels. Variations in design and in decoration sometimes occurred. At this time it was generally designed without a superstructure of shelves, although it is probable that shelves were sometimes secured to it. The oak dresser was gradually superseded in wealthy homes by the long walnut side table. The dresser continued to be made along traditional English lines for country use, and in the 18th century was usually designed with a superstructure of shelves.

Cupboards   The three-tiered oak court cupboard and the hall and parlor cupboard with a canted front resting on a stand, which were introduced during the Elizabethan style, were made throughout the Late Jacobean style. These two varieties generally lacked the fine quality of workmanship both in form and in carved decoration which had characterized the Elizabethan examples. They usually had turned baluster supports and were decorated with flat carving. They were largely supplanted early in the 18th century in the more important homes by long side tables and alcove cupboards (311) built into the panelling of the dining room.

After the Restoration the oak hall and parlor cupboard having the upper and lower portions fitted with cupboard doors was no longer used in the more fashionable houses. It was made by the village cabinetmaker along traditional English lines until early in the 18th century, when it was gradually supplanted by the popular farmhouse dresser, with its superstructure of shelves.

The large oak cupboard usually called a press or wardrobe displayed little change. It was tall, rectangular and massive, and was fitted with two long cupboard doors beneath which was a row of two drawers. It was simply panelled and was sometimes further decorated with flat carving of a coarse quality. Occasionally for the wealthy home the wardrobe was made of veneered walnut and was decorated with floral marquetry.

Bookcases   The development of the bookcase as a domestic piece of furniture is difficult to trace before the Restoration. The chest had generally served as a receptacle for books. Early bookcases were built into the wall panelling of the room. The movable bookcase was exceedingly rare until the 18th century. One early movable bookcase dating from around 1665 was fitted with glazed doors. It was rectangular and double-bodied. The upper portion, which was about three-fourths of its entire length, was fitted with two glazed doors. The slightly projecting lower body was fitted with two glazed doors and rested on ball feet.

Clocks   It is doubtful if the domestic clock was known much before the 16th century. The earliest domestic clock was driven by weights and was of the hanging variety. It required adequate space beneath the mechanism for the fall of the weights and it was generally a fixed clock and was large in size. Shortly after 1500 the domestic clock driven by springs was devised. It was first made on the Continent and was later imported into England. The spring-driven clock resulted in a compact chamber clock. This spring-driven clock in a metal case did not remain in fashion in England for any great length of time. The majority of English domestic clocks from the time of Queen Elizabeth I until the last quarter of the 17th century were weight driven. They were enclosed in a metal case, usually of brass, and were hung against the wall or set upon a wall bracket with the chains and weights exposed and hanging down. This early clock in England was known as a lantern or bird-cage clock. The introduction of the pendulum as a regulator marked a most important development in the science of measuring time. It is generally accepted that the first pendulum clock was made in Venice around the middle of the 17th century. With the introduction of the pendulum the clock assumed a different character. It resulted in the designing of the tall case clock which extended to the floor. The long case was originally designed to protect the weights from any outside interference. The tall case clock rapidly gained importance as a decorative article of furniture, and the cabinetmaker expended all his skill in decorating the case. The average height of the tall case clock was between six and one half and seven feet. The hood, enclosing the movement of the clock, was flanked by turned colonnettes and was surmounted by a frieze and molded cornice. The slightly projecting hood rested on the long trunk, which was fitted with a door. The trunk was mounted on a slightly projecting base. The early case clock was usually panelled and veneered with walnut. The more elaborate examples were decorated with floral marquetry and oysterwood parquetry.

After the short pendulum was introduced in England in 1658 small clocks of the so-called bracket or table variety were made in ever-increasing numbers. One principal variety around 1680 had a square-fronted squat case with a domed top either of wood or of pierced metal. The domed top was fitted with a metal handle in order to facilitate carrying it about. The case was usually of ebony or walnut and was decorated with elaborately pierced mounts of brass. It was mounted on small feet. This variety with some variations in design was produced throughout the 18th century and early 19th century and was decorated in the contemporary taste. Later models sometimes had a finial in place of the metal handle. It is said that the name is derived from the fact that some of the later 18th century models had separate brackets designed with the clock to be attached to the wall for the reception of the clock.

Mirrors   Mirrors were introduced from the Continent and after the Restoration they began to figure prominently in the decorative scheme of a room. The hanging mirror frame was essentially rectangular and was hung vertically. One variety of frame was carved in the manner of Grinling Gibbons. It was decorated with festoons of flowers and fruits, foliated scrolls, birds, drapes and cherubs. Other frames were made of veneered walnut and were decorated with floral marquetry. Especially striking and colorful were the lacquered frames and also rather unusual and interesting were the frames covered with gros point needlework or with a frame of stump needlework enclosed with tortoise-shell moldings.

CHAPTER FIFTEEN

WILLIAM & MARY

The study of the various styles of furniture in different countries is particularly interesting because each style mirrors the tastes, the character and the habits of those who designed it and made it and of those who used it. Each one of the great and acknowledged styles of furniture has marked characteristics peculiar to itself and represents the mode of presenting a design in a given period. The same motifs are often used in the different styles but they vary in manner and treatment according to the prevailing dictates of fashion. For example, the shell motif interpreted in a Baroque manner is different from the shell motif interpreted in a Rococo manner. A style of furniture in any given period truthfully and artistically interprets the prevailing manner of expression. As one style supersedes another there is a time of transition until the ornament and principles of design conform. The ornament which is most readily understood appears first. For that reason, around 1760 in France we find ornament in the Neo-Classic taste on furniture of Rococo form designed with cabriole legs. Gradually the ornament is perfected and the forms for furniture are designed in the new fashion and are completely controlled by that style. A true style always reflects in its manner of presentation the spirit of the period to which it belongs, whether it is in furniture, ceramics, silver or some other branch of the decorative arts. Because of its close relationship to the domestic requirements of a community furniture especially reflects the general habits of a society. The more ambitious and elegant articles of furniture were always made for the aristocracy and for the wealthy classes. These pieces expressed in their ornament and design the ultra mode of that particular fashion. The less affluent classes used furniture of similar design but treated in a more simplified manner. Much of the extant 17th and 18th century cabinetwork belongs to this latter category of which undoubtedly more was originally made.

The William and Mary style, 1689–1702, which is the second of the two picturesque English Baroque fashions of the 17th century, was largely under foreign tutelage. The two outstanding influences were Dutch and French, with the former paramount. The close commercial, political and social relationships which existed between England and Holland during part of the 16th century and the 17th century naturally led to a continuous and general interchange of ideas between these two seafaring countries. In a time of political confluence, as in the reign of William and Mary, these ties were more intensified. During this era English cabinetwork in veneered and solid walnut developed along almost parallel lines with contemporary Dutch work. Many of the veneered large pieces, such as chests of drawers and cabinets, were enriched with marquetry, which was favored in Holland. In the succeeding reign of Queen Anne the English cabinetmaker altered and improved these designs according to English tastes, and in so doing he made these articles of furniture, such as the popular Dutch model hoop-back chair, distinctively English. Although Dutch influence persisted in England as long as walnut remained the fashionable wood for cabinetwork, the influence was less pronounced from around 1700. The Dutch influence was also reinforced by the migration of Dutch craftsmen who were attracted by the prosperity in England. Included in that group was the celebrated cabinetmaker to the Royal Household, Gerreit Jensen, 1680–1715, who was of Flemish and Dutch origin. His activities extended over the reigns of Charles II, William and Mary and Queen Anne. He was a craftsman of rare skill and it seems from the Royal Household accounts that he decorated much of his furniture with marquetry and lacquer. Apparently he was the only craftsman in England at that time using the Boulle technique of decorating cabinetwork with a marquetry of metal and tortoise shell. Even in architecture the Dutch fashions were apparent under William III in the numerous houses made of red brick, the use of which was so typically Dutch.

During the reign of William and Mary a fuller French influence was apparent than in the preceding style. This was undoubtedly due to the fact that under Louis XIV all the arts were strongly organized and developed, and, as a result, France became a center of great activity and dissemination in all branches of the arts. Her influence continued to affect England and the other European countries to a greater or less extent throughout the 18th century. An impetus to the French influence in England was provided by the immigration of highly skilled Huguenot craftsmen who fled France after the Revocation of the Edict of Nantes in 1685. Undoubtedly the most celebrated of these Huguenot refugees was Daniel Marot, French architect, furniture designer and engraver of ornament, who sought refuge in Holland and later came to England in 1694. Marot's designs were based on the style of Louis XIV and his later work showed a blending of Dutch and French designs. He was taken into the service of William of Orange, who appointed him his chief architect, and later he followed him to England when he became King William III. It has not been definitely ascertained whether he worked on the interior decoration of Hampton Court Palace or not. However, the interior decoration and much of the furniture bear unmistakable traces of certain features characteristic of his engraved designs and arrangements. The corner chimneypieces surmounted with tiers of shelves, mirrors, sconces and the formal beds at the palace strongly mirrored Marot's style. It may be that he furnished the drawings to some of the French craftsmen working on the interior decorations for the palace whose names appear in the Royal Household accounts. Regardless of whether Marot did or did not work on the palace, his books of engraved designs exerted wide influence on contemporary English taste and he was undoubtedly responsible for introducing into England new forms and style of ornament from abroad. In fact, it is permissible to say that he practically founded a school. The prevailing characteristics of his style were splendor and elaboration. His designs for furniture were remarkable for their lavish display of Louis XIV Baroque motifs. Marot's work shows that he was an artist of rare capability and that he had thoroughly mastered the principles of French design. He left England to return to Holland some time during or after the year 1698. Marot, who was born in Paris around 1662, died in Holland around 1752.

The furniture of the William and Mary period may be divided into several categories. The English royalty and aristocracy had their furniture designed and decorated in the style of Louis XIV. This elaborately carved and gilded furniture was majestic and magnificent. The chairs and settees were finely upholstered, generally in imported cut silk velvets or brocaded damasks. Also included in the elegant cabinetwork were such articles of furniture as cabinets and chests of drawers veneered in walnut and skillfully decorated with delicate seaweed or arabesque marquetry. Lacquered furniture, either imported from the East or decorated in

England in imitation of the Oriental lacquer, composed another important group. Contemporary with the gilded, marquetry and lacquered furniture was a large quantity of plain, well-designed useful furniture generally made of veneered and solid walnut and in some instances of oak. This furniture was chiefly designed for the prosperous middle class who could not afford the more ambitious and richly decorated pieces of cabinetwork. It included such articles as bureaux, side tables, various small tables, chests of drawers, cabinets, stools, chairs and settees. Turned legs were substituted on this furniture for the richly molded, capped and carved tapering quadrangular pillar legs which were characteristic of the Louis XIV style, and shaped stretchers of X-form were substituted for the elaborate Louis XIV style X-form stretchers made of four consoles or brackets with a scroll-shaped profile. The furniture was well proportioned and its simplicity and restraint were a welcome change from the florid Baroque treatment of the preceding Carolean style. Finally, there was the oak furniture still constructed and decorated according to traditional English methods. Such oak furniture had largely been relegated to the more humble surroundings of the farmhouse and cottage. It was made chiefly in the outlying districts by the village cabinetmakers. Its carved and inlaid (if any) decoration was coarse and had little or no artistic merit. Included among the oak pieces of furniture were the tridarn cupboards, court cupboards, settles, stools, benches, chairs and chests.

Furniture remained essentially rectilinear during the William and Mary style. However, there was a pronounced tendency to introduce more curvilinear lines in the contours. This was discernible in the frequent appearance of certain features in design, such as the hooded and double hooded top outlined by a boldly molded cornice on the secretary cabinets, the valanced apron on tables, the shaping of the top of the upholstered chair backs and settees and the curved or serpentine shape of the X-form stretchers. The hooded top, either in a single or double arch, outlined in a boldly molded cornice, was adopted in the last decade of the 17th century and was chiefly employed on the secretary cabinet. An important milestone in chair design occurred around 1700 when the shaped or spooned chair back designed to fit a person's back and having a splat extending to or almost to the seat rail was introduced. Early in the reign of William and Mary the straight leg was revived and it almost completely superseded the scroll-shaped leg introduced in the preceding style. The molded and fluted tapering quadrangular pillar leg with its boldly gadrooned capital was typical of the Louis XIV style. In England turning was generally substituted for the elaborately capped and carved French leg. The wide flaring capital was turned in the form of an inverted cup and the tapering leg was turned in the form of a vase or trumpet. In addition to this tapering trumpet or vase-shaped leg, baluster turned and columnar turned supports were also favored. Sometimes the leg was spirally turned as in the preceding Carolean style. The leg commonly terminated in a ball or bun foot, and occasionally in a scrolled Spanish foot.

The cabriole leg was in the process of evolution during the reign of William III. It is generally accepted that this distinctive form of leg originated in China. It seems that the word *cabriole*, which is a French dancing term meaning a leap, was taken from the Italian word *capriola* meaning a goat's leap. The leg is a decorative form of a four-footed animal's front leg from the knee downward. The top curves outward as a knee and then curves inward toward the lower part just above the foot where it curves outward again and forms the foot. The cabriole leg has the contour of a cyma curve with the convex part at the top. It was introduced in French furniture late in the Louis XIV style. This early cabriole leg terminated in a cloven hoof foot or pied de biche. It was introduced in England from the Continent around 1700 and for the next fifty years all the fashionable furniture, both on the Continent and in England, was designed with a cabriole leg. In England the cabriole leg most frequently terminated in a claw-and-ball foot and in France in a French whorl foot. Due to the vogue for Gothic and Chinese ornament and detail in England from around 1750 to 1760 the straight leg supplanted the cabriole leg in some of the cabinetwork. However, the cabriole leg continued to be used on furniture designed in the French taste. As a result of Adam's influence the cabriole leg was generally discarded around 1770 in favor of the straight leg based on the style of Louis XVI. Nevertheless Hepplewhite and his school occasionally employed the cabriole leg on a few fashionable models, such as chairs, designed in the French taste. A decidedly attenuated cabriole leg persisted longest in France on the very small occasional table.

From the time of the Restoration there was evident an ever-increasing appreciation for Chinese porcelain, lacquer work, embroideries and all kinds of Chinese bibelots, such as carved ivories, jades and bronzes. Advertisements appeared in the English newspapers late in the 17th century announcing the arrival of porcelain and lacquer wares, proving the demand for these articles. The reign of William and Mary was marked by a mania for collecting porcelain. This fashion came to England from Holland, and Queen Mary with her enormous collection of Chinese porcelain and Delft faïence was particularly instrumental in developing this taste in England. After Queen Mary died in 1694 the inventory of the contents at Kensington Palace reveals that in the Garden Room alone there were 143 pieces of Chinese porcelain displayed on shelves above the chimneypieces and above the doors. This manner of arranging porcelain was shown in one of Marot's designs. In addition to the tiered shelves, brackets were also fashionable for displaying porcelain. China cabinets with glazed doors and hanging corner cupboards became more numerous. Lacquered articles also enjoyed great popularity. Practically every home of any importance had an Oriental or English lacquered cabinet mounted on a stand. The English lacquering or japanning was more often the raised variety rather than the Chinese incised or cut variety. Another interesting feature resulting from the contact with the Orient was the custom of drinking tea. This, although not entirely new, became an accepted social custom during the reign of William and Mary. In the ensuing century tables especially designed for serving tea were introduced and the tea caddy, for containing the tea, became a distinctive and decorative English accessory.

Apart from the direct influence of imported wares was the more diffused interest in the Orient to which can be attributed the fantastic European chinoiseries. These fanciful compositions depicting an imaginary world of pseudo-Chinese figures and scenes became fashionable as a decoration in all branches of the decorative arts. Motifs drawn from a Chinese fairy-tale world were employed on lacquered woodwork, furniture, silver, pottery, wallpaper and on cotton and linen prints. Their origin was due to the influence of imported Chinese wares and also to the travel books, largely Dutch, purporting to portray the life and habits of the Chinese, published around the third quarter of the 17th century. Numerous engravings by Peter Schenck of Amsterdam and several German houses inspired some of the earlier chinoiseries in the late Baroque taste. Pseudo-Chinese figures appear in rich Baroque compositions in some of the late 17th century designs of Daniel Marot. Jean Bérain, the French designer and engraver of ornament, was instrumental in developing the taste for chinoiseries in France in the Baroque style. Chinoiseries in the Rococo taste were principally attributed to the French school of decorative designers led by François Boucher. The vogue for chinoiseries was not as consistently developed in England as on the Continent. After Queen Mary's death the inventory for Kensington Palace shows that practically all the furniture in her bedroom was decorated with "India Japan" and included chests of drawers, corner cupboards and screens. The term *India* or *Indian*, which was often used to describe anything pertaining to both China and Japan, undoubtedly had its origin in the name of the various East Indian importing companies.

Marquetry, veneering and lacquering were particularly favored as decorative processes for ornamenting the surface of furniture in the reign of William and Mary. Carving was used less frequently than in the preceding style. The florid leaf carving, which had characterized the Carolean style, was seldom employed, and the walnut frames were not as over-elaborated with carved detail. Carving, however, was much in evidence in the gilded court furniture inspired by the contemporary Louis XIV style. The carved decoration on these gilt wood chairs, settees, side tables and decorative accessories was in the taste of Daniel Marot. During the William and Mary style turning was extensively employed and was a favorite substitute for carving. Turned supports were generally employed on the veneered and solid walnut furniture and on the cabinetwork decorated with marquetry and parquetry. Especially praiseworthy was the seaweed or arabesque marquetry, which was so fashionable during this era and which superseded the Carolean floral marquetry. This type of marquetry was principally found on oblong cabinets, chests of drawers, tall case clocks and small decorative tables. It consisted of an over-all design of minute delicate scrolls cut from box or holly and laid in a veneered walnut ground. Seaweed marquetry represented the culmination of the marquetry cutter's skill, and it is generally considered to be the finest of all English marquetry.

Richly figured veneered walnut surfaces were a distinctive and meritorious feature of William and Mary cabinetwork. Cross-bandings and herringbone banded borders were employed on the fronts of drawers and other flat surfaces and provided an interesting contrast to the veneered surface.

Cross-bandings, which are border bands of veneer inlaid transversely to the grain in the main surface, were introduced in the preceding reign of Charles II and were used to a greater or less extent throughout the 18th century. The veneered herringbone border, which produced a herringbone or feathered effect, was made by placing together two strips of veneer with the grain of each running diagonally. Parquetry and oystering were also used to decorate the veneered surface of cabinets, tables and other similar articles. Needlework was especially characteristic of the age of walnut, when the tall backs of chairs and settees gave ample surface for displaying elaborate designs. Some of the finest needlework was made during the reigns of William and Mary and Queen Anne, such as the fine floral designs enclosing panels of landscapes and stories from mythology. These ambitious figure subject pieces were generally omitted under the succeeding Georgian kings. The Baroque ornament during the reign of William and Mary was more refined than in the preceding style, with many of the fashionable motifs being of French origin. The lion motif was occasionally found on some late 17th century cabinetwork of French inspiration. The shell motif, which was introduced from Holland and which was so popular in the succeeding style, was just beginning to be used in England at the end of the 17th century. Included among the favorite motifs were pendants of husks, female masks, acanthus foliage and scrolls, arabesque foliage, ornamental drapes and vase forms.

Chairs   The carved and turned walnut armchair designed with a tall back was less elaborately carved than in the preceding era. The richly scrolled broad front stretcher disappeared on certain models (FIGURE 295). In place of this the four legs were usually joined with a molded serpentine X-form stretcher, often centering a decorative finial (295). The leg varied in design, but from around 1690 it was almost always straight (294, 295), and it tapered from a broad cap or inverted cup-form to a small bun foot (295). Occasionally the straight leg terminated in a Spanish scroll foot (294). A distinctive feature of the chair was the fine meshed caning (294, 295). Frequently the caned back panel was joined to the two uprights (294, 295). A characteristic feature was the elaborately carved and pierced cresting which often surmounted the back of the chair (294, 295). This chair with its half-hoop cresting was often popularly called a periwig chair. It derived its name from the fact that the cresting was designed to provide a flattering background for men's periwigs and ladies' head-dresses, which were unusually high at that time. The finials which surmounted the uprights disappeared toward the end of the century. The arms were scroll-shaped. The chair was also designed as a side chair. Variations occurred both in the form and in the decoration. This tall and narrow cane-back chair was made in the 18th century; however, it was gradually supplanted by newer chair forms.

Some of these chairs dating from the reign of William III were in the taste of Daniel Marot and were distinctive for their elaborate carvings (296). The back panel and cresting were finely carved and pierced with foliage, shells and scrollwork. In some examples the chair had a carved and pierced front stretcher, which was frequently recessed, while other models were designed with inverted cup-turned tapering legs joined with a shaped X-form stretcher centering a finial.

An important development in the evolution of the chair occurred in the reign of William III. Around 1700 curved lines were introduced in place of the former straight lines (297). The uprights were undulating and the chair back was spooned or shaped to a person's back (297). A shoulder was formed on the uprights which merged into the cresting and nearly resembled a hoop shape (297). The outline of the carved and pierced splat more or less suggested a vase (297). The cabriole leg was introduced and it terminated in a cloven hoof foot or pied de biche (297). Stretchers were still employed. In some examples the splat for the first time joined the seat rail. In the following reign of Queen Anne these changes in chair design were further developed and improved, resulting in the characteristic Queen Anne splat-back chair.

The upholstered walnut armchair with open arms and with a high rectangular raked back, which had been introduced in the Charles II era, remained fashionable in the subsequent William and Mary style. As a rule, as in the preceding era, the well-padded and upholstered back extended almost to the seat rail. The inverted cup-turned tapering legs which terminated in bun feet were joined with a molded serpentine X-form stretcher, often centering a finial. The arms were scroll-shaped. The back and seat were upholstered in a rich fabric. The chair was also designed without arms. Sometimes the upholstered back of the chair had an arched or shaped top in place of the earlier straight top and towards the end of the century the front of the upholstered seat was often shaped or valanced.

Stools   Stools were still used in large quantities. Essentially the stool and the bench were similar in form and in decoration to the chair. The seat was usually upholstered and finished with fringe. The rectangular stool was the prevailing form, although some circular stools were also designed. The long bench was generally designed with eight inverted cup-turned tapering legs, joined with molded serpentine X-form stretchers, each one of the three centers often being ornamented with a finial.

Settees   The upholstered settee during William and Mary reflected a diversity of designs. Several types of backs were in vogue. The back shaped and divided into typical chair form was the prevailing type (298). There was also the straight back with the chair form omitted and the elaborately shaped back, also made without division, the latter being relatively rare. The back of the settee was always high and it was designed either with or without the high projecting wings. The typical upholstered settee was divided into two shaped chair backs, the closed arms being outscrolled (298). The six legs were joined with serpentine X-form stretchers, each one of the two stretchers centering an ornamental finial (298). When the settee was of greater length it was supported on a stretchered frame with eight legs.

Beds   The richly draped bed (299, 300), with its framework entirely covered in silk fabric, was an imposing and sumptuous piece of late 17th century furniture. Especially remarkable were the lavish beds in the Baroque style inspired by the designs of Daniel Marot (300). The cornice of the tester was frequently surmounted with an ornately carved and pierced cresting of arabesque foliage (300).

Day Beds   The form of the day bed revealed little difference from that of the preceding style. The back rest slanted outward and was permanently fixed. The seat and back rest were well padded and upholstered. It was supported on a stretchered frame with eight legs. Tapered legs gradually supplanted the scroll-shaped legs.

Tables   The dining table essentially remained the same as in the preceding style. The principal variety had a round or oval top. It was made of oak or walnut and was generally of gate-leg construction.

The long ornate side table of carved gilt wood was designed in the contemporary French taste. It was characterized by tapered pillar legs with gadrooned capitals, an elaborately scrolled and carved openwork apron and a richly carved X-form stretcher. The small side table was also designed in the same ornate French Baroque style. The greater number of side tables both large and small were of walnut. The small walnut side table was either plain, or was decorated with marquetry. Occasionally it was decorated with lacquer work. It usually had a frieze drawer. The small side table designed "en suite" with a mirror and a pair of candlestands or guéridons was extremely popular.

The small table designed to stand in the middle of the room was decorated in the prevailing fashion. The small ornate table of carved and gilt wood essentially followed the Louis XIV style (301). The small and plain table with turned supports enjoyed a great vogue and served a variety of purposes, such as for tea, writing and needlework. This table made of walnut or oak had a rectangular top over a straight or valanced frieze (302) which was often fitted with a drawer. Frequently there was a detail in the turning of each tapered leg resembling an inverted cup (302). The legs were commonly mounted on bun feet and joined with a flat, shaped X-form stretcher (302). One popular variety provided with a tray top was probably used for needlework or tea (302). The small table was also designed in the gate-leg variety. One characteristic form of gate-leg construction had a hinged circular or rectangular folding top, which when opened was supported by double gate-legs (303). This apparently was a popular table for card playing. The top when open frequently had a velvet panel inset.

Toilet Tables   The toilet table (304) as a characteristic piece of furniture was introduced late in the 17th century. Prior to that time it is difficult to ascertain the nature of the toilet table. One variety was completely covered in elaborate draperies. Around 1690, when the swinging toilet mirror on a box stand became fashionable, a table made of walnut and sometimes of oak was designed to stand against the wall. The rectangular top rested on a valanced apron fitted with a row of drawers (304). The four or six turned tapering legs were joined with a shaped X-form stretcher and were mounted on bun feet (304). Variations in design occurred. This type of dressing table or side table is called a lowboy in America, the word *lowboy* being purely an American term. The design for this variety of table essentially followed the design for the stand fitted with drawers upon which a chest of drawers was mounted and which is called a highboy in America.

Stands   The candlestand or torchère toward the end of the century was often richly ornamented in accordance with the style of Louis XIV. It was frequently made of carved gilt wood. One principal variety of walnut candlestand had a molded octagonal top supported on a carved and tapered shaft, which rested on a carved and scrolled tripod base.

*Writing
Furniture*

Writing furniture developed several new forms. The walnut bureau and writing table were found in many English homes by the end of the 17th century. The early form of the slant-front desk during the William and Mary era was mounted on legs. It was sometimes decorated with seaweed marquetry, although more commonly it was plain and was made from solid or veneered walnut. One form of slant-front desk was on a gate-leg frame. The shallow slant-front desk with its hinged flap was over a frieze with lateral drawers, which was supported on four baluster tapered front legs and two rear legs. When the slant-front was let down it rested on the two center front legs which swung outward. The interior was fitted with pigeonholes and small drawers. When the slant-front was closed the two pivoted legs fitted into the frieze. In another variety slides were provided in place of the gate-legs to support the hinged writing board. The exterior of the slant-front was sometimes provided with a book ledge in order to support a book. Around 1700 the legs were supplanted by a series of superimposed drawers, comprising a row of two small drawers over three graduated long drawers. It was mounted on a bracket base or ball feet. This slant-front bureau or desk was usually made of veneered walnut and frequently the drawers were inlaid with a feather or herringbone banding.

The secretary cabinet or bureau cabinet (307), which is a form of double-bodied writing furniture, was introduced late in the 17th century. The upper section was designed as a cabinet and the lower section as a slant-front bureau (307). The upper portion, which was fitted with two doors and opened to reveal a series of small drawers and compartments, rested on the narrow shelf at the top of the slant-front bureau (307). The lower portion was designed with a hinged slant-front over a row of one or two narrow drawers and three graduated long drawers (307). The slant-front opened to an interior of pigeonholes and small drawers (307). Variations in design sometimes occurred. For example, in place of the slant-front it was occasionally designed with a long false drawer, which could be pulled out and the hinged front of the drawer could be let down to serve as a writing flap. This false drawer was fitted with pigeonholes and small drawers. During the time of William and Mary the secretary cabinet was usually either lacquered (307) or made of veneered walnut. It was mounted on ball (307) or straight bracket feet. The characteristic feature of the secretary cabinet designed in the William and Mary style was the boldly molded double-hooded or double-arched and sometimes double flat-arched (307) cornice. The cabinet doors were sometimes fitted with bevelled mirror panels.

The term *secretary bookcase* or *bureau bookcase* is usually reserved for a similar piece of writing furniture which has the upper section fitted with adjustable shelves for books. Later, the secretary bookcase was always fitted with glazed doors. Such a piece was rare until after the middle of the 18th century.

The walnut oblong fall-front writing cabinet of the William and Mary period generally rested on a chest of drawers, mounted on ball or straight bracket feet. The frieze of the cabinet was frequently fitted with a pulvinar drawer. The more ambitious examples were sometimes decorated with seaweed marquetry or oysterwood parquetry.

A popular form of writing table (308) had a rectangular folding top on an arcaded and stretchered gate-leg frame. The two center front turned legs swung out to support the folding top when opened.

During the William and Mary period the kneehole form of writing table was introduced (306). The typical kneehole writing table had a flat oblong top, over a long drawer, which surmounted a recessed center cupboard flanked by two sets of three and occasionally four drawers each (306). The deeply recessed center compartment was so designed to accommodate the knees of the writer. Each set of drawers rested on either four ball or four straight bracket feet (306).

Cabinets   The demand for oblong lacquered cabinets (308) increased toward the close of the 17th century. The lacquered cabinet around 1690 often exhibited finer detail and less raised work than the Charles II examples. The cabinet, as in the preceding era, had ajouré or pierced brass hinges, lock plates and matching angle mounts. This brasswork represented the highest quality of contemporary English metal work. The cabinet was usually mounted on a richly carved and gilt wood stand decorated in the French taste (308). Especially typical of the Louis XIV style were the molded, capped and carved tapering quadrangular pillar legs and the X-form stretchers made of four carved and molded consoles or brackets with a scroll-shaped profile arranged in an arched manner (308). Around 1700 another form of lacquered cabinet was introduced. In this later type the cabinet was mounted on a lacquered chest of drawers. The cabinet section had a double-hooded or double-arched top outlined by a boldly molded cornice, over two conformingly shaped panelled doors.

The oblong walnut cabinet, mounted on a chest of drawers or on a stand, was fitted with two doors, above which were a pulvinar frieze and cornice (310). The two cabinet doors opened to an interior of small drawers, doors and secret compartments. The stand was fitted with a row of frieze drawers and was mounted on four, five or six legs joined with a shaped and flat stretcher, resting on bun feet (310). The legs were sometimes S-scrolled in form (310), as in the preceding Carolean style. The luxury examples were often decorated in seaweed marquetry (310).

The walnut china cabinet, with its two glazed doors, was usually mounted on a chest of drawers. Occasionally the china cabinet rested on a stand, fitted with a frieze drawer. It was mounted on bun feet. The china cabinet was sometimes decorated with arabesque foliage marquetry.

Chests   The lacquered chest either imported from the East or made in England was a popular piece of furniture. It was commonly mounted on a low, carved and gilt wood stand. One variety of lacquered chest had a domed lid and was often mounted on bracket feet. There was still considerable demand for the oak or walnut chest. In the large households it was used for storage and in the farmhouse it still served many purposes. The chest was usually fitted with a row of drawers in the base and was mounted on ball feet.

Chests of   The chest of drawers during the reign of William and Mary was
Drawers   principally made of walnut. One characteristic variety of walnut chest of drawers had an oblong molded top over a row of two small drawers and three graduated long drawers. It was mounted on either ball or straight bracket feet. In the more ambitious examples the top, drawers and sides were often enriched with cartouches of arabesque marquetry. Contemporary with the marquetry examples were the lacquered chests of drawers. Veneered walnut chests of drawers were much in demand. Occasionally the veneering was further enhanced with an inlay of lines of holly or boxwood worked in simple geometrical patterns. As a rule geometrical moldings constituted the only decoration on the oak chest of drawers.

The chest of drawers mounted on a stand was introduced around 1680 (312). As a rule it was seldom more than five feet in height, which made the top drawers easily accessible. Unfortunately, this feature of accessibility was lost in the later tallboys. Chests of drawers mounted on a stand were made into the early years of the 18th century, and the earlier turned legs were replaced by four legs of cabriole form. The stretcher also disappeared. As a rule the chest of drawers mounted on a stand had a flat oblong molded top. The arrangement of drawers in the stand varied.

The tallboy or chest-on-chest or double chest of drawers was introduced around 1700. Both chests of drawers were of conforming design with the upper chest slightly narrower. The upper section was designed with a row of two or three small drawers over three or four graduated long drawers. The slightly projecting lower section consisted of three or four long drawers and usually rested on bracket feet. The double chest of drawers retained its popularity until around the middle of the 18th century, when other forms of bedroom furniture, such as the clothespress, were introduced. However, some demand for these tallboys continued throughout the second half of the 18th century.

Cupboards   The oak court cupboard with its three tiers of shelves was gradually superseded in fashionable homes by the long side table, which served as a sideboard table.

The hall and parlor cupboard, like the court cupboard, was no longer found in the fashionable homes, although it was still made and used in the outlying districts. One variety of oak cupboard which was of Welsh and Welsh Border origin was called a tridarn or three section cupboard. This variety of cupboard was introduced in the second half of the 17th century and with slight variations was made throughout the 18th century. It was essentially similar to the hall and parlor cupboard designed with a closed upper portion and a closed lower portion. The tridarn cupboard had an additional third section which surmounted the closed upper portion. This additional section consisted of a canopy which rested on a turned or carved support at each front corner. The back was panelled and occasionally the sides were also panelled. The additional shelf space formed by the canopy was used for the display of pewter vessels. The middle section had two turned pendants in place of the two front supports and the three panelled doors were straight. The tridarn cupboard was simply decorated along traditional English lines.

The earliest form of corner cupboard was of the hanging variety, its average height being about four feet. The hanging cupboard was freely used during the time of William and Mary as a receptacle for porcelain. It was usually decorated with lacquer work. The top of the cupboard was often surmounted with a boldly molded hooded or arched cornice in accordance with the taste of the period.

The large oak cupboard usually called a press or wardrobe was essentially similar to the wardrobe of the preceding style. It usually had two long cupboard doors and a row of drawers in the base.

Clocks   The cases for many of the fine English tall case clocks after 1685 were designed and decorated by French Huguenot craftsmen. The tall case clocks with arabesque marquetry were especially outstanding. The preeminent position held by England in the history of horological art for about one hundred years beginning with the last quarter of the 17th century is generally credited to Thomas Tompion, 1638–1713, celebrated English clock and watch maker. He was clock maker to Charles II and was the maker of many fine clocks for William III. Several important inventions are credited to him. He made some of the first watches with balanced springs. The work which Tompion so ably began was carried on by his immediate successors. Especially noteworthy was the work of Daniel Quare whose reputation in the art of horology is second only to that of Tompion's. He made an outstanding contribution to horological art by producing a clock with a one-year time piece. One of these clocks is a tall case clock which he made in 1705 and which is in Hampton Court Palace.

Mirrors　　　　Carved and gilt wood wall mirrors were very fashionable in the late 17th century. The top of the frame was usually arched and was surmounted with an elaborate and perforated cresting. The mirror was sometimes enclosed in a border of glass, bevelled and framed in a carved gilt molding. Due to the increased height, the mirror was often made in two or more plates. The mirror frames were distinctive for their fanciful style of ornamentation which was often of French inspiration.

The dressing table mirror or toilet mirror was not in general use until late in the 17th century. The principal type was the mirror in the silver toilet set which came into fashion after the Restoration. The mirror was enclosed in a silver frame and was supported by a brace. The frame essentially followed the shape and style of ornament of the contemporary wall mirror. Some of the finest silver toilet sets were made by Huguenot refugees. Around 1700 the swinging toilet mirror on a box stand was introduced (309). The mirror was enclosed in a frame which was attached to two uprights by swivel screws (309). The uprights were secured to a stand which often resembled a miniature bureau (309). The stand was designed with a slant-front, which opened to an interior of small drawers, over a long drawer (309). The toilet mirror and stand were usually veneered or decorated with lacquer or marquetry work. The average height was about three feet and the width about one foot and six inches.

Accessories　　　The detachable wall bracket was used as a ledge or shelf for the support of some object such as a clock, vase, bust or candelabrum. The bracket did not come into general use until the time of William and Mary, when it was chiefly used to display porcelain. It was made in all sizes and was usually painted or gilded. During William and Mary, as well as in the succeeding reigns, it was elaborately carved with the prevailing French motifs. Especially distinctive were some of the ornate brackets decorated in the style of Daniel Marot. Marot made many remarkable designs for wall brackets enriched with Baroque ornament and freely introduced their use into rooms for accommodating porcelains.

Crudely constructed hanging shelves for books were known as early as the Middle Ages. Hanging oak shelves for domestic use were made in the 16th century; however, it was not until William and Mary that shelves came into general use. The vogue for hanging shelves was largely due to the mania for collecting Oriental porcelain. Hanging shelves were designed and decorated in the prevailing fashion. Marot made many designs for elaborately decorated hanging shelves in the Baroque style.

Sconces were known on the Continent by the beginning of the 16th century. Until late in the 17th century wall sconces in England were made of metal. During William and Mary sconces were often gilded and were elaborately carved and decorated with characteristic French motifs. Contemporary with the carved and gilt wood sconces were the metal sconces having the back plates fitted with mirrors. Sconces were an important decorative appointment and craftsmen devoted much time to their designs for sconces and to the execution of these designs.

The tall hinged or folding type of screen did not come into general use until after the Restoration, when the lacquered screens were imported in large quantities from the Orient. Sometimes panels of rich fabric were used in place of the lacquer panels. Some of the large folding types were composed of twelve panels.

The cheval fire screen was introduced in England from the Continent after the Restoration. This variety of fire screen is composed of a decorative vertical upright frame resting on short arched supports. The frame encloses an ornamental panel generally made from a rich and colorful fabric. The panel slides in grooves on the inner side of the uprights; however, in some examples the panel was fixed. During William and Mary the cheval fire screen was made with an elaborately carved frame of gilt wood. The top of the frame was generally surmounted with an ornately carved and pierced cresting. Another variety of fire screen was the pole screen having a small rectangular or shaped frame which was fitted with a fabric panel and which was attached to a pole or rod. The pole was usually mounted on a tripod base. The framed panel could be adjusted to any height on the pole. The pole screen did not come into general use until the first half of the 18th century.

The spoon rack was probably first used in the time of Queen Elizabeth I. The oak spoon rack was chiefly a utilitarian piece and little thought was given to its design. A principal variety toward the end of the 17th century had a solid wooden back to which were attached two rows of slotted rails for spoons and a box below either with or without a lid for the knives.

The pipe rack was introduced toward the end of the 17th century. It was designed to hold clay tobacco pipes with long slender stems. This type of pipe was popularly called a churchwarden. One common variety of pipe rack designed to stand on a table consisted of a turned shaft which rested on a turned circular base. The shaft was fitted with a disc which was pierced with holes through which the stems of the clay pipes could pass. The base was fitted with one or more spill holders. Another variety was designed to be hung on the wall. It had a solid wooden back to which were attached two rows of slotted rails for the pipes. The bottom was fitted with an open small bin for spills, below which was a drawer for tobacco.

The early spinning wheel consisted of a revolving wheel, supported on a stand, driven by hand or by a foot treadle. The wheel rotated a single spindle on which the yarn was spun. After the wheel with an attached treadle was invented in the second quarter of the 16th century, spinning became a popular occupation for women of all classes. Hand spinning continued as an industry throughout the 18th century. A spinning wheel could be found in almost every English farmhouse and cottage. It was usually constructed of several woods, oak and beech being one of the more frequent combinations. The supports and spindles were baluster turned.

CHAPTER SIXTEEN

QUEEN ANNE & EARLY GEORGIAN

The 18th century is often referred to as the golden age of English cabinetwork. During this century the English cabinetmaker achieved a high standard of technical excellence in his craftsmanship. From the time of the accession of Queen Anne, in 1702, England witnessed a rapid growth and development in her national life. More people had money than ever before, which naturally raised the general standards of domestic comfort and led to the introduction of many new types of furniture. All kinds of furniture for specialized purposes, such as tea tables, card tables and breakfast tables, as well as many new forms for chairs and writing furniture, were introduced from the Continent and were found in the English 18th century home. The century was marked by the introduction of numerous styles of furniture, each one rapidly succeeding the other, in response to the constant demand from the aristocracy for new fashions. The opening years of the 18th century were conspicuous for a wider diffusion of building activity. Many great houses were built throughout England in the Palladian style, as well as many comfortable and functional houses of a less pretentious type, which are known as Queen Anne and Georgian. These houses were suitable for the needs of the middle class. All this activity in building naturally led to a greater demand for furniture and the status of the cabinetmaker was greatly improved. Cabinetmaking became a profitable business which was reflected in the size of many of these establishments. Contemporary records show that these shops employed journeymen, cabinetmakers, chairmakers, upholsterers, glass grinders, makers of frames for mirrors, carvers for chairs and tester posts, workers or smiths for the brass mounts and many other craftsmen connected with the making of furniture. Around the middle of the 18th century such very lucrative and enterprising establishments as Chippendale's also listed in their employment engravers, designers and draftsmen.

By the time of George I Continental travelling and the collecting of works of art had become the fashion among the aristocracy. The so-called Grand Tour was practically a necessity for a young gentleman after he had completed his formal education. France and Italy, and especially Paris and Venice, Florence and Rome, held the greatest allure for the travelled dilettante. Colorful and worldly Venice with her fine Palladian buildings was the playground of Europe. Since these tours often extended over a period of several years, many of these English gentlemen acquired a knowledge of art and architecture, as well as a discriminating taste in collecting, and they frequently qualified as amateur connoisseurs. A knowledge of architecture was an accepted accomplishment among this group. This taste for collecting objects of art, especially classical sculptures, was also extended to include books, which resulted in the formation at this time of some of the great libraries, for a knowledge of classical literature was equally esteemed. Naturally, this interest in the arts and literature influenced the interior planning of a house. The statue gallery in the great Palladian mansions, niches for the reception of busts or bronzes, and libraries with architecturally designed bookcases were all pronounced features of the Early Georgian era.

Italian influence, particularly Venetian, was evident in English architecture from early in the reign of George I. The chief source of inspiration was the works of Palladio, whose books were regarded as the indisputable authority on all rules of taste in architecture. To build in the Palladian manner was considered the last word in fashion. Praise was also showered on the works of Inigo Jones, who had originally introduced the Palladian style in England. In the Palladian treatment the ground floor was the basement and the first or main floor, which became the Italian *piano nobile*, was reached by a flight of steps built on the exterior. Elegant formality rather than comfort was the keynote for the interiors of these Palladian mansions, which were characterized by their lofty proportions and rich materials. The great hall was often of monumental scale, and in one particular mansion the walls for the great hall were fifty feet in height. Some of these halls with their great height, alabaster columns and rich stuccoed decoration were reminiscent of the Italian Baroque style of grandeur. The great hall led to the salon, which was a feature of these houses, borrowed from the Italian *salone*. The arrangement of a line of reception rooms opening out of one another was strictly followed. The state apartments were all on the principal floor, which sometimes comprised as many as nineteen rooms. Venetian windows were introduced by the Palladian architect and were an interesting feature. Stuccoed walls, with much of their modelled classic ornament the work of Italian stucco workers living in England, were almost always found in these Palladian mansions. The quality of these interiors depended upon the capability of the craftsmen to carry out details of Palladian architecture. From around the middle of the 18th century, aside from the influence of these Early Georgian architects, French Rococo, Gothic and Chinese influences also affected the interior decoration. However, the taste for these rapidly changing fashions was generally confined to one room and was chiefly expressed in ornamental detail.

From about the time of the accession

of George I practically all of the wood panelling in a natural finish was done in mahogany and there was very little of that. Early Georgian wood panelling, which was almost always employed only in the smaller houses and not in the Palladian mansions, was generally of pine or deal, the surface being disguised either by painting or graining. The wall was usually arranged into a system of wide panels, which were very often separated by narrow panels. The fashion of hanging pictures in the wide panels and above the chimneypiece and in the over-door panels was still observed. The panels, instead of being applied to the face of the framing, were recessed and the moldings were either plain or carved with such repetitive classic ornament as the egg and dart. This recession of the panels and the more delicate moldings exemplified a return by the Early Georgian architects to the style introduced by Inigo Jones. The shelved recess or cupboard with its pilaster framing was a distinctive feature of the Early Georgian work. After the middle of the 18th century the vogue for walls hung with either silk or paper steadily gained in popularity. And, as a result of this new fashion, wood panelling was less and less employed until finally, by late in the 18th century, it was practically obsolete. Early Georgian pine panelled rooms have always radiated a singular charm of refined gentility. In America, where the English initiative in styles of furniture and architecture was always assiduously observed in the 18th century, if we omit William Kent and most of the work of Robert Adam, wood panelling in the Early Georgian manner was quite common in the first half of the 18th century. Due to the vogue for paper-hung walls during the second half of the 18th century wood-

work was largely discarded. The close similarity existing between the Colonial style in America in architecture and furniture and the current work in England was undoubtedly due to the wide distribution of English architectural publications and handbooks of designs for furniture.

William Kent, 1684–1748, architect, landscape gardener and designer of ornament and furniture, was an important member of the Palladian movement in England. Kent, who was the son of a Yorkshire carriage painter, studied in Rome from around 1710 to 1720, where he attracted the interest of the Earl of Burlington. Through the recommendation of his patron he gained a considerable reputation in England as an architect and decorator. His name is identified with the designing and decorating of a number of the great mansions. From around 1725–30 to 1745 his influence predominated in the furniture designs and decoration for these Palladian mansions. It seems that his chief contribution was that he designed furniture to be an ordered part of the architectural scheme of the interior decoration. He constantly introduced pediments, pilasters and other architectural members in the wall surfaces, over-doors and windows of each room. These same architectural principles he incorporated into his designs for furniture so that they would harmonize with the interiors. This architectural treatment was more pronounced in the wall or stationary pieces, such as massive mahogany bookcases, and also in the massive mahogany library tables of pedestal form. His designs for furniture such as chairs, settees, side tables and consoles were largely treated in a heavy Venetian Baroque manner. This furniture was exuberantly carved and gilded. The forms for much of this furniture were ponderous and heavy with ornament, which was often marred by its cumbrous composition. Very characteristic of his style were the massive gilded side tables with their marble tops and sphinxes and figures of putti used in conjunction with boldly scrolled supports. Swags of fruit or flowers, broadly handled acanthus leaves, pendent shells and lion and human masks were used freely in his repertory of ornament. It must be remembered that this style of Baroque classicism of which Kent was the most prominent exponent was planned for the great Palladian houses and was in harmony with their sumptuous Baroque decoration. Naturally this furniture in its more extravagant form when associated with other styles and in other settings appears incongruous.

Although Dutch influence and the influence of Marot persisted in English cabinetwork as long as walnut remained the fashionable wood, the cabinetwork became more Anglicized from the early years of the 18th century. From early in the second quarter of the 18th century French taste gradually began to dominate the fashionable furniture made in England. French ascendancy in the arts under the Bourbon monarchs influenced to a greater or less extent the style of ornament and the designs for furniture in all the European countries throughout the 18th century. French furniture was first imported into England in any noticeable quantity from around 1715, and this importation continued with little interruption throughout the 18th century. The first two decades of the 18th century revealed a gradual development in English furniture without introducing any striking innovations in furniture design or in ornament. The use of graceful curving lines was characteristic of the Queen Anne style and the cyma curve, which the English painter Hogarth referred to as the "line of beauty," was much in evidence. The straight lines of the William and Mary style had begun to yield to curved lines late in the reign of William III. The development of the Dutch model chair with its vase-shaped splat and cabriole legs was a marked feature of the Queen Anne style. Social customs introduced several new characteristic pieces of furniture, such as the card table. Queen Anne furniture was praiseworthy for its charming simplicity, its fine proportions, its graceful curving lines and its richly figured veneered walnut surfaces. Walnut veneer was so effectively used under Queen Anne that the fine examples of chairs had about the same amount of veneered surface as solid surface, with the carved ornament sometimes being applied. During the first few years following the death of Queen Anne the cabinetmaker continued to produce typical Queen Anne furniture. In fact, it is generally accepted that this style of furniture was made to some extent until around the middle of the century. However, from the accession of George I the development in fashionable furniture was from the plain to the decorated.

The Early Georgian style, which lies between the style of Queen Anne and the Chippendale style, had certain distinctive features. William Kent is particularly associated with one phase of the Early Georgian style. In direct contrast to the furniture designed in the Kent manner was the furniture designed by the Early Georgian cabinetmakers which carried on the traditions inherited from the Queen Anne style. The contour of this furniture remained essentially the same as in the Queen Anne style. The chief differences were in the elaboration of the style of ornament and in the more massive character given to practically all of the pieces. This furniture was found in the less pretentious homes of the prosperous middle class. Another distinctive feature of Early Georgian cabinetwork was the architectural style given to some pieces of furniture. This architectural influence was especially apparent in the massive mahogany bookcases, secretary cabinets and the mahogany library tables of pedestal form. The stiles of the bookcases were generally ornamented with fluted pilasters adorned with Corinthian capitals and the cornices were surmounted with different kinds of pediments, such as a broken pediment, scrolled pediment or triangular pediment. The classic moldings were often carved with repetitive classic ornament, such as the egg and dart. The pronounced architectural influence seen in these imposing articles of furniture indicates the serious interest in architecture taken by the cabinetmaker and also by the well-educated English gentleman during the Early Georgian period. Some of the trade catalogues of furniture designs issued around and after the middle of the 18th century included plates of the Five Orders with detailed notes as to their proportions and principal parts. Chippendale's devotion to architectural principles can best be ascertained by what he wrote in the DIRECTOR: "Of all the arts which are either improved or ornamented by architecture, that of cabinetmaking is not only the most useful but capable of receiving as great assistance from it as any whatever. I have, therefore, prefixed to the following designs a short explanation of the Five Orders. These, therefore, ought to be carefully studied by everyone who would excel in this branch since they are the very soul and basis of his Art."

An outstanding feature distinguishing Early Georgian cabinetwork from Queen Anne cabinetwork was the adoption of mahogany, which began to succeed walnut as the favorite wood from after 1720–1725. Sir Robert Walpole repealed the import duty on mahogany in 1733 and after that date it became plentiful. Sheraton in his CABINET DICTIONARY in 1803 mentions three kinds of mahogany, namely, Cuban, Spanish and Honduran, and states that of these three Spanish is the finest. Mahogany is notable for its strength and durability and is unsurpassed as a medium for carving. A greater elaboration of carved detail can be achieved in mahogany than in walnut. In England the use of mahogany did not affect the design of furniture to any great extent until around 1740–50, with the exception of the massive and imposing bookcases and library tables designed in an architectural style for the Palladian mansions. As a result of the increased supply of mahogany around 1740 a style of mahogany furniture began to evolve that was indigenous to England. This style, which was based on English principles of design, reflected French influence in its simplified carved ornament. This French influence became more pronounced in both the form and ornament during the Rococo phase, 1745–1765. These new designs, with their distinctive Rocaille ornament, belong to the Chippendale style and are illustrated in the plates of his DIRECTOR of 1754. With the ascendancy of mahogany in cabinetwork the use of veneering was at least temporarily halted to some extent, since much of the cabinetwork was done in solid mahogany. Veneered mahogany was commonly laid on a framework of red pine. Mahogany continued to be used throughout the 18th and early 19th centuries for library and dining room furniture, while satinwood and other light colored woods became fashionable from around 1770 onwards for drawing room furniture.

The cabriole leg, which had been introduced around 1700, was the characteristic leg employed in Queen Anne and Early Georgian cabinetwork. During Queen Anne the cabriole leg had rather long slender lines while in Early Georgian cabinetwork the cabriole leg became wider and more massive. The cabriole leg in the Queen Anne and Early Georgian cabinetwork commonly terminated in a club foot or in a claw-and-ball foot. The club foot, which was disc-shaped and rounded on the bottom, was introduced about 1705 and superseded the cloven hoof foot. The claw-and-ball foot had its origin in the Orient and was derived from the Oriental design of a dragon's claw holding a ball or pearl. It was introduced in England around 1710 and succeeded the club foot; however, the latter continued to be used until around the middle of the 18th century. The eagle's claw was occasionally substituted for the dragon's claw. The claw-and-ball foot remained in fashion until around 1765. Sometimes the cabriole leg terminated in other forms of feet, such as a lion's paw or a French whorl. The French whorl foot was introduced around 1735–40 and remained in fashion for at least the ensuing two decades. It was found especially on mahogany chairs designed in the French taste.

The esteem accorded to Queen Anne furniture is undoubtedly due to some extent to its richly figured veneered surfaces. Cross-bandings and herringbone banded borders were widely used on the fronts of drawers and afforded an interesting contrast to the plain veneered surfaces on some of the larger pieces of furniture.

Carving was practically limited to the shell motif which was the favorite carved ornament during the reign of Queen Anne. It was sometimes combined with a small husk pendant or acanthus pendant and was frequently found on the knee of the cabriole leg. Marquetry was seldom employed and its use was chiefly confined to the solid splat in the characteristic Queen Anne splat-back chair. Due to the vogue for carving, which steadily increased in the Early Georgian era, marquetry became obsolete and was not revived until around 1765. As the Early Georgian cabinetmaker became more skilled in working in mahogany he elaborated on his carved detail which was noteworthy for its vigor and rich quality. Cockbeading, which is a small projecting molding applied around the edges of drawers, was introduced during the Early Georgian style and was skillfully used. The taste for lacquered furniture reached its peak in the early years of the 18th century. And, although lacquering was employed during the Early Georgian style it was less in evidence until around the mid-18th century when the Chinese taste became a prevailing fashion. In addition to the richly carved and gilded furniture in the taste of William Kent, parcel gilding was also employed on Early Georgian cabinetwork. In this practice the carved enrichments on mahogany and walnut furniture were enhanced with gilding. Much of the finest furniture made from around 1725 to 1740 featured gilded enrichments. Turning was seldom employed, except for the shafts on tripod candlestands. In furniture mounts the brass bail handle, which superseded the drop handle early in the 18th century, was attached to a shaped and flat solid back plate. After 1710–15 the center of the shaped brass back plate was cut away and it resembled a narrow flat band of scrollwork. The escutcheon or keyhole plate was commonly cartouche-shaped during the 18th century.

The shell motif, which had been introduced from Holland, was employed to a greater or less extent throughout the Early Georgian period. It was extensively used by the architectural school on their elaborately carved and gilded Baroque furniture. A large Baroque double shell carved motif was one of William Kent's favorite enrichments. With the ascendancy of the Rococo style around the middle of the 18th century, the shell motif was considerably altered and was often perforated. This carved Rococo motif of shell form is generally called a coquillage, being derived from the French word *coquille*, meaning a shell fish. We have already mentioned that from the reign of George I the tendency was to enrich the surface of furniture with more carved detail. The carved ornament employed during the Early Georgian style is often classified into several phases or developments. Naturally, any attempt to classify the different phases of ornament within dates is arbitrary, since the style of ornament overlapped and some of the motifs, especially the shell motif and acanthus foliage, were used during the entire era. The term *Decorated Queen Anne* is sometimes given to the era between 1715 to 1725, when the traditional Queen Anne forms were the forms most commonly found. The distinguishing feature of the Decorated Queen Anne style was the greater elaboration of carving. Included among the fashionable motifs were the shell, honeysuckle, rosettes, husk and acanthus pendants, acanthus foliage and various floriated and foliated scrolls. Carved mask motifs in a variety of forms, such as lion, female, Indian and satyr, figured prominently on furniture between 1720 and 1740. The dolphin motif

was revived late in the reign of George I. The legs of gilded chairs sometimes terminated in dolphins' heads with the legs frequently being scaled.

Around 1720 the carved lion mask became the newest development in fashionable furniture and largely superseded the shell motif. During those years the head, legs and hair of the lion chiefly composed the decorative carvings on chairs. The lion mask furniture was praiseworthy for its vigorous and realistic carvings. The lion phase attained its richest development around 1725. The lion motif was frequently combined with acanthus foliage. No consistency was followed in the use of the lion motif; sometimes the arms of the chairs terminated in eagles' heads and the legs in lions' paws. The eagle motif, one of great antiquity, was contemporary with the lion motif and was almost equally characteristic of this era. It was especially prominent from 1725 to 1745. The eagle motif was also remarkable for the realistic quality of its carvings. Around 1730 the use of carved grotesque motifs became more pronounced. The satyr's mask was often used between 1730 and 1740 as a carved decorative motif. After 1735 the French influence became more apparent in the style of ornament, and coincided with the growing demand for mahogany furniture. Ornament of French inspiration, such as the cabochon and leaf or ribbon motif, became increasingly popular and largely supplanted the motifs which had up to that time been in vogue. Other motifs, such as the shell and acanthus foliage, were gradually modified and were interpreted in the French Rococo taste. Thus towards the middle of the century the lavish Baroque ornament yielded to the Rocaille, which was its complete antithesis. In the process of adaptation this new style was unmistakably Anglicized.

Chairs   Late in the reign of William III the walnut chair with straight constructional lines was superseded by one of curvilinear form. The splat-back was shaped for the back of the occupant. The design of this chair was undoubtedly inspired by contemporary Dutch models (FIGURE 88) and by the designs for chairs by Daniel Marot. During Queen Anne further improvements were made in the construction to afford more comfort. In fact, the splat-back chair was so comfortable that relatively few chairs with upholstered backs were made at this time. The curved line dominated the form of the characteristic Queen Anne splat-back walnut chair (313). The spoon-shaped curve was a distinguishing feature of the profile of the back (313). The cresting was practically eliminated and the corners of the chair back were rounded off (313). The uprights and the top rail were constructed as one continuous arch (313). Sometimes there was a concave curve in the center of the top rail. The uprights were usually ramped or undulating (313). As a rule the plain solid splat, which joined the seat rail, was vase- or fiddle-shaped (313). The front of the seat rail was sometimes valanced or shaped (313). The corners of the seat rail were rounded off (313). It was fitted with a slip seat (313). The chair rested on cabriole legs (313) which usually terminated in club feet. Around 1710 the chair was sometimes designed with a broken cabriole leg. In this form of cabriole leg there was a break in the curve beneath the knee of the cabriole leg and the lower part of the leg was straight and flared out just above the foot. The broken cabriole leg was frequently collared at the cleft. Also around 1710 the cabriole leg was designed with a claw-and-ball foot (313) and it was used as an alternative to the club foot (316). The latter, which had evolved from the hoof foot, or pied de biche, continued to be used throughout the first half of the 18th century. In the early examples the cabriole legs were relatively narrow and were joined with turned H-form stretchers; and although stretchers were sometimes used after 1710 they are essentially a feature of the early Queen Anne splat-back chair. The extreme plainness of the chair during the early 18th century was sometimes relieved by a carved shell motif, often combined with a small carved husk or acanthus pendant, on the knee of the cabriole leg (315). It was designed as an armchair and as a side chair, the latter being the more common. The open arms were scrolled and extended beyond the conformingly shaped armposts. Particularly after Queen Anne the arms frequently scrolled over and the underneath part of the curve joined the scrolled armpost (315). The chair was sometimes lacquered (316) and occasionally it was decorated with marquetry work. It is doubtful if the enriched examples (313) of this chair were made before the accession of George I in

1714, and that any of the very enriched examples (323), which mark the initial phase of Georgian design, were made much before 1720. From around 1725 mahogany was first widely employed in chair design.

The vogue for this Queen Anne splat and hoop-back walnut chair with cabriole legs extended into the age of mahogany. After the accession of George I the seat was usually wider. The cabriole legs lost their long slender lines and they were usually wider and were of stronger construction to compensate for the discarded stretchers. The knees of the cabriole legs were frequently designed with scrolled brackets (313). In the armchairs of this period the arm supports were set back on the seat rail, supplanting the earlier manner of rising immediately above the front legs. The chair was usually decorated according to the taste of the different phases of the Early Georgian style of ornament. From about 1715 to 1725 the chair was marked by an elaboration of the traditional Queen Anne carved ornament. The hoop-back sometimes had a carved foliage cresting. The front seat rail frequently centered an elaborately carved shell motif. The knees of the cabriole legs were carved with a rich shell and pendant motif or with graceful pendant acanthus foliage, and the legs frequently terminated in vigorously carved claw-and-ball feet (313). From around 1715–1720 the vase-shaped splat was occasionally decorated with acanthus-carved volutes (313). In the lion phase furniture from about 1720 to 1735 the knees of the cabriole legs were frequently ornamented with carved lions' masks and the legs terminated in lions' paws (323). On these enriched specimens the carved ornament was often parcel-gilded. Variations in contour from the characteristic Queen Anne form began to occur in the latter part of the Early Georgian style. By 1740 the influence of the Chippendale school was discernible in the Early Georgian mahogany chair. The chair was usually lighter in form and the vase-shaped splat was pierced and often richly carved. The carving on the chair was marked by an elaboration of detail, which the use of mahogany made possible and which was now understood by the cabinetmakers. This chair, which began to develop all the characteristics peculiar to the Chippendale style and to mahogany chair design, will be treated in the chapter on Chippendale furniture. One principal plain variety of an open back chair around 1740 had slightly flaring uprights which supported a serpentine-shaped crest rail. The vase-shaped splat was pierced. It had open scrolled arms and conforming supports. The two front corners of the seat rail were well defined. The cabriole legs which terminated in claw-and-ball feet were carved with a characteristic motif.

The Queen Anne walnut upholstered chair had a tall back in the manner of the preceding William and Mary style. It was designed with open arms and also as a side chair, the latter being the more common. The upholstered back almost always joined the upholstered seat. The cabriole legs were relatively narrow and were frequently joined with a shaped H-form stretcher. The legs usually terminated in club feet. After the accession of George I the height of the upholstered back was reduced and the cabriole legs were more massively designed. The knees of the cabriole legs were often finished in wide brackets under the seat rail. The stretcher was discarded. The seat was wider, in fact it was sometimes extremely wide. It is generally believed that the very wide chair seat was designed for the enormous hoop skirts which were then fashionable. One principal variety essentially retained the contour of the characteristic Queen Anne splat-back chair (324). In accordance with the prevailing fashion the terminals were sometimes in the form of the heads and claws of eagles (324). In another characteristic variety the sides and top of the slightly raked back were straight, although occasionally the top was shaped (325). The seat with its pronounced corners narrowed toward the rear (325). The favorite lion motif, comprising the head, mask and paws, realistically rendered and vigorously carved, was occasionally used on these chairs (325). This type of chair, when designed with open arms, developed into an exceedingly comfortable Georgian armchair. After the death of George I, in 1727, French taste again began to influence the designs for fashionable furniture. After 1730 chairs with upholstered backs sometimes incorporated French lines and motifs in their designs. The tops of the backs of these chairs were frequently serpentine-arched and the padded open arms often rested on incurvate arm supports (325). After 1740, when the French influence became more discernible in Early Georgian furniture, the form of the chair became lighter and more French motifs were employed.

Around 1730 to 1745 many armchairs and side chairs with upholstered backs were designed in the manner of William Kent for the large Palladian mansions. These ornately carved chairs were generally gilded. They were often marred by a ponderous style which is characteristic of much of the work of William Kent. These chairs both in form and in style of ornament were inspired chiefly by Venetian models in the florid Baroque style.

The winged armchair became more popular in the 18th century. The Queen Anne walnut wing chair (314) had out-scrolled sides and was generally upholstered in floral needlework. It was fitted with a loose seat cushion. The top of the back was commonly straight (314), and occasionally it was arched. The cabriole legs were slender and usually terminated in club feet (314). The knee of the cabriole leg was sometimes ornamented with a carved shell motif and a small leafage pendant (314). During the Early Georgian style the cabriole leg was more massive and richly carved and very often terminated in a vigorously carved claw-and-ball foot. In the Queen Anne and Early Georgian wing chair the arms extended only to the wings (314), while in the later 18th century styles of Hepplewhite and Sheraton the arms extended to the back of the chair and the wide wings rested on the arms. The arms and wings having the appearance of one continuous piece as featured in the earlier models afforded a more graceful and pleasing line. The contour of many of the Queen Anne and Early Georgian wing chairs was often remarkably fine.

Another variety of a Queen Anne walnut upholstered chair was also in the form of an easy chair. It had an upholstered back of medium height. The top of the back was straight, rolled over or serpentine-arched. The closed arms were slightly flaring and out-scrolled. The knees of the slender cabriole legs were sometimes carved with a shell motif and commonly terminated in club feet. During the Early Georgian style the cabriole legs lost their slender appearance and commonly terminated in claw-and-ball feet. The knees were often acanthus-carved in accordance with the taste of that time.

The reading chair (326), which was a distinctive variety of chair, was introduced around 1705–1720 for use in the library. The seat was almost pear-shaped (326), with the narrow part in the rear, and was joined to a shaped narrow back which had a horseshoe-shaped crest rail supporting an adjustable wooden rest or board for reading (326). The seat, back and arm rest were generally covered in leather. Sometimes beneath the arms were hinged trays with three circular wells, with brass candlesticks folding underneath (326). Very often there was a drawer in the seat rail. Variations in design occurred. Such chairs with crest rails were popularly associated with cockfighting and were used by the judges; however, there can be no doubt as to their primary purpose. Sheraton in his CABINET DICTIONARY of 1803 observes that these chairs are "intended to make the exercise of reading easy and for the convenience of taking down a note or quotation from any subject. The reader places himself with his back to the front of the chair and rests his arms on the top yoke."

A variety of chair of Dutch origin (89) was popularly called the burgomaster chair. It was introduced in England around 1700 and was first made in walnut and later in mahogany. The chair had a circular frame. It was designed with a flaring semi-circular back composed of four turned uprights and traverses enclosing three oval panels carved and pierced with leaf scrolls. It usually had a caned compass seat mounted on six legs generally of cabriole form. The six legs were joined with turned cross stretchers generally resembling in arrangement the spokes of a wheel.

The corner chair or roundabout chair (327), which was a kind of open back armchair made of walnut and later of mahogany, was designed in such a manner that it could be placed in the corner of a room or could be used as an occasional chair. It was introduced in the early 18th century and was principally designed in the Queen Anne, Early Georgian and Chippendale styles. It was fitted with a slip seat. The characteristic variety usually had a semi-circular or horseshoe-shaped arm rail, which frequently had a rear raised portion, over two vase-shaped splats, flanked by three turned supports, which joined at the three corners and continued to the three rear legs (327). The seat rail rested on four legs, one at each corner (327). The four legs were often cabriole in form (327). Sometimes the front leg was cabriole in shape, and the remaining three were columnar turned. In a few examples where the chair had only one leg of cabriole form, the four legs were joined with a turned cross-stretcher. In a rare example one arm terminal was fitted with a brass swivel arm which supported an easel bookrest.

The name *writing chair* is given to several types of chairs with solid or open low wooden backs. One characteristic Early Georgian variety was originally made in walnut. It had a plain, cartouche-shaped, solid wooden, spooned back with open scrolled arms which looped onto incurvate supports. The seat rail was circular and was fitted with an upholstered slip seat. The cabriole legs had scrolled brackets beneath the seat rail and terminated in claw-and-ball feet. The knees of the two front cabriole legs were boldly carved with shell motifs combined with acanthus pendants.

The hall chair, which is a variety of wooden chair, was introduced in the early 18th century and commonly had a wooden seat. It was particularly designed for the large Palladian mansions and was used in the hall or corridor. Sheraton in his CABINET DICTIONARY of 1803 states that the chair was generally used by strangers or servants waiting to see the master of the house. As a rule it was made of mahogany and very often had the family crest painted or carved on the solid wooden back. This special variety was also designed as a hall settee. Both the chair and settee designed in the manner of William Kent looked as heavy and uncomfortable as the characteristic Gothic oak chair and settle.

Another unusual form of chair especially identified with the stately Palladian mansions was the so-called porter or page chair. It was also found in the halls of the large houses and was used by the manservant whose duty it was to open the door. It was a tall commodious upholstered leather chair having deep wings or side pieces equal to the depth of the seat and continuing to form an arched top, the purpose being to protect the occupant against the drafts.

No description of early 18th century English chairs would be complete without referring to the Windsor chair, for which there has been a demand in England from the commencement of the 18th century until the present time. Windsor chairs were first made in Buckinghamshire in the 17th century. The Windsor chair is characterized by its slender, turned spindles, its wooden saddle seat and turned splayed legs, which are usually joined with an H-form turned stretcher. The back of the Windsor chair was designed in several characteristic varieties. One of the earliest types is now usually referred to as the combback type of Windsor chair. It had a horseshoe-shaped arm rail and the center rear spindles extended through the arm rail to a higher, shaped crest rail. During the first half of the 18th century another variety was designed to which the name *hoop* or *bow-back* is generally given. This type also had a horseshoe-shaped arm rail upon which a bow or hoop back made from a continuous piece of bent wood was joined at each end of the center rear portion of the arm rail. The center rear spindles extended through the arm rail to the higher bow-back. At a later date the form of the back displayed further variations. During the first half of the 18th century the legs were sometimes of cabriole form. The English Windsor chair was commonly designed with a pierced central splat between the spindles. The frame of the chair was generally of yew, while the seat was of elm and the spindles of either birch or ash.

Benches   The benches and stools were essentially similar in design and in style of ornament to the chairs during the Queen Anne and Early Georgian era. They were frequently designed "en suite" with the chairs and settees. The oblong seat was usually upholstered in needlework, which generally covered the seat rail, and was fastened to the frame with a solid row of brass nailheads.

Settees   The walnut settee (315) essentially followed the development of the upholstered back variety of chair both in form and in style of ornament during the first half of the 18th century. Shortly after the accession of Queen Anne the cabriole legs (315) supplanted the various forms of tapered legs which had been fashionable during the preceding style. The back gradually became lower and the top of the back was usually straight (315). The settee was designed with either open scrolled arms and arm posts (315) or closed out-scrolled arms. It was commonly covered in floral needlework (315) and frequently had a long, loose seat cushion. The typical Queen Anne settee was characterized by the simplicity of its form and woodwork. After 1730 the settee was sometimes made of mahogany (329). Contemporary with the walnut and mahogany settees were the ornately decorated and gilded settees designed in the taste of William Kent (328). Swags of fruit or flowers centering pendent shells, seat rails carved with the key pattern or the Greek fret, acanthus leaves, lion masks and scrolled supports were all fashionable Baroque ingredients found on these settees (328).

The smaller type of settee, which is popularly called a love seat or courting chair, was also designed. Essentially it resembled a chair wide enough to hold two persons and is sometimes described as a double chair. The courting chair was in vogue throughout the 18th century. Although some were made with open backs, as a rule the backs of these chairs were generally upholstered until around the middle of the 18th century.

The chair-back settee, which was made in England as early as 1680, was reintroduced toward the end of the reign of Queen Anne and continued in vogue throughout the 18th century. It was generally designed with either two or three chair backs and an upholstered seat. This form of open chair-back settee, which rivalled the upholstered type of settee in popularity, essentially followed the development of the contemporary chair with an open back both in form and in style of ornament.

The term *sofa* is not found in English inventories much before the year 1700. It is rather difficult to define the difference between a sofa and an upholstered settee, since basically they were often of similar construction. The term *sofa* is generally reserved for a less formal piece. It is usually larger in size and generally has the appearance of being more over-stuffed. In a broad sense it could be used for reclining. The sofa, as it would be recognized and described as such to-day, was a relatively rare piece until after the middle of the 18th century.

Beds   The Queen Anne bed was practically the same as in the preceding style. The tester, which was usually surmounted with a boldly molded and scroll-shaped cornice, was supported by very tall, slender posts. Fine silk damask was pasted to the entire framework. The bed was richly draped, in fact the upholstery of beds was carried to the extreme limit early in the 18th century. Occasionally the bed was designed with a half tester and without the two front posts; this type of bed with a half tester is generally called an angel bed. From around 1740 the bed was sometimes made of mahogany. The panelled headboard and tester were in the early style of Chippendale. The cornice of the tester was often carved with acanthus foliage. The delicately carved slender posts of mahogany rested on short cabriole legs which commonly terminated in claw-and-ball feet.

Day Beds   The Queen Anne day bed was similar in construction to the day bed of the preceding style. The cabriole legs, which replaced the tapered legs of the preceding era, were usually joined with plain turned stretchers. The top of the upholstered back was occasionally rolled over. It seems that the day bed lost some of its popularity in the Early Georgian period.

Tables   The characteristic Early Georgian drop-leaf dining table generally had an oval or circular top and cabriole legs. It was so constructed that one cabriole leg swung out at each side to support the flaps. Shortly after the accession of George I the cabriole leg was decorated with acanthus foliage and occasionally with a lion's mask. The more elaborate carved ornament employed on chairs was rarely found on the dining table. The large drop-leaf dining table was generally designed with six legs. This variety was also made in pairs with square flaps, so that two could be placed together when an exceptionally long dining table was required.

The sideboard table (331), which is a kind of long side table, was a characteristic and important piece of Early Georgian dining room furniture. During the first half of the 18th century the dining room was practically devoid of drawer and cupboard furniture. The principal variety of oblong sideboard table almost always had a top of marble or scagliola, which is a composition imitating marble. The frieze was without drawer space and rested on four cabriole legs. Its style of ornament to a large extent followed the different phases which have already been described. Especially typical of the grandiose Baroque style developed by the Palladian architects was the sideboard table with boldly handled acanthus leaves, lion mask ornament and a pendent shell centered in the frieze (331). Other sideboard tables made of mahogany illustrated this style in a modified form and were notable for their rich and sculpturesque carvings. From around 1745–50 the Baroque solidity so characteristic of all these tables gave way to the influence of the French Rocaille.

Probably the side table represented the greatest diversity of treatment of all the different types of furniture designed during the first half of the 18th century. It was essentially a decorative piece of wall furniture and was placed beneath mirrors and between windows in the reception hall, the drawing room and salon, and it also served as a sideboard table in the dining room. It almost always had a marble top; occasionally scagliola or mosaic was substituted. The marble top was used even on the plain Queen Anne walnut variety. The side table with its carved "frame" for its marble top is often regarded as an English innovation. It was also called a slab table. The marble top rested on a carved frieze. The carved and gilt wood side table (330) figured prominently in the works published by the architectural designers, such as William Kent. It was richly ornamented with Baroque motifs and usually had an ornately carved pendant or apron under the frieze (330). The supports were of various form, such as massive S-scrolls with heads of eagles (330), female terms and sphinxes. Many of the monumental gilt side tables were of a Venetian Baroque character. After 1740 the vogue for the carved and gilt wood side table, designed from foreign models, declined. Contemporary with the elaborately decorated side table was the plainer variety of Early Georgian side table, made of walnut and later of mahogany. This table also displayed an interesting variety of design. The frequent use of such motifs as large acanthus scrolls, masks and scallop shells reflected the influence of the English architectural school of designers. The frieze was also often carved with a running pattern of wave scrolls. This wave motif, which is called a Vitruvian scroll (333), consisted of a series of scrolls forming a continuous pattern. It bore a resemblance to waves, and was widely used by the architectural designers, especially as a decoration for the friezes on various types of side tables (333).

The console table, which is a form of side table, was introduced in the Early Georgian era. The term *console* is used to describe a variety of table whose top is supported by one or more brackets or consoles. The console table was fixed to the wall, being often placed under a mirror, and was without legs in the back. At the present time the term *console* is applied, although erroneously, to any decorative table, with one or more supports either in the form of brackets or legs, which is fixed or placed against the wall. The principal variety of Early Georgian console table was the carved and gilt wood eagle console table (333). It had an oblong marble top over a richly carved frieze which was supported by a finely executed spread eagle standing on a rock (333). It rested on a molded oblong or shaped plinth. Eagle console tables were often designed in pairs and were an important feature in the symmetrical architectural treatment of the drawing room or salon. Also praiseworthy were the dolphin console tables (332). Console tables figured prominently in the works published by the architectural school of designers.

Tables of gate-leg construction were made during the first half of the 18th century, although they were no longer in vogue after the accession of George I. Early in the second half of the 18th century there was a revival of the gate-leg table but in a much lighter form. Due to their very slender turned supports, this lighter variety of a gate-leg table is usually called a spider leg table.

Gaming Tables The walnut card table (320) assumed its definite and well-known form in the reign of Queen Anne. The card table was an important and popular piece of furniture due to the fashion for card playing which developed in England early in the 18th century. The characteristic Queen Anne card table had an oblong hinged top with outset rounded corners (320). It had a conformingly shaped frieze which rested on cabriole legs terminating in club feet (320). When opened the interior was fitted with four round dished candle discs, one at each corner, and four sunken counter wells or money pockets. The interior was usually lined with needlework, damask or green baize. The cabriole leg followed the characteristic evolution, the slender cabriole leg being gradually replaced by one of bolder form. Later the cabriole leg generally terminated in a claw-and-ball foot. Until around 1715 the hinged flap was supported on a swing leg which was hinged to the back framework. At that time a folding frame with hinges was introduced, which provided greater stability when the table was open, for then a leg was at each corner. The part of the underframing on each side, which was to support the flap, was hinged and folded inward, so that when the table was closed the two legs traveled forward to the two rear corners of the fixed part of the table top. This form of construction, which is called a concertina movement, and the swing-leg form of construction were both used during the first half of the 18th century, with the former prevailing in the second half of the 18th century. After 1720 the table was sometimes made of mahogany. Occasionally the table was decorated with lacquer work. The carved decoration essentially followed the different phases of the Early Georgian style of ornament. From about 1720 to 1735 the lion mask became fashionable, and the cabriole leg frequently terminated in a lion's paw. Around 1730 the card table with outset square corners was introduced. After 1735 the front was occasionally serpentine-shaped and rested on a conformingly shaped frieze. This type was usually lighter in form and reflected French influence in its design and ornament.

Toilet Tables   The small veneered walnut dressing table or side table, which is also called a lowboy in America, was a characteristic piece of Queen Anne furniture. It was also used in the early 18th century by ladies for writing letters. The principal variety had a molded oblong top over a valanced front which contained one long drawer and a row of three smaller drawers, the two lateral drawers often being deeper. It rested on cabriole legs which terminated in club feet. Variations in design, especially as to the number of drawers, occasionally occurred. The drawers were fitted with back plates and bail handles and were frequently inlaid with a herringbone border. During the Early Georgian period the lower central drawer was often decorated with a recessed shell motif. The cabriole legs, which were of bolder form, were often carved with acanthus foliage and terminated in claw-and-ball feet. The drawers were frequently cockbeaded. The more elaborate carved ornament found on chairs was not employed on the walnut dressing table.

The dressing table with a hinged lid, which when opened revealed a framed mirror and a fitted interior for toilet articles, was introduced in the early 18th century. One type was of a kneehole form. However, relatively few designs for dressing tables with complex fittings were made in the first half of the 18th century, and the lowboy and small kneehole table retained their popularity as dressing tables until the second half of the 18th century.

Tea Tables   Tables primarily made for serving tea came into general use around the end of the 17th century. However, due to the popularity of tea gardens among fashionable society in the first half of the 18th century, tea tables did not become plentiful until around the middle of the 18th century, when cabinetmakers, due to the fashion for tea-drinking at home, devoted their time to the designing of suitable decorative tables. It seems that tea, coffee and chocolate were first introduced in England around 1650. Coffee was never as popular as tea, while chocolate was chiefly considered to be a morning drink. Around 1740 a small tripod stand was introduced which was especially designed to support the silver tray on which the tea and coffee service were placed. The circular top, which usually tilted, was notched to receive the feet of the silver tray that belonged to it. It rested on a turned shaft which was supported on a tripod base. The tripod stand was slightly over two feet in height. One type of walnut table used in the early 18th century for tea and coffee equipage had an oblong molded and tray-shaped top over a frieze which was supported on four cabriole legs. The average height of this type was about two and one half feet. Another type, generally made of mahogany, had a circular or oblong tray-shaped top supported on a turned shaft, which rested on a tripod base. It was also about two and one half feet high.

Writing Furniture

The massive library or writing table of pedestal form did not come into general use until late in the reign of George I. The characteristic variety of open pedestal table had an oblong molded flat top, over a row of frieze drawers, supported on a pair of pedestals, each containing a bank of three or four drawers. Each set of drawers characteristically rested on a molded base, and occasionally on feet. It was usually decorated on all four sides since it was generally designed to be placed away from the wall. A smaller form of pedestal table was occasionally used as a dressing table. After 1730 it was frequently made of mahogany and was parcel-gilded.

The architect's or artist's table (352), introduced in the first quarter of the 18th century, was especially designed to serve the needs of draftsmen, artists and architects. This specialized table was suitable for drawing, reading and writing. One characteristic variety was designed with an oblong molded top on a ratchet easel over a frieze resting on a turned standard and tripod support. This table frequently displayed great ingenuity in its construction. The more complex and elaborate specimens often had pull-out fronts fitted with many small compartments and adjustable rising tops (352).

The Queen Anne walnut slant-front writing desk or bureau (317) was a characteristic and favorite piece of early 18th century furniture. It had an oblong top and a hinged slant lid over a central and two small supporting drawers and three graduated long drawers (317). It rested on a molded base with straight bracket feet (317). The drawers were usually fitted with cartouche-shaped back plates and bail handles (317). The slant lid opened to reveal an interior of small shaped drawers, pigeonholes and compartments. It was usually veneered with a fine quality of walnut and was often inlaid with a crossbanding or herringbone border of a lighter wood.

During the first half of the 18th century the slant-front secretary-cabinet (318) was usually veneered with walnut, and occasionally it was decorated with lacquer. The lacquered secretary-cabinet followed the contemporary walnut examples. The characteristic Queen Anne secretary-cabinet had a double-hooded or double-arched top outlined by a boldly molded cornice over two conformingly shaped doors, having serpentine-arched and beveled mirror plates. The hooded top was usually surmounted with two or three finials. Usually beneath the two doors were two pull-out candle slides (318). The interior was fitted with small drawers, doors and compartments. The under portion had the slant lid, which enclosed a fitted writing interior, over a row of two small and two or three rows of long drawers (318). It usually rested on a molded straight bracket base (318). Variations in design sometimes occurred. Occasionally the cabinet portion was surmounted with a molded broken arched pediment centering a low plinth (318). Sometimes in place of the slant-front it was designed with one long false drawer which could be pulled out and the front could be let down to serve as a writing flap. The drawers were fitted with cartouche-shaped back plates and bail handles (318) and were often inlaid with herringbone bands. From 1730 to 1745 the Early Georgian secretary-cabinet often incorporated architectural features in its design principles. It was usually surmounted with a molded swan neck or broken pediment, centering a low plinth. The panelled doors were frequently flanked by fluted pilasters. It was sometimes made of mahogany and the carved moldings and other carved enrichments were frequently gilded.

Another variety of Queen Anne writing furniture was the walnut writing cabinet (319). It had a molded cornice and a pulvinated or cushion frieze, frequently with a drawer, over a fall-front, which, when let down, revealed a nest of drawers, doors and pigeonholes (319). The cabinet rested on a chest of drawers mounted on a molded straight bracket base (319). The cabinet portion was sometimes fitted with two doors in place of the fall-front. In this type the lower section was equipped with a pull-out writing board.

The secretary tallboy or secretary chest-on-chest was designed as the name implies as a chest on a chest. The upper chest of the characteristic Queen Anne walnut secretary chest-on-chest had a cavetto cornice over a row of three small drawers and three long drawers. The lower chest contained four long drawers and was mounted on a molded bracket base. The upper drawer in the lower chest was false and could be pulled out and let down to serve as a writing board. The interior of the drawer was fitted as a desk. The drawers were fitted with brass escutcheons and bail handles and were sometimes inlaid with panel bandings. The stiles or corners on both chests were sometimes canted and fluted.

The characteristic Queen Anne walnut kneehole writing table had an oblong top over a long drawer, which surmounted a recessed cupboard flanked by two sets of three small drawers. Each set of drawers rested on a molded bracket base. The drawers were fitted with brass bail handles and occasionally inlaid with cross-bandings in a lighter wood.

Cabinets   The oblong cabinet during Queen Anne and the Early Georgian era was usually veneered with walnut or lacquered. At a later date it was occasionally made of mahogany. The oblong lacquered cabinet was usually mounted on a stand of table form and height. In another variety the lacquered cabinet surmounted a lacquered chest of drawers. In this type the cabinet portion was frequently topped with a molded double-hooded cornice, with the sides sometimes conformingly arched. The principal variety of Queen Anne walnut cabinet had a molded cornice and a pulvinated or cushion frieze drawer over two doors which opened to reveal a series of small drawers and doors. The oblong cabinet rested on a chest of drawers mounted on a molded bracket base. Its features of design were marked by extreme simplicity.

The walnut cabinet designed for the display of china during Queen Anne and the early years of George I was distinctive for its simplicity of form and fine proportions. The upper section had a cavetto molded cornice over two glazed doors. The lower section contained a double bank of six drawers, fitted with back plates and bail handles. It rested on a molded bracket base. Occasionally the underbody was fitted with two doors in place of the drawers. It was also designed in a more narrow variety; in this type the upper portion was fitted with one glazed door. The china cabinet after 1730 frequently incorporated architectural features in its design principles. The top was usually surmounted with either a broken or swan neck pediment. The doors were frequently flanked by fluted pilasters. The carved enrichments were often gilded. The china cabinet was sometimes made of mahogany.

Bookcases   The Queen Anne walnut bookcase was essentially similar to the Queen Anne walnut china cabinet with glazed doors. One characteristic variety of Early Georgian mahogany bookcase was rendered in a majestic architectural manner and reflected the influence of William Kent (334). It was a very massive piece of furniture and usually had a richly molded cornice and broken pediment. Its classic moldings and other carved enrichments were frequently gilded. The bookcase having a broken-front was also made before the middle of the century and was an early indication of the characteristic break-front bookcase which is identified with the second half of the 18th century.

Chests   The lacquered chest for the first half of the 18th century was frequently mounted on a low carved and gilt wood stand. The walnut chest was chiefly a utilitarian piece of bedroom furniture and was used for the storage of linens and blankets. It was simply designed and was usually fitted with a row of drawers in the base. It was generally mounted on short cabriole legs which commonly terminated in claw-and-ball feet. In the second half of the 18th century chests were to a large extent superseded by other types of bedroom furniture, such as the chest of drawers.

Chests of   The demand for chests of drawers steadily increased during the 18th
Drawers   century. A characteristic variety of Queen Anne walnut chest of drawers had a molded oblong top. The front contained a row of two small drawers over three long drawers. The graduated drawers, which were enriched with herringbone bands, were fitted with back plates and bail handles. It rested on a molded bracket base. A similar bedroom chest of drawers during the Early Georgian era had the front fitted with four cockbeaded and graduated long drawers. Although some mahogany chests of drawers were made, it was not until after the middle of the century that they were made in any considerable quantity.

The bachelor chest, which was a form of a low chest of drawers with a folding top, was introduced early in the 18th century. Occasionally it was designed in pairs. As a rule, the top, when open, was supported on runners and served as a writing board. Occasionally the bachelor chest was provided with candle brackets hinged at the corners.

The tallboy (322) or chest-on-chest as a variety of bedroom furniture also became more plentiful. One characteristic Queen Anne chest-on-chest had a cavetto molded cornice over a row of three small drawers and three long graduated drawers (322). The lower chest contained three long graduated drawers and was mounted on a molded straight bracket base (322). The stiles or corners on both chests were canted (322) and sometimes fluted. The drawers were inlaid with a herring-bone banding and were fitted with brass escutcheons and bail handles. The underbody was often fitted with a pull-out slide above the top drawer. Occasionally the bottom drawer centered a recessed lunette inlaid with a handsome stellate motif (322). This motif was of Dutch origin. A cavetto molding was widely used on the cornices of china cabinets and similar pieces of furniture when made of veneered walnut in the Queen Anne style.

Dressers   The oak dresser was a popular piece of 18th century cottage furniture. It is frequently called a Welsh dresser since it was especially identified with Wales and the border counties. The sideboard portion of the dresser was usually surmounted with a superstructure of shelves. A principal variety during the first half of the 18th century had a molded cornice and a valanced frieze over three shelves secured to a wooden back. The valanced front of the sideboard portion had a row of three drawers and rested on cabriole legs. Sometimes the sideboard portion had three cupboard doors below the three drawers and was mounted on a molded bracket base. Other variations in design also occurred.

Cupboards   During the first half of the 18th century a shelved recess or cupboard commonly formed a part of the painted panelling of a room. All types of movable cupboards were relatively rare. A characteristic Georgian built-in cupboard was the corner or alcove cupboard (311) often surmounted by a semi-hemispherical head which was very often fluted, painted or carved with a shell. It was built in the dining room and was used for the disposition of silver, glass and porcelain. It was frequently constructed in two parts. Each part was fitted with a pair of panelled cupboard doors, the upper pair being longer and arched. The upper doors opened to reveal a half-round interior fitted with three shaped shelves, sometimes supported by pierced and carved brackets, surmounted by a handsome shell niche with ribbings radiating from a decorative motif, such as a demi-star motif. The interior was usually painted the same color as the exterior. This alcove cupboard, which was so called in 18th century records, was also described as a buffet in contemporary literature.

Clocks   The tall case clock in the Queen Anne period (321) was generally veneered in walnut and was frequently enhanced with a herringbone inlay. The hood, which was often surmounted with two or three finials, was usually arched and boldly molded and the top of the dial was conformingly arched (321). Frequently the arched hood was surmounted with a domed superstructure upon which was mounted two or three finials (321). Tall case clocks decorated in lacquer were in vogue from about 1710 until the middle of the 18th century (321). The lacquer decoration on these clocks was often finely executed.

The cartel or wall clock, which was introduced early in the reign of George II, was of French origin. The French bronze doré cartel was a veritable masterpiece of the ciseleur's art. The English cartel emulating the French cartel was generally made of carved and gilt wood. The round dial was frequently enclosed in carved foliage scrolls and was sometimes surmounted with a realistically carved spread eagle.

Accessories   Wall brackets during Queen Anne and George I chiefly followed the style of Louis XIV and the style of the Régence. Carved and gilt wood wall brackets were a prominent decorative appointment for the Palladian mansions. William Kent is identified with the designing of many brackets, which served for the reception of busts, candelabra and vases. This type was usually of a large scale due to the size and weight of the object it was to support. Brackets carved with flamboyant acanthus foliage or with a spread eagle were characteristic of the Early Georgian style.

The Early Georgian carved and gilt wood candlestand or torchère reflected the influence of the Palladian architects in its style of ornament. The mahogany candlestand was richly carved in accordance with the taste of the period.

At the beginning of the Early Georgian period the pedestal was introduced by the architects as a piece of movable decorative furniture.

The pedestal, which in classical architecture is the support of a column, was a development of this same substructure. The pedestal consisted of a base, dado and cornice. It was generally used to support a marble or bronze sculpture. The architectural character of the pedestal distinguishes it from the candlestand. The Early Georgian pedestals were commonly either short and columnar in form or of term shape. A term or terminal figure usually consisted of a quadrangular pillar which often tapered downward and was adorned with the figure of a head or the upper part of the body. The term had its origin in classical antiquity and the pedestal of term shape was introduced into England from the Continent. The carved and gilt wood terminal pedestal consisted of a small molded top which rested on a classical female bust surmounting a quadrangular pillar. The pillar, which usually tapered downward, rested either on four ornately scrolled feet or on a molded square plinth.

Mirrors
During the 18th century the mirror often accompanied the side table, although each was used separately. Mirrors were commonly hung between windows, facing windows or over the fireplace. A mirror especially designed to be hung between two windows is called a pier mirror, since the term *pier* is the architectural name given to that part of a wall between two windows. A mirror designed to be hung over a fireplace is called an overmantel mirror, and its length generally exceeds its height. The characteristic Queen Anne mirror had an upright arched or serpentine-arched frame, often surmounted with an elaborate openwork cresting. The beveled mirror plate was generally in two parts. During the Early Georgian period mirrors, like other wall furniture, such as side tables and bookcases, were favorite subjects for the architect and many were designed by them. One characteristic Early Georgian variety is commonly referred to as an architectural wall mirror (336). This type was distinctive for the refined treatment of its Baroque style of classic ornament (336). The frame was made of walnut or mahogany and was parcel gilded (336). The upright frame, with its gilded moldings carved with classic ornament, was surmounted by a pediment (336). The pediment was either broken or swan neck (336) and centered a low plinth which was surmounted by a gilded eagle, a shell or some other decorative carving (336). Occasionally the mirror was surmounted by a triangular pediment in place of the other types of pediments. The base of the frame was frequently valanced (336). Sometimes the base was fitted with two brass candle arms. This variety with candle arms is called a girandole mirror, since the term *girandole* is used to describe a bracket of any kind to hold candles or some other lights. In another variety of Early Georgian mirror the wood frame was ornately carved and gilded (335). Its Baroque style of classic ornament was similar to that employed on the elaborately carved and gilt wood side tables executed in the taste of William Kent.

CHAPTER SEVENTEEN

CHIPPENDALE

Two important monographs appearing in the Metropolitan Museum Studies in 1929 on the Creators of the Chippendale Style by Fiske Kimball and E. Donnell are largely responsible for clarifying Chippendale's present place in 18th century cabinetwork. Chippendale's reputation as a cabinetmaker has for many years eclipsed the reputation of all other 18th century English cabinetmakers, and the principal source of this reputation was his publication of the GENTLEMAN AND CABINET MAKER'S DIRECTOR, the first edition of which appeared in 1754. Due to these monographs and subsequent research Chippendale's position has been completely reappraised. It has now become patent that Chippendale was responsible for only a few, if any, of the designs appearing in the DIRECTOR and his claim as an original designer cannot be fully upheld. Evidence now suggests that Matthias Lock and Henry Copland were retained by Chippendale and that Chippendale was indebted to both of these furniture designers

for a large portion of the designs appearing in the DIRECTOR. Present evidence points out that Copland was responsible for a majority of the designs for carver's pieces in the DIRECTOR and that Lock made sketches for the same type of work commissioned by individual clients. These two craftsmen were aptly called in the monographs by Fiske Kimball and E. Donnell, 'Chippendale's ghosts.' Since the designs in the DIRECTOR essentially established the English Rococo style, and in view of this evidence, it was really Lock and Copland and not Chippendale who were the true creators of the Rococo or Chippendale style in England. Naturally new evidence resulting from future research could easily alter the importance of Lock and Copland.

Regardless of who did or who did not do the designs in the DIRECTOR everyone agrees that it is a valuable record of 18th century English cabinetwork. The practice of publishing designs for furniture was far from new, for it had been done in Europe since around the middle of the 16th century.

However, nothing had been attempted up to that time on such a grand scale as the DIRECTOR. Chippendale's book was entirely devoted to furniture design and illustrated practically every type of furniture in general use. The earlier books devoted only a few pages to furniture design, the bulk of the book being concerned with architecture, ornament and other related subjects. A list of subscribers published only in the first edition of the DIRECTOR included many names of the aristocracy, such as the Duke of Norfolk and the Earl of Chesterfield, as well as the names of cabinetmakers, upholsterers and many other craftsmen. Trade publications of a similar type were also issued in England around the mid-18th century by Ince and Mayhew, Robert Manwaring, Lock and Copland, Darly and Edwards, as well as by other designers. These works were not as complete as Chippendale's DIRECTOR, and, although some possessed considerable merit, they are generally considered to be much inferior to it. Thomas Sheraton at a later date, in criticizing Ince and Mayhew's book, entitled THE UNIVERSAL SYSTEM OF HOUSEHOLD FURNITURE, states that Chippendale's DIRECTOR was "a real original as well as more extensive and masterly in design."

Undoubtedly Chippendale's great reputation was chiefly founded on the DIRECTOR. Until relatively few years ago Chippendale was given credit for practically every fine piece of mahogany furniture made in England around the middle of the 18th century. Even at the present time his name is still popularly connected with this work. He has also been given credit as a practical craftsman for making some of the finest examples of cabinetwork produced at his establishment. He is even supposed to have been a wood carver of great ability, although there is no evidence that he himself ever carved at all. Recent research has gone far to clear up much of this misunderstanding. It is now clear that Chippendale spent much of his career as the organizing head of a very large and successful business which undertook the entire furnishings of a house. Chippendale possessed a fine sense of business acumen. His firm completely furnished and decorated many of the important mansions throughout England. It seems apparent that he also simplified many of his elaborate designs for chairs and other furniture for the English gentry who could not afford the more ambitious pieces of cabinetwork. In comparing extant examples of his cabinetwork in the Rococo taste, which are exceedingly fine, they are now considered to be inferior to the authenticated work of William Vile, executed in the Rococo style. However, the Rococo style represents only part of Chippendale's work. In his last phase, from 1770 to 1779, Chippendale discarded the style exemplified in the DIRECTOR, and, under the influence of Robert Adam, he produced furniture in the Adam style which is unrivalled in contemporary cabinetwork. Thus Chippendale now achieves his eminence in a style which is the antithesis of the style with which his name is popularly identified.

Thomas Chippendale, c.1718–1779, was the son of Thomas Chippendale I, a cabinetmaker and wood carver of Worcester. He moved to London with his father around 1727 and opened his own shop in 1749, and in 1753 he moved to No. 60 St. Martin's Lane, where he remained for the rest of his life. He had as his first partner James Rannie, who died in 1766, and as his second partner Thomas Haig. In 1754 he published the first folio volume of the GENTLEMAN AND CABINET MAKER'S DIRECTOR. A second edition, which was virtually a reprint, was issued in 1755 and a third enlarged edition in 1762. In the preface Chippendale indicated his great appreciation of architecture as giving the most useful assistance in the designing of furniture. The DIRECTOR contained one hundred and sixty engraved plates of designs for furniture. The third edition, which was issued in weekly parts between 1759 and 1762, had two hundred engraved plates. The majority of the designs were in the French Rococo, the Chinese or the Gothic taste. Some of the designs were of a fantastic character and were not adaptable for developing into actual furniture. Some of the finest were derived directly from the French. He undoubtedly owed the inspiration of his famous ribband back chair to the artistic work of a French designer. Many of the Chinese designs with their geometrical latticework were remarkable for their elegance and effectiveness. It is erroneous to believe that all these designs were meant to be executed in mahogany. Some were to be finished with lacquering, gilding or painting. From Chippendale's accounts it seems that he often favored gilded furniture for the salon, mahogany for the hall, dining room and library, and lacquering for the bedroom. The designs in the DIRECTOR displayed to a large extent the traditional style of the mid-Georgian period, which was chiefly an Anglicized version of the French Rococo. Upon these Anglicized French forms were grafted extravagant Rococo ornament, Chinese or Gothic detail. The other books of designs by contemporary cabinetmakers displayed even more fanciful ideas than the DIRECTOR. Fortunately, due to innate English conservatism, these designs never materialized, and the furniture of this period remains one of the great periods in English furniture design. The features of design appearing in the third edition were essentially the same as in the earlier editions and were typically Rococo in their development. Some of the plates of the earlier volumes were omitted and some new designs, especially for hall chairs, basin stands and dressing tables, were added. It is doubtful if the third edition enjoyed the same success as the earlier editions, since these designs were gradually becoming old-fashioned. The influence of the Adam brothers was first beginning to assert itself in interior decoration, and it was not too long before Chippendale began to execute many of the ideas for furniture developed by the Adam brothers.

In order to determine the merit of the cabinetwork executed at Chippendale's shop it is necessary to examine the finished pieces. It has always been exceedingly difficult to distinguish the work executed in Chippendale's shop from that of other contemporary cabinetmakers. Complete furnishing accounts for work done by Chippendale's firm are available but it has not been possible to identify the furniture. In only a few cases has the work been conclusively identified as having been made at his shop, the two most valuable sources being the furniture at Nostell Priory and that at Harewood House. The accounts for Nostell Priory date from 1766 to 1770 and include examples in the Rococo style. It can be ascertained from these invaluable accounts that the furniture made at Chippendale's shop was praiseworthy for the beautifully selected woods, for the fine constructural methods and the quality of craftsmanship in general, and for the use of refined moldings. The beautiful crisp quality of the carving shows that Chippendale employed highly skilled craftsmen. The furniture was graceful and elegant, and was substantial in appearance without conveying any feeling of heaviness. The accounts from Harewood House in Yorkshire date from 1772 and represent the post-DIRECTOR phase of Chippendale's work, which is regarded as his most perfected. It must be remembered, however, that some of the pieces were designed by Robert Adam and were executed by Chippendale's cabinetmakers. This furniture, designed in the Adam style, was frequently decorated with superb marquetry and with handsome ormolu mounts and was executed with the highest quality of craftsmanship.

Thomas Chippendale Jr., 1749–1822, succeeded to the business of his father at No. 60 St. Martin's Lane, and for some years the firm continued to trade under the name of Chippendale and Haig until the latter retired in 1796. In 1814 he had premises at No. 57 Haymarket and in 1821 he was found in No. 42 Jermyn Street. He became bankrupt in 1804 and his entire stock was sold at auction. Thomas Chippendale Jr., as his father had formerly been, was a member of the Society of Arts and exhibited five paintings at the Royal Academy between 1784 and 1801. The firm under his supervision enjoyed a good reputation despite his financial embarrassment and was very active at the end of the 18th century and at the beginning of the 19th century. He maintained the high standard of workmanship which had been established by his father. He supplied furniture to both Harewood House in Yorkshire and Harewood House in Cavendish Square, London. Some of these pieces executed in the style of the Regency are of a less extravagant nature and

really show the Regency style at its best.

From around 1740 a style of mahogany furniture began to evolve which was peculiar to England. This style, which is popularly called the Chippendale style, was the last style of the Early Georgian period. The development of this style resulted largely from the increased demand for mahogany furniture and the predominance of the Rococo influence. In this new style the forms became lighter, and, as mahogany grew more plentiful, the cabinetmaker became more skilled in executing the carved detail which the use of mahogany made possible. In addition to the French influence, as well as the earlier influence of the Early Georgian architect, Chinese and Gothic influences were also evident in cabinetwork from around 1750. However, French influence was by far the most important. Since France was the arbiter for fashions on the Continent during the 18th century, it was inevitable that England should also be affected, but she was not as completely permeated with French influence as the countries on the Continent. French taste appealed especially to the wealthy classes in England from which group Chippendale and the other designers drew their patronage. Although French taste was discernible in fashionable furniture shortly after the death of George I, it was not too pronounced until after 1735–40. The earlier furniture reflecting French influence was not of an extravagant Rococo nature. Frequently such French motifs, as the cabochon and leaf or ribbon motif, were simply grafted on characteristic mid-Georgian forms. It was not until around 1750 that the Rocaille style was intensified in England.

The term *Rococo*, which was borrowed from the French, was first used in England around 1830 to describe any fashion in dress or art that was antiquated, whimsical or freakish. At the present time, however, it is used interchangeably with the French word *Rocaille*, meaning rock work or grotto work, which is the name given to a very singular form of asymmetrical ornament that evolved in France after the death of Louis XIV. This Rocaille or Rococo style was fashionable in France from about 1720 to 1760. Certain natural forms were used as the foundation for the style of ornament which was richly fantastic. It was marked by a profusion of rock work, or rocaille, and shells, or coquillage, with flowers, foliage and fruit. It included all kinds of whimsical and extravagant forms of birds, animals and human figures. A pronounced feature was the use of broken curves for straight lines. The ornament was entirely separated from the constructional requirements and the lines ran in free curves; symmetry was avoided. In many decorative appointments, such as mirrors, sconces and wall brackets, the dominating lines were never visible but were suggested by means of related curves which were broken and irregular. As a result of this treatment, decorative appointments frequently developed many unexpected and astonishing new shapes. The development of this style of ornament could not be successfully executed in such pieces as chairs, chests and tables for they required a rectangular basis. In these articles the ornamentation, which was in the form of bronze mounts, expressed the style in its wealth of vigorous and extravagant curves. The Rococo style, which is virtually synonymous with the Louis XV style, was most suitable for interior decoration and the decorative arts, because in this style the Orders were generally omitted or modified until they were hardly recognizable.

The Rococo style, like the earlier Baroque style, was never completely assimilated in English furniture design. English designers and cabinetmakers lacked the imagination and the daring spirit to develop the Rococo style in a manner similar to the French. The English draftsmen, Lock and Copland, were the principal pioneers in this style in England, which was in vogue from around 1745 to 1765. Lock and his collaborator, Copland, issued several publications of engraved ornament interpreted in the Rocaille style, in the decade preceding the publication of the DIRECTOR by Chippendale. Their designs in the Rococo style, as well as the subsequent designs by Chippendale and other contemporaries, lacked the inventive elegance identified with the artistic work of the French designers, who were unrivalled in their ability to combine novelty of design with good taste. However, the majority of English cabinetwork in the Rococo style, with its typical cabriole leg, was of meritorious design and of enduring excellence in its fine selection of materials and in its quality of workmanship. A pronounced difference between the English and French Rococo furniture was in the absence of bronze doré mounts, which were seldom used on English furniture. French influence was particularly evident in drawing room furniture. The Rococo style in England found its most suitable expression in such elaborately carved pieces as side tables, console tables, torchères, mirrors, sconces, wall brackets and similar articles. English mahogany Rococo furniture carved in low relief and designed in a more conservative manner compares favorably with some of the finest extant examples of English cabinetwork. After the accession of George III in 1760 the Rococo style began to decline in popularity and it was gradually supplanted in fashionable furniture by the Neo-Classic style of Robert Adam, in which the superiority of the straight line was again firmly established.

Gothic taste was a phrase used by the admirers of the pseudo-medieval forms which they attempted to introduce into architecture, interior decoration and furniture. Horace Walpole, 1717–1797, the English author and wit, was one of the leaders of this Gothic cult. The effort to revive the Gothic style was restricted to a few. Furniture designed in the Gothic taste was negligible and was not carried out seriously. Designers of Neo-Gothic furniture made no pretense of adhering either to the form or to the materials actually employed by the makers of the original Gothic furniture. Leading designers, such as Chippendale, rarely did more than introduce details which they regarded as Gothic into pieces of furniture essentially of mid-Georgian contour. Tracery work, trefoil and cinquefoil motifs, Gothic cusping and cluster columns were included in the repertory of ornament and detail reminiscent of the medieval Gothic style. The legs of chairs and tables designed in the form of a cluster column were a typical feature of this Georgian Gothic fashion. Carved Gothic detail enjoyed its greatest vogue from around 1750 to 1760. Furniture designed in the Gothic taste had little artistic merit, since neither Chippendale nor his contemporaries possessed a scholarly knowledge of Gothic architecture or forms. Another later effort to revive the Gothic style occurred during the English Regency. The Georgian Gothic taste in interior decoration was generally confined to one room, the exception being Strawberry Hill, the home of Horace Walpole, which was entirely decorated in the Gothic taste.

A widespread revival in Chinese taste occurred in England around the middle of the 18th century and reached its peak around 1760. Contemporary English newspapers commenting on this prevailing whim stated that everything is Chinese or in the Chinese taste. This fashion for Chinese decoration was evident in the ornamental detail on chairs, tables and mirrors, and in fabrics and wallpaper with their chinoiseries of landscapes, figure subjects, flowers and birds. In France the taste for chinoiseries had been well developed by the end of the 17th century. The French school of decorative designers led by Watteau, Boucher and Pillement were chiefly responsible for the Rococo phase of chinoiseries which were so fashionable in France. Travel books, especially J. B. du Halde's fine work on China published in 1735 in Paris and later translated into English, stimulated this Chinese interest in England. Sir William Chambers, 1726–1796, the well-known English architect, was instrumental in disseminating Chinese taste, although the vogue had already been established in England before his important work, DESIGNS OF CHINESE BUILDINGS AND FURNITURE, was published in 1757. Chambers, who had travelled in the Orient, also published in 1772 A DISSERTATION ON ORIENTAL GARDENING. The vogue for Chinese fashions in English architecture was generally confined to interior decoration, with perhaps one or two rooms in the large mansions being hung with Chinese wallpaper and with the woodwork conveying an Oriental feeling in its carved detail and painted decoration. Before the 18th century had expired another revival in the Chinese taste occurred in England. The chinoiseries of this late 18th century revival are identified with the style of the English Regency and were partly due to the influence of the Prince of Wales, who had his drawing room at Carlton House treated in a Chinese manner, with some of the furniture designed by Henry Holland. Later work at the Brighton Pavilion around 1815 in the Chinese taste was rather ostentatious and displayed little or no elegance in its style.

Chippendale and other prominent contemporary furniture designers in their effort to conform to the prevailing fashion produced designs for furniture in the Chinese taste. These designs were often of an extravagant nature and were overloaded with ornament. Fortunately, the majority of these designs were never developed beyond the drafting board. However, as a result of this Chinese taste, the Rococo ornament of this era was augmented by an assortment of Chinese detail, which was generally simply grafted on characteristic mid-18th century Georgian forms. Pagoda motifs and fretwork figured prominently and their use often produced charming results. Carved pagoda motifs were often found on many articles of furniture and a carved repetitive pagoda motif was introduced in a wide molding. Pagoda motifs were frequently substituted for the architectural pediments on bookcases and secretary cabinets. Fretwork, either pierced or cut on a solid ground, was freely used both in the structure and in the ornament of mahogany furniture designed in either the Chinese or Gothic taste. The open fret gave the cabinetwork a light and airy feeling, while the blind fret gave the mahogany furniture additional richness. Occasionally both kinds of fretwork were found on the same article of furniture. The term *card-cut fretwork* is generally reserved for a fret pattern carved in low relief and interpreted in the Chinese taste. Card-cut lattice-work was a pronounced feature in the repertory of Chinese ornamental detail. Especially noteworthy were the chairs designed with arm and back panels of fretwork. Chinese figure subjects, birds and bells were also introduced as carved enrichments to produce an Oriental touch. In some of the decorative accessories, such as mirrors, sconces and wall brackets, the Rococo and Chinese fashions were skillfully blended. These pieces with their surprising asymmetrical forms were often praiseworthy for their light and fanciful carved decoration.

Lacquered articles of furniture achieved their greatest popularity in England early in the 18th century, and amateur japanning was regarded as a fashionable hobby. Naturally, like all hobbies, it gradually lost its appeal and by the second quarter of the 18th century the enthusiasm for japanning had greatly diminished. However, undoubtedly due to the revived interest in Chinese art, lacquered articles again became fashionable around 1750. Their popularity can easily be appraised from the numerous publications issued around the middle of the 18th century containing instructions for amateurs in the art of japanning or lacquering, as well as designs appropriate for lacquering. Especially popular was a book of engravings published by Robert Sayer around 1760 entitled THE LADIES' AMUSEMENT OR WHOLE ART OF JAPANNING MADE EASY. This book contained a charming kind of chinoiserie, invented by the French engraver Jean Pillement, which was very popular in England in all the different branches of the decorative arts. Chippendale, in order to meet the current demand, also stated in the DIRECTOR that some of his designs were suitable for lacquered decoration. He particularly favored bedroom pieces, such as Louis XV commodes, for lacquered decoration. Although some of the japanning was still executed in the earlier method with a priming or undercoating, much of the japanning by Chippendale and the later 18th century cabinetmakers could scarcely be distinguished from painting. It was more often simply paint and varnish. Frequently the colors were laid on with gum water in place of varnish. Practically all of the English lacquered articles of furniture belonging to the second half of the 18th century were essentially meretricious specimens of the earlier method.

Of all the vast quantity of furniture made in England during the Georgian period only a small portion of it can be assigned to individual cabinetmakers. This is largely explained by the fact that signed furniture was rare in England. In making a study of the authenticated furniture, the authorities have now decided on present evidence that William Vile, who was cabinetmaker to the King, was the leading mid-18th century cabinetmaker working in the Rococo style from around 1750 to 1765. He and his partner, John Cobb, conducted a large and successful business at No. 72 St. Martin's Lane. Authenticated pieces by Vile, which date from the early years of the reign of George III, are superbly finished and reveal an individuality in design. Some of the pieces are remarkable for their exuberant carvings, which are vigorously executed and skillfully finished. The veneered mahogany was selected for its fine and brilliant figure. The pieces are praiseworthy for their well-balanced lines and excellent proportions. Especially outstanding is the fresh and original quality

found in the principles of design and in the treatment of the decorative detail. It is impossible to estimate the degree of individual responsibility of Vile and Cobb for this cabinetwork. Suffice it to say that Vile was the senior partner and the known pieces for which Cobb was responsible are in the Neo-Classic style and are decorated with marquetry. After Vile retired, Cobb carried on the business until his death in 1778 and continued to supply furniture to George III and to the nobility and aristocracy. Authorities on English furniture have fully recognized the singular ability of these two partners.

In studying Georgian cabinetwork, with its high standard of design, fine materials and excellent proportions, it is patent that the time abounded with many capable designers and cabinetmakers. A fine sense of balance, harmonious lines, unity in design and suitability of ornament are all mirrored in this work. Undoubtedly this high level of design, which requires that the ornament, moldings and structure harmoniously complement and be in scale with each other, was chiefly due to a better understanding of and a closer adherence to the principles of classic architecture. The work of such mid-18th century craftsmen as William Hallet, Giles Grendey, Benjamin Goodison, and William Bradshaw exemplified these traditions associated with fine cabinetwork. William Hallet, 1707–1781, who had his establishment on St. Martin's Lane next door to William Vile, is considered to be one of the eminent cabinetmakers working at that time and he is sometimes regarded as the most fashionable cabinetmaker during the reign of George II. Benjamin Goodison, working around 1727 to 1767, at the Golden Spread Eagle, Long Acre, is considered to be one of the most outstanding cabinetmakers of the Georgian era. Authenticated pieces are distinctive for their masterful design and excellent craftsmanship. Included among the Late Georgian furniture makers were such craftsmen as John Linnell, George Seddon, and William Gates, the latter succeeding John Bradburn as cabinetmaker to His Majesty in 1777. It seems evident from the Royal accounts, 1777 to 1783, that Gates specialized in inlaid furniture, such as inlaid satinwood commodes. The marquetry work produced in his shop compared favorably with the finest examples of contemporary work.

Sinuous lines, which are a feature of the Rococo style, were freely introduced into the structure of many articles of furniture by Chippendale and his contemporaries in order to obtain a more graceful outline and to conform to the fashionable Louis XV style. Serpentine curves and reverse serpentine curves figured prominently. Serpentine curves were evident in the crest rail of the open back chair, in the top of the upholstered chair back and settee and in the seat rails of chairs and settees. The tops of certain kinds of tables, such as card tables and side tables, were often of serpentine contour, with a conformingly shaped frieze. The horizontal surface of chests of drawers and commodes were frequently serpentine-shaped, particularly when they were designed in the French taste. The vertical surface of these pieces in the French taste was sometimes bombé-shaped, as well as being of serpentine contour. From around 1750 straight quadrangular legs, often joined with a stretcher, were widely used, especially on articles of furniture designed in the Chinese or Gothic taste. The cabriole leg continued to be used in a more graceful and slender form on furniture designed in the French taste. It was often referred to as a French cabriole leg in distinction to the earlier cabriole leg of the Early Georgian style which was quite massive. Chippendale illustrated in the DIRECTOR both the cabriole leg and the straight leg for the open back chair designed in the Rococo taste. He seemed to be partial to a straight leg for dining room furniture. The French cabriole leg commonly terminated in a French whorl foot. The claw-and-ball foot continued to be used on the cabriole leg until around 1765; however, it was not illustrated in Chippendale's DIRECTOR.

Carving was by far the favorite enrichment for decorating the surface of furniture designed in the Chippendale style and it was remarkable for its crisp and sharp quality. Although the mid-Georgian cabinetmakers relied upon their careful selection of woods to produce a rich surface effect, they occasionally employed parcel gilding on the carved detail of their mahogany furniture. Chippendale in the DIRECTOR recommended that some of his Rocaille designs, in particular decorative accessories and console tables, be entirely gilded. Turning was largely restricted to the central pillars of tripod tables and to the baluster turned galleries on tea tables. During the mid-18th century the veneered panels were set flush with the framing and were outlined by small projecting moldings. This form of surface decoration was frequently found on the doors of clothespresses and wardrobes. Finely executed classic moldings were a pronounced feature on bookcases and secretary cabinets of architectural design. These moldings were often enriched with a carved repetitive classic pattern, such as the egg-and-dart, gadrooning and key fret. Dentils, which have their origin in classic architecture, were frequently placed in the cornice moldings. Bead, bead and reel, and cockbeaded moldings were also employed, the latter being frequently found around the edges of drawers. The drawers were fitted with chased brass bail handles, which were attached either to a pierced brass back plate or to two small circular or oval chased brass plates. The fashionable materials in upholstery work were tapestry, needlework, Spanish leather, damask and brocade. When the fabric covered the seat rail of a chair or settee it was usually finished with a row of brass nailheads. French tapestry was regarded as the most fashionable, while needlework gradually declined in popularity, and after 1770 needlework was largely superseded by tapestry coverings and silks.

Marquetry was revived around 1765. The finest English marquetry in the French taste was produced in St. Martin's Lane around 1770 where the shops of Thomas Chippendale and John Cobb were located. The light colored, exotic woods, which were worked in realistic designs in the manner of contemporary French floral marquetry, were laid in a ground of mahogany, satinwood or harewood veneer. Satinwood, which has a yellowish tone and varies from a plain grain to a rich figure, was often used in much fine furniture, especially drawing room furniture, after 1760. Chippendale produced veneered satinwood furniture in the French taste, shortly after its introduction, such as his marquetry satinwood commodes in the Louis XV style. Later, due to the influence of Adam, the marquetry work was in the Neo-Classic taste and was generally in panel arrangement. After 1775–80 marquetry was gradually supplanted by painted motifs; sometimes the two were combined on the same article of furniture. Although Matthew Boulton probably supplied some of the handsome ormolu mounts employed on this marquetry furniture, undoubtedly the majority of the mounts were of French origin, for as a rule English furniture mounts were much inferior to the French.

ARTICLES OF FURNITURE

Chairs   The outstanding feature of the mahogany chair with an open back designed in the Rococo taste around the middle of the 18th century was the variety of design of the back. The openwork splat, which was always joined to the seat and which generally retained its vase-shape outline (FIGURE 337), was manipulated in many ingenious designs by Chippendale and his contemporaries. It was frequently pierced with interlacing strapwork ornament. As the cabinetmaker's skill increased in handling mahogany the splat was pierced in more delicate designs and was often finely carved with Rococo foliations, scrollwork and cabochon ornament. Undoubtedly the most famous was the ribband-back (342) of French origin, which was executed in the highest degree of delicacy and grace. In this design the splat, which was formed of two long C-scrolls, was interlaced with crisply carved ribbon fastened at the top in a bow and tassel (342). The seat frame was usually straight on all four sides (337, 338, 339). The seat was either of the slip seat variety (338) or the seat rail was covered in fabric (337, 339). The top of the seat rail was sometimes carved with a small classic molding and the seat rail was often finished with a richly carved valance in the Rococo taste (340). There were two principal kinds of crest rails. One kind is usually referred to as a cupid's bow (337). This serpentine-shaped top rail was so-called because it strongly resembled the bow used by Cupid in representations of Roman mythology. A marked feature of this crest rail was the turned-up extremities (337, 338, 339), which sometimes extended one or more inches beyond the uprights (337). These ends were often twisted in a manner to form whorled terminals (337). Variations in design frequently occurred in this form of crest rail. The other kind of crest rail, which was also serpentine-shaped, had the ends curving downward to form a continuous rounded end where they joined the uprights (342). The carved legs were of cabriole form and terminated in claw-and-ball (337) or French whorl feet (340). Around the middle of the century straight quadrangular legs, usually chamfered (339), were introduced and were generally joined with stretchers (338, 339). Chippendale illustrated in the DIRECTOR both the cabriole and straight leg, the latter generally being the preferred type for the dining room. This chair was designed as a side chair and also as an open armchair. The straight arms were shaped and they rested on incurvate supports (342).

The mahogany chair with an open back designed in the Chinese taste was characterized by its pagoda-like ornament, the delicacy of its fretwork and the brackets beneath the seat rail (338, 341). A principal variety designed in the Chinese taste had an open back filled with Chinese fretwork or lattice-work (338). The crest rail sometimes had a pagoda-shaped carved cresting (341). The quadrangular legs, which were frequently headed by fretwork brackets, were often carved with card-cut lattice-work and were joined with stretchers (338). When designed as an armchair the space enclosed by the arms was also filled with fretwork. A caned seat with a loose cushion was often used in place of an upholstered seat. The chair was sometimes lacquered. Chippendale regarded chairs in the Chinese taste as being especially suitable for the bedroom.

The mahogany chair with an open back designed in the Gothic taste was chiefly a combination of the contemporary English Rococo type with some trace of Gothic detail (339). Occasionally the pierced splat was designed to simulate a Gothic traceried window. The straight quadrangular legs were usually joined with a stretcher.

The mahogany ladder-back chair was a popular design from about 1750 to 1790. With the exception of slight modifications the chair displayed little variation in its design. In a characteristic Chippendale variety the slightly flaring uprights supported a serpentine fret-pierced crest rail over three conformingly shaped and pierced cross rails. The quadrangular chamfered legs were connected with plain stretchers. Occasionally some of the later ladder-back chairs reflected the prevailing Neo-Classic influence in the carved detail, such as a carved patera appearing on the crest rail, as well as in a modification of the shape of the crest rail.

From around and after 1760–65 chair design began to reflect the influence of the Adam brothers. Some of the early examples were executed in a transitional style, with Neo-Classic motifs grafted on English Rococo frames. Chippendale, working under the influence of Robert Adam, gradually abandoned his earlier style for the more fashionable designs in the Adam or Neo-Classic taste.

The mahogany upholstered armchair with open padded arms, incurvate arm supports and a broad seat was termed "French" by Chippendale, and was a free adaptation of contemporary French models. The back was slightly raked and often serpentine-arched. The chair frequently had a valanced apron and the cabriole legs commonly terminated in French whorl feet. The undulating curves of the exposed frame were noteworthy for their vigorous execution. The chair was richly carved in Rococo motifs and the carvings were praiseworthy for their crisp quality. Some of the elaborate examples of this chair were gilded. It was also designed as a side chair. This type of "French" chair design was also made in a plainer variety. After the middle of the 18th century this plainer type of open arm chair was commonly designed with straight quadrangular chamfered legs joined with a stretcher. It had little or no carved detail. This plainer chair was notable for its fine proportions and excellent lines and it was exceedingly comfortable, which fact further increased its popularity. Apparently Chippendale continued to favor the Rococo influence, for he gave new designs for "French" chairs in the third edition of the DIRECTOR (340).

Chippendale gave six designs for hall chairs in the third edition of the DIRECTOR. He also suggested their use for summer houses as well as in the halls of the great mansions.

Settees   After 1740 French influence became increasingly evident in the design and carved decoration of the upholstered mahogany settee. Gradually the arms of the settee became higher and formed a continuation of the serpentine-arched back. This treatment of back and arms (450), which was borrowed from the French canapé designed in the Louis XV style, was characteristic of the English Rococo settee. Chippendale's indebtedness to contemporary French taste was even more obvious in the third edition of the DIRECTOR in which he gave several new designs for settees. Extant examples based on these designs are remarkable for their graceful elegance and have an entirely curvilinear framework with slender cabriole legs terminating in French whorl feet (345). Chippendale illustrated designs for settees with either cabriole or straight legs. Settees in the Chinese taste displayed a mixture of carved detail in the Chinese and Rococo taste.

The mahogany chair-back settee (341, 342) with an upholstered seat rivalled in popularity the upholstered variety of settee throughout the 18th century. This type of settee essentially followed the development of the contemporary open back chair so closely that a detailed description is not necessary. Undoubtedly it was due to this fact that this variety of settee was not illustrated by Chippendale. The chair-back settee almost always took the shape of two or three combined chairs, the arms, back and legs being similar to those of the contemporary open back chair. The back was executed in a variety of designs. Although Chippendale did not illustrate chair-back settees in his DIRECTOR, it is reasonable to assume that many were made in his establishment.

Benches   The legs of the stool and bench essentially followed the same development as the legs of the open back chair. One variety of bench, which was designed for a window recess, was frequently referred to as "French." There was a large demand for this bench in Georgian homes. It was designed with outscrolled sides and the front of the narrow seat was often serpentine-shaped. It usually rested on six legs of either straight or cabriole form. Some of the smaller examples of this variety were used as music benches.

Beds   Around 1740, when the style of Chippendale began to influence furniture design, the tester bed with tall, slender, delicately carved posts of mahogany superseded the tester bed completely covered with fabric. The mahogany headboard was richly carved and the cornice of the tester was ornately shaped and often carved with acanthus foliage. The mid-Georgian bed, which was always handsomely draped, was remarkable for its elaborately carved detail in the Rococo or Chinese taste. A pagoda-shaped tester frequently occurred on the bed designed in the Chinese taste (346). Occasionally the bed was lacquered (346), parcel-gilded, or gilded.

Tables   The mahogany dining table was not illustrated by Chippendale in his DIRECTOR. A variety of extension dining table, which came into general use in the mid-Georgian era, consisted of a center table with two oblong drop-leaves and two semi-circular end tables. The end tables, when not in use, could be detached and placed against a wall and used as side tables. The table frequently had a valanced apron, which was often sparingly carved, and the legs were commonly straight. This variety of extension table, with its obvious advantages, continued in favor until the 19th century. The dining table was essentially plain. It afforded less scope for the furniture designer than the many varieties of side tables.

The mahogany sideboard table (360), which was a long side table, as illustrated in Chippendale's DIRECTOR was designed either with or without a marble top and was without drawer or cupboard space. It was lighter in form than the Early Georgian sideboard table and it was designed either with straight or French cabriole legs. The frieze, valanced apron and legs were carved with the fashionable Rococo motifs. Frequently Chinese detail, especially card-cut lattice-work, was applied to the frieze and to the solid quadrangular legs in combination with the Rococo ornament.

The custom of having breakfast served in the bedroom led to the introduction of the small mahogany breakfast table (348) around the middle of the 18th century. It was designed to correspond with the furniture in the bedroom. One principal variety was of the Pembroke type and had an oblong top with drop-leaves (348). The frieze was fitted with a narrow drawer and it rested on four slender straight legs, which occasionally were joined with a stretcher (348). Essentially it was generally a plain piece of furniture. Sometimes in accordance with the prevailing Chinese taste fretwork detail was introduced (348). Its average length when the leaves were raised was slightly less than three feet. Designs appearing in the DIRECTOR were frequently of the Pembroke type (348).

The mahogany decorative side table designed in the Rococo taste generally had French cabriole legs, while the side table in the Chinese or Gothic taste had straight legs. It was designed either with or without a marble top. The frieze and legs were richly carved. The side table in the Rococo taste often had an ornately carved valanced apron. In addition to the mahogany side table the DIRECTOR also illustrated a number of ornately carved side tables in the Rococo taste which Chippendale recommended for gilding. Extravagantly decorated console tables of a pronounced Rococo nature were also represented in Chippendale's designs for side tables. They were often carved with a fantastic assortment of C-scrolls, shells and foliage. Under the influence of Robert Adam the straight tapering leg and classic ornament gradually and completely changed the appearance of the side table.

Many mahogany center tables, suitable for general use, were also made. The form and style of ornament essentially followed that of the contemporary side table. One principal mahogany variety around 1760 had a serpentine-shaped top over a conformingly shaped frieze which was carved with fretwork. It rested on four slender cabriole legs carved with acanthus foliage enclosing a cabochon ornament, with the legs terminating in French whorl feet.

The night table, or pot cupboard as it was called in 18th century trade catalogues, was introduced early in the 18th century. A popular variety during the second half of the 18th century was similar to the enclosed washing stand of that period. It was a small oblong table provided with a removable tray top, fitted with handgrips, which was over a cupboard with one or two doors. Sometimes a shallow drawer was beneath the cupboard compartment. It was mounted on four quadrangular tapering straight legs. The night table and close-stool chair which was also introduced early in the 18th century supplanted the close stool which was found in England from around the end of the 15th century. At a later date Sheraton in his DRAWING BOOK writes that night tables or pot cupboards intended for "genteel bedrooms are sometimes finished in satinwood and in a style a little elevated above their use."

The Pembroke table was a small oblong English table with a drop-leaf on each side. The drop-leaves were supported by hinged wooden brackets and the frieze was fitted with a small drawer. The table was supported on four slender legs which were almost always straight. The table of the Pembroke pattern was introduced around the middle of the century. Sheraton states that the table derived its name from the lady who first ordered one and who probably submitted the idea for the table to the cabinetmaker. It is assumed that the lady was the Countess of Pembroke, 1737–1831. After 1770 the table was often made of inlaid satinwood and was decorated with painted motifs in the Neo-Classic taste. The legs were of taper form. The average length of the table when extended was around three or three and one half feet. The Pembroke table was always distinctive for its delicate and restrained lines and its elegant simplicity.

Tea Tables   The social custom of inviting friends for tea at one's home resulted in the designing of numerous suitable decorative mahogany tea tables around the mid-18th century. The principal variety was of tripod form (351) and had either a shaped oblong or circular top (351) mounted on a carved shaft which rested on a carved tripod base terminating in claw-and-ball (351), whorled or padded snake feet. The top was made with a carved raised edge or with either a delicately pierced gallery of fretwork or a gallery of baluster turned spindles. The top generally tilted (351) so that the table could be placed against a wall when not in use, and it very often revolved. The circular top having an average diameter of between 25 inches and 30 inches was extremely popular, and it was also a favorite length for the oblong top. A structural feature, which was sometimes employed on this variety of table, is commonly referred to as a bird-cage (350). It consisted of two small square pieces of wood joined together by four baluster turned posts. Two long parallel pieces of wood on the under side of the table top were attached to the upper part of the bird-cage by pivots which allowed the top to tilt. The base of the bird-cage fitted over the columnar shaft of the table by means of a round hole which permitted the table to revolve. Sometimes in this variety of circular tripod table the edge was carved in a series of curves, and because of its supposed resemblance to the edge of a piecrust, it is now popularly called a pie-crust table. The top of the pie-crust table was cut from a single piece of wood. Another characteristic variety of a mahogany tea or china table was very often designed in the Chinese taste (349). This model frequently had an oblong top with a delicately pierced fretwork gallery over a frieze, carved with card-cut lattice-work, which rested on four straight quadrangular legs mounted on plinth feet (349). The legs were either pierced or carved with card-cut lattice-work and were headed with fretwork brackets (349). Occasionally the leg was in the form of a triple cluster column and was mounted on a plinth base. Frequently the legs were joined with a serpentine X-shaped stretcher pierced with openwork ornament (349). Occasionally the top lifted off and could be used as a separate tray. The average length of this table was around 33 inches. Chippendale illustrated an oblong table designed with a gallery, frieze and four legs in his DIRECTOR and observed that these tables are "for holding each a set of china and may be used as tea tables." It is apparently from this observation made by Chippendale that these tables are frequently called china tables. During the second half of the 18th century each guest was sometimes provided with his own small table for drinking tea, which also served for other purposes. This custom apparently explains the many small tables found for that period.

The term *supper table* (350) is generally given to a variety of a mahogany circular tilting top tripod table introduced around 1750. It continued to be made until about 1780–1790. The difference between a tea table of tripod form (351) and a supper table (350) was that the top of the latter was divided into compartments which were used to hold plates or cups and saucers for an informal supper. One variety had a shaped molded top fitted with eight circular dished compartments for plates. It was mounted on a turned shaft which rested on a tripod base. In another variety the eight compartments were not completely separated from each other. The circular top had a molded edge of eight scallops and had a raised center portion. The outer edge of the raised center portion was in eight concave arcs. The inner part of the central portion was dished to form a central quatrefoil depression. Sometimes it was designed with ten compartments and had a central cinquefoil depression (350). The average diameter was about 30 inches.

Gaming Tables The design for the mahogany card table during the mid-Georgian era was frequently inspired by contemporary French specimens. One characteristic variety was designed with a serpentine-shaped and molded folding top. The conformingly shaped frieze was sometimes valanced and richly carved. It rested on four slender carved French cabriole legs which commonly terminated in French whorl feet. This type of card table was distinctive for its graceful curving lines.

Toilet Tables The table particularly designed for dressing came into general use about the middle of the 18th century. An early variety of dressing table designed in the Chippendale style was in the form of a kneehole writing table. The top drawer was fitted with a hinged mirror and was divided into compartments for toilet articles. Sometimes the entire top lifted up to reveal a hinged framed mirror and a fitted interior for toilet articles. The top drawer was often provided with a writing board while in other examples the top of the table was finished in baize. Occasionally the hinged mirror was reversible and served the dual purpose of a book rest. Chippendale in the DIRECTOR referred to this variety as a "buroe dressing table." The majority of these bureau dressing tables were made of either walnut or mahogany and some were occasionally japanned. The dressing table with a fitted interior was designed in other distinctive types by Chippendale and his contemporaries, such as the commode dressing table which was a chest of drawers designed more or less in the French taste. The dressing table with a hinged box lid, which opened outward—that is, left and right—was in vogue in the second half of the 18th century. When it was closed it resembled a table; however, when the folding lid was open the interior contained a rising framed mirror and compartments for toilet articles. This table was also designed with a lifting top hinged at the rear in place of the hinged box lid. This form of dressing table with either a hinged box lid or with a lifting top was the most popular in the second half of the 18th century.

The small mahogany or walnut dressing table or side table, called a lowboy in America, could not compete in popularity with the more fashionable dressing table with its complex fitted interior. It was essentially similar in design to the lowboy of the preceding style. It was frequently decorated with inset quarter-round fluted stiles, and the central lower drawer was commonly carved with a recessed shell motif. The cabriole legs were often acanthus-carved and terminated in claw-and-ball feet.

The shaving table (401), which was so-called in contemporary catalogues and which was illustrated by Chippendale in the third edition of the DIRECTOR, was a smaller and more compact variety of a dressing table with a hinged box lid. It was provided with a framed mirror rising upward at the rear and was designed with compartments for the reception of soap, razors, bottles and other similar toilet accessories. As a rule the portion beneath the top of the table was fitted with one or two rows of shallow drawers and perhaps a shallow cupboard compartment flanked by several rows of small drawers. It was generally mounted on four legs. This shaving table became fashionable from around the middle of the 18th century onwards.

Writing Furniture   Numerous designs for the large mahogany library or writing table of pedestal form appeared in Chippendale's DIRECTOR and in the other trade catalogues. The carved decoration was usually in the Rococo or Chinese taste. Occasionally the pedestals were of bombé contour. The trade publications of the mid-Georgian era featured a number of designs for other varieties of writing tables of lighter form. A popular piece of furniture designed for writing was the mahogany writing table of kneehole form.

A characteristic variety of mahogany writing table was the so-called rent table of polygonal form, which was introduced about 1750 and which retained its popularity until early in the 19th century. Although it served different purposes it was essentially used to keep legal papers concerning the properties of an estate. It had a molded hexagonal top inset with tooled leather over six frieze drawers fitted with bail handles. The top revolved on a quadrangular pedestal fitted with a cupboard door. The drawers were commonly marked with the different letters of the alphabet; the letters were sometimes of ivory and were inlaid. The average diameter was about 52 inches. Variations in design occurred.

The principal variety of the mahogany slant-front writing desk or bureau during the time of Chippendale had an oblong top with a hinged slant lid over four graduated long drawers. The drawers were sometimes flanked with inset quarter-round reeded or fluted colonnettes. It rested on a molded base with ogee bracket feet. The slant lid when opened rested on pull-out slides and revealed an interior fitted with arcaded pigeonholes over small drawers and a central cupboard door. The four long drawers were fitted with bail handles and escutcheons and were frequently cockbeaded.

The mahogany slant-front secretary-cabinet displayed a variety of treatment in its decorative detail. One characteristic variety had an upper cabinet section with a molded cornice, commonly surmounted with a scrolled and fret-pierced pediment centering a low plinth, and a frieze over double doors. The double doors were usually glazed for the display of china. The mullions or glazing bars were arranged in an endless variety of designs. Sometimes when the secretary cabinet was decorated in the Chinese taste, the glazed doors were overlaid with delicately pierced fretwork. The under section contained a slant-front, which enclosed a fitted writing interior, over four graduated and cockbeaded long drawers. The molded base was frequently mounted on scrolled ogee bracket feet. This same piece of furniture when designed with adjustable shelves for the reception of books was called a secretary-bookcase. Sometimes in place of the slant-front it was designed with one long false drawer which could be pulled out and the front could be let down to serve as a writing flap. Variations in design frequently occurred.

The mahogany break-front secretary bookcase was a characteristic and popular piece of furniture during the second half of the 18th century. The projecting central portion was frequently surmounted with either a broken or scrolled pediment centering a low plinth. The molded cornice and frieze were over four glazed doors which enclosed adjustable shelves. The glazed doors were distinctive for the interesting and varied designs of the mullions. In some examples the mullions simulated Gothic traceried windows. The underbody contained a similar arrangement of four cupboard doors surmounted by two lateral drawers and a fall-front fitted writing drawer. It rested on a molded plinth. Occasionally the underbody was designed with two banks of drawers in place of the two lateral cupboard doors. The drawers were fitted with brass bail handles. The moldings, in particular the cornice moldings, were sometimes enriched with carved detail, and the frieze was sometimes fluted.

The mahogany secretary tallboy or secretary chest-on-chest was designed either with or without a pediment. In one principal variety the molded cornice was over four graduated long drawers. The lower chest usually contained three graduated long drawers; the upper drawer was false and was fitted with a writing interior. It rested on a molded scrolled ogee bracket base. The drawers were fitted with brass bail handles and were frequently cockbeaded.

Low China
Cupboards   Occasionally china was displayed in a rectangular standing piece of furniture of entirely open construction formed of Chinese fretwork and fitted with several shelves (347). As a rule it was about the height of a commode and was usually mounted on short legs. This article of furniture is sometimes referred to in English furniture literature as a chiffonnier although the reason for the ascription is not clear. Occasionally it is also described as a cabinet or low open cupboard. Judging from the numerous extant examples it must have been relatively popular and was apparently used chiefly for the display of porcelain. As a rule it was an ambitious piece of cabinetwork. Essentially it is a hybrid piece of furniture. Perhaps these are the pieces referred to in contemporary French literature as "commodes ouvertes dans le goût Anglais" (198, 199). (*See pages* 158, 295, 354.)

Cabinets   The mahogany china cabinet was a popular piece of furniture during the mid-Georgian era and was designed in a variety of forms and sizes. In one characteristic variety the upper section was designed either with or without a pediment; when the pediment occurred it was often scrolled and was filled in with fretwork. It had a molded cornice and frieze over two glazed doors, which were noteworthy for the various designs of their mullions. The underbody contained either two cupboard doors or two banks of drawers, and rested on either a molded plinth or a molded ogee bracket base. The carved detail was in the Rococo, Chinese or Gothic taste. The corners of the room were also sometimes fitted with china cabinets with glazed doors but these were recessed or built in. Chippendale made many elaborate designs for china cabinets in the Chinese taste, in which traces of the Rococo were frequently discernible. This variety of china cabinet, which was often mounted on a stand of varying height having straight quadrangular legs, featured a pronounced use of the pagoda motif and Chinese fretwork. The top of the cabinet was often finished with a pagoda top and the pagoda motif was introduced in the wide moldings. The frieze and legs were carved with card-cut lattice-work. The glazed doors were often overlaid with delicately pierced fretwork and the top was often surmounted with a fretwork gallery centering a pagoda motif. Many of these cabinets were lacquered. There was also a vogue for the mahogany hanging china or wall cabinet in the Rococo or Chinese taste (362).

Bookcases The architectural character given to the mahogany bookcase by the Early Georgian architects was maintained by Chippendale and other contemporary designers. These bookcases were enriched with finely carved classic moldings, copied from sections of moldings in classical architecture, and with other architectural detail. In contrast to this imposing type of bookcase numerous bookcases of a plainer variety were also made. This simpler variety was serviceable and functional and was notable for its fine principles of design and for the interesting treatment of the mullions in the glazed doors. Another form of bookcase was the break-front bookcase. It was essentially similar to the break-front secretary bookcase, except that it was not fitted for writing.

Commodes The commode or chest of drawers, which was of French origin, had its greatest period of development in France during the 18th century. It was always an elegantly designed and generally a richly ornamented piece of furniture and was often fitted with a marble top. It was designed chiefly with drawers and sometimes with drawers and doors, or with doors enclosing drawers. During the second half of the 18th century the French commode was an important piece of English furniture. No fashionable Georgian drawing room was correctly furnished without one. The English commode was sometimes decorated with applied ormolu mounts in accordance with the French taste. Carved mahogany commodes in the Rococo taste enjoyed a great vogue (354). The drawers were usually fitted with ormolu escutcheons, back plates and bail handles. Contemporary with the mahogany commode was the lacquered commode of Louis XV contour. The lacquered commode was generally found in bedrooms which were decorated in the Chinese taste. Numerous satinwood marquetry commodes inspired by contemporary French models were made from around 1760–65 to 1775 (355, 356). Undoubtedly the finest English marquetry furniture in the French taste was produced at that time. Especially praiseworthy were the satinwood commodes decorated in floral marquetry which had a delightful free-flowing quality. It is generally accepted that these satinwood commodes are unrivalled in the history of English cabinetwork not only because of their marquetry but also for their masterful design and technical perfection. The classical influence of Robert Adam was occasionally apparent in the ornament, especially in the classical friezes inlaid with paterae copied from the antique. Commodes in which the classical influence is apparent (357) represent Chippendale's final phase of development, the time at which he attained his greatest achievements.

Chests of Drawers

Chippendale made numerous designs for chests of drawers (358) which did not follow the contour of the Louis XV commode. The mahogany chest of drawers designed in the Chippendale style usually had a serpentine (358), reverse serpentine or a straight front. When the front was serpentine-shaped the corners or stiles were often canted and sometimes enriched (358). The majority of chests of drawers had four graduated long drawers which were often cockbeaded (358). The bail handles on the drawers were frequently in the French taste. The chest of drawers was very often mounted on a molded and valanced base with scrolled ogee bracket feet (358).

Clothes-presses

Although the wardrobe and clothespress were more plentiful during the mid-Georgian era the mahogany tallboy or chest-on-chest continued to be a popular variety of bedroom furniture. The molded cornice was carved with classic detail and the frieze was often carved with fretwork. The corners were sometimes canted and their carved decoration complemented that of the frieze. It usually rested on a molded base and ogee bracket feet. The drawers were frequently fitted with Rococo escutcheons and bail handles. Sometimes when the architectural design was more pronounced the stiles were enhanced with inset quarter-round fluted columns and carved capitals. Numerous designs for the mahogany clothespress (359) were illustrated by Chippendale and his contemporaries. The most popular variety had an oblong molded top over two long doors which usually enclosed sliding shelves or trays. The lower portion contained one or more rows of long drawers and rested on a molded base with ogee bracket feet. The clothespress was much preferred to the tall mahogany wardrobe which was designed with two cupboard doors. Variations in design frequently occurred.

Clocks

The mahogany long case clock designed in the Chippendale style usually had a scrolled pediment centering a low plinth over a molded cornice which was often arched (361). The top of the dial was arched and the door of the hood was conformingly shaped and was flanked by two fluted colonnettes (361). The top of the pendulum door of the trunk was often shaped and the door was flanked by fluted pilasters (361). The base of the clock was frequently mounted on scrolled ogee bracket feet (361).

Stands

The washing stand was not designed as a specialized piece of furniture until about the middle of the 18th century. Chippendale illustrated designs for the basin stand in his DIRECTOR. A principal variety of basin stand was the mahogany circular tripod basin stand (353). It had a molded basin ring on three scrolled supports joined by a median trilateral shelf containing two narrow drawers and often surmounted by a covered urn (353). The lower three (scrolled) supports rested on a dished trilateral base with three cabriole legs (353). The top of the base was dished to receive the pitcher when the bowl was filled with water. The covered urn was to hold the soap. Its average height was about 30 inches and its diameter about 11 inches. Variations in design occurred. Sometimes it was larger and had a shaped oblong top. Other later designers, such as Hepplewhite and Sheraton, made numerous designs for this category of furniture. The washing stand, when it was closed, frequently resembled a small bedside table.

The introduction of the tea table around the end of the 17th century led to the designing of a small mahogany stand for the reception of the silver teakettle and its burner. An early variety, which undoubtedly served many other purposes, was designed with a small circular top mounted on a turned shaft, resting on a tripod base. Chippendale and other designers illustrated this variety to be used as a teakettle stand. A characteristic variety of mahogany kettle or urn stand during the Chippendale style had a small quadrangular top with a raised rim. The front of the shallow frieze was fitted with a small pull-out slide. It rested on four slender legs. The width of the table averaged from around 12 inches to 15 inches. Its carved decoration was in accordance with one of the prevailing fashions. Occasionally the legs were in the form of triple cluster columns and terminated in plinth feet.

Designs for candlestands or torchères were plentiful in the mid-18th century pattern books. The majority were in the Rococo taste and were distinctive for their wealth of carved ornament. Some were designed in the Chinese taste and others combined Gothic detail in their style of ornament. In addition to the mahogany examples Chippendale recommended some of his candlestands to be gilded, painted or lacquered. In contrast to the ornately carved candlestand many were of a plainer and more serviceable character. The design for the candlestand with its shaft and tripod base was transformed by Robert Adam. His designs for candlestands were inspired by the antique Roman tripods. In this variety the top instead of being mounted on a shaft rested on three slender tapered supports which flared slightly outward at the feet. It was often mounted on an incurvate trilateral plinth. A large number of these candlestands were intended to support candelabra.

Relatively few designs for pedestals were made during the Rococo era because of their classic character. Under the influence of Robert Adam pedestals were again widely used, especially in the interior of houses decorated in the Adam taste. Pedestals were particularly suitable for classical treatment.

Mirrors   After 1740 carved and gilt wood wall mirrors in the French taste began to supplant the mirror of architectural design (343). Pendants of naturalistic fruit and flowers and C-scrolls sometimes dripping with stalactites were favorite motifs for the carved and gilded frames of mirrors decorated in the Rococo taste between 1750 and 1765 (343). Mirrors in the Gothic taste were also designed. The most extravagant and fantastic frames were those designed in the Chinese taste blended with a generous assortment of Rococo motifs. Long-beaked and long-necked birds, pagoda tops, mandarins, bells, stalactites, shells, rock-work and C-scrolls were all familiar motifs. Many of these frames were remarkable for the skillful technique displayed in blending Oriental motifs with French motifs. In this type of frame the mirror glass panel was sometimes delicately painted with a Chinese landscape and figures to further instill an Oriental feeling. Another variety of mirror designed in the Rococo style had a mirror of asymmetrical form framed in pronounced carved C-scrolls and broken curves.

Accessories   Wall brackets were an important decorative appointment in the second half of the 18th century. Pattern books by Chippendale and his contemporaries illustrated numerous symmetrical and asymmetrical designs for gilded or painted wall brackets. The majority combined a blending of Rococo and Chinese ornament and were enhanced with such favorite motifs as rock-work, C-scrolls, stalactites, exotic birds and pagoda tops. Another variety was made of mahogany and was composed of delicately pierced fretwork. This type, which was commonly used for the reception of porcelain figures and vases, was especially popular. Wall brackets were often used to hold candelabra for augmenting the illumination and were also frequently used for the reception of clocks.

Carved gilt wood sconces were also a distinctive and important decorative appointment. The majority were in the French taste. Rococo ornament was often extravagantly combined with architectural columns and Chinese motifs. Occasionally the sconces were designed with mirrors. The name *girandole,* in addition to its usual connotation of a branched candlestick, was generally given in mid-18th century English trade catalogues to a fixed wall appliqué provided with branched supports for candles. These appliqués or sconces were properly wall-lights; however, the term has been extended to include mirrors provided with candle-branches which supplemented the lighting of a room. The wall-light girandole (344) was designed with either an open-work background or with a mirror enclosed in scroll work to reflect the light. Chippendale illustrated both types in his DIRECTOR.

It seems that movable shelves for either china or books did not come into vogue in the 18th century much before the time of Chippendale, who gave eleven designs for china shelves, seven of which were of the hanging variety. Except for one described as "Gothic", they were all in the Chinese taste. Some of the standing shelves somewhat resembled the so-called chiffonnier (*see page* 290).

Designs for screens of the cheval, folding and tripod pole varieties were all illustrated by Chippendale in his DIRECTOR. The cheval fire screen was generally decorated in the Rococo taste and was recommended for gilding. The mahogany tripod pole-screen with its needlework panel was extremely fashionable. Around the middle of the century small mahogany candle screens were frequently used to protect the lighted candle from drafts. The candle screen was usually designed either as a miniature tripod pole-screen or as a cheval fire screen. Its height was slightly over a foot and it was made entirely of wood.

There was a vogue for small mahogany folding screens consisting of two sections often fitted with panels of Chinese printed paper. These screens, which were mounted on slender straight quadrangular legs, were very often reduced to the proportions of a fire screen.

The mahogany dumb-waiter was chiefly designed to take the place, to some extent, of that of a butler in the dining room. Sheraton in his CABINET DICTIONARY writes about the dumb-waiter as "a useful piece of furniture, to serve in some respects the place of a waiter, whence it was so named." The dumb-waiter was introduced in England around 1740, and it is generally believed that the variety of dumb-waiter consisting of three circular trays increasing in size from top to bottom was an English innovation in design. The trays revolved on a shaft which rested on a tripod base. Variations in design occurred. Sometimes it was designed with two tiers. It served a number of purposes in the dining room. One of its main uses was to hold dessert plates, knives and forks as well as the dessert. It was also useful for after-dinner drinking.

Wooden trays were known as early as the Middle Ages. The social custom of tea drinking rendered necessary the designing of suitable decorative wooden trays. Chippendale in his DIRECTOR illustrated designs for decorative mahogany trays. The tray was generally oblong and had a finely pierced fretwork gallery with two scrolled handgrips. Trays designed at a later date in the Adam style were frequently oval. Circular trays were relatively rare. Lacquered trays were popular throughout the 18th century. Shortly after the middle of the 18th century plain, oblong, sturdy, mahogany trays were made for the butler's use, and were set upon folding stands of X-form.

The mahogany box knife-case (363) was generally designed in pairs and was placed at each end of the sideboard table in the Georgian dining room. It was of vertical box form and had a sloping lid and a shaped front (363). The interior was divided into many small oblong partitions (363). The knives and forks were so inserted that the handles were exposed and the spoons were of opposite arrangement. The vase knife-case of graceful vase form was introduced later in the 18th century and was in the Neo-Classic taste.

The mahogany plate pail was used to carry the plates from the kitchen to the dining room. The more elaborate examples were often octagonal in form and the sides were of pierced fretwork. One of the eight sides was usually left open in order to facilitate the handling of the plates. The pail was fitted with a brass bail handle. Plate pails were often designed in pairs and were placed near the fireplace in order to keep the plates warm.

The plate warmer, in addition to being designed as one of a pair of sideboard pedestals, was also designed as a separate piece of furniture. It was in the form of an enclosed mahogany stand and had a metal lined interior and was fitted with a heater. It was used in the dining room.

The wine cooler or wine cistern, which is a portable container for holding wine bottles during the meal, has been used since the Middle Ages. It was made of various materials, such as stone and all kinds of metals. The mahogany wine cooler lined with lead was first designed shortly after 1730. Chippendale illustrated several designs for wine coolers. The mahogany wine cooler, with its lead lining, was often tub-shaped or of oval form and was mounted on four cabriole legs. Its average height was generally slightly less than two feet. The wood was bound with wide brass bands, which were either chased or plain. It was fitted with two side bail handles and a lower drain cock. Mahogany wine buckets of coopered construction were also used. The round flaring bucket, which was bound with brass bands, was fitted with two side bail handles. Its average height was about 16 inches and its diameter about 14 inches. The wine cooler was generally placed under the sideboard table or sideboard. It seems that when the wine cooler was furnished with a cover it could also be used as a case for bottles or a cellarette.

The mahogany cellarette, which was designed as a receptacle for the storage of wine bottles in the dining-room, was introduced in the Early Georgian era. It was usually placed under the sideboard table. The interior had a lead lining and was divided into partitions for the bottles. It was fitted with side handles and a lock and key to safeguard the contents. Later it was often fitted with casters so it could be readily wheeled out. It was designed in different forms; one characteristic variety was octagonal.

Terrestrial and celestial globes mounted on decorative stands, made either of wood or metal, were found in the libraries of Continental houses as early as the 16th century, and almost a century later globes mounted on stands were in use in England. In the 18th century English craftsmen provided elaborately carved stands for the celestial and terrestrial globes. These stands, which support the globe within a wooden ring called the horizon, were designed with three legs, with four or more legs or with a tripod base. This latter stand of tripod form consisting of a shaft mounted on a tripod base was especially fashionable. An orrery and an armillary sphere were frequently found among the furnishings in a large library, and were also mounted on stands similar to the globe stands.

Mahogany library steps, which were designed to facilitate the accessibility of books on the upper shelves, were seldom used before the middle of the 18th century. Their use was largely restricted to Georgian homes having a large collection of books in the library. Although library steps were a utilitarian piece of furniture they were usually of elegant design and conformed to the other library furniture. Sometimes the library steps were ingeniously designed to conceal their real purpose such as in the form of an oblong stool.

CHAPTER EIGHTEEN

ADAM

The last four decades of the 18th century were marked by a vital movement of investigation and appreciation of antique culture and its application to all phases of contemporary art. This renewed revival of interest in the arts of Greece and Rome and the new classic style based on them is believed to have been largely due to the excavations begun in 1738 at Pompeii and Herculaneum. These excavations resulted in discoveries arousing great interest in antique classic art. Italy, as in the Renaissance, once again became the center of archaeological activities, and Rome abounded with scholars from all parts of Europe. Undoubtedly the Classic Revival was accelerated by the publication from 1752 to 1767 of the great illustrated works on the Herculaneum frescoes by the Comte de Caylus and in 1766–67 of the books on Greek and Etruscan vases and antiquities by Sir William Hamilton. Of greater importance were the archaeological researches by Johann Winckelmann and his eulogies of antique art. The Adam brothers

and Giovanni Piranesi were also noteworthy figures in this new classic movement, as well as Michel Angelo Pergolesi, Giocondo Albertolli and others who supplied original designs in the new classic style. In all probability the success of this Neo-Classic movement was equally due to a reaction or revolt against the Rococo, for France began to show signs of tiring of her Louis XV style around the middle of the 18th century. In France the light and graceful Louis XVI style is the early phase of the Classic Revival while the pompous Empire style is the later phase. In England the animating spirit of the Classic Revival was the architect Robert Adam and his brother James. Robert Adam was virtually the creator of a new classic style known by his name. The Neo-Classic movement was also associated with a sentimental mode that is rather difficult to explain. This taste for plain forms, seen in the art works of such painters as Greuze and Angelica Kauffmann, seems to have resulted from an idealistic attempt to sentimentalize the ancient classic world.

The long reign of George III, 1760–1820, can easily be divided artistically into two well-marked divisions; the earlier half from 1760 to 1793, ending with Pitt's declaration of war on France, was completely influenced by the style of Robert Adam. These three decades in Georgian art were imbued with an extraordinary refinement and finish. A certain formal elegance inclining to coldness of expression pervaded much of this work. During this era the Grand Tour was more fashionable than ever among a small cosmopolitan group. The taste for works of art and classical antiquities was greatly encouraged. Many of the houses belonging to the aristocracy had their sculpture or picture galleries. Sculptures from Rome, paintings from Venice, as well as Dutch, Flemish and French works of art, rare books, collections of medals and gems were all a part of this cosmopolitan taste. Furniture and household decoration were a serious pursuit among cultured society. The culmination of this perfection of taste materialized in the work of Robert Adam. When Robert Adam first returned from Italy he was in the process of forming his style. His earlier work, which was of short duration, reflected the influence of the Anglo-Palladian style. However, Robert Adam thoroughly believed in the elegance of the ancient manner and he soon began to interpret it in his work. In his fully developed style he completely revolutionized the taste in architecture and in the decorative arts and he successfully routed the Rococo style. In Adam's matured style the moldings were smaller and lighter and the painted and stucco ornament was inspired from Italian Renaissance grotesques having their origin in ancient Roman frescoes. Adam always kept in close touch with

Italy and he retained modellers at Rome who copied bas-reliefs and ornament for him. From around 1770 younger architects as well as older members of the Palladian school adopted his style, and sometimes it is difficult to distinguish their work from the work of Adam himself.

Robert Adam, 1728–1792, was the second son of William Adam, a successful architect in Scotland. He was born at Kirkcaldy and he had three brothers, John, James and William. Robert Adam received his early architectural training from his father. In 1754 he went to Italy, and, in the course of his itinerary, he visited the ruins of Diocletian's palace at Spalatro. With the assistance of an architect and two draftsmen he secured sufficient information to produce a restoration of the entire building which he published in a splendid work in 1764, entitled THE RUINS OF THE PALACE OF DIOCLETIAN AT SPALATRO. Much of his subsequent work reflected the influence of these studies and was to a large extent based upon them. Upon his return to England in 1758 he embarked upon his architectural career in London. His success was almost immediate, and in 1762 he was appointed sole architect to the King. He resigned this office six years later, and was succeeded by his brother James, who shared the office with another. James Adam had also studied at Rome and was later closely associated in business with Robert Adam. His brother John succeeded to his father's architectural practice in Edinburgh, and his brother William is reputed to have been at different times both a banker and an architect. In 1773 Robert and James Adam began publishing an illustrious series of folio engravings and descriptions of designs for many of their more celebrated works. It was entitled WORKS IN ARCHITECTURE, and was instrumental in popularizing the Adam style of ornament. It also included numerous illustrations of different articles of furniture designed by the Adam brothers. It would be practically impossible to list all their works. In addition to public buildings, they designed many town houses in London's fashionable West End as well as a number of famous country estates. Many fine homes were remodelled and redecorated under their supervision. Robert Adam's position as architect was undisputed, and when he died he was buried in Westminster Abbey.

Although the 18th century produced a number of distinguished English architects, such as Kent, Gibbs and Chambers, undoubtedly Robert Adam was the outstanding fashionable architect. Robert Adam through his extraordinary ability created a new treatment for classic ornament which was distinctive for its singular graceful elegance and for its refined and finished detail. Out of simple curvilinear forms, of which he favored the oval, he had the genius to create combinations of remarkable beauty and variety. He never permitted decorative details to conceal the principal lines of a design. He believed that decoration should contribute its share but no more than its share to the entire effect. It was to be a part of a harmonious scheme. Robert Adam believed and successfully practiced that the smallest details of decoration and furnishings were within the field of the architect and that only in this manner could a complete and accordant result be achieved. In his vast collection of drawings, in addition to the designs for furniture, he illustrated designs for such pieces as carpets, lamps, wall brackets, fire grates, andirons and the metal hardware for doors and windows. He also provided designs for articles of

silver, including tea services, candlesticks and épergnes. He designed his furniture to form an essential part of his decorative scheme. Each piece was placed in its correct position. Although this deliberate arrangement banished all feeling of warmth and casualness it gave the rooms an atmosphere of formal elegance and spaciousness. Adam designed only for his enormously wealthy clients. An Adam home or an Adam drawing room is an individual English product and there is nothing to parallel it in all of English art. Of all his work, his richest designs were undoubtedly executed for Robert Child at Osterley.

The large decorative paintings for ceilings, fashionable during the Early Georgian period, were discarded by Adam. In his treatment of the ceilings he used small panel pictures framed in stucco and worked in the form of lunettes, circles, squares or oval compartments. Occasionally these panels and medallions instead of being painted in different colors were painted en grisaille. Sometimes as an alternative to these small scale panel pictures he decorated his ceilings with arabesque motifs in the manner of Renaissance artists. The majority of artists executing these decorative schemes developed by Adam were foreigners. Occasionally these decorative artists did paint the actual panels in the ceilings, but as a rule the work was generally carried out by lesser artists from the original designs. Probably the best known of all these painters was the Swiss artist, Angelica Kauffmann, working in London from 1766 to 1781. Her work had a distinctive decorative quality and she developed paintings of pictorial subjects in the sentimental classical manner. The work of the Italian artist Zucchi, who later married Angelica Kauffmann, was outstanding for its excellent composition and effective coloring. The Florentine artist Cipriani, who came to England in 1755, was responsible for much decorative work during his thirty years in England. He was an accomplished draftsman, but his manner of coloring lacked warmth. Biago Rebecca resided in England for many years and he painted with typical Italian facility. The Italian artist and designer Pergolesi was much in demand for designing mural decorations. His treatment of antique and Renaissance motifs in the Neo-Classic manner was skillful and finished. Undoubtedly much of the inlaid and painted decoration in the Neo-Classic manner used in contemporary cabinetwork was inspired by designs of this group of decorative artists.

The vogue for stucco walls, which had superseded wood panelling in the early 18th century Palladian mansions, continued throughout the 18th century. In Adam's matured style the plasterwork detail became much lighter. His plasterwork duplicated the delicacy and refinement so characteristic of the flat and elegant Roman stucco work. His designs reveal how thoroughly he had studied the stucco decoration in Roman villas, especially Hadrian's Villa at Tivoli. The flowing lines of delicate ornament, festoonings of husks enriched with such Renaissance motifs as urns, candelabra and sphinxes were remarkable for their flat, light and graceful elegance. Occasionally naturalistic motifs such as sprays of ivy or bay leaves and interlacing trails of vine branches appeared in this style of stucco decoration developed by Adam. Since marble was so costly Adam used a composition known as scagliola for his columns. He also used this composition resembling marble for some table tops and pedestals as well as for some very elegant floors.

Gilding, which Adam favored in his earlier work, was largely discarded in his later work. The fashionable tints during the later part of the 18th century were various light secondary colors, worked either singly or in combination, such as pale green, pink, lavender and light blue. The walls were sometimes hung with paintings symmetrically arranged. Since the decorative value was of primary importance, many of these paintings were done by contemporary artists for the space they were intended to fill. The Italian school was very fashionable and paintings by such artists as Pannini, Canaletto and Zuccarelli were the inspiration for much of this work.

After the publication of WORKS IN ARCHITECTURE Adam's influence on the decorative arts was well established. His style of light and elegant classic ornament inspired by the ornament in ancient Roman baths and villas was soon imitated by designers and cabinetmakers. Adam produced many designs for furniture appropriate for the houses he decorated. These designs for furniture were praiseworthy for the classic simplicity of their contour, for their excellent proportions and for the graceful delicacy of their ornament. It is important to remember that Robert Adam and his brother were architects and designers and not cabinetmakers. The actual cabinetmakers of Adam furniture were Chippendale and numerous other talented contemporary cabinetmakers who carried out the Adam designs. The classic contour and the light and delicate style of ornament developed by Adam was the inspiration for and dominating factor in English furniture design for practically all of the remaining years of the 18th century. Both Hepplewhite and Sheraton derived much from the designs of Adam.

Although they modified and adapted the style in order to bring it within the financial reach of the middle classes, the influence of Adam was mirrored in their work. Every field of the decorative arts from 1760 to 1800 was indelibly stamped with good taste largely due to Adam's far-reaching influence. The era was notable for the ceramic work of the illustrious potter Josiah Wedgwood, who was also instrumental in fostering the Neo-Classic movement. Although Adam's influence is undisputed, care must be given neither to exaggerate his position nor to overlook the fine work of other contemporary architects, such as James Wyatt and James Stuart, who also contributed to the development of the Neo-Classic spirit in England.

In the period between 1760 and Adam's death in 1792 his style showed considerable modification. Adam's earlier designs for furniture, which covered only a few years and were also few in number, reflected the Early Georgian style of William Kent and also some traces of the Rococo. Upon such characteristic forms he grafted his new style of classic ornament. Adam's matured style in furniture design completely revolutionized the taste in contemporary cabinetwork, resulting in the abandonment of the Rococo style. From about 1775 the influence of the Louis XVI style was evident in Adam's designs for furniture. Such pieces for the drawing room as chairs, settees and commodes were close adaptations of contemporary French models. The furniture designed by Adam was essentially rectilinear in form. Occasionally curvilinear lines, generally in the form of gracefully swept curves, were introduced. Console tables and commodes were often semicircular or semi-oval in plan. When serpentine

curves were used they were less pronounced. Occasionally they appeared in the front seat rails of chairs and settees and in the front of the sideboard table. As a result of Adam's influence the cabriole leg was generally discarded by 1770 in favor of a straight slender tapering leg of either quadrangular or cylindrical form. The quadrangular leg frequently terminated in a molded plinth. Moldings were smaller and lighter. The tops of bookcases and other similar articles of furniture were either straight or were surmounted with a shallow pediment. Finials in the form of classic urns were freely introduced. The oval form sometimes appeared in the frames of mirrors and in the backs of chairs and settees. The furniture was lighter in form than in the preceding Chippendale style and reflected graceful elegance in its general design. The delicate lines of some pieces, especially the later drawing room chairs with openwork backs, often conveyed a feeling of great fragility.

Adam, to a greater or less extent, remained partial to mahogany for dining room and library furniture because it afforded an excellent medium for his distinctive style of flat carving. However, the tendency in the later 18th century cabinetwork was toward hardwoods of a lighter tone, in particular satinwood and harewood. Robert Adam's preference for satinwood was largely responsible for its popularity and for its extensive use by other contemporary designers and cabinetmakers. In fact this era is often referred to in the literature on English furniture as the Age of Satinwood, in the same manner as the preceding era is known as the Age of Mahogany. It seems that the finest quality of satinwood came from Puerto Rico and was especially liked for its oily appearance and superb figure. Satinwood, which varies in color from a pale to a deep amber yellow, takes a fine polish and is better adapted for veneering than as a solid wood. Satinwood veneer was generally used in conjunction with contrasting veneers of other colored or stained woods, such as mahogany, tulipwood, kingwood, rosewood, ebony, harewood and stained holly. Undoubtedly from around 1770 veneering in satinwood and other exotic woods with the typical inlaid or painted decoration in rich polychrome coloring was the fashionable practice during the prevalence of the Adam style. Gilding was also much favored, especially for drawing room furniture such as chairs, settees, window benches and pier tables and pier mirrors. Parcel gilding was also used by Adam on the painted furniture.

Carving, which had been so universally practiced during the Early Georgian and Chippendale styles, was relegated to a role of secondary importance from the time of Robert Adam, and by late in the 18th century it was well in the background. This was primarily due to the fashion for veneering and for inlaid and painted decoration. Undoubtedly much of the beauty of late 18th century cabinetwork was in the use of contrasting veneers. Veneering was effectively employed on the cabinetwork designed by Robert Adam. The careful selection and arrangement of choice contrasting veneers gave an unusually rich and beautiful effect. Bandings of veneered wood became broader and more decorative. Stringing, in which a narrow line of wood is laid into a contrasting veneered ground, was also employed for decorative effects. The early carved detail on furniture designed by Adam was rather bold and vigorously executed. How-

ever, in Adam's matured style, from around 1775, the carving was in low relief and was generally in the form of such fashionable motifs as paterae, husks, urns and festoons worked in repetitive designs. Fluting was a popular decorative detail in friezes, pilasters and legs. The carved detail was minute and exact and its smooth, flat and precise quality resembled Wedgwood's cameo plaques. Later in the painted and gilded furniture such detail was generally made of composition, which was a mixture of whiting, resin and size. This composition was pressed into molds while still plastic and when the ornament was removed from the molds it was affixed to the surface of furniture with glue or pins. Especially characteristic of Adam's later work was the use of festoons or swags made of composition strengthened by a core of wire. This composition ornament on wire was often used on mirrors and under the friezes of decorative side tables. In this manner an exceedingly delicate and fragile effect could be achieved, for wood carvings of such fragility would not be serviceable.

Marquetry was revived around 1765. The different light colored exotic woods were generally laid in a ground of satinwood or harewood veneer. In the marquetry pieces designed by Adam and executed by Chippendale the ornament was inspired by contemporary French marquetry, with Neo-Classic motifs of Renaissance derivation combined with bouquets of flowers tied with ribbons. The later marquetry work covered a much smaller surface and was generally arranged in panels and in the friezes. It was treated in Adam's light and delicate style and included such favorite decorative motifs as ribboned paterae, festoons of husks, urns, radial fans and medallions enriched with husks. Occasionally in some very ambitious examples of marquetry work classical figure subjects were introduced. The fashion for decorating furniture by painting was revived around 1770 and in the ensuing decade painted decoration and marquetry were often combined on the same piece of furniture. This taste for painted furniture resulted from Adam's desire to make the furniture a closer part of the decorative scheme, in which the furniture would harmonize with the painted ceilings and with the tinted stucco walls. As a result of this new vogue, painting almost entirely superseded marquetry work by the last decade of the 18th century. The painted decoration, which was in the form of borders, floral festoons, garlands, interlacing vine trails, sprays of leafage and medallions of classical figure subjects, was found on satinwood or harewood veneers and occasionally on an entirely painted wood surface. The painted decoration was most often in natural colors and occasionally en grisaille, and as a rule it was painted directly on the wood surface. However, medallions of classical figure subjects were sometimes painted on copper panels and then inserted into the furniture. These painted copper medallions were especially found on the façades of commodes and cabinets. It is believed that the painted decoration on furniture was generally done by lesser artists who copied the style of such talented decorative artists as Cipriani, Zucchi and Angelica Kauffmann. Ambitious pieces of cabinetwork, particularly commodes and decorative side tables, were painted with figure subjects and mythological scenes copied from the painted ceilings. A large quantity of furniture was made of beech and other soft woods and its surface was entirely painted in pale colors to harmonize with the delicately colored walls.

Sometimes Robert Adam and other contemporary designers and cabinetmakers decorated their furniture designed in the French taste, especially commodes and cabinets, with finely chased bronze doré or ormolu mounts. It is reasonable to assume that the majority of these applied mounts were of French origin, for the English bronze work was inferior to that of the French, the one exception being the work of Matthew Boulton who was active around this time. During the last quarter of the 18th century continuous back plates of brass were reintroduced for the brass bail handles. These back plates of oval, circular or octagonal form were decorated with stamped detail in the Neo-Classic taste. Sometimes the fine cabinetwork of this era, such as commodes and the friezes on decorative side tables, was enriched with Wedgwood's jasper panels and medallions. The delicate coloring and classical composition of these jasper plaques harmonized with the comprehensive scheme of the interior decoration. For the same reason scagliola was occasionally inset in the panels of furniture. Undoubtedly Robert Adam's Italian training accounted for his effective use of scagliola in cabinetwork to provide a touch of coloring. The practice of painting wood to simulate marble was also occasionally used. Decorative side tables and pedestals were among the principal forms of furniture treated in this manner so that they would be in accord with their background. In the upholstering of furniture the use of French tapestry had almost completely superseded needlework by 1770. English tapestry coverings made at Fulham and at Soho were also used. Flowered silks, leather and horsehair were also favorite fabrics for upholstery work. Horsehair first became popular around 1780 and its use was recommended for furniture subjected to hard wear, such as dining room chairs.

The style of ornament developed by Robert Adam was exceedingly rich in variety and was essentially borrowed from Italian Renaissance and antique Roman ornament. The motifs were remarkable for their exquisite delicacy, for their classic refinement and for their light and graceful elegance. Included among the motifs that Robert Adam repeatedly used for enrichment were paterae, swags or festoons, especially festoons of husks, the anthemion or honeysuckle, wheat sheafs, husks, the lunette filled with a radiating design, ovals filled with radiating lobes, medallions with classical figure subjects or trophies of armor, especially of Roman body armor, rosettes, a radial fan motif, delicate arabesques, candelabra, grotesques, palmettes, water leaf, acanthus scrolling, urns often of tripod form, vases, wreathes and garlands, drapery swags, interlacing trails of vine branches, sprays of ivy and bay leaves, classical figure subjects, masks, real and imaginary animal motifs such as the ram's head, griffons, lions and birds, sphinxes, and repetitive patterns such as the egg and dart, guilloche, husk and beadwork chains. Although Robert Adam made designs for all the various forms of furniture in each of the different categories, the description of the following articles will be restricted to his better known pieces such as chairs, tables, commodes, sideboard tables and some decorative appointments.

ARTICLES OF FURNITURE

Chairs   After 1760 the influence of the Classic Revival was often perceptible in chair design. In the beginning the change was essentially restricted to the ornament rather than to any change in structure. Neo-Classic motifs were grafted upon frames of Rococo form. Some chairs recalled the grandiose style of the Palladian architects. Chairs designed by Adam around 1760–65 reflected this transitional phase (FIGURE 364). The form of the chair was gradually altered to harmonize with the Adam brothers' unique style of classic architectural decoration. Chairs became lighter. Open armchairs as well as side chairs designed by Adam were notable for their excellent proportions. In Adam's fully developed style he abandoned the cabriole leg for the straight tapering leg (365, 366) based on the fashionable Louis XVI leg. Mahogany chairs with open backs designed by Adam in the Neo-Classic taste were praiseworthy for the reserve of their forms and for the appropriateness of their carved decoration which was harmoniously related to the structural design. Husks, honeysuckle (366), urns, paterae (366) and above all the lyre, the shape of which was ingeniously varied in Adam's designs (365, 366), were all included in the repertory of classical ornament. The back was rectilinear (367), hooped (366) or serpentine (365), and the openwork splat was of lyre form (365, 366).

As the style developed, oval-, heart- and shield-shape backs became fashionable and occasionally drapery festoons or slender radial ribs replaced the openwork splat. Straight cylindrical or quadrangular legs, fluted and tapering, and terminating in a small molded foot, were typical (365, 366, 367, 368, 369). The arms in the early examples were secured to the side seat rails (364) as in the preceding Rococo style, and later as a rule they finished directly above the front legs (366, 369). The majority of arms were straight and shaped and rested on incurvate supports (366, 369). Arms joined to the uprights in a down-sweeping curve, found in Louis XVI chair design, were also employed (367). The seat rail was frequently fluted (365, 366). Satinwood was seldom employed in chair design at this time.

From around 1770–1775 the drawing room chair with open arms and an upholstered back designed by Adam was, in the majority of examples, a close adaptation of the contemporary Louis XVI chair (368, 369). However, in the English examples the carving on the molded frame was executed in a slightly larger scale than on the French models. It was made of a soft wood and was painted in pastel colors or in gilt and was generally upholstered in French tapestry or damask. An oval back was typical of this type and the straight legs were commonly cylindrical and fluted.

Adam's ability to logically conceive and consistently carry out a single style of decoration is evidenced in a set of painted beechwood chairs designed in the Etruscan taste (367) for the Etruscan room at Osterly. He writes in the WORKS OF ARCHITECTURE that he was unable to find any information about the interior decoration of the Etruscans and states that "the style of ornament and coloring" was derived directly from vases and urns. Undoubtedly the fashion for finishing chairs with painted or japanned decoration which prevailed in England in the late decades of the 18th century resulted chiefly from Adam's use of this medium of decoration.

Settees Settees essentially underwent the same development as the chair. Early settees designed by Adam were of Rococo contour and were decorated with Neo-Classic motifs. Sometimes settees as well as chairs based on Adam's early designs recalled the ponderous exuberance of the type made by William Kent (370), while other settees and chairs, such as the drawing room pieces for Moor Park (373), anticipated Adam's fully developed Neo-Classic style. Delicate moldings and straight tapered legs, which were often fluted, were characteristic features of settees designed in Adam's mature style. After 1775 the designs for his sofas as for his chairs were chiefly borrowed from contemporary Louis XVI models. The materials employed and the method of decorating were similar to those used in the chair. One characteristic variety of upholstered settee had a gracefully swept arched horseshoe-shaped frame, continuing to form incurvate arm supports. It rested on round or quadrangular fluted and tapered legs. Another variety had an oval-shaped upholstered back with open arms. The front seat rail was often serpentine-shaped and was commonly fluted. It was designed with straight tapering legs.

Benches   Adam was partial to very long benches and window seats (379) for he felt that they added to the formal effect of the drawing room. The legs were similar to those of the chair and settee and were of tapered form. The window seat generally had outscrolled sides (379) and the front of the seat was either straight or of slight serpentine contour (379). The seat rail was frequently fluted (379). The benches were generally designed en suite with the chairs and settee.

Tables   Dining rooms designed by Adam were distinctive for the richness and splendor of their furnishings. His dining room furniture was varied and in every case it was designed to be an accordant part of the room in which it was to be placed. It is generally believed that the arrangement of the sideboard table flanked by pedestals surmounted with urns was introduced by Robert Adam (376). It was designed as a group and was usually arranged in a recess at one end of the dining room. The straight tapered leg and Neo-Classic ornament employed by Robert Adam completely changed the appearance of the sideboard table (376). The sideboard table was often fitted with a brass gallery for the support of plate. The front of the table was straight, broken-fronted (376) or of serpentine contour, and the frieze, which rarely was fitted with a drawer, was of conforming shape (376). The frieze was often fluted and enriched with paterae (376) and frequently centered a tablet decorated with leaf scrolls flanking a classic urn or some other form of decoration, such as drapery swags depending from the frieze (376). It generally rested on six legs (376). The legs were commonly fluted and occasionally inlaid, and of quadrangular form, terminating in plinth feet (376). The pair of urns were usually fitted with lead liners, one was filled with ice water and the other with water for rinsing the silver knives and forks. The practice of rinsing table silver in the dining room continued until the 19th century. Occasionally the interior of one of the urns was fitted for the reception of knives. The pedestals were often used as plate warmers and cellarettes. This arrangement of sideboard table, pedestals and urns continued to be used in the spacious dining rooms until the end of the century. The pedestals and urns were generally made of the same material and were designed to accord with the sideboard table with which they were to be grouped. They were usually made of mahogany, rosewood, inlaid satinwood or painted wood; the latter were occasionally painted white with gilt enrichments.

The side table was particularly affected by the influence of Adam because this category of furniture formed an important part of the mural decoration. The straight tapered legs and the Neo-Classic ornament employed by Adam completely altered the appearance of the side table. The majority of oblong side tables were gilded, although some were occasionally made of mahogany. The gilding was often executed in subtly contrasting golden and lemon yellow tones. Gilding in two shades of gold was in accordance with the contemporary French manner of gilding. The tops were generally of marble or scagliola. The frieze was often fluted and enriched with paterae and a central plaquette, and a pendent carved festooning. It rested on four or six quadrangular tapered legs which were commonly fluted. The side table of semicircular or semi-oval form, often enriched with a central frieze tablet and having four straight tapered legs, provided the foundation for some of Robert Adam's most artistic work. This variety was usually designed in pairs and was commonly found in the drawing room under the large mirrors that filled the window piers. It was usually made of inlaid and painted satinwood or of gilt; occasionally it was painted and parcel-gilded. The original designs by Adam for the semicircular pier table indicated his preference for the square tapered pillar legs which were often fluted. The satinwood marquetry pier table usually had a top veneered in rich contrasting tones and was delicately inlaid in the classic taste. The marquetry was stained and shaded in a great variety of delicate colors. The gilded pier table sometimes had a scagliola top which was inlaid with colored composition; the later gilded examples usually had an inlaid and delicately painted satinwood top. The painted designs were sometimes in the manner of Pergolesi or Cipriani and were further enriched with a painted medallion of classical figure subjects in the style of Angelica Kauffmann. After 1770 Robert Adam generally designed his gilded pier tables for composition ornament. Festoons of wirework composition often depended from the frieze, which usually centered a plaque enclosing a painted medallion. These tables enjoyed great popularity and the fashion for the semicircular pier tables lasted throughout the 18th century. In addition to the colorful and elaborate inlaid and gilt examples, pier tables were also made in mahogany to harmonize with other mahogany furniture. They were usually ornamented with carved classic motifs and fluting.

Commodes   In the late 18th century the commode (377) was an important and elegant piece of decorative wall furniture and was frequently placed beneath a tall pier mirror. Commodes designed by Adam were notable for their delicate coloring and fine proportions, for the superlative composition of their designs and for the fine disposition of their ornament. The majority of satinwood marquetry commodes designed by Adam had a straight front and incurvate sides. The front was often fitted with a frieze drawer over two cupboard doors. It usually rested on four short straight tapered or splayed feet. These commodes were often enriched with ormolu mounts (357). Around 1775–1780 the commode of semicircular contour was in fashion (377). These semicircular commodes generally veneered in satinwood or harewood were usually designed in pairs. The principal variety had a semicircular top over a frieze and a single large front door (377). It rested on four short tapered legs which were commonly fluted and quadrangular and terminated in plinth feet. Variations in design occurred. Occasionally the front was designed with two cupboard doors, and each rounded side was sometimes fitted with a cupboard door. After 1775 marquetry was gradually superseded by painted decoration. At first painted decoration and inlay were often combined on a satinwood ground. The top was often richly inlaid with a semicircular fan motif. The frieze and front were inlaid with drapery swags, husk festoons, urns and other classic ornament. The large door and the two rounded sides were each enhanced with a medallion of classical figure subjects in the manner of Angelica Kauffmann. The painted decoration on commodes, like other painted furniture, was largely influenced by the style of such decorative artists as Angelica Kauffmann, Zucchi, Pergolesi and Cipriani. When painting had almost entirely superseded inlay work, the ground of the commode was painted a light color and was enhanced with gilded enrichments and oval or circular painted medallions.

Writing Furniture
In wall furniture, such as cabinets, secretary cabinets and bookcases, there was a return to the architectural pediments and entablatures of the Palladian school of architects, but more care was given to the proportions and the moldings were more accurate. The design for the mahogany secretary cabinet underwent certain changes. The lower portion was composed of a false drawer, which had a fitted writing interior, over two cupboard doors. The lower portion designed with a slant-front, which had been in vogue from the time of William and Mary through the Chippendale style, was no longer fashionable. The cornice of the upper portion, which was often surmounted with a shallow pediment carved with the familiar classic urn and festoons of husks, was over a frieze and two doors, generally glazed.

Bookcases
Bookcases designed by Adam were notable for their faultless proportions and their refined narrow moldings and classic ornament. Their proportions and ornament harmonized with the architectural treatment of the room in which they were to be placed. The central portion, which commonly projected, was often surmounted with either a broken or triangular pediment. Adam frequently filled the doors in the upper section with a wire trellis in place of glass. Various colored silks were used as a decorative backing for these brass trellis-work doors. The underbody of the bookcase was commonly fitted with

cupboard doors and occasionally with drawers and rested on a molded plinth. Sometimes the bookcase consisted entirely of open shelves. The majority of bookcases were of mahogany. Some were painted white, with gilt enrichments. Bookcases were sometimes permanently built into the room.

Mirrors   Gilt mirrors were an important part of the decorative scheme in an Adam-designed room. The position of the mirror was very carefully chosen. The majority of mirrors were placed between the windows with console tables below them, or over the chimneypiece (378). The tall pier mirror was usually over six feet in height. The mirror plates were now seldom divided, for the English were learning how to cast longer single plates. By the last quarter of the 18th century they could cast single plates over ten feet in length. Mirror frames designed by Adam were remarkable for their graceful delicacy and elegance. The frames were ornamented with such fashionable classic motifs as urns, medallions, paterae and festoons of husks. The frame was invariably crested; the cresting comprised such favorite decorative ingredients as delicate acanthus scrolls, husks and a draped vase or medallion. After 1770, due to Adam's interest in gesso ornament, the gilt wood frame was often ornamented with fragile husk chains of wirework composition. Later, painted decoration in the manner of such leading decorative artists as Pergolesi was employed on the mirror frames.

Stands   The designs for decorative appointments, such as torchères, sconces and wall brackets, in common with every other variety of furniture, were influenced by the classic manner of Adam. Torchères (372), which were essentially used for the reception of candelabra and vases, were especially suitable for classic treatment. Adam's designs for torchères were close adaptations of the tall and slender metal tripods found at Pompeii and Herculaneum. The legs of these were frequently headed with animals' heads, such as the favorite ram's head (372). Torchères designed by Adam were usually of tripod form and consisted of three slender long uprights which supported the top (372). The uprights flared slightly outward at the base and often rested on an incurvate molded plinth (372). Adam's torchères were always praiseworthy for their fine classic design and ornamental detail. Torchères were very often made of satinwood and decorated with marquetry, others were gilded and painted, while some were made of mahogany.

Pedestals (371) were freely introduced in the houses designed by Robert Adam. They were especially used for the reception of antique statues and busts, bronze sculptures and vases. They were made of scagliola, mahogany, inlaid satinwood or of a soft wood which was gilded or painted. Pedestals were sometimes painted to simulate marble.

CHAPTER NINETEEN

HEPPLEWHITE

The high quality of design and the technical excellence displayed in the cabinetwork of the Rococo era were maintained for the remaining four decades of the 18th century. Every branch of the decorative arts was permeated with a remarkable finish and refinement. The cabinetwork was marked by restraint, sobriety and good taste, and reflected the influence of an educated public taste. The Grand Tour, taken by a small group of cosmopolitan Englishmen, afforded a fine training in the arts as well as in polite Continental living. These travelled virtuosi formed collections of paintings, antique and Renaissance sculptures, gems and medals and rare books. This appreciation of classic art was also shared by many talented artists and architects, who were zealously engaged in studying the ruins of ancient Rome and Athens. It was in these several groups that the classic reaction was fostered in England. The era was distinguished by numerous fine furniture designers and cabinetmakers. Their work reflected the influence of the Neo-Classic movement as developed in England under the aegis of Robert Adam, and also in France in the contemporary Louis XVI style. The practice of publishing illustrated trade catalogues became a marked feature during the last quarter of the 18th century. These pattern books exerted a wide influence in spreading Neo-Classic taste, for they showed the prevailing taste in fashionable furniture and they also exhibited a rich repertory of designs to tempt the potential customer. The name *Hepplewhite* is given to a particular style of furniture fashionable from 1780 to 1795. As with Chippendale and later with Sheraton, the popular conception of the Hepplewhite style is based upon a book of designs, entitled, in this case, the CABINET MAKER AND UPHOLSTERER'S GUIDE.

Biographical information relating to Hepplewhite is exceedingly meager. Of his personal history the only known facts are that he served an apprenticeship with the firm of Gillow of Lancaster, and later came to London where he conducted a business in Redcross Street, St. Giles, Cripplegate. After his death in 1786 the administration of his estate was given to his widow, Alice, who continued to conduct the business under the name of A. Hepplewhite and Co. It is not known how long the company remained in business. The administration's accounts revealed that Hepplewhite's property was of considerable value. In 1788, two years after his death, the CABINET MAKER AND UPHOLSTERER'S GUIDE was published. It comprised almost three hundred designs engraved on one hundred and twenty-eight plates from the drawings of A. Hepplewhite and Co., Cabinetmakers. New editions of this folio volume were published in 1789 and in 1794. Ten designs signed "Hepplewhite" appeared in the second edition of the CABINET MAKERS' LONDON BOOK OF PRICES, published in 1788. These ten signed designs were similar to the designs of the other contemporary contributors and revealed that Hepplewhite did not introduce any innovations in design. The designs in the GUIDE were not signed and it is probable that they were drawings by several contemporary contributors. The GUIDE gave several designs for many of the different pieces of furniture in the various categories. These designs enjoyed great popularity and were extensively copied by cabinetmakers in America as well as in England. Undoubtedly the GUIDE, by its splendid and practical interpretation into the vernacular of the prevailing fashion in furniture design for the use of the cabinetmaker, merits the esteem accorded to it in the history of English cabinetwork.

The purpose of the GUIDE was explained in the preface. It was "to unite elegance and utility, and blend the useful with the agreeable." There was no claim made for originality. It stated that "we designedly followed the latest or most prevailing fashion." The character of the Hepplewhite style is based on the designs in the GUIDE. These designs were not the creation of any one particular person, but represented collectively the prevailing taste in furniture design. Consequently it would be exceedingly difficult to designate any piece of furniture as the actual work or design of Hepplewhite, since the name is accepted as expressing the prevailing fashion rather than the individual. In fact, there has never been a single piece of furniture which has been definitely known to have been made by Hepplewhite. The GUIDE undoubtedly enhanced Hepplewhite's reputation. In determining the value of the GUIDE it can be stated without any reservation that it was the finest English interpretation of the Neo-Classic style and that it adapted the style for the use of the cabinetmaker. Elegance was the keynote of the style. The designs were reasonable, consistent and simple, and at the same time elegant and refined. They were marked by a lightness of touch and were praiseworthy for their graceful delicacy. A large part of the furniture based on these designs was to be carried out in satinwood inlaid with other exotic woods. Gilding was also a pronounced feature. All the designs in the GUIDE were not of the same high quality, for some were rather mediocre and commonplace. Due to the fleeting fashions in furniture design during the late 18th century, some of the designs illustrated in the GUIDE were regarded several years later by other leading contemporary designers and cabinetmakers, such as Sheraton, as no longer in vogue. The first two editions of the GUIDE were essentially the same; however, in the third edition there was evident a certain amount of change, especially in chair design. There was a wide selection of chairs with square backs, which were then in vogue and were also featured in Sheraton's DRAWING BOOK, 1791–94. This was a marked departure from the shield and heart-shaped chair backs so closely identified with the Hepplewhite style.

The cabinetwork executed in the Hepplewhite style mirrored the influence of the designs of the Adam brothers, as well as the French Louis XVI style. Robert Adam's light and elegant style of classic ornament was paramount at the time when Hepplewhite was most active and it exerted a pronounced influence on the work of Hepplewhite. It was only a natural development that there should be a great demand for furniture harmonizing with Adam's singular style of classic ornament, whether the interior decoration had been executed under the Adam brothers' supervision or by one of the other architects who had adopted their style of interior decoration. As a result, Hepplewhite and his contemporaries designed furniture that would form an integral part of an Adam-inspired interior. Then, too, it is reasonable to assume that Hepplewhite executed commissions for the Adam brothers and that probably on some occasions he simplified the designs for his own later use. The graceful and perfected elegance prevailing in French furniture design on the eve of the French Revolution was also apparent in contemporary English cabinetwork. Illustrations for drawing room furniture in publications by such eminent designers as Adam, Hepplewhite and Sheraton revealed the ascendancy of France in the decorative arts. This French

taste was apparent not only in the ornament but also in the forms, such as in the contour of the backs of drawing room chairs and settees and in the contour of commodes. It was reflected in the use of tapestry coverings for drawing room furniture, in the use of large pier mirrors as decorative accessories and also in numerous other customs.

The contour of the furniture designed in the Hepplewhite style was notable for its light and elegant simplicity and for its excellent proportions. Although Hepplewhite adhered to straight structural lines he occasionally introduced curved lines into many pieces of furniture. However, the curvilinear lines were essentially subordinated to the rectilinear lines and were handled with reserve and refinement. Examples of curving lines were found in the shaped backs, arms and seat rails of chairs, in the gracefully swept curving lines for the tops of settees, in the commodes with semicircular fronts, in the bow fronts for chests of drawers, in the serpentine fronts for sideboards, in the oval-shaped tops for small tables and in the valanced aprons on the chests of drawers. Concave curving lines were emphasized in some of Hepplewhite's designs. This was especially apparent in his designs for the fronts of sideboards. Hepplewhite preferred a slender straight tapering leg, which was commonly of quadrangular form and occasionally cylindrical. The tapered leg was plain, fluted or reeded. The quadrangular leg commonly terminated in a spade foot, which is a form of rectangular foot slightly tapering toward the base. Naturally, variations in design sometimes occurred, and slender French cabriole legs were occasionally found on drawing room chairs, tables and desks designed by Hepplewhite in the French taste. Chests of drawers and other similar articles often rested on French bracket feet and occasionally on straight bracket feet, the former being by far more typical of the Hepplewhite style. Chair backs illustrated in the GUIDE were remarkable for the rich fertility of their designs, the familiar shield-back and heart-shaped back being worked in a variety of ingenious and artistic designs.

Hepplewhite, following in the footsteps of Robert Adam, frequently employed mahogany for library and dining room furniture as well as for general household articles. However, much of the furniture illustrated in the GUIDE was to be made in satinwood and was to be enriched with either inlaid or painted decoration. This tendency toward light colored woods, decorated with gay and graceful motifs, had its inception in the style of Adam and was further developed in the subsequent cabinetwork of the 18th century. The use of marquetry was especially pronounced in the Hepplewhite satinwood furniture inspired by contemporary French models. In the GUIDE designs for inlaid tops for dressing tables, commodes and pier tables were remarkably graceful and delicate. Foliated scrolls, festoons of husks, wreaths, garlands and streamers and bowknots of ribbon were provocatively gay and charming. In the less ambitious pieces of cabinetwork marquetry was more sparingly employed. The taste for painted furniture, which was revived around 1770, almost entirely supplanted toward the end of the century the marquetry decoration on the fashionable furniture made of satinwood. The painted decoration in the form of borders, delicate floral festoons, garlands and medallions was gracefully elegant and richly colorful. Painted decoration was also widely employed on furniture made of soft wood, with its entire surface painted in a pastel color to harmonize with the delicately colored walls. Especially popular and very characteristic of this era were the so-called japanned chairs and settees painted in lamp black and decorated in either polychrome colors or en grisaille. Frequently these japanned articles of furniture, which were often made of beechwood, were also enhanced with a touch of gilding to provide an effective contrast to their black ground. This furniture was relatively inexpensive and its popularity was undoubtedly due to the vogue for colorful decorative effects.

Gilding was a fashionable decorative process. The GUIDE frequently recommended that drawing room chairs, settees and benches should be entirely gilded. Pier mirrors and pier tables were favorite articles for gilding. Sometimes the carved detail on mahogany furniture and on the painted furniture was parcel-gilded. Veneering, which was the special talent of late 18th century cabinetwork, was extensively employed on Hepplewhite furniture. Bandings of contrasting veneered woods, such as kingwood, rosewood, mahogany, satinwood and harewood were effectively inlaid as borders on veneered satinwood and mahogany furniture and were richly decorative. Shaped panel bandings were also inlaid on the large surfaces, such as on the doors of bookcases, china cabinets and other similar articles of furniture. Hepplewhite showed a preference for rectangular panel shapes, although he also employed panels of oval and circular form. Stringing lines were often inlaid on the veneered surfaces for decorative purposes. The fashion for veneered surfaces and rich polychrome coloring reduced carving to a minimum. The carved decoration on mahogany furniture was in low relief and was notable for its smooth and finished workmanship. Fluting and reeding were characteristic details and they appeared on the posts of tester bedsteads and on the legs of chairs. The brass back plates mounted on drawers were commonly oval in shape, although circular and oblong back plates were also used. Furniture designed in the contemporary French taste, such as commodes, generally used French mounts. Hepplewhite gave very clear instructions in the GUIDE on the subject of upholstery. He favored French tapestry, figured silks and satins, linen, leather and horsehair, which could be plain, striped or checkered.

The style of ornament employed on Hepplewhite furniture was distinctive for its graceful delicacy, elegance and refinement. The ornament included all the classic motifs introduced by Robert Adam and the prevailing motifs of the Louis XVI style of ornament. Included among the favorite motifs were paterae often filled with acanthus rosettes, the water leaf motif, delicate acanthus scrolling, the husk motif, especially pendants or festoons of husks, honeysuckle or the anthemion, rosettes, the lyre motif, drapery swags, the wheat ear motif, the three Prince of Wales feathers, the radiating fan motif, ovals and circles filled with radiating lobes, delicate ovoid covered classic urns often flanked by festoons of husks, medallions, the vase motif, floral swags, wreaths, garlands, festoons, interlacing vine trails, sprays of foliage, interlacing ribbons, streamers of ribbon and graceful bowknots. It is probable that Hepplewhite was the first to use the Prince of Wales feather emblem as a decorative motif. It was a familiar motif on splat back chairs of the Hepplewhite type and was illustrated in the first edition of Hepplewhite's GUIDE. The wheat ear, which was another popular motif, was composed of ears of wheat realistically treated and rising from the leaves. It was often employed as a filling for the backs of chairs.

Certain examples of cabinetwork for about the last two decades of the 18th century reflected in their designs the influence of both Hepplewhite and Sheraton. This was largely due to the fact that cabinetmakers sometimes combined in one piece such features of the two styles as they desired. This trait of design was especially apparent in some examples of sideboards, secretary cabinets, china cabinets and bookcases. Since it would be practically impossible to determine which one of the two styles would be the more correct appellation, cabinetwork displaying this feature is sometimes called Hepplewhite-Sheraton. Other examples combining the style of Adam and Hepplewhite are frequently called Adam-Hepplewhite pieces for the same reason. Sometimes the term *Neo-Classic* is simply used. Then, too, cabinetmakers also made a large number of pieces, especially bookcases and china cabinets, which were more or less in accordance with the prevailing fashion, but did not possess the true characteristics of that style either in the contour or in the style of ornament. Since it would not be possible to identify these pieces except in a rather broad manner, they are often classified as George III pieces in present-day catalogues. The term *George II* is given in the same manner to such earlier pieces made during his reign. The fact that an article was not made in one of the prevailing styles, such as Hepplewhite or Sheraton, does not impair the quality of the piece being considered. There were other fine contemporary cabinetmakers and designers, such as Thomas Shearer, who were adept in introducing innovations

in furniture design, but who have unfor- publicity given to Hepplewhite and Shera-
tunately been overshadowed by the greater ton.

ARTICLES OF FURNITURE

Chairs   In appraising extant examples of chairs designed around 1775–1780,
it is apparent that some are still closely representative of the classical
style and dignity identified with the designs of Robert Adam. These
chairs are notable for their excellent proportions and fine craftsmanship (FIGURES 382, 383). One type of chair, which displayed transitional
features of design, is often called a camel-back chair (380). It had a
serpentine-arched or triple-arched crest rail with rounded ends continuing into the uprights (380). The curving arm supports were
secured to the side seat rails and the uprights of the back joined the
rear seat rail (380). The splat was very often of pierced tripod form
headed by a pierced honeysuckle or anthemion motif (380). Although
many strong and serviceable chairs were made for daily or ordinary
use in the dining room and library, the taste in chair design, in the
last quarter of the 18th century, was inclined to extreme lightness
(387, 388). This feeling of fragility and feminine grace became more
evident in the designs of Sheraton, and was especially pronounced in
the designs for drawing room chairs. Hepplewhite's designs for chairs
were praiseworthy for their elegant simplicity and for their graceful
delicacy. His designs, which were notable for their rich diversity, have
served as an inspiration for the designs of a large number of modern
chairs. Hepplewhite expended the utmost ingenuity in designing his
chair backs. Credit for creating the distinctive shield-back form (384,
386, 388) has been assigned at different times to both Adam and Hepplewhite. Although it has never been conclusively proven who was the
originator of the shield-back it can be stated without reservation that
Hepplewhite employed the form most successfully and most constantly
of all the designers. He used it in a great variety of designs all of
which were artistically pleasing. The most characteristic shapes for the
open back chairs of the Hepplewhite style were the familiar shield
(384, 386) and heart-shaped backs (391); however, oval (382, 383,
385), circular or almost circular (387), square and cartouche-shaped
(381) backs were all employed. The cartouche-shaped back was commonly restricted to chairs designed in the French taste (381). The
square back chairs were often designed either with an arched or flat-
arched crest rail. Chair backs no longer joined the seat rail but were
supported by the extension of the rear legs rising above the seat rail
(384, 385, 386). Among the favorite decorative motifs employed on
the splats in the open back chairs were drapery festoons suggesting
the heart shape (382, 391), wheat ears (384), honeysuckle or the

anthemion (380), urns, medallions (387) and the Prince of Wales emblem of three ostrich plumes (382). An oval patera, either carved (383) or inlaid (384), was especially favored as an ornament. The pierced splat, which usually resembled to a greater or less extent the outline of a beaker (385), vase (384) or lyre, was frequently discarded in favor of different filled-in designs (383, 386). A fashionable filled-in design for the oval back comprised three bar splats equally spaced and each centering a patera (383). One characteristic shield-back had five slender radial bar splats converging on a segmental rosette patera. The name *banister-back* is often given to this particular variety of chair back designed with a series of three (386), four or five upright pieces called banisters, bars, or balusters, the latter being the correct English term. Circular backs filled with radiating designs and centering an oval were also much favored (387). In fact at this time the treatment of the back presented an almost endless variety. Sometimes these chairs had upholstered backs in place of the pierced splat or filled-in designs. Oval and shield-shape upholstered backs were especially fashionable. Backs having inner ovals inserted with medallions printed or painted on silk of a natural color were illustrated in the GUIDE.

Hepplewhite preferred the straight tapering leg (384, 385, 386, 387). It was commonly quadrangular in form and often terminated in a spade foot (384). Occasionally it was cylindrical and ring-collared (385). The leg was plain, molded, fluted or reeded (384), and occasionally it was carved with a delicate beading (386) or enriched with painted decoration (387). Chairs designed in the French taste usually had cabriole legs (381). Hepplewhite still illustrated in the first edition of the GUIDE cabriole legs of attenuated form terminating in French whorl feet. Sometimes the slender quadrangular tapered legs were reinforced with stretchers. The armchair was frequently designed with graceful undulating arms which scrolled outward and rested on incurvate supports (383) which were almost always joined to the tops of the legs (386, 387). The arms were either straight (382) or slightly sloped forward (387). The front seat rail was straight (385), slightly rounded (386) or serpentine-shaped (383). Caning, which had been reintroduced, was sometimes employed on the seats, especially on mahogany and lacquered chairs. Caned seats were usually fitted with a loose cushion. The dipped seat (380), introduced around 1760, continued in vogue and was frequently used. Chairs were made of mahogany (384), satinwood (388), painted and japanned wood (387). The ornament was generally carved (386), carved and gilded or painted (387). A large majority of chairs were made of mahogany (384, 385, 386) as this wood was still the finest medium for chairs enriched with carved decorative detail. The frames of mahogany chairs were often delicately molded, and occasionally the moldings were carved with repetitive classic detail (385). The vogue for rich color effects so characteristic of the last quarter of the 18th century resulted in the production of a large number of decorative and graceful inexpensive chairs, made of beech or other soft woods which were japanned in color or in black. Hepplewhite designed a number of chairs suitable for japanning.

Although designs for winged armchairs (389) dating from the second half of the 18th century were relatively scarce, Hepplewhite gave a design for one which he called a saddle cheek or easy chair. It had an arched back and wide shaped wings. It was designed with a straight front seat rail and straight quadrangular legs terminating in spade feet and joined with a plain stretcher. He recommended that it should be upholstered in either leather or horsehair, or a "linen case to fit over the canvas stuffing."

Settees   There was a wide variety in the form of seats for two or more persons. Hepplewhite's GUIDE gave four designs for settees. Essentially the characteristic features of design found in the chairs were also employed in the settee. The upholstered settee was often a close adaptation of the contemporary French model. One variety of settee of the Hepplewhite type, which resembled a Louis XVI model, had an arched horseshoe-shaped back continuing to form the arms which rested on incurvate supports (390). The front seat rail was generally slightly rounded (390). Another variety had a straight top rail or a straight flat-arched top rail. The back of the arms were of the same height as the top rail and slightly sloped forward in a concave curve. The arms rested on incurvate supports. The dimensions of the settee were in accordance with the size of the room. It was commonly designed with eight tapered legs of cylindrical or quadrangular form. One of the settees illustrated by Hepplewhite freely employed curved lines and was designed with slender French cabriole legs. Chippendale illustrated a similar type (345) in the third edition of the DIRECTOR.

The chair-back settee (391) of the Hepplewhite style essentially followed the design of the contemporary open back chair. Shield and heart-shaped backs (391) were the favorite designs. The chair-back settee was generally made in mahogany, satinwood or a painted soft wood and as a rule it rested on eight tapered quadrangular legs.

Another lighter type of settee was the caned settee. It had a caned seat and back, and the arms were filled in with caning. The seat was fitted with a long loose cushion. It was very often made of painted or japanned wood.

Stools   Several designs for stools were illustrated in the GUIDE. They were designed with both straight tapered and cabriole legs. One had a round seat which was recommended as especially suitable for a dressing table stool. Several designs were also given for window seats, with out-scrolled sides, which were distinctive for their elegant simplicity. The window seat was designed with four straight tapered legs. The GUIDE stated that the height of the window seat was not to exceed that of the chairs in the same suite and recommended that the frame match the chairs with which it was to be used.

Day Beds   The fashionable upholstered day bed for the last two decades of the 18th century was similar to the French duchesse brisée, comprising two bergères and a stool. Hepplewhite describes a duchesse as a "couch with tub-shaped ends" and writes in the GUIDE that it was usually used in large and spacious ante-rooms.

Beds   The characteristic bed for the remainder of the 18th century continued to be the type enclosed with draperies and surmounted by a tester. Throughout the 18th century great care was given to the selection of the draperies enclosing the bed in order that they should harmonize with the decorative scheme of the room. The mahogany bed which was in general use by the end of the century is usually credited to both Hepplewhite and Sheraton. The height of the slender mahogany posts was determined by the height of the room. The pedestals of the posts were usually plain since they were concealed by the draperies. The posts, which tapered toward the top, were commonly reeded or fluted. At the base of each post there was generally a vase-shaped enlargement which was carved with wheat ears or upright foliage. The cornice was often of mahogany and was enriched with carved detail. During the vogue for painted furniture the cornice was often painted and enhanced with painted decoration. Characteristic of these painted cornices were the painted and tabbed wooden valances beneath the cornices which were illustrated in the GUIDE. Hepplewhite showed a preference for stuffed headboards crested with carved detail, for he felt that they gave an air of elegance to the bed.

Hepplewhite's GUIDE also had one plate entitled "Sweeps for Field Bed Tops" which gave five ways in which the tester could be arched. According to medieval records this type of bed was originally designed for use in war and travelling. Several of the designs illustrated in the GUIDE were hinged in order that the framework could be folded. According to the drawings it seems that this type of bed differs from the usual tester bed in that the latter had a more elaborate and elegant tester. The field bed simply had a light and plain framework of varying arched form secured to the tops of the four posts and covered with fabric.

Tables   The mahogany dining table continued to be made in three sections. It consisted of an oblong center table with drop leaves and two semicircular end tables, each generally designed with a drop leaf. Each section was designed with a frieze and rested on four slender tapered quadrangular legs. The frieze was often inlaid with tulipwood cross-bandings, stringing lines and paterae. The semicircular end tables when not in use often served as side tables.

A practical development during the last quarter of the century was the sideboard designed by cabinetmakers having a shallow central napery drawer, usually over a valanced or arched apron piece, flanked by two deep lateral wine drawers or cupboards (399). The GUIDE illustrated two sideboards with drawers of this variety. In some specimens the exterior of one lateral drawer was panelled to represent two drawers and served as a cellarette, while two drawers balanced it on the other side. The wine drawers contained divisions for bottles and were lead lined. Sideboards of this variety were most frequently made with serpentine or bow fronts, the former being the shape illustrated in the GUIDE. The sideboard usually rested on six quadrangular tapering legs with the four front legs continuing from the stiles (399). It was usually veneered with mahogany. The top was often inlaid with a cross-banding of tulipwood and stringing lines. The drawers were conformingly banded and the legs were inlaid with stringing lines (399). Variations in design occurred. Side tables were designed to correspond with the sideboard and were used in the dining-room for serving purposes.

The sideboard table having a frieze without drawers was also designed in the Hepplewhite style and was decorated in the prevailing taste. Hepplewhite illustrated four sideboard tables in the GUIDE. Three were designed with a straight front and the other with a serpentine front. The frieze was either fluted or was decorated with repeating classic motifs and centered a plaquette decorated with a classic urn, which in two of the illustrations was flanked by leafage scrolls. The ornament was to be carved, inlaid or painted. The sideboard table flanked by pedestals surmounted by urns continued to be found in many spacious dining rooms until the close of the century.

Decorative pier tables for drawing rooms were usually of satinwood and were inlaid or painted (392). The majority were semicircular and were usually designed with straight quadrangular tapered legs (392). They were generally made in pairs and were placed beneath the pier mirrors between the windows (392). Hepplewhite stated that they were very fashionable and were suitable for "much elegance and ornament." Pier tables were also made in mahogany to harmonize with other mahogany furniture. They were often inlaid with cross-bandings of tulipwood and stringing lines, and were embellished with fan paterae commonly made of shaded holly wood.

The Pembroke table was often made of satinwood and was enhanced with inlaid or painted ornament. Hepplewhite referred to these tables as the most useful tables of their class and considered them suitable for "elegance in the workmanship and ornament." He stated that the top could be of various shapes; however, he regarded the square or oval to be the most fashionable. It was designed with slender quadrangular tapered legs commonly terminating in spade feet. The Pembroke table was sometimes veneered with mahogany and cross-banded. It served many purposes, such as a tea or breakfast table.

Gaming Tables The card table was usually made of satinwood or mahogany and was commonly designed with quadrangular tapered legs. The folding tops were made in a variety of shapes, such as square, oval, circular and serpentine. The interior was covered with green baize. As a rule, the dished compartments for candlesticks and the money wells were omitted. Hepplewhite gave four designs for card tables in the GUIDE. He recommended that the tops and fronts of these card tables should be decorated in an elegant manner with inlaid or painted ornament. Card tables veneered with mahogany were often inlaid with crossbandings and stringing lines and shell paterae.

Toilet Tables Small dressing tables fitted with toilet equipage and ingeniously planned were among the most remarkable of the specialized types of furniture illustrated in contemporary trade catalogues. The dressing table with a hinged folding lid, which when opened revealed a framed rising mirror and a fitted interior for toilet articles, retained its popularity throughout the 18th century. Dressing tables in the French taste having a shaped frieze drawer curving into slender cabriole legs and decorated with a marquetry of delicate classical ornament were especially praiseworthy (397). In one type the drawer pulled out and the top pushed back, disclosing a mirror on a ratchet flanked by two compartments (397). Another variety of dressing table, termed a commode dressing table (402), was designed as a chest of drawers and was to a greater or less extent of French contour. Hepplewhite illustrated this variety in the GUIDE with a serpentine front and a valanced base curving into French bracket feet (402).

Work Tables The work table, a small delicate table fitted with the accessories for needlework, was introduced in the second half of the 18th century and was distinctive for the elegance of its design. It was usually designed with one or two small shallow drawers or with a top which lifted up to reveal a well. The pouch variety of work table was a characteristic and favorite type. It was fitted with a fabric work bag suspended under the top of the table, in which the ladies kept their fancy needlework. Work tables of the Hepplewhite type were generally of satinwood or mahogany and were delicately ornamented with inlaid or painted decoration. They had slender quadrangular tapered legs. Many varieties of work tables were made by the cabinetmakers during the late 18th century. Some were fitted with a screen with a fabric panel which pulled up at the rear of the table. The purpose of the screen was so that one could enjoy the benefit of the fire and at the same time deflect the heat from the face.

Writing
Furniture

The library or writing table of pedestal form was commonly made of mahogany, and its enrichment largely depended upon the careful selection of contrasting veneers. It was designed in a variety of shapes, such as straight, slightly convex, serpentine and kidney-shaped. As a rule the shape was selected which could most advantageously display the figure of the wood. The top was usually inset with leather or green cloth. One pedestal was often designed with drawers and the other with cupboard doors.

The term *tambour writing table* was given in the GUIDE to a variety of desk or secretary with a tambour top which enclosed drawers and pigeonholes (393). Hepplewhite stated that it "answered all the uses of the desk and had a much lighter appearance." The principal variety had an oblong top with a tambour cylinder over a frieze fitted with drawers (393). Frequently below the frieze was an arched apron piece flanked by two small lateral drawers. It rested on four tapered quadrangular legs. Occasionally the tambour cylinder was over four long drawers and rested on a molded bracket base and was fitted with a pull-out writing slide. The oblong top was sometimes surmounted with a bookcase or cabinet. Undoubtedly the design for these tambour cylinder desks was inspired by the contemporary French bureau à cylindre, designed with a solid wood cylinder. Only occasionally was the cylinder made of a solid piece of wood in the English examples. Tambour writing secretaries were also designed in the subsequent Sheraton style.

The secretary cabinet at this time was commonly designed with a fall-front writing drawer disclosing the usual writing equipment when opened. As a rule it had a straight cornice which was often surmounted with either a shallow arched pediment or a shallow pierced foliated scrollwork centering a vase or bust. The upper body was recessed and was fitted with two glazed doors. The upper drawer of the projecting lower body was deep and was over three graduated drawers or two cupboard doors. The top drawer pulled forward and the front opened downward and was held by means of quadrants, which are curved metal supports. It was often designed with a valanced base with French bracket feet. Hepplewhite illustrated in the GUIDE the secretary cabinet with a fall-front writing drawer. He also showed the slant-front variety of secretary cabinet which was now generally out of fashion. He termed the latter *desk and bookcase*. The secretary cabinet was generally made of either mahogany or satinwood, veneered with contrasting woods. Secretary cabinets with fall-front writing drawers displayed a wide variety in their designs; the general tendency was to make them lighter in form. Extant examples in the Neo-Classical style are often remarkable for the novelty of their designs (394).

Cabinets The china cabinet of the Hepplewhite type was commonly made of mahogany, although other woods were sometimes employed. The cabinet doors and underbody were often enriched with inlaid panel bandings of satinwood. It had a straight molded cornice which was sometimes surmounted with a shallow arched pediment with dies supporting classic urn finials. The upper body was fitted with two glazed doors, while the lower body commonly had panelled cupboard doors. It often had a valanced base with French bracket feet.

Bookcases The bookcase with a glazed upper portion was essentially similar in design to the china cabinet and was made of the same materials. The large library bookcase was generally break-fronted and was designed with either two or four winged sections. It rested on a molded plinth. Hepplewhite illustrated a break-front bookcase in the GUIDE with the wing on each side of the projecting central portion being of lower height. Hepplewhite devoted a plate in the GUIDE to "Doors for Bookcases." In one design the glazing bars were in the form of covered urns with drapery festoons and possessed great decorative merit. As a rule, the glazing bars in Hepplewhite furniture were designed with straight lines, especially those of polygonal form.

Commodes The commode of semicircular contour (395, 396) mounted on short quadrangular legs was regarded as the most fashionable form from about 1780 and was illustrated in the GUIDE. Inlaid festoons of husks, medallions and paterae, which were all fashionable Adam motifs, were adapted on a smaller scale to ornament these commodes which were commonly veneered with satinwood or harewood (395, 396). Painted decoration gradually superseded the marquetry work and some extant examples combine both marquetry and painted decoration (395).

Chests of Drawers The Hepplewhite style chest of drawers was designed with a bow, serpentine or straight front. It was generally designed with four graduated long drawers and it often had a valanced base curving into French bracket feet. Occasionally it had straight bracket feet. The chest of drawers was generally made of mahogany. The oblong top was often edged with cross-bandings and stringing lines and the drawers were conformingly banded. The drawers were often fitted with oval back plates and bail handles. Chests of drawers shown by Hepplewhite in the GUIDE were exceedingly simple. Chests of drawers having the top drawers fitted with toilet articles for dressing were usually of a more elaborate nature. Hepplewhite also illustrated the chest-on-chest. It had a straight cornice, the upper chest had two top drawers over three long drawers and the lower chest contained three long drawers. It rested on bracket feet. Other designs had fluted corner pilasters and the straight cornice was surmounted with three classic urns.

Clothes-presses The clothespress as illustrated in the GUIDE was severely simple in its design. It had a straight molded cornice over two long doors. The lower portion contained two or three drawers and was mounted on bracket feet. Hepplewhite pronounced the clothespress to be a necessary piece of furniture. He stated that it was usually plain and made of the best mahogany.

Stands
The teakettle or urn stand as shown in the GUIDE was designed with a slide for the teapot (400). The top was made in a variety of shapes, such as circular, serpentine and octagonal. The delicate quadrangular tapered legs were slightly splayed (400). The urn stand was generally made of satinwood or mahogany. Hepplewhite stated that it could be enriched with marquetry or painted decoration. By the end of the century the urn stand was no longer fashionable.

As a rule the candlestand or torchère was of tripod form and consisted of three slender long uprights supporting the top.

Pedestals for the reception of busts and vases were not generally shown in the later pattern books. Their designs were regarded as being within the field of the architect.

Mirrors
Hepplewhite gave six designs for gilded pier or wall mirrors in the GUIDE. He stated that the mirror with a rectangular frame was more fashionable than the mirror with an oval frame. The frame invariably had an elaborate openwork cresting which usually centered a classic urn or medallion. The cresting was composed of such favorite motifs as delicate acanthus scrolls, draperies, floral festoons and sheaves of wheat. The base of the frame was usually decorated with matching ornament. Girandoles or mirrors with candle branches were used during the 18th century to augment the lighting of rooms.

The swinging dressing mirror or toilet mirror on a box stand, which was designed throughout the 18th century in all the prevailing styles, was illustrated in the GUIDE. The frame was usually oval or shield-shaped, and the uprights were curved to harmonize with the contour of the frame. The stand commonly had a serpentine or bow-shaped front and was fitted with a row of drawers. It was usually made either of mahogany banded with satinwood or of satinwood with inlaid or painted decoration.

Accessories
The sconces illustrated in the GUIDE were distinctive for their light and graceful designs. They were generally made of carved and gilded soft wood and were often decorated with delicate ornament of wirework composition.

Designs for wall brackets shown in the GUIDE reflected the classic influence of Robert Adam. They were usually of carved and gilded or carved and painted soft wood. The painted wall brackets were to harmonize with the painted walls.

The cheval and tripod pole screens were made in all the fashionable materials and were decorated in the prevailing taste. Both varieties were of lighter and more delicate contour. The adjustable panel of the pole screen was generally oval, circular or shield-shaped. The cheval fire-screen was designed with either a fixed panel or with an adjustable sliding panel, the inner sides of the uprights being grooved. During the second half of the century adjustable screens were sometimes fitted into the structure of the backs of small pieces of furniture, such as work tables and small writing tables.

Knife-cases were made either of mahogany or of satinwood and were distinctive for their finish and refined detail. The box knife-case with a sloping lid and serpentine front and the vase knife-case of graceful vase form were the two characteristic varieties. Hepplewhite stated that the vase knife-case should be made of satinwood or of some other light wood and that it should be placed at each end of the sideboard or on the pedestals which flanked the sideboard table. The vase knife-case was often inlaid with vertical stringing.

The name *tea caddy* is given to a small box or case to hold tea. The word *caddy* is believed to have been derived from the Malay word *kati* or the Chinese word *catty* which means a measure of weight equal to about one and one third pounds avoirdupois, and signified the small box in which the tea was sent to Europe. During the 18th century tea caddies were made in a great variety of materials, including wood, pewter, ivory, tortoise shell, brass and silver. However, the favorite materials were various woods, especially mahogany, rosewood and satinwood. The tea caddy was fitted with a lock and key, for originally tea was an expensive commodity. The interior of the tea caddy was either partitioned and lead lined for black and green tea or was fitted with canisters for the two types of tea. Wooden tea caddies were commonly square, oblong, hexagonal or octagonal. Hepplewhite illustrated tea caddies of oblong, circular and oval form and recommended that the ornament be inlaid in various colored woods or painted. The tea caddy was praiseworthy for the high quality of its craftsmanship. From an artistic standpoint those of the late 18th century with their delicate inlays and refined and graceful lines were especially pleasing and elegant.

Designs for the wooden tea tray of oval form were given in the GUIDE. It was generally fitted with brass handgrips. Hepplewhite stated that the tops were to be inlaid in various kinds of colored woods or to be ornamented with painted decoration. Hepplewhite's tea trays closely followed the style of ornament found on the contemporary decorative table tops of console tables or commodes. These tea trays were notable for the fine quality of their workmanship and for their light and graceful decoration.

Accessories for drinking, such as wooden wine coolers and cellarettes, were designed throughout the early 19th century in the different prevailing styles. The name *wine table* or *drinking table* was given to a specialized table introduced toward the end of the 18th century to be used for after-dinner drinking. It was designed in various forms. One characteristic type had a horseshoe-shaped top, which averaged around six feet in length. A metal rod was attached across the open center portion and was fitted with coasters to hold wine bottles. A long narrow network bag was also stretched across the open portion and was used to hold biscuits. The two ends of the table faced the fireplace and were sometimes fitted with a rod to hold a curtain to deflect the heat of the fire.

Clocks The majority of tall case clocks (361) made from about the middle of the 18th century and at the beginning of the 19th century were marked by certain features of design. They usually were designed with a shaped pediment, very often in the form of a scrolled pediment centering a low plinth, and the top was usually surmounted with two or three brass finials. The cornice was arched or straight, and the hood door and pendulum door were generally arched. The fluted or reeded colonettes flanking the door of the hood were very often decorated with gilded brass capitals and bases. During the Hepplewhite and Sheraton styles the tall case clock was often ornamented with panel bandings and with inlaid shell and fan paterae.

CHAPTER TWENTY

SHERATON

Thomas Sheraton is one of the great names in the history of English cabinetwork. His style was the last of the five great styles of the 18th century, often referred to in furniture literature as the golden age of English cabinetwork. Biographical information relating to Sheraton is meager. He was born in 1751 at Stockton-on-Tees and died in 1806 in London. He was reared in humble surroundings and apparently was trained as a cabinetmaker. His life was one of sordid poverty and disappointment largely due to his own eccentric character. Even his books of furniture designs, which have accorded him an eminent place in English furniture history, were not a financial success. His varied career as Baptist preacher, inventor, mechanic, mystic, author, artist, teacher and furniture designer discloses the strange blend of his character. He was a man of much ability and resource and he possessed great artistic talent, but unfortunately he was his own enemy. Around 1790 he settled in London; he was married

and had two children. A few years later he was living in a humble residence in Broad Street, Soho, where he spent his time in writing and in giving drawing lessons. He apparently converted half of his home into a shop. It is not known to what extent, if any, he carried on the business of cabinetmaking. Such evidence as is available reveals that from about 1793 he supported his family by his various publications. From 1791 to 1794 he published his first book on furniture, entitled THE CABINETMAKER AND UPHOLSTERER'S DRAWING BOOK in four parts. A third edition appeared in 1802. He published in 1803 THE CABINET DICTIONARY CONTAINING AN EXPLANATION OF ALL THE TERMS USED IN THE CABINET, CHAIR AND UPHOLSTERY BRANCHES, WITH DIRECTIONS FOR VARNISHING, POLISHING AND GILDING. In 1805 he published the first part of his last work, which he never lived to finish, entitled THE CABINET-MAKER, UPHOLSTERER AND GENERAL ARTIST'S ENCYCLOPAEDIA. This was to be completed in one hundred and twenty-five parts of which the author lived to publish only thirty. He also published at different times a number of religious and philosophical pamphlets. In 1812 there was published a volume entitled DE-SIGNS FOR HOUSEHOLD FURNITURE EXHIBIT-ING A VARIETY OF ELEGANT AND USEFUL PATTERNS IN THE CABINET, CHAIR AND UP-HOLSTERY BRANCHES ON EIGHTY-FOUR PLATES. By the late T. Sheraton, Cabinet-maker. This work consisted chiefly of plates from his earlier CABINET DICTIONARY and his ENCYCLOPAEDIA.

The popular conception of the Shera-ton style, as with the earlier styles of Chippendale and Hepplewhite, is based upon a book of designs entitled THE CABINET-MAKER AND UPHOLSTERER'S DRAW-ING BOOK. The Sheraton style was in vogue from around 1790 to 1805 and much of the fine furniture, especially that veneered in satinwood, made in England in the last decade of the 18th century is generally referred to as Shera-ton. However, this appellation is used to designate a certain style rather than a personal attribution. It is important to un-derstand that, according to present evi-dence, Sheraton was not a practical cab-inetmaker who worked out his designs in the actual wood. This DRAWING BOOK, as were his subsequent publications, was in-tended chiefly for the use of contemporary cabinetmakers. Then, too, in his later pub-lications Sheraton's drawings were not confined to the typical veneered satin-wood furniture of the late 18th century. These designs followed the change in Eng-lish furniture style and showed some of the characteristics of the French Direc-toire and the incoming French Empire style. Certain characteristics of the Di-rectoire style became fashionable in Eng-land while the Sheraton style was still in

vogue and Sheraton adopted some of its special features of design in his later books. In order to distinguish between this change in his designs, the terms *Early Sheraton* and *Late Sheraton* are often ap-plied to the two different phases of his work. When the term *Sheraton style* is used it generally refers to the early and fine Sheraton work.

The DRAWING BOOK was undoubtedly Sheraton's most important work and his fame largely rests upon it. The first half of the book was devoted to an elaborate treatise on perspective, architecture and drawing, which, although it afforded Sheraton an opportunity to display his knowledge on these subjects, is relatively unimportant to the main subject of the book. The second half of the book or Part III contains the drawings for the furni-ture. These designs are praiseworthy for their splendid draftsmanship. The excel-lent descriptive notes accompanying these designs are generally both technical and practical. In the introduction Sheraton states, "The design of this part of the book is intended to exhibit the present taste of furniture, and at the same time to give the workman some assistance in the manu-facturing part of it." Later he continues, "I have made it my business to apply to the best workmen in different shops, to obtain their assistance in the explanation of such pieces as they have been most ac-quainted with." The book is marred by his conceit and self-satisfaction, and his re-fusal to appraise in a fair manner the achievements of his predecessors and con-temporaries. The author does not make it clear whether the illustrations are his own innovations, or whether they were modi-fied and adapted or simply copied from the work of other designers and cabinet-makers. Although Sheraton did not acknowledge his indebtedness to the earlier designs of the Adam brothers, it is easily discernible in his drawings that he used many of them. This was especially apparent in his designs for chairs and in his choice of decorative motifs. The influence of Hepplewhite is also patent in his drawings. However, there is a noticeable difference in the interpretation of the Neo-Classic style as developed in the GUIDE and as represented in the DRAWING BOOK. Regardless of the source of Sheraton's drawings, the DRAWING BOOK presented a splendid summary of the prevailing fashion in furniture design between 1790 and 1800. His book was extensively employed by cabinetmakers both in England and in America, and like the earlier pattern books of Chippendale and Hepplewhite it served as an important formative factor in contemporary cabinetwork. In the different parts of England more than six hundred cabinetmakers, joiners and upholsterers subscribed to the book, which shows the wide distribution of these designs.

The CABINET DICTIONARY, which was Sheraton's second publication, contained eighty-eight copper plate engravings in addition to supplementary articles on drawing and painting. In these designs Sheraton often adopted and interpreted special features of the French Directoire style. Some of these designs began to show deterioration and did not display the same high quality of draftsmanship as the designs appearing in the DRAWING BOOK. Nevertheless, the book possessed merit and some of his designs in the prevailing French Directoire taste captured the spirit of the style with considerable dexterity. In Sheraton's third and unfinished publication, the ENCYCLOPAEDIA, the signs of deterioration evident in the CAB-INET DICTIONARY became more pronounced and sometimes bordered on the bizarre. The drawings, which were in color, were of mediocre draftsmanship and showed specimens of the Empire style as developed in England. The graceful delicacy, lightness and finished detail so characteristic of Sheraton's earlier work was completely lacking in the cumbrous and often grotesque features displayed in his drawings of the French Empire style. Both of these books, however, afford an important source in studying certain phases of the English Regency style, which succeeded the Sheraton style.

Sheraton's fame depends upon his designs. The Classic Revival as developed in the style of Robert Adam and in the Louis XVI style was evident in his designs in the DRAWING BOOK. His greatest asset was his adaptability. He studied French furniture fashions with the utmost care and he produced many close adaptations of the Louis XVI style. Although he freely adapted the works of others, he was able through his special genius, especially his sense of style, to impart an original beauty and grace to his drawings. Sheraton's designs in the DRAWING BOOK were remarkable for their refined elegance and excellent proportions, for their light and graceful forms and for the delicate charm of their ornament. Sheraton possessed a finely developed sense of proportion, much more so than Hepplewhite. This fine sense of balance was evident in the contour and the distribution of the ornament. The delicate and finished forms and detail introduced by Sheraton in his drawings have never been surpassed in English furniture design. Naturally, all the designs in the DRAWING BOOK were not of the same perfected draftsmanship. His later designs incorporated certain features of the French Directoire and French Empire styles. Some of the drawings in the Directoire taste frequently had many pleasing qualities but they did not match the high level of design found in his early work. His drawings based upon the French Empire style were of a decadent nature. As a rule the forms were heavy and dull and the ornament, such as lions, sphinxes and imaginary animals, was fantastic and freakish. Sheraton's inventive ability led him to design many ingenious pieces of harlequin furniture for which the late 18th century displayed a strong predilection. Many small tables were ingeniously designed to conceal their real purpose of a dressing table, a writing table or a washstand. Sheraton illustrated in his DRAWING BOOK library steps enclosed in a library table. The top of the table was hinged and the library steps were skillfully designed to fold into the frieze. Other pieces were operated by springs and various mechanical devices, such as folding beds and couches which could be converted into tables.

The contour of Sheraton's designs, as in the earlier work of Hepplewhite, mirrored the influence of Robert Adam and the Louis XVI style. Sheraton greatly admired the finished elegance permeating the Louis XVI style of cabinetwork and he constantly endeavored to identify his work with the Louis XVI style of furniture design. Sheraton abandoned to a large extent the curved lines which Hepplewhite had introduced in many of his designs for different pieces of furniture. Sheraton favored the straight line and his designs were essentially rectangular with emphasis on the vertical lines. However, some of the work of Hepplewhite and Sheraton was quite the contrary, for Hep-

plewhite favored straight lines for the glazing bars in his bookcases and china cabinets and also preferred rectangular panels, while Sheraton showed a preference for curved lines in his glazing bars and for panels of oval form. Both designers used straight tapering legs of either quadrangular or cylindrical form. Quadrangular legs are more typical of Hepplewhite's work, while rounded legs are more closely associated with the Sheraton style. The cylindrical tapered legs were often vertically fluted or reeded and sometimes spirally turned. The legs were often finished with brass toe caps and wheel casters. The quadrangular leg often terminated in a spade foot. Occasionally the legs were joined with stretchers. Sheraton's work was characterized by its slender forms, distinctive for their elegance and refinement. As a rule his work was more delicate than the work of Hepplewhite. Sheraton's designs for bookcases and china cabinets were marked by their tall and narrow proportions. In order to make his designs for bookcases and other pieces of a similar nature more elegant he often employed scrolled or swan neck pediments and finials in the form of classic urns.

Sheraton continued to recommend for his designs in the DRAWING BOOK the same woods preferred by Adam and Hepplewhite. Golden-toned satinwood was more extensively used on furniture designed in the Sheraton style than in any of the preceding styles. It was even used for such large articles as secretary cabinets and china cabinets. Sheraton states in his DRAWING BOOK that satinwood had been much used during the last two decades of the 18th century and that he liked its "cool, light and pleasing effect in furniture." Veneered satinwood furniture was either inlaid or painted with gay and graceful Neo-Classic motifs interpreted in Sheraton's light and delicate style. Satinwood veneer was very often used in combination with veneered woods, such as mahogany, tulipwood, rosewood and ebony. Mahogany was still a popular wood for library and dining room furniture as well as for such general household articles as chests of drawers and wardrobes. It was principally used as a veneer; however, when a surface was to be enriched with carving it was also used, for mahogany has always been one of the finest mediums for carved decoration. The prevailing taste for furniture light in tone and decorated with rich polychrome colors greatly reduced the use of wood carving. Nevertheless, an examination of Sheraton's DRAWING BOOK reveals that he employed more carved detail, especially on his tapering chair legs, than is usually associated with the Sheraton style of furniture. The carved detail, executed in low relief, was distinctive for its symmetry and for its finished and delicate detail. Especially praiseworthy was the composition, as well as the disposition, of the carved classic ornament on his designs for chair backs. Sheraton showed a preference for reeding and fluting which emphasized the perpendicular effects of his designs. He used it on such members as the bedposts on tester bedsteads, on the arm supports of chairs and settees, on pilasters and on the three-quarter round stiles found on chests of drawers and other similar pieces. Sheraton was also partial to gilding. His illustrations for drawing room chairs and settees designed in the contemporary French taste were usually either entirely gilded or painted. He said that the painted examples should be partially gilded to "give a lively effect." He preferred an en-

tirely white ground with gilt enrichments. Torchères were usually gilded and the pier table except for its satinwood top was often gilded.

Sheraton displayed a preference for decorating his more elegant satinwood cabinetwork, such as chairs, commodes and pier tables, with marquetry. Sheraton's style of ornament to be carried out in marquetry was spirited and graceful and displayed exquisite detail in its composition. Floral garlands, festoons, pendants of husks and flowers, foliage scrolls, vine trails, shells, fans, rosettes, paterae, urns of blossoms, bowknotted floral stems were all imbued with a singular sprightly charm. Veneering in late 18th century cabinetwork attained a high degree of excellence. The veneer was carefully selected to show the greatest amount of figure. Richly toned satinwood and mahogany veneered surfaces were freely inlaid with decorative bandings and borders of contrasting woods, such as rosewood, kingwood, tulipwood, satinwood, harewood and mahogany. Shaped panel bandings were also inlaid in the veneered surfaces. Graceful oval panels of richly figured veneered wood were especially characteristic of Sheraton's work. Delicate stringing lines frequently appeared on the legs of chairs and tables for decorative purposes. Doors on china cabinets, sideboards and other similar pieces were often inlaid with oval or circular stringing lines, while border bandings were frequently enclosed in stringing lines. Sheraton also illustrated in his DRAWING BOOK exquisitely painted border designs for pier tables. He also showed finely painted oval medallions of classical figure subjects as well as other Neo-Classic ornament appropriate for use in painted panels. His motifs for painted decoration, like his motifs for marquetry, were notable for their delicate and finished composition. Japanned beechwood chairs and settees were also characteristic of the Sheraton style. They were generally japanned in lamp black enriched with painted decoration either in polychrome or en grisaille. The top rail of the chairs and settees often centered a delicately painted oblong tablet. This inexpensive painted furniture was charmingly colorful and it satisfied the prevailing fashionable taste for rich color effects.

The style of ornament employed on Sheraton furniture was noteworthy for its graceful and charming delicacy and for its refined elegance. The motifs were interpreted in a light and spirited manner, so typical of the Louis XVI style of ornament. The principle of symmetry was carefully observed both in the composition and in the distribution of ornament, giving the best of the designs a faultless balance. The ornament included the classical motifs developed by Robert Adam and the prevailing motifs of the Louis XVI style. Included among the fashionable and favorite motifs were paterae generally filled with rosettes, fans or shells, the water leaf motif, segmental paterae, delicate acanthus scrolling, foliage scrolls, the lyre motif, three Prince of Wales feathers, slender and graceful classic urns often decorated with festooning, shells, rosettes, fans, delicate pendants or festoons of husks, honeysuckle or the anthemion, drapery swags, lozenges, graceful floral or drapery festoons, entwined floral garlands, pendants of flowers, wreaths of flowers, interlacing vine trails, bowknotted baskets of flowers, urns of blossoms, the vase motif and medallions of classical figure subjects. Sheraton's later motifs in the French Directoire and French Empire styles are included in the subsequent English Regency.

ARTICLES OF FURNITURE

Chairs   The fragile delicacy which was a distinguishing feature of chairs designed in the Hepplewhite style became more pronounced in the early Sheraton examples. His early designs were admirable in their fine proportions and their splendid distribution of ornament. Sheraton through his reserved treatment of ornament and skillful manipulation of straight lines was able to impart a singular beauty to his drawings for chair backs. One principal difference between the form of chair backs of these two men is that Hepplewhite freely used curved lines in his chair backs, such as shield, heart-shaped and oval, while the early Sheraton style chair backs are rectangular or square (FIGURES 403, 404, 405, 406). However, Sheraton did occasionally use curved lines as can be seen in several shield-backs which were included in his DRAWING BOOK. The splats were often flanked by delicate fluted columns or banisters (403) which were sometimes slightly prolonged above the top rail. The splat was often headed by the three Prince of Wales plumes (403) which in some instances were decorated with drapery swags (405). Chair backs were also designed with three, four or five slender upright pieces, called banisters or bars. In another fashionable variety the chair back was designed with trellis work panels (404). In this type the back panel was sometimes filled with crossed diagonal or diamond lattice-work (404). The treatment of these trellis work panels was ingeniously varied. The top rail of chairs with trellis work panels often centered a slightly projecting plaquette (404). In Sheraton's designs for chair backs the splat, the banisters or the trellis work panel did not extend to the seat rail but were supported on a horizontal crosspiece raised several inches above the seat (403, 404, 405, 406). The crest or top rail of the chair back was commonly straight (404), and sometimes it was flat-arched (403, 406). Occasionally the straight top rail centered a raised oblong plaquette (404). In a few examples the top rail was slightly curved. The arms were frequently straight and slightly shaped and rested on incurvate arm supports. Other arms sloped downward almost from the top rail (404, 406). The arms often rested on vertically reeded vase-shaped supports (404). Arm supports of more or less vase form were a feature of sofas and chairs designed by Sheraton (409). The arm supports were either directly above the two front legs (406) or were joined to the side rails of the seat frame (404). The slender tapered legs were either of quadrangular (403) or cylindrical form (404). The quadrangular leg often terminated in a spade foot (403). The round leg was often vertically reeded and ring-collared (404); sometimes it was spirally fluted.

Chairs were principally made of mahogany (403, 404) or a soft wood (406, 407, 408) which was painted to accord with the colored walls and soft-toned hangings of contemporary rooms. This painted furniture was essentially most decorative. Sheraton recommended that his carved chairs in the prevailing French taste should be either gilded or painted white and parcel gilded (407). A large number of inexpensive chairs were made of beechwood and were japanned in black (406, 408) and occasionally in color. They were often decorated with flowers and floral garlands painted in natural colors (406), while some examples were brightened with touches of gilt (408). These chairs satisfied the demand for rich color effects. Chairs made of satin-wood were often enhanced with painted floral motifs (405). A large number of chairs were made of mahogany, with the frame of the chair being often delicately reeded or fluted.

Sheraton's later chair designs (407, 408) were influenced by the French Directoire style, which became current in England at the end of the 18th century, and the incoming French Empire style. Several new features of design introduced into these chairs often resulted in a noticeable change in their appearance. Horizontal lines were emphasized, and the top rail, which became broader in many models, rolled over or swept backwards (407, 408). Some chairs featured a broad concave crest rail. The top rail was also designed as a small round rail (407), which often had an enlarged center portion or a rectangular panel, with each side horizontally turned to resemble a vase. The backs of the chairs displayed a wide variety of design. Chair backs with horizontal slats and with latticed panels were among the favorite patterns (408). As a rule the front legs were round (407) and occasionally the lower part of the legs curved outward (408). Sheraton also designed chairs with saber legs, which are so-called because of their resemblance to the shape of a saber. In this form of concave leg the foot as a separate portion from the leg disappeared. Although the majority of these chairs lacked the elegance and refinement which characterized Sheraton's early chair designs, some of the better of these chair designs were completely pleasing (407, 408).

During Sheraton's final and so-called decadent period his chair designs based on the French Empire style were of an extravagant nature. They were characterized by eccentric novelties of design, distorted curves and fantastic ornament.

Sheraton illustrated in his DRAWING BOOK drawing room chairs which were close adaptations of Louis XVI models. The frames were richly carved and molded. The arm supports and round tapered legs were fluted or spirally turned. Sheraton recommended that they should be either entirely gilded or painted and parcel gilded. A white ground with gilt enrichments was a favorite combination. He stated that the back, seat and armpads should be upholstered in printed silk.

In the CABINET DICTIONARY Sheraton illustrated the French voyeuse and observed that "the manner of conversing amongst some of the highest circles of company on some occasions is copied from the French by lounging upon a chair. Hence we have the term conversation chair which is peculiarly adapted for this kind of idle position." It was designed with a narrow back supporting a padded and upholstered curved oblong crest panel that extended several inches beyond the sides of the back. In this conversation chair the occupant placed himself with his back to the front of the chair in a straddle position and rested his elbows on the arm rest.

The wing chair or easy chair of the Sheraton style was similar to that of the Hepplewhite style except that the legs were usually round and not joined with stretchers. The arms in both the Sheraton and Hepplewhite styles extended to the back of the seat and the wide wings rested on the arms. In the earlier 18th century styles the arms extended only to the wings, with the arm and wing having the appearance of one continuous piece. This feature of design afforded a more graceful and pleasing line. The contour of many examples of the Queen Anne and Early Georgian wing chair was especially fine.

In the CABINET DICTIONARY Sheraton wrote about an easy chair of tub shape. He observed that they are "stuffed all over and intended for sick persons, being both easy and warm for the wide wings coming quite forward keep out the cold air." It seems that in these chairs the wings and back were made in a semi-circle and were upholstered as one continuous unit. The term *tub chair* is also commonly given to a form of upholstered chair having a low, arched horseshoe-shaped back continuing to form the arms and characterized by its rounded appearance. The sides and back were rounded about the seat and were upholstered as one unit. The straight tapering leg was either cylindrical or quadrangular in form. Undoubtedly the design for this chair was borrowed from the duchesse, a form of French day bed, with its gondola-shaped ends and which Hepplewhite described in the GUIDE as "tub-shaped ends."

Settees, Sofas and Couches

Sheraton's early designs for upholstered settees were often close adaptations of prevailing Louis XVI models. He illustrated in his DRAWING BOOK a settee designed in the French taste to harmonize with his French drawing room chairs. The characteristic earlier Sheraton style settees were of rectangular form. Features of design most commonly employed included straight backs (409), vase-shaped arm supports (409) and tapered cylindrical legs, which were often reeded. One characteristic variety had a narrow top rail which often centered a raised oblong panel or plaque. The arms started from the top of the back and gently sloped forward in a concave curve (409). The arms usually rested on vase-shaped supports (409). It usually had eight and sometimes six tapered legs of cylindrical form; occasionally quadrangular legs were employed (409). The legs were often finished with brass toe caps and wheel casters (409). Settees were chiefly made of mahogany or a soft wood which was to be painted or lacquered. Mahogany settees were essentially plain, while the painted settees often had carved and gilded enrichments. The caned settee (409) was also designed in the Sheraton style. It was usually made of satinwood, painted or japanned beech wood and was decorated in the prevailing taste.

The chair-back settee continued to be made until the end of the century. It essentially followed the design of the Sheraton style open chair back and was decorated accordingly. It was most frequently designed with four connecting chair backs and with eight tapered cylindrical legs.

In Sheraton's later designs for settees he adopted some of the features of the French Directoire style. Settees at the beginning of the 19th century were often designed with scrolled arms and outward curving legs. One principal variety of settee of the Directoire type was of lyre form and had a shaped back and out-scrolled sides continuing in an unbroken curve to form the seat rail. It rested on short splayed legs shod with brass paw feet, which were castered. Sheraton illustrated in his CABINET DICTIONARY a variety of sofa and a variety of couch which he called a Grecian sofa and a Grecian couch respectively. The sofa was of lyre form and rested on short, straight unattractive legs. His different designs for Grecian couches were derived from those used in classical times for reclining on at meals or for sleeping. Due to the special features of design this variety of couch, as well as the sofa of lyre form, is regarded as belonging to the English Regency. The Grecian couch was designed with an out-scrolled side which usually continued in an unbroken curve to form the seat rail. It was fitted with a long loose seat cushion and a bolster. Sometimes the other side rail continued to curve upward and roll inward just above the seat cushion. It was often designed with a shaped back panel, extending about one half the length of the seat. It had short splayed legs. The characteristic splayed leg widened from the bottom to the top and its shape more or less resembled the form of the horn of plenty or cornucopia. The legs were commonly shod with brass paw feet which were castered. These couches were decorated in accordance with the taste of the Regency style (430).

Beds   The characteristic tester bed in general use by the end of the century is usually credited to both Hepplewhite and Sheraton. It had tapered and reeded front posts on a vase-turned section which rested on block supports. The posts were usually made of mahogany or were painted and parcel-gilded. The cornice, which was sometimes surmounted with classic urn finials, was usually enriched with either carved or painted detail.

Cradles   Although low cradles mounted on rockers continued to be made in the late 18th and early 19th centuries they were entirely utilitarian in character. The majority of fashionable cradles were of the swinging type. Especially typical was the swing cradle having sides of turned columns and cane panelling, hung on turned mahogany posts resting on splayed bridge feet. It was often provided with a hood. Sheraton in his CABINET DICTIONARY gave a design for an elaborately draped "swinging crib bed" provided with a hood in the form of a dome. He also gave a diagram for a kind of clock spring by means of which the cradle can swing mechanically. He observes that a clock spring was being perfected which would swing the cradle for an hour and a half. There is extant an English cradle which will swing with the aid of a mechanism for about twenty minutes.

Tables   The Sheraton style sectional dining table was designed with reeded cylindrical tapered legs, finished with brass toe caps and wheel casters. Each end section, which generally had a drop-leaf, had an oblong top with rounded outer corners and a reeded edge, over a conformingly shaped frieze. Toward the end of the century each of the two or more sections of the mahogany dining table was supported on a turned pedestal with a molded and splayed tetrapod base, finished with brass paw feet and wheel casters. The oblong top of the pedestal dining table had rounded outer corners and the edge was usually reeded. Sheraton stated in his CABINET DICTIONARY that "the common useful dining tables are upon pillar and claws, generally four claws to each pillar, with brass casters. A dining table of this kind may be made to any size, by having a sufficient quantity of pillar and claw parts, for between each of them is a loose flap, fixed by means of iron straps and buttons, so that they are easily taken off and put aside."

The form of Sheraton's sideboards resembled the designs of Hepplewhite and Thomas Shearer. Shearer, who was a contemporary of Hepplewhite, illustrated in the CABINETMAKERS' LONDON BOOK OF PRICES, published in 1788, the sideboard with deep lateral wine drawers or cupboards, described in the chapter on Hepplewhite, and the pedestal sideboard. This latter form of sideboard had a swell-front central section which was similar in design to the sideboard with deep lateral wine drawers and which was flanked and joined to pedestal ends, each having a single cupboard door. Each pedestal end was surmounted with an urn. The central portion was mounted on two tapered legs which continued from the stiles that flanked the central frieze drawer. Sheraton in his DRAWING BOOK illustrated both of these forms of sideboards. They were surmounted with a finely chased brass gallery which served to support large plate. The brass gallery was fitted with two or more candlebranches, which, when lighted, "gave a brilliant effect to the silver ware." Sheraton illustrated sideboards with slender tapered legs of either cylindrical or quadrangular form, with the latter usually terminating in spade feet. The front of the sideboards with deep lateral wine drawers designed in the Sheraton style was generally straight, serpentine, concave or bow-shaped. Variations in design occurred in both of these forms of sideboards. Toward the end of the century the structure of the sideboard with deep lateral wine drawers or cupboards generally became more massive. The wine drawers or cupboards became deeper and in some specimens extended almost to the floor. The long central frieze drawer was often over two cupboard doors. In the sideboard of pedestal form at the beginning of the 19th century the pedestal end sections flanked a shaped shelf over a row of two drawers. Each pedestal contained a single frieze drawer over a long cupboard door. Sideboards in the Sheraton style were usually veneered with mahogany and were very often inlaid.

Sheraton in his CABINET DICTIONARY illustrated the sideboard table, designed with a frieze and without drawers. He refers to these sideboard tables "as the most fashionable at present." They were designed in the style of the Regency.

Sheraton's two designs for pier tables in his DRAWING BOOK were richly decorative and delicate. He recommended that the top should be veneered in satinwood and have a painted and banded border and that the carved frame should be gilded or painted white with gilt enrichments. He favored the use of stretchers, which had been recently introduced. Both of his designs have shaped stretchers, one centering a classical vase and the other a basket of flowers. Extant examples of pier tables are notable for their elegance and refinement. The delicacy, finish and diversity of the decorative painting found on the tops of these tables is especially admirable (412, 413). In one of a pair of gilt wood side tables (412) the semi-elliptical top is painted yellow and decorated with medallions en grisaille in a chocolate ground. The oblong center medallion represents a chariot with classical figures adapted from a painting by Guido Reni, 1575–1642, depicting Aurora strewing flowers in front of the chariot. Oval medallions with figure subjects are on either side. In a pair of satinwood pier tables (413) the decoration on the top is painted in polychrome and comprises swags of realistically treated flowers depending from graceful bow-knotted ribbons within a decorated banded border. The painted ornament on the frieze and legs is rendered in a diminutive scale, which, at that time, was most fashionable.

Sheraton illustrated the Pembroke table (416) in his DRAWING BOOK and stated that it could be made of satinwood and could be decorated in an elegant manner. The slender tapered quadrangular legs were usually finished with brass toe caps and casters. The Pembroke table was a most useful table and many were made during the last two decades of the century. It was often used for serving meals, especially breakfast. Toward the end of the century the harlequin Pembroke table was introduced. This table was designed with an oblong structure which could be raised from the body of the table by means of weights. This structure was fitted with small drawers and compartments containing accessories needed for writing, drawing or needlework. Sheraton in his DRAWING BOOK illustrated a design for a harlequin Pembroke table, and writes, "It is termed a Harlequin Table, for no other reason but because, in exhibitions of that sort, there is generally a great deal of machinery introduced in the scenery."

The sofa table introduced late in the 18th century was a popular piece of furniture. Sheraton stated that the table was to be placed in front of the sofa. The characteristic variety of Sheraton style sofa table had an oblong top with end drop-leaves over two frieze drawers and rear mock drawers. The drop-leaves, which often had rounded corners, were supported on hinged wooden brackets. The over-all length of the table was between five and six feet and the width was about two feet, and the height from about 26 inches to 29 inches.

The legs were designed in different forms. The table was often mounted on a vase-turned pedestal with four molded and splayed supports, finished with brass paw feet and casters. Sometimes the sofa table was designed with two lyre-form end supports, joined by a stretcher. The table was generally made of mahogany and was banded in tulip-wood or satinwood.

It is generally accepted that the nest of tables was introduced in England rather late in the 18th century. These tables which were small and light in structure were also called "quartetto tables" since a complete set comprised four tables. They were graduated in size so that each one fitted under another, and were so designed that each table could be drawn out of each other. The nest of tables was generally made of either satinwood or mahogany and was designed in the prevailing taste. According to contemporary records these tables were generally found in the drawing room and were used for refreshments. In this manner the guest could be served in his chair. The nest of tables was illustrated in Sheraton's CABINET DICTIONARY.

Gaming Tables   The card table was usually veneered with either satinwood or mahogany and was decorated in the prevailing taste. The folding top was made in a variety of shapes, such as oval, broken-fronted, circular and square, the latter often having rounded corners. The frieze occasionally centered an oblong tablet. The slender tapered legs were either quadrangular or cylindrical in form. Sheraton's DRAWING BOOK illustrated a design for an inlaid card table having a shaped top with outset rounded corners. The three-quarter rounded stiles continued to form the round and tapered legs which were enriched with delicate leaf carving and vertical reedings. Due to the popular feeling against gambling and the Government's effort to curtail it fewer card tables were made during the Regency period.

Toilet Tables   Sheraton illustrated in his DRAWING BOOK a variety of designs for dressing tables, some of which were extremely elaborate and intricate. The favorite type was the dressing table with a hinged folding lid, which, when opened, disclosed a framed rising mirror and a fitted interior for toilet articles. Another variety was the commode dressing table which was essentially designed in the prevailing French taste. The chest of drawers in the Sheraton style sometimes had the top drawer fitted with toilet accessories. The dressing table of kneehole form, with rear cupboard doors in the kneehole space, was also occasionally made in the Sheraton style. Dressing tables were usually made of either mahogany or satinwood.

Work Tables   The work table or sewing table designed in the Sheraton style was distinctive for its elegance and refinement. The legs were frequently connected with a stretcher or a shaped undershelf. Sheraton gave considerable prominence to work tables in his DRAWING BOOK, some of which were remarkable for the ingenuity of their designs. The pouch variety of work table having a silk work bag attached to a pull-out frame as well as the work table designed as a combination piece enjoyed a great vogue (410).

Sheraton illustrated an oblong table with a high gallery, a portion of which fell forward to the level of the table top. It was fitted with a corresponding shelf below (417). This table, which bears a resemblance to the French work table of the tricoteuse type (177), Sheraton calls in his DRAWING BOOK a "French Work Table." He remarks that "the style of finishing them is neat being commonly made of satinwood, with a brass molding round the edge of the rim."

Writing Furniture

The library or writing table of pedestal form was generally made of mahogany and was distinctive for its finely figured veneered surface. Sheraton stated in his DRAWING BOOK that it could be sparingly ornamented with either carved or inlaid work and that the top was to be inset with either leather or green cloth. He illustrated a pedestal desk of oval form having the end frieze drawers fitted with rising easel bookrests. He also gave a design for the kidney-shaped pedestal writing table.

The drum table, a distinctive form of mahogany library table, became popular in England at the end of the 18th century. It was designed with a circular top inset with a tooled leather panel over six or eight frieze drawers. Half the number were often mock drawers. The top revolved on a turned column with four reeded quadrangular and splayed legs which were finished with either brass toe caps or paw feet and wheel casters. Sometimes the frieze instead of being fitted with drawers was designed with partitions for books. The top of the table averaged about four and one half feet in diameter. The top of the table was sometimes polygonal in form. These tables were described as library tables in contemporary records.

The knee-hole writing table was designed throughout the 18th century in the different successive styles.

The Carlton House writing table (418) introduced in the last quarter of the 18th century became very popular during the last decade of the century. The origin of the design and the reason for its name have never been ascertained; however, the name *Carlton House* was given to this variety of desk by at least 1796, when the name appeared in Gillow's COST BOOK dated this year. It had an oblong top with rounded rear corners (418). The two sides and the back of the desk were surrounded with a conformingly shaped plateau or superstructure of small drawers and cupboards surmounted by a three-quarter ormolu gallery (418). The plateau was fitted with a small drawer at each end and with two central tiers of three small drawers each, flanked by incurvate cupboard doors (418). Frequently the plateau had a tier of three small drawers at each end and was of the same height as the back portion. The writing surface was panelled in leather and centered a rising easel rest (418). The frieze was fitted with three drawers. It was designed with four quadrangular and occasionally cylindrical tapered legs finished with ormolu toe caps and wheel casters (418). The drawers were most frequently fitted with ormolu bail handles (418). Sheraton illustrated in his DRAWING BOOK a Carlton House writing table and recommended that it be made of either mahogany or satinwood. Some were finely inlaid with cross-bandings and delicate stringing lines. The desk generally averaged about fifty-six inches in length, although smaller desks of the Carlton House type were also designed. The design in Sheraton's DRAWING BOOK was dated 1793, and he described it as a lady's drawing and writing table.

The finest examples of wall furniture of the late 18th century, such as bookcases (420), secretary bookcases (421), cabinets and secretary cabinets (424), were made of satinwood often combined with a variety of costly veneers. Sheraton's constant striving for lightness and elegance in his forms was also apparent in his designs for these pieces. They were usually characterized by their tall and narrow proportions. This effect was largely achieved by reducing the width, by employing pediments surmounted with finials and by emphasizing vertical lines, such as the skillful manner in which the glazing bars were designed. Sheraton in his DRAWING BOOK illustrated different designs for pediments and for glazed doors to be used on bookcases. The glazing bars, which emphasized the long, vertical effect, were often designed to form interesting arches and arcades. Others were designed with upright oval and elliptical forms. Although curved glazing bars were more typical of Sheraton's work, he also occasionally employed straight glazing bars to form different elongated and polygonal forms.

Due to the prevailing taste for furniture light and delicate in form, many writing cabinets were made in the Sheraton style with low recessed cabinets, fitted with one or two solid wood cabinet doors, and mounted on slender tapered legs. These writing cabinets were usually of satinwood and were distinctive for the elegant and delicate quality of their designs and classical decoration. One fashionable variety was similar to the French bonheur du jour.

Commodes   Satinwood (422) and pastel-painted (411) commodes decorated with painted ovals of figure subjects and mythological scenes after designs of Angelica Kauffmann, Zucchi or Cipriani were most fashionable. Paterae, festoons and pendants continued in vogue; however, they were often executed on a diminutive scale. Floral compositions, painted in natural colors, were also included among the fashionable decorative ingredients.

Chests of   The chest of drawers was generally made of mahogany and was
Drawers   usually designed with a straight or bow-front. It had three or four long graduated drawers which were often finished with cock beading.

The top and the drawers were frequently inlaid with panel bandings and stringing lines. The chest of drawers was often designed with a valanced base curving into French bracket feet. Sheraton illustrated a chest of drawers in his DRAWING BOOK having outset rounded front corners and reeded front columnar stiles continuing to form the round and turned tapered feet. Sheraton gave two designs for the chest of drawers having the top fitted with toilet accessories, which he called a dressing chest. The chest-on-chest was also designed in his style.

Clothes-presses

Sheraton in his DRAWING BOOK gave a design for a wardrobe consisting of a clothespress flanked by two slightly recessed winged sections. Each wing section was fitted with a long cupboard door, panelled to simulate two doors. Sheraton stated that the upper central portion, which was fitted with two doors, should contain six or seven clothespress shelves. The lower central portion was fitted with three long graduated drawers. The slightly recessed wings were to be used for hanging clothes. The wardrobe rested on a molded plinth or bracket base.

Stands

The term *canterbury* is generally given to a stand or rack surmounted with upright openwork partitions which was designed early in the 19th century to hold bound volumes of music. In his CABINET DICTIONARY Sheraton explained that the term *canterbury* had been applied to some pieces of cabinetwork reputed to have been ordered by the Archbishop of Canterbury. One was a plate and cutlery stand with a semi-circular end and with three partitions crosswise to hold the knives, forks and plates. The other was a small music stand.

During the second half of the 18th century numerous mahogany tripod stands were made to support books and were designed in accordance with the prevailing fashion. One principal variety of reading stand had an oblong hinged top with a ratchet easel, mounted on a turned shaft with a molded tripod base. The reading stand was frequently designed with lateral metal candle arms.

The designs for gilt candlestands or torchères illustrated in the DRAWING BOOK were exceedingly fragile. The delicate scrolls were to be made of wirework composition. Sheraton stated that candlestands were very useful for augmenting the lighting facilities in a room. Mahogany candlestands of a less elaborate character were also designed in the Sheraton style.

Mirrors

Wall mirrors were not illustrated in Sheraton's DRAWING BOOK. Toward the end of the century the familiar French Empire style with a circular convex mirror (441) in a carved and molded gilt wood frame was introduced. It had a circular molded deep cavetto frame to which were applied gilt spherules or small balls (441). The convex mirror plate was encircled with an ebonized reeded fillet (441). The cresting was surmounted with a spread eagle (441). Frequently the base of the mirror was ornamented with a carved foliage pendant (441). It was very often designed with lateral candle arms. These convex circular mirrors became extremely fashionable.

During the last quarter of the 18th century a variety of mirror was introduced having a mirror plate long enough to reflect a person's full length. This standing type of mirror is called a cheval dressing glass (423) or a horse dressing glass, the term being derived from the frame or horse on which it was suspended. The mirror was enclosed in a rectangular frame which was attached to the uprights by swivel screws (423). The uprights rested on splayed bridge feet (423). Sometimes the cheval mirror was mechanically designed with lead weights so it could be raised or lowered. Frequently candle arms were attached to the uprights. The cheval mirror was illustrated in Sheraton's DRAWING BOOK and remained popular throughout the Regency style.

The swinging dressing mirror on a box stand designed in the Sheraton style generally had an oblong framed mirror attached to turned banisters. The width of the mirror exceeded its height. The stand was often designed with a bow-front. Another form of late 18th century table dressing mirror often had an oval framed mirror attached by swivel screws to shaped uprights that rested on splayed bridge feet. The uprights were connected at the bottom and often at the top with a shaped bar. The principles of design found in this dressing mirror were similar to those found in the long cheval mirror.

Accessories   Mahogany bed steps designed in the Sheraton style generally consisted of a set of three steps. The upper tread was hinged and opened to a well which was often fitted with a wash basin and a soap cup. Sometimes the bed steps were designed with a drawer under the middle tread. The bed steps rested on four short tapered legs of cylindrical form. Sheraton gave two designs for bed steps in his DRAWING BOOK.

The DRAWING BOOK contained designs for knife urns and knife boxes. The difference between Sheraton's designs and those of Hepplewhite's was negligible and it would be difficult to differentiate between the two styles. According to Sheraton the finest knife cases were made by those cabinetmakers who specialized in such work.

The name *nest of drawers* was given to a miniature form of a chest of drawers. They were made throughout the 18th century and their design followed the different successive styles for the chest of drawers.

In addition to the many pieces of furniture already mentioned as being illustrated by Sheraton, many other articles were also illustrated, including such articles as tall case clocks, sconces, tripod fire screens, architects' tables, night tables, corner basin stands, corner night tables, washing stands and library steps.

CHAPTER TWENTY-ONE

ENGLISH REGENCY

The second phase of the Classic Revival came into existence late in the 18th century. This last phase of the Neo-Classic movement is known on the Continent as the Empire style, while in England it is generally known as the Regency. This differentiation seems more appropriate since the English development was not a close version of the French Empire style. The Regency taste was in vogue in the decorative arts from about 1795 to 1820, although historically the Regency covers the years from 1811 to 1820 when George, Prince of Wales, acted as Regent for his father, George III. This revolution in taste, which occurred both on the Continent and in England toward the close of the 18th century, was based upon a closer and more profound classic revival. It fostered the cult of antiquity and was essentially an archaeological revival in which antique Greek and Roman interior decoration and material remains were copied. The talented architect Henry Holland was the principal leader of the early phase in Eng-

land, in which the elements were essentially borrowed from the French Directoire. After Holland's death in 1806 the leading designers were completely engrossed in an archaeological approach inspired by the French architects Percier and Fontaine, who wrote in the preface of one of their publications that "the style does not belong to us but to the ancients." This zeal in investigating and in copying antique ornament and forms eclipsed practically all attention to the earlier traditions developed by Robert Adam. The Regency style was marked by an eclectic character, with the principles drawn from Roman, Greek and Egyptian civilizations. In the final phase the style became dogmatic and the emphasis was placed on Grecian severity. During the Regency style some English designers renewed their interest once again in Chinese as well as in Gothic art. All these various sources employed by the Regency designers pointedly pronounce its miscellaneous character.

The gifted English architect Henry Holland, 1746–1806, was influential in developing the early phase of the Regency style in England. He was much in demand and among the famous houses in which he made alterations was Carlton House for the Prince Regent. His style of interior decoration in which he combined Louis XVI motifs with details of the French Directoire was praiseworthy for its refined simplicity. His designs, which were rare, included drawings for interior decoration and for furniture, such as bookcases, pier tables and mirrors. Holland was a brilliant decorative artist and his skillful and delicate manipulation of ornament was unrivalled in the contemporary work of other architects. Through his style of decoration he was able to introduce certain Greek and Roman details, found in the French Directoire style, into the contemporary English decorative arts.

Thomas Hope, 1769–1831, the son of a wealthy Dutch banker and merchant, was instrumental in impressing the later classic phase on English taste. In pursuing his studies of architecture he had traveled extensively in Greece, Egypt, Syria and Sicily. He was a close friend of Percier, one of the architects of the French Empire style, and he showed a strong predilection for his work. He settled in England in 1794. He used a large part of his fortune in collecting paintings and antique sculptures and in designing the decoration and furniture for his London house in Cavendish Square and for his country house in Surrey, called Deepdene. In 1807 he published his furniture designs for Deepdene in a book entitled HOUSEHOLD FURNITURE AND INTERIOR DECORATION. His furniture designs were closely derived from the French Empire models and were also inspired by archaeological ideals. Although his designs, especially those based on his

archaeological conceptions, were frequently extravagant, they were handled with more restraint than was evidenced in Sheraton's later drawings in the Empire style. His furniture was often massive and ponderous and was not practical for general use, and his drawings were marred by a certain lifeless and uninspiring quality. His book, like Sheraton's drawings in the Empire style, presaged ill for Victorian art.

In addition to the work of Holland and Hope other phases of the Regency style may be studied in Sheraton's CABINET DICTIONARY and in his ENCYCLOPAEDIA and in George Smith's COLLECTION OF DESIGNS FOR HOUSEHOLD FURNITURE AND INTERIOR DECORATION, published in 1808. This latter work contained one hundred and fifty-eight colored plates, which included numerous designs for rooms showing the interior decoration and the arrangement of the furniture. He stated that he was guided by the finest ancient specimens of the Egyptian, Greek and Roman styles. He also included some ornament in the Gothic and Chinese taste. Smith stated that an exact examination of antique examples of sculptures and paintings was required, "taking not so much the mere pattern or imitation but the spirit and principle on which the original was composed." Unfortunately, a large part of his work was inconsistent and completely lacking in harmony. He also published two later books. According to his own statement, Smith produced a considerable amount of furniture for some of England's "most exalted characters." Numerous other books were published by different persons containing collections of antique vases, tripods, altars and antique ornament. Especially praiseworthy were the issues of Ackerman's REPOSITORY. Thomas Chippendale Jr. designed and made many pieces of cabinetwork in the style of the Regency. His furniture was of a less extravagant nature and showed the Regency style at its best.

The ascendancy of France in the decorative arts was evident throughout the style of the English Regency. The severe taste, implicit in the fashion for plain forms, paramount in the French Empire style, was also the goal of the English designers. As in France, the development of this classic movement in England under the influence of Thomas Hope was founded in the imitation of Roman forms of furniture and in the adaptation of Roman motifs. It was the aim of Hope to change these bronze and marble antique remains, such as tripods, legs of tables and couches and frames of folding stools and chairs into 19th century furniture. Other articles of which there were no material remains the designers studied from representations in bas reliefs, from paintings on vases and from bronze sculptures. As a result of this taste for imitating the ancients the fashionable ornament, such as dolphins, swans, lion masks and hocked animal legs for supports, was interpreted in an archaeological manner. Classical furniture forms were reproduced, including couches with scrolled head rests, folding chairs and stools of X-form, the Grecian klismos and tripods. Hope in his book illustrated tripods that folded in a manner similar to those of the ancients. Naturally, since any close imitation of antique furniture presented numerous problems, the designers had to do a great deal of compromising and adapting. Then, too, all the many 18th century articles unknown to the ancients also had to be considered. With these problems in view the French architect Fontaine stated in one of his publications, "We have followed the models of antiquity not blindly but with the discrim-

ination entailed by the manners, customs and materials of the moderns. We have strived to imitate the antique in its spirit, its principles and its maxims, which are of all times."

Toward the end of the 18th century there was apparent in England a general interest in Greek architecture and everything pertaining to Greek art. This was evident in the Grecian style of ornament employed in architecture. Grecian vases and other objects of art, as well as furniture copied from the same classical sources, were found in many wealthy English homes. The work of Henry Holland, who developed his style essentially from contemporary French classicism, was an important factor in this transitional phase. During the first quarter of the 19th century not only were the forms of furniture changed to harmonize with antique classic ideals but the furniture designers and cabinetmakers adopted a new ideal of Grecian severity. They repudiated such traditions of the 18th century as elegance, gracefulness and delicacy. In order to achieve this new ideal of Grecian severity in furniture, the ornament was restricted and the lines were simplified and subjected to a rigid and formal discipline. The principle of symmetry was zealously followed. This ideal of Grecian severity reduced comfort to a minimum, in fact much of the furniture had little semblance of comfort. The word *Grecian* became an important one in the English cabinetmakers' vocabulary. Sheraton in his CABINET DICTIONARY illustrated Grecian couches having an outscrolled side. Early in the 19th century the so-called Grecian chair was introduced which was a reproduction of the ancient Grecian klismos.

Late in the 18th century for a short space of time an attempt was made to introduce certain Egyptian ornamental features and symbolism in furniture and in decoration. This fashion for Egyptian detail was established in France after Napoleon's Egyptian campaign in 1798 and it soon spread to England. Denon's VOYAGE DANS LA BASSE ET LA HAUTE EGYPTE published in 1802, which contained many fine examples of art based on the ancient history of Egypt, was largely responsible for creating a taste for this style of ornament. George Smith, who illustrated drawings in the Egyptian taste, freely borrowed from Denon's book. Unfortunately Smith's work was lacking in harmony. Thomas Hope employed the Egyptian style of ornament as an appropriate background for his Egyptian antiquities. He also illustrated designs for furniture in the Egyptian taste in his HOUSEHOLD FURNITURE. This Egyptian taste was largely restricted to that style of ornament, which included such favorite motifs as Egyptian figures, especially used as terminal figures, sphinxes, the winged sun disc, lion masks in the Egyptian taste and the lotus flower. The era was also marked by a Chinese revival, which was essentially represented by the use of a few characteristic chinoiseries, such as pagodas and Chinese figure subjects, birds, flowers and landscapes. Occasionally light chairs and tables made of soft woods were japanned and were decorated with painted chinoiseries. Sometimes in order to introduce an Oriental touch the beechwood frames of chairs and the legs of small decorative occasional tables were bamboo turned and were painted in imitation of bamboo. The taste for hand-painted wallpapers from China persisted to a greater or less extent throughout the second half of the 18th and early 19th centuries. These wallpapers generally depicted flowering shrubs with birds or scenes from Chinese life, such as lantern processions. Since the imported papers were very expensive they were copied in England. In the 18th century when wallpaper was to be applied, the walls were covered with a wooden framework over which canvas was stretched. Then the paper was fixed to the canvas, insuring its durability.

Regency furniture was characterized by its eclectic quality. The designs for furniture were essentially based upon a vernacular interpretation of classic ideals, certain features of the French Directoire, a simplification of 18th century traditions and a coarse version of the French Empire. Structural simplicity and the ideal of severity and seriousness were the pronounced aim of the designer and cabinetmaker. Many of the early pieces of Regency furniture with their dignified simplicity were skillfully designed and exhibited a high quality of craftsmanship. Chairs and settees frequently incorporated certain pleasing features of design. This was especially evident in the chair of Grecian pattern copied from the Greek klismos. Other varieties of furniture, such as commodes, in which a rectangular plan was substituted for the earlier semicircular plan, fared badly in this new style of classic severity. Much of the later Regency cabinetwork was marred by a mania for novelties. Unfortunately, the Regency designers and cabinetmakers did not possess the talent for combining all these novelties of design with good taste, a talent which was always so characteristic of French work. As a result, the Regency furniture in its later phase became cumbrous and dull and at times even ugly with its meaningless ornament and distorted lines. The great number of small articles introduced at this time, such as what-nots and flower stands, with their resultant air of confusion and stuffiness were an unhappy omen of things to come in the Victorian era. Cabinetwork in the Regency taste continued to be made in a more or less desultory manner into the reign of Queen Victoria, until it gradually assumed the character of a debased Rococo style, which ultimately dominated the mid-Victorian furniture. During the Regency style woods of dark color, such as mahogany and rosewood, were generally used. Mahogany, either solid or veneered, was most frequently employed. Rosewood became a very fashionable wood for cabinetwork after 1800 and many Regency pieces were made entirely of it. Satinwood was still used, especially during the early phase of the Regency. The practice of graining wood, in which a more expensive wood is simulated, was extensively used in early 19th century cabinetwork.

Metal mounts and metal inlays were the prevailing fashion for decorating the surface of furniture. The dominance of metal for decorative purposes was established by the French designers, who realized the necessity for decorating the flat uninterrupted surfaces of polished mahogany. Applied bronze mounts were more extensively used in the French Empire style than in any of the preceding French styles. The English Regency designers employed bronze mounts in a more restricted sense, and their metal mounts could not be compared with the finely designed and skillfully executed French metal work. Included among the typical English applied mounts were rosettes, paterae, bosses and anthemion palmettes. Female masks, lion masks and terminal figures were also made of bronze and were sometimes found as decorative accessories on bookcases and other furniture of a similar nature. Brass inlays cut from thin sheets of brass came into favor and were extensively employed by the Regency designers. Rosewood and mahogany furniture was frequently inlaid with narrow bandings, stringing lines and fretwork ornament cut from brass. Later the decorative brass inlays laid in a ground of a dark colored veneer became more elaborate. From around 1810 the ambitious cabinetwork featured veneered surfaces with foliated ornament and scrollwork cut from brass and different patterns of ebonized wood. Applied metal moldings were also occasionally used, and pierced galleries were sometimes found on small tables, cabinets and sideboards. Especially characteristic were the metal paw feet employed on the legs of chairs and tables. Some articles of furniture, such as hanging book shelves, featured brass colonettes and balusters as supports for the shelves. Bookcases, low cupboards, commodes and other pieces of furniture of a similar nature were sometimes flanked with freestanding fluted colonnettes made of metal. Doors, such as the doors of commodes, were often filled with brass trellis work backed by silk curtains. Drawers were very often fitted with small bronze or brass knob handles, either ornamented or plain, in accordance with the contemporary French Empire style. Loose-ring handles, some with lion masks, were also fashionable.

As a result of this taste for all kinds of decorative bronze accessories wood carving was sparingly employed. Frequently the carved detail was finished in gilt or bronze paint to simulate the fashionable metal mounts. The ambitious marquetry work and the elegant painted decoration so characteristic of the Adam style completely disappeared. Sheraton in referring to inlay work in his CABINET DICTIONARY states that "in cabinet making it was much in use between 20 and 30 years back but was soon laid aside as a very expensive mode of ornamenting furniture, as well as being subject to a speedy decay. The present mode of inlaying with brass is more durable and looks well let into black woods of any kind." Broad veneered bandings, panel borders and stringing lines laid in a contrasting mahogany or satinwood veneered surface was also a popular practice for enriching the surface of furniture. Painted furniture was restricted to inexpensive chairs and settees made of a soft wood and japanned in black with some modest decoration of flowers or geometrical designs. The style of classic ornament employed by the Regency designers was characterized by the symmetry of its composition. The ornament, which was cold, stiff and formal, was borrowed from antique Greek and Roman sources. Included among the favorite motifs and details taken from classical antiquity were archaic lion masks, the lion monopodium, the hocked animal leg as a support, lion and other paw feet, terms, caryatids, swans, dolphins, lyres, trumpets, stars, bosses, rosettes, paterae, antique heads of helmeted warriors, winged classical figures emblematic of freedom, lances, the Phrygian cap of liberty, the winged thunderbolt of Jupiter, the water leaf motif, anthemion, acanthus foliage of a stiff and formal character, tight woven wreaths, laurel leaves, Greek palm leaves, scrolls, and the Egyptian and Chinese decorative motifs already mentioned.

During the Regency some English designers renewed their interest once again in the Gothic style. This second Gothic revival in England was stimulated by the considerable amount of building in the "Gothic Castle" style in the first quarter of the 19th century. Sir Walter Scott's baronial mansion, Abbotsford, completed in 1824, with its ideas of medieval furnishings, was typical of the taste and exerted wide influence. This return to the Gothic style of architecture, which continued to express itself during a great part of the Victorian era, was upon the whole unsuccessful because in pursuing the letter of Gothic detail these devotees of the Gothic frequently neglected the qualities of right proportion and organic design which justified the utility of all this detail. They overlooked one of the outstanding merits of the Gothic style, namely, that the origin of each ornamental feature may be traced to a structural purpose. Augustus Welby Pugin, 1812–1852, who was the son of Augustus Charles Pugin, 1762–1832, a Frenchman, who settled in London as an architectural draftsman, was one of the contemporary architects who firmly believed in the glories of medieval Gothic and became a leader in the movement. He also designed furniture in the medieval manner (PLATE 477). Concerning a set of Gothic chairs he designed for Windsor Castle he wrote, "although the parts were correct and exceedingly well executed, collectively they appeared a complete burlesque of pointed design." Pugin preferred the Perpendicular style of Gothic architecture, when, as he wrote, everything became "excessively rich" and "every space was fitted with tracery and ornaments." In his book on Gothic designs for furniture, comprising twenty-seven colored engravings, practically all of the work was executed in what he called a "florid style". Many of the articles of furniture were given modern forms of light construction and were too often carried out in mahogany, rosewood and other materials unknown to the medieval world. The excessively rich carved Gothic detail, which was delicate and fanciful, was precisely and skillfully executed, but much of it seemed to be simply added and unnecessary. Unfortunately, the composite designs were a travesty on medieval cabinet-work. They presented a romantic phantasy no less exotic than some of the chinoiseries originating in England in the preceding century. The early Victorians along with their legacy of Regency classicism also inherited this Gothic tendency which was destined to invade many Victorian homes.

ARTICLES OF FURNITURE

Chairs   Chairs made during the Regency displayed a marked emphasis on horizontal lines (FIGURES 425, 426, 427, 428, 429). Saber-shaped front legs (427, 428), arms set high on the back uprights (428), the backward sweep of the top rail forming a continuous curve with the rear legs (428), were all typical features of chair design. A free use of ornament conforming to the archaeological spirit and drawn from the Egyptian, Greek and Roman civilizations was also a characteristic. Thus chairs were designed with lion terminals in the Egyptian taste (425) and with terminal figures in the Grecian taste (426). But the ideal of Grecian severity was the dominating influence. Especially typical of this Grecian taste was the Regency chair deriving from the Greek klismos (3), with its broad and flat concave crest rail, concave legs and graceful simplicity. This chair of Grecian pattern with its low back, rolled-over uprights, saber or concave front legs and other special features of design was especially fashionable (428). It was designed as a side chair and as an open armchair. The open arms were set relatively high on the uprights and generally swept downward (428). In one design the open arms scrolled downward and touched the side rail (428). In another design the open arms scrolled over the concave arm supports (427). The horizontal treatment of the chair was emphasized by its horizontal slats and cross bars (428). This chair was usually made of rosewood or mahogany. In this same spirit of imitating the antique, chairs of ancient curule or X-form with their uprights and legs terminating in archaic animal heads and feet were also made. A characteristic light chair was made of a soft wood, such as beechwood, and was most frequently painted black and brightened with brass appliqués or touches of gilt (427). Many chairs of fine craftsmanship were designed in a variety of forms during the early phase of the Regency. Straight tapered legs of either quadrangular or cylindrical form (429) were also used and were frequently finely reeded. Stringing lines, foliated patterns and paterae of brass largely replaced the carved, inlaid or painted decoration employed in the 18th century (428, 429). During the later phase of the Regency the mania for innovations in design resulted in many bizarre creations with fantastic ornament and exaggerated curves.

Sofas and Couches

The antique classic couch inspired the characteristic design for Regency sofas and couches. The sofa of lyre form with its cornucopia-shaped legs and the couch designed with an out-scrolled side have already been described in the preceding Sheraton chapter. It is generally accepted that the Regency designers derived their inspiration for these sofas and couches from the designers of the French Empire, who in turn copied the designs from antique classical sources. Sofas had become increasingly fashionable as an article of furniture used for reclining; it was practically mandatory to have at least one and very often two sofas in a room. Some of the sofas were of very large size and they usually had a bolster at each end and several loose cushions placed against the back. Their use was especially recommended when one was fatigued from reading or writing. In the more ambitious examples couches and sofas were sometimes made with animal supports (430). Thomas Hope in his HOUSEHOLD FURNITURE, 1807, gave a number of designs for couches in the Egyptian taste.

Stools

The designs for stools and window seats essentially followed the designs for chairs and sofas. Some stools were designed with hocked animal legs for supports. Stools of X-form were also fashionable.

Beds

In addition to the popular tester bed a new variety of mahogany bed was introduced by the Regency designers who borrowed the model from the fashionable French Empire lit en bateau (215). The more elaborate English specimens were ornamented with applied bronze mounts or carved and gilded decoration. Later examples of Regency beds were ponderous and had little artistic merit.

Tables

The pedestal dining table of two or more sections with each section supported on a turned pedestal with a splayed tetrapod base was in general use in the early 19th century. It was usually characterized by more massive supports during the second decade of the century. Round dining tables, which were extensively employed in France at the time of the French Empire, were revived in England early in the 19th century.

During the Regency the sideboard table designed with a frieze and without drawers was regarded as most fashionable and was characterized by its massive treatment. The supports were often of "lion monopodium" form. In this form of leg each support was composed of a head and chest of a lion resting on an elongated leg terminating in a paw foot.

The sideboard with the deep lateral wine drawers and the pedestal sideboard were also in general use and were characterized by their heavier forms. In some extant examples of sideboards the frieze was decorated with carved lion mask ornament and the tapering legs ended in paw feet (432).

The archaeological character of Regency furniture was plainly declared in some examples of pier tables, circular tables (434) and stands (437). Other tables in this category displayed a more rational form and were notable for their dignified and massive simplicity (433).

The sofa table was a popular and satisfactory piece of Regency furniture and was often finely made. The oblong top with its end drop-leaves was frequently mounted on trestle-end supports often of lyre form. Sometimes the top was mounted on a group of four short turned pillar supports which rested on a small heavy oblong median shelf supported on four splayed legs finished with brass paw feet and wheel casters. The card table with its folding top was often mounted on this same form of support.

The massive library table designed to hold bound folio volumes was introduced about this time and was regarded as a necessary piece of furniture in the large houses. It had a long oblong top over two frieze drawers. The back and sides were of wood while the front was entirely open. It had a floor shelf resting on four paw feet. The height of the opening corresponded to the height of a folio volume. It was designed in the taste of the Regency, and it frequently had four freestanding metal fluted columns headed with metal leaf capitals. These library tables were often supplemented with circular open-shelf revolving bookstands. They were designed with two or more circular shelves revolving around a central column.

An interesting variety of small table having an oblong top over a shallow frieze drawer mounted on four legs was the cheveret (439). This table which came into vogue late in the 18th century was designed with a movable book stand having an open shelf for books over one or two rows of shallow drawers. It was provided with a bracket-like handle. It has been called a cheveret because it was listed as such in Gillow's COST BOOK. Late 18th century models were frequently of satinwood, while examples dating from the early 19th century were sometimes of rosewood combined with metal mounts.

Work Tables Especially typical of the Late Georgian era were the combined game and work tables. In one variety the work or sewing table with its silk work-bag was designed with folding flaps which, when opened, revealed a chess or backgammon board. It often rested on open lyreform trestle-end supports. The work table was also frequently constructed with a hinged lid rising on an easel rest flanked by half round lids, with pierced brass galleries, which opened over wells fitted with compartments. This variety was designed with a pull-out chess or backgammon board. The table rested on open scrolled end supports with arched bridge feet terminating in brass paw mounts and casters.

Toilet Tables Early in the 19th century larger dressing tables fitted with drawers (431) became very popular and to a large extent supplanted the dressing table with a hinged box lid or lifting top. A movable dressing mirror was usually placed on top of the dressing table. George Smith in his HOUSEHOLD FURNITURE illustrated a dressing table having shaped trestle-end supports, and he writes that the drawers are to be without handles and are to be locked with spring catches (431). This omission of hardware is in accordance with the contemporary French taste for flat uninterrupted surfaces. The shaped trestle-end supports were a free adaptation of those found on certain ancient Roman tables (17).

Writing Furniture

The pedestal library or writing table and other furniture made for writing were designed in the prevailing fashion. The pedestal writing table often had reeded columns and was sometimes further enriched with brass bandings and ebonized inlay. The oblong writing table with its frieze drawers was frequently supported on massive reeded legs headed by lion masks and finishing in paw feet. It was also designed with straight tapered legs of either cylindrical or quadrangular form. There was much demand for the drum table with its turned column and splayed tetrapod base. During the later phase of the Regency the turned column of the drum table became more massive, and rested on a flat and massive shaped base, mounted on paw or winged paw feet.

Although in France the secrétaire à abattant enjoyed a great vogue from the time of Louis XVI onwards, it was never especially popular in England. George Smith in his HOUSEHOLD FURNITURE, 1806, tried to arouse an interest in this fashionable piece of French writing furniture with its fall-front writing panel, but without much success. Extant English examples are relatively scarce (435).

Wall furniture, such as secretary bookcases (436), cabinets and bookcases, frequently afforded excellent examples of the more ordinary Regency style, since to a large extent antique classical detail was simply applied to traditional 18th century forms. Bronze terminal figures and pilasters mounted with a bronze head and two feet (436) were among the favorite motifs. Brass trellis-work, backed with silk curtains, was often used in place of the glazed doors during the late 18th and early 19th centuries. Smith, writing in his HOUSEHOLD FURNITURE, 1808, observed that the silk backing "gives repose to the eye for nothing can distress the eye more than the sight of a countless number of books occupying one entire space."

Low Bookcases

Especially fashionable were the low bookcases of elbow height which revealed considerable variety in their design. Sometimes they were entirely open and frequently the open shelves were flanked by panels or doors. Gilt columns and applied metal ornament were characteristic forms of decoration for these low bookcases. Smith writes of the type with center shelves flanked by cupboard doors that they were calculated to contain all the books required in a sitting room without reference to the library. He illustrated designs for bookcase doors in

Chinese, Gothic and Egyptian taste. According to Smith, one of the principal advantages of the low bookcase was the space afforded above for hanging paintings.

Closely related in purpose to the low bookcase is the so-called chiffonnier (440). The term *chiffonnier* has never been too clearly defined in English furniture literature. An inventory of 1771 mentions a small chiffonnier table with drawers and a brass rim. It seems reasonable to assume that this refers to a type of French work table called a chiffonnière. Apparently the term does not appear in English trade catalogues until early in the 19th century when George Smith in his HOUSEHOLD FURNITURE, 1808, illustrates an article of furniture of elbow height and of open construction fitted with shelves which he calls a chiffonnier and about which he writes, "in almost every apartment of a house these articles will be found useful, . . . their use is chiefly for such books as are in constant use, or not of sufficient consequence for the library; on the same account they become extremely serviceable in libraries for the reception of books taken for present reading." He continues that "the most simple are manufactured in plain mahogany, or japanned in imitation of various woods; the more elegant in mahogany with decoration in imitation of bronze metal." Extant examples of chiffonniers depicted in English furniture literature having a frieze drawer, open framework and rounded ends bear a resemblance in general plan to the commode ouverte or open commode designed by Riesener and other contemporary French ébénistes which is now often called a commode desserte (197, 198). They are shown in English furniture literature serving a dual purpose, that is for the reception of china as well as for books. Apparently this category of furniture varied considerably in design and was sometimes fitted with metal trellis-work panel doors. In some of the longer specimens the central portion was fitted with two grille doors flanked by open sides. Their use also appears to be at least twofold.

Commodes

The subtle lines and beautiful surface decoration which gave the 18th century commode its great artistic value was lost in this new classic style. As a result, Regency commodes were marred by their massiveness and had little artistic merit, except for a few examples which were finely inlaid with brass work. Frequently the commodes were flanked by columns.

Chests of Drawers

The chest of drawers was often designed with a bow-shaped front and had the characteristic outset rounded front corners, with the drawers flanked by three-quarter round reeded columns continuing to form the short round tapered legs. The drawers were often mounted with either bronze knob or lion mask loose-ring handles. During the later Regency style the chest of drawers became increasingly ponderous.

Mirrors   The characteristic and popular wall mirror was the gilded circular convex mirror (441) already described in the preceding chapter. The swinging dressing mirror on a box stand was usually made of mahogany, rosewood or satinwood. It had an oblong mirror and the stand was generally straight or bow-fronted and frequently had projecting corners in accordance with the Regency taste. In Sheraton's CABINET DICTIONARY he discusses the decoration of glass by painting on the back as well as the simpler method of transfer-printed decoration on the back of glass.

Accessories   The what-not, a small open shelf stand introduced during the Regency, was designed with slender uprights supporting the two or more shelves. In the succeeding Victorian period the what-not was regarded as an indispensable article of furniture and was used for displaying all kinds of small curios.

The term *teapoy* is given to a small tray-top table generally supported on three legs or on a central shaft resting on a tripod base. George Smith, who illustrated the teapoy in his HOUSEHOLD FURNITURE, stated that "they were used in the drawing room to prevent the company rising from their seats when taking refreshment." Because the word *tea* appears in the word *teapoy* it has been erroneously associated with tea. Due to this imagined connection with tea the term is sometimes given to a tea chest (438), fitted with canisters, mounted on legs or on a stand. During the Regency it was often supported on a turned pedestal with a splayed tetrapod base ending in brass paw feet (438).

In the early 19th century hanging wall shelves were often designed in pairs. The tiers of each set of shelves frequently diminished in depth as they approached the top.

The flower stand was a fashionable decorative accessory. Pugin writes in his book on Gothic furniture designs, "Among the various decorations of modern apartments, we can reckon none perhaps more pleasing than a flower stand." He submitted designs in the Gothic taste for flower stands to be executed in either wood or metal.

In addition to the articles of furniture already described, many other of the characteristic forms of furniture, accessories and decorative appointments were designed in the Regency taste.

CHAPTER TWENTY TWO

AMERICAN COLONIAL & FEDERAL

Since the great majority of early settlers in America came from England it is only a natural development that we have inherited the fundamental qualities in our culture from the English. In order to be sufficiently cognizant of the gradual development of the common cultural ties existing between England and America, their transmission to the young colonies across the Atlantic and their expansion and interpretation as they were modified to the conditions in America, it is necessary for us to take a long perspective on our history, tracing it at least as far back as the Late Gothic period. We should not disregard certain influences from France, the Netherlands, Germany, Italy and Spain, for these countries had some effect in molding American life and customs. There were also influences from the Orient and from the Near East. However, the vigor of English culture was such that it eclipsed and assimilated all others. We cannot escape the fact that the majority of our ancestors were British subjects un-

til 1776. For that reason we inherited, through transmission to the colonies, English principles and traditions in architecture, in furniture design and in the other decorative arts. Much of this transmission was carried by immigration through both laymen and craftsmen who had absorbed the new styles and traditions of their native land. Little was acquired through the importation of furniture since the cost made that practice almost prohibitive.

The close similarity existing between the art styles of England and America can be attributed to a great extent to the wide circulation of architectural publications, builders' handbooks and pattern books of engraved ornament and designs for furniture. These pattern books, which were a great formative influence in the adoption of a new style both in England and in America, created a high standard of knowledge among the craftsmen, making the 18th century a period of remarkable achievement. Copies of these different publications appeared in America often within a few years of their original issue in England. In this manner every new English fashion was mirrored in the colonies. Extant examples of American cabinetwork show in many cases how closely these engraved plates with their plans and details were followed as sources by the American cabinetmaker. The rapidity and the amount of success with which these fashions were absorbed in America were essentially about the same as in provincial England for cabinetwork representing the same social standards. The very elegant and ambitious cabinetwork made in London for the aristocracy was not found in colonial America. This dependence on pattern books tended to give much of the important American cabinetwork a style common to all the colonies. Naturally, certain variations occurred both in the form and in the ornament in some of the colonial cabinetwork from the prevailing English styles. The practice of taking designs from pattern books was not conducive to developing individual designers or striking personalities, since little personal quality is embodied in this form of work. However, through this medium of pattern books, American cabinetwork achieved a high level of design and the American cabinetmaker produced many notable pieces displaying excellent taste and craftsmanship.

The early years in America were marked by the persistent struggle of the pioneers to convert a vast wilderness into a new home. As in every pioneer venture the physical labor was great, for there was the task of clearing the lands, of sowing the crops, planting the vegetables and raising the cattle. There was the work of building the houses and making them habitable. As soon as a permanent home was provided the early settlers gave their attention to the problem of furniture, which in the beginning was simply of a utilitarian nature. Gradually through their prodigious industry the newcomers began to acquire wealth, for this land was rich in vast natural resources. With their newly acquired wealth the colonists were slowly able to indulge in certain comforts and luxuries necessary to more polite living and upon which the development of the arts is dependent. Much of the wealth was attracted to cities, and such cities as Philadelphia became important centers for colonial crafts. It should be remembered that America was settled by different classes of people, who, because of their financial status, were accustomed to different modes of living in their native land. There were the well-to-do settlers in the southern colonies, the impecunious Pilgrims and prosperous Puritans in New England and the affluent Dutch and Quakers in New York and Pennsylvania respectively. In America as in Europe a wide gulf existed between the rich and the poor. This difference was reflected in the style of dress and in social customs, as well as in the manner in which the homes were furnished. The early Pilgrim settlers in New England could not afford to buy the better pieces of furniture. They made plain, substantial furniture, which was simple and crude in character and which undoubtedly was similar to the furniture that they had used in England. The Pennsylvania colony from the time of William Penn fared much better and enjoyed many of the refinements to which the colonists had been accustomed in England. Much of the fine furniture found in America was made in that colony, and the leadership of Philadelphia has long been recognized in cabinetwork from the days of William Penn to those of George Washington.

The American styles of furniture are sometimes divided into historical groups, namely the Colonial and the Federal. In American history the term *Colonial* refers to the thirteen original British colonies which subsequently became the United States of America and to that period. When the term *Colonial* is applied to cabinetwork and the other decorative arts it refers to the style prevailing before and at the time of the American Revolution. In furniture it includes the Jacobean, William and Mary, Queen Anne and Early Georgian, and Chippendale styles. The term *Federal* includes those styles in vogue after the Federal government was established in 1789. Thus the Federal group includes the Hepplewhite, Sheraton, American Directoire and American Empire styles. It is interesting to note that the earliest furniture brought to America as well as the earliest made in America was in the Jacobean style. Early Jacobean furniture was very scarce, while the Late Jacobean articles were slightly more plentiful. The Jacobean style was superseded by the William and Mary style, which, like all the subsequent English styles, was adopted in America from about five to ten years after it became the prevailing fashion in England. During this era the furniture gradually became lighter and the carved decoration was not as over-elaborated as in the preceding style. The highboy and lowboy were introduced around 1690–1700 and remained in vogue in America for almost the next one hundred years. Gate-leg tables were especially popular. Turned trumpet-shaped legs, flat, shaped stretchers and globular or Spanish feet were all characteristic features of design. Some marquetry and japanning were occasionally found on a few examples of ambitious cabinetwork.

The William and Mary style was succeeded by the Queen Anne and Early Georgian style. From around 1710 certain principles of the Queen Anne style occasionally appeared in American furniture design and the new style was adopted around 1720. In America that particular development of cabinetwork found in England in the three decades after the death of Queen Anne was seldom if ever found in America. Even in English cabinetwork those years are difficult to ascribe. Such phases occurring in English cabinetwork during that period as the lion mask and satyr mask furniture were practically unknown in America. Furniture of a pronounced architectural character was also limited, although numerous examples of secretary cabinets displayed pilasters or fluted columns. The elaborate gilt furniture in the taste of William Kent was unknown. The lack of this furniture in America is not difficult to explain, since in England it was found only in the Palladian mansions then being built for the aristocracy, and in America neither the mansions nor that class of society existed. The Queen Anne style with its graceful curving lines remained fashionable in America until around 1755–60 when it was supplanted by the Chippendale style. From about 1745–50 some of the American cabinetwork was executed in the pre-DIRECTOR or early Chippendale style and this overlapping of the two styles continued in America for the next decade. The cabriole leg first appeared in American furniture design early in the 18th century and continued in vogue throughout the Queen Anne and Chippendale styles. However, during the Chippendale style the straight quadrangular leg, sometimes terminating in a plinth foot, was employed on many chairs, settees and tables. The cabriole leg commonly terminated in a Dutch or club foot, and, although the claw-and-ball foot appeared around 1735–40, it is chiefly identified with the Chippendale style in America and was in general use from about 1750–55 to 1785. Mahogany was introduced in the first quarter of the 18th century and it was increasingly employed. Black or Virginia walnut was the other fashionable wood and essentially the principal wood of this period. The Windsor chair, which became popular very early in the 18th century in England, was later found in America and was a characteristic type of Philadelphia cabinetwork. Many fine examples of chairs, highboys, lowboys and tables were made throughout this period in America. The gate-leg table was gradually superseded by another form of drop-leaf table designed with a swing-leg. The graceful cyma curve, referred to by Hogarth as the line of beauty, was skillfully handled by American cabinetmakers working in the Queen Anne style.

The Chippendale style was in vogue in America from around 1755 to 1785, and came into full expression around 1760. Philadelphia achieved its high rank in American furniture history during the Chippendale era, which is generally referred to as the golden age of Philadelphia cabinetwork. The mahogany pieces produced in the Philadelphia cabinet shops of that time excel those of the earlier and later years in the quality of their workmanship, in their masterful designs and richly carved ornament. Philadelphia-style highboys and lowboys are ranked among the finest specimens of American cabinetwork and are equalled only by the block-front furniture of Townsend and Goddard. The city of Philadelphia, which was a leading center of wealth and fashion

in Colonial and Federal times, naturally attracted a large number of skilled craftsmen. Since the number of wealthy people in America was limited, the demand for the more ambitious contemporary cabinetwork made in England was restricted and it is obvious that the very elegant English cabinetwork made in the Chippendale style for the Royal household and the titled aristocracy was not found in America. For the same reason the style of the Adam brothers, who only made designs for the interior furnishings of their very wealthy clients, had little effect in America until around 1785 when the Hepplewhite style became the prevailing fashion and interpreted the Adam style in the GUIDE for the use of the cabinetmaker. Decorative motifs of the Adam style, such as classic urns, anthemions, rosettes and paterae, occasionally appeared in some contemporary work, such as in the frames for mirrors, but the Adam style found in England was never really developed in America. The lack of Adam style cabinetwork in America is also due to some extent to the suspension of commercial relations between the two countries during the Revolutionary War. When normal trade relations were resumed between the two countries the Hepplewhite style was the prevailing fashion in England and the American cabinetmaker changed from the Chippendale style to the Hepplewhite. The fact that the Adam brothers never issued a pattern book for the use of the cabinetmaker cannot be overlooked as an important contributing factor.

Especially praiseworthy in American cabinetwork are the so-called block-front articles made from around 1750 to 1780, which are characterized by a singular feature of design. The pieces of furniture made with block-fronts were chiefly chests of drawers, slant-front desks, secretary cabinets, chests-on-chests and kneehole dressing tables or kneehole writing tables. In a block-front article of furniture the front of each drawer was cut in such a manner as to form a raised flat surface at each end and a depressed flat surface in the center. As a rule the block-front was cut from a single thick piece of wood. However, there are certain specimens of block-front furniture in which the raised flat surface was attached by means of glue. Except for the block-front feature of design these articles essentially followed the style of the contemporary unblocked articles. As a rule block-front furniture was made of solid mahogany. Practically all the block-front articles of furniture were made in New England and the finest in quality of design and workmanship were made at Newport, Rhode Island. It is generally accepted that block-front furniture was originally developed in the cabinet shops of John Townsend and John Goddard at Newport. Block-front pieces made by Townsend and Goddard or by other New England cabinetmakers who copied their designs had certain features distinguishing them from the block-front pieces made by other cabinetmakers. The carved shells were the most distinctive feature of Townsend and Goddard block-front furniture. The shell on the end of each top drawer was raised and the center shell was depressed.

The Hepplewhite style, which became popular in London around 1780, remained in vogue in America until around 1800. This style with its refined and graceful elegance was interpreted in many fine pieces of American cabinetwork. Shield-back chairs, upholstered settees, testered beds, sectional dining tables, sideboards, card tables with hinged tops, chests of drawers and secretary cabinets are included among the principal articles designed in America in the Hepplewhite style. Carving, inlay and veneering were the favorite decorative processes employed in the Hepplewhite and in the succeeding Sheraton styles. Veneering, which was the forte of late 18th century English cabinetwork, was extensively employed and the veneer was carefully selected to show the greatest amount of figure. Mahogany continued to be the fashionable wood. There was a pronounced tendency to combine occasionally in some articles of cabinetwork, such as sideboards, secretary cabinets and beds, certain features peculiar to both the Hepplewhite and Sheraton styles. This can be partially explained by the relatively close publication of the pattern books of these two designers and for a few years their simultaneous use. Due to this fact it is practically impossible at times to determine in which one of the two styles certain articles of cabinetwork should be classified. This cabinetwork is often simply referred to as Neo-Classic or in the Classical taste.

The Sheraton style became increasingly popular in America after 1795 and every form of furniture fashionable in America from around 1795 to 1820 was made in the Sheraton style by Duncan Phyfe and other contemporary American cabinetmakers. Many fine pieces of American cabinetwork were made in the Sheraton style and were praiseworthy for their excellent proportions, their delicate ornament and their refinement. Undoubtedly the fine proportions displayed in Federal cabinetwork contributed greatly to the real merit of this furniture. Sheraton in his DRAWING BOOK showed a marked preference for rectangular forms, generally with an emphasis on the vertical effect. This was evident in his designs for open back chairs and settees. The lyre form was a favorite decorative feature in Sheraton's designs and was much used by Duncan Phyfe. Paterae, delicate festoons of flowers and husk pendants were fashionable motifs, and both large and small delicate inlaid ovals were extensively employed. Reeding and also fluting were fashionable decorative processes and they were freely used, especially on the legs of chairs, settees and tables, and also on bed posts. Sheraton stated in his writings, "Reeding amongst cabinetmakers is a mode by which they ornament table legs, bed pillars . . . and is certainly one of the most substantial of any yet adopted. It is much preferred to fluting or cabling in point of strength; and in look, much superior to the latter; and almost equal to the former . . . When reeding is introduced on a flat surface there ought always to be three, five or seven and so on, and the odd one should be in the centre. . . . Reeds look with additional beauty in some cases when a small fillet is introduced between them. . . ." Fine examples of reeding were often found in the cabinetwork of Duncan Phyfe and other contemporary American cabinetmakers.

At the present time literature pertaining to the history of American furniture often gives the name *American Directoire* to a style of furniture made in America from around 1805 to 1815. Occasionally this style is included in either the Late Sheraton or in the Early Empire style. The American Directoire style is best exemplified in the chairs and settees made by Duncan Phyfe and other contemporary American cabinetmakers. Horizontal lines were emphasized in the typical American Directoire chair. As a rule the top rail became broader and swept backwards. In some instances the chair featured a broad concave top rail. This chair, which had its origin in the Grecian klismos, was designed with saber legs or legs of concave form. The sofa or settee in which the Directoire style predominated was inspired by the ancient Greek and Roman couches used for dining and reclining. It was of lyre form and it was designed with out-scrolled sides continuing in a graceful unbroken curve to form the front seat rail. It generally rested on short splayed legs of cornucopia form. This same fine continuous curve was also the special feature of the graceful type of Grecian couch designed in the American Directoire style. In England this variety of chair, sofa and couch designed in the Directoire style is considered to be in the style of the English Regency. Numerous American Empire chairs, settees and couches continued to display variations of these design features which characterized these Directoire style pieces.

The term *American Empire* is given to the cabinetwork made in America from around 1810–15 to 1830, while the term *Late Empire* is given to the furniture made from around 1830 to 1840, at which later date Victorian furniture came into vogue, 1840 to 1901. The furniture made in this decade between 1830 and 1840 was coarsely designed and was characterized by its massive and cumbrous forms. The suitability of calling the furniture of this entire era the American Empire style has often been questioned, since few American articles of furniture were made which closely followed the style of the French Empire. It is true that certain decorative features of the French Empire style became popular in America at that time, such as the round wood columns employed on sideboards, chests of drawers and other pieces of a similar nature, and the lion paw feet and the shaggy paw feet of other animals found on sofas and couches and on the splayed tetrapod bases of tables. The exquisite applied bronze mounts so characteristic of the Empire style in France were seldom found on American cabinetwork. The French Empire style of ornament, which was frequently inspired by the different phases of Napoleon's campaigns and was often of a war-like and triumphant nature, was seldom used on American Empire pieces. The American cabinetmakers working in the Empire style showed a pronounced preference in their style of ornament for eagles, fruits, flowers, foliage and horns of plenty signifying the abundance of this new land. The American eagle became a much favored decorative motif after the adoption of the Constitution when it became the national emblem. Carved and gilded eagles serving as a finial on wall mirrors and clocks were much in evidence. Many brass eagles were imported from France and England. When the eagle was used in inlay work it was generally enclosed in an oval medallion and often had streamers in its mouth with marks representing stars. Inlaid or painted stars were also a fashionable form of ornament and were frequently used to indicate the number of states in the Union at the time the piece was made. It must be remembered, however, that they were also used for decorative purposes only and that their number is not any positive indication of the date. Coarsely carved acanthus leafage and pineapple designs were much used, especially on the posts of bedsteads. The American Empire furniture was made of fine mahogany, but unfortunately the mahogany was often stained a too brilliant red. The English interpretation of the Empire style was also apparent in some of the American cabinetwork.

In the literature relating to American cabinetwork the year 1825 or around that year is generally accepted as the fixed time which separates the antique furniture from the cabinetwork produced in the ensuing years. The term *antique* as it is used in American furniture has a rather interesting origin and meaning. In one sense the term *antique* refers to a point of time. An early Act of Congress which was passed to regulate the duties on foreign furniture stated that all furniture over one hundred years old at the time of importation was regarded as antique and could be entered duty free. Although this Act did not refer to American furniture, the popular conception of an American antique as any article of furniture over one hundred years old was undoubtedly based on the Act. In 1930 this Act was revised to read as follows, "Works of art (except rugs and carpets made after the year 1700), collections in illustration of the progress of the arts, works in bronze, marble, terra cotta, parian, pottery, or porcelain, artistic antiquities and objects of art of ornamental character or educational value which shall have been produced prior to the year of 1830" shall be admitted duty free. Although this Act did not refer to American furniture either, it became the popular conception in America to classify as antique almost all furniture made until about 1830. And so in point of time some of the American Empire may be regarded as antique. In the other and more correct sense the definition of the term *antique* has been decided by the connoisseurs who have studied the styles of furniture and understand what constitutes a true style. They regard as antique any article of furniture made in an approved style at the time that style was the prevailing fashion. The connoisseurs do not generally recognize any style beyond the Sheraton style which remained in fashion in America until about 1820–25, and so they consider around 1825 as the fixed time which separates the antique furniture from the later cabinetwork. However, it should be remembered that in the 18th century and earlier all of the furniture did not embody the requisites necessary for fine cabinetwork, namely, fine materials and workmanship and designs possessing artistic merit. This thought is expressed in a Treasury decision of June 19, 1930. "By the use of the term 'artistic antiquities' in paragraph 1708, associated as it is with works of art, collections in illustration of the progress of the arts, works in bronze, etc., the Congress had in mind something more than the mere ordinary work of an artisan. It intended by the word 'artistic' to include only antiquities which were the production of the artists and which had an aesthetic appeal, as contradistinguished from those of artisans of mere mechanical skill." In other words the article must have an aesthetic appeal; merely age does not authorize free entry.

There was an abundance of fine lumber in America which enabled the American cabinetmaker to make generous use of the majority of desirable woods employed in English cabinetwork. The use of walnut as the principal wood in American cabinetwork corresponds approximately with its use in England. However, in America oak continued to be employed to some extent throughout the first quarter of the 18th century, while the use of walnut continued much longer in America than it did in England after the introduction of mahogany. There was white walnut and even larger quantities of black or Virginia walnut which were exported to England from Virginia and also from Maryland, Pennsylvania and New York. While the tendency in England from around 1760 onwards was to use woods of lighter tone, such as satinwood and harewood especially for drawing room furniture, mahogany remained the fashionable wood in America until around 1840. Bilsted, which is the wood of the American sweet gum tree, was frequently used as a substitute for mahogany because of its pronounced resemblance. It was much used in the Revolutionary War period when mahogany from the West Indies was not available. The golden-toned satinwood furniture made in England never existed in America where the use of this wood was generally restricted to border bandings, panels, stringing lines and delicate inlaid motifs of paterae, festoons, husk pendants, eagles, stars and similar ornament. Holly, tulipwood and maple were also favorite woods for inlay work. Rosewood was extensively used for American Victorian furniture from around 1845 to 1860. From early Colonial days, plain maple, curly and bird's-eye maple were used in New England, where there was an abundant supply, for furniture which was not as fine as walnut or mahogany nor as common as pine. Cherry, which was first used toward the end of the 17th century, and other fruitwoods were used for general household articles. Applewood and pearwood were found in many well designed pieces. Hickory and ash, which are strong but not heavy woods, were favored for the spindles of Windsor chairs. Birch was used for spindles and legs and occasionally for the entire framework. Both hard yellow and soft white pine were very plentiful; the latter was especially abundant and it became the principal wood for all kinds of simple household furniture. Furniture of a modest or inexpensive character generally had seats made of rush, flag, splint or basswood, which essentially served as a substitute for the upholstered or the early caned seats found on the more ambitious mahogany or walnut cabinetwork.

The traditional decorative processes, such as carving, turning, veneering and inlay work, employed in English cabinetwork, were also found in American cabinetwork. Naturally the limited number of wealthy people in America restricted the demand for the more ambitious examples of cabinetwork. Carving was a favorite decorative process in America. It is generally believed that the finest quality of carving in America was found on the cabinetwork made between 1755 to 1785 when the Chippendale style was in vogue. Acanthus leafage was always a fashionable form of carved decoration, and carved shells were also widely used. The fan motif was also popular, and was sometimes practically the only carved decorative feature found on New England highboys in the Queen Anne style. Separately carved pieces, such as finials in the form of flaming torches and classic urns, were used to decorate secretary cabinets and other pieces of a similar nature. The carved and gilded American eagle was a favorite ornament during the Federal era for mirrors, clocks and other articles. Fluting and reeding were employed as carved decorative detail on furniture designed in the Hepplewhite and Sheraton styles. Reeding was particularly characteristic of the Sheraton style. Applied carved ornament, such as circular and oval rosettes, was occasionally used in the late 18th and early 19th centuries.

Veneering as a characteristic method for decorating the surface of furniture was practiced in America from around the reign of William and Mary. During the Hepplewhite and Sheraton styles veneering was extensively employed, and, as in English cabinetwork, it attained a high degree of excellence in the late 18th century. Inlay work, which was sparingly used in America, was employed on cabinetwork designed in the Hepplewhite and Sheraton styles. Especially fashionable were inlaid festoons of flowers, husk pendants, stars, shells, fans, rosettes, paterae and the American eagle. Inlaid oval, circular and rectangular panel bandings and delicate stringing lines were particularly featured. The decorative value of the different kinds of turning was fully appreciated by the American cabinetmaker. The different kinds of turning, such as baluster, spool, ball and many others, derived their names from their supposed resemblance in shape to the original objects. Gilding, which was occasionally used in England for drawing room furniture, was seldom used in America with the exception of gilded frames for mirrors.

Painted decoration was used only to a limited extent in American cabinetwork. Occasionally some articles of furniture designed in either the Hepplewhite or Sheraton styles were ornamented in this manner. Stencil work, which is a less expensive method than painting, was found on some American Empire pieces, especially on chairs. Occasionally the entire surface of a piece of furniture was painted. As a rule the painted furniture in America was restricted to simply designed chairs and to plainer inexpensive household articles. The elegant painted drawing room furniture found in England was never made in America. Generally the American painted furniture was enriched with some decorative painting such as flowers or with designs executed in stencil work. Lacquered or japanned articles of furniture were relatively few in America. Virtually all the japanned furniture done in a manner similar to that found in England with raised designs was made in New England, especially in Boston where advertisements appeared in the newspapers as early as 1712 stating that several cabinetmakers specialized in japanning. During the late 18th century the japanning in America was similar to the contemporary English work, which was essentially little more than painted furniture with a coat of varnish. This later work was inferior in quality to the earlier and very little of this so-called japanned furniture is extant in a good state of preservation. Of interest was some papier mâché work made in America during the Victorian era. This decorative process, which had been introduced into England from France around the middle of the 18th century, was particularly used for such small articles as snuff boxes, needlework boxes and trays. Occasionally it was made into small tables and sometimes the papier mâché was molded over a wooden framework in order to make it more durable.

Brass handles were employed on the drawers of practically all the better American cabinetwork from around 1685–90 to 1825, when knobs, either of brass or later of glass, became the prevailing fashion. Many of the brass mounts, which also included the escutcheons as well as the handles and back plates, were imported from England. From around 1685–90 to 1720 drop handles were in vogue and the small back plate, to which the handle was attached, was commonly circular, oval or lozenge-shaped. From around 1720 handles of the bail type superseded the earlier drop handles. Generally the bail handle from around 1720 to 1780–85 was attached either to a solid shaped brass back plate, which was occasionally pierced, or to two small rosettes; the latter type was especially identified with the Chippendale style. As a rule the back plates of the Hepplewhite style furniture were oval in form and the bail handles, which were conformingly shaped, were attached on each side to the oval back plates. These back plates were stamped out with dies and the impressed motifs included such favorite patriotic subjects as stars and eagles, as well as acorns, flowers, cornucopia and oak leaves. The drawers on Sheraton style furniture were also frequently mounted with oval bail handles and back plates as well as circular and octagonal. Another favorite handle for the Sheraton style furniture was the loose-ring handle attached to a round back plate at the top. Oval and octagonal brass handles attached at the top to a conformingly shaped back plate also occurred. Another form of handle was the lion-and-ring handle, with a ring suspended from the mouth of a lion mask. Although the Sheraton type handles were used on the Early Empire style furniture, brass knob handles were more typical of the Empire style. Some Sheraton style furniture, especially the drawers of tables, were also fitted with knob handles. These knob handles were round and projected about an inch from the surface of the drawer and were frequently ornamented with decorative motifs of a patriotic character, such as American eagles and the head of George Washington. Glass knobs, either of pressed or cut glass, were much used from around 1815–20 to 1840. Wooden knobs were especially identified with the Late Empire and Early Victorian cabinetwork.

The different forms of metal hinges found on cupboard doors and chests in American cabinetwork, like the brass handles and back plates found on the drawers, were borrowed from the English. It is generally believed that the butterfly hinge, which superseded the early wooden pin hinge in English cabinetwork toward the end of the 13th century, was the earliest form of hinge used in America. It was so named because of its supposed resemblance to a butterfly. The H-hinge, with its two vertical plates treated symmetrically and used in England during the 16th, 17th and 18th centuries, was very popular in America. The H L hinge, which was in the combined form of those two letters, was another characteristic decorative American hinge. Another principal form was the rat-tail hinge, which was so named because of the supposed resemblance of the lower part of the hinge to the tail of a rat. The strap hinge, having the half of the hinge attached to the door in the form of an elongated strap, was found in England in the 15th century where it was frequently quite elaborate in outline. The characteristic strap hinge in America was less elaborate and its strap terminated in either a point or a round end. Although other forms of hinges occurred, such as the butt hinge with only the barrel showing, these five forms were much favored for decorative hinges in American cabinetwork. It seems that all these hinges with the exception of the butterfly hinge were used on cupboard doors while the strap hinge was chiefly found on chests.

Upholstery in America essentially followed the prevailing fashions in textiles found in England. It is generally accepted that upholstered furniture dates from the reign of Queen Elizabeth I, although isolated examples of upholstered chairs and stools are mentioned in the inventories of Henry VIII. Extant examples of early 17th century English upholstered chairs frequently show the entire framework covered in fabric and finished with straight loose fringe. After the Restoration in 1660 upholstered furniture began to figure more prominently. A great variety of materials are used in upholstery, and in practically every period some of these coverings were of needlework, which has been a fashionable, as well as a practical, pastime for women for many years. Because imported textiles, such as silk velvets, brocades and damasks from Italy and embroidered silks from China, were so costly the principal material used during the so-called age of walnut was needlework on canvas worked in gros point or petit point. Some of the earliest furniture in America was covered with needlework on canvas. In the 18th century, when upholstery reached its zenith, cut silk velvets, brocades, brocatelles, damasks, French tapestry, satins, taffetas, Spanish leather, horsehair, chintz and other printed cottons and linens were included in the fashionable textiles used in English upholstered furniture. The general tendency for the last four decades of the 18th century was towards textiles of lighter weight and of more delicate designs and colors. The Italian velvets with their large formal patterns, which had been so fashionable, were practically abandoned, and from around 1770 French tapestry largely superseded the gros point needlework. The principal method for attaching the fabric to the framework of a chair, bench or settee was with a row of brass nailheads.

During the 18th century fine imported textiles, such as silk velvets, brocades and damasks, from France and England were extensively used in America. Due to the fact that England had to import almost all her silk, the textiles produced in the English manufactories specialized in mixed wool and silk, and as a result they were not as highly esteemed as the French silk textiles either in England or in America. The vogue for chintz, which was so pronounced both in England and in France from early in the 18th century that both countries enacted laws to prohibit its importation as well as its domestic manufacture for a period of years, was also evident in America, where it was advertised in newspapers as early as 1712. Other cotton and linen painted or printed fabrics, such as toile de jouy with its charming and captivating designs, enjoyed great popularity in America. Hepplewhite in the GUIDE recommended the use of printed cotton or linen for bed hangings, stating, "the elegance and variety of which afford as much scope for taste, elegance and simplicity, as the most lively fancy can wish." He also advised the use of white dimity for bed hangings because it gives "an elegance and neatness truly agreeable." Plain, striped or checkered horsehair was also favored by Hepplewhite and other contemporary cabinetmakers as a covering for furniture subject to hard wear. The vogue in France during the late 18th century for satin with delicately painted decoration was reflected in England and in America where both plain and figured satins were in fashion. However, damask and brocade were considered to be more fashionable 18th century textiles than satin.

The development of wallpaper, which originated in France, was chiefly inspired by the vogue for Chinese paintings on paper imported to Europe in large quantities in the 17th century as well as by the necessity to reproduce in a less costly manner the tapestries, silks and velvets used for wall coverings. The earliest wallpapers were the so-called illuminated or hand-painted papers found in France and also in England late in the 16th century. The vogue for wallpaper was not firmly established until early in the 18th century when painted papers with their designs inspired by contemporary chintz patterns became extremely fashionable in France. Around 1750 the method of making wallpaper printed in colors from wood blocks was developed in France and as a result the illuminated papers with their painted decoration done by hand became obsolete. This process of printing in colors from several superimposed wood blocks came into general use in England, Germany and Holland from around 1765–70 onwards. Flock paper, which is another variety of wallpaper, originated in France around 1620. In this process the designs were stenciled in an adhesive mordant, and then a colored flock, which is the same as a powdered wool, was scattered over the entire surface. After it was sufficiently dry the flock was brushed from the untreated surface. In this manner almost perfect imitations of Italian figured velvets with their large formal patterns, which were so fashionable as wall coverings and furniture coverings in the first half of the 18th century, were achieved. Especially fine were the red flock designs on a white or ivory ground having a velvet-like texture and a slightly raised surface. Flock papers did not become popular in France until after they were perfected in England, where the finest were made from around 1720 to 1750. Silk flock papers using a silk waste were also made in France. The vogue for flock papers continued in France until around 1780. Hand-painted papers from China were always highly prized and were regarded as a great luxury. These papers generally depicted either flowering shrubs with birds and butterflies or scenes from Chinese life, such as lantern processions or stories from the Chinese theater. Wallpapers in imitation of these Chinese papers were made in both England and in France. Also much favored were the chinoiseries made in France from the engraved designs of such gifted French artists as Boucher. At the end of the 18th century the vogue for scenic paper was well established in France.

In America the early wallpapers were imported from England or France and essentially the prevailing European fashions in wallpaper were observed in America. Of particular interest are the scenic wallpapers which were especially fashionable in America and of which many examples are extant in American homes. Undoubtedly their excellent state of preservation is due to the quality of the paper, which was made of pure linen rags, and to the method employed in hanging expensive papers. In this method the walls were covered with a wooden framework over which a canvas was stretched. Then the paper was fixed to the canvas. Occasionally in a less expensive method the wallpaper was backed with canvas before it was pasted to the wall. The practice of pasting paper directly on the wall was a later and cheaper method. The most celebrated scenic papers were printed in Paris from around 1804 to 1840. The pictorial designs for these papers chiefly illustrated subjects from history, such as Napoleon's Egyptian campaign, subjects from mythology and panoramic views of famous cities or countries. As a rule these scenic papers, which

required more than a year in preparing the wood block engravings, were hung in an unbroken line above the chair rail around a room and were without repetition. Generally they had much sky so that if the ceiling was low they could be cut off without impairing the value of the scene. Undoubtedly the most popular scenic wallpapers in America were printed by the Frenchman Joseph Dufour. The Monuments de Paris and Vues d'Italie were especially favored. His most celebrated series was the Cupid and Psyche series of which some original sets are found in America. Another popular series by Jean Zuber first printed in France in 1834 was called Scenic America and the recognition implied by France in this series was quite complimentary to a young country who had only recently won her independence. In addition to the printed scenic papers, painted scenic papers were also employed in America, which were less expensive and quite effective, although they lacked the finished details found in the printed papers.

A Brief Résumé of a few outstanding
AMERICAN CABINETMAKERS
AND CLOCKMAKERS

Extant examples of 18th century and early 19th century American cabinetwork conclusively prove that there were many skilled cabinetmakers working in America during Colonial and Federal times. Unfortunately, as in the history of English cabinetwork, it is difficult and often impossible to assign correctly much of this cabinetwork to any particular cabinetmaker. Paper labels pasted on some of this cabinetwork have been an important source for authentication for they are often the labels of the original cabinetmaker. It must be remembered, however, that a label is not always a true indication of the original maker for it may be the label of a dealer or a repairer, and there is also the possibility that a label could be removed and pasted on another piece of furniture. Through careful research additional information is constantly being gathered on the different cabinetmakers which in many cases has altered the opinions previously held on the merits of certain cabinetmakers. At one time, for example, William Savery was regarded as the paramount figure in Philadelphia cabinetwork designed in the Chippendale style. More Philadelphia pieces were attributed to him than to anyone else. However, it has now been conclusively established that many of these pieces which did not bear the Savery label were the work of other cabinetmakers. In all probability further discoveries will be made which will make or unmake the reputation of other cabinetmakers and raise some relatively unknown cabinetmaker to a commanding position.

Names of 17th century cabinetmakers are exceedingly rare. Two of the better known 17th century cabinetmakers were Nicholas Disbrowe and Kenelm Winslow. Nicholas Disbrowe, who was born at Waldon, Essex, England, in 1612 and died in Hartford, Connecticut, in 1683, was working in Hartford around 1639. He was the maker of chests and other oak furniture. Kenelm Winslow, 1599–1672, was working at Plymouth, Massachusetts, and he also made early oak furniture.

It is generally agreed that the finest American cabinetwork designed in the Chippendale style was produced in Philadelphia. The Philadelphia style highboys and lowboys represent the acme of American cabinetwork. At the present time Thomas Affleck, who was born in Scotland and came to Philadelphia in 1763, is regarded as the outstanding figure among Philadelphia cabinetmakers. Affleck, who died in 1795, had a shop on Second Street. A few years before this leading position was held by William Savery and later by Benjamin Randolph. William Savery, 1721–1787, also had a shop on Second Street. Authenticated Savery pieces retain the high position which has always been accorded them. Benjamin Randolph, who was working around 1762–1792, had his shop at the Sign of the Golden Eagle, on Chestnut Street between Third and Fourth Streets. He was a carver of great skill and made some of the finest furniture in the Chippendale style. Other Philadelphia cabinetmakers who produced furniture in the Chippendale style of the highest quality were Jonathan Gostelowe, James Gillingham, Edward James and Thomas Tufft. James Gillingham, who was born in 1736, was working around 1760 to 1775. He had his shop on Second Street between Walnut and Chestnut Streets. Jonathan Gostelowe, who was working from around 1744 to 1795, had his cabinet shop on Church Alley between Second and Third Streets. In 1790 his shop was at 66 Market Street. Thomas Tufft, who was working around 1750 to 1793, had his shop on Second Street. Edward James was working around 1783. Other prominent Philadelphia cabinetmakers producing fine pieces in the Chippendale style were John Folwell, David Evans, Daniel Trotter, Charles Pickering, Samuel Walton, William Wayne and many others.

It has already been mentioned that the block-front furniture produced by Townsend and Goddard, of Newport, Rhode Island, was equal to that made by the most talented of Philadelphia craftsmen working in the Chippendale style. The high position accorded to Newport in American furniture history is due to the ability of these two men who were cousins-in-law. John Goddard was born in Newport in 1723 and died there in 1785. John Townsend was also born in Newport in 1721 and died there around 1809. In the beginning Goddard was regarded as the creator of block-front furniture; however, it is now generally conceded that the credit for originating block-front furniture with its singular feature of design should be shared by both men.

Samuel McIntire, 1754–1811, the prominent architect and builder of Salem, Massachusetts, was also a most skillful carver. At the present time it is generally accepted that he was employed to execute the fine carvings on furniture made by other cabinetmakers, such as the Sandersons, who were well-known Salem cabinetmakers. It is also generally believed that he did make some few pieces of furniture. After his death, the carving business was carried on by his son, Samuel Field McIntire, whose carved work has often been mistaken for that of his father.

John Elliott, the well-known maker of mirrors, came to Philadelphia from England in 1753. After his retirement from business in 1776, the business was continued by his son, John Elliott Jr., who was joined by his two sons in 1804. The firm remained active until 1809. Apparently from the labels, which were often placed on the mirrors, he first had a store on Chestnut Street and later on Walnut Street. The Elliott family specialized in fretwork mirrors from around 1753 to 1809. During that long span of time only slight, if any, variations occurred in their designs for these fretwork mirrors. They also made the Early Georgian architectural mirror, which was called a Chippen-

dale-style mirror in America, and also a few carved and gilded mirrors in the Chippendale style. Their advertisements stated that they also handled imported mirrors and sconces from London and that they repaired mirror frames. Apparently the senior John Elliott also had some experience in cabinetmaking, in all probability in England, for one of his early advertisements stated that he was a cabinetmaker.

Duncan Phyfe, one of the most celebrated of American cabinetmakers, was born in 1768 at Loch Fannich, Scotland. He arrived with his family in America around 1783 and he settled in Albany, New York. He was apprenticed to either a coach builder or a cabinetmaker. He was later listed in the New York City Directory of 1792. His first shop was at Broad Street, and in 1806 he moved his shop and home to 34 and 35 Partition Street. Later, in 1811, he bought the property at 33 Partition Street, and in 1817, when Partition Street was renamed Fulton Street, his shop and home were at 168, 170 and 172 Fulton Street. He retired from business in 1847 and died in 1854. It is important to remember that Duncan Phyfe did not create a style of furniture. He followed the prevailing styles which were fashionable during his career, namely the Sheraton, Directoire and Empire styles. His best cabinetwork was done in the first quarter of the 19th century and displayed many features of the Sheraton and Directoire styles. This furniture was distinctive for its excellent proportions, for its graceful and elegant forms and for its refined decorative details, which were always in good taste. The furniture was made from the highest quality of mahogany. His later work was characterized by large and massive forms and followed to a greater or

370

less extent the French Empire style. The terms *early* and *late* are often used to distinguish his early and best work from his later and inferior work.

The names of the many craftsmen recorded in America who made the 18th century a period of fine achievement in cabinetwork are almost endless, and no attempt can be made in this book to cover even all the better known cabinetmakers working around New York, Boston, Providence, Hartford and Baltimore during the Colonial and Early Federal era. Clockmakers were also almost equally numerous. Undoubtedly every American is familiar with such popular names as Simon Willard and Eli Terry. The Chandlee family was an outstanding family of American clockmakers working in Philadelphia and Nottingham, Maryland. The first member of this family was Abel Cottey, 1655–1711, who was born in England and was working in Philadelphia around 1682 and later. His son-in-law, Benjamin Chandlee Sr., 1685–1745, who was his apprentice, carried on the business and moved to Nottingham in 1711–12. His son, Benjamin Chandlee Jr., 1723–1791, succeeded to his father's business. Several other members of this well-known family were also noted clockmakers. They produced fine tall case clocks with eight-day movements and with finely engraved dials. Daniel Oyster, 1764–1845, working at Reading, Pennsylvania, was also the maker of many fine tall case clocks. Thomas Harland, 1735–1807, working around 1773–1806, at Norwich, Connecticut, is considered to be one of the most important American clockmakers. In an advertisement of 1800 he offered, "spring and eight day clocks with enamelled and silvered faces completely finished and regulated, in mahogany and cherry cases." David Rittenhouse, 1732–1796, American scientist, astronomer, mathematician and clockmaker, is regarded as an outstanding figure in the history of American horology. He was born in Germantown, Pennsylvania, where he studied and began his noted work of producing technical instruments and clocks. In 1770 he moved to Norriton, Pennsylvania, where he continued this work at his shop located on his father's farm. He was the maker of many fine tall case clocks.

ARTICLES OF FURNITURE

Chairs   Among the early chairs found in America around 1660 were the crudely constructed, heavy and massive Carver and Brewster chairs with their turned members and vertical spindles. The Brewster chair, which is now in Pilgrim Hall, Plymouth, Massachusetts, belonged to William Brewster, 1560–1644, of the Plymouth Colony and it is said that he brought this chair with him on the *Mayflower*. It has an open back with two rows of spindles and four spindles in each row. Each open arm is also filled in with a row of four spindles. On one side beneath the seat there are two rows of four spindles each extending to the floor. In the front and also on the other side there are just the single upper rows of four spindles each. It is generally accepted that the chair should have forty spindles but that some are missing. The Carver chair, which is an armchair belonging to John Carver, 1571–1621, the first governor of Plymouth Colony, is also in Plymouth Hall. The open back has a row of three spindles and above the row of spindles is another turned crosspiece. The front legs are joined by two turned members and each side has two turned members joining the front with the rear leg. It is generally accepted that the Carver chair and Brewster chair were made in England from Dutch prototypes. Chairs of this variety, which are called Brewster and Carver chairs, were made in America, particularly in New England, without much change in form except for some variation in the number of spindles, at least until the end of the 17th century. The chief difference between the Brewster and Carver chair is that the former had more spindles. These chairs usually had rush seats.

The tall slat-back chair, introduced in England in the Late Jacobean era, was found in America at the beginning of the 18th century. This turned chair was designed as an armchair and as a side chair. The turned uprights were joined with four, five or six shaped horizontal slats. The legs were connected with turned stretchers. As a rule the American slat-back chair had a rush seat and was made of maple. It was a popular chair, and chairs of the slat-back pattern are still used to-day in farmhouses.

Another popular early American chair was the tall banister-back chair. This tall turned chair was introduced in England in the Late Jacobean era and came into use in America at the beginning of the 18th century. It was designed as an armchair and as a side chair. Usually the American banister-back chair was made of maple and had a rush seat. The turned uprights were joined with a top cross rail which was commonly crested and with a lower cross rail which was several inches above the seat. The two cross rails were connected with split banisters, usually four in number. The term *banister* is the corrupt form of the English word *baluster*. Undoubtedly both the banister-back chair and the slat-back chair were variants of the elaborately turned and carved Restoration chair or Charles II chair with its caned back panel and caned seat. Chairs of the Charles II variety were also made in America; however, they were generally much plainer and were not as richly turned and carved.

The development of the chair with an open back in America essentially followed the special features of design and the style of ornament as developed in the English chair with an open back during the Queen Anne, Chippendale, Hepplewhite and Sheraton styles. Some of the finely carved mahogany open chair backs made by the leading American cabinetmakers in the Chippendale, Hepplewhite (461) and Sheraton styles bore a very close resemblance to the original designs of chair backs illustrated in the trade publications of Chippendale, Hepplewhite and Sheraton, indicating how closely the English models were followed in America. The Early Georgian chairs with their lion mask and satyr mask decoration were not made in America. Chairs in America continued to be made in the Queen Anne style until the Chippendale style came into vogue around 1755. The corner or round-about chair was principally made in the Queen Anne and Chippendale styles in America. The ladder-back chair designed in the Chippendale style was quite popular. Among the celebrated chairs designed in the Chippendale style are the so-called sample chairs attributed to Benjamin Randolph, cabinetmaker of Philadelphia. They are called sample chairs because it is generally believed that they were used as models for his fine workmanship as well as an exhibition of skill. They include five side chairs and one wing chair (446, 447, 448). Chairs designed in the Adam style were apparently not made in America. Hepplewhite style chairs were fashionable from about 1785 to 1800 (461). Many fine American chairs were made by Duncan Phyfe and other leading cabinetmakers from about 1800 to 1825 in the Sheraton, American Directoire (466) and American Early Empire styles. Especially familiar are the chairs made by Duncan Phyfe in the American Directoire style with a lyre-shaped splat in the back. A large number of the American Empire chairs reflected the influence of the American Directoire style chair in their curving lines. Numerous features taken from earlier styles, such as Queen Anne vase-shaped splats and Gothic detail in the manner of Chippendale, were incorporated in the designs of American Empire chairs. Many American Empire chairs were painted and stenciled, included among which were some later fancy chairs and Hitchcock chairs.

The term *fancy chair* was given in America to an inexpensive painted open back chair made of a light wood and enriched with painted or stenciled decoration. It was popular in America in the first half of the 19th century and was designed in the Sheraton style and later in the American Empire style. The majority of these chairs were painted black and they usually had either a cane or rush seat. The front legs were generally cylindrical and ring-collared. The top rail, any design in the open back, the front of the seat rail and the front stretchers were often enriched with decorative painted panels. The painted decoration chiefly consisted of floral and leaf designs and was generally gilded. After 1820 these chairs were chiefly decorated with stencil work. The best quality of fancy chairs both in principles of design and in decoration were made in the Sheraton style. The cabinetmakers who specialized in these chairs were called fancy-chair makers.

The name *Hitchcock* is given to a particular type of painted American Empire open back chair made from around 1826 to 1843. It was so called because a cabinetmaker by the name of Hitchcock first made a large number of these chairs. Lambert Hitchcock was born at

Cheshire, Connecticut, and later moved to Barkhamsted. At a later date the settlement around his shop was called Hitchcockville. At first Hitchcock conducted the business by himself and the chairs carried the label of L. Hitchcock, Hitchcockville, Conn. In 1829 the business became a partnership and the label was changed to Hitchcock, Alford and Co., Hitchcockville, Conn. After Hitchcock left the firm in 1843 the label was changed to Alford and Co. During the period from 1826 to 1843 the term *Warranted* was also printed beneath the seat. Due to the popularity of these chairs, similar chairs were made by other chair makers. Because of this similarity the term *Hitchcock* is usually given to all chairs of this kind, rather than to those made only by Hitchcock. The Hitchcock chair, which was a variety of small open back side chair, was almost always painted black and was enlivened with painted and stenciled decoration. The stencil designs, which were chiefly composed of fruit, flowers and leaves, were painted in polychrome and in gilt. Although this chair varied in design, the characteristic Hitchcock chair had a turned crest rail with an enlarged center portion and a wide median slat which was usually plain but was sometimes cut in a design. At times a narrow slat was placed beneath the wide one. The uprights, which continued to form the round plain rear legs, were flat on the front in order that they could be better decorated with painted lines. The round front legs were often horizontally reeded, and were frequently splayed and tapered. The legs were connected with a plain round stretcher in the rear, two on each side and a turned one in the front. Originally the seat was made of rush; later the seat was frequently either caned or made of wood. As a rule the stencil decoration was applied on the turned top rail, on the median slat, on the front of the seat rail and on the front legs and front stretcher. Hitchcock chairs were always distinctive for their lively and decorative quality.

It is generally accepted that the American Windsor chairs were first made in Philadelphia around 1725. In addition to the comb-back and hoop-back already described in the Queen Anne and Early Georgian chapter the other principal types included the low-back, fan-back, New England armchair and loop-back. There were also numerous Windsor chairs whose backs displayed further variations in design from the above mentioned types. The chief difference between the American and English Windsor chairs was the pierced splat. The back of the American Windsor chair was composed entirely of spindles. The American Windsor chair invariably had turned splayed legs which were placed in from the edge of the chair seat. The majority of seats were saddle-shaped. In this form of seat the wood is slightly cut away in a sloping manner from the center front. The various bent parts as well as the spindles were usually of either oak or hickory. The seat was made of pine and the legs and stretchers were of either maple or birch. It is important to remember that the type of Windsor chair depended entirely upon the construction of the back. The low-back, which was an early and not especially popular form of Windsor chair, had a horseshoe-shaped arm rail centering a flat-arched crest section. In the fan-back variety the spindles flared outward in a fan-shaped manner and were surmounted with a crest rail which was shaped on the upper edge. In the New England Windsor armchair the back and arms were made from one continuous piece of bent wood. In the loop-back variety the back was made from a continuous piece of bent wood which was joined to each rear corner of the seat. When the loop-back was made as an armchair the arms were joined to the sides of the loop-back. The loop-back type of Windsor chair was also sometimes called either a balloon-back or bow-back. The Windsor chair has always been a characteristic type of Philadelphia furniture.

The upholstered open armchair and the upholstered side chair were principally made in the Chippendale style (449). Some were later made in the Hepplewhite, Sheraton and American Empire styles. The name *Martha Washington* was given to an upholstered open armchair, which, according to tradition, was used by Martha Washington at Mt. Vernon. The term is now applied to armchairs displaying similar features of design. In a general sense the armchair combined certain features of design from the Chippendale, Hepplewhite and Sheraton styles. This variety of armchair had a tall upholstered back. The top of the back was usually serpentine-shaped. The scrolled open arms, which rested on incurvate arm supports, were not upholstered. The legs were slightly tapered and were either cylindrical or quadrangular in form. In the majority of chairs the legs were joined with plain stretchers.

Wing chairs or easy chairs were fashionable in America throughout the 18th and early 19th centuries. They were made in the Queen Anne (445), Chippendale (448), Hepplewhite and Sheraton styles.

Settees, Sofas and Couches

Few upholstered settees were made in America prior to the Chippendale style. Although some Chippendale settees were elaborately carved and were designed with cabriole legs terminating in claw-and-ball feet, the greater majority had plain straight quadrangular legs connected with plain straight stretchers. The Chippendale settee was characterized by its serpentine-arched back and out-scrolled sides which were of the same height as the back and formed a continuation of the curved line of the back (450). One variety of American settee in the Hepplewhite style (390) had an arched horseshoe-shaped back continuing to form the arms which rested on incurvate arm supports that were directly above the quadrangular tapered legs. This settee generally had eight legs and was not stretchered. Sometimes the back was designed with several gently swept curves. Hepplewhite settees were in vogue from about 1785 to 1800. A large number of American settees were made in the Sheraton style from about 1795 to 1825. They were characterized by their rectangular forms. The special features of design most commonly employed in the Sheraton style settee included straight backs, which often centered a raised oblong panel, vase-shaped arm supports and reeded and tapered cylindrical legs (462). The arms usually started from the top of the back and sloped gently forward in a concave curve (462). The arm supports were directly above the legs (462). Sometimes shaped panels flanked the oblong center panel surmounting the straight top rail (462). This feature was illustrated in one of Sheraton's designs for settees appearing in his DRAWING BOOK. Certain features of the Directoire style, such as top rails having a backward sweep, were introduced in some of the early 19th century settees (467).

Both in the American Directoire sofa and couch the French Directoire style was much in evidence. The sofa was of lyre form and was characterized by the fine continuous curve extending from the top of each out-scrolled side to the front seat rail. It was generally designed with cornucopia-shaped legs. The couch also displayed the same fine unbroken curve. It had an out-scrolled side and was generally designed with a shaped and upholstered back panel that extended about one half or more the length of the seat. The other side rail continued to curve upward and very often rolled inward just above the upholstered seat. The legs were of cornucopia form. These two varieties were illustrated in Sheraton's CABINET DICTIONARY and were called a Grecian sofa and Grecian couch respectively. The characteristic curve, which was the distinguishing feature of the Grecian sofa and Grecian couch, was found with variations in the American Empire sofa and couch (471); however, in the majority of examples the curve had lost its gracefulness and the out-scrolled sides were inclined to be heavy and stiff. The cornucopia leg was supplanted by a massive winged animal paw (471) and later by a heavy plain scroll that scrolled inward.

The chair-back settee, which became fashionable in England in the reign of Queen Anne, was made in America throughout the 18th century and early 19th century in each of the successive styles. The majority were designed with either two or three open chair-backs. In America, as in England, the chair-back settee essentially followed the evolution of the contemporary open chair back both in form and in style of ornament.

Benches   The window bench, which was designed for a window recess and which was much in demand in England from the time of Chippendale, was found only seldom in America. Those made in America were principally in the Chippendale, Hepplewhite and Sheraton styles.

Day Beds The day bed was made in America from about 1650 to 1785 and was designed in each of the fashionable styles, namely Late Jacobean, William and Mary (442), Queen Anne and Chippendale. It seems that day beds were not designed in either the Hepplewhite or Sheraton styles. The so-called Grecian couch was often used for reclining in the early 19th century.

Beds Although a few high post beds were made in America in the Queen Anne style (444), the high post bed with its tester and draperies was not made in any appreciable quantity until around the middle of the 18th century. The majority of fine beds were of mahogany. The richly carved cornice, which surmounted the tester and was commonly found on English beds, was seldom used on American beds. As a rule, the style of the bed was determined by the tall slender posts, the legs and the feet. Since the tall headposts were concealed with draperies they were generally in the form of plain round columns. In America the tall footposts during the Chippendale style were usually slightly tapered but not to the same extent as in the succeeding Hepplewhite style. They were fluted and sometimes further enriched with carving. They were mounted on either cabriole legs terminating in claw-and-ball feet or on square legs resting on square feet. In the following Hepplewhite and Sheraton styles the characteristic tall post bed displayed similar details in its design. It had tall slender tapered posts that were generally reeded. As a rule at the lower part of the post there was a vase-shaped enlargement which was often finely carved with upright foliage. The post was usually mounted on either a square leg terminating in a block foot or on a quadrangular tapered leg terminating in a spade foot. Apparently the only time this bed was regarded as being in the Sheraton style was when the post was mounted on a cylindrical tapered leg. The field bed with its variously designed arched tester was also made in America and was extremely popular (463). In the American Early Empire style the posts became more massive and were often spirally carved. Toward the end of the first quarter of the 19th century the fashion for the high post bed greatly diminished, and the low post bed without a tester and draperies became fashionable. This low post bed was largely superseded around 1830–1840 by a variety of bed having a low headboard and low footboard made with an open frame and filled in with turned vertical members, such as ring-turned or spool-turned members. Many beds of this variety were made around the middle of the 19th century in America. It seems reasonable to assume that these beds had their provenance in the French provincial lit à barreaux. For a few years after 1820 the American Empire style sleigh bed made of veneered mahogany enjoyed considerable popularity. This bed, which derived its name from its supposed resemblance to a sleigh, was rather heavy and ponderous and consisted of a panelled rolled-over headboard and footboard which curved upward and rolled either outward or inward. The design for this type of bed was inspired by the contemporary French Empire lit en bateau.

Tables   The earliest American tables date from about the middle of the 17th century. American table design both in the introduction and in the development of new forms, such as card tables, tea tables and sewing tables, essentially followed English table design during the second half of the 17th century and the entire 18th century. Among the early types of tables found in America after 1660 were included the table of trestle construction with its removable top, the so-called tavern table, the gate-leg and the butterfly table. The massive and long rectangular English table with its elaborately carved bulbous-shaped legs and continuous floor stretcher was apparently not made in America.

The name *tavern table* is often given to a small, plain and sturdy table with turned legs, made from about 1675 to 1725. It had a rectangular, octagonal, round or oval top extending well over the apron which was often fitted with a drawer. The legs were often splayed and were connected with a stretcher close to the floor. As a rule the legs terminated in small ball or bun feet. Because of the convenient size of these tables they were used in public inns and in the kitchens and in other rooms of private homes. It is probable that some of the larger ones served as small dining tables.

The butterfly table was a small, plain, drop-leaf table. It was found in the different New England states and was made in the first quarter of the 18th century. In this table the two drop-leaves were supported by two large wooden wing brackets. The table has been so named because of the supposed resemblance in the shape of the solid wooden wing brackets to the shape of butterfly wings. The design for this table is generally regarded as an American innovation. The table was small and its average height was about 26 inches. The top of the table was usually of either maple or cherry and the rest of the table was of different woods. The table had a fixed oblong top and when the leaves were raised to its level the top was generally either oval or rectangular in shape. The oblong top rested on four either plain or turned splayed legs, generally terminating in small ball feet. The legs were usually connected with a plain continuous stretcher which was close to the floor. A small drawer was generally fitted beneath the top of the table, and the lower part of the drawer was wider than the upper part since it fitted between the splayed legs. Each of the two leaves was supported on a large wing bracket which was pivoted at the upper end to the under side of the top and at the lower end to the stretcher.

The gate-leg table with its drop-leaves and swinging gate construction was in use in America from about 1660. It retained its popularity to a greater or less extent until about the middle of the 18th century. The gate-leg table varied greatly in size. The larger gate-leg table was the principal variety of dining table until about 1725. After 1720 the gate-leg variety of dining table was supplanted to a large extent in the more fashionable city homes by the table with drop-leaves and cabriole legs designed in the Queen Anne style. In this variety of table the drop-leaves were supported by swing-legs of cabriole form.

The principal American dining table throughout the 18th century essentially followed the English dining table designed in the Queen Anne, Chippendale, Hepplewhite and Sheraton styles. The pedestal dining table designed in the American Empire style was characterized by its massive pedestal supports.

The richly carved English sideboard table and side table with a marble top were seldom made in America. These tables which have been found in America were relatively plain, and the majority were made from around 1740 to 1785 (452).

The name *hunt board, hunter's table* or *hunting board* is often given in certain parts of the South to describe a form of long sideboard table, designed with a frieze and generally without drawers, and a form of sideboard designed with drawers or with cupboard doors that was used for the service of refreshments. These tables varied considerably in quality and in design. Undoubtedly its most distinguishing feature was its height. The hunt table had to be tall enough so that the huntsmen could stand comfortably around it and enjoy their liquid refreshments. When it was fitted with drawers or cupboards it was generally called a hunt sideboard.

The features of design and the style of ornament for the sideboard with its shallow napery drawer and two deep lateral wine drawers or cupboards as developed in England in the Hepplewhite and Sheraton styles were essentially followed in the contemporary American sideboard. In the following Empire style the sideboard became more massive. The principal decorative features of the sideboard designed in the American Empire style were the heavy wooden columns which were either plain or spirally carved and the feet which were commonly in the form of some animal's paw.

The name *butler's sideboard* is given to a variety of Sheraton style sideboard that was surmounted with a recessed china cabinet, fitted with glazed doors. In one characteristic type the center drawer in the projecting lower sideboard portion was designed with a fall-front writing flap, which opened to reveal a fitted writing interior. This writing compartment was used by the butler for his household accounts. This type of butler's sideboard is also sometimes called a Salem secretary (464).

The side table in America was principally made in the Chippendale, Hepplewhite and Sheraton styles. It was generally made of mahogany and was finely designed and decorated with carved, painted or inlaid decoration in accordance with the taste of the period. The elaborately decorated English side tables and pier tables were seldom if ever found in America. Occasionally some of the more decorative American side tables are referred to as pier tables, based on the belief that they were originally designed to stand between two windows. Pier tables and pier mirrors were used only in a restricted sense in America for decorative purposes. The mahogany side table designed in the American Empire style became more massive and frequently had a white marble top. The table had an oblong top over a frieze that was mounted on four plain round columns resting on shaggy paw feet. It often had a heavy low recessed shelf. The design for this table was borrowed from the French Empire style. In the more ambitious examples bronze figural supports were used in place of the front round columns and the table was further enriched with gilded bronze appliqués (470).

A large number of occasional or center tables with drop-leaves suitable for general use were made from about 1760 to 1840 in the different successive styles. They were mounted on legs, trestle-end supports or pedestals. Especially characteristic were the Pembroke and sofa tables. The small Pembroke table with its hinged wooden brackets and short drop-leaves was made in America from about 1760 to 1815 in the Chippendale, Hepplewhite and Sheraton styles. As in England tables of the Pembroke type were designed in the Chippendale style and were used as breakfast tables (348, 456). The long sofa table, which was introduced in England late in the 18th century, was made in America from about 1800 to 1840. It was characterized by its drop-leaf at each end supported on a wooden bracket and by its two frieze drawers. It was often designed with two lyre-form end supports which were connected with a stretcher.

The name *corner table* is sometimes given to a form of a drop-leaf table with a triangular-shaped top which was over a conformingly shaped frieze. In all probability the design for this table was borrowed from an English Early Georgian card table with a triangular folding top. The corner table had three stationary legs and a movable leg, supporting the drop-leaf. The drop-leaf was triangular in form and was of the same size as the top, forming a square top when the drop-leaf was raised. The corner table was made in the different 18th century styles. Essentially it was a plainer type of table and many were relatively small.

Card
Tables
The card table was designed in the Queen Anne, Chippendale, Hepplewhite and Sheraton styles. A card table having a shaped top with outset rounded corners was illustrated in Sheraton's DRAWING BOOK (468). The three-quarter rounded stiles continued to form the cylindrical tapering legs (468). The so-called lyre card table designed in the Sheraton style was a favorite design at the beginning of the 19th century. The standard upon which the table top was mounted was designed in the form of two parallel lyres and rested on a tetrapod base. The strings of the lyres were often of brass. In the Empire style the lyres lost the graceful simplicity of their lines and were more coarsely carved (469).

Toilet
Tables
Included among the characteristic dressing tables made in America were the dressing table of kneehole form and the dressing table known as a lowboy in America. The dressing table with a hinged box lid, which, when opened, revealed a fitted dressing interior and a rising framed mirror, was also made in limited numbers.

Tea
Tables
The tea table of rectangular form was introduced around 1725 and was designed in the Queen Anne and Chippendale styles. The rectangular top was designed with a rim or raised edge giving the appearance of a tray. The frieze of the table was sometimes fitted with a drawer, and it was mounted on four cabriole legs. The tea table of tripod form became fashionable in America around 1760 and was designed in the Chippendale style (453). The table consisted of a top, a pedestal or column and a tripod base generally terminating in either snake or claw-and-ball feet (453). The top generally tilted and frequently revolved. Some were made with the structural feature called a bird-cage (453). The majority had circular tops (453), although some had square, serpentine-square, octagonal or rectangular tops. As a rule the tea table had a pie crust edge or a dish-top with a molded edge. Especially praiseworthy were the pie crust tea tables, the finest examples of which were made in Philadelphia (453). The English tripod tea tables with their spindled galleries or pierced fretwork galleries were apparently not made in America. Some tripod tea tables were made with a plain top; that is, they were not decorated with a raised edge. The Chippendale style china table with an oblong top and mounted on four legs was also made in America (451). It was designed with either a pierced (451) or solid gallery. In the succeeding Hepplewhite and Sheraton styles, Pembroke tables became the fashionable form for tea tables.

Work
Tables
Although some work tables or sewing tables were made in the Hepplewhite style the majority were made in the Sheraton and Empire styles (469). Of especial interest is the type popularly called the Martha Washington sewing table. It has been so named because a sewing table of this type was reputed to have been used by Martha Washington at Mt. Vernon. This variety of sewing table had an oval

or almost oval top over two or three rows of single small drawers flanked by ends which served as bins and conformed in shape to the top. The oval top was either in one piece or was divided into three parts. When it was made in one piece the entire top could be raised. When it was made in three parts the central portion was fixed while the part over each end could be raised. The sewing table was made in the Hepplewhite, Sheraton and Empire styles and had a fitted interior with sewing accessories.

Writing Furniture
The writing table of kneehole form was found in America as early as 1725. Especially notable are the block-front writing tables of kneehole form, usually mounted on ogee bracket feet and distinctive for their crisply carved convex and concave shells (455).

The slant-front writing desk with drawers came into general use after 1725 and continued in vogue until late in the 18th century. The principal variety had an oblong top and a hinged slant lid over three or four rows of graduated long drawers. The slant lid opened to reveal an interior of small drawers, pigeonholes and compartments. It was chiefly mounted on a bracket base; during the Chippendale style it was frequently mounted on claw-and-ball feet. This variety of desk was no longer fashionable after the Chippendale style and such later examples made in this variety incorporated certain features of design from both the Hepplewhite and Sheraton styles.

Another type of slant-front writing desk designed in the Queen Anne and Chippendale styles had a separate desk section mounted on a stand. The desk section had an oblong top and a hinged slant lid over a long drawer. The stand or frame was designed with a frieze, which was sometimes fitted with a drawer, and with four legs of cabriole form.

Tambour desks were made in the Hepplewhite and Sheraton styles. However, due to the fact that similar features of design frequently appeared in both the Hepplewhite and Sheraton tambour desks it is often difficult if not impossible to differentiate between these two styles. One form of tambour desk had an oblong top and a tambour cylinder or roll-top over a row of drawers. It was mounted on four slender tapered legs of either cylindrical or quadrangular form. Undoubtedly the favorite type of tambour desk had two slides or shutters of tambour construction that moved horizontally (465). It had a hinged writing lid which was before a low, oblong, deeply recessed superstructure fitted with two tambour slides opening to small drawers and pigeonholes (465). The hinged writing lid and superstructure were over two rows and occasionally three rows of drawers which were mounted on slender tapered legs (465). Occasionally the lower section was designed with four graduated drawers which were mounted on bracket feet.

As a rule the slant-front secretary bookcase in the Chippendale style was mounted on either claw-and-ball or ogee bracket feet (458). Gracefully scrolled pediments with the inner end of each scroll centering a carved rosette and quarter round fluted columns on the corners of both the upper and lower sections are interesting features occurring on some extant examples (458). The secretary bookcase in the Hepplewhite (460) and Sheraton styles frequently featured a fall-front writing drawer. Although the upper section with its glazed doors is sometimes used for the reception of china, it is often felt that it was originally intended to be used for books. The majority of these secretary bookcases were characterized by a valanced base curving into French bracket feet (460).

An interesting article of American writing furniture was the Salem secretary, which was also known in New England as a Salem desk. It was a form of secretary bookcase designed in the Sheraton style. The recessed upper section was designed with four, and occasionally only two, glazed doors enclosing bookshelves. The projecting lower section was fitted with two or three rows of drawers. In one type the top center drawer in the lower section was designed with a fall-front writing flap which opened to a fitted writing interior. In another type the lower part of the upper recessed bookcase section was fitted with small drawers and pigeonholes. The butler's sideboard having the lower section in the form of a sideboard is also called a Salem secretary (464).

Cabinets and Bookcases   Only a relatively few tall china cabinets and bookcases were made in America in the 18th century. Occasionally china cabinets surmounted the tops of sideboards designed in the Hepplewhite and Sheraton styles. China was also kept in tall corner cupboards or corner cabinets. The movable corner china cabinet, with its glazed upper section, was principally made of mahogany. It came into use around 1730 and retained its popularity for almost one hundred years. The corner china cabinet displayed little variation in its shape; however, the decorative details were in accordance with the prevailing styles. As a rule it was made in two sections with each section fitted with a pair of doors enclosing shelves. Sometimes the upper section had a single door and the lower section had either one or two doors. The doors in the upper section were frequently longer and in the Queen Anne and Chippendale styles these upper doors were often arched. When the doors in both sections were of wood this article of furniture is regarded as a cupboard. It was generally mounted on a bracket base.

Cupboards   In the second half of the 17th century such early forms of cupboards as the English hall and parlor cupboard and the Dutch kas were found in America. Movable corner cupboards were in general use throughout the 18th century. Many of these were made of pine and were intended for use in the kitchen. The built-in alcove and corner cupboards often formed a part of the wood panelling of rooms and were painted to harmonize with the panelled walls. These cupboards, which were generally made of pine, were extremely fashionable in the Queen Anne and Chippendale styles. The upper doors were almost always arched. The inner upper section in the finely made examples usually consisted of a half round interior fitted with shaped shelves surmounted by a carved half-shell cupola. The two lower panelled doors enclosed one or two shelves. The built-in cupboard generally displayed architectural features in its principles of design.

The name *press cupboard* was given in America to a form of cupboard resembling the English hall and parlor cupboard. It was first made in America in the second half of the 17th century and retained its popularity into the early 18th century. It was a large rectangular article of furniture in which the upper section had three recessed panels, fitted with one or more cupboard doors, the two end panels frequently being canted, surmounted with a projecting frieze and cornice which rested on two bulbous form supports. The lower portion was fitted with either drawers or cupboard doors. The name *press* is given to these cupboards because it is thought that the drawers or compartments served as a clothespress.

Chests   Chests were made in America from about the middle of the 16th century. The development of the chest in America was essentially similar to the development of the chest in England. Chests mounted on a stand or frame were quite popular in America in the 18th century and because they were primarily used to store blankets they are commonly called blanket chests. The Hadley chest, which is an early variety of American chest, received its name from the town of Hadley in Massachusetts, where a number of chests of this type were found. It was a rectangular chest with a hinged top, enclosing a deep well. The front of the Hadley chest was designed with three sunken rectangular panels, beneath which were generally one, two or three long drawers. The short legs were formed from a continuation of the stiles. The chest was decorated with an over-all flat carving of simple designs. The carved decoration, which was crudely executed, was generally composed of a tulip pattern with vines and leaves. As a rule the initials of the owner were carved in the design and very often they were inscribed in the center panel.

The Connecticut chest or Connecticut sunflower chest was another variety of early rectangular oak chest principally made in Connecticut. The front of the chest was usually designed with three rectangular panels which were generally over two rows of drawers. The short legs were formed from a continuation of the stiles. The panels were ornamented with a carved decoration. The center panel was commonly decorated with three carved circular designs, each enclosing either stylized sunflowers or asters. The end panels were generally carved with a tulip pattern. The other distinguishing decorative feature was the applied split banisters on the stiles and the applied circular or oval bosses on the drawers. These applied ornaments were generally painted black.

The Pennsylvania Dutch chest, with its peasant-like painted decoration, is identified with the Pennsylvania Dutch, who began to migrate from Germany around 1680 and settled in the southeast portion of Pennsylvania. As a rule, the front of the chest was ornamented with two or three shaped panels decorated with painted flowers, fruit, foliage and birds. The tulip was a favorite floral motif. The initials of the owners were often found on these chests. Many of them were made as dower chests. The almost primitive quality of these chests displayed in their construction and their folk art decoration gave them a singular charm.

Chests of Drawers   Chests of drawers were found in America prior to 1700; however, they did not become plentiful until after the middle of the 18th century. The mahogany chest of drawers was principally designed in the Chippendale, Hepplewhite and Sheraton styles and essentially followed the special features of design developed in the English chest of drawers during those styles. Due to the popularity of the highboy and lowboy, the chest of drawers was not especially popular until around the last quarter of the 18th century. The ambitious and decorative 18th century English commodes based upon the contemporary French styles were apparently not made in America. The chest of drawers designed in the American Empire style became more massive.

The tall chest of drawers was designed in America from about 1740 to 1810. At first the tall chest of drawers was generally mounted on a low frame with a valanced frieze which rested on four short cabriole legs. From about 1760 the tall chest of drawers simply rested on bracket feet and except for its added height and more rows of drawers was essentially similar in design to the chest of drawers.

The chest-on-chest was made in America in the second half of the 18th century. The majority were designed in the Chippendale style.

The highboy was introduced in America around 1700 and retained its popularity for almost one hundred years. It was designed as a chest of drawers mounted on a stand that invariably was fitted with drawers. The upper section of the American highboy was generally designed with a row of three and sometimes two small drawers over three or four graduated long drawers (443, 459). The arrangement of the drawers in the lower section varied. It most frequently had one long drawer over a row of three small drawers (459), with the two lateral drawers often being deeper. The design for the stand essentially followed the design for a type of side table which was called a dressing table in England and a lowboy in America. The highboy was designed in the William and Mary (443), Queen Anne and Chippendale styles (459). The William and Mary highboy was characterized by its flat molded top, its six turned and tapering legs and its flat, shaped stretcher (443). The characteristic Queen Anne highboy was designed with either a flat molded top or a scrolled pediment top and with four slender cabriole legs terminating in club feet. The valanced stand, which was designed with either one or two rows of drawers, often had acorn pendants. Sometimes the top central drawer and the bottom central drawer were carved with a fan or sunburst motif. During the Chippendale style the highboy commonly had a scrolled pediment (459); however, some highboys were made with a flat molded top. The four cabriole legs, which were often heavier and shorter and acanthus-carved, terminated in claw-and-ball feet. The claw-and-ball feet were the principal indication of the Chippendale style. The valanced apron frequently centered a carved recessed shell motif and the top center drawer was often decorated in a similar manner. Sometimes the stiles were decorated with fluted pilasters. The term *Philadelphia style highboy* is given to a highboy made in Philadelphia from about 1760 to 1775 (459). Essentially the Philadelphia highboy was a more richly carved example of the highboy surmounted with a swan neck or scrolled pediment designed in the Rococo Chippendale style. For example, the inner ends of the scrolled pediment terminated in carved rosettes, the stiles were often enriched with quarter-round fluted columns, the carved recessed shells were flanked with foliated scrolls in relief, the valanced apron was often embellished with carved Rococo leaf ornament and the cabriole legs were richly carved with acanthus leafage (459). The development of the highboy and lowboy in the Philadelphia school of Chippendale Rococo furniture has no counterpart in any other country.

The lowboy which is called in England either a dressing table or a side table was a favorite piece of American 18th century furniture. The design for the lowboy was essentially similar to the lower portion of the highboy. It was designed in the William and Mary, Queen Anne and Chippendale styles. The term *Philadelphia style lowboy* was given to a richly carved lowboy made in Philadelphia from about 1760 to 1775 in the Chippendale Rococo style.

Clothes-presses

The tall wardrobe or press, generally fitted with two long cupboard doors, was in use in America in the first half of the 18th century. The clothespress, which was very often fitted with two cupboard doors in the upper section and with one or two rows of drawers in the lower section, was principally designed in the Hepplewhite and Sheraton styles.

Mirrors   The earliest wall mirrors in America were imported from England and date from around 1700. One principal type of Queen Anne wall mirror had an upright arched or serpentine-arched frame, frequently surmounted with either a fret-scrolled cresting or a pierced cresting. The mirror plate was usually in two parts. It was generally made of walnut or mahogany and was often parcel-gilded. Only a relatively few richly carved and pierced upright gilded Chippendale mirrors embellished with C-scrolls, shells and other Rococo ornament were made in America. The Early Georgian upright architectural wall mirror was made in America during the Chippendale era and is called a Chippendale style mirror in America. It was made of walnut or mahogany and was parcel-gilded. The fretwork mirror was a favorite wall mirror in America. The majority were made of mahogany during the second half of the 18th century. It had an upright molded frame with a fret-scrolled cresting, which was commonly arched, and a conformingly shaped fret-cut base. Essentially it was a plainer type of mirror and the variations in shape and in decoration were slight. Occasionally there was a narrow gilded molding next to the mirror plate. Frequently the cresting and valanced base centered a carved motif, such as a shell. Sometimes the fret-cut cresting was in the form of two scrolls and centered a low plinth upon which was surmounted a carved and gilded bird. These fretwork mirrors are generally regarded as Chippendale style, unless they display some characteristic design feature of a later style.

Rectangular or oval carved and gilded wall mirrors with wirework composition ornament designed in the Adam style were relatively rare in America. Some carved and gilded rectangular upright wall mirrors designed in the Hepplewhite style were made in America. They often had an elaborate cresting composed of a classic vase or urn and festoon of flowers and husk pendants made of wirework composition. A favorite rectangular upright gilded mirror designed in the Sheraton style was the tabernacle mirror, having a carved cornice supported by columns extending the length of the frame. Often gilt spherules or acorns were attached beneath the cornice. The mirror plate was surmounted by a rectangular panel of wood or glass which was decorated with a painted design, very often depicting a patriotic event in American history. During the American Empire style this form of mirror was characterized by its coarsely painted design and more massive frame. The majority of circular convex wall mirrors with their carved and molded gilded frames which were found in America were actually imported from England.

Included among the wall mirrors found in America were the so-called courting mirrors and Bilbao mirrors. The small courting mirror had a rectangular upright molded wooden frame which centered a continuous strip of small pieces of glass crudely painted with exotic leaves and flowers. The cresting was also decorated in a similar manner. It is generally accepted that these mirrors originally came from China. Occasionally the mirror was enclosed in a shallow box which was supposed to represent its original shipping box. The Bilbao mirror also had a rectangular upright wooden frame. The frame was entirely covered with various colored pieces of marble. It had a carved and gilded openwork cresting. The mirror plate was enclosed in a gilded molding. It is generally believed that this mirror derived its name from the Spanish city of Bilbao, from where it was originally shipped to America.

The use of long pier mirrors and overmantel mirrors for decorative purposes was limited in America.

The swinging dressing mirror or toilet mirror on a box stand was a popular form of mirror throughout the 18th century. They were principally used on the tops of dressing tables, such as lowboys, or on chests of drawers. The special features of design developed in the English dressing mirror in the successive 18th century styles were also found in the American dressing mirror. It was also designed in the American Empire style.

A few tall cheval dressing mirrors were made in the Sheraton and American Early Empire styles.

Stands   Candlestands were made throughout the 18th century. The majority of candlestands were designed in the Chippendale style. They were generally made of mahogany and were often finely carved. The small top, which was usually circular, rested on a turned shaft mounted on a tripod base generally terminating in either snake or in claw-and-ball feet.

The majority of teakettle or urn stands with their pull-out slides were designed in either the Hepplewhite or Sheraton styles; however, a few early ones were in the Chippendale style. These urn stands were designed with four very slender legs.

The principal variety of washing stand found in America was the corner washing stand. The front of the triangular top was generally rounded and the two straight sides of the top were generally surmounted with a shaped wooden back piece, serving as a protection for the wall. The frieze and median shelf, the latter being often fitted with one or two drawers, conformed in shape to the top. It was designed with three or four legs. The center of the top was very often cut out for the reception of the washing bowl. Only a few washing stands designed with hinged box lids, which, when closed, resembled small night tables, were found in America. Those that were made were designed in the Hepplewhite or Sheraton styles. The small basin stand of tripod form with its molded basin ring and with its

Accessories

median trilateral shelf was also found in America in limited numbers.

Carved and gilded sconces and wall brackets were seldom if ever made in America. Apparently the few employed for decorative purposes in early American homes were almost always imported from England or France.

Although some knife urns and knife boxes were made in America in the Hepplewhite and Sheraton styles the majority were imported from England.

Such accessories for drinking as mahogany wine coolers and mahogany cellarettes were made only occasionally in America.

As a rule the mahogany dumb-waiter was designed in the Chippendale style. It usually had three circular trays increasing in size from top to bottom. The trays were on a central shaft resting on a tripod base which usually terminated in claw-and-ball or snake feet.

The cheval fire screen was seldom if ever made in America; however, the pole fire screen was a popular piece of American furniture. It was designed in the Chippendale, Hepplewhite and Sheraton styles.

Clocks

The tall case clock was first made around 1730 and continued in vogue until about 1840. As a rule the tall case clocks were made of mahogany and a few were made of veneered walnut. The finely decorated English marquetry and lacquer tall case clocks were apparently not made in America. Case clocks were not made in any considerable quantity in America until around 1775, when the case clock with a scrolled pediment centering a low plinth became fashionable. As a rule after 1775 tall case clocks were surmounted with either a scrolled pediment or other forms of shaped pediments. The influence of the Chippendale style was often evident in the open fretwork cresting. The American tall case clock essentially followed the contemporary English models. Tall case clocks during the Hepplewhite and Sheraton styles were often ornamented with inlaid stringing lines and shell paterae. Miniature tall case clocks are frequently referred to as grandmother's clocks.

Undoubtedly the favorite American bracket or mantel clock was the Terry clock of rectangular form. It derived its name from Eli Terry, 1772–1852, who was the maker. The Terry clock was an inexpensive one, for Eli Terry by using wooden works instead of the customary brass works was able to produce a cheaper clock. The mahogany Terry style clock as a rule was characterized by a scroll-top case generally centering a low plinth. The scroll-top was usually surmounted with three finials. The glass door was flanked by slender round pillars and the wooden dial was painted white. The lower part of the glass door had an oblong painted panel. It was mounted on a valanced base terminating in very slender bracket feet. The great majority of Terry clocks were made between 1815 and 1837, the later date marking the beginning of the production of machine-made clocks with brass works. Terry style clocks were made by others as well as by Eli Terry and his family. Seth Thomas, who was in partnership with Eli Terry for a year in 1809, bought the rights to make similar clocks.

The mahogany banjo clock was the favorite form of American wall clock. Simon Willard, 1753–1848, who was the most famous of the celebrated clock-making family, was the inventor of the banjo clock, which he patented in 1802. It had a circular dial with a brass bezel mounted on a flaring shaft or shank which was flanked by brass open scrolled brackets. Beneath the flaring shaft was a rectangular pendulum door. The shaft and pendulum door were decorated with églomisé panels. The dial was generally surmounted with a gilded cone finial made either of brass or of wood. In Willard's more elaborate specimens the top of the dial was often surmounted with a gilded brass eagle, the front of the wooden case was entirely gilded and beneath the pendulum door there was a fluted base finished with a pendant. Banjo clocks were widely copied by other members of the Willard family and by other clockmakers.

Spice Chests

Spice chests, especially designed to hold spices, were an interesting category of American cabinetwork (454). Some extant examples dating from the 18th century are praiseworthy for their fine cabinetwork (454). One variety was designed like a chest of drawers mounted on a stand, except that the upper section was fitted with either one or two doors, which, when opened, revealed an interior fitted with many small drawers (454). The stand, which was mounted on cabriole legs of varying length, was fitted with a row of drawers. Variations in design occurred. Extant examples vary in height from 27 to 58 inches (454). Since spices brought from the East Indies were an expensive luxury in colonial times, these chests were provided with a lock and key.

Deception Furniture

Deception furniture, especially various forms of concealed beds, was found in America in the 18th century (457). A form of half tester bed folding against a wall and concealed with a curtain was popular in New England early in the 18th century. Chests of drawers with removable fronts allowing a frame for the bedding to unfold were also made (457). Apparently deception beds were in general use in the 18th century, for a Philadelphia upholsterer, William Martin, advertised all kinds of chairs, couches, deception beds and other articles of furniture. The term *deception* was also found in contemporary English records, for Sheraton in his CABINET DICTIONARY refers to a deception table and writes that it "is one made to imitate a Pembroke table, but to answer the purpose of a pot cupboard, or any other secret use, which we hide from the eyes of a stranger."

CHAPTER TWENTY-THREE

ENGLISH VICTORIAN
and the Arts and Crafts Movement

EARLY VICTORIAN

It is only in recent years that the Victorian period, 1837–1901, has been treated as a serious study, as it is now sufficiently remote to be viewed as a whole. Now can be seen the continuous and logical process of evolution throughout the period which projected many new ideas and slowly and painfully led what had been a purely local craft through the risks of the Industrial Revolution, guided and warned by men like Pugin, Ruskin and William Morris. To the modern eye some of the furniture may seem grotesque, if not merely ugly, but the development of new techniques, the adaptation to machine processes and factory production methods, and the creation of ideas leading directly to 20th century furniture design make this a period which no one interested in the history of furniture can ignore.

Historicism, the excessive fondness for past styles, was the great weakness of the 19th century, as it stifles all attempts at original creation. From about 1820 to 1890 all the styles in Western Europe had been copied, transformed and re-created; and, in addition, toward the closing decades of the century influences had been felt from other parts of the world. It may be said that the 19th century was a repository for the artistic ideas of all countries and all other centuries. In fact, this copying of other styles should be regarded as an independent expression of the age, as a typical stylistic phenomenon belonging to the realm of art history.

The eclectic quality of Regency furniture, described in Chapter Twenty-One, reveals that the quest for novelty was well established before the reign of Queen Victoria, in the words of J. C. Loudon, writing in his comprehensive work, AN ENCYCLOPAEDIA OF COTTAGE, FARM AND VILLA ARCHITECTURE AND FURNITURE, published in 1833, "The principal styles of design as at present executed in Britain may be reduced to four, viz., the Grecian or modern style which is by far the most prevalent; the Gothic or Perpendicular style, which imitates the lines and angles of the Tudor Gothic architecture; the Elizabethan style, which combined the Gothic with the Roman or Italian manner; and the style of the age of Louis XIV, or the florid Italian, which is characterized by curved lines and excess of curvilinear ornaments."

Mr. Loudon's actual knowledge of styles and stylistic development, like most of his contemporaries', was, at least as compared with present standards, very far from first class. In a general sense, however, his description suits all the furniture known to have been made. The boundary line between the French Louis XIV or Baroque style and Louis XV or Rococo style was very confused. The Victorians were equally vague in their usage of the Elizabethan style which they sometimes applied to the late 17th century English Baroque—the Late Jacobean and William and Mary styles—as well as to the late 16th century English Renaissance. The style of a carved oak sideboard made by Jackson and Graham of London from the designs of Eugène Prignot, the firm's chief designer, shown at the Great Exhibition of 1851, is described in the official catalogue as "A happy adaptation of the English revival of antique art most generally known under the name of Elizabethan . . ." (FIGURE 472) In a word, styles were rarely understood or clearly separated, as research into art history was a later 19th century development.

Apart from Loudon's book there were other contemporary books, such as FURNITURE WITH CANDELABRA AND DECORATION by R. Bridgens, published in 1838, which attest to the prevailing fashion in the 1830's and 1840's for furniture in the Grecian, Elizabethan and Gothic styles. Henry Whitaker's book, HOUSE FURNISHING, DECORATING AND EMBELLISHING ASSISTANT (1847), comprised, in the author's own words, "original designs in the Grecian, Italian, Renaissance, Louis XIV, Gothic, Tudor and Elizabethan styles." His elaborate versions of the popular Victorian styles illustrate a marked feature of the period, that is, the similarity of the basic, classic-inspired structure, which was applied to different styles of ornament—Grecian, Elizabethan and Gothic. Only in Old French was the structure composed of scrolls and curves (473, 474).

The simple solid mahogany forms popular in the early decades of the 19th century, the Grecian or modern style, continued to be much admired and used during the first half of the 19th century. Domestically it was especially favored as a dining room style. The typical dining room chair was of klismos derivation, but now the saber-shaped front legs identified with the style of the English Regency were supplanted by legs that were straight and tapering. The usual drawing room chair was of similar form, but lighter in weight and more elegant in appearance. It was the rounding or softening of the form of this "Grecian" chair that developed into the balloon-back chair, one of the most English of chair forms. Around the mid-19th century it was given cabriole legs (507, 508), and in this form it remained the typical drawing room and dining room chair for the ensuing two decades. The Bourbon Restauration of 1814 renewed once again the English taste for French fashions in furniture, which was especially favored for the drawing room and boudoir. A superficially Rococo style of curvilinear form, elaborately carved and gilt, was much in demand. In fact, the taste for gilt furniture in one or another style continued in vogue for the drawing room until the close of the century.

Interest in early oak furniture developed as a natural consequence of the 19th century revival of Elizabethan architecture and decoration. It was Henry Shaw's SPECIMENS OF ANCIENT FURNITURE (1836) in which he gave detailed drawings of English furniture, ranging from a few medieval examples to the very late 17th century, that furnished the main source for so many so-called Elizabethan details. This was followed by Joseph Nash's MANSIONS OF ENGLAND (1839–49) with its reasonably accurate but fanciful and picturesque romanticized colored illustrations of interiors in "ancient times." These illustrations possessed the same quality as the Elizabethan furniture which recommended itself mainly as conforming with the romantic literary writings of the time and especially with the novels of Sir Walter Scott published between 1814 and 1832. Not only were Scott's novels a main inspiration for the revivalism in medieval and Renaissance art, but also his library at Abbotsford was the precursor of countless picturesquely furnished English houses replete with carved oak and stained glass.

Practically all early Victorian Gothic or Elizabethan furniture was rarely designed in the usual sense of the word, but was assembled from old pieces of carving. The practice of using quantities of "ancient fragments" was so widespread that these styles were recommended as especially economic. As J. C. Loudon writes in 1833, "It is seldom necessary to manufacture objects in this manner farther than by putting together ancient fragments which may be purchased at the sale of old buildings. . . ."

The Elizabethan style so fashionable in the 1840's was to be supplanted by the medieval style of the 1860's. Perhaps the most familiar piece of Elizabethan furniture is a short-legged upholstered side chair described as a prie-dieu, vesper or devotional chair characterized by a tall back and a very low seat. Some of these late seventeenth century Baroque-inspired chairs with spirally turned uprights and legs were intended for use in the drawing room (475), but others with a padded crest rail extending well beyond the tall and narrow upholstered back were particularly meant for family prayers.

The fashion for Gothic furniture persisted throughout the 19th century. Early Victorian furniture in this style lost something of the amateur character of the Regency Gothic but it was still far from being an authentic reproduction. The architect Augustus Welby Northmore Pugin (1812–1852) tried to establish a real understanding of the principles of Gothic construction through the publication in 1835 of his GOTHIC FURNITURE IN THE STYLE OF THE FIFTEENTH CENTURY. Although the designs encouraged a more academic approach they appear to have had little or no effect on furniture designs in general. Pugin despised the "glaring, showy and meretricious ornament" then in fashion. He scornfully attacked the trade Gothic furniture, on which "we find diminutive flying buttresses about an armchair; everything is crocketed with angular projections, innumerable mitres, sharp ornaments and turreted extremities. A man who remains any length in a modern Gothic room and escapes without being wounded by some of its minutiae may consider himself extremely fortunate." Pugin's actual designs are reasonably simple and are mainly concerned with structure, not with ornament. Perhaps the most admired pieces of the day were those made from Pugin's designs for Abney Hall, Cheadle, in Cheshire (476).

The Great Exhibition of the Works of Industry of All Nations of 1851 was the first of the international exhibitions which punctuated the second half of the 19th century. All the better-known cabinetmaking firms felt obliged to participate as a matter of prestige, with the sole object of winning an award. Although these spectacular exhibition pieces shown at the Great Exhibition of 1851 and its international successors both in Europe and in the United States led to the production of a class of furniture made for display and which at first sight may seem remote from furniture in daily use, they were the main source of Victorian taste in interior furnishings and decoration. Exhibited, illustrated and commented on, these pieces of technical virtuosity were intended to attract as purchasers persons of immense wealth or museums where they would be displayed for the edification of the public who then furnished their houses with smaller and much less costly versions. An imposing Adam style satinwood cabinet richly decorated with a marquetry of colored woods, gilt mounts and Wedgwood plaques made by the short-lived firm of Wright and Mansfield caused considerable interest at the Paris Exhibition of 1867 where it won English honors (477).

No doubt this cabinet, which belongs to the Victoria and Albert Museum, encouraged the use of plaques for decoration in the general furniture trade as well as the making of a great quantity of eighteenth century English reproductions, which were found in many late Victorian drawing rooms. Some of the pieces were virtual facsimiles; others simply made a passing allusion. It is generally accepted that after the Paris Exhibition of 1878, the production of extravagant exhibition pieces came to an end, owing to a steadily increasing sphere of interest in a genuine domestic style of furniture that blended more naturally with furniture in current use.

The Great Exhibition of 1851 affords an excellent understanding of Victorian tendencies and characteristics. It is obvious that the copying and mixing of past styles accompanied by a straining after novelty in trivial details is a striking characteristic. Standing out in the general confusion is a marked emphasis on rich and flamboyant carving of a sculpturesque quality; ornamental motifs were crammed together as if a horror existed for an empty space (472). The profusion of ornament was more often than not executed with a certain coarseness. The Victorian must have found it intoxicating to produce with the new tools the exuberant carving which, when done by hand on the costly models, was the hallmark of all fine furniture at this time.

The age is distinguished by a strong pride in inventions; the Victorians were delighted with their advance in scientific knowledge and technical skill. Thus machine-carved ornament had many admirers, who considered it an achievement for the human mind to invent machinery that could do the same work as the hand in less than one hundredth of the time and do it more perfectly. In many cases this pride in inventiveness supplanted aesthetic appreciation. For example, one could be proud of the imitation of one material by another—wood painted in imitation of mahogany, ebony or marble; panels painted in imitation of inlaid wood; glass imitating various kinds of marble, semi-precious stones, lapis lazuli and malachite that were used for decorative purposes, as in pietra dura. Frankly fascinated with these substitute materials, the originals of which were associated in the past only with wealth, the Victorians reveled in their display of commercial prosperity.

There was a considerable delight in new materials, the reproduction of things familiar in one material by means of another newly developed or unusual material, for example, the enthusiasm for metal furniture. Loudon in his ENCY-CLOPAEDIA (1833) urged the introduction of iron into the furniture of cottages and farmhouses, which would be "attended with considerable economy, at least in the article of dining tables, sideboards, bedsteads and hall chairs." The popularity of brass and iron beds, the first design for which was registered at the Patent Office in 1849, grew by leaps and bounds. In the 1880's retailers' catalogues were filled with highly decorative brass beds and swing cots with curtain scrolls for infants. Indeed the taste for metal beds became so firmly entrenched that it almost required a small revolution at the end of the century to reintroduce wood. Cast iron furniture of the type that was rarely moved, such as garden chairs and benches and hall furniture, in particular the ubiquitous rustic umbrella stand, was produced in great quantities throughout the Victorian period. About half of it was exported. Originally it was painted not in the white so fashionable today but in black, bronze or in imitation of light oak. Another class of metal furniture produced in the brass foundries of Birmingham, apart from the beds in brass tube, was a variety of chairs in both tube and strap metal. Still another class of metal furniture was made of wire, bent cold and usually gilt, which was quite light in appearance.

Perhaps the best known and most popular of the unusual materials used for Victorian furniture is papier mâché, which was suddenly made available for furnishings on a large scale because of new patents. The renowned firm of Jennens and Bettridge, who made the bulk of all papier mâché furniture, exhibited a piano with an entire case of papier mâché, decorative but nonplaying, as the manufacturer had overlooked the fact that papier mâché was acoustically not adequate. Though entire pieces of furniture such as chairs were made of papier mâché, the material proved quite unsuitable for the frames of furniture, and much that is still extant has a wood or metal frame covered with japanned papier mâché and only the nonstructural parts are made of papier mâché (478).

As the Victorians loved novelty and gadgets, ingenious devices for making furniture multipurpose—from the functionally sound to the most futile—were improved and their number increased. There was a wide range of intelligently designed furniture for invalids such as a couch on which the patient "can be raised from a horizontal to a sitting position without being disturbed." Numerous chairs were designed on the principle to be later reintroduced by Le Corbusier and Marcel Breuer (Isokon chair) for the able-bodied in a less formal age. For example, William Ryan's reclining chair designed "so that the degree of inclination is regulated with facility by the weight of the body."

Another outstanding feature of mid-Victorian design is the preference for broken outlines; the straight line was replaced by a medley of Regency scrolls, Louis XIV Baroque scrolls and Louis XV Rococo curves—generous, full and bulgy (473). Even Gothic pieces were given a restless outline. A peculiar topheaviness stamps most of the furniture owing to the fashion for abundant protuberances. The blown-up Victorian curve appealed to a prosperous, well-fed, self-confident middle class, whose tastes dictated the dominant flavor of the 19th century.

An overwhelming interest in ornament that tells a story or has an allegoric or symbolic meaning is another distinguishing feature. The Victorians by no means stand alone in their love of these and other ornament or in their reverence for the beauties of nature and their pleasure in its minute imitation; what is disturbing is their lack of taste in exploiting these subjects. Countless examples might be cited. One expressing the spirit of 1851 is a daydreamer easy chair in papier mâché made by Jennens and Bettridge, "decorated at the top" according to the description in the Official Catalogue, "with two winged thoughts—the one with bird-like pinions, and crowned with roses, representing happy and joyous dreams, the other with leather bat-like wings—unpleasant and troubled ones. Behind is displayed Hope, under the figure of the rising sun . . . "

Less famous but of far greater significance in the history of furniture, interior design and the general tide of 19th century taste was the International Exhibition held in London in 1862. It marked the first Japanese exhibit in Europe and it was the first time that the newly established firm of Morris, Marshall, Faulkner and Company participated in an exhibition and had its first success.

WILLIAM MORRIS AND ASSOCIATES

The entire life of William Morris (1834–1896), who is perhaps the most important single figure in the establishment of 20th century design, was a crusade against the debased standards of mid-Victorian mass production which he traced to the influence of machine manufacture and the disappearance of honest and satisfying handcraftsmanship. Morris' philosophy was founded entirely on the joy of the creative process which he believed had been sacrificed in the commercial conceptions and standards of art in the nineteenth century. For this reason he objected on principle to the entire system of mechanical production of any work in the arts. Everything Morris preached and practiced was inspired by medievalism, for he felt that the Middle Ages more than any other period in history exemplified his belief that good craftsmanship can only grow from joy in work.

Though Morris' own interest and talent was in the design of flat pattern which he applied successfully to embroideries, wallpapers, woven and printed textiles, carpets and tapestries, this did not prevent his having likes and dislikes with regard to furniture and interior decoration in general. His taste was set on simplicity in this as in most other matters. Simplicity, however, did not mean meagerness, for in his own words "if we really care for art we shall always feel inclined to save on superfluities, that we may have a wherewithal to spend on works of art." (THE LESSER ARTS, 1887) Nor did simplicity rule out luxury providing it was done for beauty's sake and not for show. Morris' golden rule which set the standard for all his opinions on this matter—have nothing "for mere finery's sake or to satisfy the claim of custom" (MAKING THE BEST OF IT, 1879); and above all, "have nothing in your houses which you do not know to be useful or believe to be beautiful." (THE BEAUTY OF LIFE, 1880)

Morris felt that there should be no more furniture in a room than what was really needed for daily use; namely shelves for books, chairs and seats to sit on, tables to eat and write at. In addition to these simple joiner-made pieces which he called "workaday furniture" there was also to be "state furniture," which he thought was "proper even for a citizen." In his own words, "Moreover I must needs think of furniture of two kinds . . . one part of it . . . the necessary workaday furniture . . . simple to the last degree . . . But besides this there is the other kind of what I shall call state furniture; I mean sideboards, cabinets and the like . . . we need not spare ornament on these but may make them as elegant and elaborate as we can with carving or inlaying or painting; these are the blossoms of the art of furniture used architecturally to dignify important chambers and important places in them." (THE LESSER ARTS, 1877)

Unlike Pugin who regarded Gothic to be the ideal design, Morris supported and admired it for what seemed to him

more practical reasons, for he regarded it as the ideal construction and characteristic of all that was best in handcraftsmanship. "As to matters of construction, it should not have to depend on the special skill of a very picked workman, or the super excellence of his glue, but be made on the very proper principles of the art of joinery; . . . " (THE LESSER ARTS, 1887) Furthermore, except for some movable pieces as chairs he liked substance in his furniture; it should be made of "timber rather than walking sticks."

For Morris, trained as an architect and painter, it was a first-floor flat of three unfurnished rooms at 17 Red Lion Square leased in 1857 by Morris and Sir Edward Burne-Jones (1833–1898) which marked his beginning as a designer and craftsman. Unable to buy furniture characterized by good materials and sound joinery, Morris and his good friend, the architect Philip Webb (1831–1915), designed the furniture themselves. They made rough sketches of the essential pieces and gave them to a local carpenter to execute. The Pre-Raphaelite painter Dante Gabriel Rossetti (1828–1882) described the furniture as being "intensely medieval . . . tables and chairs like incubi and succubi." There was a large round table "as firm and heavy as a rock" and chairs "such as Barbarossa might have sat in."

The same experiment was repeated at Red House, Bexley Heath, Kent, which was designed by Webb in 1859 and completed in 1860, for Morris and his bride, Jane Burden. Apart from the oak furniture, much of which was designed by Webb, tiles were designed and made to line the fireplace, cloth or paper for the walls, a jug to hold the wine and glasses to drink it out of. A remarkable feeling of respect for materials which was to be the guiding spirit of all Morris' work, pervaded the furniture and furnishings at Red House.

In 1861, the year after Morris moved into Red House, he organized a firm with offices at 8 Red Lion Square— Morris, Marshall, Faulkner and Company, Fine Art Workmen in Painting, Carving, Furniture and the Metals. Here at Red House in almost rural surroundings, worked William Morris, Philip Webb, the Pre-Raphaelites Sir Edward Burne-Jones, Ford Madox Brown (1821– 1893), who associated with the Pre-Raphaelites but did not join them, and sometimes Dante Gabriel Rossetti, as well as the expert mathematician Charles J. Faulkner. The seventh member was Peter Paul Marshall, originally an engineer but like the others vitally absorbed in arts and crafts. At Red House, in accordance with Morris' beliefs, simplicity, honest craftsmanship and cooperation between artist and artisan became the watchwords, inspired by a profound admiration for the work of the Middle Ages.

For financial reasons Morris had to give up Red House in 1865 when he moved his firm to 26 Queen Square. In 1875 the firm was reorganized as Morris and Company and in 1881 the workshops were removed to Merton Abbey at Hammersmith. From 1877 to the 1920's the firm of Morris and Company maintained showcases in Oxford Street; in 1940 it went into voluntary liquidation. Morris' influence on the contemporary trends and tastes in the arts of decoration was chiefly exercised through the company, whose production from the 1870's comprised practically every branch of applied art.

Furniture was never the most important part of the Morris firm work. It is almost a certainty that Morris never designed furniture with the exception perhaps of a few early pieces for his own use. The Morris firm produced and popularized a rush-seated light chair with turned members adapted from a rural type found in Sussex (479). The other equally popular chair is an upholstered open armchair with an adjustable back bar, the so-called Morris chair. A sketch of this chair dated 1866 by the firm's manager Warrington Taylor was sent to Webb with the following description "back and seat made with bars across to put cushions on, moving on a hinge, a chair model of which I saw with an old carpenter at Hurstmonceaux, Sussex, by name Ephraim Colman. . . ." (480)

Unlike Morris, both Ford Madox Brown and Philip Webb designed furniture. Many of the early Morris firm designs were by Madox Brown of a type described in the catalogue "of solid construction and joiner made," in brief the "workaday furniture." Madox Brown is generally credited with having originated the green stain for oak furniture which was so widely used for Art Furniture.

The most admired and widely acclaimed of the early pieces made by the Morris firm were the massive cupboards and cabinets vaguely Gothic in structure, with ample uninterrupted surfaces, as they were intended mainly as vehicles for the paintings of Morris himself and members of the Pre-Raphaelite circle. For this reason these pieces must be judged on the quality of their painting. Several such pieces were exhibited at the International Exhibition of 1862. The most elaborate was an oak cupboard or desk inlaid with various woods and designed by the architect J. P. Seddon in 1861 for his own use. Painted with subjects illustrating architecture by Madox Brown, painting and sculpture by Burne-Jones, music by Rossetti; with background painted by Morris, the whole was based on imaginary incidents in the honeymoon of King René of Anjou, as recorded in Walter Scott's ANNA VON GEIERSTEIN (481). Webb, who was the chief designer for the firm, designed a series of massive pieces in a "medieval" style, decorated by members of the Pre-Raphaelite circle with subjects from tales in the Arthurian cycle and similar epics of the Age of Chivalry. His first recorded furniture design, dated 1858, was an imposing wardrobe painted by Burne-Jones with a scene from Chaucer's "Prioress's Tale." This was Burne-Jones's first completed oil painting and was a wedding present to Morris (482).

Webb's name is especially associated with a distinctive type of austere and undecorated cottage or farmhouse furniture mainly made of unpolished or ebonized oak, possessing an air of Medievalism in its massive forms, in which the structural elements were strongly emphasized. In Webb's furniture Medievalism is reflected not in the ornamental details as in Pugin's Gothic furniture, but in the simple direct method of construction—honest joinery and honest use of materials—for to Webb furniture was first of all a common tradition of honest joinery (483). It was this same care and interest in the use of materials that laid the foundation for the revival of English furniture, which was to win the admiration of all of Europe at the turn of the century. Around 1890 Webb was succeeded by his pupil the American George Jack (1855–1932) as chief designer for Morris and Company.

ART FURNITURE AND THE AESTHETIC MOVEMENT

From the earliest days of the Industrial Revolution enterprising Englishmen had been concerned with the standards of design and most especially with the quality of ornament, as they were as ornamental in their tastes as everybody else at that time and used the words "beauty" and "ornament" almost as synonyms. In Victorian terms their problem was how to marry art to industry. Perhaps the earliest attempt to create an alliance between fine art and manufactures was Summerly's Art Manufactures started in 1847 by Henry Cole (1802–1883), whose pseudonym was Felix Summerly, and who was chiefly responsible for the Great Exhibition of 1851. Striving for improved design in objects of everyday use, Cole hoped that this commercially spirited enterprise "would promote public taste." He enlisted a great number of painters and sculptors, mostly academicians, who were willing to assist in this ambition, the intimate union of "high" art and ornament, which came to a climax in the Art movement of the 1870's and 1880's. The basic idea, to join the best art with familiar objects in daily use, was far from new, as it goes back at least to the time of the Renaissance when celebrated painters such as Raphael sometimes provided designs for intarsia or renowned painters as Botticelli or Signorelli painted the front panels on cassoni.

By the 1870's the word "art" was in current use among authors, who wrote on the subject of furnishings and decorations, to describe a particular kind of furniture, wallpaper, textiles and the like which possessed an art quality. For example, the term *Art Furniture* properly refers only to the furniture made by a firm who retained artists and architects to design for them. Thus the London Trade Directory listed Art Furniture manufacturers quite separately from ordinary furniture makers. An interesting sidelight on the use of the term is recorded by William Morris of a conversation he had with a lady who, talking about her son, said, "You know I wouldn't mind the lad being a cabinet maker so long as he made Art Furniture."

According to contemporary writings Art Furniture made use of Continental and English traditional styles. This is indicated from a comment in the FURNITURE GAZETTE (1879) in which it refers to Collinson and Lock of London who were outstanding manufacturers of Art Furniture as "Pioneers of the Backward Ho movement." Many of their designs which were widely copied by the trade were supplied by the gifted architect T. E. Collcut. Other chief designers of Art Furniture included Eastlake, Talbert and Burges, all of whom produced much well-designed furniture; practically all of it, however, was to be debased by the trade. In spite of widespread criticism the term *Art Furniture* survived well into the 1880's.

The Early English style, also sometimes called Modern English Gothic, of which Charles Lock Eastlake (1836–1906) was a leading exponent, started to gain popularity around the mid-1860's. A marked feature of this style was the rectangular form of the structure, as it followed the tradition of the medieval joiner which required a framework of verticals and horizontals (posts and rails) joined with mortise and tenon. Glue was never used. Interest in this style was roused by the publication in 1868 of Eastlake's book, HINTS ON HOUSEHOLD TASTE, which enjoyed wide popularity both in England and in America. Eastlake, who designed some furniture, none of which has apparently survived, bitterly attacks in his book the predominance of the curve in mid-Victorian furniture: "Our modern sofas and chairs aspire to elegance, not with gaily embossed silk or delicate inlay of wood, but simply because there is not a straight line in their composition. . . . The tendency of the present age of upholstery is to run into curves. Chairs are invariably curved in such a manner as to insure the greatest amount of ugliness with the least possible comfort. The backs of sideboards are curved in the most senseless and extravagant manner; the legs of cabinets are curved, and become in consequence constructively weak; drawing room tables are curved in every direction—perpendicularly and horizontally—and are therefore inconvenient to sit at, and always rickety. This detestable ornamentation is called shaping."

The furniture illustrated and designed by Eastlake was a vaguely traditional rural style based on Early English forms, somewhat Elizabethan and somewhat early Jacobean, uncomfortable but marked by sound joinery. It was simple, rectangular and practically without ornament, with a rough Gothic quality which no doubt prompted J. Moyr Smith to write later in 1887: "perhaps in decoration it was too simple . . . and in construction too much like a packing case." Regardless, it became fashionable and such was the influence of his book, for he was regarded as the chief theorist of the Art movement, that furniture produced in this manner is frequently called Eastlake. In America the furniture trade produced a debased Gothic which was far different from Eastlake's illustrations (520, 521).

Another exponent of the Early English style was Bruce Talbert (1838–1881), probably the most influential designer specializing in furniture and decoration of the whole of this period. In 1867 he published his GOTHIC FORMS APPLIED TO FURNITURE which soon found its way to the leading English designers and cabinetmakers, and countless imitations, sometimes with improvements, were everywhere made. Nine years later he published EXAMPLES OF ANCIENT AND MODERN FURNITURE in which he abandoned the Gothic for the Jacobean. In the introduction to his first book he explains why he admires the Gothic method of furniture making and why he dislikes modern cabinetwork, for "it is to the use of glue that we are indebted for the false construction modern work indulges in; the glue leads to veneering and veneering to polish." He regarded the entrance hall, dining room and library to be especially suitable for massive work in the Gothic style and which by contrast he observes will "give greater value to the elegance and lightness necessary for the drawing room." He gave numerous designs for sideboards because "being a chief piece of furniture they should receive greatest attention." Frequently his sideboards had a high back "for the purpose of displaying plate, china or porcelain." On several of his more ambitious exhibition pieces he combined enamel plaques and relief panels of figure subjects covered with

metal deposits. "The effect of this kind of decoration," according to Talbert, "was one of great richness and delicacy" and was much more enduring than the usual painted decoration. Talbert used a copper deposit of this nature on a magnificent oak sideboard which won for him his first medal at the International Exhibition held in Paris in 1867. It was made by Holland and Son and its smaller companion piece belongs to the Victoria and Albert Museum (484). Probably the classic of this period and a piece constantly illustrated at the time is Talbert's Pet sideboard with inset panels of carved boxwood and bearing a Latin inscription translated as "It is better to be summoned to a dish of herbs with love than to a fatted calf with hate." (485) The use of quotations that conveyed a mood or showed the function of the furniture no doubt stemmed in part from the strong literary attitude which was widespread in England in the second half of the nineteenth century. This fashion for the use of texts on furniture was by no means confined to England (529).

The architect and designer William Burges (1827–1881), who revived the Gothic in a highly personal style, inscribed *Venez laver* on the cold tap of a carved, painted and giltwood washstand which he designed for the guest chamber at Tower House, Melbury Road, London, 1875–1881, his own house which he built and decorated "as a model residence of the fifteenth century." The top bowl and soap dishes were of marble, the bowl being inset with silver fishes and a butterfly; the back and water tank were set with small mirrors and the taps and fittings were of bronze (486). The colorful and fanciful interpretation of

Gothic by Burges had little effect on Victorian furniture as he very seldom designed furniture other than for his clients or for his own house. Like Philip Webb, Burges designed one or two relatively plain pieces which left large smooth areas to be decorated by artists. One of these is a plain cabinet painted under his direction by E. H. Poynter which depicts the battle between the Wines and Beers. It was shown at the International Exhibition held in London in 1862, and marked the first occasion that Burges exhibited his furniture (487).

The solid joined construction of medieval times gradually gave way to an important influence from the East—the art of Japan, as Japanese wares in the form of prints, pottery and lacquer began to make their appearance in English shops shortly after 1862, the year Japan first participated in an International Exhibition. Throughout the 1860's and right up to the 1890's the general public's fast-rising interest in all things Japanese was stimulated by many books, pamphlets and magazine articles. Hand in hand with the fashion for Japanism was an interest of a more ephemeral kind for Turkish, Persian, Egyptian, Indian and Moorish art.

Probably the strongest exponent of Japanese art in England was Edward William Godwin (1833–1886) who was a friend and admirer of Burges and had started his career as a Gothic revival architect. Widely admired by the public of his day, he designed quantities of furniture not only for individual clients but for the trade, working for such firms as William Watt, Gillows of Lancaster and Collison and Lock.

Godwin as well as other contemporary designers saw in Japanese art with its highly expressive line and color and its disdain of symmetry, a chance to break the bonds of Historicism. They found in Japan a new unexplored world, an uncorrupted culture based on a different structure of thought. This revelation was to have far-reaching consequences. In brief, Japan gave them the opportunity to discover what they were seeking; it was not the parent but the godparent of the Modern movement. With respect to furniture Godwin produced new forms which, with their light rectilinear structure combined with a carefully calculated balance of form, were conditioned by oriental precepts (488, 489). In his book, ART FURNITURE, WITH HINTS AND SUGGESTIONS ON DOMESTIC FURNITURE AND DECORATION (1877) Godwin includes numerous pieces of furniture in what he calls Anglo-Japanese, all distinctive for the same rectilinear construction. The fact that a Japanese house had no furniture in the Western conception, as the Japanese live on mat level, was unimportant to Godwin. He realized that Japanese aestheticism preached the gospel of simplification as no other country did.

Thus either directly or indirectly may be attributed to the influence of Japanese art certain trends in furniture design which were to set their seal on the style of the 1890's, such as an interest in simple and rectilinear structure, a feeling for the light and airy, a more sparing use of ornament which when used contrasted effectively and clearly with the smooth surface that forms the background, and perhaps above all the values of the elegant and refined use of line.

Godwin's importance in the Aesthetic movement of the 1870's and 1880's, which like the Pre-Raphaelite movement was an expression against the current

Philistinism, has always been fully acknowledged. Founded and built on the axiom *l'art pour l'art* the aesthetes tried to make out that the only thing in life worth taking seriously was aesthetic satisfaction. The aesthetes were enchanted by the artistic charm of Japan, the Medievalism of Morris, the ideals of Ruskin, the elegance of Wilde and the free treatment of artistic ways of expression followed by Whistler.

The symbols of the movement—the lily (purity), the peacock (beauty), and the sunflower (constancy)—were much in evidence in decorative art until the trial of Oscar Wilde at Old Bailey in 1895, which banished him to oblivion. Although the symbols and other manifestations of the movement—"blue and white" or Nanking ware, introduced from Paris to London by Whistler, fans consciously disposed, furniture of bamboo, genuine or in imitation of, at times quite spidery and flimsy, and wickerwork furniture from palmstands to bookcases—are what is chiefly associated with it, there can scarcely be any doubt that in spite of everything that may be said against it, the force of the movement did much to promote a general interest in art and design.

The fashion for research into the antique and the cultivation of the past in the 19th century brought with it a tendency that was to grow into a respect and desire for furniture of early times, at least for furniture before 1830, before the age of Industrialism. Soon the fashion for collecting ceased to be the exclusive prerogative of the rich and was avidly pursued by the middle class. The taste for antiques referred to in contemporary writings as "a modern freak of fashion" grew by leaps and bounds. Antiques became a profitable business, the forger entered the field. Almost overnight the manufacture of antiques became a modern industry. Some of these fine quality, exact reproductions made in the closing decades of Queen Victoria's reign have acquired such a fine patina through the years that they would at first sight even deceive an expert.

Then too, English as well as Continental cabinetmakers liked to enrich plain pieces of furniture to make them more decorative, therefore more costly and saleable. Commenting on this practice the PALL MALL GAZETTE in 1876 writes, "There are many workmen in London who are mainly or wholly employed in enriching goods for the old furniture market. . . . The vendor probably tells his customer but the truth. He says that the furniture is old; and so it is. There is nothing new about it except the bits of decoration here and there which do not make up a hundredth part of its bulk, though they may increase its price twenty fold." Many of these English pieces which received this "enriching" one hundred years ago are most deceptive and their decoration has frequently passed as original.

ARTS AND CRAFTS MOVEMENT

In the last third of the 19th century there was a strong movement in all the countries of Europe to rejuvenate the arts and crafts. It was in England and France that the work of handling these problems systematically first began, as both countries, rich in artistic traditions, had old and reputable arts and crafts to maintain. The English Arts and Crafts movement differed essentially from the

French movement in that the former was more associated with the Middle Ages, not in form but in spirit. This developed from the art theories and ideals of Pugin, Ruskin and Morris, the triad of the Gothic revival in England. Morris was the most important single contributor, as the movement grew from Morris's insistence on the joy of the creative process.

A special feature of the English Arts and Crafts movement of the 1880's and 1890's was the establishment of guilds to raise the general standard of design through a more intimate cooperation between artist and craftsman. The Century Guild founded in 1882 by A. H. Mackmurdo (1851–1942) and Selwyn Image (1849–1930) was the first of a series of English societies of designers and craftsmen. It was followed in 1884 by the Art Workers' Guild with Walter Crane (1845–1915) and Lewis F. Day (1845–1910) as its leading originators, and in 1885 by a small organization, The Home Arts and Industries Association, which was especially interested in rural crafts and in which Mackmurdo was also actively engaged. The Guild of Handicraft started in 1888 and the short-lived Kenton and Company (1890–1892), which was a success artistically but not financially, were others. It can scarcely be surprising that from these associations of talented and individual designers different trends developed. However, although individual members were developing their own personal styles, it was not possible to work in complete isolation, as the frequency of the exhibitions and the innumerable writings by the members of the movement on all aspects of design helped to unite the movement and establish its aims.

The comprehensive term, Arts and Crafts, signifying the arts of decorative design and handicraft, came into general use when the Arts and Crafts Exhibition Society was founded in 1888, with Walter Crane the first chairman and the committee members including William Morris and Burne-Jones. The aims of the Society were outlined by Morris in the preface to a book, THE ARTS AND CRAFTS ESSAYS (1893), "Our art is the work of a small minority composed of educated persons, fully conscious of their aim of producing beauty and distinguished from the great body of workmen by the possession of that aim. . . . It is this conscious cultivation of art and the attempt to interest the public in it which the Arts and Crafts Exhibition Society has set itself to help by calling special attention to that really most important side of art, the decoration of utilities by furnishing them with genuine artistic finish in place of trade finish. . . . "

The Arts and Crafts movement encouraged a number of architects such as Leathaby, Voysey, Ashbee, Gimson and the Barnsleys to design furniture; it even encouraged a most notable example in the furniture trade itself, Sir Ambrose Heal (1872–1959). It is erroneous to believe that all the members of these organizations subscribed completely to the Ruskin-Morris school of thought. There were a number of designers such as John Sedding (1837–1891) and Christopher Dresser (1834–1904) who adopted a commercial attitude to their work and designed for machine production. But unfortunately for the growth of industrial design in England, they welcomed the machine only halfheartedly; they acknowledged it only because they felt it was futile to rebel against the inevitable. The real pioneers of the Modern movement are those who from the start stood for machine art. True to innate English conservatism, Morris and those who came after him refused any drastic break in tradition. Nevertheless it is invariably recognized that the Modern movement was built on the results which Morris and the English school had achieved from the 1860's to the mid-1890's when the initiative passed from England to America and the Continent, and after a short period to Germany. The Werkbund, composed chiefly of young architects and craftsmen, was set up in Germany in 1907. To this group the horror of the machine was unknown. The Design and Industries Association established in England in 1915 acknowledged the program developed by the Werkbund, stating in its JOURNAL in 1916 that it was "accepting the machine in its proper place, as a device to be guided and controlled not merely boycotted."

The attitude to the machine of the English school was certainly responsible for many beautiful things, especially in furniture presented by the Arts and Crafts Exhibition Society from 1888 to 1914. The original work of such men as Gimson, Scott, the Barnsleys, Walton, Ashbee and Voysey was frequently exhibited on the Continent where it was much admired for its good taste and reticence; in Italy such names as Stile Liberty and Stile Inglese were given to the Arts and Crafts work, showing that its influence was considerable abroad. Once again England became a leader in artistic cabinetwork. It must be confessed, however, that this extremely simple and constructive style of furniture which provided the impetus for the development on the Continent just after the turn of the century was little known to the British public of its own day. Ultimately an enthusiasm for Arts and Crafts inspired work led to great quantities of cheap, commercially produced fumed oak, as a substitute for the relatively limited number of these admirable but costly pieces. So in spite of their failure to produce furniture which could be bought as they had hoped by the great mass of furniture buyers, the designers within the Arts and Crafts movement created a new and significant style.

This new style of English furniture, referred to in contemporary accounts as the work of "that school of modern British designers," was so popular and so much imitated on the Continent that English cabinetmakers taking advantage of this situation shipped quantities of this furniture across the Channel. The cabinetwork of such firms as Liberty and J. S. Henry could be bought in Paris, Rome, Berlin or Vienna.

It is possible to consider here only some of the more prominent members who made the most original and influential contributions to the work of the 20th century. Among the most enterprising was Ernest Gimson (1864–1920) who together with the Barnsleys—Sidney (1865–1926) and Ernest (1863–1926) —retreated in the early 1890's from London to the Cotswolds, where it seems craftsmanship survived with more vigor than in other parts of England. The Cotswold school of furniture designers was the link between the English rural traditions of craftsmanship and the ideas of Morris. They were guided by the principles of Morris in their designing and they practiced them in their workshops. Though Gimson never actually executed any of his designs and made nothing himself but the turned ash chairs, he worked closely with his craftsmen (490). Simplicity of form, soundness of construction, and an unerring judgment in the selection of woods used are the chief characteristics of Gimson's work. The sound oak furniture made by the Barnsleys clearly acknowledges their debt to the designs of Ford Madox Brown and Philip Webb for joiner-made furniture. In 1902 Gimson and Ernest Barnsley opened workshops at Daneway House, Sapperton (491). The partnership was of short duration, lasting only a year or two, because the latter returned to practice as an architect. Sidney Barnsley, who never participated in the venture, maintained a small workshop nearby. After Gimson's death, the Daneway House workshops were closed, but craftsmen to this day keep his traditions alive in the Cotswolds. The unquestioned leader of these craftsmen is Edward Barnsley (b. 1900), son of Sidney Barnsley, whose workshop at Petersfield has produced furniture inspired by the best traditions in English design.

The precursor of the Cotswold school was Kenton and Company. All the members of this Arts and Crafts enterprise were young architects, and except for Sir Reginald Blomfield, the others—Ernest Gimson, Mervyn Macartney, Sidney Barnsley and W. R. Leathaby—ultimately gave up architecture for their craft. Perhaps the most significant contribution to the work of Kenton and Company was made by Leathaby (1857–1931) who was later to become principal of the Central School of Arts and Crafts in London. A great sideboard of unpolished oak inlaid with unpolished ebony, bleached mahogany and sycamore is representative of his work (492).

In 1888 the architect and designer Charles Ashbee (1863–1942) founded at London his Guild and School of Handicraft, with himself as chief designer in all media. Later in 1904 he moved his school to Chipping Camden in the Cotswolds. The earliest pieces made by the Guild of Handicraft were extremely simple in form and in effect differ very little from their predecessors, the so-called Art Furniture.

Probably because Ashbee recognized the hopelessness of the struggle against the forces of modern industry, he wrote in his last book that "modern civilization rests on machinery, and no system for the encouragement or the endowment of the teaching of the arts can be sound that does not recognize this," which is one of the basic premises of the Modern movement.

Charles F. A. Voysey (1857–1941), generally regarded as the most important and probably the most imitated designer before and at the turn of the century, demonstrated his versatility in the crafts—wallpaper, textiles and furniture—at the Arts and Crafts Exhibition Society of 1896. Some of his work was at the same time the most original and the most reticent at the exhibition. His furniture, like the interiors of the houses he designed, was light, airy and plain, revealing the importance of Japanese influence on his work. Voysey realized that simplicity was not easy to achieve; he expressed this idea in the incomparable phrase, "Simplicity requires perfection in all details, while elaboration is easy in comparison with it." He suggested, "Let us begin by discarding the mass of useless ornaments and banishing the millinery that degrades our furniture and fittings." The uncluttered character of his interiors inspired Continental designers. A strong vertical feeling permeates his designs. His simple furniture was made of plain oak which he frequently left unstained and unpolished, a practice he shared with designers of the Arts and Crafts movement. Voysey was especially fond of a simplified heart-shaped motif. Heart-shaped escutcheons, strap hinges terminating in hearts, and hearts cut out in the splats of his splat-back chairs are typically Voysey (493, 494). His feeling for materials and his simplicity of form furnished the initial inspiration for such English and Scottish designers as Charles Rennie Mackintosh (1868–1928), George Walton (1867–1933) and M. H. Baillie-Scott (1865–1945). The furniture made in Glasgow in the 1890's by the Scottish architect Mackintosh and the Glasgow school was the most original of any at this time, and will be treated in a later chapter.

Furniture designed by the architect George Walton owes something to the Glasgow school, but much more to the English school. From the time he opened his own decorating firm in Glasgow in 1888, his furniture was in general commercial production. In addition to his own firm, furniture from his designs was made by Liberty's and various furniture makers at High Wycombe such as William Birch. His furniture forms, pleasantly simple, reveal a penchant for constructive elements and an economy of ornament (495).

The English architect Baillie-Scott, whose work combined sound craftsmanship and a fresh approach was perhaps the best known of all English designers on the Continent, particularly in Germany where he had decorated the palace of the Grand Duke of Hesse at Darm-stadt. One of his favorite devices was to decorate the flat surfaces of his basically simple but rather massive forms of furniture with elaborate stylized natural motifs, executed in relief, in colored woods, mother-of-pearl, ivory and pewter (496, 497).

There was also the work of the architect Arthur Mackmurdo (1851–1942), one of the leading personalities of the Arts and Crafts movement, who, though less important than his friend Voysey, occasionally revealed a fresh and imaginative approach to design. The carved back of a chair he designed in 1881 with its swirling composition of flamelike leaves anticipated the ornament associated with Art Nouveau by about a decade. Mackmurdo's best designs were his simplest; his most original designs were entirely without ornament depending for their beauty on the strong contrasts of verticals and horizontals. His writing table foreshadows the Modern movement and the 20th century (498).

In summarizing this long period which covered almost a century it is apparent that a great deal of trouble had been taken to move away from Historicism. Through a host of talented men—the Pre-Raphaelites, Morris, Webb, Madox-Brown, Cole, Godwin, Dresser, Leathaby, Gimson, Voysey, and others—a simple sober style of furniture essentially rectilinear had been evolved on traditional grounds based on an honest use of materials and honest principles of joinery. In ornament, imitation that naturalistically produced the world of flowers was gradually abandoned, passing by way of stylization to simplification. It is easy therefore to understand that to the English school the Continental Art Nouveau with its sinuous lines and realistic floral motifs was like seed falling on stony ground. After the enthusiasm for Art Nouveau had dimmed on the Continent, the sober and austere aspects of the English style which Van de Velde praised in his DIE RENAISSANCE (1903) for its "systematic discarding of ornament" was zealously cultivated and developed.

With all its faults the Victorian age was an age of progress and of outstanding men who furnished the initial source of inspiration for the international style of the 20th century. Without the English impetus the subsequent creative work in Europe and the United States seems inconceivable. In their work is seen their hopes to make a fresh start. No matter how deeply Morris mourned the death of the past, he held to the belief that "all the change and stir about us is a sign of the world's life . . . it will lead—by ways, indeed, of which we have no guess —to the bettering of all mankind." (THE LESSER ARTS, 1877) No one today disputes the basic premise on which his life was built—that beautiful things should be within the reach of everyone who wants them.

CHAPTER TWENTY FOUR

AMERICAN VICTORIAN

LATE CLASSICAL
(1815–1840)

Furniture design throughout the Victorian period was one of many revivals of past styles which followed the fashion for research into the antique and was accompanied by a general decline in standards of taste as a result of the breakup of the old order of society in the new industrial age. For the most part there is no reliable rule for differentiating late Empire from early Victorian furniture. From around 1830 the already declining American Empire style showed a progressive coarsening, as the structure of furniture tended to become heavier and the carving and turning less refined. However, not all American Empire, even the early, is free from coarseness, nor all the late lacks refinement.

Furniture of the Late Classical period (1815–1840) was predicated mainly upon the plates of the English and French design books of the early nine-

teenth century and to a limited extent upon the actual pieces of imported furniture. However, the English designs are often of French inspiration as the French had long influenced taste all over Europe. Thomas Hope, in his introduction to HOUSEHOLD FURNITURE AND INTERIOR DECORATION (1807), acknowledges his indebtedness to France, and George Smith in his CABINET MAKER AND UPHOLSTERER'S GUIDE (1826) illustrates furniture designs in "The French Taste." It was from Smith that the important cabinet making firm of Joseph Meeks and Sons, active in New York City from 1797 to 1868, culled the more elaborate French examples in their advertisement of 1833. This print, which shows more than forty designs for furniture, is the earliest American publication of complete designs, as formerly only details were given in the cabinet-makers' price books (Figure 499). The designs show certain features found in the French furniture of the 1820's—large smooth surfaces devoid of ornament, free-standing columns and C and S scroll supports. The final interpretation of the Empire style was recorded by John Hall of Baltimore in THE CABINET MAKERS' ASSISTANT, EMBRACING THE MOST MODERN STYLE OF CABINET FURNITURE (1840), comprising one hundred and ninety-eight figures arranged on forty-four plates. A marked feature of the designs was the monotonous repetition of massive scrolled supports, said to be based on Grecian scrolls. Hall mentions in his introduction the great variety of scrolls, which would permit the furniture maker to produce furniture more economically.

In the decade following the War of 1812 a number of French cabinetmakers were working in New York, Boston, Philadelphia, Charleston and New Orleans. One of the earliest and most celebrated of the émigré cabinetmakers was Charles-Honoré Lannuier (1779–1819), who arrived in 1803 in New York City where he became one of the leading exponents of the French Empire style. There was also the Paris-born cabinetmaker Anthony G. Quervelle (1789–1856) who was working before 1817 in Philadelphia. He enjoyed the patronage not only of his compatriots, comprising a group of wealthy French families, who, dissatisfied with conditions in France, had been settling in the Quaker City since the days of the French Revolution, but also of the occupants of the White House. In the late 1820's he made a pair of pier tables for the dining room there. By 1846 Quervelle was listed in Watson's ANNALS OF PHILADELPHIA as a man of wealth, worth more than $75,000. Michel Bouvier, a contemporary of Quervelle, enjoyed similar success in Philadelphia from the time of his arrival in 1815 until his business was dissolved in 1861.

Among his patrons were the Philadelphia merchant Stephen Girard and Joseph Bonaparte, former King of Spain. In 1818 Bouvier was given the position of furnishing Bonaparte's house at Point Breeze, near Bordentown, New Jersey.

EARLY VICTORIAN

Victorian Classical, or Victorian Empire as it is sometimes called, was composed of the solid simple mahogany forms of the 1820's (500, 501, 502). Favored by the furniture trade, these sound pieces with little or no ornament remained in vogue into the early 1850's. Jackson Downing (1815–1852), who was an ardent admirer of J. C. Loudon and relied heavily on his ENCYCLOPAEDIA, an indebtedness he gratefully acknowledged, maintained in his ARCHITECTURE FOR COUNTRY HOUSES (1850) that the Classical or Grecian style as Loudon called it was by far the most popular for private residences. Typical of this classical taste were chairs that were modified forms of the Greek klismos, sofas inspired by the Greek couch or day bed with outscrolled ends and "French" beds (*lit en bateau* or boat bed) similar in form to a Greek sofa, placed lengthwise against the wall and intended to be seen from the side, with a single pole projecting from the wall above at a right angle, over which fabric was draped.

Of the picturesque styles there were two that were favored by the furniture trade—Gothic and Elizabethan. Downing had high regard for the Gothic, and in his ARCHITECTURE FOR COUNTRY HOUSES (1850) discusses the style in detail and gives illustrations of Gothic furniture available in America. All of it was recognizable as Gothic by the ornament or decorative detail only, for the structure was of simple classic form. Some of his illustrations were astonishingly simple, while others were elaborately carved with all the popular Gothic motifs— pointed arches, tracery, trefoils, quatrefoils, crockets, pinnacles and buttresses. He observed that the style was not as popular in America as in England and that the usual objection to furniture designed in this taste is the over-elaboration of ornament. An anonymous publication, GOTHIC ALBUM FOR CABINET MAKERS (1868), suggests that the style lingered on.

The influence of the Gothic style was much more evident in American architecture than in furniture design. Much of the most successful American Gothic furniture was designed by architects, such as William Strickland, Charles Notman, Thomas U. Walter (who together with Nicholas Biddle designed Andalusia), and Alexander J. Davis. The latter was perhaps the most prolific designer of Gothic furniture. Not only did Davis design ecclesiastical furniture for churches, but also domestic pieces for private houses, such as the furnishings for Lyndhurst. A side chair from Davis' own house, probably Kerri cottage, is in the collection of the Museum of the City of New York, a gift from Davis' son. Among the better-known cabinetmakers working in this style was John Jelliff (1813–1893) of Newark, New Jersey, who was active from around 1836 to 1890. His furniture, mainly in rosewood and walnut, was notable for its carvings (503). There was also John Needles of Baltimore (1786–1878) who worked from around 1812 to 1853. He is chiefly known for his work in the Sheraton, Empire and Early Victorian styles.

Like the Gothic, the Victorian Elizabethan style was more popular in England than in America, but the Victorians on both sides of the Atlantic Ocean were equally vague about the application of the description "Elizabethan," for example, in chairs, which although they included some of the decorative detail associated with this Renaissance period, were most of the time in a style which was not fashionable until the reign of Charles II, some seventy years later. The shape truly derives from the high-back chairs of the late 17th century, the Baroque Charles II and William and Mary styles, while spirally turned members are typically Baroque. An extant example with an ornately carved and pierced back panel recalls the designs of Daniel Marot who worked in England for several years in the service of William III (504). This type of short-legged chair was very fashionable in America and England where it was variously described as devotional, prie-dieu or vesper.

MID·VICTORIAN

No doubt the most popular style for furniture and decoration in America was the French Rococo, the Louis XV style, which flourished from around the mid-19th century for several decades. Unlike the other revived styles whose basic proportions were similar, though the applied ornament varied, this revived French style was structural; that is to say, the actual members of chairs and tables were composed of Baroque scrolls (505) and Rococo curves, the latter very much predominating (506). French Rococo characterized by its cabriole leg, sinuous curves and asymmetrical ornament was especially favored for the drawing room, and judging by the number of pieces that still exist, a great amount of it must have been made. Perhaps the most familiar of all Rococo forms was the balloon-back chair (507, 508).

The best-known exponent of the Revived Rococo style in America was the cabinetmaker John Henry Belter (d. 1863) who served his apprenticeship in Württenberg, Germany, before settling in New York City where he was first listed in the Directory for 1844. The beautiful lace-like quality of his opulent and naturalistic carvings of flowers and grapes intermingled with scrolls of interlacing foliage were skillfully executed from a piece of laminated wood, a technique which had its beginnings in antiquity. Belter's laminating process which he patented in 1856 consisted of building up thin layers of wood with the grain of the wood in every other layer running in the opposite direction, or laminated, as the method is called. The number of layers varied from 3 to 16; however, the customary number were 6 to 8 and the total thickness generally measured less than one inch. These layers were glued and pressed together and steamed in a special mold to produce the necessary curves to give the parts their shape. The layers of veneer were then ready for carvings. At the present time Belter's laminated rosewood pieces are highly prized as examples of a local style (509). A successful rival of Belter's using the laminating technique was Charles A. Baudouine who was working in New York City from around 1845 to 1900. His cabinetshop employed approximately 200 workers, of whom 70 were trained cabinetmakers. Baudouine's unpublished notebook of reminiscences, now in the library of the Winterthur Museum, relates how he circumvented infringement of Belter's patent by running a division through the center of his laminations, whereas Belter's were of single panel form. There was also Elijah Galusha (1804–1871) who moved to Troy around 1830. Working at first in the Sheraton and Empire styles, he later turned to the more fashionable Revived Rococo and Renaissance styles, which he executed in mahogany and rosewood. His realistically carved furniture compares favorably with that of John Belter and was highly esteemed in upstate New York. Still another cabinetmaker producing laminated furniture was George Henkels of Philadelphia. In 1853 he advertised "Furniture in every style, Louis XIV, Louis XV, Elizabethan and Antique with sculpture carving; and Modern style in Rosewood, Walnut, Mahogany, Satinwood and Maple." In one of his advertisments (1857) Henkels stated that "Walnut is now more used than all others. The supply of mahogany and rosewood is fast diminishing, maple has not met with much favor. Oak is in great favor for dining and library furniture." The elaborate carvings on his rosewood furniture were executed by "the best European artists."

It is interesting to note here that from around 1840 native black walnut long out of vogue once again became a fashionable wood.

In fact walnut was so widely accepted as the only wood suitable for the great and highly respected middle class, that by 1876 a critic of aesthetics depressed by the "dark look" injected a bit of rank heresy into bourgeois thinking when he questioned "whether the goodness and cheapness of black walnut had not led us into making our rooms too somber and heavy for a cheerful life."

Other leading cabinetmakers working in the Victorian Rococo include Léon Marcotte, Alexander Roux, the Meeks Brothers and Gustav Herter—all from New York, Daniel Pabst and Gottlieb Vollmer of Philadelphia, and François Seignouret and Prudent Mallard of New Orleans. The French-born Mallard (1809–1879) came to New York where he stayed briefly before settling in New Orleans in 1838. Working in the Rococo and Renaissance styles he is probably best known for his large pieces such as imposing armoires and towering poster beds with a half tester. François Seignouret, also born in France (1768), is generally regarded as the leading cabinetmaker of New Orleans where he settled in 1815 and operated a cabinetshop from 1822 until 1853, when he returned to Bordeaux. His furniture, which is scarce and in great demand, includes the favorite armoire and a Seignouret chair of gondola form with a splat back.

Still another style called the Renaissance, which turned to the classical world for its inspiration, developed around the mid-19th century. As early as the mid-1830's designs for furniture in the Cinquecento and François Premier styles were described and illustrated in pattern books that featured various current styles. The Renaissance style was evident in the Great Exhibition held in London in 1851 and two years later at the Crystal Palace Exhibition held in New York City. It continued to be admired and used in the Centennial Exhibition held in Philadelphia in 1876. Essentially it has the characteristics of a composite style and ran the gamut of

classical ornament, particularly that deriving from 16th century Italian or French Renaissance, the 17th century Baroque style of Louis XIV and the 18th century Neo-Classic style of Louis XVI. Among its easy-to-recognize features were such architectural details as pediments, generally arched or broken arched, appearing on sideboards (510); Louis XIV style tapering baluster-shaped legs with capitals seen on chairs (511), and tables (512); Louis XIV style scroll supports joined by an X-form scrolled stretcher frequently centering a classical urn seen on drawing room center tables. Also readily recognizable as Victorian Renaissance was the Louis XVI style commode or low cupboard which incorporates at each end a cupboard or shelves shaped to a quarter circle, full or re-entrant, to soften its boxlike appearance, as the rounded ends link the façade with the wall against which it is placed (513). Probably the word "florid" summarizes visually the Victorian Renaissance style. Some of this furniture, which borrowed heavily from the French Louis XVI (514) is also called Revived Louis XVI style, which illustrates only too well the confusion that surrounds an attempt to separate stylistically the Victorian revivals. Especially well-known in New York City for their furniture in the Revived Renaissance style were the cabinetmakers Léon Marcotte and Thomas Brooks (1811–1887) who was active in Brooklyn around the 1860's and 1870's. There were also the Christian brothers, Gustav and Herter, the latter exhibited at the Crystal Palace Exhibition held in New York in 1853. In nearby Newark worked John Jeliff, while furniture in the Victorian Renaissance style made in the Philadelphia workshop of Daniel Pabst is highly esteemed. The style was popularized by the furniture manufacturers of Grand Rapids. Of these, especially notable was Berkey and Gay who exhibited a set of Victorian Renaissance bedroom furniture at the Centennial Exhibition held in Philadelphia in 1876.

By 1853 the United States was ready for its own exhibition, named in compliment to its predecessor The New York Crystal Palace. Only one-fifth the size of its prototype, it was still the largest building attempted in the United States up to that time. Before it was five years old it was completely destroyed by fire, but during its brief existence European manufacturers sent to it spectacular examples of cabinetwork, ambitious exhibition pieces intended for display and not for use. It is doubtless for this reason that pieces in which usefulness was paramount or which were of unusually simple designs, obviously ahead of their times, excited no particular comment. To this latter category belongs a rocking chair made in brass tube, upholstered in plush, shown by R. W. Winfield of Birmingham at the Great Exhibition of 1851. The same chair in strap metal, which may have been made later by Peter Cooper, is in the collection of the Cooper Hewitt Museum (515). The exhibits of the American Chair Company at the Great Exhibition of 1851 were particularly enlightening, as they showed how the technically adventurous was expressed in artistic terms. The typical Victorian bulginess was applied to a chair of iron framework "with patent centripetal springs and railroad-car seats . . . capable of almost universal movement." Then too there were many prosaic objects like invalids' chairs of straightforward functional design.

Mention has been made in the preceding chapter that a marked feature of the Victorian period was a determined and continuous search for new materials, not necessarily new in themselves, but made available for the first time in furniture making. For example, in furniture wood was frequently replaced by cast iron, which in America was most commonly employed for garden furniture and umbrella stands. A considerable amount of brass furniture was also made in America in the 19th century. Still another category of metal furniture was made of twisted wire, notable for the lightness of its interesting and unusual designs (516).

The generation of the exhibition also welcomed aesthetically furniture made from organic materials. In this category is a wicker or cane chair made by John Tuph of New York exhibited at the Great Exhibition of 1851. Wicker furniture became widely popular in the United States later in the 19th century and there must have been an appreciable export trade. The LONDON FURNITURE GAZETTE of 1882 reports "A London Depot of American Furniture," which was packed like "solid timber" to save transport costs and was fitted and finished on its arrival in England. One of the American specialties was "Rattan" or cane furniture which was sold to the public by several London West End houses. Closely related to wicker furniture is that made from bamboo, an organic material.

The Victorian penchant for the picturesque manifested itself in rustic furniture in which the actual materials of Nature were used, the curves of stems and branches often possessing the scrolled and swelling character which was a marked feature of furniture made at this time. Furniture in the rustic taste simply carries on and expands a practice already established in 18th century English design when it was recommended for garden buildings. Chippendale in the THIRD EDITION OF THE DIRECTOR (1762) illustrates a seat and two chairs. Three years later Manwaring in the CABINET AND CHAIR MAKER'S REAL FRIEND shows a number of rustic seats; they were to be made "with the limbs of Yews and Apple trees as Nature produces them."

Perhaps the most striking example of Victorian naturalism is the furniture made from animal horns. No doubt it owed its popularity among Victorians to a set of staghorn furniture comprising a settee, chair and round table planned for a hunting lodge or baronial mansion exhibited at the Great Exhibition of 1851 by a firm from Hamburg. The furniture captivated Queen Victoria, who ordered a set for Balmoral made from trophies of Prince Albert's prowess. A strong note of sentimentality also dictated the staghorn furniture made in America. Two Presidents—Abraham Lincoln and Theodore Roosevelt—both received furniture made of animal horns from their admirers. The latter's home at Sagamore Hill at Oyster Bay, Long Island, still has several chairs of horn (517).

During this period the art of the upholsterer figured prominently as the improvements in metal coil springs made in the first half of the nineteenth century and the increased production of fabrics made possible by the new power looms brought into existence a new class of comfortable seat furniture with deep-sprung buttoned upholstery. In America totally upholstered furniture with no trace of framework visible and which re-

lied for effect on the rich elaboration of the upholstery belongs to the period beginning around 1870. In the Turkish frame type of chair and sofa, when the back, arms and seats were all sprung, upholstery became an art (518). The forms of totally upholstered furniture were essentially similar throughout the period and often associated with foreign design and craftsmanship. Certain firms claimed superiority of their upholstery over that of other manufacturers as they employed French and German upholsterers. Apart from the short-legged easy chair which exemplifies the constant Victorian search for comfort, the most distinctive new form of upholstered seat was the ottoman. Designed to accommodate several persons it was given a commanding position in the center of the drawing room. Its form was borrowed from the French *borne*, having a round or oval seat with a cone-shaped or cylindrical-shaped back rest, the top of which very often served for the reception of a vase of flowers, a palm or a marble sculpture (519). There were also various kinds of conversation seats, joined on an S-plan and so enabling people to sit facing each other, which went by such names as sociable, tête-à-tête or confidante.

The interiors of the mid-19th century period were filled with the products of an expanding industrial system and show the typical Victorian dislike of plain surfaces. The walls were covered with a boldly patterned paper and this in its turn was covered with pictures of assorted sizes; the carpet and the chair covers were patterned as well, and the woodwork, fireplace and gasolier were richly ornamental. Besides this multiplication of decoration, the chief characteristic is solidity of workmanship, often misapplied to the imitation of one material by another. This was the age of comfort and horsehair stuffing, of the grainer and of the decorative papier-mâché furniture of the Great Exhibition of 1851, much of which was imported into this country, as it appears to have been made here only in a very limited quantity.

AFTER THE MID-NINETEENTH CENTURY

To a remarkable Victorian, William Morris, must be given credit for creating the movement which effected a reform in public taste. Most persons had no chance to see, much less to own, any of the furniture which was produced under his supervision as it was far too costly for the average purse. Nevertheless his ideas eventually had real influence on all the arts of decoration. Had the later part of the Victorian era followed Morris' famous rule, "Have nothing in your house that you do not know to be useful or believe to be beautiful," it might have been spared much of the censure heaped upon it for its incredible lack of taste.

The gospel of "the beautiful" was first imported to the Americans in 1872 from the pages of a book, HINTS ON HOUSEHOLD TASTE, by Charles Lock Eastlake, originally published in England in 1868. Eastlake's ideas had tremendous influence, and every young couple with any pretense to culture owned a copy which they studied avidly, as the problems were handled informally in order to win friends. To meet the public demand for this non-existent style, the furniture trade, after studying the sketches which

Eastlake had drawn to illustrate his ideas of simplicity and honesty in design and construction, set its machines to work and produced woeful parodies (520, 521).

Fifty-one countries brought their art manufactures to the Centennial Exhibition held in Philadelphia in 1876 to celebrate the anniversary of American independence. Before the exhibition closed almost ten million visitors saw them. The Oriental exhibits attracted enormous crowds, and as a result countless Japanese lacquered boxes, miniature pagodas, embroideries and fans were added to the astonishing collection of bric-a-brac displayed on the étagère in the high-ceilinged Victorian parlor. Practically all the visitors saw bamboo for the first time, which was used as part of the installation in the Japanese exhibits. They were delighted with this giant grass, which in itself is quite unique, and almost overnight articles made of bamboo or shaped in imitation of it became the rage. Painted, gilded or left in its natural finish, chairs, cabinets, all kinds of stands from flower stands to whatnots, were introduced in the midst of the somber massive walnut and oak furniture.

A noteworthy 19th century development in America was the interest in antique collecting, which, as in Europe, became more popular in this country as the century advanced. Though various reasons are given to explain the antiques craze, one excellent reason is that the Victorians were snobs; they invented the term. It was Thackeray who gave it its present significance. Snobbery does not flourish in a rigid society, like that of the 18th century where everyone could tell a duke by the star of some order on his coat, but only in a fluid society where a prosperous and rising middle class presses on the heels of an established aristocracy. It is a defense mechanism, a snobbish longing for an old established background which has sold countless ancestor portraits.

Inasmuch as in England the making of fine quality reproductions of 18th century furniture was continued in varying degrees throughout the entire 19th century, it may safely be suggested that in a general sense a similar condition existed in America as she had long been influenced by European fashions. From the 1870's onward high quality copies became exceedingly popular in England; about ten or more years later this fashion was taken up by prominent Victorian furniture makers in America.

The last three decades of Victoria's reign offered a melange of revivals, as virtually every historic period was explored for design inspiration. One of the most curious developments of the 1880's and 1890's was an interest in Orientalism of Near Eastern inspiration. This dates back to the Greek War of Independence, the conquest of Algiers, the increasing activity of French relations with Constantinople, Syria and Egypt, which offered a field to painters whose talents lay in the direction of colors and picturesqueness. As France began to expand into North Africa in the 1830's, the Moorish civilization and the exotic wild life of the region attracted such celebrated painters as Ferdinand Eugène Delacroix (1798–1863) who as a member of a mission to the Sultan of Morocco acquired first-hand knowledge of this part of the world. In his "Algerian Women" (1834) the life depicted in this scene is foreign to life in France, and provided those elements of romance that were fast fading from European civilization. In America the hot stillness of the inner room portrayed in the "Algerian Women" found its counterpart in the Turkish corner of the 1890's which used the cushion-heaped divan as its center of interest. Even the most romantic devotees soon lost patience with this pseudo Near Eastern atmosphere, the final 19th century manifestation of the taste for the picturesque.

It has been discussed in the preceding chapter how in England the Arts and Crafts movement of the 1880's which grew from the ideas of William Morris brought into existence a number of Craft guilds with an emphasis on group work. The American prototype was the Art Workers' Guild of Providence, Rhode Island. Here, according to the policy of cooperative work, individual members of the guild—designers, artists and cabinetmakers—combined their talents in the production of furniture. Among the outstanding members were the architect John G. Aldrich, the painter Charles B. Stetson, and the cabinetmaker Sidney Burleigh.

An interesting development and one in which America has cause to feel pride, is the Louis C. Tiffany Company, Associated Artists, formed in 1879, which followed the trail blazed by Morris and his followers. Launched as a guiding hand to improve taste in the arts of decoration and to restore an interest in them, it was a notable step forward. The group comprised Mrs. Candace Wheeler (1827–1923), John La Farge (1835–1910), Lockwood De Forest (1850–1932), Samuel Coleman and Louis Comfort Tiffany (1848–1933). They decorated interiors for many private homes and public buildings including the White House, in 1882–1883.

The painter and craftsman John La Farge, through his special talent as a lecturer and writer, exerted a fruitful influence on contemporary American thought. He made accessible and intelligible much of the culture of Europe and the Far East which he had gleaned during his sojourn abroad in the late 1850's, where on different occasions he had come in contact with the Pre-Raphaelites. As early as 1863 he imported Japanese prints to America.

He and the American architect Henry Hobson Richardson (1838–1886) were close friends and worked together on certain projects. Richardson also produced a considerable body of furniture designs, a fact seldom known by most of his admirers. Much of the furniture, however, was integral with the interior wood work of the churches, libraries and other public buildings he designed. Movable pieces still extant reveal their simple and sound construction and show their relationship to the furniture made by Morris' circle (522). Like Morris, Richardson was also trying to break the bonds of Historicism.

The furniture section at the Columbian Exhibition held in Chicago in 1893, which like the Philadelphia Centennial Exhibition of 1876 gave evidence to this country's prosperity, comprised contributions from practically every style including the exotic Moorish. A newcomer to the scene and one that won a prize was a piece of oak furniture made to serve several purposes, being provided with a slant front which when let down serves as a writing board, a cupboard portion, two drawers, a tier of shelves for books

and two flat surfaces for the display of bric-a-brac. This combination piece, usually called a secretary bookcase, was made by the Grand Rapids Chair Company. Only its asymmetrical form reveals its Continental Art Nouveau origin, as the obvious Art Nouveau decorative detail had been systematically removed through the influence of the Arts and Crafts movement (523). On the whole the image suggests American Mission, a turn of the century development, its introduction coinciding with a surge of interest in California and its Spanish-built missions. Essentially an offshoot of the Arts and Crafts movement, this furniture, which in spite of its name was more American than Franciscan, was inspired by the rustic aspect of the English Cotswold group. It was characterized by straight lines and relatively plain forms; much of it was made by the furniture trade at Grand Rapids. One of these was Gustav Stickley, designer, manufacturer and publisher of the magazine THE CRAFTSMAN. His Mission style furniture, called Craftsman, was known for its good design. Comparing favorably with the work of Stickley was that of Elbert Hubbard who founded the Roycrafters.

In 1902, at the Turin Exhibition where all Europe as well as America was represented, the furniture exhibited from England and America was distinctively different from the fanciful extravagances of Art Nouveau and stemmed from the trail blazed by the Arts and Crafts movement. The same year the Grand Rapids Record commented: "It is undeniable that the people of today desire their furniture plain, the popularity of the California and the so-called Mission effects furnish abundant evidence of this taste."

CHAPTER TWENTY FIVE

ART NOUVEAU

WHAT IS ART NOUVEAU?

Art Nouveau deals with the period at the turn of the century which brought into existence one of the most controversial movements in art. Enthusiastically acclaimed at the time of its inception, and then shortly after emphatically denied any value, it has, in recent years, been in the process of re-evaluation, as this great artistic movement continues to fascinate us with its fantasy of invention and its prediction of 20th century functionalism.

What precisely is Art Nouveau which consistently refuses to be categorized and appeared about the same time as the Arts and Crafts movement and the Modern movement? Most often the term refers to designs of free flowing or organic form, based on some plant—like a floral abstraction, linear, undulating and rhythmic (Figure 524). Its whiplash curves convey the sense of powerful movement, restless, nervous and agitated

(525). In brief, the ornamental value of line is its main artistic development and dominates all other considerations. In many other designs the tender curve of Art Nouveau is hardened, is kept in check, and in some cases entirely omitted. This aspect of the movement lies in the direction of rational and geometrical construction, which strives much more for architectonic than for organic form. Thus Art Nouveau is not one style, but several movements with a wide variety, even conflict, of stylistic trends—the symbolism of some resulting in an extreme contrast to the modernism of others—which were united in a single cause, to ruthlessly crush what had preceded it and to clear the way for 20th century design.

The roots of Art Nouveau may be traced back to English stylistic trends of the early 1880's, which were an offshoot of the Arts and Crafts movement. This earlier stylistic phenomenon, often conveniently called proto-Art Nouveau, was floral in inspiration and linear in essence and came into existence in the environment of the late Pre-Raphaelite illustrators and designers. For this reason it is two-dimensional in character and mainly restricted to flat surfaces. In relation to Art Nouveau it is the English designer's attitude toward Nature and his aesthetic theories which are of particular interest. Designers such as Selwyn Image and Arthur Mackmurdo who founded in 1882 the Century Guild, which was one of the groups that influenced the abrupt flowering of Art Nouveau between 1890–1895, felt that the exact imitation of Nature was pointless unless the source itself was consciously revised and changed. In brief, Nature, which had ruled over art for the first half of the nineteenth century, would continue as a source of inspiration, with the one big difference that the new aesthetic required more than a faithful depiction of plant forms recommended in the teachings of Ruskin. Instead Nature would be restyled and transcended and finally abstracted.

Art Nouveau may be placed midway between Historicism—the infatuation for past styles—and the emergence of the Modern movement—an applied art that would be more appropriate to a machine-age existence. Already nascent in the Gothic Revival and the Arts and Crafts movements, it blossomed all over Europe by 1890. Essentially there was not one point of origin, but several, as the style sprang up almost simultaneously in several countries, the incentive in each country stemming from the work or personality of an outstanding individual, such as Mackintosh, Gallé, Tiffany or Van de Velde. Its fanciful and fiery youth covered the last five years of the century and it was in full bloom by 1900. Con-

fronted by the aesthetic bankruptcy of mechanization and the necessity for creating a new style, the Art Nouveau artists made an attempt to return to craft conditions, to revive handicraft. Like the Arts and Crafts movement, it was the style of the individual designer, who, following in Morris' footsteps, relied on the work of men's hands, not on machines. From 1890 in such capitals as London, Vienna, Paris and Glasgow craftsmanship was restored to its former eminence. In fact, this extraordinary revival of crafts and craftsmanship which happened at the end of the century brought a significant change—many artists turned away temporarily or permanently from the fine arts to the applied or decorative arts. It developed to a point where Walter Crane in England pointed out that the objective was "turning our artists into craftsmen and our craftsmen into artists."

As a consequence of Art Nouveau, and a most important contribution, a sense of unity in the art of interior design was reestablished. To conceive of a room and its contents as a unified whole was perhaps the one feature found in each country's interpretation of the new art. The desire to free itself from the tyranny of styles was as much a notable feature of Art Nouveau as was its striving for unity. But Art Nouveau hailed in Europe and America in its own time as new and revolutionary in its emphasis on the use of decorative form, line and color, and rich in its symbolic meaning, was never entirely free from the bondage of the historical past, which indirectly inspired her existence. Gothic, Baroque and Rococo, each in its own manner contributed to mold Art Nouveau. Gothic contributed theory; Baroque its plastic conception of form, and Rococo its principle of asymmetry. Art Nouveau also found timely inspiration in the highly linear and colorful art of Japan and freedom from the bonds of symmetry and the Greek Orders. The fascinating fluidity of the East was everywhere evident in it. Then also the marked individuality of the new art shown in the various countries is brought about in part by a special interest in certain traditions; for example, the influence of Celtic art on the Glasgow school or Rococo art on the Nancy school.

To free themselves from Historicism, the furniture designers threw accepted principles of design to the wind. They were scarcely aware of the nature of materials. Wood was twisted into strange shapes and metal writhed in tortuous curves inspired by the flowing interlacings of Nature, for the style as a whole is based on Nature, not only its decoration but also its structural conception. An awareness of this fact is necessary to the understanding of the new art, as it was in Art Nouveau that Nature as an aesthetic expression reached its highest point. Under its influence, sensuous undulating lines of growth twine and spread across the structure, taking entire possession of it (526). Chairs and tables appear as if they were molded in a taffy-like substance (527). Straight lines are erased whever possible, while natural structural divisions are no longer definable, flowing into one another to maintain a continuous linear movement. In some instances Nature is less extravagant than Art Nouveau's interpretation of it. But Art Nouveau at its best, rich in linear rhythm, as angularities disappear in a mystical blending of surfaces, can assume its place among the masterpieces of cabinetwork of all ages (528).

The Turin Exhibition of 1902 marked the decisive point as well as the crossroads of Art Nouveau. It was evident to everyone that the style was already declining. Although a number of artists continued to use it up to the outbreak of the First World War, the main artistic development after 1902 tended toward simplicity, more emphasis on structural function and less on ornamentation. The real underlying reason for the abrupt rejection of Art Nouveau was the rumblings of a new movement—the Modern —which was gradually developing in Germany and Austria, where the English influence was particularly strong. All the time Art Nouveau was in fashion, the names of certain English designers— Voysey, Walton, Ashbee, Baillie-Scott and others—were constantly mentioned on the Continent. It was their constructive principles, a rational feeling for form and its fitness, that attracted wide interest, and not their contribution to the development of ornamentation. On the other hand, the Continental Art Nouveau artists first turned their attention to ornament, since they believed decoration necessary. The problem as they saw it was to find an appropriate form for the decoration, and when they found it, they would have created a new style. However, the problems at the beginning of the 20th century reached beyond the bounds of art. Gradually the artists realized that the answer to the stylistic problems, which social and economic evolution had brought forth, lay in constructive principles, that is, simplicity of form and honesty toward materials and working processes—ideals for which the Arts and Crafts movement fought. It was then that the leading Art Nouveau artists discarded Art Nouveau in order to give their creative energy to a wide movement supporting these ideas. Their interest focused on new shapes; decorative problems were subordinated.

As this new international movement spread and attained popularity as the style of fashion and the avant-garde, it became so protean in its manifestations that it demands to be studied country by country.

FRANCE

The new style became most firmly established in France where it retained its popularity the longest. As Rococo and Neo-Rococo achieved their culmination in France, the latter appearing twice in the 19th century, it is only natural that the most important influence of Rococo on Art Nouveau occurred in this cultural area. Two distinct centers of Art Nouveau developed in France, one in Paris around S. Bing and the other in Nancy under the aegis of Emile Gallé (1846–1904). The closest ties between Rococo and Art Nouveau occurred in Nancy, where in the 18th century, during the reign of the Polish king Stanislaus (1735–1766), this university town had been transformed by Rococo façades and sinuous grillwork into a veritable maze of linear fantasies. When the Bourbon king, Louis XVIII, ascended the throne in 1815, after Napoleon I's downfall, the earliest Neo-Rococo furniture was made at Nancy and flourished until it was supplanted by Napoleon III's Neo-Classicism in the 1860's. The artistic revival of the 1890's once again brought Rococo into the foreground, as Nancy's artists blended it with the new art.

The undeniably important position held by France in Art Nouveau was chiefly won by Gallé and a host of other artists and designers. Gallé, whose reputation to a large extent is based on his work in glass, was the first great exponent of Art Nouveau in France. He was one of the most interesting of all Art Nouveau designers, as well as France's outstanding naturalist. By around 1900 Gallé's workshop employed approximately three hundred workers, who were busy making glass and furniture. To a certain extent Gallé's designs for furniture were in the French stylistic traditions, such as Louis XIV, Louis XV or Louis XVI. In a word, the construction and design were traditional. Only the decoration—carving which he developed two-dimensionally and marquetry which was Gallé's specialty and varied from plant forms to verses—displayed dramatic Art Nouveau tendencies. Gallé believed that the function of furniture should find expression through decoration and not construction. Gallé's inscriptions gave a symbolical expression to the idea of his furniture; for example, a work table inscribed "Travail est Joie." (529) This class of furniture bearing inscriptions, which induced an aesthetic experience beyond what was innate in the piece of furniture itself, was much in fashion in France, where it was called *meubles parlants.*

None of Gallé's furniture ever achieved the daring unconventionality of his contemporary Louis Majorelle (1859–1926), who may be assigned a position among Art Nouveau furniture designers which corresponds to that of Gallé in art glass. Shortly after Majorelle inherited his father's furniture business in 1879, he began to design furniture in the fashionable Louis XIV, Louis XV and Louis XVI styles. However, he worked mainly in the Louis XV style or Neo-Rococo, until around the end of the century, when, under Gallé's influence, he started to design in the Art Nouveau taste. Less bound by tradition in construction and more plastic in conception than Gallé, the main characteristic of his furniture is the graceful but powerful dynamic line (530). The plastic conception was so important to him that he worked in clay as a sculptor and molded his most important furniture forms, later translating the model into carved wood. In his best work the extraneous Neo-Rococo or Neo-Baroque decorative details were removed or discreetly restrained and confined to certain areas which permitted the undulating dynamic flow of line to dominate the entire character of his furniture. No doubt his finest work ranks among the most perfected achievements of Art Nouveau (531).

Unlike Gallé and Majorelle the other Nancy furniture designers were architects. Among the outstanding members were Emile André (1871–1933) who was Nancy's most important architect, Jacques Gruber and Eugène Vallin (1865–1925). The furniture designs of the latter are more in the manner of Majorelle than any of the designers belonging to the Nancy school (532). He adopted a similar sculptural and dynamic form language based on floral and Neo-Baroque inspiration. Later, in the first few years of the 1900's, he, like Majorelle, discarded the floral elements in favor of a more abstract decoration or no decoration at all, relying on the graceful flow of the structure to provide the decorative accent or element. This style with large and smooth surfaces was simple, sober and more international, and lasted to a certain extent until just about

the beginning of the First World War. After Gallé's death in 1904 the Nancy school, devoid of his leadership and inspiration, faded from the limelight, as Nancy returned once again to the province's own enduring style, Louis XV.

In contrast to the Nancy school, Parisian Art Nouveau furniture is less ponderous, more refined and restrained. The Nature-inspired decoration is more stylized, at times abstract and often restricted to small areas. Unlike the Nancy school, where the artists followed in Gallé's footsteps, the Parisian designers were completely individual personalities, each presenting his own form of Art Nouveau. S. Bing, a native of Hamburg, opened his first shop, Maison de l'Art Nouveau, at 22 Rue de Provence, in December 1895. This was to become the focal point in Paris for the new style. Apart from the three most prominent who worked for Bing—Georges de Feure (1869–1928), Eugène Gaillard and Eugène Colonna—there were a number of other well-known representatives, such as Alexandre Charpentier (1856–1909) (524) and Felix Aubert (b. 1866), Tony Selmersheim (b. 1871), and Hector Guimard (1867–1942). This group produced some of the finest examples of Art Nouveau furniture. No doubt the leading Art Nouveau architect was Guimard. The symbolical plant conception that clearly influenced the construction of his famed Métro stations in Paris is also evident in his furniture (527, 528). Art Nouveau was frequently dubbed Style Métro by the general public.

Of all Bing's artists Georges de Feure appears the most conservative, for although his furniture is certainly Art Nouveau it assumes a traditional French character (533). Until 1900 the form language he uses for his constructive elements is always derived from plants and flowers with stalks, and is notable for its elegant and delicate execution. In contrast to de Feure, the work of Eugène Gaillard is more virile; at times ponderous. His plastics and dynamic approach conveys a quality of forceful and powerful movement that relates to Majorelle. One of his important and striking pieces at the Paris Exhibition of 1900 was a tall cupboard with completely abstract and plastic ornament (534). As a furniture designer Eugène Colonna may be placed midway between the two. He can be either elegant or dynamic, as well as being more austere, more severe in his decoration than either one of them (535).

After the Paris Exhibition of 1900 when the Parisian artists were faced with the exaggerations of the style, they retreated and made a subtle return to a quiet, restrained form of Art Nouveau, which with its inventive and graceful elegance was more in accord with the true traditions of French period furniture. In fact, the situation is the same as existed in the mid-18th century, when the perfected Louis XV style made its debut freed from the exaggerations of rocaille. Then it was rocaille subdued and simplified. Now it is the form language of Art Nouveau. Also now as then, it is the perfected final phase, not the youthful extravagances which brought forth the noblest. This final phase was of short duration, as a feeling of tradition asserted itself more and more. And as the rocaille surrendered to the Neo-Classicism of the late 18th century, so now before 1910 there was a return to a simplified and modernized Classicism, especially in the direction of Directoire and Empire (536).

BELGIUM

In Belgium, generally regarded as the epicenter of Art Nouveau, there was a tremendous reaction in the 1880's against the imitation of period styles and an intense search for something new, something different. Here, as in France, architecture and the decorative arts were markedly influenced by the Neo-trends —Gothic, Renaissance, Baroque and Rococo. Finally, in the early 1890's Art Nouveau emerged from the Neo-Rococo which had exerted a powerful influence in the previous decade. In contrast to French Art Nouveau, the Belgian style, with its plastic and noticeably three-dimensional treatment, offers a much more heavy and ponderous impression of the new art than any that appeared in France, while the ornament in the hands of the Belgian designers was presented in an abstract manner. Several aspects of Art Nouveau were presented in Belgium.

First there was Victor Horta (1861–1947), the son of a Belgian cobbler and Belgium's leading architectural figure at the turn of the century (537). Horta, with his plant-inspired abstractions and his Neo-Baroque idea of form to which were added certain Gothic and Louis XV ingredients, was the first to achieve a fully developed mastery of the new style. It is generally agreed that Horta launched the new style in his now celebrated house designed for Professor Tassel, No. 6, rue Paul-Emile Janson, Brussels, completed in 1893. In contrast to Horta's dynamic and plastic forms, the work of Gustave Serrurier-Bovy (1858–1910) is strongly committed to the influence of the English Arts and Crafts style, even to its note of rusticity.

It seems that during his year's stay in England in 1884, he traveled extensively and fell under the spell of William Morris and his followers. Refreshingly simple in a "rustic" Arts and Crafts manner, his furniture possessed a feature that was more distinct in his work than in that of the English artists, namely asymmetry, which had been evident in English furniture since the Anglo-Japanese furniture of Godwin. A practical aspect of this asymmetry permitted him to combine several pieces of furniture in the one construction, for example, an open bookcase over a slant-front desk mounted on a chest of drawers flanked on one side by a low cupboard. Another notable feature, also introduced by Serrurier-Bovy, but one that he could not have possibly borrowed from the English, was his use of slightly arched trusses, always placed diagonally and freely where they were or were not needed (538). These gently curved trusses, which were less constructive than elegant, were to be adopted and transformed by Van de Velde to become one of his most typical design principles, as well as one of the outstanding features of Belgian Art Nouveau.

Both aspects of Belgian Art Nouveau—the dynamic and plastic and the constructive striving—are seen in the work of Henri Van de Velde (1863–1957). Quite apart from the role he played in the Modern movement he has been considered the creator and theoretical founder of Art Nouveau. Deeply absorbed in the doctrines of Ruskin and Morris, he was perhaps the most prolific writer of Art Nouveau, and the leading theoretician among the men of the 1890's. After renouncing his career as a painter, Van de Velde made his debut as a decorative designer in 1893. To Van de Velde the line was all important, and as

a result of his conscious and continuous struggle to find beauty in the fitness and eloquence of the line, it is felt too much in most of his work. Taken as a whole his furniture designs are marked by eclecticism. The undecorated slat-like furniture, which he designed for the first house he built at Uccle, near Brussels, in 1896, is reminiscent of English work (539), while a writing chair made in 1897 with its bent laths is in the Serrurier-Bovy tradition. Often heavy in its form, Van de Velde's furniture never achieves the sophisticated elegance of that by Majorelle or Gaillard (540).

In Belgium both in architecture and decorative arts (and Belgium is the only country where it is possible to speak of Art Nouveau architecture) the new style was of short duration, being abandoned around 1905. Van de Velde had already left the country in 1899. Two years later, in 1901, he accepted an invitation from the Grand Duke of Saxe-Weimar to head the Weimar School of Arts and Crafts, the immediate predecessor of the Bauhaus, which was opened under the tutelage of Walter Gropius in 1919, in a building designed by Van de Velde.

SPAIN

Art Nouveau may be seen with notable clarity in Spain—where it was called Modernismo—in the extraordinary architecture and furnishings of the Catalonian architect, Antonio Gaudi y Cornet (1855–1926). One of the most imaginative artists, he succeeded in fusing most of the style elements of the 19th century—Neo-Gothic, Neo-Baroque, Neo-Rococo and the most fanciful naturalism into a decorative rhythmic whole. His furniture with its markedly plastic shapes exemplifies the style of this most outstanding innovator and original genius of Spanish Art Nouveau. Despite the wildly imaginative, eccentric shapes he incorporated in his furniture, he also had constructive ideas in mind (541).

ENGLAND

Though England had helped to furnish the precursors of Art Nouveau and to prepare the ground, and though English influence was considerable on the Continent, it was clear that the Continental style had no chance of winning popularity in England. The principal reason was her own Arts and Crafts movement. It had taken tremendous effort on the part of English designers to move away from Historicism, and to develop, on traditional grounds, a simple sober style of furniture based on simple sound construction principles, partly of a rectilinear character. Thus it is easy to understand that the linear rhythm of Art Nouveau was like seed falling on stony ground.

HOLLAND

The main development of Art Nouveau in Holland is markedly two-dimensional. Her architecture and furniture were completely untouched by the linear rhythm of the new art. The sober, rational and constructive principles of the Arts and Crafts movement proved of far greater interest to the Dutch designers than the decorative. Furniture designed by Holland's most advanced architect and one of the pioneers of the Modern movement, H. P. Berlage (1856–1934), with its very simple lines and rectilinear construction illustrates

the main development in Holland (542). The results of Berlage's attempt to lay the foundation for a new style became clear twenty-five years later at the Paris Exhibition of 1925, in the furniture designed by the architect Gerrit Rietveld (1888–1964), who kept the integrity of the flat rectangular plane advanced by Berlage. In contrast to Berlage, furniture designed by the Dutch painter Johan Thorn-Prikker (1868–1932) reveals a simplified and modernized classicism.

GLASGOW

The English corollary of the Continental Art Nouveau had its center in Glasgow with the architect and designer Charles Rennie Mackintosh (1863–1928) as its most important artistic personality. The other three artists, who with Mackintosh comprise the Glasgow group—"The Four" as the group were often called—were Herbert MacNair and the MacDonald sisters, Margaret (1865–1933) and Frances (1874–1921). Margaret married Mackintosh and Frances married MacNair. The Glasgow school is a result of a great many overlapping trends—the Arts and Crafts movement, the Pre-Raphaelites and the literary and symbolical tendencies, the art of Japan and the Celtic revival with its nationalistic spirit. Mackintosh, with his great creative power, molded these tendencies and gave them independent form.

Mackintosh treated each room or building as a unity, designing every decorative detail to produce a unified impression. Each piece of his furniture was meant for a particular setting in which it would complement the consciously created atmosphere of a room. When seen in context his furniture is entirely justified, but when isolated it has a peculiar strangeness. As in his architecture, Mackintosh's furniture is often straight-lined, markedly linear, and makes much decorative use of structural elements. The decoration is never permitted to overflow, but is confined to a strictly bound and austere form. The Glasgow school is generally associated with very simple pieces of furniture with broad plain surfaces contrasted with comparatively small areas of rich pattern. Moldings are dispensed with to increase the effect of the large smooth surfaces. Characteristic of this style with its linear and symbolic features, is a severely plain white enameled rectilinear cupboard designed by Mackintosh around 1902. The projecting cornice devoid of moldings is remarkably simple. When the cupboard doors are open a kind of decoration with a distinct tendency to verticalism is revealed, which is so typical of the school. Against a pearl-gray background stands a strange, slender, elongated figure of a woman wrapped in a white robe, holding in her outstretched arms a pink stylized full-blown rose. The decoration is inlaid with opaque colored glass in white, dark blue and pink (543, 544).

Mackintosh is especially remembered for his chairs, with extremely tall backs, often as much as six feet high, characterized by oval insets, the pierced pattern of squares or crescents, as they exemplify his peculiar inventiveness (545, 546). The attenuated lines of these chairs and the use of decorative motifs in the form of eerie, elongated, tapering figures wrapped in white robes, led to the Glasgow school being dubbed the Spook school in England. No doubt the vertical and austere character that prevails in most of Mackintosh's interiors evokes a lighter, more airy, even if not spooklike, feeling.

The light and airy quality of Mackintosh's interiors reveals the importance of Japanese influence on his work, and is reminiscent of Voysey's design for interiors with their sense of spaciousness brought into existence by sparse furnishings. Mackintosh's lively rectilinearism— the interplay between verticals and horizontals, squares and rectangles and their value as a decorative element—stimulated the Austrian artists, who had close contacts with the Scottish school, far more than the fashionable floral experiments of the French. In the capable hands of Josef Hoffmann the square developed into a much-admired motif around 1900. While Mackintosh was acclaimed at exhibitions held at Vienna, 1900, Dresden, 1901, and Turin, 1902, he was never appreciated in England. Soon the Glasgow school was to fade from the scene owing to the developments in Germany and Austria just after the turn of the century.

GERMANY

Compared to England, Belgium and France, Germany and Austria were both late arrivals on the battlefield against stylistic tyranny. Apart from the Neo-trends, particularly Neo-Renaissance, which flourished in Germany in the 1870's and 1880's, the Germans were especially interested in folk art which resulted in a simple rustic furniture painted in various colors in imitation of peasants' furniture. In the years just preceding 1900, the young German designers became enamored with Van de Velde, whose unequivocal theoretical doctrines appealed to the German mind. His beliefs about the relationship of art to daily life had noticeable influence. Perhaps above all, to conceive of a room as a unified whole—the space it encloses, all the furniture and objects belonging to it, no matter how important or modest—injected new meaning into the work of these designers.

By 1900 Germany was almost entirely under the spell of Art Nouveau, her ornamentation showing unbounded exuberance, as so often in past centuries. The movement was called Jugendstil, after a ribald and lively periodical, JUGEND, first published in Munich in 1896. There were two principal centers, Munich and Darmstadt, which played an important role in the development of Jugendstil and where it was to have a brief but golden interlude before it was renounced by the leading designers. It was only natural that Darmstadt would be a center of much activity for it was here that the Grand Duke Ernst Ludwig of Hesse, who was an ardent patron of the arts, had his residence.

The nucleus of the Munich school, as it was generally called, was composed of seven young artists: Hermann Obrist (1863–1927), Otto Eckmann (1865–1902), Richard Riemerschmid (1868–1957), Bernhard Pankok (b. 1872), Bruno Paul (b. 1874), August Endell (1871–1925), and Peter Behrens (1868–1940). In 1897 Obrist, Pankok, Paul and Riemerschmid founded the Münchener Vereinigte Werkstätten für Kunst im Handwerk, an organization whose purpose was to create a national German art free of stylistic imitation, through the medium of cooperation between the artist and the skilled worker.

Obrist and Eckmann were the first two German artists to create decorative

motifs with a linear rhythm. The former, whose work is mainly two-dimensional, started an embroidery workshop at Florence in 1892, which, two years later, he moved to Munich, where it attracted wide attention. Eckmann, like a number in the Munich group, was originally a painter who turned to the decorative arts after the decline of easel painting in Germany and became one of Germany's leading Art Nouveau graphic artists. During his short lifetime Eckmann was also a prolific designer of textiles, wallpapers as well as furniture. Furniture designed by the Munich group is distinctively constructive; its wealth of superfluous curving ribs, joints and struts is reminiscent of the work of Serrurier-Bovy and Van de Velde. There are, of course, exceptions; some pieces have sculptural undulating shapes with all elements flowing into one another.

In the first years of the 20th century these designers had already seen beyond the purely decorative aspects and were moving toward a more rational construction. Stimulated by the work of the tireless writer, Hermann Muthesius (1861–1927), they began to experiment with construction and function. Thereafter their dominant interest was to simplify designs, to create new forms. Riemerschmid's furniture around the turn of the century is occasionally so simple and modern in appearance that it can readily pass for mid-20th century (547).

A special event in the history of Art Nouveau occurred in 1899 when the Grand Duke of Hesse invited a group of young artists, also seven in number, to build an artists' colony on Darmstadt's Mathilde-Höhe. Among those invited were Behrens, the leading figure of the Munich group, and Olbrich, one of the founders of the Secession in Vienna. It is hardly surprising that these two significant artists established the tone for the Darmstadt group. The colony was officially opened in 1901 with an exhibition called a Document of German Art. Instead of the customary temporary buildings designed for an exhibition it was the colony's permanent houses that were under consideration and which the Grand Duke had so generously financed. Except for Behrens, who was the only member to design and furnish his own house, Olbrich designed all the other buildings, while the other members had shared in the design of the interiors. Behrens was by far the most advanced. Essentially he had cut through the pastry and pastiche of Jugendstil and had taken a decided step toward rational functionalism. Briefly, Jugendstil moved still further away and was to be rapidly transformed into what its theoreticians—first and foremost Van de Velde—had meant it to be. In 1904, a critic describing the interior design exhibition held at St. Louis that year write "The sins of the Jugend style have been completely overcome."

AUSTRIA

It is generally accepted that Art Nouveau arrived so late on the scene in Austria, that it was possible for her to see more clearly the outline of a more radical and fruitful development. She was to develop her own style which had no conventional connection with Art Nouveau, and this style is the principal reason why there was no strong Art Nouveau movement in Austria. Then, too, the Austrians were in close contact with the English in the 19th century and it was apparent that they found the ideals of the Arts and Crafts movement far more provocative than the symbolical, floral and plant-abstracted forms used in France and in other European countries.

The Secession style, as the Austrian version of Art Nouveau is called, signifies its independent and even rebellious character. The term was derived from a union of radical Viennese painters and sculptors founded in 1896 under the name of Wiener Sezession. It was concentrated almost entirely in Vienna, with its headquarters in Olbrich's cube-shaped building erected in 1898, the same year its publication VER SACRUM, notable for its square format, made its first appearance. The new style is irrevocably connected with Otto Wagner's two pupils, the architects Josef Hoffmann (b. 1870) and Joseph Maria Olbrich (1867–1908), who were among the founders of the Vienna Secession. The goal of the Secessionists was to start entirely anew. "It was for this reason," writes Hoffman in 1954 in a letter to Stephen Tschudi Madsen, whose book, SOURCES OF ART NOUVEAU, is the definitive work on the subject, "that the pure square and the use of black and white as dominant colors especially interested me, because these elements had not appeared in former styles." (548) As both Hoffman and Olbrich were architects they were more interested in architectural and constructional problems than in ornament. Furniture had to express function in architectural terms rather than in linear ones suggesting growth and organic life, the typical Art Nouveau form. The simple geometrical ornament, the the square and the circle which they developed in the late 1890's was sparingly but elegantly employed and was subordinate to a strict ornamental order in an entity composed of simple planes. The simpler relationships of flat surfaces, such as Hoffmann preferred, showed the way to the next generation's stylistic ideals of undecorated geometric form. Hoffmann preferred the square motif arranged in twos or threes or in rows horizontally or vertically. In the following decade, owing to Hoffmann's influence, squares enjoyed a great vogue in Vienna and in large sections of Europe. Olbrich adopted as his favorite ornament the circle—circles in rows or in clusters, circles enclosing flames.

The Viennese school of interior design agrees remarkably well with that of the Glasgow school. This, naturally brings up the question: What was the actual relationship between Glasgow and Vienna? The similarity between the two schools is a popular subject, and accord is still to be reached. It seems a reasonable assumption that if the two schools developed independently in each respective country, which is possible as two advanced architects may have had the same solution to the existing stylistic problems, then such influence as the Glasgow school may have exerted, at least at the start, was more in the nature of a stimulus, as incentive, rather than a direct influence.

So to sum up the new style in Austria: As a result of the work of Hoffmann, Ol-brich and others, such as the architect Adolf Loos (1870–1933) who is reputed to have said "Ornament is a crime," (549) Vienna rapidly gained world recognition as one of the most progressive centers of the new movement in Europe. Even before 1900, Vienna had mapped out a course that bypassed Art Nouveau and created her own style which with its constructive search and desire for agreement with the material was to lead directly to the completely new stylistic ideals of the Modern movement. "To try to find beauty in form instead of making it rely on ornament," a principle recommended by Loos in a series of articles written in 1897–1898, was to be propagated across Austria and Europe by the Wiener-Werkstätte, an organization founded by Hoffmann in connection with Koloman Moser (1868–1916) and others.

In conclusion it is interesting to note here what the UPHOLSTERER AND INTERIOR DECORATOR (April 1928) had to say about this era. "A quarter of a century ago all Europe was watching the Vienna art movement, the Munich school, the Glasgow and other theories of art interpretation, which ignoring the vagaries of Art Nouveau progressed steadily along a given path of simplified ornamentation." Frequently the Vienna work anticipated the Art Décoratif of the Paris Exhibition of 1925 (550, 551, 552).

CHAPTER TWENTY-SIX

THE TWENTIETH CENTURY
and the Modern Movement Today

TO THE FIRST WORLD WAR

It is not hard to find fault with the name Modern movement, as all movements are modern when they start, that is to say they relate to or are characteristic of the present. But scholars such as Sigfried Giedion, Brun-Zevi, Henry-Russell Hitchcock, Thomas Howarth and Nikolaus Pevsner have in their work given international approval to this name, to describe the trend that resulted in entirely new stylistic ideals. This trend which made a clean sweep, allowing a constructional and rational form to emerge by mercilessly removing all ornament, paid full attention to the utilization and particular qualities of the material, coupled with honesty in the use of it, though without in any manner ignoring aesthetic considerations.

No doubt what makes an object look modern to most people is the quality of simplicity, providing this kind of simplicity meets with their approval. Otherwise they might find such descriptive words as bare or cold more appropriate. If they have thought about the subject in any manner, they most likely associate it with the word *functional.* Many people who deride Modern and regard it with hostility would be surprised to learn how much of the teachings of the movement —a preference for clean lines, for pleasing proportions, for the rejection of useless ornament—has already entered their lives and has helped to mold their tastes. The doctrine of functionalism has swept away considerable Victorian clutter and in some respects has greatly simplified our lives.

According to Morris' teachings it was necessary in a civilized community for everyone to have pleasant things to use. Morris clearly expressed his ideas in the thirty-four lectures which he delivered between 1877 and 1894 on artistic and social questions. "I don't want art for a few," Morris preached, "any more than education for a few, or freedom for

431

a few." Then he asked that all-important question, "What business have we with art at all unless all can share it?" In this respect Morris was the father of the Modern movement. But this was only one-half of Morris' teachings. The other half remained firmly rooted in the 19th century, for in his plea for the revival of handicraft, the "joy of the maker," he looked backward into the times of medieval primitiveness. Though Morris wanted an art "by the people and for the people" and admitted that cheap art is impossible because "all art costs time, trouble and thought" his attitude of hatred toward modern methods of production remained unchanged. The machine was Morris' arch enemy.

The solution, of course, was to learn what the machine could do, for it was apparent that manufacture could not be organized on any other basis. Some designers, awakening to the potentialities of the 20th century and the marvels of modern industry, shared the belief that industrial design and the products made by the machine might be as legitimate a form of artistic expression as those made by the human hands. Van de Velde, expressing his belief on the beauty inherent in machines, asserted, "The powerful play of their iron arms will create beauty as soon as beauty guides them." Hand in hand with a belief in the machine was an appreciation for designs of a classically pure perfection; that is, the desire to simplify or to eliminate decoration and to preserve the qualities inherent in natural materials. The American architect, Louis Sullivan (1856–1924), in his ORNA-MENT IN ARCHITECTURE (1892), stated that "ornament is mentally a luxury not a necessity."

The Viennese architect, Otto Wagner (1841–1918), said in 1894 that a new style compatible with modern requirements would stress "horizontal lines . . . great simplicity and an energetic exhibition of construction and materials." (Figure 553) Also from Vienna, the architect Adolf Loos (1870–1933) pointed out that "the lower the standard of a people, the more lavish are its ornaments. To find beauty in form instead of making it depend on ornament is the goal towards which humanity is aspiring." (549) To Loos pure beauty in an individual work of art is "the degree to which it attains utility and the harmony of all parts in relation to each other." A few years later similar views were expressed with the same forceful conviction, though in a more comprehensive manner by Sullivan's greatest pupil, Frank Lloyd Wright (1869–1959), who in 1901 read a manifesto on The Arts and Crafts of the Machine in which it eulogizes the Machine Age (554).

As Nikolaus Pevsner writes in his PIONEERS OF MODERN DESIGN (1949), these five men (Van de Velde, Sullivan, Wagner, Loos and Wright) were "the first architects to admire the machine and to understand its essential character and its consequences on the relation of architecture and design to ornamentation. . . ."

The achievement of a wide movement promoting these ideas, the art of the 20th century, undeniably belongs to German architects and writers. The movement which they nurtured proved strong enough to bring forth a universal style of thinking and building. Foremost among the German writers who helped to create a "pure art of utility" was Hermann Muthesius (1861–1927) who served as a connecting link between the English style of the 1890's and Germany. He became the recognized leader of a new trend toward Sachlichkeit which followed the short-lived Jugendstil in Germany. The word *Sachlich*, which has no English equivalent but means relevant or applicable to the matter at hand, became the slogan for the ever-growing Modern movement. Reasonable Sachlichkeit is what Muthesius extols in English architecture and crafts; from the modern artist he asks for "perfect and pure utility, creation for use."

Partisans of Sachlichkeit pleaded for practical undecorated furniture in smooth, polished light forms as a boon to housewives; for wide horizontal windows and floods of light and for fresh flowers in the rooms. Some of the earliest results of this campaign were shown at an exhibition of industrial art held in Dresden in 1906, where the Deutsche Werkstätten exhibited their first quantity-produced, machine-made furniture designed by some of the leading German architects such as Bruno Paul. The next problem the German industrial designers met and overcame was the standardization of parts. Their first unit furniture—an idea originating in America where it was introduced for bookcases—was shown in 1910. This new furniture developed from the spirit of the machine was as a whole neat and comfortable, of a simple classical character free of all gingerbread, for the Deutsche Werkstätten did not frown upon a note of tradition. These characteristics which were not revolutionary but reasonable popularized the new furniture in Germany and were conducive to a change of taste throughout the country.

Undoubtedly the most important step to coalesce the various individual experiments into a universally recognized style was the founding in 1907 of the Deutscher Werkbund. The aim of this new association which comprised a number of adventurous manufacturers with some architects, artists and writers, was to promote industrial work of high quality. The main idea—quality—was defined as meaning not only excellent durable work, the use of flawless genuine materials but also "the attainment of an organic whole rendered Sachlich, noble and, if you will, artistic by such means." From the start this group felt no horror of the machine. Though no machine can reproduce the delicacy and sensitivity of hand craftsmanship, the machine can produce an altogether different kind of excellence, providing the particular limitations of machines are closely studied and designs are created in terms of machine processes.

The program developed by the Werkbund—the acceptance of the machine in its proper place—was adopted by other countries: Austrian Werkbund, 1910; Swiss Werkbund, 1913; the Design and Industries Association, England, 1915; while the Swedish Slösdsförening was organized into a Werkbund late in the First World War. In Germany the Werkbund was not the only center to spread the ideals of the Modern movement, for the art schools through their appointment of new teachers and principals were equally progressive.

Nevertheless, no matter how progressive in spirit the Werkbund and these art schools were, the essential problem facing the industrial designers was still not settled. This problem—where the emphasis should be placed in the future on standardization or individualism—was resolved at the Werkbund Exhibition at Cologne in 1914. Van de Velde, the standard-bearer for individualism, yielded to Muthesius and his principles of standardization. It was the buildings at this exhibition and particularly the model factory by Walter Gropius (b. 1883) the most adamant German innovator, who regards himself as a follower of Morris, Van de Velde and the Werkbund, that won the day and the future for Muthesius. This factory, revealing as never before the exciting architectural potentialities of new materials—steel, concrete and glass, in contrast to buildings using traditional methods and materials, wood, brick and stone—cast the die for a new style, one that would take advantage of modern methods of construction and equipment and the mass production of building parts. Thus from the efforts of a relatively small group of men of genius—from Morris who had laid the foundation of the Modern style to Gropius who finally determined its character—Victorian Historicism, the legacy of the Romantic movement, was abandoned for an international style attuned to modern life and its scientific basis. Honesty, fitness of purpose and contemporary expression became the watchwords.

BETWEEN THE TWO WARS

The First World War brought economic, social and cultural changes which rapidly and radically reshaped the conditions and patterns of people's lives and thoughts. The time was ripe for a change and changes there were, as modern designers who had become increasingly aware of the challenge of an industrialized society, and the striking beauty of engineering, whose famous monument was the Eiffel Tower, centered their interests on industrial materials and processes. A very new potent synthesis of modern design ideals sprang up and became embodied in the work of artists' groups in the various European countries, such as in Holland, Germany and France. By 1920 modern designers were developing three elements which up to this time had been kept in the background, namely, the acceptance of mass production, a predilection for geometric shapes and the forms and materials of engineering. The aim of the functionalist movement of the 1920's and 1930's—to bring design into line with social and technical development—was initiated.

De Stijl, a movement primarily concerned with functionalism and the integration of painting and sculpture with architecture, flourished in Holland from 1917 to 1928. Initiated by Dutch painters, it developed unifying concepts affecting all the arts. Three elements formed the fundamental basis of the work of de Stijl: in form the rectangle; in color the primary hues, red, blue and yellow; in composition the asymmetric balance. In 1917 Gerrit Rietveld, who was one of its leading exponents, designed a chair without dovetailing and in which comfort has yielded to geometry. The framework of the chair consists of square members simply screwed together. They cross one another, but do not penetrate; in this manner their overlapping distinctness is stressed, which is the basic aesthetic conception behind the chair. Rietveld's chairs show the influence of Wright's chairs of a dozen years before (554, 555). In 1924 Rietveld built the Schröder house at Utrecht, together with all its furniture and furnishings, which today is regarded by many as "still the youngest house in Europe." Here the partition of space into cubic units by means of freely interpenetrating planes is emphasized as never before in Western architecture. Flexible walls or moving partitions further demonstrate the radical and consistent principles of the design.

The years 1920–1925 saw a notable expansion of the influence of de Stijl, first in Belgium, then in Germany, France, Eastern Europe and even in Russia. De Stijl influence upon French architects is not as apparent as upon German. But it may be noted that in France no building, not even by Le Corbusier, was as advanced in design as Rietveld's Schröder house. Then, too, Le Corbusier's famous device of painting the walls of the same room in different colors had been anticipated by de Stijl designers.

In 1921 the Stijl painter, writer and architect and its leading spirit, Theo van Doesburg (1883–1931), began to divide his time between the Bauhaus schools at Weimar and Berlin. Though the degree of his influence is still a matter of controversy, the Bauhaus more and more turned toward clarity, discipline and the desire for a uniform and consciously developed style in architecture and the allied arts such as the Dutch movement had already inaugurated.

More will be said about the Bauhaus in a moment, meanwhile a word about the furniture designed by the Swiss architect Charles Edouard Jeanneret-Gris (1887–1965) who is much better known by his pseudonym, Le Corbusier. This great architect believed that the sphere of architecture embraced every detail of household furnishing. "My intention," he stated, "is to illustrate how, by virtue of . . . standardization . . . industry cre-

ates pure forms, and to stress the intrinsic value of this pure form of art that is the result." Proceeding on this premise, Corbu furnished the Pavillon de l'Esprit Nouveau which he and Pierre Jeanneret designed for the Paris Exhibition of 1925, with chromium-plated tubular-steel furniture until then seen only in offices and with standardized unit furniture (in America the so-called "storage-wall" units) also very much like utilitarian office furniture. Apart from these pieces, which Corbu redesigned to suit his own needs and taste, he introduced Thonet bentwood chairs in which one piece of bentwood formed the rear legs and uprights. This feature simplified the design and increased the continuity. Of these chairs selected by Corbu for use in the buildings he designed in the 1920's perhaps the most notable is the circular bent beechwood armchair, which in Corbu's own words "possesses nobility." (556) In 1928–29 Corbu in collaboration with Pierre Jeanneret and Charlotte Perriand designed a small group of chairs, tables and built-in cabinets made to suit a certain internal space that were artistic achievements of proportion and detail. Of great interest are three types of chairs designed for the interiors at Ville d'Avray, which have brought forth complete schools of furniture design since their introduction. All three were in tubular steel, either chromium-plated or enameled and upholstered in leather or in black and white cowhide. First there is the reclining chair or chaise longue consisting of two completely separate parts; namely, an H-form cradle which in turn supports a long, form-fitting frame that can be freely adjusted to any angle. This delightful chair, perhaps the most relaxing chair that has ever been designed, recalls one of Corbu's characteristic architectural devices, that is, the lifting of the main part of a building off the ground by columns of distinctly sculptured character to convey a weightless look. In this chair Corbu has tried to minimize the strength it takes to support a relaxed human being (557). Second and equally delightful is a modern version of the traditional British officer's armchair with a pivoting backrest (558), and finally a heavy upholstered easy chair. The table tops of the dining and work tables were usually of glass in order to keep the table from obstructing visually the free flow of space; sometimes they were of polished marble.

For the model room in the Salon d'Automne the built-in cabinets or storage walls were framed in delicate sections of chromium-plated steel which formed a modular grid into which were fitted units of shelving, rows of drawers, cabinets with mirrored sliding doors, and display boxes with glass fronts.

Though tubular steel furniture was nothing new, as men such as Breuer had designed tubular steel chairs and tables at the Bauhaus in Weimar and Dessau since 1923, Corbu's furniture was to inspire a number of furniture designers for many years to come. In addition to the conscious use of simple geometric forms, his pieces displayed one other marked feature of functionalism; that is, the separation of functionally different parts of the same object. For example, in chair design Corbu went to great lengths to differentiate in form and material between what you sat on and what does the hard work of supporting your weight (soft leather against hard steel). This basic doctrine of functionalism had been clearly and firmly recognized at Gropius'

Bauhaus. Corbu carried this principle even further in one of his dining tables in which the marble top instead of resting on the H-form frame of steel is supported by very thin pieces of steel that extend above the frame.

A symbol for functionalism on the Continent was the Bauhaus school in Germany established successively at Weimar, Dessau and Berlin. The first school was opened at Weimar in 1919. The main workshop at Dessau, designed by Walter Gropius, its founder and first director, was itself one of the great buildings of the 1920's. The purpose of this new school, which combined an academy of art and a school of arts and crafts, was to teach experimental methods of designing for the machine. For more than a decade it became a focal point of energy in Europe as well as a storm center of propaganda for and against the machine until it was abolished by the National Socialists in 1933. Essentially it was a workshop and a school; a laboratory for handicraft and for standardization. The students were urged to explore industrial materials and processes, to experiment freely and boldly, but always to bear in mind the purpose their design should serve; namely, creation for use, i.e. form should follow function. Indeed the emphasis on functionalism was so great as to suggest that all the furniture made throughout the ages was hopelessly nonfunctional. Their functional solutions for furniture were expressed in geometric forms influenced by Stijl concepts of rational simplicity. These Bauhaus designers were, however, far more preoccupied with problems of function than were the Stijl artists. Among the Bauhaus ideas that broke with European precedent were the use of chromium-plated metal tubes in the design of furniture; highly polished surfaces made interesting by textures rather than ornament, and stacking furniture to facilitate storage. Many Bauhaus designs were bought and manufactured by industry. Though most of the Bauhaus products were made by hand, the precision and clarity of their geometric contours imbued them with a machine-made appearance, which was an important consideration for early modern designers.

It was at the Bauhaus that the first cantilever chromium-plated tubular steel chair was made in 1925. Designed by Marcel Breuer, this chair was a complicated armchair with seat, back and armrests of canvas stretched from a bent tubular frame (559). The first tubular chair without back legs in which the characteristic resilience of steel was utilized was designed in 1927 by Ludwig Mies van der Rohe (b. 1886) one of the great innovators of chromium-plated steel furniture, who succeeded Gropius as director of the Bauhaus. Apart from the fact that the legs were curved instead of straight, Mies' cantilever chair, in which he applied a new design principle by substituting a double S-shaped support for the conventional four legs, was identical with the modern product (560). In the following year Breuer designed his version of the cantilever chair, which achieved the production line and became the prototype for thousands of variations seen all over the world (561). Thonet of bent beechwood fame produced a countless number of cantilever chairs from Breuer's designs. Though the steel tube had important virtues as a material for furniture, it also, like sheet metal, has certain defects. Above all it is

cold to the touch; this coldness is due to the fact that steel is a much better conductor of heat than wood, leather or plastics. In contrast to wood, which is a warm and living or vital material, metal is cold to the eye, which used in furnishings produces a rather cold and sterile interior. Despite these drawbacks there was a rapid increase of production of all kinds of tubular furniture from around 1930 to 1939, which came to typify "functionalism" of the 1930's. After a period in which to forget the worst of it there is a genuine revival of interest in tubular metal furniture.

Only several years separate Mies' sleek Barcelona chair which also entrusts the sitter's weight to cantileverage from the first cantilever chairs. This chair has become a classic, and like all Mies' furniture it requires, paradoxically, faultless handcraftsmanship to produce its machine-made look. Described by its admirers as "pure" this chromium-plated steel bar chair with supporting leather straps and tufted leather cushions received its name from the International Exhibition held at Barcelona in 1929, where Mies' pavilion for the German government won world acclaim. The best qualities of Mies' work—economy of line, beauty of proportion and precision—are revealed in this chair (562).

It was at this time that the tide of functionalist Modern reverencing the influence of Germany—that is, all this geometric purity in design, which has in it something abstract, something purely rational—had its brief period. But it is important to mention here that geometry in design is not new. From the earliest times Western culture has traditionally chosen geometric shapes in preference to non-geometric forms; their superior beauty lies in their rational appeal. Plato in the PHILEBUS, declares that when he speaks of beauty of form he means "straight lines and circles, and the plane or solid figures which are formed out of them by turning-lathes, rulers and measures of angles; for these I affirm to be not only relatively beautiful, like other things, but they are eternally and absolutely beautiful."

It was inevitable, however, that a reaction set in against the cold simplification of forms of the 1920's and early 1930's—"the square, spare, bare period" —which only admits as much comfort as is compatible with its abstract notions of pure beauty. From around 1933 many designers stopped talking about the house as a "practical machine for living in" and gradually progressed to freer, more aesthetic designs.

While Gropius and his group were organizing the Bauhaus, the majority of people in America were enchanted with the past. Antiques and imitations, both good and bad, routed any trace of the Modern movement from the American drawing room. In the brief span of about two decades, shopping for antiques, for old furniture, in all seasons, had become a most popular American pastime for rich and poor alike. In the 1920's decorators and gift shops were carrying antiques, even the department stores such as John Wanamaker, Marshall Field and the Jordan Marsh Company sent their buyers to Europe to buy quantities of antiques to lure the customers. The occupants of the White House were not unaware of the importance of American antiques. In 1925 President Coolidge appointed a commission to collect for the White House examples of the work of our early American cabinetmakers, which it was hoped would "create a still deeper and more abiding interest and respect for the work of our forefathers."

Everyone in the furniture trade was busy making reproductions. There was a comfortable number of relatively small cabinetshops employing skilled cabinetmakers, such as Karcher and Rehm, Vollmer, Pottier and Stymus, Kimbel and Alavoine, where copies of period forms were faithfully reproduced to the most minute detail. Great houses built by rich Americans were furnished with carefully selected reproductions to convey a European atmosphere. Italian Renaissance and 18th century French interiors furnished the principal source of inspiration. The Vanderbilt mansion at Hyde Park built by the illustrious firm of McKim, Mead and White in 1896–1898, gives evidence of this taste. The elaborate furnishings for this mansion were selected with exacting care by Stanford White, Ogden Codman, Jr., and other noted decorators. No doubt many of the copies of French antiques that furnished these mansions came from France. Commenting on furniture-making in France, the UPHOLSTERER AND INTERIOR DECORATOR (April, 1925) notes that "the copies of antiques of which there are many are often as solidly made as the actual old furniture itself. There are more cabinetmakers in Paris who reproduce antiques than there are furniture factories in France."

In contrast to the costly copies being made in America, the folly of indiscriminate machine production was glaringly revealed in the imitations made to meet the demands of the mass market. All this showy furniture of indifferent design, construction and materials, was produced in answer to the increasing demand for cheap "effects." Furniture in mock Tudor and Stuart versions, Italian and Spanish Renaissance are typical of this era. The worst of this vulgar "machine art" with grimacing griffons and leering masks is the "borax" class, so-called because hawkers of this cleanser offered premiums, and the word became associated with "extra" values, which commercial furniture manufacturers often offered in words or in "extra" large forms, "extra" carving, "extra" glossy finish. The era of quality reproductions made for commercial distribution, when more accurate copying became important, was initiated in the 1930's.

Apart from brief flirtations, the first genuine interest in modern furniture in America was inspired by the Paris Exhibition of 1925, which was a resounding success and brought into existence the style known as Art Moderne. A quarter of a century had elapsed in France since Art Nouveau, and in the meanwhile Modern art had arrived. All too long French decorative art had been confined to the making of isolated objects of artistic interest, certainly very precious from every point of view, but not in step with modern industrial development. The time had come to conform to the necessities of modern life and to bring the work into line with current taste, individual and collective, and with new architectural conceptions. The process of manufacture having become entirely different from those of earlier days, the first necessity of all was to break with the older ornamental traditions. By encouraging her designers to adapt new designs to the possibilities of machine tools, to industrialize in the best sense of the word without in the smallest degree neglecting their

artistic quality, the French hoped to give new orientation to their arts and their use could be considerably spread. Depending on the French reputation for luxury craftsmanship, their goal was to create a new style that could play an important role in the new order of things. The outcome was the Exposition Internationale des Arts Décoratifs, covering more than seventy acres along the right bank of the Seine, which opened in May, 1925. That the exhibition stood for modern decorative and industrial art is clearly conveyed in a paragraph which barred from the exhibition "copies, imitations, or counterfeits of ancient styles." Every class of industry was represented since the most simple and everyday objects are capable of being made with as much beauty as articles of luxury. In its determination to belong to its own times, to reject anachronisms, to bring more beauty into everyday life, this great exhibition was related to the program laid down by William Morris. More than twenty countries took part in the exhibition, and though America did not participate (neither did Germany or Russia), American furniture manufacturers and designers attended in the thousands. Writing on the exhibition THE STUDIO (1925) observes, "the will to modernism which dominates the craftsmen is regulated by the same essential principles— consideration of the medium, adaptation of the shapes to the material used and to the purpose of the object being made and an almost total suppression of ornament (563, 564)—there is, however, a very great difference between the salient characteristics of the furniture made by the different countries. . . . It appears quite clearly that Sweden, Poland, Denmark, England, and Switzerland, however anxious they may be to be modern in their decorative art seek to do so without breaking entirely with the past; while France, Holland, Austria, Czecho-Slovakia and Belgium up to a certain point having made a clean sweep of all the traditional styles are trying to create a modern style which shall possess as much novelty as possible. . . ." (565, 566)

THE UPHOLSTERER AND INTERIOR DECORATOR (June 1925) in answer to its own question "What is this new art?" maintains that "The new art cannot be defined because it has no limitations, no definition of character. Every designer has a law unto himself. One can describe a Louis XVI chair but not a new art chair." (567, 568)

The French art of 1925 called New Art or Art Moderne was not strictly new. Admittedly the elements of the style—a predilection for geometric forms (569) and a marginal interest in the Nature forms popular in Art Nouveau, but now noticeably refined—were not after all such unheard of novelties in the history of French furniture. Art Moderne, unconsciously indeed, for it cherished a fine contempt for the furniture that went before it, merely took up the old French classicism. It fastened by instinct on the point where an earlier generation had stopped; but now it was interpreted according to the ideals and philosophy of the 20th century—a complete new attitude of mind. Thus once again the old visibly influences the new; the new the logical outcome of it. Briefly, in essence new arrangement of old "studio properties." (568, 569, 570)

Commenting on the relatively few French decorators who specialized in this new field, THE UPHOLSTERER AND IN-TERIOR DECORATOR (July 1925) writes, "Of course Jacques Ruhlmann is preeminent (568, 570). His work is remarkable . . . Many of the tables are no higher than chair seats. It is one of the characteristics of this New Art. [In addition to Ruhlmann there is] the work of a very progressive young organization, Suë et Mare, some of whose pieces have been acquired by the Metropolitan Museum of Art (571) . . . these two firms . . . best typify the last word in New Art."

Ruhlmann, a great French furnisher, exercised a wide and beneficial influence on the arts of furnishing and interior decoration in France. Writing on Ruhlmann, his talent and success, THE STUDIO (1926) comments that "Up to about 1911 the most serious reproach which could be leveled at modern French furniture was the predominance of ornament over shape, which latter was also often lacking in simplicity, logic and quietude. Ruhlmann was one of the first who had the courage to conceive and carry out works which were strictly rational in construction and which relied for their beauty chiefly on the general harmony and balance of lines and volumes dictated by the purpose to be served by the article. . . . Ruhlmann's simple and sumptuous art has been greatly aided in its success by the remarkable clearness, precision, economy and sobriety of the forms to which modern machine production has accustomed us. . . . But furniture thus conceived requires fine material and perfect execution. Ruhlmann realized this at the outset. . . . Some of Ruhlmann's chairs as well as his desks and sideboards have the legs partly included as part of the body of the piece itself. This device was inaugurated by Ruhlmann and since much imitated."

(572) "He does not, like so many others, force himself to appear 'modern' but is so instinctively."

In contrast to Ruhlmann's work and a few other decorators, extravagant excesses and arguable taste (573) marked much of the work at the exhibition which passed at the time for the latest word in French decorative art. Less than five years after the exhibition, the French moderated Modern.

The public in America as in France first became acquainted with Art Moderne through various exhibitions given at leading department stores. In May 1927 R. H. Macy sponsored an exhibition of New Art furnishing which showed furniture designed by Paul T. Frankl, Jules Bouy (574), John Helmsky and other modern designers, In the following year numerous department stores, such as Lord and Taylor and B. Altman, sponsored New Art exhibitions. But the exhibition of the year, and of great importance in promoting Modern in America, was the International Exhibition of Art in Industry sponsored by R. H. Macy from May 14 to 26. The purpose of the exhibition was to encourage further interest on the part of the American public and the American designers in modern art as applied to industrial design and to present examples of the best European and American schools, so the public might see the complete picture; to give an opportunity to make comparisons and to determine their individual preferences for the modern art of the various countries. Three hundred exhibitors were selected from the foremost designers and craftsmen in France, Germany, Italy, Austria, Sweden and the United States to create rooms in the spirit of their national art. The work of such famous architects and designers as Josef Hoffmann of Vienna, Bruno Paul of Germany, Jules Lelu of Paris and Giovanni Ponti of Milan was displayed. Among the American exhibits was a city apartment by Kem Weber of Los Angeles, a living room by Eugene Schoen of New York, and a penthouse studio by William Lescaze also from the same city.

At the January 1928 furniture market of the Grand Rapids Market Association, an association which at that time comprised 450 exhibitors, American designers created some furniture showing Art Moderne influence which was well received. It was a memorable occasion because the market, held semi-annually, celebrated its 100th birthday. In honor of the occasion a panorama of furniture spanning the past fifty years had been arranged—Victorian Renaissance, Eastlake, Golden Oak and Mission—to mention but a few. At the summer market of the same year Art Moderne attained the peak of its sudden popularity.

It can hardly be surprising that at the Chicago Century of Progress which opened on June 1st, 1933, modern furniture in harmony with the ultramodernism of this international exhibition was given prominence. However, it was a modified Modernistic and distinctly removed from the bizarre Art Moderne of the past. In the following year a fleeting phase of Modern designated as Classic Modern with more emphasis on classic and less on modernistic was introduced to dispel a sameness, a heavy dullness, that hovered over Modern. It was hoped that Classic Modern which was chiefly white and gold would drive away the clinical look—a look strenuously resisted by the public. In 1937 a new "homey" look, a crafted look for Modern was forecast by Widdicomb with its new collection of Swedish Modern designed by Carl Malmsten, whose furniture had been exhibited at the Swedish Pavilion of the Paris Exhibition, 1925.

For a deeper understanding of modern design in the 1920's and 1930's too much credit cannot be given to the Museum of Modern Art, New York, founded in 1929, and the fifteen exhibitions of American Industrial Art held at the Metropolitan Museum of Art between the years 1917 and 1940. Each of the exhibitions held at the Metropolitan Museum strongly emphasized the value of art in industry, as it was the museum's belief that "the hope of industrial art design lies in America, that our manufacturers and designers have not only the technical but also the artistic ability to produce objects of applied art of high type, especially on the basis of 'quantity production' which is the only basis calculated to meet the requirements of current life." By quantity production is understood "the making of a number of pieces at a time from a single design or of a number of identical pieces from time to time, but from a model or drawings retained for the purpose." Apart from the highest calibre of design, one interesting condition upon entries required that the product exhibited must be or represent the regular work of the exhibiting firm. In a word, no display pieces. Exhibitors of furniture to the first exhibition included such manufacturers as W. and J. Sloane, Orsenigo Company, Inc., and A. Casiraghi Inc. Newcomers to the third and fourth exhibitions were the Grand Rapids Furniture Company and Elsie de Wolfe respectively. Especially noteworthy was the eleventh exhibition, The Architect and the Industrial Arts (1929), in which distinguished American architects—Ely Jacques Kahn, Ralph T. Walker, Joseph Urban, John Wellborn Root, Eugene Schoen, Eliel Saarinen, Raymond M. Hood, Armistead Fitzhugh and the ceramic designer Léon V. Solon—made the exhibition practically their own by planning every detail. Among the lenders to the twelfth exhibition (1931) were Baker Furniture, Aluminum Company of America, Gilbert Rhode and four well-known designers of tubular steel furniture—William Lescaze, Eugene Schoen, Donald Deskey and Paul Frankl, the latter also familiar for his so-called skyscraper furniture. In the preface to the catalogue for the fifteenth and final exhibition which ran from April 29 to September 15, 1940, Richard Bach, who initiated this unique program, stated: "In the present exhibition it is clear that modern design has come a long way in the brief span of its life."

The New York World's Fair as well as the Golden Gate Exhibition in San Francisco, both held in 1939, brought to a climax the upsurge of Modern. Swedish Modern enjoyed a great vogue after its resounding success at the New York World's Fair, and was to have a fruitful influence on American furniture design.

SCANDINAVIAN FURNITURE

Of great importance in the study of modern furniture is that made in the four Scandinavian countries—Denmark, Finland, Norway and Sweden—which fulfills many of the demands that a modern way of life has placed on furniture. It runs the gamut from handmade furniture in wood to completely industrialized furniture in metal, laminates and plastics. The history of modern furniture in each of the four countries does not entirely coincide. Sweden took the lead at the start of the current renaissance in the 1920's and early 1930's. At that time the byword was Swedish Modern. Since the mid-20th century Denmark has been preeminent. From the time laminated techniques were pioneered in Finland by Alvar Aalto, Finnish furniture has been a product of the machine. Finally, Norway has in recent years made marked progress, particularly with export furniture. The best in Scandinavian furniture is the result of a reasonable attitude toward things which takes into account construction, choice of material, function and expressiveness. Steeped as these countries were in handicraft tradition they believed and practiced that beauty and quality can be achieved only through the close cooperation of the furniture architect, as they call the designer, and the manufacturer. Made for people who lead modest and orderly lives, their goal is to produce furniture possessing everyday excellence within the economic reach of every citizen.

An engaging honesty has always characterized Swedish furniture. In the 18th century when French influence was paramount, the Swedish craftsmen blended this influence into a native Swedish style with clean lines and a sound conception of ornamentation which during the latter part of the 18th century received fittingly the name Gustavian, in honor of the popular king, Gustavus III (1746–1792). Under Napoleon's Marshal Bernadotte (1763–1844), who became King of Sweden (and also Norway) in 1818 as Charles XIV, the country had an attraction for Empire, especially Biedermeier.

The plain but agreeable, wholesome and homey quality of Biedermeier, conveying a feeling of well being, had a formative influence on Swedish modern with which the general public first became acquainted on a considerable scale at the Stockholm Exhibition of 1930.

Truly modern furniture production developed first in Sweden, especially if it is viewed in connection with the attempts to raise the household standards of the masses. For the first time in the world the Swedish were making furniture designed to meet the physical and aesthetic needs of mankind as a whole, and not of special estates and classes. Briefly, aesthetic consideration of designs was tempered by social and economic conditions.

At this point it seems appropriate to say a few words about the English "utility" furniture scheme, of standard specification and design, which was introduced by the government during the Second World War to meet the timber shortage. The interesting feature of this wartime control was a definite and conscious effort to improve design. Through it the public became accustomed to a simpler type of design of good proportions and clean lines than was available before the war. Of course, permanent government control of design in any consumer trade is scarcely likely to be beneficial.

The Swedes prefer to think of Swedish Modern not as a style but as a movement —the growth of an idea—a new conception of the place of furniture in the scheme of modern life. A movement based on universal need, capable of infinite development and adaptability to all conditions so long as the fundamental idea is not lost sight of; that is, the human form and the arrangement of the interior so as to give the individual the greatest freedom for his activities in a harmonious atmosphere within the limited space which he calls his home. This idea has been maintained, as is evident, for example, in Swedish chairs and unit furniture. A chair should be designed so that the occupant sits in a posture which gives most rest and the typical Swedish chair is built just for the purpose (575). The Swedes have been leading exponents of unit furniture as well as "knock down" or "package" furniture. The advantage of unit furniture is, of course, that extra pieces can be bought as needed and it fits more easily into a room than the customary type, and in this latter respect it shares the virtue of built-in furniture without its immobility. Like the Swedish prefabricated house, which was a great success, the package furniture also results in great economies in labor costs.

One of the pioneers and leading figures for Swedish Modern is Carl Malmsten (b. c. 1880). An extreme reactionary against sterile functionalism, Malmsten has fought for more than four decades for a more personalized home environment. Achieving a fine harmony between the old and new, Malmsten has followed, in his own words, " the classic Swedish line of unpretentious simplicity for the furtherance of peace-filled home and work milieu." Another leading pioneer also born in the 1880's but whose approach is international is Josef Frank, who came from Vienna where he was one of the leading progressive architects of the 1920's.

After the Stockholm Exhibition of 1930 leading designers such as G. A. Berg, Einar Dahl and Axel Larsson abandoned geometric functionalism and turned their attention to the creation of practical utilitarian furniture. They tried to develop lighter lines for furniture, and by attaching shelves and cupboards to the walls they hoped to increase the free flow of space. These designers made progress in creating comfortable chairs by studying sitting positions, and they also studied the possibilities of using different materials and colors in standard furniture in order to increase the combination potentials. Bruno Mathsson, whose ideas have been reflected in the greater part of Swedish furniture production, is generally regarded as the most typical representative of this group. He started to experiment with laminated wood furniture around the same time as Alvar Aalto of Finland, and he occupies a distinguished position for his chairs with laminated wood frames which he has been continually developing and refining for a period of over twenty years (575). He is also well known for his extension dining table provided with four drop-leaves and four gates. This remarkable table, which when closed is only nine inches deep and opens to one hundred ten inches, was exhibited at the New York World's Fair, 1939 (576). During the 1940's such furniture designers as Carl-Axel Acking and Elias Svedberg based their designs for furniture on the findings of the furniture function studies already mentioned. Yngve Ekström has been the source of design inspiration at Swedese. Among the younger generation is Nils Strinning, who is known for his string series in which he combined plastic-covered wire supports with wood shelves, and Hans Johansson who has carried out some interesting experiments with wood construction without screws or glue, as the tension of the material holds the different parts together. In the opinion of the Swedish author Ulf Härd af Segerstad, which he gives in his book, MODERN SCANDINAVIAN FURNITURE (1963), "Current furniture production is more comprehensive and more differentiated in Sweden than in the other Scandinavian countries. It ranges all the way from the exclusive handmade pieces of wooden furniture to the industrially produced item in various materials."

In Finland the Modern style began to evolve around the turn of the 19th century, with the search for a Finnish national style. Apart from the mainstream was the furniture designed by several of the leading architects of the period such as Eliel Saarinen and Lars Sonck which bore the indelible marks of their forceful personalities. In the Iris factory, Finland's first producer of industrial art, Louis Sparre created around 1900 a kind of well-designed furniture not unlike the English and Austrian furniture of this time. This was followed by a period of plain, practical classicism of German inspiration. The social revolution and housing reforms following the First World War period finally gave rise to the simplicity and practicality which today characterizes the furniture of this country. Acting as intermediaries between the old and the new is the work of the furniture designers Carl Johan Boman and Werner West. Boman, who is still active, possesses remarkable knowledge about the production of furniture from both the handicraft as well as the technical side. From the technical aspect he has designed chairs which can be adjusted by means of a simple device to different sitting positions, and also stackable, folding

and row chairs. Space-saving furniture for the small apartment also received his attention.

Undoubtedly Finland's great exponent of Modern is the architect Alvar Aalto (b. 1888), who was the first to exploit the spring-support principle to laminated wood. Using native birch he not only designed a number of chairs and stools made entirely of plywood and laminated wood, but he also invented some of the methods for making them (577). He made his first laminated birch chair in 1929. Through the years Aalto has continued to develop the possibilities of laminated birch. Working with the Helsinki manufacturer Artek, he has designed armchairs, stools, tables, and even shelf-unit brackets. Aalto's furniture has interesting details which can be singled out. Especially notable is his method of shaping the laminated birch leg where it joins with the seat or table top. The leg fans out with a soft and refined organic movement, suggesting the re-creation of a living tree (578).

Currently furniture production in Finland is developing along two main lines; one follows the tradition of wood, chiefly native birch, while the other employs steel construction often of a very advanced type. Among the designers working in wood are Olavi Hänninen, Reino Ruokolainen, Olof Ottelin, Carl Gustav Hiort af Ornäs and Runar Engblom. No doubt the pioneer in the metal group is Ilmari Tapiovaara, a versatile designer, who is greatly interested in the problems affecting industrial production. Specializing in metal and plastic furniture, he has in recent years designed furniture for offices, hospitals and other public buildings. There are also Antti Nurmesniemi, one of Finland's best all-around designers; Olli Borg who works in plastic as well as in metal, and Yrjö Kukkapuro, a young representative for metal furniture who prefers to work with light pliant furniture which can be used advantageously on terraces, in public waiting rooms and the like.

The furniture fair held at Stavanger in Norway in 1961 clearly showed that the younger generation of Norwegian furniture designers are eager to put their country on an equal basis with the other Scandinavian countries. By tradition Norwegian furniture is heavy and robust. This feature is best expressed in a sturdy, practical type of rustic "cabin" furniture —the cabin in the mountains or by the sea which plays an important part in the Norwegian way of life. Around the beginning of the 20th century a characteristic and romantic version of the Jugend style appeared, the so-called dragonesque style. Its leading exponent was Gerhard Munthe, Norway's first designer in the field of modern applied arts. In the 1920's Norwegian furniture designs reflected a simplified classical influence, while in the following decade under the tutelage of such functionalistic designers as Herman Munthe-Kaas and Knut Knutsen, functionalism prevailed. Early in the 1940's Alf Sture helped to lay the foundation for a modern traditional interpretation. Much of his wood furniture has a warm, livable and modest look. Also using wood as his medium is Torbjörn Afdal whose furniture designs reflect the influence of such Danish designers as Kaare Klint and Ole Wanscher. There is also metal furniture designed by Tormod Alnaes who teaches at the State School of Handicrafts and Industrial Art at Oslo, a school that has contributed tremendously in the renaissance of Nor-

wegian furniture. One of the finest designers in Scandinavia is Björn Ianke, a skilled cabinetmaker and a former student of Carl Malmsten. Of the group of younger Norwegian furniture designers, Sven Dysthe has had considerable success with his export furniture combining wood and metal.

Danish designs have exercised perhaps the greatest single influence on American interiors and furnishings. Indeed modern Danish furniture which retains the sparsely seasoned flavor of contemporary Swedish design has become almost as familiar in the American home as the Boston rocker. Its transatlantic success appears to rest on two Danish virtues—a graceful practicality and livability, a simple and natural vocabulary of form that looks handmade. For this reason it mingles easily with such perennial American favorites as the pine furniture of New England, Pennsylvania farmhouse or the furniture made by the Shakers.

It is often said, and quite rightly so, that the Danish handicraft tradition has been a very significant factor in the remarkably rapid development of Danish Modern. That the Danes succeeded in establishing a certain standard for the aesthetic design of everyday furniture is due no doubt to the less explosive character of industrial development in this country which made it possible for the Danes to preserve the handicrafts as the formative factor in quality standards. In other words they were able to transfer the sound tradition of their handicrafts as regards treatment of material, good constructive design and careful attention to details, to a more industrialized production. However, it should not be overlooked that Germany in the first years of the 20th century was not alone in seeking simplicity and functional form for objects of everyday use. The Danish contribution also began in the first decade of the 20th century, and it was to gather strength until some forty years later Denmark had become one of the most important countries in the world in the field of the crafts and industrial design. From the start Denmark had clearly formulated in accordance with the new times the theoretical precepts and social goals essential for modern furniture production.

The basic work for the design of light modern types of Danish furniture was laid in the 1930's when Danish cabinetmakers employed the leading designers in Copenhagen to free them from the stagnation of derivative styling. An important influence on the development in this period is due to the architect Kaare Klint (1888–1954) who in 1924 was appointed to lead the newly created class in furniture design at the Royal Academy's School of Architecture. Through his teaching there he exerted influence on an entire generation of Danish furniture designers. "It is hardly wrong to say," writes Esbjørn Hiorth in his book, MODERN DANISH FURNITURE, "that Klint was the first Danish furniture designer who founded his design on a purely rational basis. Each piece was designed only after a systematic study of the various functional demands made on that particular type of furniture, and he required the same thoroughness of his students. That which we now take for granted was positively revolutionary thirty years ago. Under the leadership of Klint, the Academy's Furniture School was more than a school for furniture designers; it became a laboratory in which the functional basis of the design of

modern furniture was investigated and registered." (579)

The young designers received a chance to put their ideas into practice, when, in 1930, the Copenhagen Cabinetmakers Guild, which is more than 400 years old, initiated an annual competition for new types of furniture. Toward the end of the 1940's, as a result of a fruitful collaboration between designers and cabinetmakers, a number of simple types of furniture had been created which have since become the models on which almost the entire production of the Danish furniture industry is based.

But before considering such famous examples of these prototypes as those designed by Hans Wegner and Finn Juhl, some of the furniture designers of the 1930's and early 1940's, apart from Kaare Klint, deserve special mention as their ideas have notably influenced the greater part of Danish furniture production. Among these are O. Mölgaard-Nielsen, Arne Jacobsen, Ole Wanscher, Rigmor Anderson, Edvard and Tove Kindt-Larsen, Peter Hvidt and Börge Mogensen (580).

Now for an example of these prototypes; namely the chair with open arms designed in 1945 by Finn Juhl (b. 1912) for the cabinetmaker Niels Vodder, which was one of the first examples of a lightweight modern chair. The practical elegance of this chair with its sensitively molded, sculptured frame and its sparsely upholstered seat and back aroused great admiration. Since then several variants of the type have been created both by Finn Juhl and some other designers, and today it is one of the most popular types of armchair. As is clearly shown in this chair, Juhl especially likes to emphasize the separation between seat and frame—an ingenious way to shed weight. The carrying structure is stressed as one thing and the seat and back are simply surfaces to give rest (581). To divide a chair and other forms of seat furniture into components is one of Juhl's characteristic design principles (582). Some of his case pieces, such as chests of drawers, reveal a similar independence between the drawers and frame. Table tops (583) and legs are often treated in a like manner, and in this respect recall Le Corbusier. The use of sparse upholstery as well as cane or rush which frequently replaces the upholstery give a general impression of airiness.

Another example is the familiar chair designed in 1949 by Hans J. Wegner (b. 1914) for the cabinetmaker Johannes Hansen which he simply called "the chair." (584) According to Wegner it was inspired by a chair in the Copenhagen Museum, a Chinese child's chair having a solid splat and arched horseshoe-shaped crest rail, a typical Ming design. Wegner rarely uses the "floating" device—having the back and seat suspended or held away from the frame—a device associated with Juhl and widely adopted in America after his work became better known. Although these two completely simplified chair types by Juhl and Wegner are handmade, they became the basic models for numerous variants produced by industrial methods. It may appear inconsistent for industry to carry on the forms and aesthetic standards of handicrafts, but Danish industrial art is predominantly based on production in small factories and the borderline between handwork and industrial methods of production is very fluid. While the basic frames and other uniform parts are machine made, a major part of the working processes—for example, the sculptured shaping of the crest rail, arms and tapering legs, the intricate joinings and soft oil rubbing—are done by hand.

In furniture production there are only a few factories based totally on a definitely industrial production in which such materials as light metals and artificial materials as plastics are employed exclusively, just as they are in the manufacture of automobiles. Only a few Danish designers have worked with modern furniture of this type. Examples of purely industrial manufacture are Arne Jacobsen's two chairs, the "egg" (585) and "swan" dating from 1957. Each is a pivoting chair with leather or wool-covered foam rubber upholstery over a molded reinforced plastic shell mounted on a chromium-plated steel pedestal. These pieces show the stringent simplification that characterizes the industrial line of Danish furniture design. An exponent of this type of design is Poul Kjaerholm, one of the younger furniture designers, whose work is reminiscent of Mies' steel furniture of the late 1920's (586). It is mainly a combination of steel and "natural" materials, such as leather or wicker for chairs, while his tables generally have massive tops of wood and occasionally stone. It is interesting to note here that the tide of functionalist modern that in the 1930's swept over countries as close to Denmark culturally and geographically as Sweden, Finland and Germany, found no ready response among Danish furniture designers. Machine art apparently seemed too sensational in a community where industry was less influential than rural occupations.

The "Danish mania" began in the United States almost from the day Edgar Kaufmann, Jr., of the Museum of Modern Art, New York, returned from Europe in 1948 with photographs of Finn Juhl's chairs. In the course of the 1950's this fashion gathered impetus, culminating in an exhibition of the Arts of Denmark which opened at the Metropolitan Museum of Art on October 14, 1960. The interest in Danish furniture led not only to a collection designed by Finn Juhl for the Baker Company and introduced in 1951, but more importantly it created among American designers a new respect for the treatment of wood—that is, its structural and decorative possibilities when woods of various colors and grains are combined. Meanwhile the two polarities in Danish design, the sculptured handcrafted quality in wood and the international expression using new materials and new techniques continue to win admirers in America each year.

FROM THE SECOND WORLD WAR TO THE PRESENT

Modern architecture has changed the concept about furniture by emphasizing a closer relation between indoors and outdoors and recommending a freer use of interior space. The cupboard and other forms of storage furniture, which had been so important at one time, are now often built into the walls themselves or are simple rectangles obviously related to the architecture of the room. Storage walls, room dividers, demountable partitions and modular case furniture virtually unknown in 1940 are found in every kind of interior today. These practical ideas and functional innovations can be attributed to the industrial designers who are a phenomenon of the United States unparalleled elsewhere. Of this group of designers the architect-designer George Nelson (b. 1908) is outstanding. A substantial part of Nelson's designs are furniture "systems" rather than individual items of furniture (587). The storage wall system set up as a wall or against one, conveniently provides the storage space formerly handled by a bookcase, cupboard, desk, chest of drawers and the like.

With storage pieces thus simplified and often absorbed by the architecture and with seating units built in or which appear as if built in, the chair has offered 20th century furniture designers their most interesting problem. Architects and designers have concentrated all their ingenuity to design chairs having agreeable silhouettes, relative transparency, portability, durability and comfort. It is for this reason that chairs predominate in this chapter as they clearly portray new ideas, forms, techniques and materials. In a word, they are the hub of the Modern movement.

Space will permit only a brief outline of the main materials and techniques developed during the last one hundred years. First to be considered is bentwood furniture. The principles of wood bending have been known and practiced for many years. In furniture bentwood shapes have always been important. A familiar early example is the traditional Windsor chair with a bow-shaped back which is still being made in large quantities. Undoubtedly the most famous example of the use of bentwood is the Thonet chair, the invention of Michael Thonet (1796–1871) who was born at Boppard in the Rhineland. Thonet's earliest successful experiments were in bent plywood. Thousands of miles away, in New York City, Belter was working on much the same principle in his ornately carved rosewood chairs. Prince Metternich of Vienna became acquainted with Thonet's bent plywood chairs and invited him to live in Vienna, an invitation Thonet accepted. There he continued his experiments. In 1856 Thonet perfected a process by which solid lengths of beechwood could be steamed and bent to form long curved rods looking like the proverbial willow. He used Carpathian beech because of its singular tight parallel grain; other woods not possessing this quality are apt to splinter at the point of greatest strain. Bentwood made it possible to produce chairs without complicated carved joints and contours, paving the way for the first mass production of standardized furniture. Thonet fashioned bentwood chairs that ran the gamut from the fancifully curved and curled rocking chair which exploited all the possibilities of steamed bentwood (588) to such simple models as the Vienna café side chair, geared for the mass market which Thonet had foreseen. Millions of bentwood chairs—one of the lightest, strongest chairs ever designed—have been sold by Gebrüder Thonet throughout the world. The Vienna café model catalogued in 1876 as Chair No. 18, which is still in production with slight modifications, has sold well over fifty million copies (589).

Next to be considered as a principal machine material is plywood and laminated wood, and unlike metal or plastic it retains some vestige of a traditional material. The decorative process of veneering and possibly some form of plywood was known to the ancient Egyptians. Though veneering continued to be used to a greater or lesser extent through the centuries, plywood was not rediscovered until the end of the 18th century. In 1830 Michael Thonet, at the beginning of his career, was making chairs from narrow strips of veneer bent and glued together under pressure in a wood mold. He failed, however, to take advantage of this invention. In 1865 the first American patent was taken out for plywood, and thirteen years later at the Paris exhibition of 1878, the Americans showed thin, bent and perforated plywood for backs and seats of chairs and benches. This thin plywood began to appear in many parts of the world as a cheap substitute for ordinary wood—for example, as a backing for mirrors and chests of drawers and cupboards, or as paneling in cupboard doors. A sudden demand created by the First World War for war purposes brought about notable improvements in plywood structure. After 1918 plywood was joined by the products of related techniques—laminated board and blockboard, both of which are extensively used in furniture. Each has a core of wood built up of thin strips or blocks respectively, faced on both sides by plywood, which makes the material rigid and of a heavier gauge than the usual type of plywood, and thus offsets its chief defect—a lack of stiffness. Originally known as "veneered wood," the name *plywood* only came into common use after the First World War. It was hoped that the new name would erase the popular prejudice against its poor start, when it was generally regarded as a rather second-rate material, an attitude that sometimes persists even today. The production of reliable plywoods, blockboards and laminated boards in the inter-war period revolutionized the methods of furniture making. In a very short time it became evident that the new materials offered an alternative to paneled framing, which since the 15th century has remained preeminently the soundest method of construction, and more significantly this alternative was simpler and more adapted to mass production.

The next step was to learn how to bend plywood permanently. Even before the First World War, a Finnish plywood manufacturer in collaboration with his designer, the Finnish architect Alvar Aalto, began a series of experiments to try to make furniture entirely out of bent plywood. Their efforts were so successful that by the late 1930's their Finmar furniture made of native birch, which abounded in Finnish forests, was becoming well known. It was Aalto who first exploited the natural springiness in the material, which in some of his designs for chairs he used to the full extent, so that they became in effect one large spring which flexed downward when sat on. For example, in 1934 Aalto introduced an armchair having a continuous seat and back bent in sweeping curves and formed from a single sheet of plywood, using birch veneer as a facing, suspended within a bent, cutout, laminated birchwood frame (577). There is also his cantilever armchair with a seat and back of bent plywood, with spring arms and legs of laminated birch. In a word, Aalto used the natural spring in the material, as Breuer and Mies a few years earlier had used the spring of steel in their tubular steel furniture. No doubt the well-known long chair (chaise longue of laminated wood designed by Breuer in 1936 for Isokon) illustrates how easy the material was to his hand (590).

Laminated wood, not to be confused with laminated board, is a cross between plywood and bentwood. While the veneers in plywood are usually laid with the grain of each layer running in alternate directions, the layers in laminated wood are commonly thicker than plywood veneer, and are laid so that the grain of each runs in the same direction. This difference in construction is evident in the properties of the two materials; that is, plywood is equally strong in both directions, but laminated wood as ordinary solid wood is strongest along the length of the grain. For this reason plywood is used for the seat and back (as in the Finnish chair) where the stresses are almost the same in all directions; laminated wood is used for the thicker arms and legs where the stresses run parallel to the length of the wood. Laminated wood is stronger than bentwood. Its springlike quality can be used advantageously over the best of ordinary solid wood in production, as imperfections and weaknesses in the grain are either greatly reduced or cancel one another out in successive layers. Then too the impregnation of the wood with synthetic resins which form the material and set it into shape provides greater strength.

Bent plywood can produce only the kind of shape which can be made out of a flat piece of material; that is, its shape can curve in only one direction at a time. Double-curved or molded plywood, that is plywood bent in two directions, was intensively and rapidly developed during the Second World War by the aviation industries in Europe and America. In this manner plywood could be used in a softer, more undulating way rather than simply bent for chair backs and seats. This new technique was used by Charles Eames (b. 1907) and Eero Saarinen (1910–1961) for a molded plywood chair entered in the Organic Design competition conducted by the Museum of Modern Art in 1940. Their entry won and even though their molded plywood chair never went into production the era of the molded chair had arrived. It was only after the Second World War that Eames and Saarinen each independently produced molded chairs, Eames of plywood (1945) and reinforced plastic (1951) and Saarinen of reinforced plastic (1946).

In 1945 Charles Eames, one of America's most genuinely industrial architect-designers, introduced his shock-mounted chair with its two separate pads or "petals" of molded plywood serving as a back and seat and its skeleton-like steel tubing frame. Making use of the springiness of the materials, this chair, first produced by Herman Miller in 1946, with its rubber shock mounts electronically welded to the wood and steel, is a notable product of machine technology. Though Eames' furniture is known and used around the world, it is this comfortable, flexible, and almost indestructible chair that the general public remembers whenever Eames' name is mentioned (591). Ten years later, in 1956, Eames, using the experience he acquired through production trials, designed one of the great chairs of the 20th century, a lounge chair and ottoman of laminated wood on a metal swivel base with down- and foam-filled leather cushions (592).

About the same time in England

Ernest D. Race created a whole new English style out of laminates, steel and aluminum. Race carried on in the tradition of Sir Gordon Russell (b. 1892) who with Sir Ambrose Heal (1872–1923) were the major influences in English furniture design through the first forty years of the 20th century. Their firms, Heal & Son and Gordon Russell, dominated the furniture market. Russell was chiefly responsible for continuing the tradition of rural designs reminiscent of Gimson, while Heal's furniture was more receptive to the influence from Europe. It was not until the reaction of the 1950's to the war years of utility furniture that English design was able to compete again in the international sphere. Race had worked in the British aircraft industry during the Second World War, where he became aware of the potentialities of its techniques if applied to furniture design. Combining lightness with economical use of materials, Race designed for the Festival of Britain in 1951 an occasional or garden chair made from steel rod with a molded plywood seat painted in bright colors which was widely popular. Perhaps the leading English designer today with a wide reputation abroad is Robin Day, who pioneered in England the use of more complicated shapes in plywood in the Festival Hall, and has been the principal source of design at the firm of Hille, which dominates the progressive market as Heal & Son had done before the war. Another interesting development dating from around the early 1950's has been a renewed interest in the Windsor chair and variations of it. The designer Lucian Ercolani has been responsible for this revival in country-style furniture which is made by Ercol Furniture, Ltd., at High Wycombe in

Buckinghamshire, where the presence of large beech forests encouraged the early growth of the chair industry.

During the 1950's and 1960's Italian designers working for such leading furniture firms as Arflex, Gavina and Padova have with typical Italian fecundity and boldness created a number of distinctive chairs and tables in plywood and laminated wood.

Compared to ordinary wood, plywood is a very stable material, which is perhaps its most important advantage in relation to machining. Then, too, no matter in what form plywood is used, it lends itself to broad and simple surfaces on which to display the figure of the wood. There is an almost unbelievable number of beautiful plain and figured veneers available for plywood furniture, the selection of which is an important aesthetic consideration. Wood has always been one of the most rewarding of materials and in its new form it should go on to new potentialities of beauty and usefulness.

Then there is the invention of chromium-plated steel furniture which has been treated already in this chapter. Chromium-plated steel chairs and tables, pieces designed by modern architects such as Breuer, Le Corbusier and Mies van der Rohe, have spawned entire schools of furniture design since they first appeared. Perhaps the most significant of modern American furniture is of metal. Of particular interest is the Catenary furniture designed by George Nelson in 1963 for Herman Miller, Inc. Each chair consists of eight horizontal pillows hung on cables swung from the chromium-plated steel framework. In all countries —England, Denmark and Italy, to mention but several—young designers are attracted to the clarity of metal, and if their work is not new in concept it is frequently original in detail.

A distinctive related class are the molded steel wire chairs. In 1951 Eames introduced his version of a wire shell chair and a year later the American, Italian-born sculptor, Harry Bertoia (b. 1915) introduced his wire mesh chair. In spite of a superficial likeness, the two chairs are fundamentally different. One basic difference is that Eames' seat cradle is supported on legs (593) while in Bertoia's chair the seat cradle is suspended by triangular side braces over the base (594). "This suspension of the seat cradle," comments INTERIORS, October 1952, "gives the chair flexibility, automatic adjustment to two positions by means of an effortless shift of body weight." In 1966 Knoll Associates introduced a collection of nine pieces comprising chairs, tables and stools, all made of steel wire, designed by the American-born architect, Warren Platner (595). The seat cushions in the chairs are "floated" on suspended platforms and all upholstery is of molded latex.

There is also the light alloy furniture. Light alloys are divided into two groups: those with aluminum as the main metal and those with magnesium; the latter are occasionally known as ultra-light alloys. Both aluminum and magnesium alloys have one important characteristic in common—their extreme lightness combined with strength. They possess little of the elasticity or springiness of steel, and under the same weight they bend much more than steel. This extra "give" must be considered when designing furniture. Outdoor furniture is one promising field for aluminum. A Swiss firm for the Zurich Exhibition of 1939 offered outdoor chairs of aluminum that were graceful, imaginative, comfortable and durable. Shortly afterward Marcel Breuer designed a garden chair in solid aluminum which, as in all this designer's work, the natural properties of the material seem to suggest the finished form of the design.

In 1868 the first commercial plastic, cellulose nitrate, was created in the United States. Called celluloid, this first American plastic was soon found to have many uses. Forty-one years passed before the plastics industry took its second major step forward. In 1909 Dr. Leo Henrik Baekeland introduced phenolformaldehyde resins. The first phenolic in this country was given the trade name Bakelite coined from his name. From 1909 to 1926 two more plastic materials were developed—cold-molded and casein. Familiar products for these two types of plastics were knobs and handles, and knitting needles, respectively. From that time onward the tempo of plastics development increased consistently. Cellulose acetate was the next large volume plastic to be developed commercially in this country. Launched in 1927 it was available only in sheets, rods and tubes until 1929, when it appeared as a molding material and became the first injection-molded plastic. Acrylic, or polymethylmethacrylate, plastic was commercially introduced in the United States in 1936. Acrylics offer exceptional clarity and are strong, rigid and resistant to sharp blows (596). They may be colorless or in a full range of transparent, translucent and opaque color. Both polyethylene, which was originally produced in England, and the polyesters were introduced commercially in the United States in 1942. Fifteen years later in 1957

polypropylene was first used commercially in the United States by Hercules and in 1960 in England by Imperial Chemicals.

Plastics are man-made materials, in contrast to nature's materials such as wood and metal. A generally accepted definition is: "Any one of a large and varied group of materials consisting wholly or in part of combinations of carbon with oxygen, hydrogen, nitrogen and other organic and inorganic elements which, while solid in the finished state, at some time in its manufacture is made liquid, and thus capable of being formed into various shapes most usually through the application, either singly or together, of heat and pressure." Plastics are a family of materials—not a single material—each member of which has its special advantages. Whatever their properties or form, plastics fall into one of two groups—the thermoplastic or the thermosetting. The former are plastics that become soft when exposed to sufficient heat and harden when cooled, no matter how often the process is repeated, while the plastic materials belonging to the thermosetting group are set into permanent shape when heat and pressure are applied to them during forming. Reheating will not soften these materials. Injection-molding is the principal method of forming thermoplastic materials. (Modifications of the injection process are sometimes used for thermosetting plastics.) In injection-molding, plastic material is put into a hopper which feeds into a heating chamber. A plunger pushes the plastic through this long heating chamber where the material is softened to a fluid state. At the end of this chamber there is a nozzle which abuts firmly against an opening into a cool, closed mold. The fluid plastic is forced at high pressure through the nozzle into the cold mold. As soon as the plastic cools to a solid state, the mold opens and the finished plastic piece is ejected from the press.

With the rapid development of plastics, of "engineered" materials since the Second World War, it was only a matter of time until furniture designers would turn to plastics. In chair design they have made possible new shapes that possess a new type of comfort, while their new profiles have a fluidity, a grace, a technological beauty of line that immediately strikes the eye. In 1946 the architect-designer Saarinen introduced a molded plastic shell armchair. The capacious molded shell, upholstered in foam rubber and provided with loose seat and back cushions, was held up cradle fashion in a skeleton-like tubular steel framework mounted on four conventionalized steel legs. This skillfully designed easy chair, in which the average person can sit comfortably in a variety of positions, offered such pleasant protection to the sitter that Florence Knoll (b. 1917) the architect-trained designer for whom the chair was designed, popularly dubbed it the "womb chair." (597)

Saarinen, who always designed imaginatively and soundly within the new aesthetics that the machine demands and allows, achieved a great triumph in his chalice-like pedestal chair introduced in 1957. It was designed with a single stem and base in place of the customary four legs. In contrast to the other molded chairs, that is, plastic, plywood or wire mesh, where the distinction between the shell and supports is quite apparent, this chair presents a more truly unified design whereby the seat and support, the two essential parts, seem to be of one and the same material. In this instance the shell is of a molded plastic reinforced with fiberglas, while the stem and base are of spun aluminum. It seems that it was Saarinen's intention to make a completely plastic chair, but no plastic exists which when used in such fine dimensions will retain its form under direct weight (598). Then there are the already mentioned "egg" and "swan" chairs designed by the Danish designer Arne Jacobsen with hide or wool covered foam rubber upholstery over a reinforced plastic shell mounted on a chromium-plated steel pedestal.

Up to this time the costs of materials and methods were so high as to set these chairs apart. All used reinforced plastics, that is plastic reinforced by some fibrous material, in this instance fiberglas. Or conversely, all used glass fiber "mats" reinforced with certain resins or plastics in which the mats are soaked. Regardless, handwork was involved and the process could not be mechanized sufficiently to reduce costs significantly.

However, the discovery of the plastic, polypropylene, a product of gases, made possible the utilization of the technique of injection molding, which up to this time was not capable of being applied to chair design for the lack of a suitably tough material. Polypropylene makes strong rigid industrial moldings without need for reinforcement and costs no less than half as much as plastic fiberglas moldings. Its shining clear surfaces which can be solid colored are stainproof, chip proof, and do not scratch easily. Under the design supervision of Robin Day, the London firm of Hille produced a chair seat which could be mass-produced at low unit cost by injection-molded polypropylene. In less than a year this stacking chair, comprising a colored shell and a simple tubular metal frame, was either being made under license by, or exported to, almost every leading country in the world. Stack and gang chairs of injection-molded technique were a notable development. Their low price and high comfort have come to be taken for granted. In 1965 Knoll Associates introduced a new stack and gang chair of injection-molded plastic and die-cast aluminum designed by the American-born Don Albinson (b. 1921). Instead of the more usual one-piece plastic seat, the back and seat are separate pieces that "give" with the body and are therefore comfortable for long periods of sitting (599).

An important contribution in plastic furniture is the "Seggio" chair designed by the Italian Joe C. Columbo (b. 1933) for Kartell. It is unique in that it is the first chair on the market of the four-leg variety that is completely made by the injection-mold process. This chair, which will both stack and gang, first appeared on the market in 1967 (600). In 1966 Hille launched an armchair version of the original injection-molded stacking chair, which was also designed by Robin Day. The tooling for these chairs involves very high financial investment. An especially high degree of responsibility is placed in the designer, calling for an attempt to obtain the highest level in all aspects of the design. These aspects fall into three broad categories: those of technology and production, function, including the intricacies of anthropometric considerations, and the more intangible ones of aesthetics or good appearance. These three areas of design are indivisi-

ble and the attempt to encompass them satisfactorily is very exacting. Meanwhile, in plastic reinforced fiberglas the Finnish designer Eero Aarnio (b. 1932) has designed noteworthy models, including the Gyro chair, an entirely plastic egg-shaped chair of sinuous curves, comfort and rocking motion, molded in two parts without legs or pedestal (601) the Ball chair in the form of an all-enveloping plastic shell or ball molded in two parts that rests on a very low metal base. There is also the Dutch designers' Pierre Paulin's "amoeba" chair and the Danish designer Verner Panton's (b. 1926) chair which entrusts the sitter's weight to cantileverage. (602)

At the present time Italy, one of the triad in the international sphere of modern furniture, the other two being the Scandinavian countries and the United States, leads the field in creating new forms and fresh uses for plastics in furniture design. One of the great post-war producers is Kartell, located near Milan. Owned by a husband and wife team, Anna and Giulio Castelli, this firm has placed Italy two giant steps ahead in plastic design for the home.

Since the years immediately following the Second World War when Gio Ponti (b. 1891) together with several other architects from around Milan put Italy back in the furniture world with the "floating look," Italian furniture has run the gamut from simple classicism in wood to notable and sometimes dramatic demonstrations in laminates (603), metals (604), plastics (605) and gigantic upholstered units.

With new and not so new materials (606) and technology as their tools, designers are continuously creating new furniture in various media. Foam rubber, either solid polyurethane foam or a combination of the spongy plastic and foam rubber commonly thought of as substitute material for seat cushions, is now looked upon as a total furniture form. In contrast to the easy chairs and sofas in the form of chunky cubes which virtually require no support or framing with metal, wood or rigid plastic, are such pieces as the undulating chaise longue designed by the French-born designer Olivier Mourge, which hides its steel frame and foam rubber padding under a zip-on stretch jersey slipcover (607). At this time all foam furniture requires a fabric covering. Even paper and the air we breathe have become useful materials for the designer's craft—air-filled clear plastic furniture or inflatable seating, and disposable paper furniture.

In summary, Modern furniture is the result of many influences; among them is the art of Japan, the Arts and Crafts movement, Art Nouveau, de Stijl, Le Corbusier, the Bauhaus, Marcel Breuer, Alvar Aalto, Charles Eames, the manufacturers of Scandinavia, Italy, and the United States.

Throughout its entire development art, and furniture is art, has been an expression of contemporary life and modern points of view. Through the centuries each style has sought its nourishment from the life about it, and consequently during its whole development it has always been modern, expressing in its form the changes of contemporary life and thought. A wise designer studies all past styles, for in them he finds principles similar to those which must underlie his own work if it is to be successful— design quality, workmanship and the fact that it meets a demand. Only the future can show how much creative power our age possesses for the development of its own style. If future generations can say that this age founded its style on true, logical and organic principles, then this age has been proved strong and creative, and future generations will have received a firm foundation on which they can build further and develop. It will be called the style of the 20th century and will be included in the sequence of categories of design which constitutes the history of art. It will be a machine art, as the 20th century has brought an almost unbelievable concentration upon technology due to the advance of science and it has not finished growing or changing.

CHINESE

CHINESE FURNITURE

Although direct trade has existed between China and the West for practically four centuries it has been only in the present century that we in the West have begun to understand the real art of China. When we first became interested in Chinese art through the foreign merchants of the 17th and 18th centuries, the art of China was already decadent. Unfortunately, these later and less desirable features of Chinese art attracted the fancy of the Europeans, and the Chinese anticipating a lucrative market emphasized such features. This created a false impression of Chinese taste among Europeans. At a later date this same desire to please and to create a market for their wares led the Japanese to produce ornate lacquer wares with masses of mother-of-pearl, which are so incongruous with their own taste. These misguided ideas on Chinese art have finally been erased by the splendid pioneer research of students and scholars who travelled to China to study ancient cities, after China became open to the West through the building of railroads. Illustrated works by these scholars on Chinese art and tomb furniture threw an entirely new light on Chinese civilization. For the first time the West realized that China had a great and glorious art history that reached far into the past. The untold quantities of funeral furniture revealed in the opening of tombs, which occurred during the construction of railroads, gave new significance to the industry and life of ancient China. Painting, sculpture, textiles, jade carving, ceramics and bronze casting were all a part of that great past. The tomb furniture, which was of immeasurable value in reconstructing Chinese culture, owed its origin to the Chinese custom of burying with their loved ones models or pictorial representations of objects which they had used in this life, to enable them to pursue their earthly occupations in their future life. Models of their homes, images of their family and animals, vessels for cooking and utensils for food were all included among the articles placed in the tombs.

The arts in China made rapid technical and aesthetic development during the Han dynasty, 206 B.C.–A.D. 220. This was the time when Chinese traditions in the arts were being formed. It has been conclusively established that China had cultural contact with the Roman Empire during this period, which entirely dispels the old theory that Chinese art developed behind closed doors. In fact, Chinese culture has always welcomed foreign influence. During all the great periods in Chinese history, the Chinese were generally borrowing and assimilating foreign culture. However, due to their peculiar genius, whatever the Chinese borrowed they generally through the years made their own. For example, the pagoda was adapted in such a manner that it became distinctively Chinese and it is extremely difficult to discern its resemblance to its Hindu prototype, the Indian stupa. The T'ang dynasty, 618–906, is often justifiably called the Golden Age or Augustan Age of Chinese art. All the arts flourished during this classic period and there is no reason to believe that the craft of cabinetwork did not make similar progress. Bronze work, pottery, textiles and jades revealed a singular strength and vitality plus a superb mastery of technique. The Sung dynasty, 960–1279, is frequently described as a prolonged Golden Age for artists, poets and craftsmen. Marco Polo's description of the capital city of Hangchow in 1280 relates the amenities of life enjoyed by its citizens and gives us reason to believe that China was perhaps the most civilized of all nations. The art work of this second classic period reflected a direct and refined simplicity free from over-elaboration, which imbued it with a singular nobility and strength. During the Ming dynasty, 1368–1644, art as an entirety possessed admirable strength and vigor. There was a tendency to return to earlier work both in form and decoration. The art of the Ch'ing dynasty is directly associated with its three great emperors, K'ang Hsi, 1662–1722, Yung Chêng, 1723–1735, and Ch'ien Lung, 1736–1795, who were all patrons of the arts. The Emperor K'ang Hsi founded the Academy for the decorative arts at Peking, which flourished for more than a century. The art of this era with its sophisticated refinement was unrivalled for its perfection of technique. Although this exhibition of skill merits lavish praise, the ornamental detail is often wearisome, for it lacks the spontaneity and originality which great art always possesses. That touch of genius found in the young and virile art of China was gone, and in the absence of fresh sources of inspiration the inevitable signs of decadence became increasingly patent. In later times their finest work, which still displayed superb craftsmanship, became purely imitative.

Western collections of Chinese art, which are especially rich in Chinese ceramics, afford an excellent source for studying Chinese craftsmanship. Bronze casting, jade carving, textiles and ceramics have always been handled by the Chinese with consummate skill. In wood and ivory carving and in lacquering they are also remarkably talented. Although much less is known about their cabinetwork from early times it is a reasonable assumption that their furniture was of similar distinction. Recurring political crises and social upheavals have been responsible for the loss of much of the fine furniture, for it is so difficult to safeguard in time of peril or flight. Vast quantities must have been destroyed in the looting and burning of great palaces which occurred with regularity at the end of each dynasty. Unfortunately China's troubled history with its resulting vicissitudes has continued into the 19th and 20th centuries. Despite the limited amount of extant Chinese furniture of which practically none exists prior to Ming, it can be stated with confidence that the same manipulative power and unerring instinct for form, which the Chinese have so admirably expressed in other materials, are also found in their cabinetwork. Fine Chinese furniture will satisfy the most exacting taste. The same splendid dexterity, which is the inheritance of centuries of craftsmanship, is also revealed in their articles of furniture. In fact, so much

of all their art work is good and so little is bad, that the Chinese undoubtedly rank among the most gifted of nations. Perhaps the supremacy of Chinese craftsmanship is best exemplified in ceramics. The polychrome and monochrome wares, unsurpassed for form and color, and the magnificent blue and white wares, which are fully appreciated in Europe and little understood in America, will always rank among the treasures of the world.

Chinese furniture made in hardwoods is perhaps the last of all Chinese forms of art to attract the understanding and appreciation of the Western world. Although records are available for a history of Chinese furniture, the literature is relatively sparse in comparison to the available literature on the other branches of Chinese art. The reason seems to be that the craft of cabinetwork was not as highly esteemed by the Chinese as the other handicrafts. The theory has been advanced that bronzes dating from around and prior to 1000 B.C. were probably metal prototypes of forms made of wood, such as a box-like form of platform construction that could serve as a low seat, a table or a platform. Whether these were ever made of wood will probably remain a matter of conjecture. It is generally believed that much of the Chinese furniture was adapted from the West, especially from the region now known as Turkestan. Traces of Hellenistic and Roman influences are also evident. However, the Chinese with their peculiar genius assimilated the foreign influences, and their furniture as it finally developed was distinctively Chinese in form and in feeling. Chinese records tell about the Emperor Ling, who in the second century of the Han Dynasty was known for his great interest in foreign furniture, especially chairs and couches. It is generally accepted that the chair was introduced in Early Han, since ceramic models of chairs have been found in Han tomb furniture. Apparently one of the earliest chairs was in the form of a contemporary stool which was large enough to serve as a platform for sitting cross-legged or kneeling and to which was simply added a back. The Chinese chair as it finally developed was an adaptation of the Indo-Central Asian armchair to the Chinese architectural style. Early extant examples of Chinese cabinetwork are found at Nara, Japan, in the Shosoin, the Imperial treasure house. These pieces, which chiefly comprise small articles such as stands and boxes, were brought to Japan from China prior to the second half of the 8th century and are remarkable for their refinement. There is practically no Sung furniture in existence. However, representations of Sung furniture occurring in paintings show that it was not too unlike that of Ming.

Perhaps it should be explained here that the Chinese originally lived on mats or platforms before and during the T'ang dynasty. The Japanese, who borrowed heavily from Chinese culture during their formative period, which corresponds to the T'ang dynasty, adopted this manner of living on a mat level and still live at the present time in the same manner. They sit on rush mats called tatami which are mounted on a rice-straw ground and are approximately three feet by six feet in area and two inches thick. The tatami cover the entire floor and are soft and pleasant to walk on. The Japanese sometimes use various types of low supports for back or arm rests. Guests are provided with a cushion or zabuton to sit on. Round or oblong dining tables of various sizes, small oblong writing tables and dressing tables, which generally resemble the western swinging toilet mirror on a box stand, are all low pieces. Actually there is only a very small amount of Japanese furniture. Individual dining trays or ozen are often used instead of a large dining table. The ozen is placed on the floor or on a low stand. The Japanese use no beds. In the evening a futon, which resembles a thick quilt, is spread on the tatami and in the morning the futon and covers are folded and put in the oshi-ire which is a kind of built-in cupboard provided with a pair of sliding doors. (An oshi-ire is found in almost every room in a Japanese house.)

This living platform in China is called a k'ang. In a very broad sense a Japanese house may be said to be all "k'ang." Members of the family as well as guests when they enter a Japanese home remove their shoes in the entrance hall before they step up to the mat level. The difference between living on a mat level or platform and sitting on chairs determines the kind as well as the amount of furniture used. In parts of China both levels were retained and used together and as a result both high and low furniture suitable at each respective level is found. The built-in or permanent k'ang found in North China is a part of the construction of the house. This mat-covered platform is generally slightly lower than the height of a chair seat and usually extends the length of one side of each room. It is generally deep enough to recline on comfortably. It is faced with brick, and in one way or another it is generally mildly heated for the winter months. In addition to the low table, which is the most characteristic piece of k'ang furniture, the other typical pieces are low cupboards or chests, which are primarily used to hold quilts, cushions and bedding. Among the peasant classes the built-in brick k'ang is the chief center for living in each home, and the heat from inside the k'ang rising to the platform level makes it the most comfortable place in a Chinese house during the long and cold winter. The hibachi or charcoal brazier is the only heat-producing unit in a Japanese home. It is placed on the floor and on a cold day the members of the family sit around it in order to warm their hands.

Undoubtedly the finest Chinese furniture was made during the classical period of Chinese domestic culture, or approximately from around 1400 to 1600 in the Ming dynasty. The restraint in design and in ornament evident in this cabinetwork bears a striking resemblance to the best of contemporary Western furniture design. The furniture, with its purity of line and its graceful but inconspicuous details, is praiseworthy for its dignified and elegant refinement. The designs possess a timeless beauty and reveal an unerring instinct for proportion and balance. The superb woods handled with consummate skill are an outstanding feature. The structural honesty, strength of line and cubic proportions, which are important characteristics of Chinese furniture design, give the cabinetwork a nobility of form and an almost pristine severity that are in accordance with the finest Chinese classical traditions. In a Ming home belonging to one of the cultured class, the measured and forceful simplicity of the chairs, tables and cupboards was in unison with the interior architecture, both with their rectangular symmetry being part of a well-disciplined plan. Formalism and regularity, symmetry and the straight line are the essence of a Chinese room. The furniture was never arranged in an informal or casual manner. The arrangement was subject to a rigid discipline that did not permit any deviation and the decorative appointments were also placed with studied care. The rich color of the enamelled porcelains, the beautiful patina of the bronzes, hanging scrolls of paintings or calligraphies revealing the fertile artistic imagination of the Chinese, magnificent jades, the lovely hues and satin-like finish of the woods and the exquisitely embroidered silk cushions created an air of subdued luxury that was completely in harmony with the character of a Ming interior. The aesthetic and moral ideal of simplicity of home cherished by the Chinese from the early days of their civilization was indelibly stamped on these Ming interiors. From around the late 17th century onwards the cabinetwork began gradually to lose those qualities that made it great. A sophisticated refinement noticeable in the form and selection of detail replaced the strength and vigor invariably associated with the acme of Chinese craftsmanship.

The craft of cabinetmaking in China was guided by several well-established principles which imbued it with a singular distinction. Chinese joinery which is unique can be studied advantageously in the drawings appearing in Dr. Gustav Ecke's book entitled CHINESE DOMESTIC FURNITURE. These joints which never were investigated technically before were studied with exacting accuracy by Dr. Ecke in old furniture repair shops in Peking. In traditional Chinese joinery wooden dowel pins were never used unless they were positively essential. The use of glue was also dispensed with as much as possible. Turning was completely avoided, since it was deemed unworthy of a skilled craftsman. Veneering was generally limited to less costly cabinetwork. It seems probable that the Chinese preferred furniture made of solid wood because of its more lasting qualities. Moldings, beadings and any decorative detail were carved in the surface of the furniture and were not applied. Carved ornamental detail, which was used only in a limited manner on Ming furniture, was admirable for its clarity and exactness. In the subsequent Ch'ing dynasty the furniture as a rule displayed a more liberal amount of carved detail which often detracted from the linear composition of the furniture. The use of caning for chairs, benches, stools, beds and couches was a feature of Chinese cabinetwork. Of interest, especially to the Western student, is a type of cabinetwork generally referred to as the bamboo style, which simulates to some extent in wood a type of South China work executed in bamboo. Bamboo style chairs, couches and other articles of furniture often have a lighter quality and seem to be ideal for summer use and garden pavilions. A marked feature of this work is the use of additional members in the form of thin canes of bamboo outlining the framework, much of which also has a rounded character. For example, a straight rounded chair leg is flanked by two slender bamboo-like members. Other features of Chinese cabinetwork, such as the curving braces used diagonally under the tops of some tables and stools, will be considered in the description of the articles of furniture. It appears that lacquered articles of furniture were relatively few. Stands, often lacquered in red, were used for the reception of bronzes and porcelains. Any use of lacquered furniture in a more lavish manner was apparently restricted to princely palaces. It is generally believed that the magnificent patina with its subdued color and luster found on ex-

tant examples of Ming and Early Ch'ing furniture was acquired naturally through the centuries rather than from any original special treatment. The finest and most costly woods were simply finished with a wax polish free from any coloring ingredient. Sometimes a thin transparent lacquer was also employed.

The high esteem accorded to Ming furniture is partly due to the magnificent hardwoods with their admirable mellowed tones and satin-like luster. Much of the fine furniture was made from imported woods. The Chinese preferred tzu-t'an above all other woods, which according to some authorities is unsurpassed for beauty. The genus of tzu-t'an, which is more commonly called red sandalwood or palissandre, is a matter of controversy. It is generally identified as either *pterocarpus santalinus* or *dalbergia*. The latter is indigenous to China, while the former is imported. It seems reasonable to assume that both genera, which are closely related, were used. Some of the cabinetwork at the Shosoin Imperial treasure house is made of tzu-t'an. It is a hard and compact wood, having little or almost no figure, and varies in color from a reddish brown to red. Through the centuries tzu-t'an acquires a beautiful patina and becomes a deep violet color ranging from a brownish to a blackish violet tone. At least from the time of the Sung dynasty, hua-li, which is not unlike our Western rosewoods, was used for much of the best cabinetwork and is highly regarded by the collectors of Chinese furniture. Hua-li comprises several varieties of which the yellow or huang hua-li, employed in Ming and Early Ch'ing cabinetwork and belonging to the genus *pterocarpus indicus*, is regarded as the finest. It appears that the huang hua-li was imported, but other varieties found in this group of rosewoods were of native growth. Huang hua-li is a close-grained wood of amber tone with very interesting and unusual markings. A lovely golden glow almost seems to exude from its satin-like surface. The generic name of hung-mu is given to certain rosewoods, also belonging to *pterocarpus indicus,* having a reddish quality sometimes streaked with black. It is a smooth compact wood, occasionally having beautiful markings and noted for its durability. It is often believed that these woods, which came into general use from the 18th century onwards, were originally used as a substitute for the choicer red sandalwood as well as for some of the scarcer rosewoods.

Furniture made of chi-ch'ih-mu, popularly called chicken-wing wood, is also highly prized by the connoisseurs of Chinese cabinetwork. In durability it is superior to oak. It has a rugged character and is more coarsely grained than the woods already described. Through the years its varying tones of greyish brown often darken to a rich coffee-brown. It has been suggested that the term "chicken-wing" refers to the typical greyish-brown tones and dark streaks found in this wood. The botanical ascription for chicken-wing wood is an open subject. This problem of botanical names for woods used in Chinese cabinetwork is due to the fact that in China the woods are known only by their commercial names. The problem is further complicated by the lack of distinction between indigenous and imported varieties, the latter being often imported from the tropical forests of southeastern Asia. Then, too, the history of the woods in that part of the world is not as familiar to the Western world as that of the woods common to Europe and America. Before mentioning a few of the lesser woods employed

in Chinese cabinetwork, it should be stated here that teak was never used as a wood in traditional Chinese cabinetwork. Wu-mu or ebony is occasionally used, in particular for inlay work on furniture of a more ornate character. Hu-mu or burl displaying a rich figure was much favored by the Chinese for inlay work. Nan-mu, generally identified as a kind of cedar native to China and with lighter tones shading in color to yellowish-browns, was a durable and useful wood. Yu-mu or elm and chang-mu or camphorwood were also native and familiar woods. Altogether there were about twenty indigenous woods, including chestnut, pear, cypress and oak, used in the average cabinetwork. It appears that such furniture was the Oriental counterpart of the European provincial work executed in native woods.

The metal mounts on Chinese cupboards, wardrobes, cabinets and similar articles of furniture are in complete harmony with the pieces they ornament and contribute greatly to the beauty of the early cabinetwork. The same forceful and elegant simplicity and flawless balance evident in fine Chinese cabinetwork is reflected in the design and distribution of the metal mounts. The early metal mounts were made of an alloy comprising copper, zinc and nickel. This copper alloy in the West is generally called paktong, which is the Canton name for white copper, and corresponds to German silver, the difference being in the varying proportions of its three ingredients. Paktong was cast in sheets by the Chinese metalworkers, and after it was cold it was cut and hammered. The singular beauty of its soft and warm luster has never been duplicated in modern Chinese metal mounts. Many of the shapes for the handles and back plates were geometrical, such as oblong, diamond, square and circular, and were either solid or cut out with simply an outline resembling a narrow band remaining. Of particular interest is a solid back plate in the form of a bat, which later appeared in many variant and elaborated forms in 18th century English brass mounts. Drop handles, loose-ring handles and bail handles of either rectangular or curved form attached to one large or two small back plates were all included. The austerity and boldness of design unmarred by little if any ornamental detail was a conspicuous feature of these metal mounts and gave them a striking simplicity that was completely and artistically satisfying.

ARTICLES OF FURNITURE

Chairs　　It has already been mentioned that the chair as a domestic article of furniture was introduced in China in the early centuries of Buddhism. Whether the chair came from the South and India with Buddhism, or from the North, being transmitted by other Asiatic peoples, or perhaps from the ancient classical Western world, being transmitted across the entire distance of Asia, remains a matter of conjecture. It does seem, however, that the chair in its final evolution most strongly reflected Indo-Central Asian influences. Chinese chair design is principally based on two fundamental types. One type has its provenance in the Chinese yoke rack pattern, which is represented in its archaic form in the Chinese shan-lan gate or Japanese torii with its yoke and very slightly splayed posts. This Chinese yoke pattern, which is similar to the Indian yoke design, was adapted for one of the principal open chair back designs displaying a yoke-shaped crest rail extending beyond the uprights which usually have a very slight splay (FIGURES 609, 610). The rectangular-shaped seat rests on four legs joined with stretchers (609, 610). The splat, which is most commonly solid and with straight sides, extends from the crest rail to the seat (609, 610) and was substituted for the cross rail or connecting tie under the yoke in the original yoke design. The back of the chair is very often spooned, that is, it is shaped to fit the back of the occupant (609, 610). The center-front of the crest rail is sometimes slightly concave serving as a neck-rest. It is designed as either an armchair (609) or a side chair (610). The treatment of the open arms and armposts is subservient to the chair back design and is in complete harmony with it. The front stretcher is very close to the ground since it serves as a foot-rest and for the same reason it is often heavier and flattened (609, 610). The side and rear stretchers are usually at higher levels, with the rear stretcher generally the highest (609, 610). As a rule the seat of the chair is generally higher than the standard European model in order to keep the feet from the cold and damp polished brick floors by using a footstool or the front stretcher as a foot-rest. Extant Ming examples of the yoke type splat-back chair, which still remains the principal form for the ordinary domestic chair, are admirable for their interesting and varied treatment of line and detail, dispelling any feeling of monotony.

The other principal type of chair has an arched horseshoe-shaped crest rail continuing to form the arms (611). Perhaps the principal difference between this chair and the upholstered French chair with a gondola-shaped back or the so-called English tub chair is that the seat in the Chinese model remains rectangular. The open back has a solid splat and two uprights, one being at each corner of the seat directly above the two rear legs (611). The arms are either rounded off and continue to form the armposts or curve outward and rest on the armposts (611). The four legs are joined with stretchers (611). This splat-back chair is generally believed to be a Chinese adaptation of an Indian or Indo-Central Asian chair with a circular-shaped back and seat.

In addition to these two principal varieties there are several other characteristic types. In another very common type of splat-back chair the ends of the crest rail are joined to the uprights, with the sharp corners generally slightly softened or rounded. An interesting feature of Chinese chair design is the structural detail introduced beneath the seat, such as bracketed straight (609) or shaped aprons, horizontal rails with broken lines (610) and solid brackets with cut-outs outlined in a bead molding (611). Chairs in the so-called bamboo style furnish another distinctive form of Chinese chair design (612). Extant examples of bamboo-style chairs have a rectangular framework of rounded members with the back and arms filled in with slender vertical round members (612). The legs are often flanked with slender round members simulating thin canes of bamboo (612). The folding type chair of X-form, commonly having a yoke type back, is still another early type of Chinese chair.

Couches   The large and massive couch with its low back and arm rests is an impressive and choice piece of Chinese domestic furniture (615). The couch was derived from the Chinese mat-covered platform to which was added at a later date the low back and arm rests. In extant examples probably dating from Ming the back and arm rests are either of solid wood or are filled in with lattice-work or bars executed in simple Chinese repetitive patterns, such as the square or swastika. The short legs commonly terminate in the so-called horse-hoof foot, which is characterized by a slight inward curve (615). This foot, which is peculiar to the square leg from the beginning of the Ming period, was replaced by a weak conventionalized scroll toward the end of the 18th century. The Ming square leg and horse-hoof foot were admirable for their strength and vigor. Sometimes the leg and foot were outlined in a strong bead molding emphasizing the sweeping and unbroken line (614). The elegant simplicity of the low rectangular k'ang table (614), which was placed on the couch, complemented the geometrical purity of the Ming couch, a quality always highly esteemed by the Chinese. One principal variety of k'ang table was designed with a straight or shaped apron continuing in an unbroken line to the quadrangular legs terminating in horse-hoof feet (614). There are also extant examples of early k'ang tables with valanced aprons and with short massive cabriole legs. The k'ang table was also designed in the bamboo style. The couch was also designed without the back and arm rests (613).

Beds   Beds with four tall posts and canopies of separate construction are found in early Chinese illustrations dating from around 400 A.D. Extant examples of testered beds (617) probably dating from the Ming period are essentially similar in principles of design to the couch with its low back and armrests. The rectangular platform rests on short quadrangular legs terminating in horse-hoof feet and is enclosed on three sides and occasionally partially on the fourth side, which is the front and also one of the long sides, by a low railing filled with lattice-work (617). The tester with its lattice-work valance is supported by four posts. When the front of the bed is partially enclosed there are two additional tall posts extending to the tester and flanking the opening (617). Apparently during the day the bed hangings or draperies were often loosely tied to the four tall posts. It seems that a thick quilt similar to the Japanese futon was placed on the bed or platform and in the morning the quilt and covers were folded and put away. In this manner the bed with some cushions placed on it served as a day bed or a platform on which to sit and recline during the day and which in all probability was its principal purpose. A very low and long bench is frequently placed in front of the bed as well as in front of the k'ang in order to help the occupant step up to or down from the platform level.

Stools   The designs for rectangular stools usually follow one of three principal forms. One type is characterized by its quadrangular legs terminating in horse-hoof feet. Another type has slightly splayed legs with high side stretchers derived from the "post and rail" of the Chinese yoke design and a third type is in the bamboo style (616). The elaboration of structural design introduced in these three fundamental forms is always interesting and varied and remarkable for its functional clarity. The stool was always a much used article of Chinese furniture. Of particular interest is a barrel-shaped seat (618), in the form of an ancient drum, made of various materials, especially porcelain, and also of granite for garden use. According to Chinese records seats of barrel shape were highly esteemed from early times. Barrel-shaped seats made of wood are a choice article of Chinese domestic furniture and are notable for the forceful and striking simplicity of their designs.

Tables   The high rectangular table as distinct from the low k'ang table was introduced in China shortly after the chair. According to illustrations the legs of the early tables were mounted on a rectangular framework that rested on the floor. This feature of structural design was still used at least as late as Ming. One principal variety of table dating from Ming is characterized by its four quadrangular legs terminating in horse-hoof feet (619, 620).These tables were made in a wide variety of sizes, and the top was square or almost square or oblong (619, 620). The apron, which is generally straight, is of varying depth and continues into the leg (619) Frequently stretchers or a horizontal railing beneath the apron are incorporated into the design. Of particular interest is a method of table construction, generally credited as a Chinese innovation, which was occasionally employed on these tables. This method features a braced table top with four oblique braces extending from the under side of the table top to the upper part of the leg (619, 620). When the four braces are long enough to meet at the center of the under side of the table, the table is designed with a deep apron to conceal the joining and to make a more aesthetic design. This table was also designed devoid of any form of securing members. Undoubtedly this variety of table with its horse-hoof feet served many purposes, such as a writing, library or game table. The very small square table resembled a stand and in all probability it was often used for the reception of porcelains or bronzes.

Another variety of table apparently generally having a square or almost square and occasionally an oblong top of varying length is designed in the bamboo style (623). These tables often have a rather block-like quality softened to some extent by their rounded members (623). Generally the edge of the table does not extend beyond the legs (623). In some examples the legs are carved in imitation of thick bamboo canes, while in other tables this bamboo design is conveyed in slender rounded members simulating thin canes of bamboo, which are often worked in simple geometrical patterns, such as an open frieze band of oblongs under the top of the table (623). Many extant examples although adhering to the bamboo style prototype display a more free and independent adaptation revealing the fertility of the Chinese craftsman (625). Occasionally the square leg was adopted in place of the rounded leg. Also of interest is a table of hybrid design, chiefly displaying features of the bamboo style and always characterized by oblique brackets (626).

The structural design for an interesting and principal variety of oblong Chinese table (624, 627) of varying length is seen in the Chinese shan-lan gate with its yoke, splayed posts and connecting tie or rail beneath the yoke joining the two posts. The legs for these tables splay outward and forward and are connected sometimes with one but more often with two side stretchers, which are always placed very high since they represent the connecting tie of the yoke rack (624, 627). The front of the table top, which is one of the long sides, represents the yoke and therefore extends well beyond the legs at each end (624, 627). This so-called yoke table is generally designed with a narrow bracketed apron (624, 627). Sometimes the top of the table is designed with up-turned ends. Occasionally and especially in some of the early examples a rail either mortised into or pierced through connects the two front legs directly under the bracketed apron (624). Variations in design and detail occur, but the splayed legs, the connecting side ties and the idea of the yoke in the longitudinal top frame are invariably present. These tables, depending upon their length, undoubtedly served numerous purposes in the Chinese home. They are frequently referred to as side tables, probably because as a rule their length obviously exceeds their width and their aesthetic appeal is chiefly derived from the long side. However, the "backs" of these tables are finished in a similar manner and in that respect they do not necessarily have to be placed against a wall. Perhaps in the Chinese home they traditionally occupied a position in which the backs were as much in evidence as the fronts.

A distinctive and important variety of long and narrow table is characterized by its trestle-end supports which are notable for their boldly carved openwork panels (629, 630, 631). This table is generally referred to as a side table or sideboard table although the "back" of the table is similar to the front. The table top, which generally but not always has up-turned ends (630, 631), extends well beyond the trestle supports and in that respect is similar to the so-called yoke table. As a rule the trestle-end supports are perpendicular; however, a very slight splay can be detected in some examples. The table top is over a bracketed apron generally designed with graceful cut-outs outlined in a bead molding (629, 630). Related to this variety of sideboard table and probably of much earlier origin is the trestle table with a plain, very long and narrow removable top board (628). Each trestle-end is designed with a rectangular top and four straight legs and resembles a small table or stand, for which in all probability it was used when not serving as a support for the table board. In addition to the tables already described there was also the rectangular lute or psaltery table, a small table or stand, with a circular top, designed with either cabriole or straight slender legs, and numerous other forms.

Chests   An interesting variety of Chinese furniture is the oblong chest or coffer with its slightly splayed front and sides, being mounted on splayed legs continuing from the stiles (632, 634). The oblong molded top, which commonly has up-turned ends, extends well beyond the sides and this extended portion is supported by brackets (632, 634). The upper part of the front of the chest is fitted with a row of two or three drawers (632, 634). In order to have access to the lower portion of the chest it is necessary to remove the drawers. It seems that originally it was designed as a chest with a lid and that the drawers were added at a later date. Beneath the chest compartment is a shaped apron (632, 634). Essentially the façade is divided into three more or less equal portions, namely the drawers, the inner compartment and the apron (632, 634). Each drawer is provided with a back plate and handle. Apparently these splayed chests were frequently used as bridal chests and were generally designed in pairs. The back of these chests is also finished.

Cupboards   One type of low cupboard (635) is closely related in its principles of design to the splayed coffer mounted on four splayed legs. It is fitted with a row of frieze drawers above two or four cupboard doors and is mounted on short splayed legs connected with a bracketed shaped valance (635). The oblong top with its up-turned ends projects well beyond the sides (635). The low cupboard is also designed with straight sides and is characterized by its cubic appearance. The treatment of the panels and stiles contribute to this block-like quality. The drawers of both the splayed- and straight-sided low cupboards are mounted with back plates and handles, and the cupboard doors with hinges, back plates, drop handles and padlock (635).

One principal variety of cupboard, praiseworthy for its austere simplicity, is characterized by the slight splay of its sides and front (636). The oblong molded top extends slightly beyond the stiles, which are frequently rounded and clustered. However, the top molding does not project beyond the base (636). The legs are a continuation of the stiles and are therefore slightly splayed (636). It is designed with two long panelled doors and a bracketed straight valance (636). The bracketed valance is a classical structural feature of Chinese design and is used in practically every category of Chinese furniture, such as in the designs for some chairs and tables. The hardware comprises an oblong back plate, the decorative drop handles and the rings through which is passed the rod of the conventional padlock (636). The doors swing open on pivots furnished by lengthening additional uprights. Since these serve as hinges no metal hinges are required (636).

Another type of tall cupboard (633) with two long cupboard doors, is designed with straight sides, and is generally characterized by an angular or cube-like appearance. The façade is mounted with metal hinges and back plates with drop handles and padlock.

The tall rectangular cupboard generally in two or four parts is an imposing as well as necessary article of Chinese furniture, since the Chinese stored many of their choice possessions in its capacious compartments (637). The upper cupboard with its two cupboard doors is about one third of the total height (637). The lower or principal piece with its two long cupboard doors, beneath which is often a horizontal panel, is mounted on short legs which are a prolongation of the stiles

(637). The lower cupboard is frequently designed with either a bracketed straight or shaped valance (637). These cupboards were designed in different standard sizes and were an essential part of every well-established Chinese household. Occasionally two of the double-bodied cupboards were placed side by side forming a four-part cupboard and sometimes one and even two additional cupboards were placed above each two-part cupboard. The cupboards were symmetrically arranged along the wall. The impressive metal hinges and back plates with their drop handles and padlocks are praiseworthy for their excellent disposition, contributing greatly to the richness of the façade (637). The interiors of these cupboards are generally ingeniously designed with concealed drawers and shelves in addition to the open sliding shelves and drawers.

The description of the articles of furniture has been essentially restricted to a few traditional forms in each of the principal categories belonging to the classical Ming period. The numerous forms introduced in each category dating from around the 18th century onwards is not within the scope of this work. In addition to the principal categories, which include seat furniture, beds and couches, tables and case pieces, there are several other distinctive categories, such as various types of carved wood screens with decorative panels, and different kinds of carved wood stands, such as basin stands, tall stands for the reception of lanterns, and clothes racks derived from the yoke design. The purpose of this chapter has been three-fold, namely, to familiarize the general reader with traditional Chinese cabinetwork, to point out that classical Chinese furniture and Chinese Chippendale have little if anything in common other than the word *Chinese,* and that Ming hardwood furniture with its structural honesty and simplicity of form is especially adaptable to modern domestic Western architecture. The practicality and refined severity and the flawless proportions evident in traditional Chinese furniture design provide invaluable material for the contemporary designers of modern furniture.

PLATES

2

3

1. Wood Folding Stool, Egyptian   2. Wood Chair, Egyptian   3. Fragment of a Red
Figure Ware Kylix showing a Klismos, Greek   4. Marble Throne Chair with sculptured relief decoration, Etruscan   5. Marble Throne Chair, Roman

5

6

7

6. Bronze Folding Stool, Roman   7. Detail of Bronze Couch and Head-rest from Pompeii
8. Detail of a Bronze Couch and Head-rest from Pompeii   9. Detail of a Bronze Couch showing the Fulcrum inlaid with silver, from Amiterno   10. Bronze Couch and Head-rest from Boscoreale

9

10

11

12

ouch decorated with bone carvings
lass inlay, Roman   12. Footstool
ated with bone carvings and glass
belonging to couch, Roman
ronze Bed, Etruscan   14. Marble
e or Couch Legs, Roman

13

14

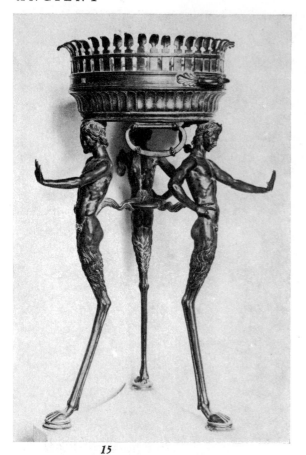

15

16

15. Bronze Tripod from Pompeii 16. Bronze Tripod in the Grecian style from Pompeii
17. Marble Table Support, Roman 18. Marble Tripod from Tavola

17

18

21

22

19 20

19. Walnut Chair with pierced tracery and linen-fold panels, having a hinged seat, French, *15th century*   20. Carved Oak Chair, having the back panel carved with the Tree of Jesse, French or Flemish, *15 century*   21. Oak Stool of trestle form with Romayne medallions, English, *about 1535*   22. Carved Oak Food or Livery Cupboard, English, *late 15th century*   23. Carved Walnut Coffre with Flamboyant tracery, French, *15th century*

23

24

25

24. Carved Oak Side Table, E[ng]lish, *about 1500*   25. Oak[en] Chest-Stool with Romayne [Me]dallions, English, *about 15[..]* *1550*   26. Oak and Lin[en] Folding Table, French, *15th c[en]tury*   27. Oak Ambry with foliated ironwork, English, *ab[out]* *1450*

27

28

Oak Bench with linen-fold panels, Eng-
about 1520

Walnut Dressoir carved with Flamboyant
ic tracery, French, *late 15th century or
16th century*

29

30. Oak Armoire, with linen-fold panels, French, century

31. Carved Oak Crédence with pierced Flamb tracery, French, *late 15th century*

30

33   34

32. Walnut Savonarola inlaid with certosina work, Lombardy, *about 1500*   **33.** Carved Walnut Dantesca, *second half of 16th century*   **34.** Carved Walnut Sgabello, Urbino, *about 1500*

35. Walnut Armchair, Tuscan, *first half of 16th century*   **36.** Carved and Inlaid Walnut Chair, Venice or Brescia, *late 16th century*   **37.** Carved Walnut Armchair with ornate front stretcher, *late 16th century*

36   37

38

38. Carved Walnut Cassapanca with Medici arms, Florentine, *mid 16th century*

39. Walnut Writing Cabinet with "picture" intarsia made for Charles V, probably at Mantua *in 1532*

39

40

. Walnut and Rosewood Chest inlaid with
rtosina work, North Italian, *about 1500*

. Marriage Cassone decorated with gilt pas-
lia partly enriched with color, Florentine,
st half of 15th century

. Carved Walnut Cassone, North Italian,
id 16th century

41

42

43

44

43. Carved Walnut Chest of Drawers, *late 16th century*   44. Carved Walnut Credenzina, Tuscan, *about 1575*

45. Carved Walnut Refectory Table with trestle-end supports, Florentine, *1500–1550*

46. Carved Walnut Prie-Dieu, *about 1580*

46

45

47

50

48

47. Carved Walnut Credenza, *second half of 16th century*   48. Folding Beechwood Monastery Chair, Tuscan, *16th century*   49. Carved Walnut Mirror, *third quarter of 16th century*   50. Walnut Sacristy Cupboard with intarsia work, Tuscan, *second half of 15th century*

49

51

51. Carved Walnut Armchair, Venetian, *second half of 17th century*

52. Carved and Gilt Wood Chair, Venetian, in the manner of the Italian sculptor, Antonio Corradini, *about 1700–1752*

52

54

53. Carved Wood Lantern with Sansovino forms, Venetian, *about 1570*   **54.** Painted and Parcel Gilded Secretary Cabinet, Venetian, *early 18th century*

53

55.

56

55. Painted and Carved Bombé and Serpentine-shaped Commode, Venetian, *mid 18th century*   56. Painted and Carved Bombé and Serpentine-shaped Commode, Venetian, *mid 18th century*

57. Painted and Carved Chair, Venetian, *mid 18th century*   58. Painted and Carved Table, Venetian, *mid 18th century*

57

58

SPANISH

59
60

59. Inlaid Walnut Sillón de Caderas, *16th century*   60. Walnut Sillón Frailero with collapsible frame, *16th century*   61. Walnut Sillón Frailero, *17th century*

62. Upholstered Walnut Chair, *17th century*   63. Carved Walnut Chair, *17th century*
64. Carved Walnut Chair, *17th century*

62
63

65

65. Walnut Chest-Bench with linen-fold panels, *late 15th century*

66. Carved Walnut Chest-Bench, *late 15th century*

66

67

67. Walnut Chest carved with tracery *15th century*

68. Walnut Armario in the Mudéjar style used as an archive, *13th century*

68

69

9. Upholstered Walnut Bench with
  hinged back, *17th century*

0. Inlaid and Polychromed Arma-
  o, *16th century*

70

71

71. Walnut Papelera with inlaid decoration in the Mudéjar style mounted on a trestle stand, *16th century*   **72.** Walnut Vargueño with inlaid decoration in the Mudéjar style mounted on a puente stand, *16th century*   **73.** Walnut Table, *16th century*

73

74

74. Carved Walnut Table,
17th century

75. Inlaid Walnut Vargueño
with ivory colonnettes mounted on a taquíllon, *17th century*

75

76

76. Carved Walnut Table with a base of H-form and a
colonnaded traverse, *late 17th century*   77. Carved
Oak Stand fitted with water vessels and lavabo, *early
18th century*   78. Walnut Armario probably from a
church sacristy, *16th century*

78

77

79

79. Carved and Polychromed Walnut Chest with painted lid, *16th century*
80. Walnut Chest with inlaid decoration of Moorish design, *16th century*

80

81

82

83

81. Carved Palissandre Armchair with applied ebony bosses, North Netherlandish, *first quarter of 17th century* **82.** Palissandre Chair with lion finials, North Netherlandish, *first half of 17th century* **83.** Folding Palissandre Chair with arcaded back, North Netherlandish, *about 1650*

84. Spirally Turned Walnut Armchair, North Netherlandish, *about 1650* **85.** Carved Walnut Armchair with scrolled supports, North Netherlandish, *late 17th century* **86.** Carved Walnut Armchair with scrolled supports, North Netherlandish, *about 1700*

84

85

86

87   88   89

87. Carved Walnut Chair, North Netherlandish, *about 1700*   **88.** Carved Walnut Chair, North Netherlandish, *first quarter of 18th century*   **89.** Carved Walnut Burgomaster Chair with cane seat, North Netherlandish, *first quarter of 18th century*

90. Carved Oak Chest, North Netherlandish, *first half of 17th century*

90

91. Tester Bed with damask hangings, back being partly covered with Chi embroidered silk, North Netherland *about 1700*

92. Built-in Bed, being part of the geometrical panelling inlaid with eb Dordrecht, *1626*

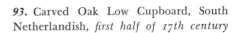

93

93. Carved Oak Low Cupboard, South Netherlandish, *first half of 17th century*

94. Veneered Walnut Serpentine-shaped Commode, North Netherlandish, *first half of 18th century* **95.** Veneered Walnut Table inlaid with stars and circles, North Netherlandish, *second half of 17th century*

96. Veneered Walnut Kettle-shape Secretary Bookcase, North Netherlandish, *about 1753*

96

94

95

97

97. Carved Oak Table with vase-shaped supports, North Netherlandish, *first half of 17th century*   98. Carved Oak Double-bodied Cupboard, South Netherlandish (?), *first half of 17th century*   99. Carved and Veneered in part Ebony Cupboard, North Netherlandish, *second half of 17th century*

98

99

101

100

00. Veneered Walnut Kettle-shape Cabinet, North Netherlandish, *about 1750*

01. Oak Linen Press, probably North Netherlandish, *early 16th century*

02. Veneered Cabinet with floral marquetry, probably North Netherlandish, *last quarter of 17th century*

102

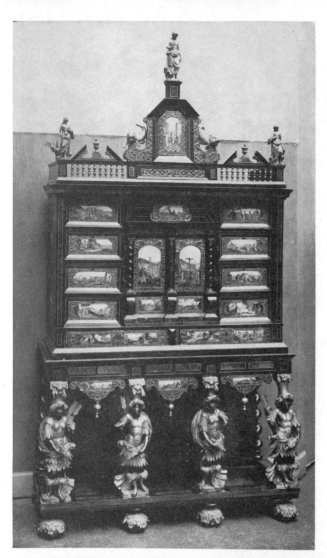

103

103. Veneered Ebony Cabinet with painted panels mounted on a richly carved stand, Antwerp, *17th century*

104. Veneered Ebony Cabinet with painted panels, Antwerp, *first half of 17th century*

104

106

107

105. Oak Chair carved with Renaissance ornament, *second half of 16th century*
106. Carved Walnut Armchair with arms terminating in a ram's head, *second half of 16th century* **107.** Carved Walnut Armchair with arms terminating in a ram's head, *about 1590* **108.** Carved Walnut Caquetoire, *about 1575* **109.** Walnut Chaise à Vertugadin with upholstered seat and back panel, *about 1600* **110.** Walnut Armchair with spirally turned members, *first quarter of 17th century*

109

110

108

111

112

111. Carved Walnut Dressoir in the style of Jacques Androuet Du Cerceau, *second half of 16th century*

112. Carved Walnut Armoire à Deux Corps in the style of Jean Goujon, enriched with veined marble plaques, *second half of 16th century*

113. Walnut Draw-Top Table with seven columnar legs, *first quarter of 17th century*

113

114

114. Carved Walnut Coffre in the style of Hugues Sambin, *second half of 16th century*

115. Carved and Parcel Gilded Walnut Armoire à Deux Corps in the style of Hugues Sambin, probably a wedding gift to Diane de France, daughter of Henri II, upon her marriage to Orazio Farnese *in 1555* **116.** Carved Walnut Dressoir in the style of Hugues Sambin, *second half of 16th century*

115

116

117

117. Carved Ebony Cabinet with gilded bronze mounts the interior designed with cabinet drawers inlaid with ivory, *about 1650*   118. Carved Walnut Table with colonaded ends in the style of Jacques Androuet Du Cerceau, (end view), *about 1560*   119. Carved Walnut Armoire à Deux Corps, *late 16th century*

119

118

121

122

120. Carved and Gilt Wood Armchair, *last quarter of 17th century*   **121.** Carved and Gilt Wood Armchair, *late 17th century*   **122.** Carved Walnut Armchair, *late 17th century*

123. Carved Walnut Armchair, *about 1700*   **124.** Carved and Gilt Wood Table, *last quarter of 17th century*

123

124

125

126

127

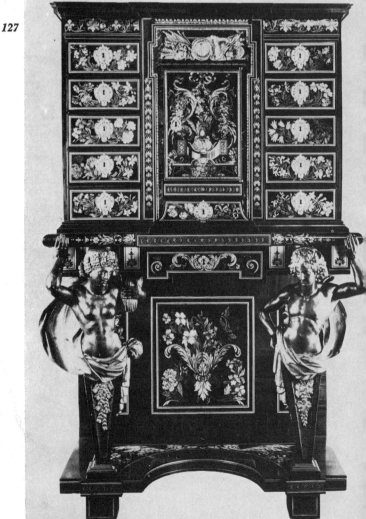

125. Veneered Ebony Table with th[e]
cupboard compartments decorated w[ith]
a Boulle marquetry of engraved b[rass]
on tortoise shell depicting fantastic [de]
signs in the manner of Jean Béra[in]
mounted in chased and gilded bro[nze]
early 18th century

126. Carved and Gilt Wood Guérid[on]
last quarter of 17th century

127. Cabinet on Stand veneered w[ith]
ebony, violet wood, tortoise shell an[d]
marquetry of various woods, pew[ter]
brass and copper. The support[ing]
carved wood terminal figures are stai[ned]
and parcel gilded. Mounted in cha[sed]
and gilded bronze. The cabinet is p[os]
sibly an early work of André Cha[rles]
Boulle; however, it may be the work [of]
one of his predecessors.

128. Veneered Ebony Coffret de Mariage with a marquetry of engraved brass on tortoise shell, mounted in chased and gilded bronze. One of a pair. Probably made in the atelier of André Charles Boulle for a member of the French royal family, *late 17th century or early 18th century* **129.** Veneered Ebony Low Cabinet with a marquetry of engraved brass on tortoise shell and having a medallion of Henri IV, mounted in chased and gilded bronze. Similar to original cabinets with a medallion of Louis XIV from the atelier of Boulle which were in the 17th century placed on stands. Attributed to a successor of Boulle working in the period of Louis XVI. **130.** Pedestal Clock and Pedestal veneered with a marquetry of engraved brass on tortoise shell and mounted in chased and gilded bronze in the manner of André Charles Boulle, *early 18th century*

128

129

130

131

131. Bibliothèque Basse veneered with coromandel wood and a Boulle marquetry of tortoise shell on brass and mounted in chased and gilded bronze. The center oval medallion chased with a design of the Rape of Helen. Stamped E. Levasseur and made in the period of Louis XVI.

132. Veneered Ebony Armoire with tortoise shell panels inlaid with engraved brass and mounted in chased and gilded bronze. Probably made by André Charles Boulle from designs by Jean Bérain for Louis XIV, *late 17th century*

132

133

133. Veneered Ebony Bureau Plat decorated with a marquetry of tortoise shell on brass and with chased and gilded bronze mounts. Probably from the atelier of André Charles Boulle. *Late 17th century or early 18th century.*

134. Table Commode en Tombeau in the style of André Charles Boulle, one of a pair. The two original commodes were made by Boulle for the use of Louis XIV at Trianon in 1708–1709. Attributed to an imitator of Boulle working at the time of Louis XVI or perhaps later.

135. Carved and Gilt Wood Guéridon, *late 17th or early 18th century* 136. Bureau Semainier of kneehole form veneered with a marquetry of tortoise shell, mother-of-pearl, ivory, ebony and brass in the style of André Charles Boulle, *late 17th century or early 18th century*

134

135

136

137   138   139

137. Carved and Gilt Wood Armchair, *early 18th century*   **138.** Carved Oak Fauteuil, *first quarter of the 18th century*   **139.** Carved Walnut Bergère Confessional, *second quarter of the 18th century*

140. Carved Walnut Bergère en gondole, stamped J. B. Tilliard (ME 1752), *about 1755–1760*   **141.** Carved Walnut Chaise à Bureau, *mid 18th century*   **142.** Carved and Gilt Wood Fauteuil, stamped I. Lebas (Jean Baptiste Lebas, ME 1756), *about 1760*

140   141   142

143

144

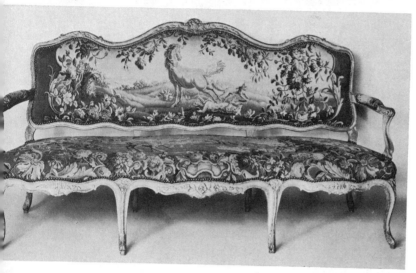

145

143. Carved and Painted Beechwood Fauteuil, stamped Bara (Charles Vincent Bara, ME 1754), *about 1760*

144. Carved Walnut Duchesse Brisée, with the chair in the form of a bergère en gondole, *mid 18th century*

145. Carved and Painted Canapé, *about 1750*

146. Carved Beechwood Turquoise, *about 1750–1760*

146

147

147. Veneered Guéridon-Table decorated with a cube parquetry and with chased and gilded bronze mounts, stamped L. Bouden (Leonard Bouden, ME 1761), *third quarter of the 18th century*
148. Mahogany Guéridon-Table with gilded bronze gallery and mounts, stamped C. Tompino (Charles Tompino fl. about 1745–1789), *third quarter of the 18th century*   **149.** Carved and Gilt Wood Console in the style of Meissonnier, *about 1735*
150. Veneered Kingwood and Acajou Bureau Plat mounted in chased and gilded bronze with espagnolettes, in the style of Charles Cressent, *early 18th century*

148

149

150

151

Veneered Bureau à Cylindre
rated with marquetry and
nted in chased and gilded
ze, having a deep drawer
d with toilet accessories,
t 1765

Bureau du Roi Louis XV,
ered with a marquetry of
ous woods and mounted in
ed and gilded bronze. Begun
760 by Jean François Oeben
finished in 1769 by Jean
ri Riesener, signed Riesener
769 à l'arsenal de Paris. The
zes are by Jean Claude Du-
sis, père (d. 1774), Sieur Wi-
and Louis Hervieux.

153

153. Veneered Bureau à Dos d'Âne, decorated with marquetry and mounted in chased and gilded bronze, stamped J. Tuart (Jean Baptiste Tuart, fl. mid 18th century), *about 1750*
154. Veneered Bureau à caissons latéraux or a writing table with lateral compartments decorated with marquetry and mounted in chased and gilded bronze, attributed to Jean François Oeben, *about 1750*   **155.** Veneered Palissandre and Tulipwood Poudreuse decorated with marquetry and with chased and gilded bronze mounts, *about 1750–1765*
156. Veneered Pedestal Secrétaire having a drop-front writing panel, decorated with marquetry and mounted in chased and gilded bronze, *about 1755*

155

156

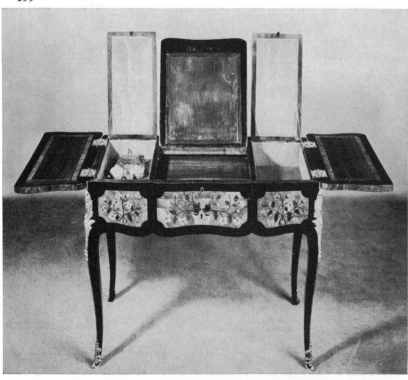

157

157. Veneered Bonheur du Jour decorated with a marquetry in the Chinese taste and mounted in chased and gilded bronze, *about 1760*   158. Veneered Tulipwood Commode mounted in chased and gilded bronze, *first quarter of the 18th century*

158

159

159. Veneered Kingwood Commode with lavish Rococo mounts of chased and gilded bronze, perhaps after designs by Nicolas Pineau. Attributed to Charles Cressent (1685–1768), *about 1730–1735*   **160.** Veneered Commode decorated with marquetry and chased and gilded bronze mounts. Stamped I. M. Chevallier (Jean-Mathieu Chevallier, 1694–1768, fl. mid 18th century), *about 1745*

160

161

161. Veneered Commode decorated with marquetry and mounted in chased and gilded bronze by Jacques Caffieri. Stamped Joseph (Joseph Baumhauer, d. 1772, fl. mid 18th century), *1750–1755* **162.** Veneered Ebony Commode decorated with panels of black and gold lacquer in the Chinese taste and mounted in chased and gilded bronze. Stamped B V R B (Bernard Van Risenbourgh, fl. before 1767), *about 1750–1760*

162

163

163. Veneered Ebony Commode decorated with panels of black and gold lacquer in the Chinese taste and with chased and gilded bronze mounts after designs by Jean-Charles Delafosse, *1734–1789, about 1760–1770, transitional period*   164. Veneered Ebony Commode decorated with panels of black and gold lacquer in the Chinese taste and mounted in chased and gilded bronze. Stamped I. Dubois (René Dubois, ME 1755), *about 1765–1770, transitional period*

164

165

165. Carved Oak Armoire, *early 18th century*

166. Carved Oak Buffet à Deux Corps, Aix, department of Bouches-du-Rhône, *first quarter of the 18th century*

166

167

168

169

167. Carved and Gilt Wood Chaise, stamped I. B. Lelarge (Jean-Bapt
Lelarge), *about 1775*   **168.** Carved Beechwood Fauteuil, *about 1*
169. Carved and Gilt Wood Bergère, stamped G. Iacob (Georges Jac
ME 1765), *about 1775–1785*

170. Carved Walnut Bergère, painted and parcel gilded, attributed
Jean Baptiste Claude Sené, 1748–1803, *about 1788*   **171.** Carved a
Gilt Wood Canapé, by Georges Jacob, ME 1765, *about 1775–1785*

170

171

172

172. Carved and Gilt Wood Lit à la Duchesse with tapestry bed hangings, stamped G. Iacob (Georges Jacob, ME 1765), *about 1775–1785*

173. Carved and Gilt Wood Lit à la Turque, *about 1775*

173

174

174. Carved and Gilt Wood Console Table in the taste of Jean-Charles Delafosse, *third quarter of the 18th century*   **175.** Veneered Chiffonnière decorated with a marquetry of tinted dark green and light yellow boxwood worked in a diaper design, *about 1775–1785*

176. Veneered Tulipwood Table à Ouvrage of the tricoteuse type inset with a soft paste Sèvres plaque and mounted in chased and gilded bronze, attributed to Georges Jacob, ME 1765, *about 1785–1790*   **177.** Table à Ouvrage of the tricoteuse type veneered with satinwood, tulipwood and ebony, decorated with a network of lozenges and blue and white earthenware plaques in imitation of Wedgwood and with chased and gilded bronze mounts. One side of the uppermost tray may be lowered. Stamped A. Weisweiler (Adam Weisweiler, ME 1778 and working c. 1774–1809), *late 18th century*

176

178. Veneered Ebony Table à Pupitre having a drawer fitted with writing equipage, decorated with panels of black and gold lacquer and mounted in chased and gilded bronze, stamped M. Carlin (Martin Carlin, ME 1766), *about 1775–1780*

179. Table à Dejeuner decorated with marquetry and inset with a Sèvres porcelain plaque dated 1775, mounted in chased and gilded bronze. Stamped M. Carlin and I. Pafrat (Martin Carlin, ME 1766 and Jean-Jacques Pafrat, ME 1785), *about 1785*

180. Veneered Tulipwood Table à Pupitre with elaborate mechanical fitments, having two drawers fitted with sewing accessories concealed by a drop-front and an easel to form a reading or writing stand. Decorated with Sèvres plaques, 1783, and with chased and gilded bronze mounts. Stamped M. Carlin (Martin Carlin, ME 1766), *about 1783*   **181.** Guéridon-Table made of chased and gilded bronze and inset with a lapis lazuli plaque, attributed to Adam Weisweiler, ME 1778, *about 1790*

178   **179**

182. Guéridon-Table veneered with tulipwood and a floral marquetry of various woods and mounted in chased and gilded bronze, the top being fitted with a gilded bronze candelabrum. Possibly by Jean Henri Riesener, ME 1768, *late 18th century*

180

181

182

183

183. Secrétaire à Abattant veneered with tulipwood and violet wood, decorated with marquetry and mounted in chased and gilded bronze. Stamped J. H. Riesener. Made by Riesener in 1780, although the style is generally characteristic of the mid 1760's. Originally delivered for the use of Marie Antoinette at Versailles and transferred to the Château de Saint-Cloud in 1785

184. Veneered Secrétaire à Abattant decorated with a marquetry network of lozenges enclosing narcisses and mounted in chased and gilded bronze; the trapezoid centering a chased and gilded bronze medallion. Made by Riesener for the use of Marie Antoinette at the Château de Saint-Cloud and having the written signature, Riesener, fe. 1790

184

185. Veneered Ebony Cabinet having a drop-front writing panel. Decorated with panels of black and gold lacquer and mounted in chased and gilded bronze in the style of Adam Weisweiler, ME 1778, *about 1785–1790* 186. Secrétaire à Abattant veneered with thuya wood and violet wood and having a marble top. Decorated with chased and gilded bronze mounts in the manner of Gouthière and gilded plaques in the manner of Clodion. The center oval plaque is chased with a scene of a sacrifice to Love. Stamped J. H. Riesener and delivered at Versailles on February 12, 1783 for the use of Marie Antoinette.

187. Marquetry Régulateur mounted in gilded bronze, case stamped B. Lieutaud (ME 1748), dial signed Robin à Paris (Robert Robin, clockmaker to Louis XVI), *about 1780*

185

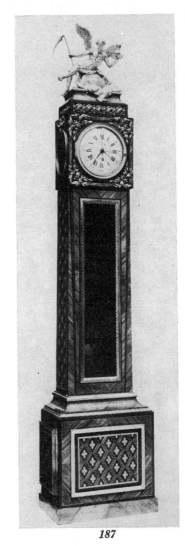

187

186

188

188. Veneered Jewel Cabinet having a hinged lid opening to a shallow compartment and a fall-front panel enclosing a cabinet of drawers. Decorated with a marquetry forming a diaper design enclosing roses and mounted in chased and gilded bronze. Signed J. H. Riesener, *about 1780*

189. Veneered Secrétaire à Etagère having a drop-front writing panel, decorated with Sèvres plaques and chased and gilded bronze mounts. The interior fitted with pigeonholes and drawers. Stamped M. (Probably by Martin Carlin, d. 1785), *about 1775–1785*

190. Régulateur veneered with tulip wood, violet wood and other woods and mounted in chased and gilded bronze, made by Martin Carlin, ME 1766, *about 1775–1785*

190

189

191

191. Veneered Ebony Commode decorated with panels of black and gold lacquer and mounted in chased and gilded bronze. The cipher of Marie Antoinette occurs in the frieze. Attributed to Jean Henri Riesener, ME 1768, *about 1784*

192. Commode veneered in mahogany and mounted in chased and gilded bronze and centering a medallion of biscuit de Sèvres, made by Guillaume Beneman (ME 1785 and working about 1784–1804), *about 1785–1790*

192

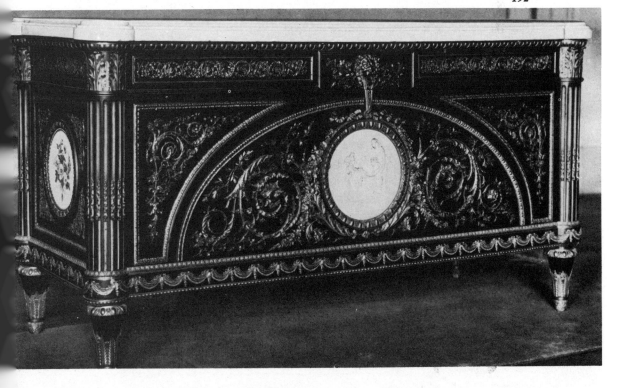

193

193. Veneered Commode decorated in marquetry with scenes from the Commedia dell'-Arte by David Roentgen. In addition to the firm's R, it also has the initials I. Z. (Januarius Zick, a Roentgen designer), *about 1780–1790*   **194.** Veneered Ebony Entre-Deux decorated with panels of black and gold lacquer in the Chinese taste and mounted in chased and gilded bronze. One of a pair. Stamped B V R B (Bernard Van Riesenbourgh, fl. before 1767), *about 1765*   **195.** Encoignure veneered with thuya wood and violet wood and decorated with mounts of chased and gilded bronze, stamped J. H. Riesener. Originally delivered en suite with the Secrétaire à Abattant at Versailles on February 12, 1783, for the use of Marie Antoinette.

194   195

196. Veneered Mahogany Mechanical or Harlequin Table decorated with marquetry forming a diaper design and mounted in chased and gilded bronze. Serving as a reading, writing and toilet table. Attributed to Jean Henri Riesener, ME 1768, *about 1778*
197. Veneered Mahogany Commode-Desserte mounted in chased and gilded bronze, attributed to Claude-Charles Saunier, ME 1752, *about 1775–1785*

196

197

198. Veneered Mahogany Rosewood Desserte mounted in chased and gilded bronze. One of a pair. Stamped J. H. Riesener (Jean Henri Riesener, ME 1768), *about 1775–1785*
199. Veneered Mahogany Desserte with chased and gilded bronze mounts in the manner of Pierre Gouthière, 1738—1813-14, attributed to Jean Henri Riesener, ME 1768, *about 1775–1785*

198

199

200

201

200. Carved and Gilt Wood Chaise, stamped G. Iacob (Georges Jacob, ME 1765), *late 18th century*   **201.** Carved and Painted Fauteuil, *about 1790–1800*

202. Carved Painted and Parcel Gilded Chaise with swan supports, *about 1803*

203. Mahogany Table in the form of an antique tripod, attributed to Georges Jacob, ME 1765, *late 18th century*

202

203

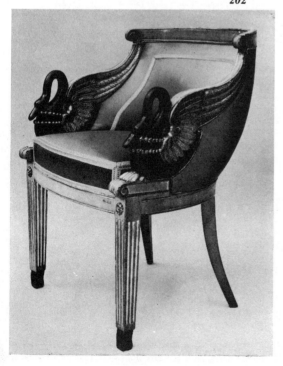

204

204. Carved Mahogany Lit with elongated terminal figures each having the bust of a woman and two human feet, *about 1790–1800*   205. Carved Palissandre Side Table, *about 1795*   206. Mahogany Commode inlaid with brass, *about 1790–1800*

206

207　　　　　　　　208

207. Mahogany Fauteuil with terminal figure supports and gilded bronze appliqués, stamped Iacob D. R. Meslée (Jacob Desmalter), *1804–1814*　　　**208.** Mahogany Fauteuil with terminal figure supports and gilded bronze mounts, *1804–1814*　　　**209.** Throne Chair designed for Emperor Napoleon I by Percier and Fontaine for the Chamber of Deputies, *about 1805*

210

210. Mahogany Chaise à Bureau with gilded bronze mounts, attributed to Jacob Desmalter, *1804–1814*　　　**211.** Mahogany Lit with gilded bronze appliqués, *1804–1814*

213

212

212. Silver Gilt Cradle designed by P. Prud'hon for the son of Napoleon I who was King of Rome and afterwards the Duke of Reichstadt, *1811*

213. Detail of the Cradle   214. Mahogany Table with elongated terminal figure supports, each having a gilded bronze bust and two human feet, *1804–1814*   215. Mahogany Lit of Maréchal Berthier, *1804–1814*

214

215

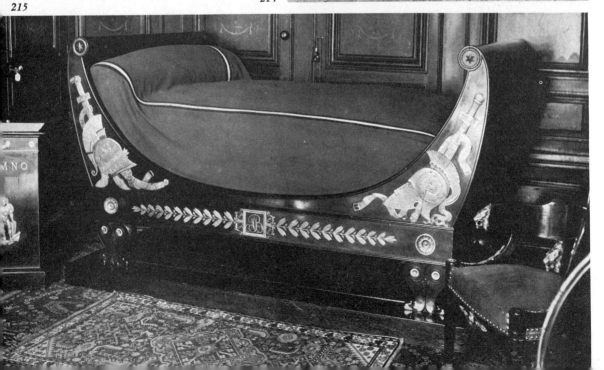

216

217

216. Chased and Gilded Bronze Table with figural supports and a malachite top, *1804–1814*
217. Veneered Fruitwood Coiffeuse with gilded bronze mounts made for Empress Marie Louise, *about 1810* **218.** Lavabo made of amboyna wood and mounted in gilded bronze. Based on a design by Charles Percier and made by Martin Guillaume Biennais, goldsmith to Napoleon I, *1804–1814* **219.** Mahogany Bonheur du Jour with gilded bronze appliqués, *1804–1814*

219

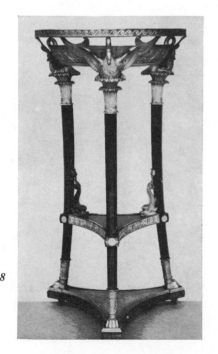

218

220

220. Mahogany Commode with gilded bronze mounts, *1804–1814*   **221.** Carved Mahogany Desserte in the Romantic or Neo-Gothic taste, *1830–1848*   **222.** Mahogany Chaise inlaid with stringing lines and mounted with bronze appliqués, *1815–1830*

221

222

223

224

223. Ebonized Chaise inlaid with mother-of-pearl, *1852–1870*   224. Veneered Palissandre Bas d'Armoire inlaid with citronnier, *1852–1870*   225. Veneered Mahogany Bureau inlaid with citronnier, *1830–1848*   226. Veneered Mahogany Secrétaire à Abattant mounted in chased and gilded bronze. Part of the mounts signed Detler (Franz Detler fl. first third of 19th century), Vienna, *about 1815. Transitional period between Empire and Biedermeier.*

226

225

227

228

227. Veneered Mahogany Center Table, Vienna, *about 1820*   **228.** Table veneered in various woods and painted in India ink, Vienna, *about 1825*

229. Chestnut Chair, Vienna, *about 1825–1830*

230. Veneered Mahogany Sofa inlaid with stringing lines and decorated with carved and gilt wood appliqués, Innsbruck, *1837*

229

230

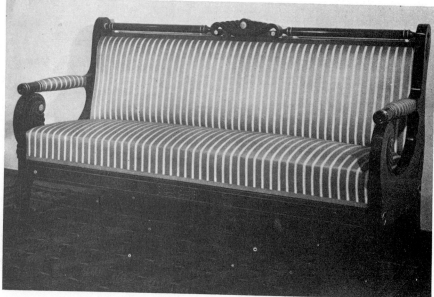

231

232

233

231. Chaise à Capucine, Province of Orléans, *18th century*   **232.** Chaise à Capucine, Burgundy, *18th century*   **233.** Chaise à Capucine, Provençal, *18th century*

234. Chaise à Capucine, Provençal, *18th century*   **235.** Chaise à Capucine, Province of Orléans, *early 19th century*   **236.** Fauteuil, Provençal, *early 19th century*

234

235

236

237

237. Lit Clos with two doors, Bretagne, *18th century*

238. Lit Demi-Clos, Auvergne, *early 19th century*

239. Lit à Colonnes, Bretagne, *early 19th century*

238

239

240

240. Table with drawers, Bretagne, *18* *century*   241. Table with drawers, Bretagne, *late 18th century*

2

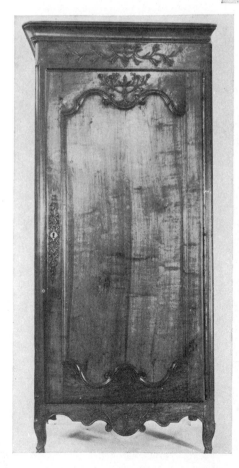

242

242. Bonnetière, Poitou, *18th century*

243. Garde-Manger, Bretagne, *mid 19th century*

243

244

244. Buffet Bas, Champagne, *18th century*

245. Armoire in the Château de Pau, Gascogne, *17th century*

246. Armoire with diamond point motif, Gascogne, *early 19th century*

245

246

247

247. Buffet-Crédence or Buffet à Glissants with steel buttress hinges and fret-pierced keyplates, Provençal, *18th century*   **248.** Armoire with steel buttress hinges and fretpierced keyplates, Provençal, *18th century*   **249.** Armoire, Bordeaux, Province of Guienne, *18th century*

248

249

250

250. Table with drawers, Alsace, *early 19th century*

251. Buffet-Vaisselier, Auvergne, *18th century*

252. Armoire, Bretagne, *dated 1756*

251

252

253

253. Maie or Huche, Bretagne, *18th century*

254. Press for Linen, Basse-Bretagne, *dated 1674*

255. Pétrin, Provençal, *early 19th century*

254

255

256

257

256. Panetière, Provençal, *18th century*   257. Panetière, Provençal, *early 19th century*
258. Etagère, Provençal, *18th century*   259. Bôite à Sel, Provençal, *18th century*
260. Bôite à Farine, Provençal, *18th century*   261. Pewter Wall Fountain and Lavabo, *18th century*

258

259

261

260

262   263   264

262. Carved and Inlaid Oak Armchair with panelled back, *about 1600*   **263.** Turned Ash and Oak Chair, *early 17th century*   **264.** Turned Oak Chair with triangular seat, *first half of 17th century*

265. Carved Oak Armchair of the Glastonbury type, *about 1600*   **266.** Carved Oak Draw-Top Table, *late 16th century*

266

265

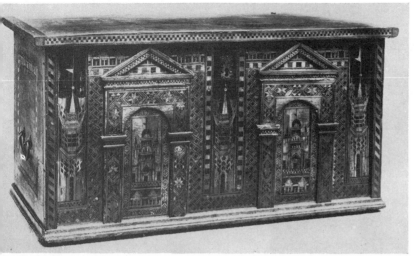

267

267. Oak Nonsuch Chest inlaid with holly and bog oak, *late 16th century*   **268.** Carved and Inlaid Oak Tester Bed, *late 16th century*

268

269

270

271

269. Carved Oak Writing De
about 1600   270. Carved Waln
Court Cupboard inlaid with ho
and bog oak, *late 16th century*

271. Carved and Inlaid Oak a
Walnut Hall and Parlor Cupboa
late 16th century   272. Car
Oak Hanging Livery or Food C
board with turned balusters, *f
half of 17th century*

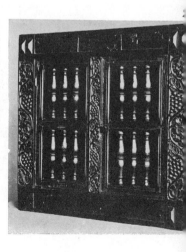

273.   274   275

273. Armchair and Footstool, with frame entirely covered in fabric, *early 17th century*
274. Walnut Chair of the Farthingale type, *early 17th century*   **275.** Turned and
Carved Oak Chair of the Yorkshire-Derbyshire type, *mid 17th century*

276. Turned and Carved Oak Chair of the Yorkshire-Derbyshire type, *mid 17th century*
277. Oak Chair with knob-turned front legs and stretcher of the Cromwellian type, *about
1650*   **278.** Oak Joint Stool with baluster-turned splayed legs, *about 1625*

276   277

278

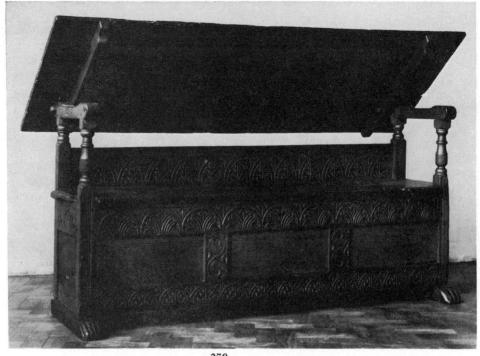

279

279. Carved Oak Table-Settle, *mid 17th century*

280. Oak Side Table with folding top resting on a gate support formed of half of the right hand back leg and framed to stretchers also of half thickness, *first half of the 17th century*   **281.** An early form of Chest of Drawers, the upper portion having two deep drawers and the lower cupboard portion enclosing three drawers. Oak veneered in part with ebony and inlaid with ivory and mother-of-pearl. *Dated 1653*

281

280

2   *283*   *284*

282. Spirally Turned Walnut Armchair, *about 1665*   **283.** Carved and Turned Walnut Armchair of the Restoration type, *about 1675*   **284.** Carved and Gilt Wood Sleeping Chair with adjustable back, *about 1675*

285. Painted and Parcel Gilt Armchair carved with dolphin motifs, *about 1675*

286. Carved and Gilt Wood Armchair, *about 1685*

285   *286*

287

288

287. Carved Walnut Day Bed with adjustable back, *about 1680*   288. Veneered Walnut Chest of Drawers with floral marquetry, *about 1675*   289. Veneered Burr Walnut Chest of Drawers on Stand, *about 1680–1685*
290. Veneered Walnut Game Table fitted with backgammon board. Top inlaid with bands and stars in wood and ivory, *about 1660–1685*

289

291

291. Veneered Walnut Cabinet with floral marquetry of various woods and stained ivory, and having an interior veneered ground of oystering, *about 1670*   **292.** Veneered Burr Walnut Writing Cabinet on a carved and turned stand, fitted with silver mounts, *about 1675*

293. Cabinet japanned in colors on a black ground in the Chinese taste, mounted on a carved wood stand, *about 1670*

293

295

294

294. Carved Walnut Chair, *about 1690*   **295.** Carved Walnut Chair, *about 1690–1695*
296. Carved Walnut Chair of the Marotesque type, *about 1690–1695*

297. Carved Walnut Chair, *early 18th century*
298. Carved Walnut Settee, *about 1690–1700*

297

298

299

299. Tester Bed with hangings of crimson Italian brocade, *late 17th century*

300. State Bed having a pinewood frame covered with velvet and silk, *about 1695*

300

301

302

301. Carved Painted and Parcel Gilded Curio Table in the French taste, *late 17th century*
302. Turned Oak Table with tray top, *about 1690–1700* **303.** Veneered Walnut Card Table with circular folding top supported by gate-legs, *about 1690–1700* **304.** Turned Oak Dressing Table, *about 1690*

303

304

305

305. Oak Writing Table with folding top and hinged gate-leg supports fitting into the framework, *late 17th century* **306.** Veneered Walnut Kneehole Writing Table decorated with seaweed marquetry, *about 1700*

306

307. Secretary Cabinet with a slant-front japanned in red and gold, *about 1700*

308. Cabinet japanned in black and gold on a carved gilt wood stand in the French taste, *about 1690*

307

308

309

311

310

309. Toilet Mirror japanned in green and gold, *about 170…*
310. Veneered Walnut Cabinet decorated with seawee…
marquetry mounted on a stand, *about 1695–1700*
311. Carved Pinewood Alcove Cupboard or Buffet, *abou…*
1700   **312.** Oak Chest of Drawers with geometrical pan…
elling mounted on a turned stand, *about 1690*

312

313

314

313. Carved and in part Veneered Walnut Chair, *about 1715*   **314.** Carved Walnut Wing Chair, *about 1715*

315. Carved Walnut Settee, *about 1710–1715*   **316.** Chair japanned in gold and silver on a scarlet ground, made by Giles Grendey, *about 1730*

316

317

317. Veneered Yew and Walnut Slant-Front Bu reau or Desk, *about 1720*

318. Secretary Cabinet with a slant-front, j panned in red and gold, *early 18th century*

318

319

320

319. Veneered Walnut Writing Cabinet with fall-front mounted on a chest of drawers, *about 1710–1715* **320.** Card Table japanned in gold and silver on a scarlet ground, made by Giles Grendey, *about 1730* **321.** Carved Tall Case Clock with japanned and silvered decoration, *about 1725* **322.** Veneered Walnut Tallboy or Double Chest of Drawers with inlaid stellate motif, *early 18th century*

321

322

323

324

323. Gilded Chair, carved and modelled in gesso with lion-mask ornament, *about 1720–1730*　　**324.** Carved Walnut Armchair with eagle's head and claw terminals, *about 1725*　　**325.** Carved Mahogany Armchair with lion-mask ornament, *about 1735*

326. Carved Mahogany Reading and Writing Chair, formerly in possession of the poet John Gay, 1685–1732, *about 1730*　　**327.** Carved Walnut Corner or Writing Chair, *about 1720*

326

328

328. Carved Painted and Gilt Wood Settee in the style of William Kent, *about 1735*

329. Carved Mahogany Settee, *about 1745*

329

330

331

330. Carved and Gilt Wood Side Table, designed by the architect Henry Flitcroft, *about 1725*

331. Carved Sideboard Table of pinewood stained mahogany, with lion-mask ornament, reflecting the influence of the Palladian architects, *about 1735*

332. Carved and Gilt Wood Console Table supported by interlaced dolphins, *about 1730*
333. Carved and Gilt Wood Eagle Console Table, *about 1730*

332

333

334. Carved and Painted Pinewood Bookcase with gilt enrichments, in the architectural style of William Kent, *about 1730*   335. Carved and Gilt Wood Mirror, probably designed by William Kent, *about 1740*
336. Veneered Burr Walnut Early Georgian Architectural Mirror with gilt-gesso ornament, *about 1730*

334

335

336

337

338

337. Carved Mahogany Chair in the Rococo taste, *about 1750*   **338.** Carved Mahogany Chair. The fretwork back resembles a design in Chippendale's *Director* 1754 for a "Chinese Chair." *About 1755–1760*   **339.** Carved Mahogany Chair in the Gothic taste, *about 1760–1765*

340. Carved Mahogany Armchair based on a design for a "French Chair" in Chippendale's *Director*, 3rd edition, 1762. *About 1760*   **341.** Carved Mahogany Chair-Back Settee in the Chinese taste, *about 1755*

340

342

343

342. Carved Mahogany Chair-Back Settee with ribband-back splats, *about 1755*
343. Carved and Gilt Wood Mirror in the Rococo style, probably by Thomas Chippendale, *about 1760*

344. Carved and Gilt Wood Sconce (Girandole) in the Rococo style. Similar to a type illustrated in Chippendale's *Director*, 1754. *About 1755*   **345.** Mahogany Settee in the French taste of curvilinear form carved with gadrooning, *about 1760–1765*

345

346. Tester Bed with japanned decoration in the Chinese style. Probably made by Thomas Chippendale, *about 1750–1755*

347. Low Open Cupboard for displaying china, japanned in black and gold with fretwork decoration in the Chinese taste, *mid 18th century*

346

347

348 **349**

348. Carved Mahogany Breakfast Table. Similar to a design in Chippendale's *Director*, 1754. *About 1755* **349.** Mahogany China Table with fretwork decoration in the Chinese taste, *mid 18th century*
350. Carved Mahogany Supper Table with bird-cage support, *about 1760* **351.** Mahogany Tea Table on a tripod stand carved in the Rococo taste, *about 1760*
352. Carved and Turned Mahogany Tripod Basin Stand, *about 1760*
353. Mahogany Architect's or Artist's Table carved with Chinese fretwork, *about 1760*

350 **351**

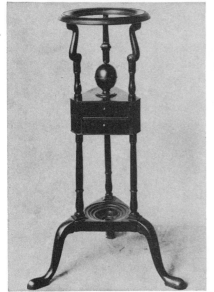

352

353

354

354. Veneered and Carved in part Commode in the Rococo taste. Bears a resemblance to a design in Chippendale's *Director,* 1754. *About 1755*   **355.** Satinwood Commode in the French taste, with marquetry decoration and ormolu mounts, *about 1775*

356. Veneered Mahogany Commode in the French taste, with marquetry decoration and ormolu mounts, made by John Cobb, *about 1770*

356

357

357. Satinwood Commode with marquetry decoration and ormolu mounts. Probably by Thomas Chippendale from a design by Robert Adam, *about 1770*

358. Veneered and Carved in part Mahogany Chest of Drawers, *about 1760*
359. Veneered and Carved in part Mahogany Clothespress enclosing sliding shelves, attributed to William Vile, *about 1760*

359

360

360. Carved Mahogany Sideboard Table in the Gothic taste. Based on a design in Chippendale's *Director*, 1754. *About 1755*   361. Veneered and Carved in part Mahogany Tall Case Clock with gilt-brass fittings, *about 1775*

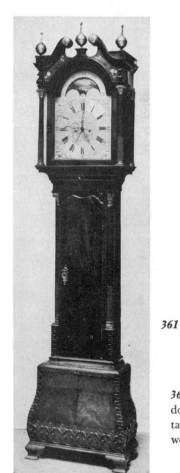

361   362   363

362. Mahogany Hanging China Cabinet with glazed doors and sides decorated in fretwork in the Chinese taste, *about 1755*   363. Veneered and Inlaid Yew wood Knife Boxes, *about 1770*

365

366

364. Carved and Gilt Wood Armchair, probably made by Samuel Norman from a design by Robert Adam, dated 1764. *About 1765* *365.* Carved Mahogany Chair with lyre-shaped splat, designed by Robert Adam for the dining room at Osterley Park, *about 1775* *366.* Carved Mahogany Armchair having a splat composed of a lyre with patera and honeysuckle motifs, probably designed by Robert Adam for the breakfast room at Osterley Park, *about 1775*

368

369

367. Beechwood Armchair painted to represent satinwood and decorated with Neo-Classical motifs. Designed by Robert Adam for the Etruscan Room at Osterley Park, *about 1775* *368.* Carved and Gilt Wood Armchair. Bears close resemblance to contemporary French models. Probably designed by Robert Adam, *about 1775* *369.* Carved and Gilt Wood Armchair, the back supported by winged sphinxes. From a design by Robert Adam, dated 1777, for Osterley Park, *about 1777*

370. Carved and Gilt Wood Sofa, similar to a design by Robert Adam and probably made by John Linnell, *about 1762*   **371.** Carved, Painted and Parcel Gilded Pedestal, designed by Robert Adam for Moor Park, *about 1765*

372. Carved and Gilt Wood Torchère, *about 1770*

373. Carved and Gilt Wood Settee. Designed by Robert Adam in 1764 for Moor Park and probably made by Samuel Norman

372

373

374

375

374. Carved Mahogany Dining Table in two sections, *about 1775*

375. Carved Mahogany Wine Cooler, *about 1770*

376. Carved and Inlaid Mahogany Sideboard Table with sideboard pedestals and urns veneered and inlaid with satinwood and mounted in ormolu, *about 1770*

376

377

378

377. Veneered Harewood Commode decorated with medallions o[f] figure subjects in light woods on a dark ground. Mounted in or[mo]lu and having a center frieze panel in ormolu. Designed b[y] Robert Adam for the drawing room at Osterley Park, *about 177[?]*

378. Carved and Gilt Wood Overmantel Mirror, *about 1774*

379. Carved and Gilt Wood Window Stool. Designed by Rober[t] Adam in 1764 for Moor Park and probably made by Samuel Nor[?]man

379

381

382

380. Carved Mahogany Armchair of the 'camel-back' type. The splat carved and pierced with a vase and honeysuckle ornament, *about 1775*   381. Carved Mahogany Armchair with cartouche-shaped back filled with 'Gothic' arcading, *about 1775*
382. Carved Mahogany Armchair with Prince of Wales' feathers, *about 1775*

383. Carved Mahogany Armchair, *about 1780*   384. Carved Mahogany Chair inlaid with boxwood paterae. The splat closely resembles a design in Hepplewhite's *Guide*, 1788. *About 1785*   385. Carved and Turned Mahogany Armchair, *about 1785*

384

385

386

387

388

386. Carved Mahogany Armchair of the banister-back type, *about 1785*   **387.** Mahogany Armchair painted black and ivory with decorative detail in color, *about 1780–1785*   **388.** Satinwood Armchair with painted decoration, *about 1790*   **389.** Mahogany Wing Chair, *about 1780–1790*

390. Mahogany Settee with applied carved detail of boxwood, *about 1785*

389

390

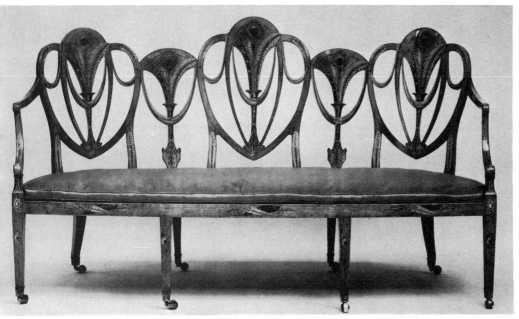

391

391. Satinwood Chair-Back Settee with painted decoration, each chair back of the 'heart-shaped' type, *about 1785*

392. A pair of Inlaid Satinwood Pier Tables, *about 1780–1785*   **393.** Inlaid Satinwood Tambour Cylinder Desk, *about 1780–1790*

393

394

394. Secretary Cabinet decorated with medallions classical figure subjects after designs by Angelica Kauf mann painted en grisaille on a cream ground and i the lower section on a black ground, with ormol moldings, *about 1780*

395. Satinwood Commode with marquetry decoratio and painted medallions of figure subjects, mounted i ormolu, *about 1780*

395

396. Marquetry Harewood Commode, by William Moore of Dublin, *about 1785*

397. Marquetry Toilet Table in the French taste having the top drawer fitted with toilet accessories, *about 1775–1780*   **398.** Marquetry Harewood Bonheur du Jour in the French taste, *about 1770–1780*

399. Veneered Mahogany Inlaid Satinwood Sideboard, *about 1780–1790* **400.** Mahogany Teakettle or Urn Stand, *about 1780–1785*

399

401

401. Veneered Mahogany Shaving Table, *about 1790* **402.** Veneered and Inlaid Mahogany Commode Dressing Table in the French taste, *about 1775*

404

405

403. Carved Mahogany Chair. The back based on a design in Sheraton's *Drawing Book,* 1791–1794. *About 1795* **404.** Carved Mahogany Armchair having a back panel filled with trellis-work, *about 1795* **405.** Satinwood chair with painted decoration in polychrome, *about 1795*

406. Beechwood Armchair with decoration painted or japanned in polychrome, *about 1795* **407.** Carved, Painted and Parcel Gilded Armchair, *about 1800* **408.** Turned Beechwood Armchair japanned in black and gold, *about 1800*

407

408

409

409. Beechwood Settee with decoration painted or japanned in polychrome, *about 1790*

410. Satinwood Work Table with mahogany stringing lines fitted with a writing drawer, *about 1790*   **411.** Painted Commode, the ovals having figure subjects after Angelica Kauffmann, the largest after a copy of her "Cupid Asleep." *About 1790*

410

413

412

412. Gilt Wood Side Table with painted decoration, made for the Prince of Wales for Carlton House, *about 1795*   **413.** The top is decorated with medallions of figure subjects painted en grisaille on a chocolate ground. The oblong center medallion is adapted from a painting by Guido Reni, *1575–1642*

414. Satinwood Side Table with painted decoration in polychrome and with ormolu mounts, *about 1795*   **415.** The top is decorated with festoons of flowers painted in polychrome.

415

414

416

417

416. Veneered Mahogany and Inlaid Satinwood Pembroke Table, *about 1790*

417. Inlaid Satinwood Work Table of the tricoteuse type. Based on a design in Sheraton's *Drawing Book,* 1791–1794, which he calls a French Work Table. *About 1790–1795*

418. Veneered Mahogany Carlton House Writing Table, *about 1800*

418

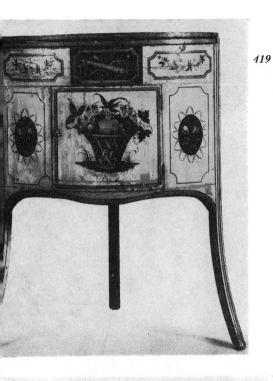

419

420

421

419. Corner Washstand painted or japanned in polychrome, *about 1790*   *420.* Mahogany and Satinwood Bookcase. Corresponds to a design in Sheraton's *Drawing Book,* Appendix, 2nd and 3rd editions. *About 1795*
421. Inlaid and Painted Satinwood Breakfront Secretary Bookcase, *about 1790*

422

422. Satinwood Commode with painted decoration in colors, *ab[out] 1790* 423. Satinwood Cheval M[ir]ror with painted decoration in [col]ors, *about 1790* 424. Secre[tary] Cabinet veneered with satinw[ood] and mahogany. The center of [the] upper portion painted en grisa[ille] after designs by Sir Joshua R[ey]nolds. *About 1790*

42[4]

423

425

426

425. Carved Wood Armchair, painted black with gilt detail in the Egyptian taste. Based on a design in Smith's *Household Furniture,* 1808, plate 56. *About 1810* 426. Carved Beechwood Armchair, japanned in dark green with gilt detail. The female terminal figures in the Grecian taste. *About 1810*

427. Beechwood Armchair japanned in black with brass mounts, *about 1810*
428. Mahogany Armchair inlaid with brass, *about 1810–1815* 429. Beechwood and Mahogany Chair inlaid with brass, *about 1820*

7

428

429

430

430. Carved and Gilt Wood Couch with lion terminals in the Egyptian taste, made by Gillow, London, *1808*

431. Mahogany Dressing Table inlaid with ebony. After a design in George Smith's *Household Furniture*, 1808. *About 1810* **432.** Mahogany Sideboard with carved lion-mask ornament, *about 1800*

431

432

434

436

433. Mahogany Table Inlaid with ebony and silver. Designed by Thomas Hope for his house Deepdene and corresponding to a design in his *Household Furniture, 1807.*

434. Rosewood Table with brass mounts having gilded lion-headed supports. Based on a design in Thomas Hope's *Household Furniture*, 1807. *About 1810*

435. Inlaid and Veneered Mahogany Secrétaire à Abattant, *about 1810*   **436.** Mahogany Secretary veneered with zebra wood and having a fall-front writing drawer. Egyptian heads and feet in ormolu. The watercolor drawings in the glazed upper section are signed J. Baynes, *1808.*

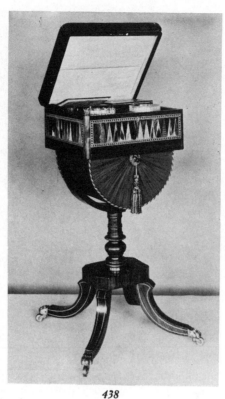

437

438

43

437. Carved Mahogany Tripod Stand supported by chimeras. Similar to a design in Thomas Hope's *Household Furniture*, 1807. *About 1810*   **438.** Rosewood Teapoy with Tunbridge work, *about 1820*   **439.** Rosewood Cheveret with ormolu mounts, *early 19th century*

440. Rosewood Chiffonnier or Low Bookcase with satinwood bandings and gilt detail and having metal trellis-work panels, *early 19th century*   **441.** Carved and Gilt Wood Convex Wall Mirror, *about 1810*

440

441

442. Maple Day Bed, New England, *1700–1725*   443. Maple and Pine Highboy with japanned decoration. New England, probably Boston, *early 18th century*

444. Maple Bed with bed hangings of homespun linen embroidered in crewels, Rhode Island, *1735–1750*

443

445. Maple Wing Chair, New England, probably Massachusetts, *1720–1740*

445

146

447

4

146. Carved Mahogany Chair. One of six sample chairs attributed to Benjamin Randolph, Philadelphia, *1760–1775*   **447.** Carved Mahogany Chair. One of six sample chairs attributed to Benjamin Randolph, Philadelphia, *1760–1775*   **448.** Carved Mahogany Wing Chair. One of six sample chairs attributed to Benjamin Randolph, Philadelphia, *about 1770*

449. Carved Mahogany Armchair in the Chinese taste, Philadelphia, *about 1770–1780*   **450.** Mahogany Settee with serpentine-arched back, Philadelphia, *about 1770*

449

450

451

452

451. Carved Mahogany China Table having a gallery formed of pointed arches in the Gothic taste, New York, *1765–1775* **452.** Carved Mahogany Side Table with marble top, Philadelphia, *1760–1775*

453. Carved Mahogany Tripod Tea Table with bird-cage support, Philadelphia, *1765–1780* **454.** Walnut Spice Chest, Philadelphia, *about 1740–1750*

453

454

455

455. Carved Mahogany Block-Front Knee-hole Writing Table, Newport, *about 1765–1775*   **456.** Mahogany Breakfast Table in the Chinese taste. Labelled by John Townsend, Newport, *1760–1780*   **457.** Mahogany Deception Bed having hinged top and false front enclosing a folding frame made of ash, Philadelphia, *about 1780–1790*
458. Cherry Wood Secretary Bookcase with a slant-front, made in a Southern colony, *about 1755–1775*

458

456

457

459

460

459. Carved Mahogany Philadelphia Style Highboy, *about 1765–1780*

460. Veneered Mahogany and Inlaid Satinwood Secretary Bookcase, Philadelphia, *about 1790*

461

46[

461. Mahogany Armchair with carving attributed to Samuel McIntire. The back resembles a design in Hepplewhite's *Guide*, 1788. Salem, Massachusetts, *about 1790–1800*
462. Mahogany Settee. The carved decoration based on a design by Samuel McIntire and probably done by him. Salem, Massachusetts, *about 1800*
463. Mahogany Field Bed, *about 1790*

463

464

465

464. Veneered Mahogany and Satinwood Salem Secretary with a fall-front writing drawer, Salem, Massachusetts, *about 1800*　**465.** Veneered Mahogany and Inlaid Satinwood Tambour Desk having two slides of tambour construction. Labelled by John Seymour and Son, Boston, *1796–1805*

466. Carved Mahogany Chair in the Duncan Phyfe taste, New York, *1805–1810*
467. Carved Mahogany Settee. Probably made by Duncan Phyfe. New York, *about 1805–1810*

468

469

470

468. Veneered Mahogany and Inlaid Satinwood Card Table, New England, *about 1800*   **469.** Carved Mahogany Work Table and Writing Table with lyre-form end supports, labelled by Michael Allison, 46–48 Vesey Street, New York, and *dated 1823*

470. Rosewood Console Table with gilded metal mounts and figural supports and gilt wood shaggy paw feet, labelled by Charles Honoré Lannuier working around 1805–1819 in New York

471. Carved Cherrywood Couch painted to represent rosewood, with gilt enrichments. Probably from the workshop of Duncan Phyfe, *about 1815–1825*

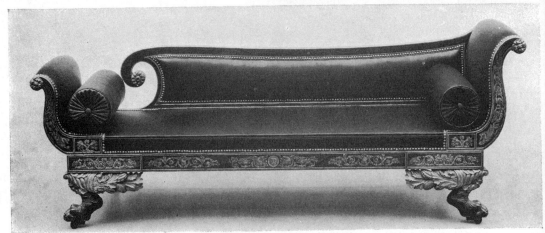

471

472. Carved Oak Sideboard designed by Eugène Prignot and made by Jackson and Graham, London, shown at the Great Exhibition, *1851*

473

474

473. Carved Walnut Armchair decorated with marquetry and set with a porcelain plaque with a portrait of Prince Albert. Designed and made by Henry Eyles, Bath, for the Great Exhibition, *1851*   **474**. Carved Walnut Armchair decorated with marquetry and set with a porcelain plaque with a portrait of Queen Victoria. Designed and made by Henry Eyles, Bath, for the Great Exhibition, *1851*   **475**. Carved and Spirally Turned Mahogany Chair, *about 1845*   **476**. Carved Oak Cabinet designed by A. W. N. Pugin for Abney Hall, Cheshire, *about 1847*

475

476

477

478

477. Satinwood Cabinet decorated with polychrome marquetry, gilt mounts and Wedgwood plaques. Made by Wright and Mansfield, London, *1867*   478. Japanned Metal Bed with papier mâché panels, *about 1850*   479. Turned Ebonized Beechwood Chair with rush seat, *about 1870*   480. Ebonized Oak Morris Chair, *about 1870*

479

480

481. Painted and Inlaid Oak Cupboard, shown at the International Exhibition, *1862* 482. Wardrobe painted with a scene from Chaucer's "Prioress's Tale", *1858*

481

482

483

484

483. Oak Table by Philip Webb, *about 1870*
484. Carved and Inlaid Oak Sideboard decorated with enamel plaques and metal panels in relief designed by Bruce J. Talbert, London, *1867*
485. Oak Sideboard designed by Bruce J. Talbert and made by Gillows, Lancaster, and exhibited *London, 1873*   486. Carved, Painted and Gilt-wood Washstand designed by William Burges, *1880*

486

485

487

487. Sideboard designed by William Burges and painted by
E. J. Poynter, exhibited at the International Exhibition, *1862*
488. Ebonized Wood Sideboard decorated with inset panels
of "embossed leather" paper and silverplated mounts. Designed by E. W. Godwin and made by William Watt, *about
1877* 489. Ebonized Oak Coffee Table designed by E. W.
Godwin and made in numbers by William Watt, *from about
1868*

489

488

490

491

493

Turned Ash Slat-Back Chair with a rush seat, de-
[signe]d and made by Ernest Gimson, *about 1888*
[491.] Brown Ebony Cabinet and Stand inlaid with mother-
[of-pe]arl, designed by Ernest Gimson and made at the
[Dane]way House Workshops, *1908* **492.** Oak Sideboard
[decor]ated with inlay, designed by W. R. Leathaby, *about
1890* **493.** Oak Desk with brass hinges and mounts,
[desig]ned by C. F. A. Voysey, *1896*

492

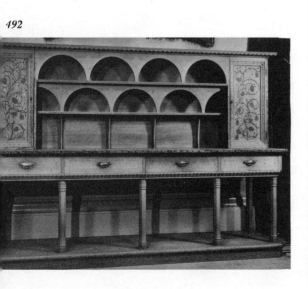

494

495

494. Oak Chair designed by C. F. A. Voysey, *1896*   **495.** Table and Arm chair designed by George Walton, *about 1898*   **496.** Oak Music Cabinet decorated with colored inlays and metal relief designed by M. H. Baillie Scott and made by the Guild of Handicraft for the Grand Duke of Hesse *1898*   **497.** Oak Child's Chair with inlaid decoration designed by M. H. Baillie Scott, *about 1901*   **498.** Oak Writing Table designed by Arthur Mackmurdo, *1886*

496

497

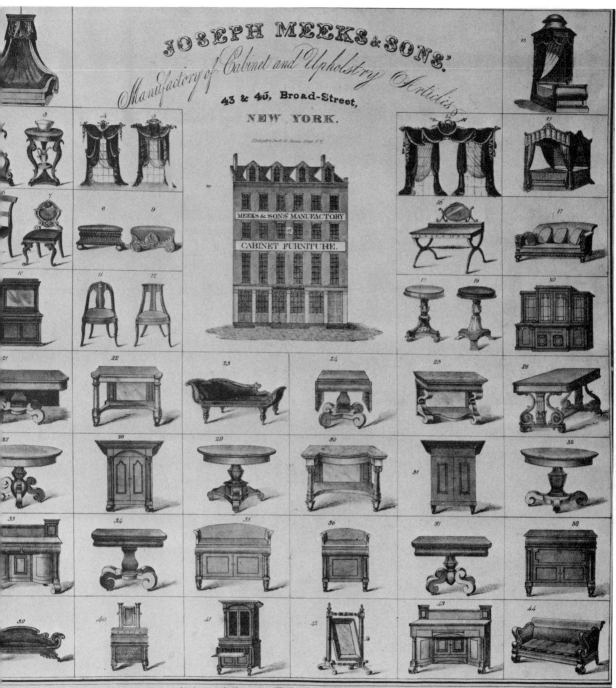

500

501

500. Mahogany Chair, *about 1840*   501. Mahogany Chest of Drawers with free-standing columns, *about 1840*   502. Mahogany Center Table on a tripod base terminating in C-scrolls, *about 1840*   503. Carved Rosewood Chair made by John Jelliff, Newark, *about 1845–55*

503

502

504

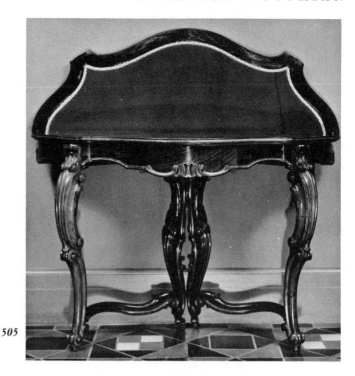

505

504. Carved and Spirally Turned Rosewood and Mahogany Chair, *about 1850*
505. Rosewood Card Table made by Charles A. Baudouine, New York, *about 1850*
506. Rosewood Secretary made by John Jelliff, Newark, *about 1850–1860*　　**507.** Carved
Rosewood Balloon-Back Chair made by Elijah Galusha, Troy, *about 1850–1860*

507

506

508

509

508. Balloon-Back Chair painted in white and parcel gilded, *about 1850–1860*
509. Laminated Rosewood Chair made by John Belter, New York, about 1850. The chairs belong to a set of furniture used by Abraham Lincoln in Illinois   510. Carved Walnut Sideboard made by Daniel Pabst, Philadelphia, *about 1886*   511. Carved Rosewood Armchair made by John Jelliff, Newark, *about 1860–1870*

510

512. Carved Walnut Side Table made by Daniel Pabst, Philadelphia, *about 1868*
513. Veneered and Inlaid Commode made by Léon Marcotte, New York, *about 1875* **514.** Ebony Chair with gilded bronze mounts made by Léon Marcotte, New York, *about 1860*

512

513

514

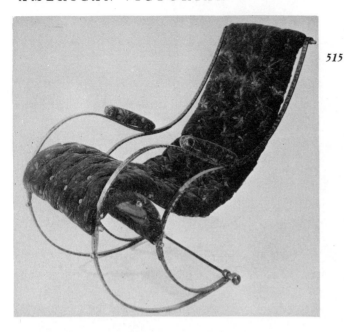

515

516

515. Wrought Iron Rocking Chair owned by Peter Cooper (1791–1883) probably made at the Trenton Iron Works, *about 1860*   **516**. Garden Chair made of iron and wire, *about 1870*   **517**. Armchair made of steerhorn, probably Western United States, *about 1910*   **518**. Upholstered Armchair from the dressing room of the residence of John D. Rockefeller, Sr., 4 West 54th Street, New York   **519**. Upholstered Ottoman from the residence of Mrs. Andrew Carnegie, 3 West 51st Street, New York

518

517

519

521

520

9. Walnut Settee in the Eastlake style, *about 0*   **521.** Walnut Chest of Drawers with dress-mirror in the Eastlake style, *about 1870*   . Oak Armchair designed by Henry Hobson chardson for Woburn Library, *1878*   **523.** Oak cretary Bookcase made by the Grand Rapids air Company, *1892*

523

522

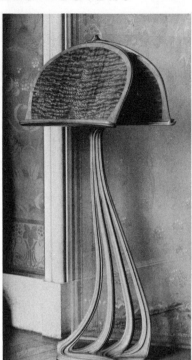

524. Revolving Music Stand by Alexandre Charpentier, *about 1901*   **525**. Veneered Cabinet enriched with carving and polychrome marquetry, signed L. Majorelle, Nancy, *1900*

526. Carved Pearwood Bed with citronwood panels enriched with marquetry by Mercier Frères, *about 1900*   **527**. Carved Pearwood Table by Hector Guimard, from the architect's house in Paris, *about 1908*

526

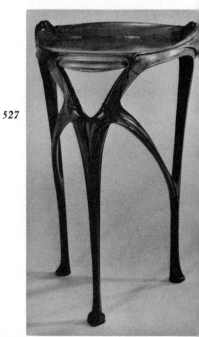

527

528

8. Carved Ashwood Writing Table by Hector Guimard, from the architect's house in ris, *about 1903* **529.** Carved and Inlaid Walnut Work Table by Emile Gallé for : Paris Exhibition, *1900*

529

530

531

530. Veneered Cabinet enriched with carving and polychrome marquetry by Louis Majorelle, *1900*   531. Walnut Armchair stained green by Louis Majorelle, *1900*
532. Walnut Chair by Eugène Vallin, *about 1900*   533. Carved and Gilded Settee by Georges de Feure, *1900*

53

532

535

534

534. Carved Walnut Buffet by Eugène Gaillard shown at the Paris Exhibition, *1900*   **535**. Palissandre Table by Eugène Colonna, *about 1900*
536. Carved Walnut Chair by Eugène Gaillard, *about 1908*

537. Carved Fruitwood Chair by Victor Horta for the Hotel Solvay. Brussels, *1895–1900*

536   **537**

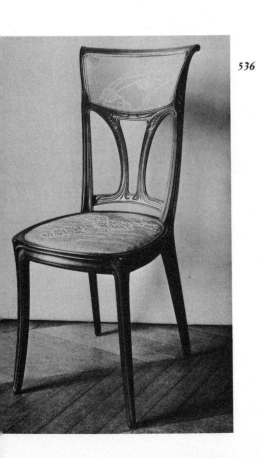

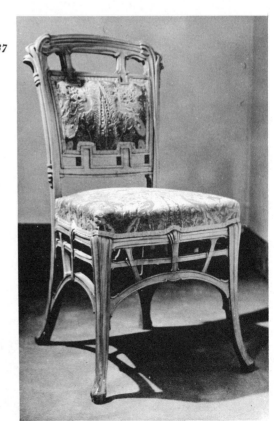

538. Walnut Sideboard by Gustave Serrurier-Bovy, *about 18*
539. Furniture by Henri van de Velde for his house at Ucc.
1896

538

540

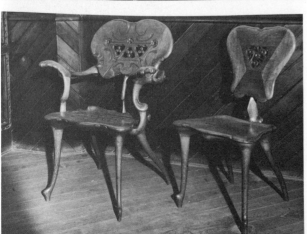

540. Jacaranda Writing Table by Henri Van
de Velde, Uccle, *about 1898*   541. Carved
Walnut Chairs by Antonio Gaudi for Casa
Calvet, Barcelona, *about 1898–1904*

541

542

543

544

542. Oak Chair by H. P. Berlage, *about 1895*
543. White Enameled Wood Cupboard by Charles Rennie Mackintosh, exhibited at the Turin Exhibition, *1902*
544. (Same as 543) but open.   545. Oak Chair by Charles Rennie Mackintosh for his apartment at 120 Main Street, Glasgow   546. Oak Chair by Charles Rennie Mackintosh, *about 1900*   547. Mahogany Armchair by Richard Riemerschmid, *1899*

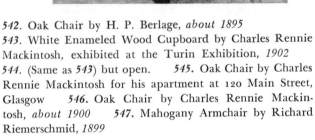

546

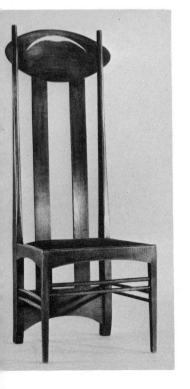

547

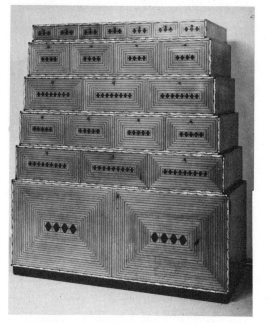

548

549

550

548. Ebony and Mother-of-Pearl Cigar Cabinet by Josef Hoffmann, Vienna *1910–1914*
549. Walnut Table and Chair by Adolf Loos, Vienna, *about 1898*   **550.** Ebony and Mother-of-Pearl Oval Chest by Karl Adolf Franz, Vienna, *about 1912*   **551.** Inlaid Miniature Bookcase enriched with enamel plaques, Vienna, *about 1904*   **552.** Veneered Cabinet on Chest of Drawers by Clemens Frömmel, Vienna, *1903*

552

551

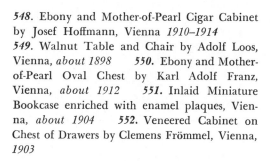

553. Armchair with metal mounts designed by Otto Wagner, Vienna, *about 1900*
554. Pine Wood Armchair designed by Frank Lloyd Wright, American, *1904* **555.**
Painted Wood Armchair designed by Gerrit Rietveld, Dutch, *1917* **556.** Armchair
of bent beechwood designed and manufactured by Gebrüder Thonet, Austria, *1870*

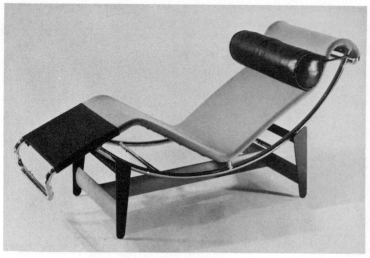

557

558

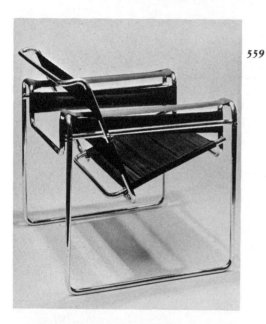

559

557. Adjustable Long Chair of chromium-plated tubular st
and steel frame, painted green and black; gray jersey; bla
leather. Designed by Le Corbusier and manufactured by Tho
Frères, France, *1927*   **558.** Armchair of chromium-pla
tubular steel; black canvas. Designed by Le Corbusier a
manufactured by Thonet Frères, France, *1929*   **559.** Ar
chair of chromium-plated tubular steel; canvas. Designed
Marcel Breuer and manufactured by Gebrüder Thonet, A.
Germany, *1925*   **560.** Armchair of chromium-plated tubu
steel and cane. Designed by Mies van der Rohe and mai
factured by Gebrüder Thonet, A.G., Germany, *1927*   5
Chair of chromium-plated tubular steel; wood; cane. Design
by Marcel Breuer and manufactured by Gebrüder Thon
A.G., Germany, *1928*

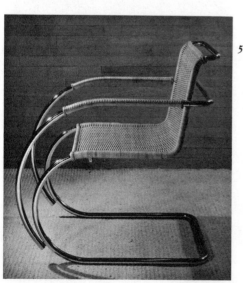

560

561

562

563

564

. Barcelona Chair of chromium-
ted steel bars designed by Mies van
Rohe, *1929*   **563.** Palissandre
ble with oak supports designed by
Legrain, *1923*   **564.** Black Lac-
ered Wood Chaise Longue with
ther-of-pearl inlay designed by P.
grain, about *1925*   **565.** Macassar
ony Writing Table and Chair de-
ned by Pierre Chareau, *1925*

565

566   567

568

566. Amaranth and Violet Wood Low Cupboard designed
Maurice Dufrène, 1925   567. Mahogany Chair design
by Blanche Klotz, 1923   568. Chair designed by Jacqu
Ruhlmann for the dining room l'Hôtel du Collectionneur
the Paris Exhibition, 1925   569. Lacquered Wood a
Parchment Bonheur du Jour, about 1920–1925

569

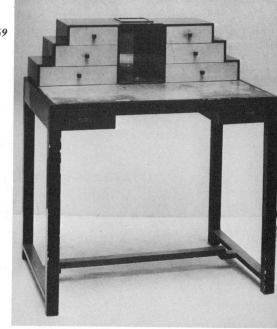

570

570. Macassar Ebony Bed inlaid with stringing lines of ivory designed by Jacques Ruhlmann, about *1920–1925*   571. Macassar Ebony Writing Table of kneehole form mounted in gilt bronze, designed by Louis Suë and André Mare for the Paris Exhibition, *1925*

571

572

573

572. Macassar Ebony Cabinet inlaid with stringing lines of ivory designed by Jacques Ruhlmann, *about 1925*   573. Armchair, the wood frame covered with white sharkskin designed by André Groult, *1925*   574. Tulipwood writing Table of kneehole form, with ebonized bandings designed by Jules Bouy, *about 1930*   575. Armchair of laminated bent birchwood; black canvas webbing and white lambskin slipcover. Designed by Bruno Mathsson and manufactured by Firma Karl Mathsson, Sweden, *1940*

575

574

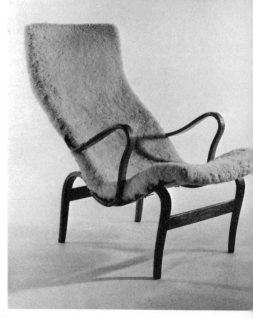

576. Teakwood Extension Dining Table with four drop leaves and four gates designed by Bruno Mathsson and manufactured by Firma Karl Mathsson, Sweden, *1938* **577.** Lounge Chair with a bent laminated birchwood frame and plywood seat and back, designed by Alvar Aalto and manufactured by Artek, Helsinki, *about 1934*

576

577

578

579

580

578. Stool of laminated birchwood; leather. Designed by Alvar Aalto and manufactured by Artek, Helsinki, *1954*   **579.** Mahogany and Rosewood Bed designed by Kaare Klint for the cabinetmaker Rud Rasmjssen, Copenhagen, *about 1930*   **580.** Pinewood Unit with built-in bed; also a table on the back wall. Designed by Børge Mogensen, *1954*

581

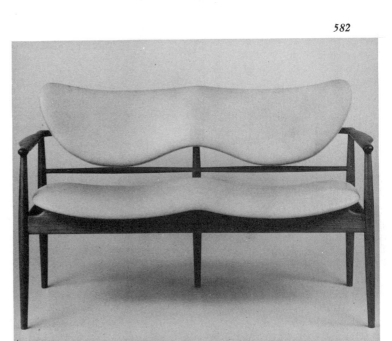

582

581. Teakwood Armchair designed by Finn Juhl for the cabinetmaker Niels Vodder, Copenhagen, *1945* **582.** Teakwood Settee designed by Finn Juhl for the cabinetmaker Niels Vodder, Copenhagen, about *1950* **583.** Teak and Maplewood Table designed by Finn Juhl for the cabinetmaker Niels Vodder, Copenhagen, *about 1950*

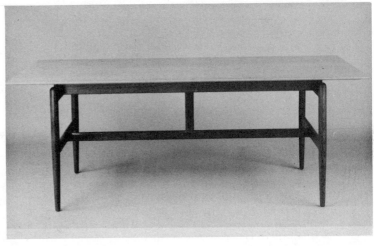

583

584

584. Teakwood Armchair designed by Hans J. Wegner for the cabinetmaker Johannes Hansen, Copenhagen, *1949*   585. "The Egg," armchair designed by Arne Jacobsen for the manufacturer Fritz Hansens, Copenhagen, *1957*
586. Chair of chromium-plated steel and wicker designed by Poul Kjaerholm, Copenhagen, *1957*

585

586

587

7. Comprehensive Storage System including a dining and writing table designed by George Nelson for the manufacturer Herman Miller, Inc., Zeeland, *about 1950*
8. Rocking Chair of Bent Beechwood designed and manufactured by Gebrüder Thonet, Austria, *about 1860*   **589.** Vienna Café Chair of bent beechwood designed and manufactured by Gebrüder Thonet, Austria, *76*

589

588

590

591

590. Long Chair of bent laminated birchwood; upholstered pad. Designed by Marcel Breuer and manufactured by the Isokon Furniture Co., Ltd., London, *1935*   **591.** Chair of molded walnut plywood, metal rod; designed by Charles Eames for the manufacturer Herman Miller, Inc., Zeeland, *1946*   **592.** Lounge Chair and Ottoman of laminated rosewood on metal swivel base; leather. Designed by Charles Eames for the manufacturer Herman Miller, Inc., Zeeland, *1956*

592

593

594

595

593. Chair of formed steel wire, painted black with a plastic slipcover designed by Charles Eames for the manufacturer Herman Miller, Inc., Zeeland, *1951*   **594.** Chair of formed steel wire designed by Harry Bertoia for the manufacturer Knoll Associates, New York, *1952*   **595.** Chair of steel wire; molded latex. Designed by Warren Platner for the manufacturer Knoll Associates, New York, *1966*

596

597

598

596. Armchair, plexiglass plastic shell on cast aluminum stem designed by Estelle and Erwine Laverne for Laverne International Ltd., New York, *1962*   **597.** "Womb" Chair, molded reinforced plastic shell, metal rod and foam rubber, designed by Eero Saarinen for the manufacturer Knoll Associates, New York, *1946*   **598.** Pedestal Chair, molded plastic reinforced with fiberglas; aluminum painted white. Designed by Eero Saarinen for the manufacturer Knoll Associates, New York, *1957*   **599.** Stack/Gang Chair, injection molded plastic and aluminum. Designed by Don Albinson for the manufacturer Knoll Associates, New York, *1965*   **600.** "Seggio" Stack/Gang Chair, injection molded plastic. Designed by Joe Columbo for the manufacturer Kartell, Milan, *1967*

599

600

1

602

601. "Gyro" Lounge Chair, molded plastic reinforced with fiberglas. Designed by Eero Aarnio, Finland, *1968*   602. Chair of plastic reinforced fiberglas designed by Verner Panton for the manufacturer Herman Miller, A.G., Basel, *1967*   603. Armchair, bent and pressed plywood; polyester lacquer. Designed by Joe Columbo for the manufacturer Kartell, *1964*   604. Bed of lacquered metal designed by Cini Boeri for the manufacturer Sarmo, Milan, *1965*

604

603

606

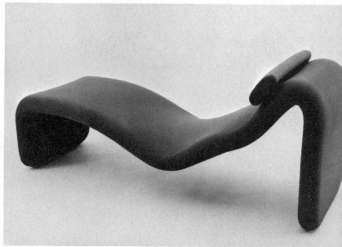

605

605. "Marema" Stacking Tables, injection molded. Designed by Gianfranco Frattini for the manufacturer Cassina, Medea, *1968*   **606.** Basket Chair of rattan designed by Isama Kenmochi for the manufacturer Yamakawa Rattan Co., Ltd., Tokyo, *1959*
607. Long Chair, nylon stretch fabric over foam rubber on steel frame, designed by Olivier Mourgue for the manufacturer Airborne International, France, *1965*

607

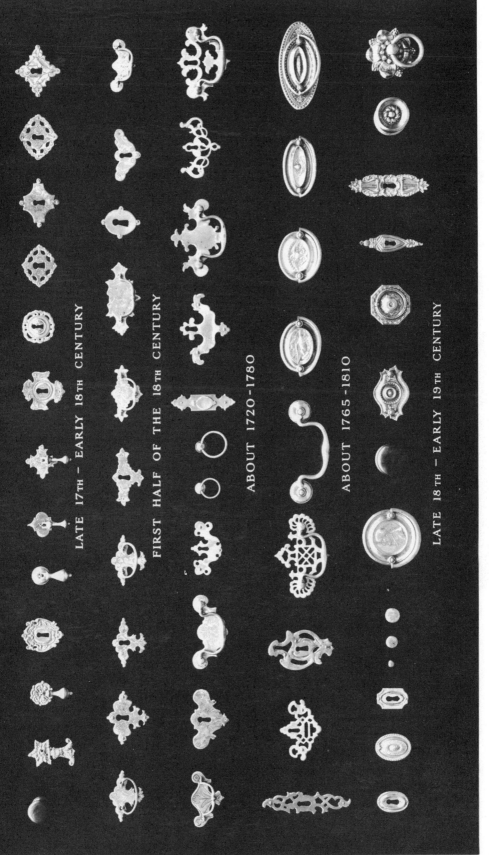

TYPES OF HARDWARE USED ON EARLY AMERICAN FURNITURE

LATE 17TH – EARLY 18TH CENTURY

FIRST HALF OF THE 18TH CENTURY

ABOUT 1720–1780

ABOUT 1765–1810

LATE 18TH – EARLY 19TH CENTURY

609

610

611

609. Rosewood Armchair with yoke pattern back, *Ming dynasty*   610. Rosewood chair with yoke pattern back, *Ming dynasty*   611. Rosewood Armchair with arched horseshoe-shaped crest rail, *Ming dynasty*

612. Rosewood Armchair in the bamboo style, *Ming dynasty*   613. Rosewood couch in the bamboo style, *Ming dynasty*   614. K'ang Table, *Ming dynasty*

612

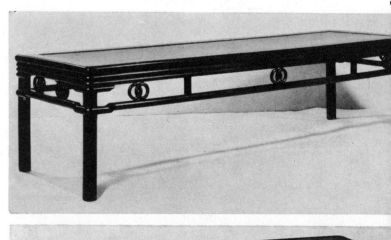

614

616

615

615. Rosewood couch with low railing, *Ming dynasty*
616. Rosewood Stool in the bamboo style, *Ming dynasty*
617. Rosewood Tester Bed or Couch, *Ming dynasty*
618. Rosewood Barrel-shaped Seat, *Ming dynasty*

617

618

619

62

621

622

619. Lacquered Table inlaid with mother-of-pearl in a tin lining, having a braced top, *Ming dynasty*

620. Rosewood Square Table having a braced top, *Ming dynasty*

621. Four Rosewood Stools in typical arrangement, *Ming dynasty*

622. Rosewood Bench with splayed trestle-end supports, *Ming dynasty*

23

624

623. Rosewood Square Table in the bamboo style, *Ming dynasty*

624. Rosewood Yoke Table, *Ming dynasty*

625. Rosewood Side Table, *Ming dynasty*

626. Chicken-wing wood Library Table with oblique corner brackets, *Ming dynasty*

625

626

627

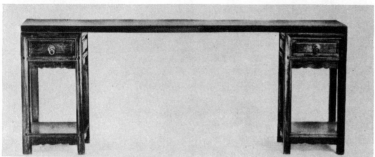

628

629

627. Rosewood Side Table of the yoke table type, *Ming dynasty*

628. Rosewood Trestle Table with removable top, *Ming dynasty*

629. Rosewood Side Table with trestle-end supports, *Ming dynasty*

630. Rosewood Side Table with trestle-end supports, *Ming dynasty*

630

631

631. Rosewood Side Table with trestle-end supports, *Ming dynasty*

632. Rosewood Chest or Coffer, *Ming dynasty*

633. Rosewood Cupboard, *Ming dynasty*

632

633

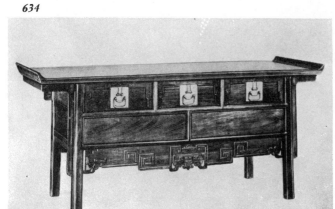

634. Rosewood Chest or Coffer, *Ming dynasty c. 16th to 17th century*   **635.** Rosewood Low Cupboard, *Ming,*

636. Rosewood Cupboard with splayed legs and bracketed valance, *Ming dynasty*

637. Rosewood Cupboard in Four Parts, *Ming dynasty*

BIBLIOGRAPHY
ARTISTS AND CRAFTSMEN
INDEX

AUSTRIA

Österreichisches Museum für Angewandte Kunst, Vienna: NOS. 226–230.
Kunsthistorisches Museum, Vienna: NOS. 212, 213.

ENGLAND

The Fitzwilliam Museum, Cambridge: NO. 14, by courtesy of the Syndics.
The Victoria and Albert Museum, London: NOS. 24, 27, 39–41, 51, 53, 114, 125, 129, 132, 136, 151, 157, 162, 169, 173, 178, 179, 187, 188, 193, 262–264, 267, 269, 270, 272–275, 277, 279–281, 284, 285, 287–294, 297–300, 303, 305, 308, 309, 311, 313, 315, 317–319, 321, 322, 324, 326–328, 330, 333–336, 338–344, 346, 348, 351–353, 355, 356, 358, 360, 361, 363–369, 371, 372, 374, 377, 378, 380–382, 384, 385, 387, 388, 396, 397, 402–404, 406, 408–410, 416, 419, 421–423, 425–434, 436–438, 441.
The Wallace Collection, London: NOS. 29, 52, 127, 128, 130, 131, 133, 159, 171, 177, 180, 182, 183, 186, 189, 195, by courtesy of the Trustees.
The Lady Lever Art Gallery, Port Sunlight, Cheshire: NOS. 307, 357, 376, 395, 411.

FRANCE

Musée Arlaten, Arles: NOS. 233, 234, 236, 247, 248, 256, 258–260 (PHOTOS E. Barral).
Musée des Arts Décoratifs, Paris: NOS. 140, 144, 166, 201, 204–207, 209, 211, 214, 217, 219–221, 223–225, 249.
Musée Nationale des Arts et Traditions Populaires, Paris: NOS. 231, 232, 235, 237–239, 241–244, 246, 250, 251, 255, 257, 261 (PHOTOS Soulier).
Musée Nationale du Louvre, Paris: NO. 5 (PHOTO Mella), NOS. 152, 190, 192

(Photos Caisse Nationale des Monuments Historiques).
Château de Gros Bois: NO. 215 (PHOTO Caisse National des Monuments Historiques).
Château de Pau: NO. 245 (PHOTO Caisse Nationale des Monuments Historiques).
Musée des Beaux-Arts, Rennes: NOS. 240, 252–254.

HAWAIIAN ISLANDS

(ALL PHOTOS: Honolulu Academy of Arts)
Mr. and Mrs. C. Wendell Carlsmith, Hilo, Hawaii: NO. 524.
Mr. and Mrs. Walter F. Dillingham, Honolulu: NO. 501.
Mrs. Gustav Ecke, Honolulu: NOS. 498, 502, 504, 506, 509.
The Honolulu Academy of Arts, Honolulu, Hawaii: NOS. 496, 500, 507, 510, 512–514, 516–518, 521.
Mrs. James R. Judd, Honolulu: NO. 522.
Mr. Frederic Mueller, Honolulu: NO. 508.
Mrs. Dorothy Clune Murray, Honolulu: NO. 523.
Mrs. Edward E. Sox, Honolulu: NO. 505.

HONG KONG

Mr. Henri Vetch, Hong Kong: NOS. 497, 499, 503, 511, 515, 519, 520 (PHOTOS Honolulu Academy of Arts).

ITALY

(ALL PHOTOS: Mella)
Museo Nazionale. Naples: NOS. 6–8, 10, 15–18.
Museo dei Conservatori, Rome: NO. 9.
Museo Gregoriano, Rome: NO. 13.
Palazzo Corsini, Rome: NO. 4.
Collection Loewi, Venice: NO. 57.
Museo Correr, Venice: NOS. 55, 58.
Raccolta Barozzi, Venice: NO. 56.

THE NETHERLANDS

Rijksmuseum, Amsterdam: NOS. *37, 50, 81–88, 90–104, 117, 185, 216.*

SPAIN

(ALL PHOTOS: *Mas*)

Barcelona Museo Arqueológico Nacional, Arquilla: NO. *72.*

Museo de Arte de Cataluña, Barcelona: NOS. *70, 71, 75, 79.*

Catedral-Museo, León: NO. *68.*

Exposición de Guadamecíes, Madrid: NOS. *59, 61.*

Museo de Artes Decorativas, Madrid: NOS. *63, 65, 78.*

Museo Lázaro, Madrid: NOS. *62, 66, 67, 80.*

Sigüenza Catedral: NO. *74.*

Museo Episcopal, Vich, Barcelona: NO. *60.*

Museo Diocesane, LaSeo, Zaragoza: NO. *69.*

Zaragoza, El Pilar Sacristéa Mayor: NO. *76.*

UNITED STATES

The Brooklyn Museum, Brooklyn, N. Y.: NO. *2.*

Yale Gallery of Fine Arts, Mabel Brady Garvan Collection, New Haven, Conn.: NOS. *399, 420.*

Cooper Union Museum for the Arts of Decoration, New York: NO. *89.*

Duveen Brothers, New York: NOS. *47, 48, 147, 148, 154, 155, 163, 164, 197, 199, 203, 210.*

Services du Conseiller Culturel, Ambassade de France, New York: NOS. *200, 222.*

The Frick Collection, New York: NOS. *42, 45, 106–108, 118, 134, 156, 175, 176, 181, 184, 194, 198.*

The Metropolitan Museum of Art, New York: NOS. *1, 3, 11, 12, 19–23, 25, 26, 30–36, 54, 105, 109–113, 115, 116, 119–124, 135, 137–139, 141–143, 145, 146, 149, 153, 158, 165, 167, 168, 170, 172, 174, 191, 196, 202, 218, 265, 266, 268, 276, 278, 282, 283, 286, 295, 296, 301, 302, 304, 306, 310, 312, 316, 320, 323, 329, 337, 359, 375, 383, 386, 391–393, 398, 405, 407, 412–415, 424, 439, 443, 462, 466–471.*

Frank Partridge, Inc., New York: NOS. *332, 345, 347, 349, 350, 362, 390, 400, 417, 440* (PHOTOS *Albert Waks*).

The Philadelphia Museum of Art, Philadelphia, Pa.: NOS. *28, 43, 44, 46, 49, 64, 73, 77, 126, 208, 271, 325, 331, 354, 370, 373, 379, 394, 401, 418, 435, 448, 450, 460, 463, 464.*

The National Gallery of Art, Washington, D. C.: NOS. *38, 150, 160, 161.*

Colonial Williamsburg, Williamsburg, Virginia: NOS. *314, 389, 447, 449, 458.*

Henry Francis du Pont Winterthur Museum, Winterthur, Delaware: NOS. *442, 444–446, 451–457, 459, 461, 465.*

PICTURE SOURCES FOR CHAPTERS 23–26, ENLARGED EDITION, 1969

AUSTRIA

Österreichisches Museum für Angewandte Kunst, Vienna: NOS. *548, 550, 551, 552.*

Österreichisches Postsparkassenamt, Vienna: NO. *553.*

BELGIUM

Bibliothèque Royale de Belgique, Brussels: NOS. *537, 538.*

DENMARK

Museum of Decorative Arts, Copenhagen: NOS. *533, 534, 579–581, 586.*

FINLAND

Artek, Helsinki: NO. *577.*

FRANCE

Musée de l'Ecole de Nancy, Nancy: NO. *532.*

Musée des Arts Décoratifs, Paris: NOS. *524, 536, 563–570, 573.*

GREAT BRITAIN
Bristol City Art Gallery: NO. *489.*
University of Glasgow: NOS. *543, 544.*
The Victoria and Albert Museum, London: NOS. *472–475, 477–481, 483–488, 490–498, 525, 529–531.*
Salford City Art Gallery: NO. *476.*

THE NETHERLANDS
Municipal Museum, The Hague: NO. *542.*

NORWAY
Nordenjeldske Kunstindustrimuseum, Trondheim: NO. *540.*

SPAIN
Mas, Barcelona: NO. *541.*

SWEDEN
Firma Karl Mathsson: NO. *576.*

SWITZERLAND
Kunstgewerbemuseum, Zurich: NO. *539, 546, 549.*

UNITED STATES
The Museum of Art, Boston, Mass.: NO. *522.*
The Henry Ford Museum, Dearborn, Mich.: NOS. *500–502, 509, 516, 517, 520, 521.*
Hank Loewenstein, Inc., Fort Lauderdale, Fla.: NO. *600.*
Grand Rapids Public Museum, Grand Rapids, Mich.: NO. *523.*

Atelier, New York, N. Y.: NO. *605.*
The Cooper-Hewitt Museum of Design, New York, N. Y.: NOS. *515, 526.*
Fritz Hansen, Inc., New York, N. Y.: NO. *585.*
Knoll Associates, New York, N. Y.: NOS. *562, 594, 598.*
Laverne International, New York, N. Y., NOS. *560, 596, 599.*
Collection of Just Lunning, New York, N. Y.: NO. *584.*
The Metropolitan Museum of Art, New York, N. Y.: NOS. *499* (Gift of Mrs. R. W. Hyde, 1943), *514* (Gift of Mrs. D. Chester Noyes, 1968), *535* (Edward C. Moore, Jr. Gift Fund, 1926), *571* (Edward C. Moore, Jr. Gift Fund, 1925), *572* (Edward C. Moore, Jr. Gift Fund, 1926), *574* (Gift of Mrs. C. A. Castle and Mrs. Paul Dahlstrom, 1968), *582* (Edward C. Moore, Jr. Gift Fund, 1961), *583* (Edward C. Moore, Jr. Gift Fund, 1961), *608.*
The Museum of the City of New York, New York, N. Y.: *504, 518, 519.*
The Museum of Contemporary Crafts, New York. N. Y.: NOS. *602, 604.*
The Museum of Modern Art, New York, N. Y.: NOS. *527, 528, 545, 547, 554, 555, 557–559, 561, 575, 578, 588, 589, 590.*
Stendig, Inc., New York, N. Y.: NO. *601.*
The Newark Museum, Newark, N. J.: NOS. *503, 506, 511, 513.*
The Philadelphia Museum of Art, Philadelphia, Pa.: NOS. *510, 512.*
Munson-Williams-Proctor Institute, Utica, N. Y.: NOS. *505, 507, 508.*
Herman Miller, Inc., Zeeland, Mich.: NOS. *587, 592.*

ENGLISH

Ackermann, Rudolph. *Repository of Arts, Literature, etc.*, London, 1809–1828.

Adam, Robert and James. *Works in Architecture.* Began publishing in parts in London, 1773, and printed for the authors, 1778–1822.

Adam, Robert. *The Ruins of the Palace of the Emperor Diocletian at Spalatro in Dalmatia.* London, 1764.

Bell, J. Munroe. *The Furniture Designs of Chippendale, Hepplewhite and Sheraton, arranged by J. Munroe Bell.* New York, 1938.

Benn, R. Davis. *Style in Furniture.* London, 1904.

Blake, J. P. and Hopkins-Reveirs, A. E. *Old English Furniture for the Small Collector, its Types, History and Surroundings from Medieval to Victorian Times.* London, 1930.

Brackett, Oliver. *English Furniture Illustrated, A Pictorial Review of English Furniture from Chaucer to Queen Victoria,* Revised and Edited by H. Clifford Smith. London, 1950.

Brackett, Oliver. *Thomas Chippendale.* London, 1924.

Burgess, Fred W. *Antique Furniture.* London, 1915.

Cescinsky, Herbert. *English Furniture of the Eighteenth Century.* 3 VOLS., London, 1909–1911.

Cescinsky, Herbert. *English Furniture from Gothic to Sheraton.* Michigan, 1937.

Chambers, Sir William. *Designs for Chinese Buildings and Furniture.* London, 1757.

Chamberlain, Samuel. *Tudor Homes of England.* New York, 1929.

Chippendale, Thomas. *The Gentleman and Cabinet-Maker's Director, being a collection of the most Elegant and Useful Designs of Household Furniture in the Most Fashionable Taste.* First edition published in 1754; second edition in 1755 and third edition in 1762, London.

Clouston, R. S. *English Furniture and Furniture Makers of the Eighteenth Century.* London, 1906.

Clouston, K. Warren. *The Chippendale Period in English Furniture.* London, 1897.

Cole, Herbert. *An Introduction to the Period Styles of England and France, with a Chapter on the Dutch Renaissance.* Manchester, 1927.

Crane, Walter, *William Morris to Whistler.* London, 1911.

Crunden, John. *Convenient and Ornamental Architecture.* London, 1770.

Crunden, John. *The Joyner and Cabinet-Maker's Darling or Pocket Director.* London, 1765.

Darly, Mathias. *The Compleat Architect.* London, 1770.

Darly, Mathias and Edwards, George. *A New Book of Chinese Designs.* London, 1754.

Dickinson, George. *English Papier-Mâché.* London, 1925.

Dossie, Robert. *The Handmaid to the Arts.* 2 VOLS., London, 1758. A second edition with improvements and additions in 1764.

Dutton, Ralph. *The English Interior, 1500–1900.* London, 1948.

Dutton, Ralph. *The Victorian Home.* London, 1954.

Eastlake, Charles Locke. *Hints on Household Taste in Furniture, Upholstery and other Details.* London, 1872.

Ellwood, George Montague. *English Furniture and Decoration, 1660–1800.* London, 1909.

Evelyn, John. *Diary of John Evelyn with an introduction and notes by Austin Dobson.* London, 1908.

Field, Horace and Bunney, M. *English Decorative Architecture of the 17th and 18th Centuries.* London, 1928.

BIBLIOGRAPHY

Foley, Edwin. *The Book of Decorative Furniture, its Form, Colours and History.* 2 VOLS., London, 1911.

Gribble, Ernest R. *Early English Furniture and Woodwork.* London, 1922.

Halfpenny, W. and J. *New Designs for Chinese Temples, Garden Seats, etc.* Published in parts between 1750–1752 in London.

Hamilton, Sir William. *Collection of Etruscan, Greek, and Roman Antiquities from the Cabinet of the Hon. Wm. Hamilton.* Naples, 1766.

Hamilton, Sir William. *Outlines from the Figures and Compositions upon the Greek, Roman and Etruscan Vases of the late Sir William Hamilton.* London, 1814.

Harvey, John. *Gothic England, 1300–1550.* London, 1947.

Hayden, Arthur. *Chats on Cottage and Farmhouse Furniture.* New York, 1912.

Heal, Sir Ambrose. *London Furniture Makers, From the Restoration to the Victorian Era, 1660–1840.* London, 1953.

Hepplewhite, A. and Co. *The Cabinet Maker and Upholsterer's Guide.* First edition in 1788; second edition in 1789, and third edition in 1794. London.

Hope, Thomas. *Household Furniture and Interior Decoration.* London, 1807.

Household Furniture in Genteel Taste, published by the Society of Upholsterers and Cabinet-Makers. First edition, London, 1760.

Ince, William and Mayhew, Thomas. *The Universal System of Household Furniture.* Published in parts between 1759 and 1763 in London.

Johnson, Thomas. *One Hundred and Fifty New Designs for carvers' pieces, frames, candlestands, candelabra, tables and lanterns.* Issued in monthly parts between 1756–1758, with a second edition in 1761. London.

Johnson, Thomas. *Twelve Girandoles.* London, 1755.

Jones, William. *The Gentleman's and Builders' Companion.* London, 1739.

Jourdain, Margaret. *English Decorative Plasterwork of the Renaissance.* New York, 1926.

Jourdain, Margaret. *English Decoration and Furniture of the Early Renaissance, 1500–1650.* London, 1924.

Jourdain, Margaret. *English Decoration and Furniture of the Later XVIII Century, 1760–1820.* London, 1922.

Jourdain, Margaret. *English Interior Decoration 1500–1830.* London, 1950.

Jourdain, Margaret. *English Interiors in Smaller Houses from the Restoration to the Regency, 1660–1830.* London, 1923.

Jourdain, Margaret. *Regency Furniture, 1795–1820.* Revised and Enlarged edition. London, 1948.

Jourdain, Margaret. *The Work of William Kent.* London, 1948.

Jourdain, Margaret and Edwards, Ralph. *Georgian Cabinet-Makers.* Second edition, London, 1946.

Jourdain, Margaret and Rose, T. *English Furniture, The Georgian Period, 1750–1830.* London, 1953.

Kimball, Fiske and Donnell, Edna. *Creators of the Chippendale Style.* Metropolitan Museum Studies, May and November, 1929.

Layton, Edwin J. *Thomas Chippendale.* London, 1928.

Lenygon, Francis. *Decoration in England 1640–1760.* New York, 1927.

Lenygon, Francis. *Furniture in England from 1660 to 1760.* London, 1915.

Lenygon, Francis. *The Decoration and Furniture of English Mansions during the 17th and 18th Centuries.* London, 1909.

Litchfield, Frederick. *History of Furniture; From the Earliest to the Present Time.* Seventh edition; revised and enlarged. London, 1922.

Lock, Matthias and Copland, Henry. *A New Book of Foliage.* London, 1769.

Lock, Matthias and Copland, Henry. *A New Book of Ornaments, consisting of Tables, Chimnies, Sconces, Clock Cases, etc.* London, 1768.

Lock, Matthias and Copland, Henry. *A New Book of Pier Frames.* London, 1769.

Lock, Matthias and Copland, Henry. *A New Drawing Book of Ornaments.* London, 1740.

Macquoid, Percy. *A History of English Furniture.* 4 VOLS., London, 1904–1908. VOL. I, *The Age of Oak,* 1904; VOL. II, *The Age of Walnut,* 1905; VOL. III, *The Age of Mahogany,* 1906; VOL. IV, *The Age of Satinwood,* 1908.

Macquoid, Percy and Edwards, Ralph. *The Dictionary of English Furniture, from the Middle Ages to the Late Georgian Period.* Revised and enlarged by Ralph Edwards, 3 VOLS., London, 1954.

Manwaring, Robert. *The Cabinet and Chair Maker's Real Friend and Companion.* London, 1765.

Manwaring, Robert. *The Chair Makers' Guide.* Revised edition. London, 1766.

Milne, James Lees. *The Age of Adam.* London, 1947.

Percival, MacIver. *Old English Furniture and Its*

Surroundings from the Restoration to the Regency. London, 1920.

Pergolesi, Michele Angelo. *Original Designs on Various Ornaments.* The plates were issued separately between 1777–1791 in London.

Pugin, Augustus Welby N. *Gothic Furniture in the style of the 15th century, designed and etched by A. W. N. Pugin.* London, 1835.

Pugin, A. *Gothic Furniture, consisting of 27 coloured engravings from designs by A. Pugin.* London, 18—.

Roberts, Henry D. *History of the Royal Pavilion, Brighton. The Original Furniture and Decoration.* London, 1939.

Robinson, Frederick Sydney. *English Furniture.* London, 1905.

Roe, F. Gordon. *Victorian Furniture.* New York, 1952.

Rogers, John C. *English Furniture.* Revised and enlarged by Margaret Jourdain. London, 1950.

Sayer, Robert. *The Ladies' Amusement or Whole Art of Japanning made easy.* London, c.1760.

Shearer, Thomas. *Designs for Household Furniture.* London, 1788.

Sheraton, Thomas. *Designs for Household Furniture exhibiting a Variety of Elegant and Useful Patterns in the Cabinet, Chair and Upholstery Branches on eighty-four plates, by the late T. Sheraton.* London, 1812.

Sheraton, Thomas. *The Cabinet Dictionary, containing an explanation of all the terms used in the Cabinet, Chair and Upholstery Branches, with directions for varnishing, polishing and gilding.* London, 1803.

Sheraton, Thomas. *The Cabinet-Maker, Upholsterer and General Artist's Encyclopaedia.* Unfinished. Part I published in London, 1805.

Sheraton, Thomas. *The Cabinet-Maker and Upholsterer's Drawing Book.* Published in four parts from 1791–94, and third edition in 1802. London.

Simon, Constance. *English Furniture Designers of the Eighteenth Century.* London, 1905.

Smith, George. *A Collection of Designs for Household Furniture and Interior Decoration.* London, 1808.

Smith, George. *A Collection of Ornamental Designs after the Manner of the Antique.* London, 1812.

Smith, George. *The Cabinet-Makers' and Upholsterers' Guide, Drawing Book and Repository of New and Original Designs for Household Furniture.* London, 1826.

Stalker, John and Parker, George. *Treatise of Japanning and Varnishing.* London, 1688.

Strange, Thomas Arthur. *English Furniture, Decoration, Woodwork and Allied Arts, 17th, 18th and 19th Centuries.* London.

Stratton, Arthur. *The English Interior, a Review of the Decoration of English Homes from Tudor Times to the 19th Century.* London, 1920.

Symonds, Robert Weymss. *English Furniture from Charles II to George II.* 2 VOLS., London, 1929.

Symonds, Robert Weymss. *Masterpieces of English Furniture and Clocks; a Study of Mahogany and Walnut Furniture.* London, 1940.

Symonds, Robert Weymss. *Old English Walnut and Lacquer Furniture.* London, 1923.

The Cabinet Makers' London Book of Prices and Designs of Cabinet Work. Thomas Shearer and Others. First edition 1788 and second edition 1793, London.

Tipping, Henry Avray. *English Homes.* 9 VOLS., London, 1920–1939.

Vallance, Aymer. *The Art of William Morris.* London, 1897.

Vardy, John. *Selection from the Works of Inigo Jones and William Kent.* London, 1744.

AMERICAN

Cornelius, Charles Over. *Furniture Masterpieces of Duncan Phyfe.* New York, 1922.

Dow, George Francis. *The Arts and Crafts in New England, 1704–1775.* Topsfield, Mass., 1927.

Downs, Joseph. *American Furniture, Queen Anne and Chippendale Periods.* New York, 1952.

Dyer, Walter Alden. *Early American Craftsmen.* New York, 1915.

Hall, John. *The Cabinet Makers' Assistant, Embracing the Most Modern Style of Cabinet Furniture.* Baltimore, 1840.

Halsey, Richard and Tower, Elizabeth. *The Homes of our Ancestors, as shown in the American Wing of the Metropolitan Museum of Art.* New York, 1925.

Hornor, William MacPherson. *Blue Book of Philadelphia Furniture, William Penn to George Washington.* Philadelphia, 1935.

Kimball, Fiske. *Domestic Architecture of the American Colonies and the Early Republic.* New York, 1922.

Kimball, Fiske. *Mr. Samuel McIntire, Carver. The Architect of Salem.* Salem, 1940.

Lichten, Frances. *Decorative Art of Victoria's Era.* New York, 1950.

Lockwood, Luke Vincent. *Colonial Furniture in*

America. 2 vols., Third edition, New York, 1926.

Lockwood, Luke Vincent. *The Pendleton Collection.* Providence, 1904.

Lyon, Dr. Irving Whitall. *The Colonial Furniture of New England.* Boston, 1924.

McClelland, Nancy Vincent. *Duncan Phyfe and the English Regency, 1795–1830.* New York, 1939.

Metropolitan Museum of Art. *American Chippendale Furniture, a Picture Book,* New York, 1940.

Miller, Edgar George, Jr. *American Antique Furniture.* 2 vols., Baltimore, 1937. An abridgement of the two-volume work, New York, 1950.

Morse, Frances Clary. *Furniture of the Olden Time.* New York, 1917.

Nutting, Wallace. *Furniture of the Pilgrim Century, 1620–1720.* Revised edition. Massachusetts, 1924.

Nutting, Wallace. *Furniture Treasury.* 2 vols. in 1928 and a 3rd vol. in 1933. Massachusetts.

Ormsbee, Thomas Hamilton. *Early American Furniture Makers.* New York, 1930.

Sack, Albert. *Fine Points of Furniture, Early American.* New York, 1950.

Singleton, Esther. *The Furniture of Our Forefathers.* 2 vols. New York, 1900.

Walpole Society. *The Arts and Crafts in Philadelphia, Maryland and South Carolina, 1721–1785,* vol. I, and *1786–1800,* vol. II, collected by Alfred Coxe Prime. Topsfield, Mass., 1929.

FRENCH

Adams, Louis. *Decorations Intérieures et Meubles des époques Louis XIII et Louis XIV; Reproduits d'après les compositions de Crispin de Passe; Paul Vredeman de Vries; Sébastien Serlius; Bérain; Jean Marot; De Bross; etc.* Paris, 1865.

Arnaud d'Agnel, G. *Arts et Industries Artistiques de la Provence.* 2 vols. Paris.

Arnaud d'Agnel, G. *Le Meuble. Ameublement Provençal et Comtadin du Moyenage à la fin du XVIII Siècle.* Paris, 1913.

Bajot, Edouard. *Encyclopédie du Meuble, du XV Siècle jusqu'à nos Jours.* 7 vols., Paris, 1901–09.

Bajot, Edouard. *Profils et Tournages; Recueil de Documents de Styles . . . Gothique, François I, Henri II, Henri III, Henri IV, Louis XIII, Louis XIV, Louis XV, Louis XVI, Empire.* 2 vols., Paris, 1898–1903.

Ballot, Marie Juliette. *Charles Cressent, Sculpteur, Ebéniste, Collectionneur.* Paris, 1929.

Benoît, François. *L'Art Français sous la Révolution et L'Empire.* Paris, 1897.

Bérain, Jean Louis. *Œuvre de J. Bérain.* Paris, 1711.

Bérain, Jean Louis. *Œuvres de J. Bérain contenant des ornaments d'architecture.* Paris, 1711.

Bérain, Jean Louis. *Ornaments Inventés par J. Bérain.* Paris, 1711.

Blondel, Jacques François. *De la Distribution des Maisons de Plaisance et de la Décoration des Edifices en Général.* 2 vols., Paris, 1737–38.

Boulenger, Jacques Romain. *L'Ameublement Français au Grand Siècle.* Paris, 1913.

Brentano's, New York. *The Interior Decorative Art of France in the 17th and 18th Centuries.* 2 vols., New York, 1917.

Caylus, Anne Claude Philippe, Comte de. *Recueil d'Antiquités; Egyptiennes, Etrusques, Grecques, Romaines, et Gauloises.* 7 vols., Paris, 1756–1767.

Champeaux, Alfred de. *Le Meuble.* 2 vols., Paris, 1885.

Clouzot, Henri. *L'Ameublement Français sous Louis XV.* Paris, 1913.

Clouzot, Henri. *Les Meubles du XVIII Siècle.* Paris, 1922.

Collection de L'Art Régional en France (a survey of Provincial Architecture). *L'Habitation Provençale,* R. Darde; *L'Habitation Basque,* L. Colas; *L'Habitation Bretonne,* J. Bouille; *L'Habitation Landaise,* H. Godbarge. Paris, 1925.

Collection de L'Art Régional en France (a survey of French Provincial furniture). *Le Mobilier Lorrain,* Charles Sadoul; *Le Mobilier Basque,* Louis Colas; *Le Mobilier Breton,* Paul Banéat; *Le Mobilier Provençal,* Henri Algoud; *Le Mobilier Bas-Breton,* Jules Gauthier; *Le Mobilier Alsacien,* Paul Gélis; *Le Mobilier Bressan,* Alphonse Germain; *Le Mobilier Normand,* Léon le Clerc; *Le Mobilier Flamand,* V. Champier; *Le Mobilier Auvergnat,* Jules Gauthier; *Le Mobilier Vendéen et du Pays Nantais,* Jules Gauthier. Paris, 1924.

Denon, Dominique Vivant, Baron de. *Voyage dans la Basse et la Haute Egypte.* 2 vols., Paris, 1802.

Dilke, Lady. *French Decoration and Furniture in the 18th Century.* London, 1901.

Dreyfus, Carle. *French Furniture, in the Louvre Museum* (Louis XIV and Louis XV pieces). Paris, 1921.

Du Cerceau, Jacques Androuet. *Œuvre de*

Jacques Androuet dit du Cerceau. 2 VOLS., Paris, 1884.

Dumonthier, Ernest. *Bois de Siéges.* Paris, 1912.

Dumonthier, Ernest. *Etoffes d'Ameublement d'Epoque Napoléonienne.* Paris, 1909.

Dumonthier, Ernest. *Le Meuble-Toilette, Poudreuses, Coiffeuses, etc.* Paris, 1923.

Dumonthier, Ernest. *Les Siéges de Georges Jacob, époques Louis XV, Louis XVI et Révolutionnaire.* Paris, 1922.

Dumonthier, Ernest. *Les Tables, Tables à la Grecque, Tables à Ouvrages, etc., Louis XVI et Premier Empire.* Paris, 1924.

Dumonthier, Ernest. *Lits et Lits de Repos.* Paris.

Félice, Roger de. *Little Illustrated Books on Old French Furniture,* 4 VOLS. VOL. I, *French Furniture in the Middle Ages and under Louis XIII,* translated by F. M. Atkinson, London, 1923. VOL. II, *French Furniture under Louis XIV,* translated by F. M. Atkinson, New York, 1923. VOL. III, *French Furniture under Louis XV,* translated by Florence Simmonds, New York, 1920. VOL. IV, *French Furniture under Louis XVI and Empire,* translated by F. M. Atkinson, New York, 1921.

Gebelin, François. *Les Châteaux de la Renaissance.* Paris, 1927.

Havard, Henry. *Dictionaire de L'Ameublement et de la Décoration depuis le XIII siècle jusqu'à nous jours.* 4 VOLS., Paris, 1887–90.

Havard, Henry. *Les Boulle* (collection des artistes célèbres), Paris, 188–.

Hessling, Egon. *Le Mobilier de la Renaissance Française, collections du Musée de Cluny.* Paris, 1910.

Hessling, Egon. *Le Mobilier du Premier Empire.* Berlin, 1910.

Hessling, Egon. *Le Mobilier Louis XV au Musée des Arts Décoratifs de Paris.* Berlin, 1910.

Hessling, Egon. *Le Mobilier Louis XV au Musée du Louvre.* Berlin, 1910.

Hessling, Egon and Hessling, Waldemar. *Die Louis XVI Möbel des Louvre.* Berlin, 1912.

Hessling, Egon and Hessling, Waldemar. *Le Style Directoire le Mobilier.* Paris, 1914.

Hessling, Egon and Hessling, Waldemar. *Louis XIV Möbel des Louvre und des Musée des Arts Décoratifs.* Berlin, 1909.

Jacquemart, Albert. *A History of Furniture,* translated from the French, edited by Mrs. Bury Palliser. London, 1878.

Janneau, Guillaume. *Les Meubles.* 3 VOLS. VOL. I, *De l'Art Antique au Style Louis XIV;* VOL. II, *Du Style Régence au Style Louis XV;* VOL. III, *Du Style Louis XVI au Style Empire.* Paris, 1929.

Keim, Albert. *Le Beau Meuble de France.* Paris, 1928.

Keim, Albert. *La Décoration et le Mobilier a l'Epoque Romantique et sous le Second Empire.* Paris, 1929.

Kimball, Fiske. *The Creation of the Rococo.* Philadelphia. 1943.

Lafond, Paul. *L'Art Décoratif et le Mobilier sous la République et l'Empire.* Paris, 1906.

Lemonnier, Henry. *L'Art Français au Temps de Richelieu et de Mazarin.* Paris, 1893.

Le Pautre, Jean. *Collection des plus Belles Compositions de Le Pautre.* Par Decloux and Dowry, Paris, 18—.

Longnon, Henri and Huard, Frances Wilson. *French Provincial Furniture.* Philadelphia, 1927.

Maillard, Elisa. *Old French Furniture and Its Surroundings, 1610–1815.* Translated by MacIver Percival. London, 1925.

Marot, Daniel. *Œuvres du Sieur D. Marot, architecte de Guillaume III, Roi de la Grande Bretagne.* Amsterdam, 1712.

Marot, Daniel. *Receuil des Planches des Sieurs Marot, père et fils.* Amsterdam, 1712.

Meissonnier, Juste Aurèle. *Œuvre de Juste Aurèle Meissonnier, peintre, sculpteur, architecte et dessinateur de la chambre et cabinet du roy.* Paris, 17—.

Molinier, Emile. *Histoire Générale des Arts Appliqués à L'Industrie du V* à la Fin du XVIII Siècle.* 5 VOLS., Paris, 1896–1911.

Molinier, Emile. *Royal Interiors and Decorations of the 17th and 18th Centuries.* 5 VOLS., Paris, 1902. VOL. I, *Louis XIV;* VOL. II, *Régence and Louis XV;* VOL. III, *Régence and Louis XV;* VOL. IV, *Louis XVI;* VOL. V, *Louis XVI.*

Mottheau, Jacques. *Meubles Usuels, Louis XVI.* Paris, 1952.

Mottheau, Jacques. *Meubles Usuels, Régence et Louis XV.* Paris, 1952.

Oppenord, Gilles Marie. *Œuvres de Gille Marie Oppenort.* Paris, 18—.

Osborn, M. *Die Kunst des Rokoko.* Berlin, 1929.

Percier, Charles and Fontaine, Pierre François Leonard. *Choix des Plus Célèbres Maisons de Plaisance de Rome et des Environs.* Paris, 1809.

Percier, Charles and Fontaine, Pierre François Leonard. *Palais Maisons et Autres Dessinés à Rome.* Paris, 1798. New edition 1830.

Percier, Charles and Fontaine, Pierre François Leonard. *Recueil de Décorations Intérieures, Meubles, Bronzes, etc.* Paris, 1812.

Ricci, Seymour de. *Louis XIV and Régence Furniture Decoration.* New York, 1929.

Ricci, Seymour de. *Louis XVI Furniture*. London, 1913.

Roubo, Andre Jacob. *L'Art du Menuisier*. 2 VOLS., Paris, 1769–1772.

Saglio, André. *French Furniture*. London, 1907.

Salverte, François, Comte de. *Les Ebénistes du XVIII Siècle, Leurs Œuvres et Leurs Marques*. Paris, 1937.

Salverte, François, Comte de. *Le Meuble Français d'après les ornementistes de 1660 à 1789*. Paris, 1930.

Strange, Thomas Arthur. *French Interiors, Furniture, Decoration, Woodwork and Allied Arts, 17th, 18th and 19th Centuries*. London, 1907.

Vacquier, Jules F. *Les Anciens Châteaux de France*. 10 VOLS., Paris, 1920–1926.

Vial, Henri. *Les Artistes Décorateurs du Bois*. 2 VOLS., Paris, 1912–22.

Wallace Collection Catalogue on Furniture. Text with Historical Notes by F. J. Watson. London, 1956.

ITALIAN, SPANISH &
DUTCH and FLEMISH

Albertolli, Giocondo. *Ornamenti diversi inventati, desegnati ed eseguiti da Giocondo Albertolli*. Milano, 1782.

Berendsen, Anne. *Het Nederlandse Interieur; Binnenhuis, Meubelen, Tapijten, etc.* van 1450–1820. Utrecht, 1950.

Bianchi, Gino. *Il Mobilio Antico Fiorentino*. Firenze, 192–.

Bode, Wilhelm von. *Italian Renaissance Furniture*. Translated by Mary E. Herrick. New York, 1921.

Borchgrave D'Altena, Joseph, Comte de. *Décors Anciens d'Intérieurs Mosans*. 4 VOLS., Liége, 1930–32.

Burckhardt, Dr. Jacob. *The Civilization of the Renaissance in Italy*. Vienna, 1937.

Burr, Grace Hardendorff. *Hispanic Furniture, with examples in the collection of the Hispanic Society of America*. New York, 1941.

Byne, Arthur and Byne, Mildred Stapley. *Decorated Wooden Ceilings in Spain*. London, 1920.

Byne, Arthur and Byne, Mildred Stapley. *Provincial Houses in Spain*. New York, 1925.

Byne, Arthur and Byne, Mildred Stapley. *Spanish Interiors and Furniture*. 3 VOLS., New York, 1921.

Byne, Arthur and Byne, Mildred Stapley. *Spanish Ironwork*. New York, 1915.

Catalogus van Meubelen en Betimmeringen Rijksmuseum, Amsterdam, 1952.

Domenech, Rafael and Bueno, Luis Pérez. *Meubles Españoles Antiguos*. Barcelona, 192–.

Eberlein, Harold Donaldson. *Interiors, Fireplaces and Furniture of the Italian Renaissance*. New York, 1916.

Eberlein, Harold Donaldson. *Spanish Interiors, Furniture and Details from the 14th to the 17th Century*. New York, 1925.

Ferrari, Giulio. *Il Legno e la Mobilia nell'Arte Italiana*. Milano, 1925.

Guérin, Jacques. *La Chinoiserie en Europe au XVIII Siècle*. Paris, 1911.

Hunter, George Leland. *Italian Furniture and Interiors*. 2 VOLS., New York, 1918.

Jonge, Carla Hermine de. *Hollandische Möbel und Raumkunst von 1650–1780*. Holland, 1922.

Labarte, Jules. *Handbook of the Arts of the Middle Ages and Renaissance*. London, 1855.

Morazzoni, Giuseppe. *Il Mobile Genovese*. Milano, 1948.

Morazzoni, Giuseppe. *Il Mobile Veneziano*. Milano, 1927.

Morazzoni, Giuseppe. *Mobili Veneziani Laccati*. Milano, 195–.

Odom, William M. *A History of Italian Furniture from the 14th to the Early 19th centuries*. 2 VOLS., New York, 1918.

Palladio, Andrea. *I Quattro Libri dell'Architettura di Andrea Palladio*. Venetia, 1570.

Palladio, Andrea. *The Architecture of A. Palladio*. 4 VOLS., translated from the Italian. London, 1715–1720.

Pedrini, Augusto. *Italian Furniture; interiors and decoration of the 15th and 16th Centuries*. London, 1949.

Piranesi, Giovanni. *Diverse Maniere D'Adornare I Camini*. Roma, 1767.

Riccoboni, Louis. *Histoire du Théâtre Italien*. Paris, 1728.

Richter, Gisela Marie Augusta. *Ancient Furniture; A History of Greek, Roman and Etruscan Furniture*. Oxford, 1926.

Salvatore, Camillo. *Italian Architecture, Furniture and Interiors during the 14th, 15th and 16th Centuries*. Boston, 1904.

Schottmuller, Frida. *Furniture and Interior Decoration of the Italian Renaissance*. New York, 1921.

Singleton, Esther. *Dutch and Flemish Furniture*. London, 1907.

Sluyterman, K. *Huisraad en Binnenhuis in Nederland, in Vroegere Eeuwen*. Holland, 1918.

BIBLIOGRAPHY

Sluyterman, K. *Intérieurs Anciens en Belgique.* Holland, 1913.

Symonds, John Addington. *Renaissance in Italy.* New York, 1921.

Terni de Gregory, Winifred. *Vecchi Mobili Italiani; Tipo in uso dal secolo XV al secolo XX.* Milano, 1953.

Vasari, Giorgio. *Lives of the Most Eminent Painters, Sculptors and Architects; newly translated by G du C. de Vere.* 10 VOLS., London, 1912–1915.

Vogelsang, Willem. *Le Meuble Hollandais au Musée National d'Amsterdam.* The Hague, 1910.

Weisbach, Werner. *Die Kunst des Barock in Italien, Frankreich, Deutschland und Spanien.* Berlin, 1924.

Weissman, Adriaan Willem. *Documents Classés de l'Art dans les Pays-Bas du Xe au XIXe Siècle.* Utrecht, 1914.

Winckelmann, Johann Joachim. *Histoire de l'Antiquité.* Paris, 1764.

Winckelmann, Johann Joachim. *Monuments Antiques Inédits.* Paris, 1766.

Winckelmann, Johann Joachim. *Réflexions sur l'Imitation de l'Art Grec.* Paris, 1754.

Wytsman, P. *Intérieurs et Mobiliers de Styles Anciens, collection recueillie en Belgique.* 2 VOLS., Brussels, 1898.

CHINESE

Dupont, Maurice. *Les Meubles de la Chine.* Second series. Paris, 1926.

Dye, Daniel Sheets. *A Grammar of Chinese Lattice.* 2 VOLS., Cambridge, Mass., 1937.

Ecke, Gustav. *Chinese Domestic Furniture.* Peking, 1944.

Ecke, Gustav. *"Wandlungen des Faltstuhls, Bemerkungen sur Geschichte der Eurasischen Stuhlform"* in *Monumenta Servica.* VOL. IX, 1944 page 34 sqq.

Hommel, Rudolf P. *China at Work.* New York, 1937.

Inn, Henry. *Chinese Houses and Gardens.* Edited by Shao Chang Lee, Revised Edition. New York, 1950.

Stone, Louise Hawley. *The Chair in China.* Toronto, 1952.

ARCHITECTURE & REPERTORIES of DESIGNS

Berliner, Rudolf. *Ornamentale Vorlage-Blätter des 15. bis 18. Jahrhunderts.* 4 VOLS., Leipzig, 1924–1926.

Bolton, Arthur T. *The Architecture of Robert Adam and James Adam (1758–1794).* 2 VOLS., London, 1922.

Byne, Arthur and Byne, Mildred Stapley. *Spanish Architecture of the sixteenth century, general view of the Plateresque and Herrera styles.* New York, 1917.

Destailleur, Hippolyte Alexandre Gabriel Walter. *Recueil d'estampes relatives à l'ornamentation des apartments aux XVI, XVII, et XVIII siècles.* 2 VOLS., Paris, 1863–1871.

Fletcher, Sir Banister Flight. *A History of Architecture on the comparative method, for students, craftsmen and amateurs.* 14th edition, New York, 1948.

Fletcher, Sir Banister Flight. *Andrea Palladio, life and works.* London, 1902.

Guilmard, Désiré. *Les Maîtres Ornamentistes.* 2 VOLS., Paris, 1880–1881.

Hamlin, Talbot Faulkner. *Architecture Through the Ages.* New York, 1940.

Hitchcock, Henry Russel. *Modern Architecture, Romanticism and Reintegration.* New York, 1929.

Hitchcock, Henry Russel. *Early Victorian Architecture in Britain.* New Haven, 1954.

Jessen, Dr. Peter. *Der Ornamentatich.* Berlin, 1920.

Jessen, Dr. Peter. *Meister des Ornamentichs.* Berlin, 1923.

Kimball, Fiske. *A History of Architecture.* New York, 1918.

Prentice, Andrew Noble. *Renaissance Architecture and Ornament in Spain, 1500–1650.* London, 1893.

Speltz, Alexander. *Styles of Ornament, from Prehistoric Times to the Middle of the XIXth Century.* Translated from the second German edition. Revised and edited by R. Phene Spiers. London, 1910.

Speltz, Alexander. *The Coloured Ornament of All Historical Styles.* Leipzig, 1915. PART I, *Antiquity;* PART II, *Middle Ages;* PART III, *Modern Times.*

Ward, William Henry. *Architecture of the Renaissance in France (1495–1830).* London, 1912.

ENGLISH VICTORIAN

Addison, Agnes: *Romanticism and the Gothic Revival.* New York, 1938.

Arts & Crafts Essays by members of the Arts & Crafts Exhibition Society with a preface by William Morris. London, 1903.

Art Journal Illustrated Catalogue of the Industry of All Nations. London, 1851.

Art Journal Illustrated Catalogue of the International Exhibition. London, 1862.

Aslin, Elizabeth: *Nineteenth Century English Furniture.* New York, 1962.

Bell, Malcolm: *Edward Burne-Jones. A Record and a Review.* London, 1892.

Blomfield, Paul: *William Morris.* London, 1934.

Bøe, Alf: *From Gothic Revival to Functional Form.* Oslo, 1957.

Clark, Kenneth: *The Gothic Revival.* London, 1928.

Cobden-Sanderson, T. J.: *The Arts and Crafts Movement.* London, 1905.

Dresser, Christopher: *Japan—Its Architecture, Art and Art Manufactures.* London, 1882.

Fischel, Oskar and Boehn, Max von: *Modes and Manners of the Nineteenth Century.* Translation by M. Edwardes. 3 vols. London, 1927.

Gaunt, William: *The Aesthetic Adventure.* Reprint Society. London, 1945.

Gaunt, William: *The Pre-Raphaelite Dream.* Reprint Society. London, 1943.

Gimson, Ernest: *Ernest Gimson. His Life and Work.* London, 1924.

Godwin, Edward: *Art Furniture.* London, 1877.

Joel, David: *The Adventure of British Furniture, 1851–1951.* London, 1953.

Hamilton, Walter: *The Aesthetic Movement in England.* London, 1882.

Harbron, Dudley: *The Conscious Stone. The Life of Edward William Godwin.* London, 1949.

Henderson, Philip: *William Morris, His Life, Work and Friends.* New York, 1967.

Ironside, Robin: *Pre-Raphaelite Painters.* New York, 1948.

Jones, Owen: *Grammar of Ornament.* London, 1856.

Joy, Edward T.: *The Country Life Book of Chairs.* London, 1967.

Lethaby, William Richard: *Philip Webb and His Work.* London, 1925.

Loudon, J. C.: *Encyclopaedia of Cottage, Farm and Villa Architecture.* London 1833, 1947, and 1857.

Mackail, John William: *The Life of William Morris.* 2 vols. Reprint. London, 1907.

Morris, William: *Decorative Arts Pamphlets.* London.

Morris, William: *Arts and Crafts Exhibition Society.* London, 1899.

Morse, Edward S.: *Japanese Homes and Their Surroundings.* Boston, 1889.

Official Descriptive and Illustrated Catalogue of the Great Exhibition, 1851. Vols. III and IV. London, 1851.

Pevsner, Nikolaus: *High Victorian Design.* Ipswich, Great Britain, 1951.

Pevsner, Nikolaus: *Pioneers of Modern Design from William Morris to Walter Gropius.* New York, 1949.

Pugin, Augustus Welby N.: *Contrasts.* London, 1836.

Pugin, Augustus Welby N.: *The True Principles of Pointed or Christian Architecture.* London, 1841.

Stafford, Maureen: *British Furniture Through the Ages.* New York, 1966.

Symonds, R. W. and Whineray, B. B.: *Victorian Furniture.* London, 1962.

Talbert, Bruce J.: *Gothic Forms Applied to Furniture, Metal Work and Decoration for Domestic Purposes.* London, 1867.

Talbert, Bruce J.: *Examples of Ancient and Modern Furniture.* London, 1876.

BIBLIOGRAPHY

Victoria and Albert Museum: *Victorian Furniture. Small Picture Book,* No. 59. London, 1962.

Victoria and Albert Museum: A Commemorative Album of the Great Exhibition of 1851. Compiled by C. H. Gibbs-Smith. London, 1950.

Victoria and Albert Museum: Catalogue. Victorian and Edwardian Decorative Arts. Loan Exhibition. London, 1952.

Watkinson, Ray: *William Morris As Designer.* New York, 1967.

Watt, William: *Art Furniture.* London, 1877.

AMERICAN VICTORIAN

Baird, Henry Carey: *Cabinet Maker's Album of Furniture.* Philadelphia, 1868.

Conner, Robert: *Cabinet Maker's Assistant.* New York, 1842.

Cook, Clarence: *The House Beautiful.* New York, 1877.

Downing, A. J.: *The Architecture of Country Houses.* New York, 1850.

Downing, A. J.: *Cottage Residences.* New York, 1842.

Hamlin, Talbot Faulkner: *The Greek Revival Architecture in America.* New York, 1947.

McCabe, James D.: *Illustrated History of the Centennial Exhibition.* Philadelphia, 1876.

McClinton, Katherine Morrison: *Collecting American Victorian Antiques.* New York, 1966.

J. L. Mott Iron Works: Illustrated Catalogue of Statuary, Fountains, Vases, Settees. New York, 1873.

Newark Museum: Catalogue. Classical America 1815–1845. Loan Exhibition. Newark, 1963.

Randall, Richard H., Jr.: The Furniture of H. H. Richardson. Loan Exhibition. Boston Museum, 1962.

Stickley, Gustav: *Craftsman Homes.* New York, 1909.

Wellman, Rita: *Victoria Royal. The Flowering of a Style.* New York, 1939.

Williams, Henry T. and Jones, Mrs. C. S.: *Beautiful Homes.* New York, 1878.

ART NOUVEAU

Ahlers-Hestermann, Friedrich: *Stilwende, Aufbruch der Jugend um 1900.* Second edition. Berlin, 1956.

Amaya, Mario: *Art Nouveau.* Paperback. New York, 1966.

Bahr, Herman: *Sezession.* Vienna, 1900.

Bajot, Edouard: *L'Art Nouveau—Décoration et Ameublement.* Paris, 1898.

Bayard, Jean Emile: *El Estilo Moderno.* Paris, 1919.

Behrens, Peter: *Ein Dokument Deutscher Kunst; die Ausstellung der Künstler-Kolonie in Darmstadt, 1901.* Munich, 1901.

Casteels, Maurice: *Henry Van de Velde.* Brussels, 1932.

Denis, Maurice: *Théories 1890–1910.* Third edition. Paris, 1920.

Fourcauld, Louis de: *Emile Gallé.* Paris. 1903.

Glück, Franz: *Adolf Loos.* Paris, 1931.

Guérinet, Edouard: *La Décoration et l'Ameublement à l'Exposition de 1900.* Paris, 1901.

Juyot, Paul: *Louis Majorelle. Artiste Décorateur. Maître Ebéniste.* Nancy, 1926.

Hoeber, Fritz: *Peter Behrens.* Munich, 1913.

Howarth, Thomas: *Charles Rennie Mackintosh and the Modern Movement.* New York, 1953.

Kleiner, Leopold: *Josef Hoffmann.* Berlin, 1927.

Lenning, Henry F.: *The Art Nouveau.* The Hague, 1951.

Madsen, Stephan Tschudi: *Sources of Art Nouveau.* English translation by Ragnar Christophersen. New York, 1956.

Museum of Modern Art, New York: *Art Nouveau.* Edited by Peter Selz and Mildred Constantine. New York, 1959.

Rheims, Maurice: *The Flowering of Art Nouveau.* English translation by Patrick Evans. New York, 19—.

Tiffany, Louis: *The Art Work of Louis Tiffany.* New York, 1914.

Velde, Henry van de: *Die Renaissance im Modernen Kunstgewerbe.* Berlin, 1901.

MODERN MOVEMENT—TWENTIETH CENTURY

Arts of Denmark: Catalogue. Loan exhibition organized by the Danish Society of Arts and Crafts and Industrial Design. United States, 1960–1961.

Bertram, Anthony: *The House, a Machine for Living In.* London, 1935.

Blake, Peter: *Le Corbusier.* Paperback. Baltimore, 1966.

Frankl, Paul T.: *New Dimensions.* New York, 1928.

Giedion, Siegfried: *Mechanization Takes Command.* New York, 1948.

Gropius, Walter: *The New Architecture and the Bauhaus.* London, 1935.

Hiort, Esbjørn: *Modern Danish Furniture.* New York, 1956.

Horta, Victor: *Moderne.* Brussels, 1926.

Logie, Gordon: *Furniture from Machines.* London, 1947.

Maki, O.: *Designers of Today.* Helsinki, 1955.

Martin, J. L. and Speight, S.: *The Flat Book.* London, 1939.

Moody, Ella: *Modern Furniture.* Paperback. New York, 1966.

Mumford, Lewis: *The Brown Decade.* New York, 1931.

Muthesius, Hermann: *Das Englische Haus.* Vols. I–III. Berlin 1904–1908.

Museum of Contemporary Crafts, New York: Catalogue. Plastic as Plastic. Loan Exhibition. New York, 1968.

Museum of Modern Art, New York: *What Is Modern Design?* Edgar Kaufmann, Jr. New York, 1950.

Museum of Modern Art, New York: *Introduction to Twentieth Century Design from the Museum's Collection.* Edited by Arthur Drexler and Greta Daniel. New York, 1959.

Museum of Modern Art, New York: Alfred H. Barr, Jr. De Stijl. Booklet. Western Germany, 1961.

Perry, T. D.: *Modern Plywood.* New York, 1942.

Plath, Iona: *The Decorative Arts of Sweden.* New York, 1948.

Read, Sir Herbert: *Art and Industry.* Third edition. London, 1952.

Segerstad, Ulf Hård af: *Modern Scandinavian Furniture.* English translation by Nancy and Edward Maze. Totowa, New Jersey, 1965.

Story of the Plastics Industry. Twelfth revised edition. Prepared under the direction of The Society of the Plastic Industry, Inc., New York. Edited by Don Masson. Booklet. New York, 1968.

Sullivan, Louis Henry: *Kindergarten Chats and Other Writings.* New York, 1947.

Teague, Walter Dorwin: *Design This Day.* American Edition, 1946.

Wallance, Donald W.: *Shaping America's Products.* New York, 1956.

Wettergren, Erik: *The Modern Decorative Arts of Sweden.* English translation by Tage Palm. Malmö Museum, 1926.

Wright, Frank Lloyd: *On Architecture. Selected Writings, 1894–1940.* New York, 1941.

Figures in heavy type refer to illustrations

INDEX

The Complete Guide to Furniture Styles

From ancient Greece and Rome, through medieval times, and up to the present day, domestic furniture has been an integral part of civilization, and its study reveals much about our history and culture. This classic guide to furniture styles discusses the development of domestic furniture in Europe, America, and China, detailing the great periods of French and English furniture from the Renaissance through the Empire and Regency periods. Furniture from every age is represented in over 600 photographs of pieces from major collections throughout the world. The book's highly readable style and extensive coverage make it ideal for both the interested novice and the experienced collector.

"Occasionally there comes from a publisher a guide to furniture styles so comprehensive that smaller and less informative volumes can be dispensed with . . . this thoroughly complete volume is an example. Beautifully written and completely informative."

—*Interior Design*

"An entertaining book for the general reader and an invaluable encyclopedia of furniture for collectors, students and artists."

—*American Artist*

Louise Ade Boger has long been an authority on furniture and the decorative arts. She is the author of *The Dictionary of World Pottery and Porcelain* and has co-written *The Dictionary of Antiques and Decorative Arts* with H. Batterson Boger. Mrs. Boger has written a monthly column on antiques for *House and Garden* magazine for the past fifteen years.

Published by Charles Scribner's Sons New York

Antiques & Collecting/Interior Design / $17.95   ISBN 0-684-17641-6

Cover photo: Cecil Bedroom, courtesy of the H.G. Du Pont Winterthur Museum.